An Introduction
to the Old Testament

Second Edition

An Introduction to the Old Testament

The Canon and Christian Imagination

Second Edition

Walter Brueggemann
and Tod Linafelt

WESTMINSTER
JOHN KNOX PRESS
LOUISVILLE · KENTUCKY

Second edition
Published by Westminster John Knox Press
Louisville, Kentucky

12 13 14 15 16 17 18 19 20 21—10 9 8 7 6 5 4 3 2 1

Book design by Sharon Adams
Cover design by Dilu Nicholas
Cover illustration: The Tower of Babel by Tamas Galambos (Contemporary Artist)/Hungarian National Gallery, Budapest, Hungary/ The Bridgeman Art Library

Library of Congress Cataloging-in-Publication Data

Brueggemann, Walter.
  An introduction to the Old Testament : the canon and Christian imagination / Walter Brueggemann and Tod Linafelt. — Second edition.
     pages cm
  Includes bibliographical references and index.
  ISBN 978-0-664-23458-4 (pbk.)
  1. Bible. O.T.—Introductions.   2. Bible. O.T.—Criticism, interpretation, etc.
3. Bible--Canon. I. Linafelt, Tod, 1965– II. Title.
  BS1140.3.B78   2012
  221.6'1—dc23

                        2011051971

Contents

PART III: THE WRITINGS

CONCLUDING REFLECTION

Preface to the Second Edition

Having been first introduced to the serious (and thrilling) academic study of the Bible as a student of Walter Brueggemann over twenty years ago, in his course on the Pentateuch at Columbia Theological Seminary, I was both pleased and hesitant to accept the invitation to collaborate with him on this revised and expanded second edition of *An Introduction to the Old Testament*. What could I add? However, while my own scholarly work remains thoroughly influenced by Professor Brueggemann, it has also moved in a slightly different direction, with more investment in traditional literary categories and in interest in the cultural history of the Bible. And my teaching for the past fifteen years has taken place almost entirely within an undergraduate context, at Georgetown University, in contrast to Brueggemann's long career teaching in seminaries. So in the end we hope that our complementary interests and teaching experiences have made this new edition of the book a worthwhile project.

The present edition has several new features. First, a substantial new chapter (chapter 2) on the literary art of the Old Testament focuses on the differing literary resources of biblical *narrative* and biblical *poetry*, respectively. There has lately been a great surge of interest in the literary workings of the Bible, but too often the very real differences between these two large genres have been flattened or ignored. Biblical prose narrative and biblical poetry (or verse) work with very different literary tool kits and are used in very different ways. It seems clear that the ancient authors were quite aware of the differing conventions and possibilities associated with narrative and with poetry, and that their audiences would have responded differently to these two primary literary forms. The better we understand these forms, the better we are as readers.

Beyond that new chapter, one finds throughout the book a series of text-boxes, which take two forms: close readings and midrashic moments. The *close readings* focus in on particularly interesting or illuminating details in the texts and suggest, briefly, lines of interpretation arising from such close attention. Anyone who has ever been in a class or a workshop with Professor Brueggemann knows that he is unrelenting in his demand that we read closely and take seriously the details and texture of Scripture, rather than relying on a vague or misleading paraphrase that attempts to reduce the text to some easily digested lesson. Though few and brief, our close-reading textboxes arise from that same spirit of collaborative classroom interpretation. "Midrash" is the traditional Jewish name for "interpretation," most especially the type of interpretation that brings the ancient text into explicit dialogue with later cultural contexts, and our series of *midrashic moments* highlight specific examples of the biblical text being put to good interpretive use. Such examples not only show the continuing generative power of the Bible but also, we hope, encourage readers toward a more active use of the Bible in contrast with a passive reading. In other words, there is a long history of creative reuse of biblical stories, images, and ideas; and reverence for the text ought not to discourage such creativity. Finally, in addition to the newly written additions to the book, each chapter has been revised and updated, some more than others naturally, and the bibliography has been expanded to take account of works published since the first edition.

I was pleased to find that the first edition of the book was dedicated to Charles Cousar, Professor Brueggemann's longtime colleague at Columbia Theological Seminary. Charles Cousar was also my professor at Columbia, and he taught me the same sort of imaginative close reading of the New Testament that Brueggemann required of the Old Testament. It is difficult to imagine two better professors to initiate one into the academic study of the Bible, and so I am happy to second that original dedication: to Professor Charles Cousar.

TOD LINAFELT
Ordinary Time 2011

Preface to the First Edition

Recent developments in interpretive perspective in Old Testament study and the emergence of newer methods in the last two decades have made a huge difference for the way in which churches (and pastors) may have access to the Old Testament as a source and norm for faith. In older scholarship that was dominated by historical-critical approaches, Old Testament studies for the most part was a highly academic enterprise for "experts," with not much obvious or intentional connection to the life and practice of the church. The resultant problem tended to be either that pastors were tempted to stay with historical-critical matters that did not connect very well, or they had to make fanciful leaps that tended to disregard the gains of historical-critical study and so to proceed in a precritical manner.

The newer approaches and methods—especially canonical, rhetorical, and sociological—permit the text to come more readily into contact with the milieu of the contemporary interpretive community of the church. There is of course still an important role for historical criticism; but other approaches now stand alongside and make the interface of ancient text and contemporary community more poignant and palpable. The present book is my effort—albeit a personal effort and at some points idiosyncratic—to mediate and make available fresh learnings of Old Testament studies that will be of peculiar force for pastors and Christian congregations. It will be evident that I have more interest in and more expertise in some parts of the Old Testament than in other parts, but such is permitted in a statement that intends to be personal and colleague-to-colleague. It will also be evident that because this book is intended for congregational and pastoral use, I have not reiterated all of the elementary critical apparatus of history, geography, and chronology that often appears in an introduction to the Old Testament. Such data will in other ways be available to pastors and congregations.

It will be evident that I have been instructed by and learned a great deal from the canonical approach of Brevard Childs, a fact gladly acknowledged in the term "canon" in the title. Childs has taught us all about the legitimacy and force of church interpretation that is formed by but not enthralled to academic, critical categories. It is difficult to overstate the importance of Childs's contribution for the field generally or for my own personal perspective on interpretive matters. It will be equally apparent, however, that I am unwilling to follow Childs all the way, that is, unwilling to conclude that the force of canonical traditioning was able to override all parts of the tradition that do not fit canonical intentions or, eventually, that do not fit the church's "rule of faith." Or alternatively, I am not willing to exclude from consideration all textual testimony that does not readily adapt itself to the categories of normative church teaching. It is my judgment that the canon, taken alone and without attentiveness to the parts that do not fit, eventuates in a process of repression, surely the last thing that a church in a technologically repressive society needs.

Thus the title of my book includes "imagination" because I believe that the text both embodies and insists on ongoing work of imaginative interpretation that does not and will not conform to the strictures, limits, and demands of church faith. To that end, I have freely cited from the book *Congregation*, a collection of essays on the books of the Hebrew Bible by urbane Jewish literary figures (Rosenberg 1987). These suggestive essays notice and celebrate nuances and dimensions of the text that fall well outside the scope of the Christian canon. My own sense is that it is the interplay between *normative* and the *imaginatively playful* that gives the text its obviously transformative energy. To be sure, the playfully imaginative by itself without the normative dissolves the text in a way that makes it of little help to a missional congregation. Thus, on the one hand, the danger of the canonical by itself is in the direction of repression; the danger of the imaginatively playful by itself, on the other hand, is to dissolve the text away from the gravitas of mission. It is my judgment that the interface between the canonical and the imaginative is exactly the way in which the most responsible and faithful interpretation takes place. I expect, moreover, that that is exactly how it is done among pastors and among congregations that take the Bible as the normative and as the live Word of God.

While I have given my own read of matters, I have quoted copiously from other authors. I have done so because I wanted the reader to be engaged in the ongoing interpretive conversation that is rich and thick well beyond my own read. It is my hope that by such engagement the text may be freshly appropriated by pastors and congregations, not simply for the next task of church study but as an alternative world of well-being, freedom, and responsibility, alternative to the world of dominant secular culture or to the conventional world of church teaching that too often has become thin and arid.

In thinking about the generative work of the text in the process of providing an alternative world that invites faithful imagination, I have had in mind the guidelines of two giants in the field of interpretation. Amos Wilder says of world-making narrative:

> If we ask a prestigious body of modern critics about the relation of story-world to real world, they will reply that it is a false question. For one thing the story goes its own way and takes us with it; the storyteller is inventing, not copying. He weaves his own web of happening and the meaning of every part and detail is determined by the whole sequence. We lose our place in the story if we stop to ask what this feature means or refers to outside it.
>
> More important, these students of language will ask us what we mean by "real world." There is no "world" for us until we have named and languaged and storied whatever is. What we take to be the nature of things has been shaped by calling it so. This therefore is also a story-world. Here again we cannot move behind the story to what may be more "real." Our language-worlds are the only worlds we know! (Wilder 1983, 361)

What Wilder says of story is surely true, mutatis mutandis, of a rich panoply of other genres as well. And Raymond Brown, in his early study of interpretation, comments: "After all, in the Scriptures we are in our Father's house where the children are permitted to play" (R. Brown 1955, 28).

Without denying the gravitas of the canonical, I have wanted to give assent as well to the "otherness" of the text that is other even beyond that canonical gravitas. Karl Barth has famously written of the "strange new world" within the Bible. Indeed! It is to be noted, however, that the strangeness and newness of the world in the text surges even beyond normative canonical categories, as Barth himself has been able to recognize. Thus I hope that this effort on my part will enhance the world-making, imaginative work of church interpretation, precisely because the flat, thin world of our dominant culture is by itself not an adequate venue for the abundant life given by the God of the gospel.

It remains for me to express thanks in many directions. This book was undertaken at the suggestion of Carey Newman, then of Westminster John Knox Press. After his departure from the press, Greg Glover has succeeded him and has done diligent, steadfast work to transpose my writing into a workable book. Tim Simpson has worked through the manuscript in detail, and has measurably corrected and strengthened the book in important ways.

David Knauert has labored mightily on the bibliography. Most of all, I express my thanks to Tia Foley, who has overseen the entire process of preparation of the manuscript with her characteristic gifts of technical competence, exegetical capacity for my penmanship, patience, and attentiveness to detail, all of which have brought the process to a good conclusion. The longer I work at writing, the more I am increasingly aware of how dependent I am on such good cohorts, and so my great appreciation to Greg, Tim, David, and Tia.

I am pleased to dedicate this book to my colleague Charles Cousar with gratitude and affection. Cousar's presence on the Columbia Seminary faculty was the primal attraction for me to come to the seminary, and I have not been disappointed in the years since that decision. In addition to his steadfast friendship and good colleagueship, Charlie is a model of church scholarship, pastoral teaching, and institutional citizenship. On all these counts I am glad for our long season of shared life on the faculty together, and now for the chance to grow old in retirement alongside him.

WALTER BRUEGGEMANN
Ash Wednesday 2003

Introductory Materials

1

Imaginative Remembering

The Theological Witness of the Old Testament

As recently as fifty years ago, there was a general consensus about an introduction to the Old Testament, about the questions to be asked and the answers to be given. That general consensus managed, in an odd way, to keep together a deep *grounding in faith* ("Christian" faith, since the critical scholarship of that era was undertaken primarily by Christian scholars) and in the *critical judgments* then operative. These scholars maintained an uneasy settlement of faith and criticism, one that at the time seemed honest and workable. In more recent times, however, that general consensus has given way to an immense pluralism of perspectives and methods that, not surprisingly, now preclude agreement among scholars. As a consequence, the offer of an introduction has become more complex and problematic. What follows is an attempt to offer a critically informed, intellectually coherent introduction that may function as a guideline for critically informed, theologically responsible Bible reading in the church. For the most part, we shall state the main contours of current scholarly opinion; but there is no point in writing an introduction unless one has the freedom to do so from a particular angle of vision. In what follows, we exercise that freedom in ways that we hope are both responsible and suggestive.

I

At the outset, readers may reflect on four themes that relate to current and recurring problems in reading the Old Testament.

1. The term "Old Testament" itself bears reflection and quickly raises a nest of difficult issues. The term refers to a specific set of "books" that constitute part of Christian Scripture. As Christian readers of this Scripture, we

3

read increasingly in the presence of and with awareness of Jews as the first to believe in the God of this Scripture and the direct descendants of the people who recorded and passed down these traditions; consequently, the term "Old" Testament is not without problems (Brooks and Collins 1990). It is a confessional term, for it asserts that Christians read this Scripture always with an attentiveness to the "New" Testament that we read as deeply and intimately connected to the "Old" Testament. Thus, for Christians, the two parts of Scripture stand together as "old and new," the "old part" coming to fruition and fulfillment in the New that attends to Jesus as the Messiah. That is an elemental claim of Christian faith, one that has been attested from the earliest time in the church. But it is not a simple claim for at least two reasons.

First, the "Old/New" connection seems to preempt completely the Old and to exclude any reading of it except a reading toward the New. While this is a long-established Christian assumption and practice, it is not one that can be sustained in the presence of Jewish reading and certainly not one assumed in this discussion. Thus in speaking of "the Old Testament," we intend to leave room to allow and affirm that as Christians read this text toward the New Testament, so Jews properly and legitimately read the same scrolls toward the Talmud as the definitive document of Judaism. This in no way compromises claims made in Christian faith, but intends to eschew any monopolistic reading that crowds out a Jewish reading that is likewise faithful to the text and is to be taken with equal seriousness by Christians. Thus in reading the Old Testament, readers of this book must ponder how Christians are "coreaders" with Jews, how far and in what ways we may read with Jews, and in what ways we read in different directions and apart from Jews. This question is not an easy one and is not served by any compromise of Christian faith or by any patronizing of Jews.

Second, the phrase "Old Testament" is unfortunately too often understood as an affirmation of "supersessionism" (the idea that the New "supersedes" the Old and thus renders it obsolete). This assumption is evident in parts of the New Testament (see Heb 8:13 for example) and unmistakable in much Christian interpretation and practice (Soulen 1996). That, however, is not a correct or helpful understanding of "Old/New," for the phrase "Old Testament" seeks to testify to the close and intimate connection between the faith of Israel and the faith of the early church that attests to Jesus. Christian faith is both continuous with Judaism and discontinuous from it, and the matter admits of no easy articulation. It is clear in Christian understanding that Christian faith and the Christian reading of the New Testament cannot be undertaken without the Old, and cannot tolerate any notion of the superseding of the Old Testament. (This point has been clear in the church since Marcion, an early teacher in the church who sought to contrast the God of the Old Testament and the God of the New. The church has early and always refused such a teaching.) The "Old-New" linkage, then, does not suggest the disposal of the Old Testament in Christian reading but rather insists that the Old Testament is indispensably important in a Christian reading of the New Testament. It is clear that the Old Testament provides the categories of faith and interpretation through which the New Testament is to be understood and without which the New Testament cannot be faithfully and intelligently read. While these issues are complex and currently under intense discussion, for now it is sufficient for the reader to recognize that the Old Testament, as in "Introduction to the Old Testament," is densely loaded with interpretive possibility and problematic. The term "Old" is not merely a convention or a convenient label, but a thick reference that bespeaks much of the difficulty and the wonder of the church's relation to Judaism, a difficulty and wonder already amply attested by Paul in Romans 9–11.

2. An introduction to the Old Testament, a study of the *literature* of the Old Testament and a consideration of the *theological* claims it makes, is not to be confused with a study of either the *history of ancient Israel* or the *history of Israelite religion*. Nonetheless, it is also clear that one cannot understand the literature of the Old Testament or its theological claims without an interest in and awareness of the history of ancient Israel and of its religion. In simplest form, it is important to know that Israel's history in the Old Testament is characteristically presented in three identifiable periods:

1. The *premonarchial* period, from the beginning of Israel to the rise of David in 1000 BCE
2. The *monarchial* period, from the rise of David in 1000 BCE to the destruction of Jerusalem in 587 BCE
3. The *postmonarchial* period, after 587 BCE, a period that encompasses both the exile and the recovery from exile that led to the formation of Judaism and, eventually, to the emergence of Christianity.

This scheme is everywhere assumed in the Old Testament and becomes a convenient way to make sense of the literature as Israel reflects on its life with God in the world under the terms of various sociopolitical-economic conditions. While a close connection between literature and historical context cannot always be demonstrated, the literature, as an act of generative imagination, characteristically purports to be intentionally linked to concrete historical contexts.

It is clear that historical dimensions of Israel's faith and literature in the Old Testament are immensely problematic. Consequently the articulation of an introduction itself is equally difficult. Not more than two generations ago it was widely assumed among critical scholars that the biblical story line closely reflected the lived experience of historical Israel (see Bright 2000; Hayes and Miller 1986). Within recent decades, however, the emergence of new critical methods, together with fresh perspectives and new questions, have led many critical scholars to conclude that the story line given in the Old Testament is itself no reliable guide for "what happened." Indeed, we have no direct access to "what happened," though scholars continue that difficult investigation. What we have in the Old Testament, rather than reportage, is a sustained memory that has been filtered through many generations of the interpretive process, with many interpreters imposing certain theological (and other) intentionalities on the memory that continues to be reformulated. This is not to suggest that the Bible is historically unreliable, but rather that different questions must be asked of the dynamic interpretive process that eventuated in the Bible. Reliance upon extrabiblical evidence such as archaeological remains and inscriptions, moreover, has led many scholars to the conclusion that much of what is claimed as history in the Old Testament has no basis in verifiable fact. This judgment makes the story line of the Bible, to say it boldly, fiction.

While this judgment will for a long time remain in dispute, it is enough for now to recognize what is likely to be a very large divergence between "real history" and "claimed history," even as we recognize that what scholars now accept as "real history" is itself not a disinterested reconstruction of the past of Israel. For purposes of literary introduction, we may attend to the proposed history reflected in the text, while being alert for signals of the way in which real historical circumstance caused purported history to be inscribed as it is. The reader may be confident in attending to the literature of the Old Testament not only that ours is not a historical study, but also that the biblical text itself does not purport to be "history" in any modern sense of the term. Thus the literary offer as a vehicle for religious claims does not rise or fall with critical historical reconstruction, for the literature is not a product of *events*, but a product of imaginative *interpretation*. It will be a relief for some readers at the outset to be able to acknowledge that this literature of the Bible stands some distance from what modern people might call "history." This is not a failure on the part of the Bible, but a failure of modern interpretive categories that have been imposed upon the literature, categories that have turned out, surprisingly, to be incongruous with the literature itself (Childs 1979).

3. While the study of the Old Testament has been a largely historical enterprise for the last several centuries, only recently has Old Testament study been freshly addressed under the rubric of *canon*, an approach that offers an alternative to study under the rubric of *history*. The term "canon" attests that literature of the Bible functions as normative and regulative for a community. In Old Testament study the term refers to the list of books that came

to constitute the scriptural corpus of literature for both Jewish and Christian communities of faith. The Hebrew canon, normative for Jewish faith, is the subject of this introduction. The Hebrew canon, that is, the normative list of books, is organized into three distinct elements:

The Torah consists in Genesis, Exodus, Leviticus, Numbers, and Deuteronomy, traditionally termed "The Five Books of Moses" (or Pentateuch). This corpus of literature is received as having the highest scriptural authority in Jewish tradition and, derivatively, in Christian tradition as well. It was likely in its completed form by the fifth century BCE, that is, by the time of Ezra.

The Prophets as a canon consists in eight "books" divided into two groups. The Former Prophets include Joshua, Judges, Samuel, and Kings; the Latter Prophets are Isaiah, Jeremiah, Ezekiel, and the Twelve Minor Prophets (the last constituting one scroll). This corpus reached its final form by the second century BCE, attested in the book of Ben Sirach, and has a lesser authority than does the Torah. This consensus judgment is somewhat called into question by the evidence of the Dead Sea Scrolls, which witness to a more fluid situation.

The Writings includes a somewhat miscellaneous collection of eleven books:

> The three great poetic books of Psalms, Job, and Proverbs
> The "Five Scrolls": Ruth, Esther, Ecclesiastes, Lamentations, and the Song of Songs
> A revisionist historical corpus of 1 and 2 Chronicles, Ezra, and Nehemiah; and a single apocalyptic scroll, Daniel

This material reached its canonical shape and status only very late, likely in the Christian era, and possesses less of a canonical authority than the Torah or the Prophets, that is, "The Law and the Prophets" (see Matt 5:17; 7:12; 11:13; 16:16; 22:40). Readers should note that there is a distinction between the Protestant and Roman Catholic/Orthodox canons in that the latter includes a series of seven works called the "deuterocanonical" (that is, "second canon") books, also known as the Apocrypha. As the name implies, these texts are widely understood to be of secondary status in terms of their significance to the development of the Christian community's faith. Thus in this present study we will concern ourselves only with the main lines of the textual tradition.

The process of canonization, whereby this varied literature reached authoritative status for these communities of faith, is largely hidden from us. But it is clear that religious leaders and communities engaged in serious debate about which books belonged in Scripture. At the core, the leading literary authorities were obvious; at the margin, however, opinion varied. While the canon eventually received something like an official acknowledgment or promulgation, it is undoubtedly the case that canonization fundamentally reflects the tried and tested usage of the religious community. These books were recognized to be the most recurringly useful, reliable, and "meaningful," that is, judged to be true teaching. This does not mean in every case that they are the "best" books from a religious, moral, or artistic perspective, but that the community of faith was drawn to them. This list of books thus became the normative starting point and literary deposit from which arises the endless process of tradition and imagination whereby the community of Judaism is constituted and, derivatively, whereby the Christian community is given the resources through which to understand, affirm, and receive Jesus of Nazareth as the defining theological reality.

The matter of canon, however, is complicated for Christian usage beyond this disciplined Jewish list. The complication arises because a different Jewish community in Alexandria by the third century BCE had developed a much more open, much more extensive list of authoritative books rendered in Greek. This version of the canon, the Septuagint, from the outset was more expansive and less disciplined than the "Jewish canon," reflective of a different cultural, intellectual climate. Christian appropriation of Jewish canonical materials, eventually reflected in Roman Catholic usage, opted for the larger Greek canon. The Protestant tradition, since the Reformation in the sixteenth century, has returned to the smaller, more disciplined Jewish canon (thus the subject of this study), but has departed from the ordering of the Hebrew canon to follow the different ordering of the Greek list. Thus the Bible familiar to Protestant Christians is a mix of the list of the Hebrew Bible ordered according to the Greek-speaking tradition. The list of books in the slightly larger, Greek-speaking canon used by Roman Catholics (and not included in the Hebrew canon used by Protestants) constitutes the Apocrypha, books that are accorded deuterocanonical ("secondary" or halfway) status in Protestant usage.

What may interest us about canon beyond an understanding of lists and order of books, however, is that since the 1970s "canon" has come to be understood not simply as a historical development or a literary decision, but as a *theological* practice. That is, the development of the literary corpus, it is now recognized, took place through a theological impulse, a concern to shape the literature according to defining theological conviction. James Sanders has shown that the "canonical process" was in the service of a monotheistic conviction, even though much of the literature that became the Old Testament would not easily serve such a belief (J. Sanders 1976). Brevard Childs has shown that the shaping and editorial process of bringing the literature to its form was in the service of the core faith of the canonizing community (Childs 1979). Childs has gone even further to propose that beyond canonical process or canonical shape we may find present in the literature itself a normative canonical interpretation that coheres with the primary dogmatic convictions of the church (Childs 1993). In this perspective, the literature itself is, from the ground up, a normative theological statement. It is formed according to passionate theological conviction.

This latter argument, variously stated and greatly disputed, may alert the reader to a key awareness about the Old Testament: The historical claims of the text are in profound tension with the canonical claims now recognized in the text. Until the 1970s the historical claims dominated critical study, and "canon" was regarded as a late and unimportant feature of the literature. Now, for some scholars, the theological intentionality of the text is more important and roughly runs over what might be taken as historical. It tends to be the case for interpreters in church venues (including seminaries) that theological intentionality claims primary attention. In other contexts, like public universities, that prize "objectivity," the matter is viewed differently. Positively, such a tilt to the canonizing process is viewed by church-inclined readers as a major interpretive achievement. Negatively, such a process is viewed by scholars who resist church intrusion into critical study as an ideological distortion of the text. Thus one's verdict on the canonizing process is likely not to be an innocent critical judgment, either positively or negatively, but a decision reflecting one's stance toward the confessional claims of the Jewish and Christian interpretive communities. The matter is unsettled in current scholarship. It is in any case clear that the "final form" of the text is some distance removed from anything like historical reportage. The reader will need constantly to attend to the interplay of historical claim and canonical impetus in the study that follows.

4. The interplay of historical reportage and canonical formation is endlessly complex. The process of that interplay is the work of tradition, the defining enterprise of biblical formation, transmission, and interpretation that we may term "imaginative remembering."

The remembering part is done in the intergenerational community, as parents tell and retell to children and grandchildren what is most prized in community lore (see Exod 10:1–2; 12:26; 13:8, 14; Deut 6:20; Josh 4:21; Ps 78:5–8). One may assume that what is remembered is rooted in some occurrence. For example, the great exodus narrative surely has behind it some defining emancipatory happening. It is, however, an occurrence to which we have no access, and we cannot make certain the claim for its "happening." Remembering, moreover, is itself shot through with imaginative freedom to extrapolate and move beyond whatever there may have been of "happening." Sometimes that imaginative reconstrual is intentional, in order to permit the memory to be pertinent to a new generation. For example, it is possible that the exodus narrative (in Exod 1–15) contains exilic materials in order that the later generation of the sixth-century exile might understand the exodus memory in terms of its own emancipation from Babylon. Sometimes, surely, the imaginative construal that goes beyond "happening" is unworthy and untenable. Either way, the traditioning process of retelling does not intend to linger over old happenings, but intends to recreate a rooted, lively world of meaning that is marked by both coherence and surprise in which the listening generation, time after time, can situate its *own* life, rather than gaining direct access to a world long past.

This act of imaginative remembering, we believe, is the clue to valuing the Bible as a trustworthy voice of faith while still taking seriously our best critical learning. Critical scholarship for a long time has tried to separate "reliable remembering" from imaginative extrapolation, thereby reducing matters to a bare minimum (von Rad 1962, 105–15, 302–5). Current scholarship is in a quite skeptical mood: many scholars increasingly judge the "historical" claim of the Old Testament to be largely unreliable, or at least not provable, and often unlikely (Dever 2001; Finkelstein and Silberman 2001), not to mention loaded with ideological freight (Barr 2000). The recognition of these critical judgments is important and warns against making irresponsible claims for historicity of the text.

At the same time, however, one can judge that the imposition of modernist tests of reliability on the text has been deeply wrongheaded and has asked of texts what they did not intend to deliver. Thus what parents have related to their children as normative tradition (that became canonized by long usage and has long been regarded as normative) is a world of meaning that has as its key character YHWH, the God of Israel, who operates in the narratives and songs of Israel that are taken as reliable renderings of reality. Given all kinds of critical restraints and awarenesses, one can only allow that such retellings are a disciplined, emancipated act of imagination. We can note in passing that current skepticism about the text in some scholarly circles is also an act of interpretive imagination rooted in modernist positivism; we have, however, no wish to linger over that awareness.

The notion of the dynamism of the traditioning process is no new awareness in Old Testament studies. In the eighteenth and nineteenth centuries, in the matrix of Enlightenment rationality, the traditioning process was worked into a defining hypothesis concerning the emergence of Old Testament historical texts according to a series of proposed "documents" or "sources," thus the phrases "documentary hypothesis" and "source criticism." According to the most influential version of the hypothesis, which is still reported in many books, the ongoing tradition of Israel's "historical remembering" is marked by fixed accent points in the tenth, ninth, seventh, and fifth centuries BCE, represented in hypothetical documents respectively designated as the

Yahwist (J), the Elohist (E), the Deuteronomist (D), and the Priestly (P) tradition. More recent versions of the theory date J and E to the ninth century BCE, P to the eighth, and D to the seventh.

Each stratum of tradition relied on what was remembered, took what it wanted and could use, neglected what it would not itself use, reformulated and resituated to make a new statement. The final form of the text is a combination of these several major attempts at reformulating the core tradition of that memory.

That hypothesis of documents was governed by a notion of the linear, evolutionary development of Israelite religion that has since been called into question; but the dynamism of the process itself continues to be recognized, albeit in very different form. It was only in the mid-twentieth century that scholarship began to move away from "documents" to "traditions," but the point of the dynamism is the same in either case. The tradition, including its final form, is a practice of imaginative remembering.

In the traditioning process of telling and retelling in order to make faith possible for the next generation, each version of retelling (of which there were surely many in the long-term process) intends, perforce, that its particular retelling should be the "final" and surely the correct one. In the event, however, no account of traditioning turns out to be the "final" one, but each act of traditioning is eventually overcome and displaced (superseded) by a fresher version. The later, displacing form of the tradition no doubt is assumed to be the final and correct one, but is in turn sure to be overcome and, in part, displaced by subsequent versions of the memory. The complexity of the text evident on any careful reading is due to the happy reality that as new acts of traditioning overcome and partly displace older materials, the older material is retained alongside newer tradition. That retention is a happy one, because it very often happens that a still later traditionist returns to and finds useful older, discarded material thought to be beyond use.

II

The traditioning process that came to constitute the church's Scripture is not an innocent act of reportage. It is, in each of its variations over time, an intentional advocacy that means to tilt the world of the next generation according to a conviction of faith. We may identify three facets of that intentionality that can be taken into account in our study.

First, we have already noted that the tradition that became Scripture is a relentless act of imagination (D. Brown 1999; 2000). That is, the literature does not merely describe a commonsense world; it dares, by artistic sensibility and risk-taking rhetoric, to posit, characterize, and vouch for a world beyond the "common sense." The theological aspect of this imagination is that the world is articulated with YHWH as the defining character, even though YHWH in all holiness defies every attempt to make this character available or accessible in any conventional mode. That theological dimension of imagination—to render a world defined by the character of YHWH—is matched by a rich artistic sensibility that renders lived reality in song, story, oracle, and law. The artistic aspect of the text, about which we will say more in the following chapter, is not uniform and one-dimensional; in the narratives of Samuel, for example, or in the poetry of Job or in the metaphors of Jeremiah, we are offered "limit expressions" that render the "limit experiences" of the generation that offers its testimony and that invites "limit experiences" in the listening generation that would not be available without this shared "limit" language (Ricoeur 1975, 107–45).

Second, it is now widely recognized that the traditioning process is deeply permeated by ideology. The traditioning generation in each case is not a cast of automatons. Rather they are, even if unknown to us and unnamed by us, real people who live real lives in socioeconomic circumstances where they worried about, yearned for, and protected social advantage and property. Indeed, the traditionists surely constitute, every time, a case study in the Marxian insight that "truth" is inescapably filtered through "interest." And while Marx focused on economic interest, it is not difficult to see in the traditioning process the working of interest expressed through gender, race, class, and ethnic distinctions (Jobling 1998; Schwartz 1997). Because the text is marked by these pressures, it is clear that the text is open, in retrospect, to critique. As David Brown has seen, the later traditioning process may indeed circle back and critique the older, established textual tradition. In doing so, it is important to recognize that each subsequent critique of older tradition (including one's own critique) is itself not likely to be innocent; it in turn reflects social location and interest.

Third, the religious communities of Judaism and Christianity that take this text to be normative will affirm in a variety of ways that this text is inspired. In this affirmation, the religious communities go beyond critical scholarship, which in its characteristic skepticism avoids any such claim. These religious communities make this claim not because they are obscurantist or engaged in special pleading of a defensive kind, but because over time these communities have found these texts to be carriers of and witnesses to the most compelling offer of a meaningful, responsible, coherent life.

The term "inspiration" is not without its own complexity. If we recall the mention of "artistic imagination," we may for starters say that the biblical text is "inspired" in the way that every gifted artistic accomplishment is inspired.

It is recognized that the artist is peculiarly gifted and is able to move beyond ordinary capacity in an extraordinary moment of rendering. To say this much is to say a great deal: that the singers and storytellers and poets who constituted the Old Testament did indeed reach beyond themselves in an extraordinary way.

But when Christians speak of the Bible as "inspired," we mean to say much more than that. We mean to say that God's own purpose, will, and presence have been "breathed" through these texts. Such a claim need not result in a literalist notion of "direct dictation" by God's spirit, as though God were whispering in the ear of a human writer; it is clear that the claim of "inspired" is an inchoate way of saying that the entire traditioning process continues and embodies a surplus rendering of reality that discloses all of reality in light of the holiness of YHWH. Through that disclosure, which happens in fits and starts by way of human imagination and human ideology—but is not finally domesticated by either human imagination or human ideology—we receive a "revelation" of the hiddenness of the life of the world and of God's life in the world. And because we in the church find it so, we dare to say in the actual traditioning process with trembling lips, "The Word of the Lord. . . . Thanks be to God."

Now it will occur to an attentive reader that these three facts of the traditioning process—imagination, ideology, and inspiration—do not easily cohere with one another. Specifically, the force of human ideology and the power of divine inspiration would seem to be definitionally at odds. Precisely! That is what causes the Old Testament to be endlessly complex and problematic, endlessly interesting and compelling. The interplay of human ideology sometimes of a crass kind, of divine inspiration of a hidden kind, and of human imagination that may be God-given (or may not be) is an endlessly recurring feature of the text that appears in many different configurations. It is that interplay of the three that requires that the text must always again be interpreted; the traditioning process, for that reason, cannot ever be concluded, because the text is endlessly needful of new rendering. (A case in point is the way in which the biblical teaching on slavery appeared at a time to be "inspired," and now can be seen to be ideology [see Haynes 2001].) It is this strange mix that is always again sorted out afresh. It is, however, always a sorting out by church interpreters and scholars who themselves are inescapable mixes of imagination, ideology, and inspiration.

The traditioning process is endless and open-ended. We can, however, make this distinction. First, there was a long process of traditioning prior to the fixing of the canon as text in normative form. Much of that process is hidden from us and beyond recovery. But we can see that in the precanonical traditioning process there was already a determined theological intentionality at work (J. Sanders 1976). Second, the actual formation of the canon is a point in the traditioning process that gives us "Scripture" for synagogue and for church. We do not know much about the canonizing process, except to notice that long use, including dispute over the literature, arrived at a moment of recognition: Jewish, and subsequently Christian, communities knew which books were "in" and which were not. But third, it is important to recognize that the fixing of the canon did not terminate the traditioning process. All the force of imaginative articulation and ideological passion and the hiddenness of divine inspiration have continued to operate in the ongoing interpretive task of synagogue and church until the present day. In Judaism that continuing traditioning process (which makes its own claims for normative authority) has taken the form of the great Talmuds, midrashic extrapolation, and ongoing rabbinic teaching. In Christian tradition we may see the New Testament as an immense act of interpretation of the Old Testament that itself became normative for the church (Moberly 1992). Beyond the New Testament, moreover, interpretation has continued both under church authority as well as in scholarly communities that regularly have had a wary relationship with church authority. This ongoing interpretation has evoked interpreters who, in every generation and in every context of the church, have rearticulated faith in the intellectual categories and cultural environment where the church has lived. Thus, for example, the core claims of faith were articulated in terms of Neoplatonic Greek philosophy in the early centuries by the Apologists, in the categories of Aristotle by Thomas Aquinas, through humanistic "new learning" by the Reformers, and, in our own time, in the categories of Karl Marx in the work of liberation theologians. It is, moreover, the case that every so often the postcanonical traditioning process has come to exercise decisive control over the biblical text itself, as is variously evident in Roman Catholic, Lutheran, Anglican, or Calvinist traditions. Postcanonical interpretation characteristically yields a certain casting of Scripture, and thus on occasion— in the crisis of reform—the ongoing developed tradition is radically called into question by a fresh attentiveness to the canonical text.

It is in the very character of the text itself to require and generate ongoing interpretation that is itself imaginative and often laden with ideology. The very presence of "the book" in these religious communities bespeaks a kind of unsettled restlessness that characteristically "makes ancient good uncouth," including ancient interpretation that is rendered "uncouth." When we ask why the text requires and generates an ongoing interpretive tradition, we may first answer with David Tracy that it is in the character of any "classic" to be a durable source for new disclosures (Tracy 1981). While not from our perspective adequate, Tracy's formulation of "classic" is immensely important and helpful, for it recognizes that the Bible participates in the properties of

great literature that defies any single explanatory reading that is eventually
exhausted.

Beyond the claims of "classic," the faith claim of the church is that the Bible
as the church's Scripture is without parallel, for it is God-given—given to be
sure through the quixotic work of human beings—as originary testimony to
the truth of God's presence in and governance of all creation. Because it is
God-given, given as God characteristically gives through the hidden workings of ordinary life, the book endlessly summons, requires, demands, and
surprises with fresh reading. The only way to turn the book into a fixed idol is
to imagine that the final interpretation has been given, an act of imagination
that is a deep act of disobedience to the lively God who indwells this text. The
only way to avoid such idolatry is to know that the lively God of the text has
not given any final interpretation of the book that remains resistant to our
explanatory inclinations.

The traditioning process, when it is faithful, must be disciplined, critical,
and informed by the best intelligence of the day. But it must be continued—
and is continued—each time we meet in synagogue or church for telling and
sharing, for reading and study, each time we present ourselves for new disclosure "fresh from the Word." There are two postures that characteristically want to terminate the daring process of traditioning. On the one hand,
there is a mood in the church—sometimes linked to what is called a "canonical" perspective—that judges that the "true" interpretation has already been
given, and all we need to do is reiterate. On the other hand, Schleiermacher's
"Cultured Despisers of Religion" who live at the edge of the church often
fail to recognize the thickness of the traditioning process, and take the biblical offer at surface meaning, run the matter through the prism of modern
rationality, and so dismiss the tradition as inadequate. Either way—by confessional closure or by rationalistic impatience—one misses the world "strange
and new" that is generously, with recurring surprise, given in the Scriptures.

2

Narrative and Poetry

The Literary Art of the Old Testament

It is hard to deny that in some respects the Old Testament is among the most unliterary works of literature that we have. Biblical Hebrew narrative exhibits a style that often seems simple, even primitive, in comparison with other great works of world literature. And Hebrew poetry, lacking the strict metrical patterns of classical verse or the rhyme of later English poetry, has more often than not gone unrecognized *as* poetry. Yet once we become aware of the distinctive elements of both biblical narrative style and biblical poetic style, we can begin to appreciate with fresh eyes the rich literary artfulness of the Old Testament. Moreover, having knowledge of and appreciation for the literary style and conventions of the Bible may well facilitate a deeper engagement with the ethical and theological dimensions of the text.

THE NATURE AND WORKINGS OF BIBLICAL NARRATIVE

Saint Augustine, already in the fourth century CE, confessed that biblical literary style exhibits "the lowest of language" and had seemed to him, before his conversion, "unworthy of comparison with the dignity of Cicero." It is easy to see what he meant. For example, biblical *narrative* especially (things are very different with biblical *poetry*, as we will see below) works with a very limited vocabulary, and it often repeats a word several times rather than resorting to synonyms. Its syntax too seems rudimentary to modern ears, linking clause after clause with a simple "and" (what the linguists call "parataxis") that reveals little about their syntactical relation, instead of using complex sentences with subordinate clauses ("hypotaxis"). Notice, for example, the

17

dogged repetition of "face" and the run-on syntax in the following very literal translation of Genesis 32:21 (where Jacob is sending ahead of him a very large gift to his estranged brother Esau, in hopes that Esau will be placated over Jacob's earlier stealing of his blessing): "For he said, 'Let me cover his face with the gift that goes before my face and after I look upon his face perhaps he will lift up my face." And if modern translations tend to obscure these features, even when one is not reading the Hebrew one is bound to notice the paucity of metaphorical description, the brevity of dialogue, the lack of reference to the interior lives of characters, the limited use of figural perspective (that is, dropping into the perspective of characters within the narrative world), and not least the jarring concreteness with which God is imagined to be involved in human history.

Many of these features are elements of biblical literature's *economy of style*, or essential terseness. We may compare, for example, Homer's use of sometimes startling metaphors in describing a scene with the practice of biblical authors (all of whom are essentially anonymous), who by and large avoid such elaborate figurative language. Contrast this description in the *Iliad* of the death of a single, obscure Trojan charioteer—"Patroclus rising beside him stabbed his right jawbone, / ramming the spearhead square between his teeth so hard / he hooked him by that spearhead over the chariot-rail, / hoisted, dragged the Trojan out as an angler perched / on a jutting rock ledge drags some fish from the sea, / some noble catch, with line and glittering bronze hook" (16.480–85; Fagles trans.)—with the blunt recounting from Genesis 34 of the massacre of an entire city by two of Jacob's sons: "Simeon and Levi, Dinah's brothers, took their swords and came against the city unawares, and killed all the males. They killed Hamor and his son Shechem with the sword" (Gen 34:25–26). Indeed, biblical narrative tends to avoid description of any sort, metaphorical or otherwise. The principle applies, with some exceptions, not only to *physical* description—so that we are rarely told what either objects or people look like—but also, and more importantly, to the *inner* lives, thoughts, and motivations of characters in the narratives. It would be a mistake, however, to take this economy of style as an indicator of the Bible's essential simplicity or primitiveness as a work of literature. Indeed, it is primarily this terseness that lends biblical narrative its distinctive complexity as literature.

In beginning to think about the narrative art of the Bible one could do no better than to read Erich Auerbach's "Odysseus' Scar," the opening chapter of his book *Mimesis*, in which he compares biblical narrative style with Homeric epic style. Auerbach offers the first and best modern articulation of how the drastic terseness of biblical narrative is not just the absence of style but is in fact a distinctive and profound literary mode in its own right. Auerbach famously describes Homeric style as being "of the foreground," whereas biblical narratives are by contrast "fraught with background." In other words, in the *Iliad* and the *Odyssey* both objects and persons tend to be fully described and illuminated, with essential attributes and aspects—from physical descriptions to the thoughts and motivations of characters—there in the foreground for the reader to apprehend. But with biblical narrative such details are, for the most part, kept in the background and are not directly available to the reader. So, as noted above, we are very rarely given physical descriptions of either objects or people in the biblical narrative. (This contrasts with nonnarrative cultic or liturgical texts where, for example, we are given quite detailed descriptions of the tabernacle and its furnishings; see Exod 25–27.) What do Adam and Eve look like? We do not know. Abraham? Sarah? Moses? We do not know. As Auerbach puts it in his comments on Genesis 22, where God commands Abraham to sacrifice his son Isaac, it is unthinkable that the servants, the landscape, the implements of sacrifice should be described or praised, as one might expect in Homer: "they are serving-men, ass, wood, and knife, and nothing else, without an epithet" (Auerbach 1953, 9). Occasionally a certain quality is ascribed to some person or object: we are told that Eve perceives that the tree of knowledge is "a delight to the eyes" (Gen 3:6), and likewise we are told that Joseph is "handsome and good-looking" (Gen 39:6). But as a rule such minimal notations are given only when necessary to introduce some element that is important to the development of the plot. In the present cases the attractiveness of the tree of knowledge leads to the eating of its fruit (but what kind of fruit? We are not told, the long tradition of the apple notwithstanding), and Joseph's attractiveness leads, in the next verse, to the sexual aggression of Potiphar's wife and thus indirectly to Joseph's imprisonment. And even here one notices that one is not told what it is that makes the fruit lovely to look at or what exactly makes Joseph so beautiful.

Beyond a lack of physical description in the biblical stories, one notices too that descriptions of personal qualities are largely absent. That is, characterization is rarely explicit, but rather must be teased out of the narrative based on what characters *do* and *say*. The presentation of Esau and Jacob in Genesis 25 illustrates this nicely. It is true that we are told that Esau is "a skillful hunter, a man of the field" (v. 27), but the essential characterization of Esau as impulsive and unreflective, indeed almost animal-like, is conveyed by action and dialogue. Thus, coming in from the field to discover that his brother Jacob has prepared a stew, Esau inarticulately blurts out, "Let me eat some of that red stuff, for I am famished" (v. 30). Alter notes that Esau "cannot even come up with the ordinary Hebrew word for stew (*nazid*) and instead points to the bubbling pot impatiently as (literally) 'this red red.'" Then, after agreeing to trade his birthright to Jacob in exchange for some of the stew, Esau's impetuous, action-oriented character is suggested by the "rapid-fire chain of verbs": "and he ate and he drank and he rose and he went off" (Alter 2004, 131–32).

The character of Esau is starkly contrasted in the story with the character of Jacob. If Esau is all instinct and action, Jacob is all calculation and deliberation. The stew is prepared and waiting for the return of Esau from the field, and one cannot fail to notice the mercantile manner in which Jacob first suggests, and then demands formal confirmation of, the trading of the birthright: "And Jacob said, 'Sell now your birthright to me.' And Esau said, 'Look, I am at the point of death, so why do I need a birthright?' And Jacob said, 'Swear to me now'" (vv. 31–33, au. trans.). These initial thumbnail characterizations of Esau and Jacob will be fleshed out further two chapters later, in Genesis 27, where the blind Isaac is deceived into bestowing his blessing on Jacob rather than the intended son, Esau. The elaborate ruse carried out by Jacob, with, to be sure, the invaluable help of his mother Rebekah, in which he impersonates Esau, confirms his calculating ambition even as it adds outright deceit to his résumé of character traits. Jacob will become a consummate trickster as the story proceeds—though he will also, as an elderly man, be tricked by his own sons—but he is never actually *described* by the narrator as tricky or deceptive, in the way that Odysseus is described repeatedly in terms of his resourcefulness or Achilles in terms of his rage, for example, but instead has his character revealed by what he says and what he does. Esau, for his part, will play a lesser role in the narrative that follows, although his reappearance in chapter 33 is striking and in some ways unexpected. However both his inarticulateness and his utter lack of calculation are revealed by his response upon hearing that Jacob has stolen his blessing: "he cried out with an exceedingly great and bitter cry and he said to his father, 'Bless me, me also, Father'" (27:34, au. trans.); and again, a few verses later, "'Do you have but one blessing my father? Bless me, me also, Father.' And Esau lifted up his voice and wept" (v. 38, au. trans.).

By not directly revealing the qualities of character of the actors in the narrative, the narrator puts the onus of interpretation on the readers, who must work out on their own—albeit with hints given—what they think of these characters. To repeat, this is not the *absence* of characterization, but is a *certain mode* of characterization, and in fact a fairly complex mode at that.

We may best see the complexity of this mode of characterization, and indeed of the Bible's economy of style more generally, when it comes to the inner lives of the characters. Readers are for the most part used to having access in one form or another to the thoughts, feelings, and motivations of the characters about whom they read. Again, Auerbach on Homer: "With the utmost fullness, with an orderliness which even passion does not disturb, Homer's personages vent their inmost hearts in speech; what they do not say to others, they speak in their own minds, so that the reader is informed of it.

Much that is terrible takes place in the Homeric poems, but it seldom takes place wordlessly" (Auerbach 1953, 6). For instance, the tragic death of Hector at the hands of Achilles near the end of the *Iliad* (in book 22) has devoted to it (in the Greek) fourteen lines of lament by Hector's father, seven lines by his mother, and fully forty lines by his wife, Andromache. We may compare this with the brief notations of grief in biblical narrative. On the death of Sarah: "And Sarah died at Kiriath-Arba (that is, Hebron) in the land of Canaan, and Abraham went in to mourn for Sarah and to weep for her" (Gen 23:2, au. trans.). On the death of Moses: "And the Israelites wept for Moses in the plains of Moab thirty days; then the period of mourning for Moses was ended" (Deut 34:8, au. trans.). One might object that since both Sarah and Moses had lived long and fruitful lives their deaths lack the tragedy of noble Hector being cut down in his prime over the affairs of his less noble brother Paris, and thus inspire less intense expressions of mourning.

But even with more obviously tragic deaths we see in biblical narrative the restraint of the narrator, who acknowledges the grief of the survivors but refrains from allowing them full expression of it. We noted above, for example, Jacob's response to what he takes to be evidence of his young, beloved son Joseph's death: "A vicious beast has devoured him, / Joseph torn to shreds!" (Gen 37:33, au. trans.). In a scene that seems intended to characterize Jacob as an extravagant mourner, the narrator goes on to describe Jacob as rending his clothes and donning sackcloth and refusing to be comforted by his other children: "'No, I shall go down to Sheol to my son, mourning.' Thus his father bewailed him" (37:35, au. trans.). Yet even here the few scant lines in Hebrew do not come close to matching the sixty lines of direct lament over the death of Hector, not to mention the extended scene in book 24 of the *Iliad* where Hector's father Priam goes to the tent of Achilles to beg for the return of his son's much-abused corpse.

Consider also the notoriously ambiguous story in Leviticus 10 of the burning of Nadab and Abihu, the sons of Aaron. The reader is told that the two young priests brought "strange fire" or "alien fire" (*'eš zarah*) before the Lord, "and fire came out from before the LORD and consumed them, and they died before the LORD" (10:1–2, au. trans.). Moses very quickly offers a sort of cryptic theodicy, cast as a line of verse, in the face of the shocking event: "This is what the LORD spoke, saying, 'Through those near me I will show myself holy / and before all the people I will be glorified'" (10:3, au. trans.). No more laconic response could be imagined, both to the death of the young men and to Moses' extemporaneous theologizing, than that attributed to Aaron: "And Aaron was silent." Surely we are to imagine Aaron's grief as real and deep—indeed, a few verses later Moses forbids Aaron and his other sons to go through the public rituals of mourning while they are consecrated for service in the temple (10:6–7)—and yet all we are given is his silence. Unless one imagines this silence to indicate a complacent assent to what has just been witnessed, the narrator gives us, to borrow from Auerbach again, "a glimpse of unplumbed depths." It is, in short, a silence that is "fraught with background," a silence that demands interpretation on the part of the reader. Is Aaron feeling pure shock? Overwhelming sadness? Anger at God? Confusion or despair? Is his silence a rejection of Moses' statement of God's intent? And if so, on what basis? We are given no access whatsoever into the inner life of Aaron, and because we do not know what he is thinking we also do not know what motivates his silence.

It is with regard to this latter issue, the question of character *motivation*, that we may see the importance of recognizing the distinctively terse mode of biblical narration. As noted above in considering the story of Jacob and Esau, the narrator reveals very little about the inner lives of characters, instead reporting mainly action and dialogue, or what the characters *do* and what they *say*. If we are given little or no access to the thoughts and feelings of the characters about whom we read, then it follows that the motivation behind what they do and say is also largely obscure. The importance of this obscurity of motivation can scarcely be overstated for any literary reading of the Torah or for biblical narrative in general, since it more than anything else is what gives the literature its profound complexity as it forces the reader to negotiate the many possible ways of imagining the characters' inner lives. Let us try to justify this claim with reference to the literature itself.

We may take Genesis 22 as a classic example of the ambiguity of character motivation in the Torah. In a story that has never failed to engage the imagination of interpreters ancient or modern, God commands Abraham to take his son Isaac and sacrifice him as a burnt offering. Although a few chapters earlier we have seen Abraham challenge the justness of God's decision to destroy Sodom and Gomorrah, here Abraham says nothing in response. Instead, there is the narrator's terse report: "So Abraham rose early in the morning, saddled his donkey, and took two of his young men with him, and his son Isaac; he cut the wood for the burnt offering, and set out and went to the place in the distance that God had shown him" (vv. 3–4). Abraham's silent obedience here is often taken to be motivated by an untroubled and unquestioning faith in God, which, depending on one's perspective, may be seen positively as an expression of ultimate piety, or negatively as an expression of unfeeling religious fanaticism. But both interpretations fail to recognize the fundamental literary convention of the refusal of access to the inner lives of characters. That we are not *told* of Abraham's inner, emotional response to the demand that he slaughter his son does not mean that he *has* no inner, emotional response. Surely we are to assume that he does, but rather than describing it for us or allowing Abraham to give voice to it, the narrator leaves us guessing as to what that response might be and thus also as to his motivation for his actions.

Now, it is possible to fill that gap left by the narrator with an inner calm that reflects absolute faith, but it is equally possible to imagine that Abraham is feeling anger, disbelief, and even disgust (with God for demanding the slaughter? with himself for not protesting?). And however one fills the gap of Abraham's inner life initially, surely it is complicated by Isaac's calling out to him in verse 7, "Father!" and by the plaintive question that follows, "The fire and the wood are here, but where is the lamb for a burnt offering?" It is precisely because we do not know what Abraham is thinking or feeling that his brief response to Isaac's question ("God himself will provide the lamb for a burnt offering, my son," v. 8) takes on a deeply ironic double meaning. On the one hand, it may be read as a ruse, if not an outright lie, to deflect any suspicions that may be dawning on the son; on the other hand, it may be read as a straightforward statement of faith that a sheep will indeed be provided. It may even be the case here that the author makes use of the ambiguities of Hebrew's seemingly rudimentary syntax in order to signal the potential irony to the attentive reader. For there is no punctuation in the Hebrew text, and one may also construe the syntax to read: "God will see to the lamb for the offering: *namely*, my son."

To go back to Abraham's initial response to Isaac, we may see how what at first instance looks like wooden repetition may be a subtly modulated use of a key word or theme. When God first calls out to Abraham to begin the episode, Abraham's response is, "Here I am"; when Isaac calls in the middle of the episode, on the way to the place of sacrifice, Abraham's response is, once again, "Here I am, my son"; and when, at the climactic moment that the knife is raised over the boy, the angel of YHWH calls out, "Abraham, Abraham!" (22:11), his response is again, "Here I am." In each case the single Hebrew word *hinneni*, "here I am" or "behold me," is repeated by Abraham. To substitute a synonym for the sake of variety is to lose a concrete expression of what is certainly a central theme for the story, namely the anguished tension between the demands of God and the ethical demands of another human being (Abraham's own child no less!). Surely every ethical impulse demands that Abraham not kill his son, and yet this is precisely what God demands that he do. He responds "Here I am" to both God and Isaac, and yet he cannot be fully "there," fully present, to both equally. It is only with the third, very late, repetition of "Here I am" that the tension is resolved and Abraham is no longer caught between these opposing demands on his loyalty. One might say that Abraham's threefold response provides the underlying armature for the story, marking the beginning, the middle, and the end. Although the single word *hinneni* is literally repeated each time, it acquires a new depth of meaning—and certainly a new tone—with each repetition. And to the end of the story it remains the case that we are never quite sure what Abraham is thinking as he first travels in silence, then responds to his son, then binds and raises the knife, and finally sacrifices the ram instead.

If we do not know what motivates Abraham in Genesis 22, it is also the case that we do not know what motivates Isaac to make his inquiry as to the whereabouts of the sheep or what he is thinking as his father binds him and lays him on the makeshift altar. But by this point we are not surprised by this fact, since we have begun to see that the biblical authors make use of this convention in order to allow for depth of character and depth of meaning. It is perhaps somewhat more surprising to note that this convention applies to God too, who is after all a character in these narratives as well, and so the *literary* art of biblical narrative has distinct *theological* implications. What motivates God to demand the sacrifice of Isaac? The narrator refuses to tell us, though for any reader, religious or not, this must certainly be a compelling question.

We are told that "God tested Abraham" (22:1); but this does not give us an answer to our question. The sense of the word "test" (Hebrew *nissah*) is something like "trial" or "ordeal," and so God decides to put Abraham through an ordeal, presumably to test his mettle. (A comparison with the opening chapters of Job is apt.) But why, and to what end? Is it to find out how strong Abraham is under pressure? To see whether he values his son more than he values God? Does God genuinely learn something new about Abraham, about humanity, or about God's self through this test ("now I know . . ." [22:12])? Without knowing what motivates God or what God is thinking as the knife is raised, we cannot finally even know whether Abraham has passed or failed the test. Most readers assume that he has passed, but a few have dared to suggest that God wanted not blind obedience from Abraham but resistance—after all, such resistance was honored when Abraham argued on behalf of Sodom and Gomorrah—and that in failing to argue with God, Abraham failed to show the strength of character that God hoped to see (Wiesel 1976, 93–94; Fewell and Gunn 1993, 52–54). If such a reading seems strained, especially in light of 22:16, that it is nonetheless possible—if only just—witnesses to the profound but productive ambiguity of Hebrew literary style, which exploits to great effect its distinctive economy of style.

We could say much more about the literary art of Old Testament narrative, especially about the patterns or structures that biblical authors and editors have used to construct both individual stories and larger blocks of material, but we want to close by pointing out one final way in which the literary and the theological are bound up. We mentioned at the beginning of this chapter the jarring concreteness with which God is sometimes imagined in the

Bible as active in the world: God walks in the garden of Eden and enjoys the evening breeze; God shows up at the tent of Sarah and Abraham to promise them offspring; God destroys Pharaoh's army at the Red Sea; God inscribes with God's own hand the tablets of the covenant at Sinai; and in the final, poignant scene of the Torah at the end of Deuteronomy, God buries Moses after allowing him a vision of the promised land that he is not finally to enter. But if the Hebrew literary imagination is relentlessly *concrete* in its workings, including its imaginings of God, it does not follow that it is without *craft* or *nuance*. Indeed, divine agency and human agency are almost always imagined in these narratives as being inextricably but ambiguously bound together in such a way that neither is autonomous or effective in and of itself. For example, God announces to Rebekah in Genesis 25 that the elder of her twins (Esau) will serve the younger (Jacob); but two chapters later, when the time has come to deliver the blessing to the proper son, God has apparently left the matter to Rebekah to work out, which she does with great effectiveness. Joseph may declare in Genesis 50 to the brothers who, thirteen chapters and many years earlier had sold him into slavery, that "Even though you intended to do harm to me, God intended it for good," but the story also suggests that it is largely his own wits and talent, rather than any supernatural intervention, that allows him to survive and prosper in Egypt.

Even in the exodus story, where God's concrete saving action seems more tangible than anywhere in the Bible, the divine plan requires human agents for implementation. Thus after the flurry of first-person active verbs by which God resolves to liberate Israel from slavery ("I have observed . . . , I have heard . . . , I have come down to deliver them . . . , to bring them up . . . [3:7–8]), God shifts unexpectedly to the second person, saying to Moses, "So come, I will send you to Pharaoh to bring my people, the Israelites, out of Egypt" (3:10). Moses quite naturally responds, "Who am I that I should go to Pharaoh, and bring the Israelites out of Egypt?" God's answer is telling with regard to the interdependence of divine and human agency: "I will be with you" (v. 12). Who is it that liberates Israel—God or Moses? It is both. But even that answer is too simple, since the liberation of Israel requires not only the cooperation of God and Moses but of *Israel* as well. Thus Moses dutifully announces to the enslaved Israelites God's plan to liberate them, which God has again stated in a flurry of first-person verbs: "I will free you. . . , and deliver you from slavery. . . . I will redeem you. . . . I will take you. . . . I will be your God . . . , I will bring you into the land that I swore to give to Abraham" (6:6–8). The response? "They would not listen to Moses, because of their broken spirit and their cruel slavery" (6:9). The point would seem to be a sociological one: the people cannot be liberated before they are ready, and after generations of bondage and hard labor it will take more than promises to get them ready; only after seeing the very real power of Pharaoh broken by repeated plagues are the Israelites able to summon the energy to come out of Egypt.

Pharaoh himself is no less a site of this fundamental tension, in this case paradox, of divine sovereignty and human agency. On the one hand, *God* claims responsibility for "hardening" Pharaoh's heart so that he refuses to allow Israel to leave (7:3; 14:4); but on the other hand, Pharaoh is said by the narrator to have hardened *his own* heart (8:11, 28). And still other times a passive voice is used, so that Pharaoh's heart "was hardened" or "became hard" (7:14; 8:15; 9:4), thereby leaving the agency behind the hardening unclear. This shifting of agency allows the narrative to retain a sense of God's sovereign activity in history, while at the same time affirming the moral culpability of Pharaoh, whose repeated promise of freedom is never fulfilled and thus represents rather realistically the psychology of tyranny. Logically, we as readers may want to know, Which was it? Did God harden Pharaoh's heart, or did Pharaoh harden his own heart? But the story refuses to put forth one answer or another, giving us a "both/and" that reflects a pronounced trend in biblical narrative to render not only the inner lives of both humans and God but creation and history itself as unfathomably complex and finally unresolvable.

THE NATURE AND WORKINGS OF BIBLICAL POETRY

"If I feel physically as if the top of my head were taken off," Emily Dickinson once wrote, "I know *that* is poetry." Dickinson was, of course, somewhat more than averagely tuned in to the effects of poetry. In truth, poetry—even great poetry—often fails to take the top of one's head off, and even sometimes goes unrecognized *as* poetry. There is no more striking example of this than the Old Testament, which contains a distinctive body of poetry that has been, for two thousand years, only rarely and inconsistently represented on the page in the form of verse rather than prose. Though some passages are lined out in ancient and medieval manuscript traditions, these include not only ones that we would now recognize as poetry but also lists of names that are clearly not poetry (in the same way that the phonebook is not poetry just because it is lined out). And printed Bibles from Guttenberg on, until the twentieth century, represent most of the poetic sections of the Bible as blocks of text indistinguishable from prose.

The question of whether biblical poetry even exists has been around since ancient times, and it has been exacerbated by the fact that our primary models for what counts as poetry are drawn from classical literature, which was highly metrical (that is, marked by the regular alternation of stressed and unstressed syllables known as "meter"). Already in the first century CE, Jewish intellectuals like Philo and Josephus, feeling the need to defend their cultural heritage in terms of Greek and Roman ideals, went looking for iambs and hexameters in the Torah. And they were followed in this task by later Christian writers such as Origen (in the early third century) and Jerome (in the fourth and fifth centuries), who also assumed that if poetry existed in the Bible then it must exist in metrical form. The search for meter in biblical literature has been revived on occasion in the modern period as well, but it has never amounted to much, for the simple fact that ancient Hebrew verse is not metrical.

This lack of conformity to classical standards—as well as to virtually all poetry in the West until the nineteenth century—has no doubt been a major factor in keeping biblical poetry under wraps and underappreciated, but so has the Bible's status as religious literature. This status means that attention to literary *form* has been a low priority for interpreters of the Bible, eager as they have been to move to the *content* or the *meaning* of any given passage. There has been very little allowance in biblical interpretation for the possibility that, as Wallace Stevens puts it, "poetry is the subject of the poem."

A major breakthrough in understanding biblical poetry came with Robert Lowth's *Lectures on the Sacred Poetry of the Hebrews*, first delivered in association with Lowth's chair in poetry at Oxford and then published in 1753. Lowth's most lasting contribution, for good and ill, was his identification of *parallelismus membrorum*, or parallelism of lines, as the primary structuring principle of ancient Hebrew verse. "Things for the most part shall answer to things, and words to words," Lowth writes, "as if fitted to each other by a kind of rule or measure" (Lowth 2005, 205). From Psalm 114:4, for example:

> The mountains skipped like rams,
>   the hills like lambs.

Or from Song of Songs 8:6:

> Love is strong as death,
>   passion fierce as the grave.

Notice that "mountains" matches "hills," and that "rams" matches "lambs." And notice the strict parallelism of "love//passion," "strong//fierce," and "death//grave." Lowth admitted that many lines of biblical poetry did not display the same equivalence of terms that we see here, but nonetheless the recognition that lineation was based on the matching of two or three short lines in a couplet (two lines) or triplet (three lines) form, which did not depend on meter, opened the way for more sustained attention to such poetry *as poetry*, rather than just repetitious-sounding prose.

For two hundred years after Lowth nearly all attention to biblical verse was on this phenomenon of parallelism, and most especially semantic parallelism (or parallelism of meaning), which too often was reduced to the idea that the second or third line in a couplet or a triplet simply restates the basic idea from the first line. But recent scholarship has shown that the relationship between lines is more intricate and more interesting than this. Adele Berlin, Michael O'Connor, F. W. Dobbs-Allsopp, and others have shown that parallelism involves not only semantic features (a parallelism of *meaning*) but also grammatical, syntactical, and phonological patterns (generally not apparent in translation), and that complex syntactical constraints underlie the ancient Hebrew poetic line, which are not in the end reducible to "parallelism." Moreover, Robert Alter and James Kugel have shown that even when the relationship between lines looks to be semantically parallel at first glance, there is often a subtle dynamism in which the second line moves beyond the language or imagery in the first by making it more concrete, more specific, more intense, or more emotionally heightened. Thus, in the matched lines quoted above from the Song of Songs, *passion* is a more specific emotion associated with *love*; *fierce* heightens and intensifies the connotation of *strong*; and *the grave* serves as a concrete symbol of *death*.

Beyond the question of line structure, however, the cluster of other features that typify biblical verse has mostly been overlooked by scholarship of recent decades. But one can get a much richer sense of the distinctive workings of biblical poetic style by recognizing these features—features that can be seen more clearly when compared with the workings of biblical prose narrative.

As we saw above, ancient Hebrew authors developed a *prose* style that was especially suited for narrative (or storytelling) and that prefigured in important respects the style and techniques of both modern novelistic fiction and history writing. Virtually all other long narratives in the ancient world—from the Epic of Gilgamesh to the Babylonian *Enuma Elish* to the Canaanite epics to the *Iliad* and the *Odyssey*—take the form of verse, reflecting the oral origins of the epic genre. By casting their stories in the form of prose, biblical authors pioneered a "writerly" form of narrative that did not depend on the rhythms of oral poetry and that allowed for the development of a genuine third-person narrator, whose voice could be distinguished from the direct discourse attributed to characters within the narrative. It also allowed for a depth-of-consciousness and an opaqueness in its literary characters so that, as we saw above, readers are seldom told what characters are thinking or feeling at any given moment, even though it is often vital to characterization and to plot development.

Biblical poetry, however, is very different. First, formal differences mark the poetry as *verse* (instead of prose): not only lineation, but also a compressed syntax that tends to drop particles and pronouns in order to achieve the conciseness of the line. And biblical poetry is, to borrow Terry Eagleton's vague but appropriate characterization of poetry in general, much more "verbally inventive" than biblical prose narrative. The terse, straightforward style of biblical narrative means that it tends to avoid elevated diction or figurative language. But the poetry is filled with figurative language, from the mostly conventional imagery found in the Psalms, for example, to the more inventive imagination of the book of Job, to the double entendres of the Song of Songs. So the troubled fate of the psalmist is, often as not, imagined in terms of "the pit" that threatens to swallow or "the flood" that threatens to overwhelm; and God is imagined as a "rock," a "fortress," or a "shield."

As the suffering Job imagines blotting out the day of his birth, he both personifies and eroticizes it, as he imagines the night longing for the day, which, in his counterfactual curse, never arrives:

> Let the stars of its dawn be dark;
>   let it hope for light, but have none;
>   may it not see the eyelids of the morning.
> (Job 3:9)

Later, Job imagines God's enmity toward him in terms of the ancient grudge between God as Creator and the chaotic force of the personified Sea:

> Am I the Sea, or the Dragon,
>   that you set a guard over me?
> (7:12)

Answering Job, thirty chapters later, God returns to this image, but redefines and repersonifies the chaotic Sea not as an enemy combatant but as an infant to be nurtured:

> Who shut in the sea with doors
>   when it burst out from the womb?—
> when I made the clouds its garments,
>   and thick darkness its swaddling band.
> (38:8–9)

The Song of Songs, erotic poetry set in the alternating voices of two young, unmarried lovers, prefers a lush, bodily-based array of metaphors. For example, the male voice proclaims:

> Your two breasts are like two fawns,
>   twins of a gazelle,
>   that feed among the lilies.
> (4:5)

Or this, from the female voice:

> As an apple tree among the trees of the wood,
>   so is my beloved among young men.
> With great delight I sat in his shadow,
>   and his fruit was sweet to my taste.
>
> (2:3)

If line structure and other formal markers are enough to establish the presence of verse in the Bible, they still do not tell us much about its use or function. Again, a comparison with biblical prose is instructive, since one of the most striking features of biblical poetry is that it is relentlessly nonnarrative. Once ancient Hebrew culture had developed the flexible prose form for recounting stories, both long (e.g., Genesis, 1 and 2 Samuel) and short (e.g., the books of Ruth and Esther), it seems that verse was reserved for more specialized, highly rhetorical uses. For example, the prophets are most often represented as casting their messages in poetic form. Note the parallelism and figurative language in, for example, Amos's well-known cri de coeur,

> Let justice roll down like waters,
>   and righteousness like an ever-flowing stream.
>
> (5:24)

This familiar parallel structure is combined with hyperbole and a striking visual imagination (both very much lacking in biblical narrative, though common in the ancient epic tradition) in the prophet Isaiah's utopian vision of the future:

> The wolf shall live with the lamb,
>   the leopard shall lie down with the kid.
>
> (11:6)

Verse also seems to have been the preferred form in ancient Hebrew, as in so many languages, for the aphorism—the pithy and often didactic observation on the nature of the world—which, like poetry more generally, aims for a maximum of meaning in a minimum of words. The book of Proverbs is filled with such aphorisms in verse form, such as,

> A soft answer turns away wrath,
>   but a harsh word stirs up anger.
>
> (15:1)

For more skeptical versions of such aphorisms, one can turn to the book of Ecclesiastes, as in:

> All streams run to the sea,
>   but the sea is not full.
> . . . .
> The eye is not satisfied with seeing,
>   or the ear filled with hearing.
>   (1:7–8)

or,

> In much wisdom is much vexation,
>   and those who increase knowledge increase sorrow.
>   (1:18)

But one of the most interesting uses of biblical verse is as an early form of what will later go by the name of "lyric poetry," that intensely subjective, non-narrative, and nondramatic form that has dominated modern poetry at least since Wordsworth. This early form of lyric foregrounds two final characteristics of biblical poetry, both of which further distinguish it from biblical prose narrative. First, biblical poetry is invariably presented as direct discourse, the first-person voice of a speaking subject (a precursor of the modern "lyric I"). Again, ancient Hebrew narrative separates the third-person *narrator* from the dialogue spoken by *characters*, which is grammatically marked (by expressive forms and deictics, to use the technical terms) as direct discourse, whereas the narrator's voice is not (see especially Kawashima 2004a). Biblical poetry is also marked in this way; it is, in other words, always presented as if it were dialogue. For example, the biblical narrator will never be represented as speaking in poetry, but characters can be, as in the deathbed blessing of Jacob near the end of the book of Genesis (chap. 49) or the Song of Deborah in the book of Judges (chap. 5).

The second way that biblical lyric poetry distinguishes itself from narrative is in its willingness to give access to the inner lives of its speakers. If biblical narrative trades in opaqueness of characterization, biblical poetry fairly revels in the exposure of subjectivity. When biblical authors wanted to convey feeling or thought, they resorted to verse form. Obvious examples of this formal preference include poetic books like the Psalms and the Song of Songs, where the expression of passion, whether despairing or joyful, is common. We find also in narrative contexts briefer poetic insets that serve to express or intensify emotion. Take, for example, Jacob's reaction to the bloodied robe of Joseph, which is rendered as a perfect couplet of Hebrew poetry: *ḥayyah ra'ah 'akalatu / taroph toraph yoseph* ("A vicious beast has devoured him, / torn, torn is Joseph!"—au. trans.). The book of Job serves as an example on a much larger scale, beginning in the narrative mode and giving precious little insight into Job's thoughts or feelings. But when the story moves to Job's anguished death wish ("Let the day perish in which I was born, / and the night that said, 'A man-child is conceived'" [3:2]), narrative gives way to the passionate but finely modulated poetic form of chapter 3, followed by many chapters in verse form of Job's impassioned defense of his integrity.

T. S. Eliot's dictum, "when we are considering poetry we must consider it primarily as poetry and not another thing," might seem like a truism, but it is a sentiment that sometimes needs repeating. This is especially true when it comes to considering the poetry of the Bible, which has so often been treated precisely as "another thing"—traditionally as theology or as ethics but more recently, under the guise of literary criticism, as narrative. But biblical poetry is, in at once the most simple and the most complicated ways, *poetry*. To consider a biblical poem as poetry is to pay attention to its line structure, its status as direct discourse and the sort of speaking voice that it presents, its diction and imagery, and its willingness to give expression to thought and emotion in a way that biblical narrative rarely does. It is, in other words, to attend not only to *what* the poem means but also to *how* it means and to how it gets used. By paying such close attention to literary *form*, in addition to *content*, we honor those authors and communities that worked so hard to produce and preserve literature of a very high quality.

PART I

The Torah

3

Introduction to the Torah

Many interpreters are now returning—after centuries of hypercriticism—
to a view that the text of Genesis–2 Kings (excepting Ruth, following the
Hebrew Bible order) constitutes the "Primary Narrative" of ancient Israel
that funded the imagination and fidelity of Judaism. Such a judgment is quite
traditional and must ignore important distinctions, both critical and canonical. It must ignore the canonical distinction between the canon of the Torah
and the canon of the Prophets that indicates a radical divide in the literature
between Deuteronomy and Joshua at the death of Moses. It must, in turn, also
disregard the common critical distinction between the Priestly material that
shapes Genesis–Numbers and the Deuteronomic theology that derives from
Deuteronomy and that dominates the corpus of Joshua–Kings.

To the extent that we may entertain the notion of such a Primary Narrative,
these nine books (counting 1 and 2 Samuel as one, and 1 and 2 Kings as one)
offer an imaginative portrayal of Israel's memory that runs from the *creation of
the world* (Gen 1) to the *exile of Israel in Babylon* (2 Kgs 25). There is no doubt
that 2 Kings 25:27–30 voices a definitive literary, historical, and theological
ending. Given that ending, whereby royal Judah winds up in deportation to
an "unclean land," the Primary Narrative is an act of uncommon imagination
that dares to claim that the *story of the world*—of heaven and earth—culminates
in the deportation of the leading inhabitants of Jerusalem to a foreign land.
This imaginative construal of the "story of the world" evidences a profound
conviction that the "story of the world" is "our story," that is, the story of the
generation of Israelite exiles. Beyond that, the canonists dare to assert that this
self-centered conviction is an inspired truth concerning not only Israel but the
God of Israel: God's intention for the world has come to a deep and sad caesura
in this moment of the sixth-century Jewish exile. In any case, such an extended

narrative exhibits a shrewd interpretive capacity to bring together the largest truth of the world with the most concrete reality of Israel's life, an interpretive capacity that is uncommon but characteristic of the text of the Old Testament.

Even when we accept this notion of a Primary Narrative, we must slow down enough to make important distinctions, and so segment the narrative into its smaller units, distinctions that are noticed in the formation of the canon itself.

The Primary Narrative (Genesis–2 Kings) is decisively interrupted by the canonical distinction of the *Torah* (Genesis–Deuteronomy) on the one hand and *Former Prophets* (Joshua–Kings) on the other. That important distinction in the literature reflects both the hidden story of literary development as well as a different theological judgment about the normative character and authority of these two quite distinct canonical pieces. As we shall see, the interruption between Torah and Former Prophets is not only formal but substantive. It is at this break in the narrative that Moses dies: by ending the Torah with the death of Moses, the tradition means to assert that Moses is the normative character and teacher who vouches for the authority of the corpus of the Torah. This does not mean that Moses was the "author" of this literature in any modern sense of authorship, but that the literature claims the unrivaled authority of this character in the tradition. At this break point, moreover, Israel enters the land of promise (in Joshua). Thus the Torah of Moses and the life of Moses must conclude prior to entry into the land, for as founder he is explicitly prohibited from entering the land of promise (see Deut 34:4).

The Former Prophets (Joshua–Kings) reflect on *Israel in the land*, in contrast to the Torah, which presents Israel as a *pre-land* people passionately enroute to the land (J. Sanders 1972). In the present chapter, we will consider the Torah and defer until later a discussion of the Former Prophets. Nevertheless, it is clear that the two bodies of literature, subunits of the Primary Narrative, are intimately connected. The pre-land Torah looks "with eager longing" to the narrative of the land, and the land narrative of the Former Prophets looks to the pre-land literature as normative for life in the land. The dialectic of *not in the land/in the land* is definitional for Israel's self-understanding as given in these texts. It is this dialectic that makes the linkage of the two units in the Primary Narrative poignant and compelling, for understanding this dialectic is crucial for the theological claims of the Old Testament.

I

The Torah comprises the first five books of the Jewish and Christian Scriptures. In Christian usage the term "Torah" is characteristically mistranslated as "law" (based on the Greek *nomos*); it is better rendered as "instruction," that is, a teaching that gives guidance. In its final, canonical form, the Torah is the normative instruction of Judaism and, derivatively, the normative tradition to which Jesus and the early church regularly appeal. The Torah instruction is constituted by a combination of narrative and commandments, though it is not clear how the two relate to each other. A great deal of scholarly energy has been used in seeking to understand this relationship. Adele Berlin writes:

> Is the Torah a series of legal collections with narrative sections serving as the glue that holds them together, or is the Torah primarily a narrative, with some blocks of legal material inserted here and there? . . . Is the narrative the background for the laws or is the law a detail of the narrative? This is like asking whether in the perceptual puzzle the image is an urn or a human profile. In the Torah, there could be no set of laws without the narrative of revelation and no narrative of revelation without the laws. The laws would have no *raison d'être* without the revelation narrative and the revelation would have no content without the laws. While we need to continue to analyze individual laws and law collections, we also need to consider the possibilities of more profound meanings that the laws together with their narratives may evoke. (Berlin 2000, 25, 30–31)

Critical scholarship has spent long years of effort on the literary prehistory of the Torah, that is, the complicated traditioning processes that eventually arrived at the five scrolls that came to constitute the canonical, normative Torah. In sum, that phase of critical scholarship over a period of 250 years reached the conclusion that the Torah is constituted (a) by the use of a rich and complex variety of traditions that derive from many contexts (including ready appropriations from non-Israelite materials and cultures) and (b) by shaping and interpreting those materials, over time, through a steady, fairly constant theological intentionality. That is, the traditioning process is a sustained practice of *appropriation* and *transformation* of available materials. The outcome is a complex tradition, a product of an equally complex traditioning process that roughly—quite roughly—serves as an attestation to the character, purpose, and presence of YHWH, the God of Israel who is the creator of heaven and earth and who is the deliverer and commander of Israel.

It is evident, however, that this steady interpretive resolve does not everywhere fully prevail in the text that became the Torah, so that the Torah itself reflects ongoing tension between a *variety of materials* that continue to have something of their own say and a *theological intentionality* that seeks to bring coherence to the complexity and variety of the materials and, where necessary, to override and trump the initial claims of extant materials. More critical study (to be found in the academy) attends primarily to the *complexity and variety* of the materials, whereas more focused "church interpretation" gives primary attention to the *theological constancy* produced by the canonical traditioning process. Our judgment is that our reading must attend to both of these tasks and to permit neither to silence or depreciate the other. It is clear to us, moreover, that neither of these perspectives is privileged as more intellectually respectable, so that the demanding part of responsible interpretation is to take seriously both the critical attentiveness to the variety and complexity and the "canonical" impetus toward constancy and coherence.

It is an old, traditional assumption of Bible reading, reflected in New Testament attribution, that the Torah is authorized (and therefore "authored") by Moses (see, for example, Matt 19:7–8; 22:24; Mark 1:44; 7:10; Rom 9:15; 10:5, 19; 1 Cor 9:9; 10:2). We must recognize at the outset that such a traditional way of speaking of the "Torah of Moses" was a device whereby Israel credited its normative teaching to its most normative teacher. The claim for Moses did not entail the notion of "authorship" in any modern sense, for the tradition is interested in authority, not in authorship. The issue of "Mosaic authorship" of the Torah has been an endlessly vexing issue over a long period of time, and critical scholars have used much energy uncovering the complexity of traditioning that is covered over by the "authorship of Moses." We may mention four ways of scholarship that have been variously important in the study of that complexity:

1. Julius Wellhausen summarized and consolidated a long effort of critical scholarship in the "Documentary Hypothesis" (also known as "Source Theory"), proposing that the Torah reached its final form in a series of successive "documents" or "sources," each of which reflected and articulated a particular mode of Israel's religion. His great book, originally published in German in 1878, was the decisive presentation of the hypothesis that has dominated Old Testament scholarship for over a century (Wellhausen 1994; see Miller 2000, 182–96). The hypothesis was an attempt, in nineteenth-century categories of German academic life, to attest to and understand the complex traditioning process evident in the text itself. (For an updated version of the Documentary Hypothesis, see Friedman 1997.)

2. Hermann Gunkel sought to go behind Wellhausen's "documents" in order to recover the characteristic genres of oral communication underlaying the material that came to constitute the hypothetical documents (Gunkel and Begrich 1998 [original German, 1933]). By introducing formal categories of "myth, legend, saga, fable, and novella," Gunkel called attention to the artistic, imaginative dimension of the material that could not be regarded in any scientific way as "history." Thus Gunkel opened the way for an appreciation and study of the text that was not contained in the dominant historical categories of Wellhausen. It is an oddity of scholarship that it has taken over a century for the insight of Gunkel to impact study in the field in a major way.

It is Gunkel who pointed the way for "traditioning" as distinct from a more exacting notion of "history."

3. William Foxwell Albright, the premier figure in U.S. "biblical archaeology," presided over a major attempt to demonstrate that the biblical materials, matched to nonbiblical evidence, in large measure can be shown to be "historically reliable" (McKim 1998, 558–62). At mid-twentieth century, the enterprise of biblical archaeology was a powerful scholarly force in which theological interpretation of the Old Testament largely proceeded (even among the most critical scholars) on the assumption that the text reflected authentic history. That judgment was highly tendentious on the part of those who held a faith claim about the Bible. In the last two decades, the immense influence of that approach has been overturned; the field is now open to a profound skepticism about the historical reliability of the biblical text. It should be noted that this *skepticism* is potentially as highly tendentious as the earlier *fideism*, and the question of history continues to remain open.

4. Gerhard von Rad was perhaps the most influential theological interpreter of the Old Testament in the twentieth century. In 1938 he published an article that laid out the main lines of his approach, a perspective that was later exposited in his two-volume *Old Testament Theology* (von Rad 1966, 1–78; 1962; 1965). Von Rad proposed that the early "historical" traditions of the Old Testament began as a short confessional credo that was then regularly modified, expanded, and reiterated in new circumstances in subsequent generations. This approach made it possible to understand the traditioning process in all its dynamism. At the same time, von Rad was able to finesse historical questions by easily assuming the congruity between the "historical confessions" of the text alongside "history" understood in more scientific terms (Brueggemann 2001b, ix–xxxi). Indeed, it is the collapse of that uneasy compromise that has made "historicity" such an acute question in current Old Testament studies.

Each of these major scholarly efforts, each reflecting a certain cultural moment, has made an important contribution to our understanding of the text. Each of them, however, also reflects a mood of scholarship and a way of putting a research question that could not subsequently be undertaken by any scholar. That is, the particular interpretive question tends to belong to and reflect certain assumptions that do not persist over time. The gain of this scholarship is to understand (a) that the textual material is uncommonly complex and variegated and outruns our best interpretive categories, and (b) that interpretation, in every cultural setting, reflects a real world of cultural practice and of contested faith.

We may identify two newer approaches that go in quite fresh different directions, but that oddly converge in surprising ways. In 1979 two definitive books on method were published. Brevard Childs, the most influential Christian theological interpreter of the Old Testament in the United States, published his *Introduction to the Old Testament as Scripture*, in which he considered the "canonical shape" of each book of the Old Testament (Childs 1979). He proposed that whatever the prehistory of the literature may have been (à la Wellhausen and Gunkel), the "final form" of the canonical text is a major theological achievement. The traditioning process is one that led to canon, the production of a normative theological statement. Childs's accent, in contrast to older critical study, is on the theological constancy of the corpus. To be sure, Childs has been much criticized for seeming to disregard the complexity of the literature that critical study has noticed, and by seeming to find theological coherence too readily in the text. Nonetheless, Childs has generated a perspective from which church interpreters are able to proceed concerning the main theological claims of the text.

In the same year, Norman Gottwald published his definitive book, *The Tribes of Yahweh*, in which he offered a sociological reading of the Moses-Joshua traditions according to the categories of Marxian analysis (Gottwald 1979). The outcome of Gottwald's work is to propose that the Torah provides a militant YHWH-based ideology for the mounting of a social revolution whereby the "tribes of Israel" overthrew and destroyed the system of Canaanite city-states with their practices of economic exploitation. In that YHWH-based ideology, YHWH is understood to be the legitimator of a social ideology that intends an egalitarian or communitarian society, a society quite alternative to the conventional practice of "Canaan." Not surprisingly, Gottwald's radical proposal has been sharply criticized, both because of his historical conjectures and because of his reliance upon Marxian categories of interpretation. As one might expect, Childs rejects Gottwald out of hand, though Gottwald himself proposes a suggestive interface of their respective works.

For all of their differences, which are enormous, we may group Childs and Gottwald together—not only as the two most inventive approaches of the second half of the twentieth century, but also because, in very different ways, both Childs and Gottwald view the Torah in its final form as an act of *interpretive intentionality* that is deliberately shaped by the traditioning process and that intends predetermined outcomes for the community that commits itself to this scripting of reality. Childs understands the interpretive intentionality of the canon of the Torah to produce a community of obedience that is singularly committed to the will and purpose of YHWH. He will have nothing of Gottwald's direct linkage of faith to socioeconomic matters. Gottwald understands the interpretive intentionality of the canon of the Torah to produce a daring community of revolutionary imagination and action. Gottwald resists any theological absolutizing that is disconnected from life in the real world of economic-political contestation.

There is room, in our judgment, for both of these perspectives and, no doubt, in the church practice of biblical interpretation some will incline variously toward Childs's or Gottwald's presentation. For now it is enough to recognize that the canon of the Torah, as the outcome of a complex and, in part, intentional traditioning process, has produced a normative text as the ground for faithful Jewish imagination and practice and, derivatively, for Christian imagination and practice as well. While an understanding of the complex prehistory is useful, it is not of compelling importance for church preaching and teaching. What counts is the way in which a relatively constant *theological intentionality* is woven through and eventually made intrinsic to the *complexity of materials*. In this imaginative remembering, the notion of "Mosaic authority" is the thick label that signals Israel's conviction concerning YHWH. It is clear that human agents have been at work through the entire traditioning process. They witness to the will, purpose, and presence of YHWH, who remains inscrutably hidden in and through the text and yet who discloses YHWH's own holy self through that same text. "Moses" is the signal of faithful traditioning that attests that these scrolls are a reliable source upon which to ground faith and life.

It is a widespread assumption that the Torah reached roughly its final form by the time of the exile or soon thereafter (587–537 BCE), most probably reflected in the usage reported in Nehemiah 8:1 wherein Ezra read "the book of the law [Torah] of Moses." It cannot be demonstrated that this event refers to the completed Torah, but it is an adequate working hypothesis and an indication that the community was by then thinking in those terms. Thus the connection we wish to accent is the linkage between *Torah* and *exile*.

It is important to pause over the usage of "exile," which is not as simple as one might think (J. M. Scott 1997). The biblical narrative itself attests that the decisive leadership of the Jerusalem community was deported by the Babylonians away from Judah to distant areas in Babylon (see 2 Kgs 24–25; Ps 137; Jer 52). There they remained an identifiable community with high self-regard (as in Jer 24) until Cyrus the Persian ruler conquered Babylon and permitted a return of some Jewish exiles after 537 (see 2 Chr 36:22–23). This notion of "exile" has been recently challenged on historical grounds, to suggest that the reality of deportation was less decisive and radical than the biblical record attests, that the notion of "exile" is an ideological term designed to establish the pedigree and assert the legitimacy of certain elements in the Jewish community as the proper leadership for the reconstitution of the community.

The historical matter is disputed and need not concern us here. It is enough that some generative elements in the community of emerging Judaism, after the destruction of Jerusalem in 587, presented themselves as "exiles" who had to live and practice faith in a landless environment without the conventional supports of city, temple, or monarchy. Indeed, if the exile is not taken at full value as "historical," then it is yet another spectacular case of "imaginative remembering," an act that is never completely disinterested.

It may be that the final form of the Torah was not reached in the brief period of the Babylonian displacement, but rather in the subsequent Persian period during which there continued to be communities of passionate Jews far from Jerusalem. Either way, after the disruption of 587, under Babylonian or Persian aegis, Jews understood themselves to be exposed, vulnerable, and at risk without the visible supports of a stable homeland. For our purposes it does not matter greatly if the exile is "historical" as given us in the Bible (as we are inclined to think), or if it is an ideological self-characterization. Either way, displaced people needed a place from which to validate a theologically informed, peculiar sense of identity and practice of life. The traditioning process that produced the Torah thus strikes us as a remarkable match for displacement, so that we may understand "the Torah of Moses" as a *script for displaced community*. This connection greatly illuminates the fact, as noted above, that the "Torah of Moses" concludes in Deuteronomy 34 with the death of Moses (thus the end of the normative period) and Israel poised to enter the land of promise but still landless. We may believe that this now normative tradition was powerfully and peculiarly germane to a community that understood itself as exiles, poised to reenter the land but still landless. Thus the Torah came to have durable validity for subsequent generations in the community as canon.

We should not, however, miss the likely fact that in what may have been the moment of the initial acknowledgment of the Torah as canon, it was known to be an immediately practical and existential resource for this community. This community, seemingly without resources, asserted that this tradition was an adequate and reliable resource for its continuing life. It need hardly be said that the Torah has continued to be the primary resource for ongoing generations in the Jewish community that are characteristically displaced people at risk. Derivatively, the same claim for the Torah as primary resource is also true for Christians engaged in radical and serious obedience.

II

The Torah is then a normative resource, rooted in the authority of Moses, for the sustenance of a peculiar community of faith and life that is displaced and without other resources. The narrative traditioning process, propelled by great theological intentionality, was able, through great imaginative maneuvers, to fashion widely variegated and diffuse memories into a more or less coherent statement upon which this otherwise resourceless community could stake its life.

Before moving on to a consideration of the particulars of the Torah materials in the chapters that follow, we may identify five interpretive themes concerning this most normative script for exiles.

1. The Torah is constituted by *narratives* and *commandments*, the relationship of which is complex and unsettled. That the Torah is largely constituted by *narrative* is a reminder that to call this corpus "law," as Christians are wont to do, is a profound misnomer. The narrative materials of the Torah, closely analyzed by Gunkel and his cohort Hugo Gressmann, are complex and variegated in the extreme. (See Gressmann in Gunn 1991.) In canonical form, however, we may suggest that all of this material is roughly thematized as a recital of miracles wrought by YHWH in which unexpected transformative miracles characteristically happen because the defining character in this tradition is none other than YHWH, to whom the entire corpus attests.

As Gerhard von Rad has seen (von Rad 1966, 53, 55, and passim), Psalm 136 is likely a quite late psalm that summarizes in doxological form the main themes of the Torah materials:

> creation (vv. 4–9)
> exodus (vv. 10–15)
> wilderness leading (v. 16)
> seizure of the land (vv. 17–22)

The psalm is framed as thanksgiving (vv. 1–3, 26), thus a response of amazed gratitude for the recited series of wonders that have made life possible. The doxological reference of every verse, moreover, attests to YHWH's abiding steadfast love toward this community of "low estate" (v. 23) that lives always in the presence of enemies (v. 24). The practice of gratitude in a context of threat is characteristic of this community sustained by the Torah.

To be sure, this psalm is a belated, highly stylized theological reflection upon the Torah; it reflects a coherence that is not explicit in the Torah itself, for there is much in the Torah corpus that does not readily or obviously serve the primary story line. From a theological perspective, however, that same theological constancy of miracle and gratitude is implicit everywhere in the Torah materials where it is not expressed, and is to be accented in church reading, preaching, and teaching. Israel's life, characteristically at risk, is grounded in miracles of fidelity that lie deeply beneath Israel's capacity to enact a life of faith. The ground of the life of this community without other resources is *wonder*; the appropriate response to such wonder is *gratitude*. It is obvious that this doxological framing of lived reality, lined out in the Torah, constitutes an immense act of counterimagination that refuses to yield to the evident harsh reality of circumstance.

2. The complex corpus of narratives in the Torah is matched by a complex corpus of *commandments*, issued, according to canonical form, to and through Moses at Sinai. It is sometimes suggested that the single command from Sinai is Exodus 20:2, "you shall have no other gods before me," and that all the rest of the commandments are exposition of that command. The God who readily enacts life-sustaining wonders is the God who summons the recipients of those life-sustaining wonders to complete, uncompromising response in obedience. The God who gives is the God who commands; Israel's traditioning process continues to exposit and interpret the singular command of Sinai in order to bring every phase of life, personal and public, under obedience to YHWH and to determine what particular form obedience may take amid the vagaries of life, where matters of obedience are not clear.

The commands of Sinai operate in the life of listening Israel as intentional and self-conscious acts of discipline whereby this community at risk may sustain itself in its wonder and gratitude, in its peculiar identity as a people living from miracles. The Israelites knew concretely that if Israel did not have specific disciplines as a way of navigating its demanding cultural environment, it would soon or late helplessly and hopelessly submit to the commands of another lord, Pharaoh of Egypt or Nebuchadnezzar of Babylon or Cyrus of Persia. And when Israel abandoned its YHWH-given disciplines and subscribed to the requirements of another lord, it would soon cease to be the people of YHWH. It is to be noted concerning the commands that a conventional Christian stereotype of "Jewish legalism" completely misses the point of what the commands intend and what they effect (E. Sanders 1977). There is little doubt that such dismissive caricatures of the commands of the Torah on the part of Gentile culture have succumbed to Enlightenment notions of freedom that culminate not in covenantal fidelity but in autonomy, a posture from which it is impossible to maintain a distinct, primal communal identity.

3. This Torah is a normative *act of imagination* that serves to sustain and legitimate a distinct community of gratitude and obedience. That distinct community, whether in the Assyrian, Babylonian, or Persian period, lived among cultural pressures and political powers that had no appreciation of its distinctiveness, no doubt found that distinctiveness at best an inconvenience and, if possible, would have abrogated it. The risk and threat to this distinctive community in exile, however, was not primarily external pressure. Much more likely the threat to the future of the community, with its peculiar wonder and its particular gratitude, was the internal reality that the world of

Jewishness, sustained by an imaginative traditioning process, was too costly and demanding for some of its members. Thus the endless pressure of the easier option of dominant culture would eventually erode Jewishness. There is evidence that some in the community readily joined the dominant culture and became economically successful in doing so. We may anticipate, moreover, that some ended in despair, no longer able to make the courageous interpretive connection from remembered wonder to anticipated wonder. Thus we may imagine that the sustained community of Jews who held to the tradition without compromise was a small, disciplined, intentional group—perhaps elite in learning or authority or economics or all of the above—who became the nucleus of emerging Judaism. Even that minority, however, could not have been sustained without this tradition of normative miracles and disciplines of command, so that we may conclude that the Torah is the God-given strategy through which a faithful community at risk is sustained.

4. If the requirements of exile were costly and demanding for adults who went deep into memory and so sustained hope (see Lam 3:21–24), we may imagine that the *transmission to the next generation* of this radical, buoyant distinctiveness was urgent and deeply problematic. The young, who did not after a while remember the ancient glories of Israel, were surely candidates for membership in the dominant culture of the empire at the expense of this distinctiveness. It is likely that the Torah is peculiarly aimed at the young, in order to invite them into this distinct identity of wonder, gratitude, and obedience.

We may notice two uses that suggest this intergenerational crisis to which the community attended:

In Exodus 12–13 there is a pause in the narrative in order to provide detailed guidance for the celebration of the Passover that will remember the exodus as here narrated. It is curious that in the very telling of this defining wonder of deliverance, the tradition pauses in that telling to provide for subsequent celebrations. It is, moreover, noteworthy that while Christians tend to glide over these two chapters of instruction easily and quickly, Jewish readers give primary attention to this material of instruction, for it is the repeated celebration of the memory of the exodus that sustains Jewish identity when it is under threat from a dominant culture (Neusner 1987). One suspects that the tradition pauses for so long and goes into such detail about celebration because the inculcation of the young was urgent and could not wait, not even until the end of the narrative of deliverance. The instruction, in its final form, aims at the young in exile who may be ready to turn away from the community into dominant culture. Thus "Moses" three times focuses precisely on the children:

> And when your children ask you, "What do you mean by this observance?" you shall say, "It is the passover sacrifice to the LORD, for he passed over the houses of the Israelites in Egypt, when he struck down the Egyptians but spared our houses." (Exod 12:26–27)

> You shall tell your child on that day, "It is because of what the LORD did for me when I came out of Egypt." It shall serve for you as a sign on your hand and as a reminder on your forehead, so that the teaching of the LORD may be on your lips; for with a strong hand the LORD brought you out of Egypt. (13:8–9)

> When in the future your child asks you, "What does this mean?" you shall answer, "By strength of hand the LORD brought us out of Egypt, from the house of slavery. When Pharaoh stubbornly refused to let us go, the LORD killed all the firstborn in the land of Egypt, from human firstborn to the firstborn of animals." (13:14–15)

The question asked by the child is highly stylized, as in contemporary Passover celebrations. Behind this stylization, however, the child may be ignorant and unaware and really want to know; or perhaps the question is posed skeptically and defiantly. Either way, the normative tradition provides what is meant to be a compelling response to the child.

In parallel fashion, Michael Fishbane has commented on Deuteronomy 6 that the children here are "distemporaries," contemporaries disinclined to embrace the defining tradition (Fishbane 1979, 81–82):

> When your children ask you in time to come, "What is the meaning of the decrees and the statutes and the ordinances that the LORD our God has commanded you?" then you shall say to your children, "We were Pharaoh's slaves in Egypt, but the LORD brought us out of Egypt with a mighty hand." (Deut 6:20–21)

Clearly the tradition of Deuteronomy aims to recruit the young into a distinct lore of wonder and a distinctive discipline of gratitude that issues in visible obedience (Brueggemann 2001a, 81–93).

5. Thus the Torah provides the materials for the social construction of reality and for socialization of the young into *an alternative world* where YHWH lives and governs. We cannot overstate that the Torah, in its final, normative form, is an act of faithful imagination that buoyantly and defiantly mediates a counterworld that is a wondrous, demanding alternative to the world immediately and visibly at hand. The world visibly and immediately at hand is characteristically a world that has no patience with Jews or with the God of the Jews, that has no tolerance for wonder when the world can be managed, no appreciation for gratitude when the world can be taken in self-sufficiency,

and certainly no readiness for obedience when the world is known to be an arena for autonomy.

While we Christians are accustomed in Western Christendom to take the Bible as the ultimate source of our given world, the Torah is recurringly a contradiction of the world we regularly regard as given. It was so in the ancient world of hostile powers with their cultural hegemony where social givenness resisted the rule of YHWH. It is, moreover, surely so in the modern world of Enlightenment rationality or in the postmodern world of fragmentation and its privatization of meaning.

It has been a characteristic task of Jewish teaching, nurture, and socialization to invite the young into the world of miracle, and so to resist assimilation. Only of late have alert Christians in Euro-American contexts noticed that the challenge that has always been before Jews is now a fresh challenge for Christians as well. As the Western world has been perennially hostile to the claims of Jewish faith, so the emerging contemporary world of commodity grows more signally hostile to the claims of Christian faith as well. As has not been the case in the long Christian hegemony of the West, now the church is having to think and act to maintain a distinct identity for faith in an alien cultural environment. While the church will characteristically attend to the New Testament in such an emergency, a study of the Torah already alerts us to the resources for this crisis that are older and deeper than the New Testament. The Jews in exile reported themselves dismayed about singing the songs of Zion in a strange land (Ps 137:1–3). And now Christians face that same issue. The liberal Christian temptation is to accommodate dominant culture until faith despairs. The conservative Christian temptation is to fashion an absoluteness that stands disconnected from the dominant culture. Neither of these strategies, however, is likely to sustain the church in its mission. More likely, we may learn from and with Jews the sustaining power of imaginative remembering, the ongoing, lively process of traditioning that is sure to be marked by ideological interest that, in the midst of such distinctiveness, may find fresh closures of reality not "conformed to this world." The preaching, teaching, and study of the Torah is in order to "set one's heart" differently, to trust and fear differently, to align oneself with an alternative account of the world (Little 1983). All this Israel fashioned and practiced—at once *imaginatively* resolved, *ideologically* driven, and *inspired* beyond interest—under the large, long, fierce voice of Moses.

4

Genesis 1–11

Cosmic Miracles in Contradiction

The materials in Genesis 1–11 constitute an especially rich theological and literary resource in the Old Testament. From the grandly resonant creation narrative in chapter 1 ("In the beginning when God created the heavens and the earth . . ."), to the paradise lost of the Eden story in chapters 2 and 3, to the tragedy of the first murder in chapter 4, to the shocking destruction by flood in chapters 6–9, to the doomed heights of human ingenuity in the tower of Babel story in chapter 11, this opening section of Genesis is filled with some of the most memorable, larger-than-life biblical stories. The talking snakes, worldwide destruction, nine-hundred-year-old ancestors, and towers reaching to heaven represent a world that would have been no less fantastic to an ancient reader than it is to us moderns. In this respect, these chapters offer an exception to the nascent realism of classical Hebrew narrative, which we explored in the introductory chapter on biblical narrative and poetry. Rather, in their final, canonical form, they function to frame the more concrete historical materials of the Old Testament in a cosmic perspective and, in sum, they constitute a brief theological history of the world. As such, they provide the complex, problematic environment in which Israel's faith and life are to be understood.

Two long-standing critical problems about chapters 1–11 need to be noted at the outset. First, it is evident that some of these materials have been appropriated by Israel from older, well-developed cultures. In some cases, we have available parallel texts that are older and that evidence the antecedents to the biblical texts. These texts, moreover, have been formed, used, and transmitted in the great cultic centers of major political powers. They functioned in those contexts, surely liturgically, as founding statements for society, authorizing, legitimating, and ordering certain modes of social relationships and certain forms of social power. For a long period, since Hermann Gunkel at the beginning of the twentieth century, scholars have referred to these materials, both in the Old Testament and in their cultural antecedents, as "myths." The usage of that term does not imply falsehood, as the term might be taken popularly. Rather, after the manner of Joseph Campbell, the term refers to founding poetic narratives that provide the basic self-understanding of a society and its raison d'être, foundational formulations of elemental reality that are to be regularly reiterated in liturgical form in order to reinforce claims of legitimacy for the ordering of society. The poetic narratives characteristically portray great founding events in which "the gods" are the key actors and the actions undertaken are primordial in that they precede any concrete historical data. The Old Testament clearly emerged in a cultural world where founding myths were commonly shared from one society to another. It is evident that Israel readily participated in that common cultural heritage and made use of the same narrative materials as were used in other parts of that common culture.

Second, as elsewhere in pentateuchal studies, scholars have been able to detect several strands of tradition that, in the terms set by Julius Wellhausen, are recognized as the hypothetical Priestly (P) and Yahwist (J) sources (Wellhausen 1994). The entwining of these two interpretive strands operates in two quite distinct ways in this material. On the one hand, in the creation materials the two strands are kept distinct from each other, each complete in itself, so that Genesis 1:1–2:4a is assigned to the P source and 2:4b–3:24 to J. The two creation traditions stand alongside each other, each with its own integrity. On the other hand, in the extended flood narrative of 6:5–9:17, the two strands are interwoven into a remarkable literary coherence with 6:5–8; 7:1–12; and 8:20–22 forming the basis of J, and 6:9–22; 7:13–16; 8:14–19; and 9:1–17a the primary articulation of P. It is not necessary for us to delineate the two traditions in detail. It is enough to recognize that the final form of the text is complex, the outcome of a long-term traditioning process wherein different interpretive moments and perspectives rearticulated the ancient memory in terms usable in different contexts.

The prehistory of these canonically shaped chapters in terms of non-Israelite antecedent materials, on the one hand, and a diversity of traditional Israelite sources, on the other hand, is well established and is not in dispute. That prehistory, while interesting, is perhaps not especially important for theological interpretation of the final form of the text beyond the important awareness that biblical literature existed not in a cultural vacuum but in lively engagement with its context. Still, one can get a sense of the distinctiveness of Israel's vision of the cosmos and of humanity's place in it by comparing the Priestly account in Genesis 1 with, for example, the Mesopotamian creation story known as *Enuma Elish*.

The materials of these chapters are rich and varied, whether stemming from two main sources (P and J) or from a variety of antecedent sources. The easiest distinction to make with regard to the form of the material is between *narrative* and *genealogy*. The genealogies are in chapters 5, 10, and 11. They reflect kinship groups as a way of establishing rootage and legitimacy. It is clear, however, that these genealogies are not to be taken simply as reportage on kinship, but that kinship is used in them metaphorically to characterize many other relationships, social, political, and religious. Thus "kinship" is a way of speaking about networks of power, legitimacy, and loyalty. In some phases of scholarship these genealogies were unfortunately misunderstood when taken with uncritical literalness, when in fact they reflect many serious and defining relationships that are not those of either family or kin. The shockingly long life spans assigned to ancestors in chapter 5, moreover, strike us as fantastic. When those ages are compared with the older sources, such as the Sumerian King List, however, it is evident that Israel's genealogies are sobered and drawn more closely to lived reality, as the life spans are radically shortened in Israelite versions.

The narratives of these chapters include several types of stories, some of which have not been especially important for subsequent interpretive reflection. Some materials are *etiologies*, that is, stories told in order to explain the cause or origin of something extant in culture (see 4:17–25 on the origins of cities, tools, and musical instruments; and 9:18–28 on the origin of wine and of culturally different peoples). The brief narrative of 6:1–4, which seems to reflect a mythical tradition left in its quite primitive form, became, in a later time, a rich source of speculative reflection, but that reflection was not much connected to the normative traditioning of the faith community. The primary accent in theological interpretation has been placed especially upon the creation texts of 1:1–2:4a and 2:4b–25 with its related narrative in 3:1–24, the narrative of Cain and Abel (4:1–16), the great flood narrative (6:5–9:17), and the account of the tower of Babel (11:1–9). Each of these narratives reflects older ancient Near Eastern traditions, so that it is impossible to ask questions about historicity. Rather, these materials may better be understood as complex, artistic attempts to articulate the most elemental presuppositions of life and faith in Israel, attempts that understood the world in a Yahwistic way. The end result of the interpretive process is a text that provided an imaginative context for the emergence of Israel in the midst of older cultural claims, visions, and affirmations.

The key issue in reading these texts according to the central traditions of church interpretation is to see that the canonizing process of editing and traditioning has taken old materials and transposed them by their arrangement into something of a theological coherence that is able to state theological affirmations and claims that were not intrinsic to the antecedent materials themselves. We may suggest that the materials have been shaped in order to make the following statements possible:

1. The two creation narratives, in very different modes, articulate that the world ("heaven and earth") belongs to God, is formed and willed by God, is blessed by God with abundance, is to be cared for by the human creatures who are deeply empowered by God but who are seriously restrained by God. The creation narratives are an affirmation of the goodness of the world intended by God (see below).

2. The narratives of 3:1–24 and 4:1–16, immediately after the affirmation of creation, attest to the profound problematic that is inherent in creation. Creation is said to be recalcitrant and resistant to God's good intention for the world. This deep, elemental disorder, narratively instigated by the serpent and rooted in disobedience, is enacted as human violence; it is, moreover, reinforced by the odd distortion reported in 6:1–4 wherein the "sons of God" and the "daughters of humans" entangle inappropriately.

3. The flood narrative sits at the center of this material as the great disruption of creation. The waters of the flood are understood to be the great primordial power of chaos that now endangers life on the earth at the behest of the Creator God. That is, the chaotic waters are here not opposed to the will of the Creator, but are an instrument of the will of the Creator. It is a remarkable and deeply freighted moment when God is "sorry" for creation and resolves to "blot out" human beings, thus promptly proposing to abrogate the initial endowment of humans in the creation story (6:6–7).

While the flood itself is an assertion of God's wholesale judgment against creation, the biblical narrative is primarily interested in the exception of Noah, "a righteous man." With his family Noah becomes the survivor of the flood and the first of the new humanity that appears post-flood and, according to 9:6, is still "in the image of God" (on which see 1:26; 5:1–2). Thus the deep disruption of the flood is not a total disruption. The flood narrative, for all of the destruction that it articulates, culminates in the divine promise that guarantees the working of creation in life-giving ways (8:22), and the divine promise of covenantal faithfulness toward the creation for all time to come (9:15–17).

4. The narrative material ends in the narrative of 11:1–9, a final statement of human arrogance that challenges God and that evokes God's harsh response. The four "narratives of contradiction"—Genesis 3, 4, 6:5–9:17, and 11:1–9—articulate a steadily intensifying recalcitrance against the will of the Creator that each time evokes God's harsh response (Miles 1995, 128–46). The generous will of the Creator will not finally be mocked and will not be overcome by creaturely recalcitrance.

For all of that narrative assertion of resistance to the Creator God, one can observe that, alongside a response of anger from God toward the disobedient, in these narratives God also acts graciously and protectively to curb the destructiveness enacted and evoked by the human creatures. Thus after the harsh judgment on the man and woman, God clothes the two of them in order to cover over their newly felt shame (3:21). After the expulsion of Cain, the murderer, God marks Cain in order to protect him from murder in turn (4:15). As noted, the destructive force of the flood willed by God is unexpectedly concluded with divine promises (8:22; 9:8–17). This sequence of narratives ends stunningly with the concluding judgment of 11:1–9 without a compensatory counterpoint from God. As Gerhard von Rad has seen, it is as though the entire narrative complex is designed so that the reading community of faith is left waiting for the appearance of Israel in the world, an appearance accomplished by Abraham and his barren wife, Sarah (11:30; 12:1–3; von Rad 1966, 67).

The sum of these narrative parts constitutes a remarkable theological statement. What may have been various myths of origin is now transposed into a theological statement of divine judgment and divine rescue, rescue and judgment being the defining categories for the God of Israel and for God's impingement upon the world in which Israel lives. In that transposed form, then, this material is no longer interested in origins and in the sort of generic religious questions that are endlessly fascinating. Now, rather, the text is an attestation to the main themes of Israel's faith in God.

Since judgment and rescue form the focal points for God's presence and activity in this material, it is important to recognize that while God readily enacts both judgment and rescue in completely free ways, alongside this theological pairing the sum of the material attests as well to the recurring disobedience, arrogance, and violence that profoundly contradict God's way in the text. The capacity to state in this (for Israel) "originary text" this elemental recalcitrance is an astonishing interpretive achievement. Thus the eleven chapters, taken all together, attest that the will and purpose of the Creator God are sovereign, but that sovereignty is deeply and categorically under assault from the outset. This assertion draws close indeed to the lived reality of the world, then and now, in which it is unmistakably clear that creation is in contradiction.

This way of beginning the Bible, moreover, by appeal to creation, prepared the way for the primal drama of the Bible, namely, redescription or the restoration and mending of a scarred, broken creation to the intent of the Creator. These chapters thus make a fundamental theological affirmation, but they also prepare the way for what is to come. In God's own way God negates recalcitrant power present in creation to bring human creatures to obedience that makes the world livable. We should note that the canonical traditions managed to make this claim precisely by the utilization of older, mythic materials that in their antecedent functions were remote from such claims and affirmations.

It will be useful to consider in some closer detail the two dominant narrative clusters in this material: the creation texts and the flood narrative.

THE CREATION TEXTS

While Genesis 1–2 draw a lot of interpretive attention because they stand first in the biblical text, they probably ought to be understood in terms of an older, already extant liturgical tradition on creation. The primary and proper context in which Israel articulated its creation faith is in doxology, the public, liturgical practice of lyrical, poetic utterance whereby Israel sings its awe and wonder about the glory and goodness of God's creation (see, for example, Pss 19, 104, 145, 148). Our term "creation stories" is to be understood in the context of that exuberant liturgical tradition.

Genesis 1:1–2:4a

This text is a solemn, stately, ordered, and highly symmetrical narrative that reads almost like a liturgical antiphon. It has some clear affinities to the well-known *Enuma Elish*, an older Mesopotamian account of creation. As indicated, however, the creation text with which the Bible begins has been shaped and reshaped as a vehicle for Israel's faith. Among the many possible interpretive dimensions of the text, we may call attention to the following:

1. It is widely agreed that Genesis 1:1–2 constitutes a remarkable premise for creation, namely, that disordered chaos (expressed in Hebrew onomato-poetically as *tohu wabohu*) was already "there" as God began to create: "In the beginning when God created the heavens and the earth, the earth was a formless void and darkness covered the face of the deep." That is, God did not create "from nothing," as the traditional doctrine of *creatio ex nihilo* suggests, but rather God's act of creation consists in the imposition of a particular *order* upon that mass of undifferentiated *chaos*. For much of the Bible, the energy of chaos (antiform) continues to operate destructively against the will of the Creator, and sometimes breaks out destructively beyond the bounds set by the decree of the Creator (Levenson 1988). It is an interesting example of imaginative remembering that much later, in 2 Maccabees 7:28, the tradition finally asserts creation out of nothing, a view that since then has predominated in later church traditions of theological interpretation. The insight of

the text as we have it, however, is a recognition of the intrinsic contradiction to God's will that is present in the stuff of creation itself. Thus the Creator makes creation possible, not by a single act, but by the endless reenactment and reassertion of a sovereign will over the recalcitrant stuff of chaos.

2. The peculiar role and character of human persons in creation has been especially important to the derivative theological traditions:

a. The "male and female" together are created to govern creation (1:26–28). This elemental assertion of the equality of men and women is at the taproot of the Bible, even if it is not always upheld in other biblical texts. This assertion has of late been an important claim for the emergence of theological feminism in an effort to subvert long-standing and deeply entrenched patriarchal assumptions that fail to recognize a God-given equality.

b. The "male and female" together are in "the image of God" (1:27). This latter phrase is not at all developed in the Old Testament, but has become central in subsequent articulations of theological understanding of human personhood. While the phrase "image of God" is open to many interpretations, it is plausible that it refers to the exercise of human sovereignty over creation as a regency for God's sovereignty (Barr 1968–1969; Bird 1997, 123–54; Børresen 1995). This role for human persons bespeaks both human freedom and human responsibility for the care of the earth.

> ### Close Reading: Genesis 1:1–2:4a
>
> The entire creation story in 1:1–2:4a is structured around the number seven and its multiples. (Seven is the number signifying completion or wholeness in ancient Israelite thought.) Not only are there seven days of creation, but if you look closely you will notice that the word "God" occurs 35 times, and the word "earth" occurs 21 times. Also, God declares a completed act of creation to be "good" seven times. What is interesting about this last fact is that the word "good" is missing on days two and seven, so it is used twice on days three and six to compensate. Why? Possibly because day two is concerned with the place of the waters of chaos, which are not exactly "good," even though they have a place in God's creation, and on day seven there is no real act of creation, since it is the day that God rests. Day three on the other hand is concerned with the creation of the livable realm of dry land and day six with the creation of humans, so perhaps these days are deemed *especially* "good."

c. The notion of "image of God" is reinforced by the imperatives that follow, "subdue" and "have dominion" (1:28). These verbs have often been understood to mean that the man and woman in the image of God are free to use the earth as they wish without restraint (White 1967). Contrary to this notion that the Bible is thus a warrant for environmental abuse and exploitation, Cameron Wybrow has shown that the "rape of the earth" has emerged

not from the Bible and this imperative, but from the impulse of Enlightenment autonomy that lacks any covenantal restraint (Wybrow 1991). More
plausibly than that misconstrual, which has been given wide articulation,
this pair of imperatives intends that human persons in human community
should be responsible for the care of the earth and its boundless, God-given
fruitfulness for the benefit of all creatures. Thus the imperatives bespeak not
unrestrained, indulgent freedom, but a mandate for the community to take
responsibility for the well-being of the earth.

3. The sustained affirmation of this liturgy of creation is that the world
(all of heaven, all of earth) is willed by and seen by God to be "good," that
is, lovely, beautiful, pleasing (1:10, 12, 18, 21). This reiterated affirmation,
which we might imagine as a congregational response to a Priestly litany,
culminates in verse 31 with the intensified phrase "very good." This affirmation of the goodness of creation has been decisive for the Jewish and Christian
traditions as a foundation for a life-affirming, world-affirming horizon with
a determined appreciation of the good of the material world in all its dimensions—including sexuality and economics. This tradition will have nothing
to do with world-denying, world-denigrating, or world-escaping religious
impulses that characterize too much popular faith in U.S. culture.

4. The liturgical characterization of creation in Genesis 1 culminates in 2:1–
4a with the authorization of the Sabbath as a God-given, God-practiced, God-
commanded observance. The day of cessation from work declares that God's
creation is, at root, an unanxious environment for life that is not defined by
energetic productivity or self-preoccupied consumption, but is defined by the
peaceableness that has confidence in the reliability of the world as God's creation without excessive exertion on the part of God or of humankind. Thus the
Sabbath is the discipline of pause that celebrates the world as God's good place
for life, and that relishes the human role in creation as "the image of God."

The Sabbath became, in the developed traditions of Israel, a primary mark
of Jewish life even as it continues to be. Whether or not this particular narrative is datable to the exilic period, as the older historical-critical consensus
had it, or to the preexilic era, as newer research suggests, it is likely that the
Sabbath became a distinctive mark of Jewishness in the Babylonian exile when
faith was practiced in an alien or hostile cultural environment. The Sabbath
became the lived testimony of Judaism that the "rhythms of cessation" as trust
in the Creator constitute a mighty alternative to the frenzy of production-
consumption that marks the world when it does not know that the world
belongs safely to the God who has called it "very good."

Even if the Priestly creation story is preexilic, the Torah itself almost certainly reached its final form during the sixth-century exile. In that context,
the claim that the world belongs to the God of Israel is a mighty and daring

alternative to the dominant, easily visible claim that the world is governed by Babylonian gods. Thus the liturgy of YHWH's goodness connects the character of the world to a particularly Jewish vision of God, articulated through the various interpreted points noted above. The text makes large theological claims to be sure, but it functions in and through these cosmic claims to sustain the specific community that relies on this imaginative tradition. That is, its purpose is concretely existential. Given that canonical reality about the final form of the text, it is self-evident that the text is not about "the origin of the world" as that phrase is usually employed, and thus it has no particular connection to the "creation versus evolution" debate or, more broadly, to the issue of "science and religion." Such expectations of the text, in our judgment, completely miss the point and function of the text in its original setting or in its durable canonical articulation. The question for the text is not so much "How did the world begin?" but rather "What *sort* of world do we have?"

Genesis 2:4b–25 (together with 3:1–24)

It is clear that this second creation narrative is quite distinct from the first, and that it characterizes the origin of the world in a very different way. The two accounts have in common an accent on YHWH's originary enactment of the world, and on the human creature as the "chief creature" who is responsible for the well-being of all creation.

This text, as the first creation text, has been material that has generated an immense amount of imaginative tradition. We may note three matters in particular from that imaginative tradition.

1. Unlike 1:26–28, the male and female creatures in this second narrative are not created equal in the image of God. Rather, the man has priority and, according to this tradition, the woman is derivatively formed from his "rib" (2:21–22). As might be expected, this narrative account has given grist for a compelling notion of female subordination, which has then been translated into model social relationships that privilege men and legitimate patriarchy. It is not surprising that this narrative point has attracted great interpretive attention with the rise of feminist consciousness. Phyllis Trible in particular has made a winsome case against subordination, a case that is of immense importance, even though her analysis has not been received everywhere as persuasive (Trible 1978, 72–143). In any case, the contrast between 1:26–28 and 2:21–22 is noticeable and has provided impetus for ongoing interpretive engagement.

2. Chapter 3 is to be read along with chapter 2. In chapter 3 the key character alongside the man and the woman is the serpent, who utters the *sly* voice of temptation that triggers disobedience and, consequently, exclusion of

---

**Midrashic Moment:
Genesis 2:4b–25**

The second creation story, unlike the first, does not say that humans are created in the "image of God," but it does portray God as breathing into the new human creature "the breath of life." Combined with the dust or dirt out of which God forms the human (2:7), this gives us an interesting picture of humanity as a peculiar combination of transcendence and materiality. That is, we are physical, earthly beings, but bear also a spark of divinity. William Shakespeare catches this paradox nicely in the line he gives Hamlet: "What should such fellows as I do, crawling between earth and heaven?" (*Hamlet*, act 3, scene 1) Shakespeare even gets the order right for a Hamlet who is more earthbound than transcendent: in the Priestly creation story in Genesis 1, the author speaks of "the heavens and the earth" (1:1), emphasizing the transcendence of God; whereas in the earthier story of Genesis 2, the terms are reversed to "the earth and the heavens" (2:4b), a slight matter of emphasis that nicely catches the theologies of the individual writers.

---

the human creatures from God's garden. The particular dramatic development of the narrative is possible only because of the *commanding* voice of the serpent; and yet the narrative expresses neither curiosity about the serpent nor explanation for it. The serpent is a given in the narrative and consequently in the garden—a voice that seeks to contradict and counter the compelling, commanding voice of the Creator God. The serpent, by verses 14–15, stands under a curse. What interests us, however, is the narrative affirmation that the serpent belongs to the creatures of the garden. Rendered theologically, this affirmation means that the seductive voice of evil is intrinsic to the creation; that is, the creation in principle is under siege from evil that contradicts the intention of the Creator. And this in a world called "good" many times in Genesis 1. Taken altogether through a combination of antecedent sources, Genesis 1–3 asserts that the good world of God is in potential contradiction to the Creator, a reality sketched more fully in what follows in Genesis 4–11.

3. As many church people know, Genesis 3 is the denouement of the creation narrative of Genesis 2. That narrative is understood in Christian interpretation as "the fall" whereby human creation (and ultimately all of creation) has fallen hopelessly and irreversibly into the power and into the habits of sin, so that human persons are irreversibly alienated from God and helpless to alter that condition. In this classical interpretation, human sin is not a series of specific, discrete acts, but it is a continuing strand of related decisions that cumulatively produce alienation from God and helplessness.

This understanding of the "fall" of humanity into the power of sin—a fall that prepares the way for the good news, the gospel—is rooted in the interpretive authority of Paul, especially in Romans 5:12–21, but see also

1 Corinthians 15:21–22, 45–49. Paul is paralleled in a recognition of the sorry state of helpless humanity in the near-contemporary Jewish apocalyptic of 2 Esdras (4 Ezra):

> It would have been better if the earth had not produced Adam, or else, when it had produced him, had restrained him from sinning. For what good is it to all that they live in sorrow now and expect punishment after death? O Adam, what have you done? For though it was you who sinned, the fall was not yours alone, but ours also who are your descendants. For what good is it to us, if an immortal time has been promised to us, but we have done deeds that bring death? And what good is it that an everlasting hope has been promised to us, but we have miserably failed? Or that safe and healthful habitations have been reserved for us, but we have lived wickedly? Or that the glory of the Most High will defend those who have led a pure life, but we have walked in the most wicked ways? Or that a paradise shall be revealed, whose fruit remains unspoiled and in which are abundance and healing, but we shall not enter it because we have lived in perverse ways? (2 Esd 7:116–124)

That interpretive venture, deeply rooted in experience and deeply insightful of profound helplessness, received in turn more systematic articulation in Augustine, powerful exposition in Luther, and lyrical voice in Milton's *Paradise Lost*. This common interpretive enterprise has impacted Western culture in powerful ways and has evoked profound probes of human character in both religious and secular modes.

This interpretive history is of interest for our study, however, precisely because the Old Testament itself features no such teaching about "the fall," nor does the textual tradition of the Old Testament refer again to the narrative of Genesis 3. To be sure, the prophetic teaching of Hosea, Jeremiah, and Ezekiel asserts that their contemporaries are hopelessly locked into recalcitrance against God; but nowhere in the Old Testament is that judgment articulated beyond existential disappointment about contemporaries into an ontological principle. The more characteristic view of the Old Testament concerning human sin and human capacity for obedience is expressed in Deuteronomy 30:11–14: "Surely, this commandment that I am commanding you today is not too hard for you, nor is it too far away. . . . No, the word is very near to you; it is in your mouth and in your heart for you to observe."

The Old Testament knows about profound sin (see Pss 32; 38; 51; 130). In these same psalms, however, there is complete confidence in the readiness of God to forgive. Thus a great accent is placed on repentance with the characteristic affirmation that humans can repent and that God is ready and able to forgive such repentance, without any lingering disability or alienation. In particular circumstances Israel is said to be beyond hope, but this is regularly a concrete, situational judgment, one never transposed into a more foundational theological claim.

Thus the dominant trajectory of interpretation around this question of sin is very different in Judaism and in Christianity. It is not the case that either interpretive trajectory can be said to be wrong. It is, however, worth noting that the dominant Christian interpretation has entailed an immense act of imaginative exposition beyond the narrative itself that makes no such universal claim out of the narrative of a particular case. Moreover, since the late twentieth century there have been probes among Christian scholars suggesting that the decisive interpretation of Paul by Augustine and Luther misconstrued Paul's intention (E. P. Sanders 1977, on "covenantal nomism"). In any case, it is clear that interpretation is not finished, but is an endless, open-ended project for those who take the text seriously and authoritatively.

THE FLOOD NARRATIVE

The flood narrative of Genesis 6:5–9:17 occupies both a disproportionate amount of space in the larger text of Genesis 1–11 and a pivotal theological position in that corpus. Three critical concerns should be acknowledged at the outset.

First, there is perennial interest in the question of the historicity of the flood, expressed especially in recurring claims that the ark of Noah has been found (Bailey 1989). These questions are at bottom futile, because it is probable that in many different social contexts there were experiences of floods that evoked flood stories, but no one of which can therefore claim to be the flood that is remembered in our text. Thus even the discovery of the ark would only indicate the confirmation of *a* flood, which in any case is not in doubt; but such a find would still be well short of *the* flood.

Second, there is no doubt that the flood narrative, as presented in the book of Genesis, has important literary antecedents in the Near East, especially in the Gilgamesh Epic. The recognition of such literary antecedents recontextualizes the "historical" question, and permits us to focus instead upon the intention of the interpreters who took over the extant flood tradition and utilized it as a means of voicing Israel's faith.

Third, the flood narrative has been a primary arena in which scholars have traced distinct literary sources, one source using the name of YHWH and one clearly avoiding that name. Thus most of the commentaries dissect the narrative into two literary sources, and no doubt there is ground for such distinctions. Bernhard Anderson, however, has shrewdly shown how the final form of the text weaves the sources into an artistic whole with 8:1 at its pivot point in an intricate design: "But God remembered Noah" (Anderson 1994, 56–74). It is that divine remembering that turns the narrative away from the destructiveness of the flood toward restoration and renewed fidelity on the part of God.

Anderson's analysis provides a way to move beyond these several critical questions that have claimed a disproportionate amount of interpretive energy to the theological exposition that bears Israel's canonical intentionality. Indeed, one may argue that the flood narrative articulates the primary claims of Israel's faith *in nuce*.

1. The theological premise of the flood narrative is YHWH's speech of judgment consisting in an indictment of a failed creation (6:5, 11–12) and a divine judgment whereby God resolves to "blot out" all creation (6:6–7) and "make an end of all flesh" (6:13). The release of the mighty floodwaters is a function of the divine resolve to terminate. The waters are the forces of chaos (see 1:2) that in this narrative function as obedient tools of God's negative intention. Thus the narrative begins as a conventional account of judgment enacted.

2. The speech of judgment and its ensuing enactment are, however, decisively disrupted by God's notice of Noah (and his family), who stands in God's favor (6:8) and who is rescued because of Noah's righteousness (6:9). Noah and his family constitute a decisive exception to the general destruction. Thus the identification of the righteous remnant becomes a decisive qualification in the general destruction. The chaotic waters are eased and withdrawn as "God remembers Noah."

3. God's willingness to nullify the threat of the flood and to reestablish well-being in the earth as God's creation arises from the presence of Noah. As a consequence, God promises "never again [to] curse the ground" (8:21). Indeed that curbing of the negation is matched by a positive guarantee of the rhythms of creation, appropriately presented in the rhythms of Hebrew poetry:

> As long as the earth endures,
>   seedtime and harvest, cold and heat,
> summer and winter, day and night,
>   shall not cease.
>   (8:22)

It is astonishing that the turn from divine judgment to divine assurance is not accomplished by any human repentance or resolve; the inclination of the human heart as "evil" at the outset (6:5) continues to be "evil" at the end (8:21). Nothing has changed in the inclination of humanity. All that has changed, decisively changed, is God's resolve to remain the faithful creator in spite of the condition of creation. That is, God is shown to be more fully gracious and positively inclined toward the earth.

4. The second conclusion to the flood narrative in 9:8–17 also revolves around God's promise that "never again" will the flood destroy the earth. The rainbow, as a reminder to God, who might otherwise forget, assures creation of God's "everlasting covenant between God and every living creature of all flesh that is on the earth" (9:16). Patrick Miller writes of this text:

> The natural environment is secured in covenant with human and natural creatures. The covenant with Noah restores and secures the creation for the benefit of the creatures, animal and human. Human treatment of the natural world, therefore, is a matter not only of the attitude toward the creation, but also how humankind receives the promise, which it shares with the animal world. . . .
>
> The nations are a part of the created order, the outcome of the blessing of God in the completion of creation. The restoration of the creation after the Flood involves also the restoration of humanity as a part of that creation and of the renewal of the blessing (Gen 8:17; 9:1, 7) through the lineage of Noah (Gen 9:19). So also the establishment of covenant with Noah is an establishment of covenant with all of humankind. The text makes this point repeatedly and thus with much emphasis. The universal covenant with humankind as a way of perpetuating and maintaining the creation incorporates the nations of which Israel is a single part. (Miller 1995, 165, 166–67)

Thus in both proposed literary sources (identified as J and as P), the dramatic movement is the same:

	judgment	*assurance*
J:	Genesis 6:5–7	8:21–22
P:	Genesis 6:11–13	9:8–17

The dominant story line concerns God's change of mind, and God's readiness to nullify God's plan to destroy (see Jer 18:1–11). The mitigating factor is Noah, who is perhaps a harbinger of faithful Israel, but such an identification of Noah with Israel is nowhere explicit (see Ezek 14:12–20; Heb 11:7). It is impossible to overstate the cruciality of Noah for the dramatic movement of the text. In the end, however, the decisive and most interesting character is not Noah but the God of Israel, who freshly embraces creation.

In its present location in the text, the flood narrative is hardly less than another creation narrative, because of the way in which God reorders the world away from chaos, just as happened in chapter 1. The flood narrative thus is a crucial text for articulating the deep tension and defining contradiction between the recalcitrance of creation and the will of the Creator. Rolf Rendtorff comments:

> Chapter 9, in particular vv. 8–11, serves as a solemn confirmation of that promise. What God has just declared will be the content of his *bĕrît*: not to bring a flood over the earth again and not to destroy living beings again. But before that confirmation, God makes it clear that this world is no longer "very good." God reconfirms his blessing of fertility (v. 1), but immediately he adds that peace no longer prevails between human beings and animals (v. 12), or among human beings themselves, so that a strict commandment is needed to prevent murder (vv. 5–6). (Rendtorff 1993, 127–28)

The flood story culminates in a recognition that God's faithful commitment to creation and to human community has prevailed, thus assuring that the world has a future. The genealogies before and after the flood narrative are articulations of continuity that survive even through the chaotic disruption. While the story of the world as God's creation is momentarily disrupted by the chaotic waters, that disruption does not and cannot prevail against the intention of YHWH to maintain the "family line" of humanity. This reassurance of continuity in the face of threat in Isaiah 54:9–10 later becomes an assurance cherished by exiles in Israel who faced a threat and a dislocation of their own.

It is evident that the process of interpretation in Israel has been able to articulate, through these diffuse materials, a steady theological affirmation concerning the

Close Reading: Genesis 9:1–7

As the flood story closes, in the beginning of chapter 9, God reiterates the basic command to humanity that was first articulated in the Priestly creation story of Genesis 1: "Be fruitful and multiply, and fill the earth." But if we look closely at what follows each command, we notice that whereas God in Genesis 1 stipulates plants and fruit as food for humanity (1:29), in the flood story God allows the eating of animals (9:2) for the first time. It seems clear that, at least in the Priestly traditions, humanity was originally created to be vegetarian, and to refrain from violence against God's other creatures. The allowance of meat after the flood seems to be a concession to the essentially violent nature of humanity. And by disallowing the eating of the blood along with the meat (9:4), the story lays the basis for later practices of animal sacrifice, where the blood must be poured out and returned to the earth as a sign of atonement for killing the animal.

interface of God's good sovereignty and the sustained recalcitrance intrinsic to creation that resists the purpose of God and that recurringly places the world in jeopardy. Given the peculiar mythical antecedents of this flood text and given the large themes now carried by these opening texts of Genesis, it is not surprising that these texts, over long generations of interpretation, have become fertile materials for rich, diverse interpretation. The transposition of these ancient materials into a relatively coherent theological statement is unmistakably a powerful act of imagination, that is, canonical imagination. It is evident that while the continuing act of communal imagination is decisive, that definitive act did not terminate imaginative interpretation that continues, perforce, in both Jewish and Christian communities.

5

Genesis 12–50

The Ancestors

The narrative materials of Genesis 12–50 present the tradition of the earliest ancestors of Israel wherein the most elemental themes of faith are rooted and paradigmatically articulated. In an earlier generation of scholarship, it was thought that the narratives, on the basis of cultural and archaeological evidence, could be well situated in the culture of the Near East in the second millennium, so that they could be regarded as historically rooted. Current scholarship, however, regards such historical data as doubtful at best, so that we must treat the materials as a product of traditional communal remembering, whatever may have been the facts behind the memory. And while the stories in Genesis 1–11 represent a less true-to-life, more mythological world, beginning in chapter 12 we encounter the more realistic style of classical Hebrew narrative: characters are complex and multilayered (just like the people we meet every day), and they move in a recognizable world shaped by the competing claims of family, God, and their own personal hopes and desires.

I

This material consists in a four-generation account of the origins of the community that became Israel: Abraham and Sarah (Gen 12–25), Isaac and Rebekah (Gen 25–27), Jacob and Rachel (Gen 25–36), and Joseph (Gen 37–50). The beginnings of this family, prior to Abraham, are traced in a traditional form in 11:10–32, all the way back to Shem, son of Noah (see 1 Chr 1:1–27; Luke 3:34–38, where the family is traced back to "Adam, son of God"). These genealogies are not to be taken historically, but are conventional devices to establish legitimacy and pedigrees of connection (Johnson 1988; R. Wilson 1977).

The materials of the first three generations have much in common. They consist in a collection of brief narrative episodes that are expressed in conventional form, that are woven together to present something of a life story; it is quickly evident that the materials presented tend to focus on the key characters in terms of interfamilial relations, the securing of land, the securing of a wife and, consequently, of sons who may be heirs. Our interest in these texts pivots on the way in which the individual stories (which may have existed before their appearance in the canon as discrete oral units) have been artfully shaped by authors and editors into a coherent and complex extended narrative. Some have argued that the Joseph materials are of a different kind, not made up for the most part of discrete narrative episodes that may have once stood alone, but rather a more tightly connected sequence of episodes. The distinction between chapters 12–26 (which sound more like family traditions) and the Joseph narrative in chapters 37–50 has long been noted, though more recent scholarship has also pointed out ways in which the Joseph story looks back to the earlier patriarchal stories (Friedman 1998, 36–45).

The important form-critical analysis of Hermann Gunkel (1997) is especially relevant in reading the ancestors' stories. This great German scholar paid attention to the artistic, aesthetic aspects of the short narrative units and concluded that this folk society had a characteristic repertoire of recurring narrative modes that it repeated in various contexts with many artistic variations. Gunkel's work has been extended by Robert Alter, who has identified "type-scenes" in which the same narrative motif is variously reiterated, such as "the endangered ancestress" (12:10–20; 20:1–18; 26:1–11) or the betrothal scene (24:10–61; 29:1–20) (Alter 1981, 47–62). The reiteration of type-scenes may sound strange to us until we recognize that such popular TV programs as *M*A*S*H*, *Seinfeld*, *The West Wing*, or *The Sopranos* broadly reiterate the same transactions episode after episode. Thus in reading this material in Genesis, one must attend to the literary conventions that are operative, a recurring set of narrative codes that frequently reappear in the material, while at the same time noting what sometimes seem like minor differences but which take on added significance precisely because of the recurring pattern.

Because of the immense influence of Gunkel, Old Testament scholars have spent enormous energy on the smallest narrative units and upon the particularity of the smallest unit of text. Theological interpretation, however, must attend to the larger narrative units as well, and to the ways in which the smaller narrative elements (which may have at some point existed independently) have been made to serve the larger theological intentionality of the whole. In reading Genesis 12–50, and particularly 12–36, it is evident that the formation of the larger text has been accomplished without smoothing out all of the disjunctions that occurred when the materials were brought together. Nonetheless, it is also evident that a larger interpretive intentionality is at work. This intentionality, according to Gerhard von Rad, may have arisen as discrete narratives were gathered together under the themes of a crucial liturgical assertion (which he termed "creed"; von Rad 1966, 1–78). But even if von Rad is not right in his proposed prehistory of the text, Brevard Childs is no doubt correct that the completed form of the text is the sustained account whereby a single childless couple (Abraham and Sarah) is blessed by the primordial care of God (Childs 1979, 152–53); consequently, by Genesis 46:26, sixty-six persons belong to the family, enough to ensure continuity and social significance. Because the family is endlessly in jeopardy, there can be little doubt, according to this telling, that the well-being of the family is the gift of God. Thus the story is told so that the *account of the family* cannot be narrated apart from the sometimes overt and sometimes hidden *work of God*, who has promised, willed, and guaranteed the well-being of the family.

It is clear that the theological theme around which all of this disparate material is gathered is the theme of *promise from God to the ancestors of Israel*. By the traditioning process that theme of promise has been imposed upon or read into texts that, in an earlier form, were not directly related to the promise. It may be, as Claus Westermann proposes, that the motif of promise was originally situated in 18:1–15, from which narrative the accent on promise cannot be removed without destroying the plot of the episode (Westermann 1980a, 11–30). This initial promise may have been concerning a child to be born, especially a son in a patriarchal society. That theme of promised son (and therefore heir) has come to dominate the entire narrative, so that in each generation a son (and heir) is by God given only belatedly to a barren mother when all human resources have been exhausted (21:1–7; 25:21–26; 30:22–24). We should especially notice that the promise is not a generic good feeling or a sense of optimism about the future. It is rather a specific utterance from God's own mouth that is remembered and quoted in the text and in the lore of Israel. That remembered utterance comes to be the core of the narrative tradition. It functions both to articulate what God must yet do in order to be reliable, and to hold Israel to trust in God's utterance as the defining resource for this family into a future of vulnerability and jeopardy.

Although the promise may have been intrinsic to some of these smaller narratives in their most elemental form, it has been handled by the tradition to become a much more powerful and more formulaic utterance that now governs the entire narrative. The clearest articulation of that more formal usage of promise is in 12:1–3, the beginning point of the ancestral story. Abraham (or Abram) is abruptly addressed by God, first of all in an imperative mandating Abraham's departure from all that is familiar and secure. In the very same initial sentence the imperative shades into a promise concerning "the land that I will show you." The ancestral narrative is preoccupied with the land of promise, a concrete piece of real estate to which this family is entitled by the utterance of God. The subsequent anxiety about a son (and heir) that recurs in each generation is in order that the promise of land may be kept alive, for without an heir in each generation the promise is nullified (see 15:1–6). So the basic narrative tension that pushes these chapters forward is the tension between promise and fulfillment: God has promised progeny and land, but it is not clear how this elderly and barren couple will generate progeny, nor is it clear how the land will become theirs. Readers keep reading in order to find out whether and how God will fulfill these promises.

The promise continues in 12:2 specifying that Abraham and his family will reach sociopolitical prominence, a promise subsequently taken to be fulfilled in the achievements of David and Solomon. The promise concludes in verse 3 with the stunning assurance that Israel's very existence will be a blessing to "all the families of the earth." That is, Israel's life in the world is itself a means and source of well-being for other nations. From this beginning point, the other nations are always on the horizon of Israel as they are upon the horizon of the God of Israel. This cluster of promises, strongly reflected in 28:13–15, becomes the originary principle for all that follows in the narrative account of the life of Israel. It may indeed be seen that this promissory utterance that characterizes the biblical God as a future-generating, future-governing God is a core theme of the entire Bible. We may point in particular to three circles of tradition that fall rightly within the vision of this passage.

First, following von Rad, many scholars see that the initial promise of God to Abraham in 12:1–3 functions as the hinge and connecting point to bring together the *history of the nations* in Genesis 1–11 and the *history of Israel* in all that follows (von Rad 1966, 65–74). As we have seen concerning the theological intentionality of Genesis 1–11, that cluster of texts testifies to a deep alienation of the nations from God, a contradiction that exists between God and the world. A popular way to speak of that malfunction of creation is as "the fall." In the text itself, the nations are said to be "cursed" (see 3:17–19; 4:11–12; and by implication 11:6–9), that is, subject to God's negating transcendence. The initial promise God makes to Israel is that Israel "shall be a blessing to the nations," so that the *blessing* carried and embodied by Israel is to counter and overcome and nullify the *curse*. In this juxtaposition, the role of Israel, according to God's intention, is in order that the other nations and the whole world will be blessed, that is, enjoy the abundance and well-being that were from the outset intended in the blessing of creation, as in 1:22 (Wolff 1966).

Second, in the formation of the Bible this narrative of promise has been drawn into relation with very different traditions associated with the book of Deuteronomy and the literature derived from it. That tradition focuses upon the commandments, and is concerned to make the claim that Israel is given the land of promise (in the book of Joshua) and must govern the land of promise (in the book of Judges) according to the requirements of the commandments. As we shall see, that same historical tradition reflects, in the books of Kings, on how the land will be forfeited by Israel when it is disobedient to the demands of the Torah. That very different theological tradition is concerned with the condition of obedience whereby the land will be held. In the full tradition, however, the accent on conditionality has behind it the ancestral promise of land. Consequently, the land of obedience (so Deuteronomy) is first of all an entitled land. Later Israel, led by Joshua, receives the land because God has initially promised it. This connection between traditions is explicit in Joshua 21:43–45, which celebrates the completion of land occupation and understands that occupation as a fulfillment of old promises. (It should also be noticed that the same promise is articulated and presumed upon even in the exodus tradition that in its original articulation was a quite different circle of memory; see Exod 2:24; 3:16–17.)

Third, the ancestral narratives receive little attention in the literature that is commonly dated to the monarchial period of ancient Israel, that is, the pre-exilic prophets. But then, abruptly, the Abraham tradition reemerges in the literature of the exile in a rather spectacular way (see Lev 26:42; Isa 41:8; 51:2; 63:16; Jer 33:26; Ezek 33:24; Mic 7:20). It is clear that after the demanding tradition of the Torah linked to Moses had led to a theological interpretation of the destruction of Jerusalem in 587, the interpretive community of ancient Israel turned from the rigorous conditionality of Moses to the free promise of God made at the outset to Abraham and Sarah. Thus the exilic community found in the memory of that promise a ground for hope when the claim of Torah obedience was no longer adequate. This promise, now rearticulated, provided, in a most general way, the assurance that God was still at work on behalf of the displaced community to guarantee a future of well-being. More particularly, the promise was important to a displaced, deported community in its conviction that it was still entitled to the land (which it did not presently possess). It is affirmed that soon or late in God's good time, God would keep the promise and Israel would be restored to the land of promise, not because of merit or obedience, but because God is faithful to God's own promise that permeated Israel's life and faith from the outset.

Thus in all three literatures, (a) the account of the *curse of the nations* in Genesis 1–11, (b) the Deuteronomic reflection on the *land in relation to the Torah*, and (c) the *exilic recovery of promise*, the ancestral narratives are of decisive importance for Israel's faith and self-understanding; they provide ballast for life in a world that kept this community endlessly off balance and in jeopardy.

II

Beyond the Old Testament itself, we may note two interpretive trajectories that are important in current ecumenical conversations. On the one hand, the ancestral promise to Abraham became a powerful resource in the interpretive work of Paul in the early church; this tradition helped to support the claim that the gospel of Jesus Christ was properly extended beyond the Jewish community of Torah keepers to Gentiles who were not subject to the Jewish Torah. Paul makes this argument in Romans 4:1–25 and, more particularly, in Galatians 3:8, wherein he regards the promise of Genesis 12:3—"in you all the Gentiles will be blessed" (au. trans.)—as an early opening beyond the Torah community. Indeed, Paul labels that remarkable promise to Abraham "the gospel beforehand" (Gal 3:8), suggesting that already in that initial utterance of God to Abraham the way is open beyond the chosen people. Thus Paul's opening of the gospel to non-Jews is commensurate with the notion that Genesis 12:3 pertains to the nations under curse in Genesis 1–11. The promise of Abraham is an immense ecumenical venture, for this promise bearer is the father of many families of faith.

While Christians have found in the ancestral promise an opening to Gentiles, on the other hand Jewish interpreters have paid particular attention to the promise of land made to this family. There is no doubt that the land is a dominant preoccupation of the ancestral narratives, and becomes an acutely important grounding when the community is later landless. Specifically, the detail of land boundaries in Genesis 15:18–21 provides a vision and sketch of greater Israel that anticipates the furthest reach for territory in Israel under Solomon. The purchase of land at Hebron, moreover, with a deal that is legally and carefully consummated has been subsequently understood in some forms of Zionist Judaism as a guarantee of ownership and entitlement to the land (see Gen 23). Thus the old memory has become a powerful ground for and ingredient of land claims even into the contemporary practices and ambitions of the state of Israel.

These two cases of a *Christian opening to Gentiles* and a *Jewish claim to the land* indicate how rich and how supple this tradition of promise continues to be for interpretation in a variety of directions. Finally, in this regard, it is important that Abraham in broadly ecumenical conversations is understood to be the father of faith for all three "religions of the book," Judaism, Christianity, and Islam. Indeed, that so much is shared by these deep interpretive traditions probably encourages the deep acrimony among them, for the children of Abraham endlessly struggle with and compete for control of the legacy of a common ancestor.

Two other matters warrant consideration. First, the above discussion pertains less directly to Joseph in Genesis 37–50 than it does to his three forebears. Unlike Abraham, Isaac, and Jacob, Joseph is presented as an Israelite who made it big in the Egyptian Empire by his readiness to submit to and accommodate the aims of his imperial overlords. While Joseph is celebrated in the narratives as a man of deep Yahwistic faith who effectively rescues his vulnerable family (as in 45:1–16 and 50:15–21), it is not often noticed that he is at the same time an accommodator to Pharaoh's acquisitive policies: Joseph is the imperial agent who accomplishes an economic monopoly for the throne at the expense of agrarian peasants (47:13–27). If Joseph's accomplishments are read in light of the exodus narrative that follows, then Joseph must be understood as an accomplice in achieving state enslavement. Thus Joseph is portrayed as an ambiguous figure who juggles his deep theological identity as an Israelite along with his pragmatic commitment to the politics of the empire. Some suggest that this narrative, like the narrative accounts of Daniel and Esther, portrays a community of faith that must live carefully, knowingly, and cunningly at the

---

Close Reading: Genesis 50:22–26

Biblical authors and editors often use repetition in order to provide a structure or design for the content of a passage, and this structure can clue us in to thematic concerns of the narrative. In this passage, notice how intentional repetition provides an envelope-like structure for the passage that emphasizes Joseph's dual identity as an Israelite who has also essentially become an Egyptian:

 a. And Joseph lived in **Egypt**, he and his father's household, and Joseph lived a hundred and ten years.

 b. And Joseph saw the third generation of sons from Ephraim, and the sons of Machir son of Manasseh, as well, were born on Joseph's knees.

 c. And Joseph said to his brothers, "I am about to die, and God will surely single you out and take you up from this land to the land he promised to Abraham to Isaac and to Jacob."

 b'. And Joseph made the sons of Israel swear, saying, "When God indeed singles you out, you shall take up my bones from this place."

 a'. And Joseph died, a hundred and ten years old, and they embalmed him and he was put in a coffin in **Egypt**.

By placing Joseph's association with Egypt as the outside terms in the design and his association with Israel as the inside terms, the passage seems to claim that his allegiance to Egypt was a surface allegiance only and that his core identity is Israelite. And at the very center of the structure, singled out for emphasis, is the reiteration of the promise of land.

delicate boundary between resistance and accommodation (Humphreys 1973; D. Smith 1989). What may be an older story thus serves as a resource for later generations of the faithful who must practice faith in a vulnerable, highly contested political environment likely in the Persian period.

Second, the mothers in Genesis, particularly Sarah and Rachel, are of immense importance to the tradition. (By contrast to these two mothers, Rebekah is not at all mentioned in the ongoing interpretive tradition.) In an earlier time, these stories were widely referred to as "patriarchal narratives," or as stories "of the fathers," with an accent only upon the sires of the next heir in each generation (Westermann 1980a). And the tradition characteristically focuses upon the male children. More recent feminist sensibility, however, has invited attention to the mothers in Israel who are indispensable to the tradition. For starters, each of the mothers is barren, thus being each time a receptor of God's miraculous gift of a son and an heir (Gen 11:30; 25:21; 29:31). In every generation, the story cannot proceed without the mother. Specifically Sarah, as the mother of faith, is present along with Abraham in the exilic memory of Isaiah 51:2; she is, moreover, undoubtedly the implied subject of Isaiah 54:1–3, a humiliated wife who will become the fecund mother into the future. Moreover, in Galatians 3–4 Sarah becomes the *type* for Paul's contrast concerning the freedom of the gospel and the slavery that negates the freedom of the gospel (see Rom 4:19; 9:9; Heb 11:11). In Galatians 4:27 Paul quotes directly from Isaiah 54:1 so that Sarah is further interpreted as the true bearer of the gospel to which Paul vigorously attests.

The figure of Rachel functions very differently in the developed tradition (Dresner 1994). She is presented as the grieving mother whose child has died in Jeremiah 31:15, the mother of lost exiles. In a remarkable twist of the tradition, Rachel in exile now becomes the one who "refuses to be comforted" (Jer 31:15), displacing father Jacob, who, in the earlier narrative account, "refused to be comforted" (Gen 37:35). The redeployment of grief from Jacob to Rachel is continued in Matthew 2:18, which quotes Jeremiah 31:15 in response to Herod's slaughter of the innocents. It is plausible to suggest that the unmitigated grief is reassigned to Rachel in the tradition (and away from Jacob) because mother love is the most intimate imaginable and, consequently, mother loss is as profound as can be articulated. Emil Fackenheim has extrapolated even beyond these usages of Jeremiah and Matthew to suggest that Rachel "will not be comforted" because the loss of her children extends to six million exterminated Jews; such unbearable loss requires the engagement of this mother of all grief to voice the unfathomable depth of loss (Fackenheim 1980).

While Rebekah is not taken up in the subsequent biblical tradition, we should notice that a third mother does figure in the tradition, namely, Hagar.

In a negative appeal to Hagar (Gal 4:21–31), Paul takes her as a metaphor for slavery in order to contrast her with the "free woman" (Sarah). That negative development in the tradition notwithstanding, in the narrative itself Hagar is an important and positive presence (Trible 1973; Callaway 1986). Thus Hagar is a vexation to Sarah and, consequently, to Abraham as well. Nonetheless, she is a mother of one of Abraham's blessed sons, Ishmael, and she is the recipient of the ministering mercy of one of God's angels (Gen 21:17–19). Hagar embodies the fidelity of God to the family of faith that persists just outside the primary genealogy of Abraham, Isaac, and Jacob. She functions in the narrative to keep the horizon of Israel open to "the other" who also has legitimate claims to make upon the promise of God. Her presence in the tradition precludes the excessive narrowing of the tradition. It is instructive that in the report of Abraham's death, "His sons Isaac and Ishmael buried him in the cave of Machpelah" (Gen 25:9). They were there together in an acknowledgment that while from different mothers, the insider and the outsider share the legacy of the one father.

That father is in the Bible the father of all faith. He is the one who ventured into the unknown at the behest of God's imperative. He had faith sufficient to trust the promise against all of the settled data at hand, to run risks upon the basis of nothing more than God's assuring utterance. While the narrative of Genesis 12:10–20 and the securing of a second wife (just in case, 16:2) measure Abraham's insecure pragmatism, he is presented in derivative tradition as the quintessential practitioner of trust in God. In the Genesis narrative itself, his radical obedience in 22:1–14 bespeaks his utter faith, a radicality celebrated in the New Testament extrapolation of the tradition. Thus Paul in Galatians 3:6 quotes Genesis 15:6 to attest Abraham's model faith (see also Rom 4:22–23), and the recital of the faithful in Hebrews 11:8–19 shows Abraham as the primal embodiment of trust in God. It is evident that the traditioning process, in a most imaginative way, has transposed what may have been folk memories into a vigorous, definitive claim and model for faith. The "gospel beforehand" is that even this dysfunctional family can be a carrier of the promise, both for its own heirs to come and for those outside the family who are included in the promised future and in God's intentionality that reaches well beyond the scope of this family. The mothers of the family are valued, but then so is Hagar, who lives at the outer edge of the family of choice.

6

The Book of Exodus

The book of Exodus contains primal material for the faith of Judaism and Christianity, and is the first testimony to the defining role of Moses in the life of Israel. It is also a classic of storytelling, with the scene of baby Moses floating in his little "ark" (the same word used for Noah's ark) on the Nile, the escalating conflict between Moses and Aaron on the one hand and the magicians of Pharaoh on the other, the recognized tragedy of the deaths of all firstborn in Egypt, and the dramatic rescue at the Red Sea. After these stories come the first extended block of legal/ethical material in the Bible, including the first articulation of the Ten Commandments (20:2–17). It is clear that the exodus story was read and reread often in ancient Israel, since later biblical authors cite it frequently, and it is our opinion that it ought to be read and reread by contemporary communities of faith as well.

The book is readily divided into three parts: the liberation from Egypt (1:1–15:21), the interval in the wilderness before arriving at Sinai (15:22–18:27), and the Sinai experience (19:1–40:38).

I

The exodus narrative itself, the account of the departure of the slave community at the behest of YHWH from the oppression of Pharaoh in Egypt, extends through Exodus 1–15. This narrative constitutes the powerful, compelling center of Israel's defining memory of faith, as is evidenced in both the noted retellings of the account in Scripture itself (see Exod 12:26–27; 13:8–10, 14–15; Deut 6:20–24; 26:5–9; Isa 43:16–19; 48:20–22; Amos 9:7), down through the continued usage of the narrative in the Seder meal of Passover in

75

contemporary Judaism. This narrative has become the defining, paradigmatic account of faith whereby Israel is understood as the beloved, chosen community of YHWH and the object of YHWH's peculiar and decisive intervention in public events (see Exod 4:22). This narrative, moreover, is a crucial component in the articulation of YHWH, the God of Israel, as the God with power to override the empire through a miraculous intervention that renders the empire helpless and impotent.

In an earlier time when scholars had more confidence in historical-archaeological data, it was usual to locate the exodus event historically in the thirteenth century, somewhere between 1280 and 1230 BCE, just at the turning point from the Bronze Age to the Iron Age. In that interpretive frame of reference, the pharaoh of the exodus narrative was thought variously to be Ramesses II, Seti I, or Merneptah, so that, in any case, the event of the exodus was securely situated in the real time of the empire. More recently, scholars have come to doubt the historicity of the event and certainly to doubt any claim to locate the event historically. Thus William Dever, a cautious archaeologist, can conclude: "The whole 'Exodus-Conquest' cycle of stories must now be set aside as largely mythical, but in the proper sense of the term 'myth': perhaps 'historical fiction,' but tales told primarily to validate religious beliefs" (Dever 2001, 121).

It is not possible to deny or affirm whatever may have been "historically" the case, though we must allow that some turn of events gave rise to the particular articulation of the miracle that we have in the biblical narrative. Given the limit of historical evidence and given the power of the narrative for the liturgical imagination of Israel, it may be best to understand this text as "paradigmatic" history after the fashion of Eric Voegelin (1956). When understood as paradigmatic, the narrative is seen to make a claim of intense particularity, but a particularity that invites and permits rereading in a variety of circumstances and contexts, with reference to any encounter with overwhelming, abusive power. Consequently, the theme of "YHWH versus Pharaoh" functions not as historical reportage, but as a retelling of paradigmatic confrontation with reference to a particular tyranny and a particular or anticipated rescue.

Such a move from reportage to paradigmatic rereading is compelling when we note that every telling or retelling of tyranny and deliverance is bound to be pertinent in any particular time and place. The imaginative remembering of this transformative event is not focused upon some past transformation now largely lost in its concreteness, but is characteristically and inescapably focused upon a contemporary or near-contemporary occurrence of tyranny and deliverance that still has pertinence to the retelling community. The vitality and authority of the exodus event and the exodus narrative—and the God who inhabits that narrative—are found precisely in the continuing and repeated retelling of the definitive emergence of Israel and the definitive characterization of YHWH. That the narrative includes a variety of literary sources attests to the fact that the retelling community, in many circumstances and in many generations, time after time, found this narrative plot as powerfully disclosing as it was in any initial telling, a disclosure about both parties, YHWH and Israel.

The paradigmatic reuse of the narrative is evident in other places of Scripture as well. The most obvious case is in Joshua 4:22–24:

> "Israel crossed over the Jordan here on dry ground." For the LORD your God dried up the waters of the Jordan for you until you crossed over, as the LORD your God did to the Red Sea, which he dried up for us until we crossed over,

so that all the peoples of the earth may know that the hand of the LORD is mighty, and so that you may fear the LORD your God forever.

> **Midrashic Moment:**
> **Exodus and Revolution**
>
> In his book *Exodus and Revolution*, the political philosopher Michael Walzer argues that the biblical story of the exodus is the paradigmatic text for political revolutions in the West, including the American Revolution: "In 1776, Benjamin Franklin proposed that the Great Seal of the United States should show Moses with his rod lifted and the Egyptian army drowning in the sea" (Walzer 1985, 6). What makes the exodus story so important for later political movements, according to Walzer, is its emphasis on this-wordly liberation—that is, one need not wait for heaven or the coming kingdom of God in order to see justice done.

The crossing of the Jordan is understood as a replication of the exodus, a replication that also attests to the sovereignty of YHWH.

There is no doubt, moreover, that the exodus narrative provides the plot and structure for the ark narrative in 1 Samuel 4:1–7:1. In both the initial defeat of the ark of YHWH and in its culminating triumph, the Philistines are said to allude to the exodus, thus making the parallel to the exodus event itself unmistakable:

> Woe to us! Who can deliver us from the power of these mighty gods? These are the gods who struck the Egyptians with every sort of plague in the wilderness. . . . Why should you harden your hearts as the Egyptians and Pharaoh hardened their hearts? After he had made fools of them, did they not let the people go, and they departed? (1 Sam 4:8; 6:6; see Exod 10:1–2)

A third usage is in the poetry of Isaiah 40–55, wherein the return home of Jews from Babylon is understood as a replication of the exodus event (Anderson 1962; 1976):

Depart, depart, go out from there!
. . . .
For you shall not go out in haste,
    and you shall not go in flight;
for the Lord will go before you,
    and the God of Israel will be your rear guard.
                                        (Isa 52:11–12)

For you shall go out in joy,
    and be led back in peace;
the mountains and the hills before you
    shall burst into song,
    and all the trees of the field shall clap their hands.
                                        (Isa 55:12)

. Each of these texts reiterates in new circumstance the central narrative claims made primally in the exodus account. There is no doubt, moreover, that in the New Testament, the wonders of Jesus are understood as parallel acts of emancipation and transformation wherein Jesus enacts the wonders that properly belong to God (see Luke 7:22).

The central material of the exodus narrative is found in the sequence of "plagues," that is, the acts of disruptive, transformative power on the part of YHWH that serve to overwhelm the power and authority of Pharaoh and, consequently, to rescue the slaves from the power and authority of Pharaoh (Exod 7–11). The plagues are occasions of immense and inscrutable power that are taken to be signs of YHWH's sovereignty, not at all to be explained naturalistically, as has been frequently attempted. They are not to be understood naturalistically because they make immediate and direct appeal to the hidden and odd power of YHWH, without which they have no force in the narrative.

The immediate effect of the plagues is in order that "the Egyptians may know that I am YHWH" (7:5, au. trans.). The verb "know" is used in a double sense of (a) having convincing data, but also (b) acknowledging as sovereign. The slow sequence of plagues evidences that Pharaoh, little by little, began to acknowledge and concede, in grudging ways, the rule of YHWH, so that Pharaoh must eventually confess his sin and ask forgiveness (10:16–17). In the end, Pharaoh even acknowledges that the power to bless resides among the Israelites (12:32). The consequence of such a show of power is that Israel also may "know that I am YHWH," that is, recognize YHWH's real sovereignty over Pharaoh's pseudo-sovereignty, and so receive the gift of freedom given by YHWH (10:1–2). Thus the plague narrative constitutes disclosure (to both Egypt the oppressor and to the oppressed slaves) of the way YHWH presides over power relations in history. YHWH's governance, it is revealed, is to the astonishing benefit of the slaves. The narrative account has no reservation in exhibiting YHWH's capacity to manage the wonders of creation in order to evoke historical newness (Israel) as an outcome of disordering and reordering creation (Fretheim 1991).

This core account of a power struggle that YHWH wins is preceded in Exodus 1–4 by (a) a characterization of Israel's circumstance of oppression (chap. 1), (b) an introduction of the person of Moses (chap. 2), and (c) the powerful intrusion of YHWH's will and purpose into the life of Moses by way of a call narrative and confrontation (chaps. 3–4). These chapters introduce the cast of characters and prepare for the dramatic confrontation of chapters 7–11. It is noteworthy that in all of chapters 1–2, YHWH plays no effective role, so that the narrative begins in a needy human world. From the outset, we are on notice of the drama to come because of the wonder of Hebrew births in defiance of Pharaoh (1:8–22), and because of the rage and passion of Moses, who is a dangerous, violent agent of the slaves (2:11–22).

The narrative account of these introductory chapters focuses upon the theophany of 3:1–6, whereby YHWH's inscrutability engages Moses and authorizes him for a dangerous confrontive mission in a challenge to the power of Pharaoh. The odd account of the burning bush is a more or less characteristic theophany, that is, a narrative report on the inscrutable appearance of YHWH in a decisive act. From this point on there is no doubt that the inscrutable YHWH, "the God of Abraham, the God of Isaac, and the God of Jacob" (3:6), is the key player in this contest with Pharaoh to determine who will control the destiny of the Israelites.

It is worth noting that YHWH has not been actively engaged in the narrative until the end of chapter 2. Before that point the narrative concerns the context and situation of the slaves. What evokes YHWH to action, moreover, is the vigorous, public outcry of the slave community that

> ### *Midrashic Moment: Exodus 1:15–22*
>
> In her novel *Moses, Man of the Mountain,* Zora Neale Hurston writes: "The birthing beds of Hebrews were matters of state. The Hebrew womb had fallen under the heel of Pharaoh. . . . The shadow of Pharaoh squatted in the dark corners of every birthing place in Goshen. Hebrew women shuddered with terror at the indifference of their wombs to the Egyptian law" (Hurston 1991, 1). Hurston catches very well the contrast in these opening chapters of Exodus between the powerful tyrant and the seemingly powerless slave camp; though as it turns out, the fundamental power of life resides with the slaves, and it will not be stopped by any tyrant.

brings to speech its suffering and distress. It is of great importance that the initial impetus for the exodus confrontation was not from YHWH but from the slaves who groan and cry out (2:23). It is Israel's cry that evokes YHWH (2:24–25). This initiating power of voiced pain is characteristic of Israel's powerful tradition of "lament," a cry that is able to evoke the power of God and so initiate the contest of the plagues that follow.

By 12:32 the deed of departure is in principle done; the resistance of Pharaoh to the emancipatory will of YHWH is broken. Before telling of the actual departure of Israel from slavery, the narrator pauses in 12:43–13:16 in order to provide detailed guidance for subsequent celebration of the event. While the narrative has reached its final form through a complex traditioning process, the placement of this material is exceedingly important. It indicates that the framers of the tradition understood from the outset that the material is not historical reportage; it is, rather, material intended for liturgical reiteration, not only that the founding, saving event can be remembered, but that it can be "represented" and reenacted in other times and places that await emancipation. The text is designed so that the memory is a generative event in subsequent generations of Israel, generative of energy and courage for the belated contexts in which God's people will again face oppression, will again cry out in pain, and will again appeal to the God of all departures.

The exodus narrative culminates in chapters 14–15 with the actual departure from Egypt. While in popular lore the emancipation from Egypt is dominated by a great wall of water, in the narrative itself the water is at best instrumental to the real miracle. Much more important than water in the narrative of chapter 14 is the series of utterances through which the Egyptians acknowledge YHWH's decisiveness (v. 25), and do indeed come to "know that I am YHWH" (v. 18, au. trans.). Commensurately, the Israelites come to see and believe in YHWH (v. 31) and know that "the LORD will fight for you" (v. 14). YHWH does indeed "gain glory" over Pharaoh (vv. 4, 17), the practical effect of which is the liberation of Israel.

The narrative of chapter 14 is matched by the poem of 15:1–18, commonly regarded as a primal scripting of the entire plot from slavery to the land of promise. The "Song of Moses" begins with a recognition of YHWH's warrior quality (v. 3) and culminates in a celebration of YHWH's kingship (v. 18). Thus Israel's travail begins in a cry (2:23) and is transposed into doxological praise and celebration (15:21), sorrow turned to joy (see John 16:20; Plastaras 1966).

It is clear that this liturgical drama has funded the imagination of Judaism through the centuries, and has provided ground for hope when circumstances on the ground would yield none, even as the circumstances on the ground in Egypt had yielded no hope. The liturgical reenactment for which this narrative is the script serves to make present in Israel's imagination and life the rule of YHWH, without which the rule of Pharaoh remains unchallenged and uncurbed.

While the narrative rendering of emancipatory counterreality is character-istically Jewish and serves Judaism in a primal way (Levenson 1993, 127–59), it is also the case that the same narrative has funded the emancipatory imagi-nation of liberation theology in many parts of the world, in circles of Chris-tian faith beyond the concrete and immediate claims of Judaism (Pixley 1987). Because the narrative itself is generative and transformative, it seems clear that *the concrete claims of Judaism*, on the one hand, and *the large liberation trajectories of interpretation*, on the other, are not mutually exclusive: the God named and known first of all by Jews is the God who, in many other venues, is also the God who enacts exoduses where none has seemed possible, even as the one in Egypt did not seem possible (see Amos 9:7; Brueggemann 1998, 15–34).

II

At the conclusion of the exodus narrative, Israel is on its way to Mount Sinai and the awesome moment of covenant making, an encounter that begins in 19:1. Between the end of the exodus narrative in 15:21 and the arrival at Sinai in 19:1, the narrative materials portray Israel en route from slavery to covenant (15:22–18:27). This so-called sojourn tradition continues after the meeting at Sinai, beginning at Numbers 10:11, when Israel "sojourns" again until arrival at the land of promise at the end of Deuteronomy. This material functions as something like travel music to transport Israel from one place to another:

> Exodus: Exodus 1:1–15:21
> *Sojourn*: Exodus 15:22–18:27
> Sinai: Exodus 19:1–Numbers 10:10
> *Sojourn*: Numbers 10:11–Deuteronomy 34:12

The sojourn material is organized around a series of encounters at different oases, as Israel moves, in stylized telling, by stages. Attempts have been made to recover the itinerary of the sojourn by identifying various oases and con-necting them in terms of realistic possibilities of travel. The narrative gives the impression, however, that the oases are only staging arenas for narratives of crisis, so that any geographical recovery of the sojourn is likely impossible and, in any case, is of little interest to the narrative community. Much more central in the tradition are the transactions in crisis that need have no locat-able historical placement, because they are relational transactions that report in paradigmatic ways on Israel's life with God. The themes that dominate the tradition include (a) the rebellious quarrelsomeness of Israel, (b) the generos-ity of God as sustainer, and (c) the anger of God at Israel's rebellion. Where

or when such encounters take place is immaterial, because they are characteristic enactments of the faith of Israel.

At the outset, it is important to understand the function of the notion of
"wilderness" in the tradition. It is easiest to take "wilderness" as a geographical reference, and that is surely what the tradition itself understood. As a geographical location, the term refers to the area traversed by Israel between
Egypt (slavery) and the promised land (secure well-being). The term signifies,
moreover, an area without visible evidence of life-sustaining resources such
as water, bread, or meat. This is clearly how the tradition presents the matter
of wilderness. Since the exodus itself is something of an act of imagination, it
is not unreasonable to suggest that the wilderness that is presented with geographical realism is an arena of imaginative construal. It is a launching pad for
God-Israel transactions in an environment of acute risk and deep jeopardy.

In the lived experience of Israel, it is plausible that the sixth-century deportation, when Israel was removed from the land, provides the historical connection of Israel to the "wilderness." That is, the concretely remembered
wilderness serves to comment upon the palpable experience of exile when
Israel found itself without the usual supports for community life—temple,
city, or monarchy. This connection of wilderness to exile is even more apt if
we remember that the pentateuchal traditions reached something like final
form in the sixth or fifth century, so that contemporary experience is read into
and through ancient remembering.

As "wilderness" may be made contemporary in exile, so "wilderness" may
be understood theologically and cosmically if wilderness as chaos is the primordial condition of disorder and the primordial force of anti-life that seeks
to negate the life of Israel and the life of the world. Such a characterization
of cosmic wilderness (chaos) is offered, for example, in Isaiah 24:1–13. The
point of understanding "wilderness" as exile and as chaos is to suggest that
while the term may be rooted in the narrative geographically, it has more
profound dimensions in Israel's interpretive tradition.

Thus the narratives of Exodus 16–18 are wilderness accounts—without
visible life-support systems—that well serve the large, imaginative enterprise
of exile and that fund a large sense of chaos. The narrative in this cluster of
texts that has drawn most interpretive energy is Exodus 16, the account of the
manna. The two principle ingredients of this narrative are Israel's desperate,
recalcitrant need, and YHWH's inscrutable, generous response of generosity. Beyond that transaction, the teaching of the narrative (a) proposes a covenantal, neighborly model of economics (vv. 17–18), (b) underscores Israel's
rebellious resistance to that model of economics (vv. 19–21), and (c) affirms
the peculiar gravity and cruciality of the Sabbath, a characteristic accent of the
Priestly interpreters who refracted Israel's memory through cultic institutions

and practices (vv. 22–26). The outcome of the narrative is the assertion of YHWH's reliability and fidelity toward Israel in its season of deep need.

III

When Israel arrives at Sinai, a new, extended, complex tradition begins, featuring (a) the making of *covenant* between YHWH and Israel, and (b) the issuance of the *commands* of YHWH that become the condition and substance of the covenant. It is not possible to know anything about the history or geographical location of Sinai. Frank Crüsemann states the decisive function and importance of the mountain for the ongoing interpretive tradition:

> Sinai is, however, a utopian place. It is temporally and physically outside state authority. The association of divine law with this place is completed by steps, which the catastrophe of Israel both enabled and compelled. Sinai became the fulcrum of a legal system not connected with the power of the state and therefore not an expression of tradition and custom. . . . The very real survival of Israel, in spite of the kind of conquest that had destroyed other nations, depends on a fictional place in an invented past. They escaped every earthly power and therefore are put ahead of those kingdoms. (Crüsemann 1996, 57)

In all its complexity, the Sinai tradition extends through the book of Leviticus and through Numbers 10:10, when Israel departs the mountain. The reason the material is so complex is that over time the tradition of commands sought to extend the rule and will of YHWH to every aspect of life, personal and public, civic and cultic. The completed literature, moreover, contains many layers of tradition and many voices of interpretation. As a consequence, one can trace the main flow of the Sinai tradition; in its final form, however, the material contains many twists and turns that cannot be read as a tight coherence. This tradition is at the core of Judaism, which is constituted by obedience to YHWH's Torah. Conversely, in Christian tradition this material has been largely downplayed, precisely because it has been erroneously understood as "law" that provides a way to earn God's grace. A reconsideration of the role and function of the commandments in their rich interpretive complexity is now of immense importance for Christians, precisely to be delivered from wrongly informed and distorting caricatures of the tradition of commandment.

In this extended tradition of command, the most important materials are in Exodus 19–24, commonly termed the "Sinai pericope." This material is perhaps the earliest in the tradition of commandment and is in any case normative for what follows. These chapters include a preparation for the meeting with YHWH at the mountain (19:10–25), the proclamation of the Ten Commandments (20:1–17), the acceptance of Moses as the normative mediator of torah (20:18–21), and a concluding narrative of covenant making, whereby Israel takes an oath of allegiance to YHWH (chap. 24). The *proclamation of commands* and the *oath of allegiance* are the defining elements of the covenant that bind Israel to YHWH in obedience. While it is not possible to establish the early date of the Decalogue, it is readily seen that this catalog of commands is the most elemental of all of YHWH's torah requirements. In a sense, all the other commands are interpretations of these ten.

Chapters 19–20 and 24 form a narrative envelope that encloses the legal corpus of 21:1–23:19. This body of commandments is commonly thought to be the earliest such "law collection" in Israel; in part it seems to represent a modest agricultural community. These chapters were likely an independent corpus that originally had no connection to the Decalogue; in its present place, however, the collection is offered as the first exposition of the Decalogue. With reference to 24:7, this collection is often termed the "Book of the Covenant," even though it likely had no primary relation to the reference. It is the earliest example of the dynamism of Israel's Torah, a process whereby older commands are endlessly reiterated, exposited, or transposed to meet new circumstances.

This collection of commandments embodies some of the primary features that recur in Israel's Torah. On the one hand, the Torah includes a so-called humanitarian tradition that is concerned for a workable communitarianism that values all members of the community. Thus it is instructive that the very first commandment in the corpus concerns the limitation on debt slavery in order that creditors and debtors in the community can function together as neighbors (21:1–11). This same concern is voiced in 22:21–24, 25–27; and 23:9 with reference to widows, orphans, resident aliens, and the poor. The commandments insist that economic transactions must be neighborly transactions. On the other hand, there are absolute formulations of law, as in 21:12–17 and 22:18–20, that rigorously uphold social order in a merciless fashion without any humanitarian qualification. These different accents are placed back-to-back in what was likely a very complex development of the tradition, so that one is able to see the tension between an absolute commitment to order and a compassion for the powerless (Hanson 1977). There is no doubt that theological-moral *absolutism* and *compassion* live side by side and in tension through the complex process of Torah interpretation.

The Sinai pericope of Exodus 19–24 ends with the ascent of Moses into the mountain for forty days and forty nights (24:18). In 25:1 a new corpus of texts begins in a quite different genre. In 25:1–31:18 Moses receives instruction directly from YHWH concerning the arrangement of a "holy place" that will be adequate for the habitation of the Holy One in the midst of Israel. These chapters constitute a series of commands that are matched, not precisely but in great detail, in 35:1–40:38, with the report that Moses obeyed the commands of 25:1–31:18 exactly, and thereby constructed an adequate shrine for YHWH. The verification of Moses' exacting obedience is the culminating report of 40:34–38, attesting that YHWH's glory did indeed come to abide in the tabernacle in the midst of Israel. Thus Moses, in addition to being the great Torah interpreter, becomes the great guarantor of YHWH's presence in Israel.

Two critical matters concerning this material are of interest. First, this material belongs to the Priestly tradition. This phrase is a scholarly usage referring to a community of interpretation in ancient Israel that was concerned primarily with practices of holiness and orderliness that would make possible the habitation of YHWH in Israel. While holiness may pertain to every facet of life, the central focus of this interpretive tradition is upon cultic matters and the arrangement of worship practices, for it is in worship that YHWH is most plausibly and most intensely present in Israel. This focus caused this tradition to exclude many other considerations from its horizon. Because of this focus, the ones who fostered this interpretive tradition are reckoned to be "priests," thus the "Priestly tradition."

It is likely that this tradition that extends from Genesis through Numbers was brought to its present form in the exile, thus a tradition of *presence* in a context of deeply felt *absence*. There is no doubt that the tradition draws upon older materials, but the present formulation is understood as an imaginative act whereby YHWH's presence would be assured in absence. This particular tradition within the Torah is easiest to identify of all the sources because it characteristically articulates matters with precision and is attentive to proper order and symmetry (as in the case of the "mercy seat" in 25:17–22, for example).

Second, it has been noticed that the material of Exodus 25–31 consists in seven speeches whereby "The LORD said [or spoke] to Moses" (25:1; 30:11, 17, 22, 34; 31:1, 12). Interpreters suggest that these seven speeches are designed to match the seven days of creation in Genesis 1, also a Priestly text (Blenkinsopp 1977, 5; P. Kearney 1977, 375–86). These seven speeches, moreover, culminate with the Sabbath (31:12–17) as does the seventh day in Genesis 2:1–4a. As a consequence, it is plausible that amid the immense disorder of history, the Priestly tradition imagined an alternative, well-ordered creation that is experienced in worship (Levenson 1988, 66–77). The tabernacle replicates creation, except without the disorder of lived reality.

While the text is rather boring to read and has been much neglected in interpretation, we should not miss the powerful theological imagination at work here or the intense pastoral concern to give access to the presence of God. It is likely that the tabernacle, as presented here, is based on the memory of an old tent where YHWH was known to be present (see 33:7–11), but the memory of the tent has been refracted through the nearer memory of the Jerusalem temple, so that the tabernacle is an imaginative construct continuing the functions of tent and temple. What matters most for theological interpretation, however, is the provision for presence, for the term "tabernacle" (*miškan*) is derived from the Hebrew verb *šakan*, which means "to sojourn, to abide provisionally." Thus the word bespeaks a provisionally abiding presence. The presence is particularly signified by the reality of "glory," a characteristic way of speaking about YHWH's palpable, powerful presence (40:34–38). The tabernacle, moreover, contains the "mercy seat" (25:17–22). This English phrase translates *kapporet*, a noun from *kipper*, a word known among us from *Yom Kippur*, the "Day of Atonement." Thus the "mercy seat" is the locus of reconciliation, forgiveness, and atonement, now structured by the priests into the center of Israel's life.

If the widely shared assumptions stated above are correct, then these materials represent a powerful example of the way in which the Torah tradition, rooted at Sinai, is extended and extrapolated to come to terms with new circumstances and new needs in the community. The circumstance of absence in exile evoked an interpretation of divine presence whereby those without a temple (for it had by now been destroyed) were given access to that presence in a more or less improvised mobile shrine.

The command to construct a suitable habitat for the divine presence (Exod 25–31) and the report of implementation of the command (Exod 35–40) have between them, in the present form of the text, a very different kind of narrative in Exodus 32–34. These three chapters constitute a dramatic articulation of one defining aspect of Israel's faith and are intimately connected to the Sinai pericope of Exodus 19–24.

In 24:18, as noted above, Moses is on the mountain for forty days and forty nights. If we read directly from 24:18 to 32:1, we can understand that it is the "delay" of Moses that evokes the crisis narrated in Exodus 32. The person of Moses dominates the tradition. In his absence, Aaron (portrayed as his brother, but perhaps the cipher for a competing priestly tradition of interpretation) seizes the initiative and produces an alternative representation of God, the calf (32:4). It is likely that the calf, at the outset, was not idolatrous, but simply a competitor to the ark of the covenant as a proper sign of divine presence. In any case, the narrative presents the rivalry of Aaron (now judged to be disobedient) and Moses (the obedient leader who can intervene with YHWH and change YHWH's mind) (32:11–14). The outcome of this encounter is (a) the breaking of the covenant of Sinai (v. 19) and (b) the legitimation of the

Levites as the true advocates of the faith of Moses (vv. 25–29). Thus the text no doubt reflects not just a brotherly exchange, but competition and conflict between rival priestly groups with their competing interpretive voices.

Moses' role as intercessor (chap. 33) evokes YHWH's self-announcement as God of mercy and judgment (34:6–7) and yields a renewed covenant granted by YHWH (34:10) with a new declaration of torah (34:11–28). In its present form, the narrative of these chapters serves to underscore the legitimate authority of Moses against other authorities (the Aaronide priests) who challenge the tradition of Moses. Beyond that rivalry resolved in favor of Moses, however, it is important to notice the theological claim of these chapters. The account concerns a covenant *broken* (32:19) and *remade* (34:10). This sequence is paradigmatic in the Old Testament, for YHWH's covenant with Israel is recurringly broken and remade, *broken* in recalcitrance on the part of Israel, *remade* due to YHWH's generosity and compassion.

It belongs to the very character of YHWH, who acts in judgment and mercy, to break covenants that have been violated in disobedience, and then to renew those covenants (see Jer 31:31–34; Isa 54:7–8); it belongs to the very character of Israel, who seeks autonomy, to violate covenant and yet to remain endlessly needy and dependent upon YHWH and who therefore willingly, eagerly returns to covenant with YHWH when invited back into that relationship. Thus Exodus 32–34 is a template for the life of Israel with YHWH; the covenant made in 34:10 is the very same covenant of 24:3–8, and yet a different, altogether new covenant because it is freshly grounded in YHWH's compassion and forgiveness. This is the pattern of the long-term drama of faith in the Old Testament.

In sum, the book of Exodus provides defining categories for the faith of ancient Israel. The three decisive motifs noted here are commensurate with the three large units of the book:

1. *Deliverance*. The God who defeats the oppressive power of Pharaoh and who thereby emancipates Israel from slavery is characteristically the God who delivers from oppression; correspondingly, Israel is characteristically a people delivered, though it is clear that YHWH's readiness to deliver is not confined to Israel (see Amos 9:7). The sojourn materials of Exodus 16–18 are congruent with the exodus materials. The God who delivers is the one who sustains the people delivered.

2. *Covenant*. The crucial material of Exodus 19–24 concerns covenant making whereby YHWH signs on as the God of Israel, and Israel submits in obedience to the commands of YHWH. This relationship of command and obedience is definitional for Israel, a relationship reflected in the later, often reiterated formula, "I will be your God and you shall be my people" (see Exod 6:7; Jer 11:4; 24:7; 30:22; 31:33; Ezek 11:20; 14:11; 36:28; 37:23, 27). Two

matters are important. First, the exodus emancipation and the Sinai covenant belong inextricably together. The deliverance is in order to establish the new obedience of Sinai; the new obedience of Sinai is possible only because of the deliverance. In these twinned events, Israel exchanges the harsh governance of Pharaoh for the new governance of YHWH that is marked by mixed components of fierceness and generosity. Second, it is clear that in the covenant the God who can say "the whole earth is mine" (Exod 19:5) is nonetheless the God who takes Israel as YHWH's own special people (19:6). This scandal of particularity is decisive for faith in the Old Testament, even though it concerns the God of all creation.

3. *Presence.* This third theme, often neglected in Old Testament interpretation, receives great attention in the text of Exodus. The Priestly tradition knows that hosting the Holy One is no small, trivial, or casual undertaking. Therefore the practice of symmetry, order, discipline, and beauty is essential to the reality of God's presence in Israel. This corpus of text on presence requires that interpretation not neglect the demanding reality of YHWH's holiness, a neglect to which a technological, pragmatic society is immensely open. As the book of Exodus ends, the Sinai meeting continues into the book of Leviticus. Israel receives much more instruction about holiness in the materials that follow. Israel is invited, under discipline, to sojourn in the midst of God's glory, a glory powerfully celebrated in the defeat of Pharaoh (Exod 14:4, 17).

7

The Book of Leviticus

The book of Leviticus is all too often skipped over by modern readers in general and by Christian readers in particular. But this is a shame. It is a rich and interesting book, albeit one that seems more foreign to modern readers than do the narratives of Genesis and Exodus, the poetry of the Psalms, or the ethical preaching of the prophets. But it is worth taking the time to read Leviticus and to take its religious vision seriously. It is a vision based on the recognition that human beings live in a physical world of bodies and the consequent claim that religion has to do with that *physical* world and not just with what one *believes*. Thus the attention to dietary rules, skin diseases, and bodily fluids, which can seem off-putting to many readers, may be seen as a systematic attempt to bring the materiality of our existence into the realm of religion. And the practice of animal sacrifice is a recognition that the killing of animals for food is a morally difficult thing, and that it ought also to brought into the realm of the religious life. Moreover, the notion of "blood atonement," which permeates Christian theological thinking on the death of Jesus, cannot be understood without reference to Leviticus.

I

In the book of Leviticus the Sinai tradition of covenantal commandments, begun in Exodus 19, continues. Indeed, this Sinai-situated material extends from Exodus 19:1 through Numbers 10:10. All of the material in the book of Leviticus that purports to be from Moses is part of the Priestly tradition, a formulation of covenantal requirements that reflect the concerns and interests of the Priestly source. This material no doubt draws upon older traditions and practices, but is perhaps given its final form in the exile. That final form is an attempt to provide a reliable way of hosting the presence of YHWH in an environment seemingly marked by YHWH's absence. The focus of all of this material is on the distinctions between "the holy" and "the common" on the one hand, and between "the unclean" and "clean" on the other (see 10:10). Chapters 1–16 focus more on the holiness of God, and chapters 17–27 (often identified as a separate source called "the Holiness Code") extend that notion of holiness to the land and to the people of Israel.

At the outset, it is important to consider the meaning of "holiness" that this text seeks to explicate (Gammie 1989). The term must be understood on a continuum of uses, so that it has no simple, single definition. On the one hand, the term "holiness" bespeaks *separateness*, almost in the manner of an elemental religious taboo, the affirmation that God is so different and distinct from Israel that Israel dare not draw near to God or be in God's presence except with the most careful preparations and qualifications (see 2 Sam 5:6–8 for a narrative concerning such a dangerous taboo). On the other hand, the term develops in Israel's usage in an ethical direction so that the term may also refer to *righteousness* or *justice* according to the requirements of the Torah. The term has such rich and varied usage precisely because it seeks to articulate what is most characteristic, and therefore most hidden and inscrutable, about God.

It is also important to consider the meaning of "clean" (*tahor*) and "unclean" (*tame'*), which are not in the first instance terms of moral judgment, as they are often taken to be. It is difficult to come up with good English translations for these terms. Sometimes "pure" and "impure" are used, but these also have taken on a moral valence that is not quite right for the Hebrew terms. For example, touching a corpse renders one "unclean," but clearly if a loved one dies, family members are expected to hug and hold and ultimately prepare the body for burial. There is no moral failure involved here, but nevertheless one is rendered "unclean" or *tame'* by such actions. Likewise, both menstrual blood and semen render one unclean, but these bodily fluids are not by any means intrinsically bad. To the contrary, the Priestly author has commanded humans to "be fruitful and multiply" (Gen 1:28), and both of these bodily fluids are indicative of the ability to fulfill that command. It is better to think of the state of uncleanness as being slightly out of the ordinary, and a state that requires some ritual activity—normally not much more than washing with water—to return to a state of normality.

The book of Leviticus is a priestly manual, that is, a set of instructions for the practice and conduct of the priestly office. The priests are charged with two primary tasks: "to instruct Israel not to cause defilement, and to purge the sanctuary whenever it is defiled" (Milgrom 1989, 63). The responsibility of the priests is articulated in two distinct ways in the book of Leviticus. In chapters 1–16 holiness is situated in the cult; in chapters 17–26 holiness pertains in larger scope to the promised land. While the fundamental issues are largely the same in the two parts of the book, they are articulated in different ways; consequently scholars have concluded that chapters 17–26, commonly termed the "Holiness Code," constitute a separate tradition and perhaps a separate literary source.

II

In the first part of the book (chaps. 1–16), we may distinguish several subunits of material. The first section of the book, chapters 1–7, consists of a catalog of different kinds of sacrifice that are authorized by YHWH and are to be enacted by authorized priests. It is likely that this is a highly schematized taxonomy of sacrifices that for much of Israel's life were conducted in a much more ad hoc and random way. These several sacrificial acts likely arose in a rich variety of historical circumstances, no doubt many such practices being appropriated from the broader religious environment of Israel's cultural context. It is a primal agenda of the Priestly tradition to order and regularize in a somewhat theoretical fashion what in practice may have been much less clearly organized and conceptualized. It is not necessary (or even possible) to understand the precise procedure or intention of each sacrifice named. It is enough to see that the complicated sacrificial system, as it is articulated in this tradition, is a gift of God to make interaction with the Holy God possible and affirmative. The sacrificial system is presented as a gift of God's grace that makes a relationship possible. It is to be noted that such interaction (communion) is understood in the tradition as a *mediated* process. Israel has no *immediate* access to God, but access is characteristically gained through authorized personnel and procedures.

While the particulars of these sacrificial procedures are rich and varied, it is likely that the procedures can be understood as (a) acts that celebrate the relationship of YHWH with Israel in its proper functioning, and (b) acts of purification, purgation, and reconciliation when the relationship has been disrupted by Israel's sin and disobedience. Moreover, all of the sacrifices except for the first—the *'olah*, or the whole burnt offering (chap. 1)—would have provided a meal for the sacrificer. An implication of the sacrificial system is thus that anytime one wanted to eat meat, the animal had to be sacrificed religiously before being consumed. This requirement connects back to the Priestly author's original vision for a vegetarian humanity (Gen 1:29), and the sacrificial context probably helps to atone for the taking of the animal's life.

In the past season of theological interpretation, it has been fashionable among Christian interpreters to critique and polemicize against the sacrificial system offered here, noting its exacting, punctilious character and suggesting that the procedures provide means of manipulation of the Deity. Such a critique was mounted from an extreme Protestant perspective that offered an explicit polemic against the practices described, but also offered an implicit critique of Roman Catholic practices that were taken to have more in common formally with the system of the priests than such a Protestant perspective could entertain. This polemic, however, fails to recognize that in its own context, such a system of sacrifice is understood as a provision given in YHWH's generosity; thus God provides the mediating means of effective communion.

> **Midrashic Moment: The "Burnt Offering" in Leviticus 1**
>
> The Hebrew term for the "burnt offering" in Leviticus 1 is 'olah, meaning "that which goes up" (i.e., up in smoke entirely). It is the only offering that is wholly burned, with no remainder. The important ancient Greek translation of the Bible known as the Septuagint translates 'olah as holokaustos, or "whole burning." It is from this Greek word that we get the modern term Holocaust, which is widely used to refer to Nazi Germany's attempt to destroy all of European Jewry in the 1930s and 1940s. This use of the term emphasizes the wholesale killing and massive destruction represented by Nazi racial policy and practices, but many have objected that the religious overtones of the word are entirely inappropriate in this context. Thus in recent years another biblical Hebrew word has come into use, shoah or "destruction," which does not have the connotation of a sacrifice to God.

Beyond that, the entire argument of the Epistle to the Hebrews is based on the claim that Jesus is, in Christian understanding, both the priest who effectively reconciles humanity to God and the sacrificial offering that effects restored communion. To be sure, such an argument claims that in Jesus the Israelite "system" of sacrifices is superseded; even that claim, however, inescapably appeals to the categories of that system as a witness to the identity, role, and efficaciousness of Jesus. Indeed, the entire popular Christian notion of "being saved by the blood" depends upon this liturgical antecedent that became the ground for a "sacrificial" understanding of Christ's atoning work. Thus these materials perform an immensely important role in Christian theology by providing categories through which to explicate the "work of Christ."

Leviticus 8–10 turns from legitimated and authorized sacrificial practices more precisely to the office of the priest who is to effect such sacrifices. The accent in these chapters is upon the priestly lineage of Aaron, who is a dominant figure in this tradition. Aaron and his sons occupy the key role in making possible Israel's access to YHWH. It is likely that this textual tradition reflects the advocacy and triumph of the Aaronide priests in the exilic and postexilic periods in what must have been a highly contested claim for sacerdotal power and authority. The claim of legitimation is further advanced as the tradition situates Aaron, the founder of the priestly order, as the brother of Moses and therefore close to the taproot of primary authority. (We should remember that Exodus 32 voices a powerful polemic against Aaron, a narrative that no doubt reflects the advocacy of a rival to the lineage of Aaron in contestation for priestly authority and preeminence.)

In a quite enigmatic narrative fragment, two of the sons of Aaron are accused of disobedience to YHWH by offering "unholy" or "strange" fire ('esh zarah), and are consequently consumed by the fire (Lev 10:1–2). This strange narrative, in any case, acknowledges that even this most sweeping claim for priesthood must take into account that Israel's best institutional provisions for religious practice are flawed and problematic. Even while marring the qualification of this priestly order, however, that acknowledgment of failure does not deter recognition of the crucial role of this priesthood in distinguishing between holy and common, clean and unclean. As a result, Israel may gain access to YHWH, but such access is always a potentially dangerous thing. (One is reminded of Exod 4:24–26, where God attempts to kill Moses in the night, right after having chosen and commissioned Moses to free God's people from Egypt.)

The provisions in chapters 11–15 permit a broader scope for holiness and the kinds of "impurities" that could endanger the community. These chapters are of particular interest because they focus on matters outside the cult itself, affirming that every aspect of the life of Israel constitutes a zone in which the practice of holiness is urgent. Particular attention may be given to the matter of "bodily discharges" in chapter 15, related to the concerns of chapter 12 as well. These texts concern, for one thing, the "impurity" of a woman in menstruation and in childbirth, and have been subject to the critique that they condemn the natural bodily functions of a woman as "unclean." In the same chapter the concern extends to the bodily discharge of a man as well. While this matter may not be evenhanded, the concern is beyond any simple judgment upon women. Mary Douglas (1996) has notably suggested that all such "discharges" upset order by having things "out of place." Characteristically the accent is on the practice, with only very lean explanation or justification for the commands, but it is important to remember that such uncleanness or impurity is by no means presented as a moral or ethical failure. Involved as they are in the good of procreation, neither menstrual blood nor seminal emissions are seen as "bad" by the Priestly writer, and they are not condemned in these texts. It seems rather that the *loss* of these life-giving bodily fluids is seen as potentially dangerous and thus requiring ritual attention.

Special attention should be given to chapter 16, the only reference in the Old Testament to Yom Kippur, the Jewish Day of Reconciliation, or, in older parlance, Day of Atonement. In this most awesome of all practices in Judaism on this most awesome of all days, Israel is forgiven its sin and is reconciled to God, a practice that continues in contemporary synagogues with great power and importance. The actual process of forgiveness seems to be the transfer of guilt to an animal, which then carries the guilt or impurity away, a process wherein the guilt is treated as having an almost material quality.

Such a procedure may strike a contemporary reader as deeply "primitive." It is to be noted, however, that exactly this same procedure and assumption are operative in some understandings among Christians of Jesus Christ as the "bearer of sin." It is in any case evident that for both Jews and Christians, forgiveness and reconciliation depend upon divine initiative and are accomplished in ways more elemental than any rational or moral explanation can provide. The provision for reconciliation here locates the graciousness of God in a liturgical act that is inscrutable and that defies theological explanation. While such a provision is beyond the ken of Christian interpretation, it must in any case be recognized that the actual operation of Christ's effective forgiveness is in parallel fashion beyond rational or moral explanation. The entire drama is deeply sacramental, that is, a visible sign affecting a theological matter that is not visible.

III

In the second half of the book of Leviticus, in chapters 17–26 (with an addendum in chap. 27), scholars have recognized a more coherent collection of commandments, which provide that "You shall be holy, for I the LORD your God am holy" (19:2). Because of this accent throughout the collection, the material is dubbed the "Holiness Code." The general concern for holiness in Israel, reflected in chapters 1–16, is commensurate with YHWH's own holiness and is continued in these chapters. As indicated, the horizon of holiness in this collection is much wider, for it concerns the entire scope of the promised land. If, as is likely, this material is dated in its final form to the exile, then a concern for the land is especially important, for it reflects an anticipation among displaced people of restoration into the land. We may note three particular matters:

1. The general provision of Leviticus 18 and 20 specifies sexual conduct that is prohibited because it violates purity, would pollute Israel and the land, and would thereby jeopardize the community. It is evident that sexual relations within the community and its extended family constitute a zone of immense urgency whereby the community can be put at risk. These texts list a variety of distorted relations that would violate purity and holiness, and so bring deep trouble upon the community and upon the land.

In particular, one prohibition among many prohibitions concerns sexual relations between males (18:22; 20:13). In recent interpretation, the prohibition of "homosexual" relations has received great attention in the church in the United States. The teaching of these verses itself is, however, ambiguous. Something is being prohibited here, but it seems clear that the text does not construct a larger category of homosexuality, which is then condemned. Rather, the prohibition seems to concern the specific idea that men not "waste their seed" in sexual couplings that will not give rise to conception. Given that prohibition, difficult questions remain about the significance of these particular prohibitions in the wider interpretive conversation on two counts.

First, the list of prohibitions reflects an intense interest in the maintenance, preservation, and enhancement of a holy community and is part of a general system of holiness that concerns every facet of life. As a result it is doubtful that these two particular verses of prohibition should be taken out of context when it is generally acknowledged that the wider holiness system advocated here is not pertinent in contemporary Christian faith. It seems unlikely that this single prohibition can be extracted from a wider notion of holiness of a ritual kind to the neglect of the rest of the system, as reflected, for example, in 19:19.

Second, in theological interpretation it is not clear how a particular prohibition mentioned nowhere else in the commandments of Sinai is to be related to the wider sweep of the gospel, that is, the interpretive question of the relation of the Bible to the gospel. It is clear that on many other issues (e.g., slavery, divorce), the interpretive practice of the church (on the grounds of the gospel) has relativized the teaching of a biblical commandment. Such a maneuver will be unsettling in many quarters; concerning other subjects, however, that same interpretive maneuver is so commonplace as to go largely unrecognized and unacknowledged. The contemporary disputatious interpretive discussion of these prohibitions concerns the same question about "Bible and gospel" that the church has faced on many other subjects.

2. Between the catalog of sexual prohibitions in chapters 18 and 20 stands chapter 19 and its remarkable vision for communal welfare in Israel. This chapter provides the commandment of love of neighbor to which Jesus refers as "the second great commandment" (v. 18):

> The first is, "Hear, O Israel: the Lord our God, the Lord is one; you
> shall love the Lord your God with all your heart, and with all your
> soul, and with all your mind, and with all your strength." The second
> is this, "You shall love your neighbor as yourself." There is no other
> commandment greater than these. (Mark 12:29–31)

This particular commandment, quoted from our verse, is reinforced in the
chapter by a provision for the poor in Leviticus 19:9–10, 15, and by a remarkable teaching on respect for those who are not Israelites:

> When an alien resides with you in your land, you shall not oppress
> the alien. The alien who resides with you shall be to you as the citizen
> among you; you shall love the alien as yourself, for you were aliens in
> the land of Egypt: I am the Lord your God. (Lev 19:33–34)

Mary Douglas has proposed that chapters 18 and 20 provide a deliberate
framing for chapter 19 so that the whole is arranged to show that *love of neigh-*
bor has become the key component of a vision of holiness. With reference to
chapters 18 and 20 in relation to chapter 19, Douglas writes:

> This impressive pair of chapters is like a great proscenium arch for a
> processional rite, or more like two carved pillars on either side of a
> shrine. Leviticus deliberately puts the laws of honest dealings at the
> center and the sexual sins at the periphery. The laws on each side
> against incest, sodomy, and bestiality are backed by twice-repeated
> warnings that the land will vomit the people out if they follow these
> practices. Defilement is the common threat for them all; it results
> from cultic violations, which makes the context inescapably cultic.
>   . . . The effect of using these unedifying sexual deviations to build
> a frame around chapter 19 is to underscore the concepts of justice
> which are expounded in the middle. The pure and noble character of
> the Hebrew God is contrasted with the libidinous customs of the false
> gods. This does not mean that the sexual deviations are not counted as
> sinful, but it does imply that they are less significant than sins against
> justice, false oaths, stealing, cheating, and false witness. . . .
>   The lesson here is not that holiness is purely a matter of the cult
> but that holiness requires in ritual contexts correspondence to what
> God's people must do for each other in secular contexts. The paral-
> lel between what people do for God and what people do for each
> other is theologically rich. The ritual laws, in short, are grounded in
> justice. . . .
>   . . . On the principle of pedimental [architectural] composition, we
> should look for the meaning of Leviticus in its middle part, chapter 19.
> And in the middle of chapter 19, we read, "You shall love your neigh-
> bor as yourself" (v. 18). The rule that astonishes Christians who did
> not remember that it came from the Old Testament is revealed as the
> cornerstone of holiness teaching. (Douglas 1999, 345, 346, 348, 349)

Thus, in Douglas's interpretation, the arrangement of the materials serves to subordinate holiness and purity to justice. Or said alternatively, holiness develops in the interpretive practices of Israel so that it comes to focus on justice; the more ethical accent on justice seems to grow stronger at the expense of the notion of holiness as taboo. It may be that Israel has taken a cultural notion of holiness and transposed it over time to conform more fully to the will of YHWH, the God of the covenant.

3. The tilt of holiness toward justice is further evidenced in this corpus of commandments in Leviticus 25, the great chapter on the practice of Jubilee. The practice of Jubilee, here given its primal biblical grounding, extends the sabbatical principle to provide that after forty-nine years (seven times seven years), the Jubilee shall be enacted whereby the land is given rest and whereby land as covenantal inheritance is returned to the "rightful owners," who may have lost the land in the rough-and-tumble of economic transactions. It is remarkable that this practice is understood as a discipline of holiness: "For it is a jubilee; it shall be holy to you" (v. 12). At the same time it cannot be doubted that the developed teaching on the practice moves toward neighborliness, in congruity with the commandments of 19:17–18, 33–34. Thus a corpus of commandments that has its focus on cultic purity whereby the holiness of YHWH can be hosted readily spills over into the secular (that is, the noncultic dimensions of life) so that holiness becomes a practice of neighborly justice.

The Holiness Code concludes in chapter 26 with a recital of covenant blessings commensurate with Torah obedience (26:3–13) and with a much longer articulation of severe covenant curses commensurate with disobedience to the Torah (vv. 14–39). This chapter underscores the cruciality and urgency of the practice of obedience, of *holiness* that takes the form of *justice*.

The book of Leviticus is yet another case in which older materials that are likely rooted in quite concrete practice are now transposed into a settled vision of a holy people in the company of the Holy God: "You shall be for me a priestly kingdom and a holy nation" (Exod 19:6; see 1 Pet 2:9).

We need to recognize that Leviticus is preoccupied with a series of concerns that are in many ways strange to modern or postmodern readers. Because the Priestly material focuses inescapably upon cultic matters and refracts their concern with attention to precision and symmetry, these materials have seemed in the context of modern secularization to be at best ancient curiosities. It is worth noting, however, that as the modern, self-sufficient world of the Enlightenment has come under threat and has been shown to be less than sufficient, there has been, at least in the United States, a return to the agenda reflected in this material.

Generally this return is reflected in contemporary preoccupation with the absence of God, as society has become increasingly profane, and conversely a new spirituality that concerns the presence of God. More specifically, when the world is seen and known to be under threat, a response in purity is newly important. Thus in the title of her influential book, *Purity and Danger*, Mary Douglas has seen that a sense of cultural danger evokes a preoccupation with holiness, thus providing one important clue to the culture wars now at work vigorously in church and in society in the United States that appeal in remarkable ways to the Bible (Douglas 1996).

The book of Leviticus articulates an old and perennial agenda in Israel in which there is an awareness of the radical otherness of YHWH, who cannot be approached casually but who can be hosted only with rigorous, disciplined intentionality. This agenda is rooted in Israel's profound sense of the character of this God who is, at the same time, faithful and ominous. That sense of God is perhaps intensified in a season of cultural danger. This reality may provide a clue for our appreciation of the codification of older materials in the exile or soon thereafter. It is curious that by the time of the exile, perhaps by the time of the final form of this text, there was no longer a temple in Jerusalem where sacrifices could be offered and cultic holiness could be practiced. This may suggest that the extended inventory of sacrifices and related materials in the book of Leviticus is to be understood not as a manual for practice, but as a liturgical, aesthetic act of imagination of what the world of Israel is like when it is known to be focused upon glad responses in obedience and sacrifice to YHWH. In this horizon there is no other chance for entry into the presence except through disciplines of holiness. While the book of Leviticus is remote from our contemporary world, its issues inescapably persist because the otherness of God persists in the world of faithful interpretation (Knohl 1995).

8

The Book of Numbers

The fourth book of the Torah contains themes we have already noticed, including more commands from Sinai and more stories of wilderness journeying. The book of Numbers has been to a certain extent disregarded, both in critical studies and in church use, because it seems to lack a clear, compelling character as a piece of literature. It has not been thought to be of decisive importance for critical understanding either of the traditions of Israel or of the foundations for biblical faith. There are, however, clearly some high points in the book, and there is much of interest to be gleaned.

With important exceptions to be noted, the book of Numbers is largely cast according to Priestly tradition. This means (a) that the primary agenda is sacerdotal, that is, the vision of Israel here is of a purified Priestly community that is kept ritually clean in order that it may host the presence of God; (b) that the book likely reached its final form in the exile, in that context providing pastoral guidance and reassurance among displaced Jehudites (exiles) who sought reformation as a "pure Israel"; (c) and that all the while it uses older materials—cultic and historical—but transforms them to serve the theological vision appropriate to a sacerdotal representation of the community of Israel.

I

Several ways of understanding this opaque material have been suggested:

1. It is most obvious that the book of Numbers divides at 10:11. The material up until this point is more instruction from Sinai through the work of Moses, instruction that concerns the proper ordering of the worship life of the community. This material thus continues the Priestly instruction that

began in Exodus 25 and continued on through the book of Leviticus. We should understand that "Moses" as guide is a belated appeal in the tradition to the remembered, "designated" guide of Sinai. The material after 10:11 and the noted departure from Mount Sinai characterizes Israel's long and vexed traverse from the mountain of commandments to the land of promise, the goal of the entire tradition. Thus the book divides between materials of *Sinai* and materials of *sojourn*, though it will be understood that in refracted form both accents of the tradition are designed for an exilic community as it ponders, (a) obedience (in the form of holiness) and (b) a projected return to the Holy Land.

2. It is possible to divide the book further by geographical reference, even though it is understood that geographical claims are now chronologically remote from actual geographical realities; they function symbolically, as do the narrative moves of Israel—in imagination—always closer to the land of promise or, in the sixth century, always closer to return to the land. In such a division, the first locus is at Sinai, as already noted, pertaining to 1:1–10:10. But then the remaining material can be divided in the suggestion that 10:11–21:9 locates imagined Israel on its way, north of Sinai, and that 21:10–36:13 moves Israel closer and situates Israel in the Jordan Valley. Thus the geographical division of 10:11–21:9 and 21:10–36:13 is a literary strategy for imagining Israel eventually closer to the land of promise. The accent on "imagined Israel" is an important one, both because it is futile to try to reconstruct the historical stages for the material and because the material in Priestly redaction is designed to serve the belated community of sixth-century exiles as a pastoral resource and guideline. Thus, belated though they may be, historical traces have been completely overridden by a later interpretive intentionality in the interest of a later community facing its own peculiar problem of displacement and loss with a theologically rooted possibility of reentering into the land and the presence.

3. A third, particularly suggestive proposal by Dennis Olson begins with the two census lists in chapters 1 and 26 (Olson 1985). These lists, which present a taxonomy of the population of Israel (from which the book derives its name "Numbers"), are to be understood not as historical reportage but as part of the interpretive staging of the book. Olson has suggested that the first list is of the "old generation," that is, the generation of Moses that had been disobedient. It is under severe judgment. The second list, in chapter 26, concerns the new generation that is reckoned to be obedient and therefore will receive the land of promise. In Olson's proposal the book of Numbers is organized in order to contrast the two generations, one failed and one faithful, to articulate the deep caesura in the self-understanding of

Israel whereby Israel's history is marked with a defining discontinuity at its defining center.

The sharp distinction between the two generations, an older one *disobedient* and a later one *obedient*, indicates a deep break in Israel's history, a break caused by the depths of disobedience to YHWH. As Olson has well noted, the only semblance of human continuity between the two generations is represented and embodied by the two faithful spies, Joshua and Caleb. Thus in 14:6–9 only Joshua and Caleb are trusting enough to rely upon the presence of YHWH for the new land in order to risk the dangers of entry. In 14:24, moreover, Caleb (even without Joshua) is marked as the carrier of continuity through his peculiar fidelity: "But my servant Caleb, because he has a different spirit and has followed me wholeheartedly, I will bring into the land into which he went, and his descendants shall possess it." It is clear that within the imaginative, interpretive venture that is the final form of the text, Joshua and Caleb function as types, albeit quite minority types of fidelity, that provide continuity for the large narrative from the exodus to the land.

4. Because the book of Numbers, in its final form, is an exilic document making use of older materials, we may see that the two-generation sequence and the two faithful Israelites (Joshua, Caleb) are not to be taken as historical realities, but are highly imaginative articulations designed precisely for the exilic crisis:

> The old fickle generation is the generation that evoked the destruction of 587 and suffered the deportation.
> The new generation is the generation of deportees that in new fidelity may reenter the land (particular reference might be made to the three generations of Ezek 18, wherein the third generation is the generation of the exile that is no longer bound by the disobedience of the previous generations).
> Joshua and Caleb are in fact the faithful remnant in exile who lived through the breach and embody what there is of continuity in the life of Israel.

In its final form, then, this way of reading the book of Numbers becomes an interpretive reflection upon the break of the sixth-century exile, and the summons to fidelity of the exilic remnant who may in due course reenter the land and take up a faithful life in the land.

All of these matters, in Priestly horizon, are understood in terms of the disciplines of holiness and ritual cleanness. These disciplines make possible the presence of the life-giving God in the midst of Israel, a presence that is in contrast to the stark absence of God, who has withdrawn (in exile) from profane, unclean Israel.

II

Thus the Priestly tradition has used older materials and shaped them imaginatively in order to offer a pastoral, theological interpretation especially geared to the realities of sixth-century displacement. In the context of that general shape for the literature, we may consider in turn several texts that are especially fruitful for theological interpretation.

1. In the materials of 1:1–10:10, the continued instruction at Sinai, the best-known text is the blessing of 6:24–26 that is entrusted to Aaron and his sons. (The reference to "Aaron and his sons" is likely recognition that in the emergent Judaism of the exile and thereafter, the priestly order of Aaron occupied a prominent position as the de facto leaders of the cultic community that Judaism had become. Thus "Aaron" here is not a remembered brother of Moses, but the acknowledged sacerdotal leader of the cult community.) The blessing may be understood as the liturgical outcome of an intense Priestly ordering of reality. That is, the enunciation and assurance of blessing is possible because Israel is now, in the Priestly horizon, ordered so that YHWH's power for life is available and assured through cultic practice. This Priestly utterance is decisive for life.

The blessing cites the name of YHWH three times; thus it is intensely focused upon YHWH as the true giver of well-being. The Priestly assurance is of YHWH's protective, sustaining presence expressed as "face/countenance," a way of speaking of a culture of presence that issues in peace (*shalom*). Thus the beginning of the benediction in "bless" and the outcome in *shalom* together bespeak a world of guaranteed material blessing from God the Creator. Between the beginning in blessing and the outcome in *shalom*, moreover, it is cultic presence, made possible through the disciplines of holiness, that become the source of an assured world of well-being as YHWH's gift.

2. Numbers 11–14 contain narratives that are usually regarded from a narrative source older than the predominantly Priestly materials of the book of Numbers. Whether older or not, these narratives clearly reflect an interpretive horizon different from the Priestly materials. These materials reflect the crisis of being in the wilderness without adequate life-support systems, a condition imaginatively redeployed with reference to the exile.

Numbers 11:4–25 reports on Israel's hunger in the wilderness and the response of sustenance. In verses 4–6 Israel is presented in a needy, demanding posture of complaint. Moses then intercedes with YHWH on Israel's behalf (vv. 10–15), and verses 16–25 report on the organized way in which YHWH responds to the crisis of hunger. The narrative is of particular interest because of the speech (prayer) of Moses on behalf of hungry Israel. In addition to demonstrating the courage and effectiveness of Moses vis-à-vis

YHWH, the particular, defiant charge of Moses against YHWH in verse 12 merits attention:

> Did I conceive all this people? Did I give birth to them, that you should say to me, "Carry them in your bosom, as a nurse carries a sucking child," to the land that you promised on oath to their ancestors?

In Moses' own denial of responsibility, it is clearly understood that it is YHWH, not Moses, who conceived, birthed, carried, and gave suckle to Israel. It is remarkable that this rhetoric employs maternal imagery, and so implies YHWH to be a mothering God. One may conclude that such extremity of expression is evoked and required by the extremity of the hunger crisis and the threat that that crisis poses to Mosaic leadership.

The threat to Mosaic leadership is reflected as well in the narrative of chapter 12. Miriam is presented as Moses' sister, though in Israel's memory she may be reckoned as an alternative voice of authority. The narrative reports on the way in which her challenge to the authority of Moses is a hazardous undertaking, for Miriam is not only smitten by leprosy for the challenge, but in the end depends upon the intervention of Moses for healing. The episode testifies to the singular authority that the figure of Moses occupies in the memory and imagination of Israel.

The narrative of chapters 13–14 concerns the case of the spies who assess Israel's chances against the resident population in Israel. This episode is a primary case in which Joshua and Caleb are singled out as carriers for a faithful future in Israel. The report on the land is congruent with the immensity of the old promise, for the spies report on the abundant fruitfulness of the land that they have surveyed. They attest to the impressive size of a "single cluster of grapes," as a measure of productivity in the land (13:23). (This single cluster of grapes being carried on a branch has become a familiar and much-used image in the State of Israel.) And they attest that the land "flows with milk and honey," as promised in the old tradition (13:27).

The issue of the narrative turns, however, on the fearfulness or confidence of the spies. The majority of the spies are fearful, because they reckon on entering the land without reference to the power and fidelity of YHWH: "So they brought to the Israelites an unfavorable report of the land that they had spied out, saying, 'The land that we have gone through as spies is a land that devours its inhabitants; and all the people that we saw in it are of great size. There we saw the Nephilim (the Anakites come from the Nephilim); and to ourselves we seemed like grasshoppers, and so we seemed to them'" (Num 13:32–33).

The trusting minority of two (Joshua and Caleb) counter that fearfulness with a bold affirmation of YHWH's guidance into the land: "If the Lord is pleased with us, he will bring us into this land and give it to us, a land that flows with milk and honey. Only, do not rebel against the LORD; and do not fear the people of the land, for they are no more than bread for us; their protection is removed from them, and the LORD is with us; do not fear them" (Num 14:8–9). Thus the story becomes a contest of trust and distrust in YHWH.

The story develops along two lines. First, Moses disputes with YHWH and presses YHWH to be faithful to Israel on the basis of YHWH's previous commitment to Israel (14:17–19; see Exod 34:6–7). When we remember that this material is not to be reread in the context of the exodus, the appeal to YHWH's gracious forgiveness is crucial for the remnant community. What may be an older memory became crucial in the context of Babylonian exile. To that later generation, the narrative assured YHWH's fidelity to the second generation of exiles. Second, the faithful and unfaithful are sorted out by YHWH, so that Caleb (here even without Joshua) is identified as the single thread into the future, for he embodies the kind of fidelity that trusts in YHWH, which is indispensable for Israel's future: "None of the people who have seen my glory and the signs that I did in Egypt and in the wilderness, and yet have tested me these ten times and have not obeyed my voice, shall see the land that I swore to give to their ancestors; none of those who despised me shall see it. But my servant Caleb, because he has a different spirit and has followed me wholeheartedly, I will bring into the land into which he went, and his descendants shall possess it" (Num 14:22–24). It is Caleb with "a different spirit" who is the wave of the future. The narrative then reports on the ways in which destructive disobedient human calculation can only lead to destruction (14:26–45).

3. Some of the most interesting and perhaps most important material in Numbers is the account of Balaam in Numbers 22–24. This account seems to be based on very old poetic material that in the final form of the text is filled out with prose interpretation and commentary. The poems purport to be prophetic response to the request of King Balak of the Moabites who wants Israel "cursed" because the "invading Israelites" constitute a threat to his regime. The response of Balaam, who has been hired by Balak precisely to curse, is that he cannot, in the end, utter a curse:

> How can I curse whom God has not cursed?
> How can I denounce those whom the LORD has not denounced?
> For from the top of the crags I see him,
> from the hills I behold him;
> Here is a people living alone,
> and not reckoning itself among the nations!
>
> (23:8–9)

He cannot curse because he has been commanded by YHWH to bless Israel, whom YHWH wants blessed:

> See, I received a command to bless;
> he has blessed, and I cannot revoke it.
> (23:20)

Thus inside the text itself we have an assertion that God's will for a blessing to Israel cannot be resisted and certainly cannot be contradicted by a curse. The text asserts the immense force of YHWH's sovereignty that will finally prevail in the face of every resistance. In context it is asserted that all the force of YHWH's sovereignty is a blessing for Israel. Thus the text is related, in its final form, to the initial blessing YHWH makes to Abraham (Gen 12:1–3). The text, moreover, picks up on the Genesis theme that not only is Israel blessed, but through Israel other peoples are blessed as well:

> Blessed is everyone who blesses you,
> and cursed is everyone who curses you.
> (Num 24:9b; cf. Gen 12:3)

It is probable that in its early telling, this sequence of texts concerns contestation between Israel and Moab. But we can imagine Israel reading this story in the context of exile in alien Babylon and, by making it their own story, understanding themselves to be marked and protected by YHWH's blessing that cannot be controverted. The text offers a wilderness report that functions as a powerful pastoral reassurance to exiles.

4. By the conclusion of the book of Numbers, the Priestly account of Israel's vexed sojourn from slavery to the land of promise is almost completed.

Close Reading: The Balaam Story in Numbers 22

Throughout the Balaam story there is quite a bit of emphasis on the theme of sight or seeing. The very first word of the story in Hebrew is the key word "saw" (ra'ah): "Balak son of Zippor saw all that Israel had done to the Amorites" (22:2). Balaam is himself identified as a seer, "the man whose eye is clear . . . who sees the vision of the Almighty" (24:3–4), and he and Balak repeatedly look out from a high vantage over the people of Israel, who are so numerous that according to Balak they "hide the face of the earth" (22:5). The author seems to have some fun with this theme in the story of Balaam and his donkey, when the donkey is able to see the angel of the Lord who is standing the road, while Balaam is blind to him (22:22–35)—the donkey is more of a "seer" than Balaam is.

The long trail to fulfillment of YHWH's initial promise is narrated by the Priestly tradition and presented by "stages" (Num 33:1). The Priestly tradition stages its telling of Israel's core memory from creation to Jordan, just short of fulfillment.

It is not doubted that the intent is the occupation of the entire land of promise, even though it is already occupied by other populations that are to be displaced:

> Speak to the Israelites, and say to them: When you cross over the Jordan into the land of Canaan, you shall drive out all the inhabitants of the land from before you, destroy all their figured stones, destroy all their cast images, and demolish all their high places. You shall take possession of the land and settle in it, for I have given you the land to possess. You shall apportion the land by lot according to your clans; to a large one you shall give a large inheritance, and to a small one you shall give a small inheritance; the inheritance shall belong to the person on whom the lot falls; according to your ancestral tribes you shall inherit. But if you do not drive out the inhabitants of the land from before you, then those whom you let remain shall be as barbs in your eyes and thorns in your sides; they shall trouble you in the land where you are settling. And I will do to you as I thought to do to them. (33:51–56)

Thus the Priestly tradition ends with hope and assurance, a hope and an assurance that are offered in the final form of the text, even to exiles who might then be able to imagine themselves in the sixth century poised for reentry into the land, but who are not yet there. It is the purpose of the exilic poetry of Isaiah 40–55 to articulate that actual return.

III

The entry (or reentry) into the land is a gift of God to be undertaken by Israel with great confidence. But for all the accent on entry into the land in this tradition, the theme is, as we might expect, refracted through a Priestly concern for purity, cleanness, and holiness. Thus, "You shall not pollute the land in which you live; for blood pollutes the land, and no expiation can be made for the land, for the blood that is shed in it, except by the blood of the one who shed it. You shall not defile the land in which you live, in which I also dwell; for I the LORD dwell among the Israelites" (Num 35:33–34).

The threat of *pollution and defilement* are consistently uppermost in the Priestly horizon. The only way the Holy Land of the Holy God can be securely entered is if the people work to maximize holiness and minimize

uncleanness, pollution, and impurity. Thus the long Priestly corpus of commandments on holiness in Exodus, Leviticus, and Numbers is acutely pertinent in a vision of the land of promise as a place of holiness and purity. We are
to believe that the holiness restriction pertains to the land. We are, however,
permitted to consider the alternative that this tradition is interested in land
only as a surface agenda, whereas the real point may be holiness. The two
accent points are held together in a way that permits considerable interpretive
maneuvering. In any case, the proper interpretive maneuver is to see that the
old resources of land and holiness, although they may have been in historical
scope, are now reread in the acute crisis of exile. The *demands of holiness* are
linked in tensive ways to the *assurance of (re)entry* into the land of promise. It
is worth noting that even in Isaiah 40–55, a very different voice of interpretation, the juxtaposition of these concerns continues to be operative. Thus in
the great announcement of the "new exodus," a concern for "unclean things"
is voiced:

> Depart, depart, go out from there!
>   Touch no unclean thing;
> go out from the midst of it, purify yourselves,
>   you who carry the vessels of the Lord.
>   (Isa 52:11)

Indeed, earlier in Isaiah the call of the prophet is in a context of admitted
"impurity" of both the prophet and the people (Isa 6:5). It is evident that
the concerns of the Priestly tradition are not marginal to Israel. In the book
of Numbers, purity, cleanness, and holiness are decisive preconditions for a
future in the land of promise, a land YHWH generously gives, a land a Holy
God gives to a holy people.

9

The Book of Deuteronomy

In the telling of the foundational story of the faith of ancient Israel in Genesis through Numbers, the narrative has moved from the creation of the cosmos (Gen 1:1–2:25) to the brink of the Jordan River and the verge of the promised land (Num 33:48–49; see vv. 51–56). This coherent narrative account, albeit pieced together in somewhat disjointed fashion from older materials, makes the claim that the very goal of God's creation, from an Israelite perspective, is the settlement of Israel in the land of promise. Thus the narrative moves from "earth" (*'eres*) to "land" (*'eres*), reflecting both the intentionality of God the Creator and the destiny of Israel as God's people of promise. This entire narrative account in its final form has been shaped by Priestly traditionists who assert (a) that the commands of Sinai occupy the crucial pivotal center of the narrative, and (b) that the commands of Sinai are decisively tilted toward holiness and purity; for it is profaneness and impurity, in Priestly perspective, that have caused the displacement and deportation of Israel in the sixth century. In reading this material, it is important to recognize both that the narrative account is a product of several already extant materials, and that it now functions as a coherent narrative with an easily discernible intentionality.

When we come to the book of Deuteronomy, the text pauses "beyond the Jordan in the land of Moab," and Israel remains there through the entire narrative account (Deut 1:5). Indeed, at the end of the book of Deuteronomy, Moses and Israel continue on "the plains of Moab . . . opposite Jericho" (Deut 34:1). As a result, the narrative of land entry is resumed only in Joshua 1–4, picking up the thread from Numbers 33. Thus the book of Deuteronomy, lodged between Numbers 33–36 and Joshua 1–4, is an insert into the ongoing narrative, an insert that in three extended speeches presents Moses as the teacher and instructor of Israel in its final preparation for entry into the land of promise that has long been the goal of the narrative.

It is of decisive importance to recognize that the book of Deuteronomy presents the voice of a tradition that is different from the Priestly voice by which we have thus far primarily been addressed in the Pentateuch. Consequently the first five books of the Bible, the Torah, are constituted in two distinct literary units: Genesis–Numbers as the voice of the *Priestly* tradition and Deuteronomy as the voice of the *Deuteronomic* tradition. These two distinct literary units reflect two quite different interpretive voices in Israel that articulate quite contrasting theological intentionalities. The canonical process has placed the two interpretive trajectories back-to-back, forming a seam between Numbers and Deuteronomy, and giving the appearance of narrative continuity. In order to appropriate the interpretive intentionality of the final form of the text, however, it is important to recognize that these two traditions do very different things with Israel's faith out of two very different fundamental assumptions.

I

The book of Deuteronomy is organized into three extended speeches of Moses, together with a concluding section that is constituted by two poems and a concluding narrative in Deuteronomy 32–34. The speeches of Moses are narratively situated at the Jordan, purporting to be Moses' final instructions for Israel as Israel enters the land of promise. The ostensive purpose of the instruction is to *warn* Israel about the seductions of the land of Canaan and to *urge* Israel to adhere to its peculiar identity as YHWH's chosen people. In the rhetorical form of warning and urging, this tradition of Mosaic instruction contains some of the richest, most important, and most eloquent theological interpretation in the entire Old Testament. Indeed, in Deuteronomy 1:5 it is said, "Moses undertook to expound this law [*torah*] as follows." The expounding and exposition that follow indicate that Deuteronomy is a foremost focal point for the ongoing dynamism of the Torah tradition of Mount Sinai, all of which is credited to the ongoing authority and imagination of Moses.

The first speech of Moses (1:6–4:49) is a quite general instruction that narrates entry into the land, and that focuses upon some of Sinai's most elemental requirements for the covenantal community, most especially the shunning of idols (4:15–20).

The third speech of Moses (29:1–31:29) articulates the transition that Israel is to make from the generation of Moses to the generation of Joshua, that is, from an accent upon Sinai commands to an accent upon the land.

This interface of Moses as the man from Sinai and Joshua as the man for the land shows the way in which the interpretive tradition of Deuteronomy is concerned precisely about the interface between Torah commandments and land occupation.

Sandwiched between these two speeches is the second speech of Moses, which constitutes the primary materials of the book of Deuteronomy and which is usually referred to as the center of Deuteronomic theological interpretation (5:1–28:68). Many scholars, following von Rad, have thought that this material is intentionally shaped in four literary components introduced in chapter 5, with a preliminary statement that provides the access point for all that follows (von Rad 1966, 26–33):

1. This central speech begins in 5:6–21 with a reiteration of the Ten Commandments from Exodus 20:1–17. This quotation from Sinai, with some interpretive variation, establishes the baseline for Deuteronomy, that is, a representation and reinterpretation of the main claims of Sinai; the reiteration of the Ten Commandments establishes Moses as the proper interpreter of that tradition. Thus all Torah interpretation that follows is credited to the ongoing authority of Moses.

2. Chapters 6–11 are a series of almost homiletical appeals whereby Moses reviews YHWH's goodness and generosity toward Israel, and urges Israel to adhere to the commands of Sinai and to Israel's proper identity as YHWH's chosen people. Particularly important is the imperative of 6:4–5, which begins with the imperative verb "Hear," in Hebrew šemaʿ. These two verses, designated in tradition as "the Shema," function peculiarly as a creedal baseline for Judaism, indicating that Judaism is a community addressed by the commanding voice of YHWH and whose life is lived in response to that imperative address. Derivatively, this is the same "first commandment" that Jesus references in Mark 12:29–30.

3. Chapters 12–25 constitute the legal corpus of Deuteronomy. Some scholars (Kaufman 1978–1979) suggest that the ordering of these commandments follows in rough outline the Ten Commandments so that the corpus is organized as a commentary on the Decalogue. That relationship between the Ten Commandments and this corpus is not clear or self-evident; it is clear, however, that the corpus in the mouth of Moses does reiterate older commandments and reinterprets them for a new context and circumstance. Thus in this corpus on the commandments, the accent falls upon the act of Mosaic reinterpretation.

While there are occasional references to matters of cultic holiness in this corpus that have parallels to the holiness concerns that preoccupy the Priestly tradition, on the whole this material has a quite different horizon. It is concerned primarily with the enactment of Torah commandments and the practice of covenant in the daily affairs of the community that pertain to sociopolitical-economic matters (Crüsemann 1996, 249–65). We may observe this propensity by citing three texts:

a. *Deuteronomy 15:1–18*, likely derivative from older material in Exodus 21:2–11, provides for a "year of release" every seven years, whereby poor debtors in the community who must work off their debts by serf labor have their debts canceled at the end of seven years and are permitted to reenter the economy of the community in a viable way. This provision is often taken as a signature commandment in Deuteronomy (Hamilton 1992). The commandment is concerned that there be no permanent economic underclass in Israel, and so it subordinates the working of the economy to the neighborly fabric of the community. This most radical economic teaching is rooted in the exodus memory, so that debt cancellation for the poor is not unlike deliverance from the pressures of Pharaoh's Egypt (see v. 15).

b. The extended text of *16:18–18:22* has been understood as a statement of polity whereby the powers of governance in Israel are divided in order to prevent an excessive concentration of power (Lohfink 1982; McBride 1987). While several offices of governance are mentioned, special attention may be paid to 17:14–20. This peculiar provision for monarchy is without antecedent in the older materials of Sinai, and appears to be a *novum* in Israel. The statute provides limitation upon the acquisitive capacity of the monarch (concerning silver, gold, horses, chariots, and wives), and seeks to situate monarchy in the context of the Torah, thus identifying the reading and study of the Torah as a primary preoccupation and responsibility of the king (see vv. 18–20).

Close Reading:
The Ten Commandments

The Bible preserves two well-known versions of the Ten Commandments—one in Exodus 20 and another in Deuteronomy 5. (A third, lesser-known version, is found in Exodus 34:10–26 and is sometimes called "the ritual Ten Commandments.") In comparing the two versions, one sees that they are very similar and clearly stem from a single tradition. However, in reading closely, one notices that the rationale for the Sabbath day is different. In Deuteronomy 5:14–15 the reason given for Sabbath rest is the historical memory of being slaves in Egypt, whereas in Exodus 20:11 the reason given is a form of *imitatio Dei*, that is, since God rested on the seventh day after creation, humans should rest as well. It might seem odd that the version in the book of Exodus does not have a reference to the exodus event, but perhaps that is the point: that event is near enough, both for the reader and for the Israelites in the world of the text, that we need not be reminded of it; whereas by the time we get to Deuteronomy it has begun to recede into the past.

c. A series of brief provisions in *24:17–21* are concerned with the protection, dignity, and well-being of orphans, widows, and resident aliens. This triad of social groups is named repeatedly and, taken altogether, designates the most vulnerable and exposed persons in a patriarchal society that depended on male advocacy. The tradition of torah in Deuteronomy is insistent on the claim that the covenant community is obligated to protect the vulnerable who are unable to protect themselves. Thus verses 17–18 advocate economic justice for those without collateral ("pledge"). In verses 19–22 the community is urged three times to leave a residue of crops in the field after harvest that they may be gathered by the poor for their sustenance. This urging pertains in turn to the harvest of grain, olives, and grapes. The leavings are an inchoate form of welfare support for the needy. In verses 18 and 22, moreover, Israel is reminded to connect the present social imperatives to its own memory of God's protection of Israel when it was vulnerable in Egypt. Thus the memory of Egypt provides motivation and energy for an economic vision in the interpretive tradition of Deuteronomy.

These three rather characteristic clusters of commands evidence the way in which a variety of commandments—some from older sources, some undoubtedly innovative, many cast in a quasi-homiletical style—are brought together in a coherent appeal. The intention of the whole of this Mosaic vision of a covenant community is to insist that Israel must act out its distinctive theological identity as YHWH's people in the concrete exercise of political-economic power. This interpretive tradition, as much as any part of the Bible, makes the definitive connection between a theological claim and a public ethic of neighborliness.

4. With the declaration of YHWH's goodness toward Israel in chapters 6–11 and the articulation of YHWH's commands to Israel in chapters 12–25, this great middle speech of Deuteronomy has as its third element a mutual taking of oaths whereby YHWH, the God of the covenant, and Israel, the people of the covenant, commit themselves to each other in an exclusive, mutual loyalty (26:16–19). Each party to the pact has "obtained the agreement" of the other in solemn oath. While this oath, as reported in the text, is now a literary report, it likely had behind it a liturgical ceremony of mutual commitment that had immense sacral, symbolic force. By this act, Israel will enjoy the peculiar blessing and protection of YHWH; and Israel, it is promised, will live out a quite distinct ethic in the world, an ethic in sharp contrast to the cultural environment all around.

5. The literary residue of a liturgical act of covenant making concludes with a fourth element of blessings and curses in chapter 28 (see also 27:11–26). This concluding element is a set of liturgical sanctions of rewards and punishments

that are commensurate with obedience or disobedience to the covenant commands. The range of blessings and curses suggests that YHWH's covenantal sovereignty pertains to every sector of Israel's life, so that the shape of every part of life is derived from covenantal disposition.

These four elements—proclamation of God's gifts (chaps. 6–11), articulation of God's commands (chaps. 12–25), mutual oath taking (26:16–19), recital of blessings and curses (chap. 28)—constitute the bulk of the middle section of the book of Deuteronomy. But the four elements also reflect what was likely an older liturgical practice of the making and remaking of covenant, whereby Israel is constituted, each time freshly constituted in the liturgical act. Thus derivatively the literature of Deuteronomy replicates liturgical practice and, in a literary mode, is a tradition that *enacts* Israel as YHWH's covenant people.

This tradition claims Moses as its key character, thus establishing the Mosaic authority of the interpretive tradition. The tradition itself asserts that this material is post-Sinai, that is, interpretation of Sinai done at another time and place. The term "Deuteronomy" derives from the Greek term *deuteros* ("second" or "copy") and *nomos* ("law") in Deuteronomy 17:18. That is, Deuteronomy is not the primal covenantal document, but is recognized as a belated replication of that tradition.

II

It is a primary assumption of critical scholarship that Deuteronomy is to be understood as the "scroll" that was reported as being found in 2 Kings 22 and that served as the impetus for the religio-political reform of King Josiah in 621 BCE. That scroll caused King Josiah to reconstitute his political realm in terms of a Yahwistic covenant. Consequently, we are able to connect the tradition of Deuteronomy to the late seventh century in Judah. By 621 the scroll tradition was already well established, so that scholars hypothesize that earlier in the seventh century, or perhaps as early as the eighth century, there arose an interpretive theological tradition in Israel that claimed rootage in older Mosaic memories and that was passionately concerned for the covenantal character of Israel. The tradition behind Deuteronomy may have old roots; it received its definitive covenantal shape, however, in the eighth and seventh centuries, precisely at the time when the Assyrian Empire dominated Judah. It is evident to many scholars that the form of the covenant in Deuteronomy coheres with the form of the political treaties found among the Assyrian rulers so that the form from Assyria was utilized to voice particularly Yahwistic convictions. Eventually this tradition of Deuteronomy, by this match of form and content, becomes the predominant voice of covenantalism in the Old Testament, a theological framework that decisively shapes much of the Old Testament and much of Jewish and Christian theology that follow therefrom.

The transformation of old Sinai memories into belated covenantal sociotheological theory and practice was not an easy or obvious accomplishment. Rather, that transformation of the tradition is the work of an interpretive community that is marked by immense interpretive imagination. It seems fair to conclude that this hugely creative interpretive act that pushed Israel's theological horizon in a covenantal direction was accomplished by a small interpretive cadre working with great intentionality. The purpose of that theological intentionality is to provide interpretive ground whereby Israel, as an intentional community of covenant, may contrast itself in its daily life with any indigenous alternative in the land of Canaan and with any temptation to submit to Assyrian cultural hegemony. This theological intentionality has been termed "YHWH alone" interpretation, a powerful insistence upon YHWH to the exclusion of any theological alternative or compromise (M. Smith 1987). Thus the book of Deuteronomy, a series of speeches by Moses between the arrival at the Jordan in Numbers 33 and the crossing of the Jordan in Joshua 3 and 4, is an articulation of the most self-conscious theological understanding available in ancient Israel. The four elements of the literature we have identified show that the tradition operates with great imaginative freedom, and is, by utterance, able to imagine, authorize, and empower a very different sense of being God's people in the world.

Although there is some evidence that Deuteronomy is rooted in northern prophetic tradition, we do not know for sure who it is who brought such self-conscious tradition to expression, so that the source of the tradition is termed the "Deuteronomists," a tautology that only distinguishes this interpretive voice from that of the Priestly tradition. Of this Deuteronomic interpretive tradition that claims Mosaic rootage, we may observe the following:

1. Because the tradition is focused upon attentiveness to and interpretation of Torah traditions, these primal interpretive voices are sometimes thought to be *Levites*, those particularly charged with Torah interpretation (see 33:8–11).

2. Alternatively, it is clear that the tradition has peculiar affinities to the *prophetic* tradition so that the corpus of Deuteronomy is something of a prophetic voice expressed in other nonprophetic genres. (See especially 18:15–18.)

3. Whatever else may be said about this theological tradition, its passionate commitment to the Torah causes it to stand outside and over against the assumptions of royal Israel that believed and trusted YHWH's unconditional promise to the house of David as the only clue to the future of Israel. The Deuteronomic tradition is not excessively inured to royal-messianic thinking,

but continues to believe that *Torah obedience* is the decisive component of faith (see 1 Sam 12:14–15, 24–25). As a result, the tradition of Deuteronomy—rooted in Moses and straining to contemporaneity—functions as a loyal opposition to the monarchy and asserts that Israel's future rests not on divine oracles to the royal establishment, but on the honoring and enactment of the Torah.

4. While we cannot know the origin of the Deuteronomic tradition, which may be priestly or prophetic, it is clear that as the tradition developed it came to be managed and led by *scribes*, that is, by learned folk who valued scrolls and who kept the teaching available through the management of scrolls. Thus Deuteronomy stands at the center of the process by which Judaism became a "religion of the book" and in the end depended upon "men of the book" to sustain its interpretive authority in Israel.

5. The tradition of Deuteronomy is not confined to the book of Deuteronomy itself, but is a larger, more expansive interpretive tradition. This is particularly evident in the book of Jeremiah, which, in its final form, is deeply impacted by Deuteronomic tradition. We may mention in particular the utilization of scribes by the prophet Jeremiah to accomplish specific ends (see Jer 36:4 on Baruch and Jer 51:59–64 on Seraiah). Thus the book of Jeremiah not only resonates with the Deuteronomic tradition, but also shows the way in which the "book" tradition is managed and kept alive.

6. It is most plausible that the tradition of Deuteronomy reached a settled form in the seventh century BCE. But it was a continuing tradition of considerable vitality. Thus it is a likely hypothesis that the interpretive categories of Deuteronomy, in terms of covenantal obedience or disobedience, were solidified in the seventh century. Only a century later, however, Judah faced the destruction of its city and the deportation of 587, an event that required energetic interpretive commentary. Thus we may imagine that the more or less settled tradition of Deuteronomy in the seventh century continued its vitality in the sixth century, especially among displaced people.

We may identify two ways in which this interpretive paradigm of covenantal obedience continued its vitality. First, in the book of Deuteronomy itself, some texts are gathered around the central speech of Moses (chaps. 5–28) to comment on this crisis of exile. Thus in Deuteronomy 4:29 "Moses" speaks of "from there" where Israel has been "scattered" (4:27). Now since "scattered" is a technical term for exile, it is likely that the "from there" of 4:29 refers to the Babylonian place of deportation. This text goes on to say that "from there," that is, from Babylonian exile, Israel may repent and come home as a new people of obedience. This means that the settled Torah tradition of 5:28 is belatedly kept current by subsequent interpretation in the next layer of tradition.

Conversely, the weighty matters of chapter 31 bespeak a recalcitrant covenant practice of disobedience of which Moses reports YHWH saying:

> On that day I will surely hide my face on account of all the evil they have done by turning to other gods. Now therefore write this song, and teach it to the Israelites; put it in their mouths, in order that this song may be a witness for me against the Israelites. For when I have brought them into the land flowing with milk and honey, which I promised on oath to their ancestors, and they have eaten their fill and grown fat, they will turn to other gods and serve them, despising me and breaking my covenant. And when many terrible troubles come upon them, this song will confront them as a witness, because it will not be lost from the mouths of their descendants. For I know what they are inclined to do even now, before I have brought them into the land that I promised them on oath. (Deut 31:18–21)

Thus chapters 4 and 31 form an envelope to the primary speech of chapters 5–28 and articulate what counted in the tradition of Deuteronomy for the next generation. In 30:1–10, moreover, the same concern is expressed concerning YHWH's resolve to "gather" Israel "from all the peoples" where they are scattered (30:3), thus a reference to deportation, exile, and homecoming. Thus the theological tradition that in an earlier setting aimed at reform of the monarchy in a later context articulates the conditions of homecoming for the entire people, in both circumstances and in the insistence upon obedience to the Torah.

Second, it is a common hypothesis among scholars that the great historical narrative of Joshua–Kings that tells of the history of Israel in the land until exile is told from the perspective of Deuteronomy and so is reckoned in some sense to be a "Deuteronomistic (or Deuteronomic) History" (Noth 1981). As a result we may observe that in a convergence of (a) the unfolding of the book of Deuteronomy itself into the second generation, (b) the final form of the book of Jeremiah, and (c) the "history" of Joshua–Kings, the interpretive tradition of Deuteronomy shows itself to be remarkably resilient and generative, emerging as a distinct voice in characterizing Israel's faith and Israel's vital interpretive tradition.

III

The tradition of Deuteronomy is to be fully appreciated by its juxtaposition to the Priestly tradition in the Torah. The two interpretive traditions together constitute a formidable interpretive enterprise. While the final form of the text of the Pentateuch juxtaposes the two interpretive traditions, we should pay primary attention to the contrasting vistas of the two traditions. The outcome of such an observation is to underscore the pluralism of Torah teaching in its most intense and canonical formulation. The Priestly tradition concerns itself more with the concrete, everyday activities of religious life, with an eye toward hosting God's holy presence through liturgical acts and religious practice. The Deuteronomic tradition is concerned with these issues as well, but it tends toward high homiletical eloquence and a fiery ethical critique. Both traditions were vital in ancient Israel, even as they may continue to be today.

The "book of Deuteronomy" is not finally to be understood simply as a fixed scroll, but as a lively interpretive tradition that continues to characterize ongoing Judaism, even as the same generative categories show up later in Christian articulation that practices the same kind of ongoing interpretation. The book of Deuteronomy stands as the primary example of the dynamism of the Torah tradition whereby old memories are endlessly re-presented and reinterpreted, rearticulated, and reimagined in ways that keep the main claims of faith pertinent and authoritative in new circumstances. This vitality of the Deuteronomic tradition was a key factor in permitting Judaism to flourish even after it lost the conventional supports of temple monarchy and city in the crisis of 587 BCE and in the ensuing period of exilic displacement.

10

Reprise on the Torah

In its final form, the Torah or Pentateuch is an immense literary-theological achievement of the concretely *historical traditioning process*. At the same time, the church and the synagogue take it to be an immense *gift of God*, who is disclosed therein as the creator of heaven and earth and as the savior and commander of Israel. It is impossible to overstate the authoritative force of this literature for Judaism, for all subsequent interpretive literature in Judaism purports to be commentary on and therefore derivative from this foundational text. The matter is only slightly different for Christians, in that the New Testament makes fresh claims around the person and work of Jesus. Even here, however, the governing themes of interpretation are, for the most part, grounded in and formed by the primal witness of the Torah. Jesus, after all, claims to come not to abolish but to fulfill the Torah (Matt 5:17).

It is certainly the case that the final form of the text has been accomplished through the gathering, appropriation, reshaping, and interpretation of a mass of already existing materials, both narrative and legal, likely both written and oral. And it is possible, as Hermann Gunkel has demonstrated, to have some understanding of and make some judgments about the earlier forms and claims of the materials; however, in the final form of these texts the earlier materials have been radically reshaped and recontextualized. The traditioning process in Israel freely appropriated materials from a variety of cultural contexts, not excluding the appropriation of mythic materials that function in ideological ways in earlier high imperial cultures. The borrowing from many quarters is unmistakable; at the same time the transformation of borrowed materials caused the same materials, reshaped and recontextualized, to voice new holy claims congruent with the interpretive intentionality of Israel. It is a matter of interpretive contestation in any particular text to determine

(a) the extent to which borrowed materials bring with them persistent borrowed meanings and, conversely, (b) the extent to which borrowed materials are so changed as to become carriers of content that is profoundly different and new. It is clear in any case that the borrowing, widespread as it was, was not nearly a cut-and-paste appropriation, but was consistently a powerful intentional interpretive act that yielded something very different from what may have been the original.

This ongoing activity of borrowing and appropriating through the interpretive process implies that it is exceedingly difficult to make judgments about the historicity of reported events. Many scholars have assumed that the later the reported event, the more possible is the claim of historicity. Because the entire traditioning process is a sustained act of interpretive imagination, moreover, it is likely that the imaginative freedom of interpreting Israel was not greatly informed by or restrained by "what happened." It is to be fully and definitionally appreciated that the traditioning process is one of interpretive imagination, that is, the actualization of an alternative world centered in YHWH's presence, the presentation of an alternative narrative account of reality with YHWH as its subject. This alternative world and this alternative narrative account of reality are quite in contrast to what we normally and modernly term "history." Thus, for the most part, posing the question about "history" in these materials is a futile one. Consequently, popular suggestions of historical evidence for reported events are largely whimsical, subjective, and misleading, whether they move in a credulous or in a skeptical direction. The upshot is a recognition that the Torah is canonical imagination, though there remains to inquire about the extent to which "canon" is normative truth and the ways in which "canon" is ideological advocacy (Green 1989). The capacity to accept the textual material as imaginative rather than historical is a necessary prerequisite for reading intelligently; even given that prerequisite, however, the character of the imaginative act of interpretation is itself open to contestation between fideists and skeptics (Brueggemann 1997, 726–50; Childs 1993; Carroll 1991).

In any case, the traditioning process that pursues a canonical *intentionality* (J. Sanders 1976) and that eventuates in a canonical *shape* is a remarkable achievement whereby a complexity of "bits and pieces" of tradition of many kinds is drawn together in a more or less coherent unity (Childs 1979). The "more or less" quality of that unity is to be taken seriously in the interpretation of any particular text, because some texts adhere to canonical coherence *more*, wherein the original meaning of the tradition readily yields to interpretive imposition. Conversely, some adhere to that "canonical coherence" *less*, wherein the original meaning of the tradition persists. The traditioning process itself, over a long period and through many efforts, was not able to

be singularly consistent about transposition and transformation of appropriated materials. For that reason an attentive reading of the material must allow
for "more or less" in varying dimensions. This "more or less" quality of the
final form of the text has, on the one hand, produced rather tight and intense
church interpretation that accents unity by the "more" of canonical coherence; in response, not surprisingly, such church interpretation has produced
an academic response of "less," whereby the complexity and variation of the
tradition is more fully accented and appreciated than is the canonical coherence. This endless interpretive tension, often contrasting church interpretation and academic interpretation, is not surprising. It is in the end inescapable,
precisely because the tension of "more or less" is readily evident in the final
form of the text itself.

As we consider the shape of the Torah in its canonical coherence, we
may observe three matters that are roughly consensus in interpretive practice. First, the canonical coherence of the whole of the literature is organized
around only a few *core theological claims*, claims that continue to be central in
the interpretive life of the synagogue and the church. These themes have
been enunciated by Martin Noth in critical fashion and by Gerhard von Rad
in theological exposition (Noth 1972; von Rad 1962). The conventional catalog of such themes includes the following:

Creation	Genesis 1–11
Ancestors	Genesis 12–50
Exodus	Exodus 1–15
Wilderness sojourn	Exodus 16–18
Sinai commands	Exodus 19:1–Numbers 10:10
Wilderness sojourn	Numbers 10:11–36:13
Sinai commands extrapolated	Deuteronomy

These themes gather to themselves a rich variety of already existing materials;
for the most part the materials in their complexity serve the theological theme
under which they are subsumed.

On this list of themes, two observations are important.

1. It has been noticed, especially by James Sanders, that the Torah ends
at the death of Moses in Deuteronomy 34, looking into the land of promise,
but still short of entry into the land (J. Sanders 1972). Thus the narrative
literature serves the condition, circumstance, and hope of the landless, particularly sixth-century exiles at the time of the formation of the literature. Subsequently, many generations of Diaspora Jews have been served by the same
motif. That narrative termination, which stops short of fulfillment in the land
of promise, has been lined out, moreover, in elegant fashion in Hebrews 11
with its remarkable conclusion:

> Yet all these, though they were commended for their faith, did not receive what was promised, since God had provided something better so that they would not, apart from us, be made perfect. (11:39–40)

The tradition itself knows exactly where the narrative story should end and knows why it ends there: because the tradition is open to fulfillment for that which it awaits in hope. This open-ended hope is not "failure" (as was suggested by Bultmann 1963), but a sense of dynamism of reality in the hands of the future-creating God. This hope in such a God, moreover, coheres with the characteristic lived reality of the community of faith, Jews and Christians, that the promises are not fully kept, that hopes are not fully realized, and that history has not come visibly to the full rule of YHWH. Such fullness is well promised and well hoped, but unmistakably not in hand.

2. The Torah in authoritative form articulates the primal themes of faith for nearly all that is to follow, Jewish and Christian. There is, however, one important exception: the later emergence of the Jerusalem establishment, not situated in the text of the Old Testament until the books of Samuel and Kings (see especially 2 Sam 5:6–10; Ps 78:67–72). This achievement of David and Solomon must be held in abeyance in the telling of the normative story, though one may recognize in the ancestral narratives of Genesis some hints of anticipation of David and Jerusalem, since the makers of the final form of the texts were fully familiar with that subsequent development. In any case, the normative literature is constructed so that Israel still awaits *kingship* that will issue for both Jews and Christians in messianic hope, and *temple* that for Jews and Christians will issue an expectation of YHWH's full and palpable presence in the community. It is clear that both themes of *Messiah* and *presence*, in Christian parlance, serve the theological claims made in the church for Jesus, who is confessed to be the awaited Messiah and the bodied presence of God.

Midrashic Moment: Deuteronomy 34

Near the end of his famous "I Have a Dream" speech, delivered in 1963 at the height of the civil rights movement, Martin Luther King Jr. refers explicitly to the end of the Torah, where Moses dies outside the promised land, having been allowed to see it by God but not allowed to enter with the people. "He's allowed me to go up to the mountain," says King, "and I've looked over. And I've seen the promised land. I may not get there with you. But I want you to know tonight, that we, as a people, will get to the promised land!" In a strategy that means to fight against both hopelessness and complacency, King's speech replicates the open-ended and forward-looking nature of the Torah, which ends with the promised goal in sight but not yet in possession.

Second, while the traditioning process is complex and long-term, scholars now accept that the final form of the text reflects the work and conviction of two great *theological-interpretive trajectories* working in and around the exilic period, both of which have deep roots in earlier phases of Israel's life and faith. The final form of the text is the editorial achievement of the Priestly and Deuteronomic traditions.

The *Priestly tradition*, with primary attentiveness to holiness and the cultic institutional practices that enhance holiness, produced the final form of Genesis–Numbers. These materials, organized around a system of "generations" in order to ensure genealogical continuity in a community under threat, focused upon cultic arrangements of holiness in the Sinai traditions of Exodus 25–31, 35–40, Leviticus, and Numbers 1–10. These materials of command are prefaced by narratives that concern, for example, the authorization of the Sabbath (Gen 2:1–4a) and circumcision (Gen 17).

The *Deuteronomic tradition* that introduced covenant into Israelite interpretive tradition contributes the book of Deuteronomy to the Torah. It is a widely held hypothesis that the "historical narrative" of Joshua, Judges, Samuel, and Kings is informed by Deuteronomy and its interpretive *Tendenz* (Noth 1981). Deuteronomy, in contrast to the Priestly tradition, is concerned for the right ordering of the political-economic life of Israel, though it is not without interest in cultic holiness.

These two traditions provide very different interpretive accents and surely arise in different circles of traditionists. It is of enormous importance that the Torah, in its final form, has juxtaposed the two traditions, thereby assuring that the primal canon of ancient Israel is pluralistic, giving prominence to traditions that were in intense contestation with each other. It is, as a consequence, not a surprise that the ongoing interpretive work of Judaism and Christianity continues the vigorous contestation that is already present in the canonical text. That contestation, as a continuing enterprise in text and in interpretation, is crucial to the character of faith, because the contestation rooted in the plurality of traditions assures that the canonical claim of the text can never be safely and finally reduced to a closed, settled package of teaching. The pluriform character of the text assures an endless dynamism in interpretation that inescapably requires that interpretation should be contestation.

Third, it is evident that the plot of the Torah, constituted by the interface of Priestly and Deuteronomic traditions and shaped by the focus upon dominant interpretive themes, moves from God's creation of "heaven and earth" and the ordering of the "earth" (*'eres*) to the brink of the "promised land" (*'eres*). Thus the canonical horizon of the Torah that begins in a cosmic focus upon the earth devolved into a focus upon Israel's destiny and future, though never losing sight of the larger vista. The move from *'ereṣ* as "earth" to *'ereṣ* as "promised land" is accomplished in the ancestral narratives of Genesis 12–36, whereby the ancestors of promise are assured a special land, a land not yet received at the close of the Torah. There is no doubt, in any case, that the promised land "flowing with milk and honey" will manifest all of the blessings of fertility, fruitfulness, and abundance that belong to creation; consequently, the land of Israel is a "good land" as a representative embodiment of creation that God has called "very good" (Gen 1:31).

The move from *creation* to *land of promise*, however, is wrought in the Torah only by way of Sinai. The Sinai tradition of Exodus 19:1–Numbers 10:10 occupies nearly one-half of the material of the Torah. This corpus of commandments is complex and multilayered; like the narrative, it has been formed through a multifaceted interpretive practice that asserts the terms of land reception that are congruent with the Creator's ordering of all of creation (Crüsemann 1996). It is evident in ancient and in modern practice that the land as gift and as possession, taken by itself, generates and is generated through self-serving ideology. It is precisely the teaching of the Torah on holiness toward God and fidelity toward neighbor (so powerfully articulated at Sinai) that curbs the propensity, ancient and contemporary, to treat the gift of land as an unconditional entitlement.

Thus the large plot sequence of *creation–Sinai tradition–land* holds together the sense of entitled land so celebrated in ancient Israel and the conditionality of obedience as a precondition of the land. These two matters in some tension— *unconditional entitlement* and the *condition of obedience*—are held together in the gift of YHWH, who is disclosed as one who is generous in gift and sovereign in demand. Over the generations, Israel pondered this restless interface that is rooted in YHWH's own character. The fact that the traditioning process could never escape the tension that is definitional for Israel is, perhaps, the reason that the tradition continued to develop through layers and layers of rearticulation. Sam Balentine has nicely seen how this tradition has served as a concrete resource for communities of faith whose anticipation of the gift of land was a more powerful reality than the possession and settlement of the land itself:

> The process that leads to the canonization of the Pentateuch works intentionally to preserve a vision of another world where the hope and promise of God's creational design remain vital and attainable. In the surety of this vision, the faith community in Yehud [Judah] survives. Consigned to live at the border—between the realities that manage and extend the status quo and the enduring trust that rests in future possibilities, elusive but real—Yehud finds in the Torah's vision the foundation for building a new and viable self-identity. (Balentine 1999, 240)

The whole in all of its complex, multilayered parts is for the believing communities the Word of God/revelation/guidance for how to live in the world over which YHWH presides. As Rabbi Ben Bag Bag said of the Torah many centuries ago: "Turn it and turn it, for everything is in it" (Mishnah *'Abot* 5:22).

PART II

The Prophets

11

Introduction to the Prophets

There is no doubt that the Torah (Pentateuch) constitutes the primary, normative scripture of Judaism. While the other biblical books that follow play an important role in the religious life of the community, they are of a lesser authority. In the complete canonical tradition of the Hebrew Bible, it is conventional to divide the non-Torah parts of the text into two units, the Prophets and the Writings. In this discussion we will be following that distinction, even though it is a quite late distinction in the development of the tradition. At the outset, moreover, we acknowledge the force of John Barton's argument that the non-Torah parts of the canon are of a piece and constitute one category, thus mitigating a hard-and-fast distinction between Prophets and Writings:

> It seems to me that in an important sense the Torah was, and had been for a long time, the only corpus of material that was "Scripture" in the fullest sense, the only set of documents on which the character and integrity of Judaism crucially depended; and in saying that other scriptures formed only one category rather than two my primary concern is to argue that all other holy books, of whatever precise kind were equal in being of secondary rank by comparison with the Torah. (Barton 1988, 93)

While granting the cogency of Barton's historical judgment, we nonetheless must finally face the canonical shape of the literature. The traditioning process has impacted the literature that became the second canon of the Prophets, so that the literature is now shaped in an ordered, more or less symmetrical way.

The prophetic canon, which comprises two parts (the Former Prophets and the Latter Prophets), is understood in canonical fashion as second to and reliant on the first canon of the Torah. In canonical perspective, we may say that the Torah is the articulation—in narrative and in commandment—of the norms of faith and obedience commensurate with the rule of YHWH. The prophetic canon is a literature that articulates Israel's faith and practice in the rough-and-tumble of historical reality. The prophetic canon is an exercise in rereading the history of Israel and the history of the world according to the gifts and requirements of the God of the Torah. The simple sequence of "Torah, Prophets" is a given of the canon, though the critical situation of the literature is much more complex. There is a likelihood that the Former Prophets draws its theological perspective from Deuteronomy and is thus shaped by Torah literature. In the Latter Prophets, however, the critical reality is very different. It is commonly thought by scholars that the prophetic oracles of the eighth and seventh centuries antedate the final form of the Torah, thus suggesting that the earliest articulation of what became the canonical faith of the Torah may have been first accomplished by the prophets. This has been a lynchpin of historical-critical consensus since the time of Wellhausen (see Wellhausen 1994), though it has not gone unchallenged.

In any case, it is clear that the literature of the prophetic canon, in very different circumstances and in very different modes, seeks to do in parallel fashion what the Torah seeks to do, namely, to imagine, articulate, and evoke a world ordered by and responsive to YHWH, the Creator of heaven and earth and the Lord of Israel's covenant.

THE FORMER PROPHETS

The Former Prophets in the Jewish canon is constituted by the books of Joshua, Judges, Samuel, and Kings. (The book of Ruth, familiarly located in Christian Bibles after the book of Judges, is in the Jewish ordering of books lodged rather late in the third canon of the Bible, the Writings.) These four books (or six if we take into account the twin scrolls of 1 and 2 Samuel and of 1 and 2 Kings) are reckoned in the Jewish canon as "prophets." Such a category invites us to think again about the meaning of "prophetic." It is conventional among more conservative Christian interpreters, and indeed in popular imagination, to understand "prophetic" as an exercise in *prediction*, in foretelling the future, so that prophets become something like ancient Israelite versions of Nostradamus. In Christian interpretation, such an understanding of prophecy characteristically moves to the anticipation of Jesus. Conversely, more liberal Christian interpretation tends to understand "prophetic" in terms of a passionate *engagement for justice* in society. Although the latter comes closer to an accurate description of the prophetic role, neither of these inclinations will help us much in understanding the nomenclature for this material that is termed "prophetic."

Rather, "prophetic" refers to the character and horizon of the material in its final form. To be sure, this material contains specific references about named (and unnamed) prophets, but the canonical label "Prophets" refers to the material itself and not to specific prophetic personalities. What is prophetic is the capacity to reconstrue all of lived reality—including the history of Israel and the power relations of the known world of the ancient Near East—according to the equally palpable reality (in this reading) of the rule of YHWH. Thus James Sanders refers to the "monotheizing tendency" of the canon (J. Sanders 1976). By this he means that the interpretive work of the textual tradition in its normative form aims to reread Israel's history and faith toward the singular unrivaled reality of YHWH. The reason Sanders speaks of a "tendency" rather than a full accomplishment is that the monotheizing accent is not fully accomplished and complete; older, perhaps polytheistic traces are still discernible in the text or at any rate religious claims that do not cohere with Israel's primal Yahwistic affirmation. Thus the canonical imposition of Yahwistic monotheism, the clear intent of the conditioning process, is characteristically in tension with older inclinations in the literature that sometimes do not easily yield to that canonical intentionality. The point to observe is that the canonical framing of the Former Prophets is accomplished through a vigorous interpretive process that characteristically transposes the literature in canonical form from something that it previously was not.

From that awareness, we may readily observe two key points about the four books that constitute the Former Prophets. First, the Jewish nomenclature of "Prophets" suggests something very different from the conventional Christian habit of regarding these books as "history." There is no doubt that the interpretive process that culminates in the canonical books utilized older materials of many kinds, some of which may be historically reliable. Scholars are variously inclined to be skeptical of such utilization of sources as history or are, alternatively, inclined to give the Bible the benefit of the doubt. It is at the moment the common judgment of scholars that the "historical reliability" of this material is not very strong, and that the earlier the period reported, the less "grounded in fact" the material is taken to be (Dever 2001; Finkelstein and Silberman 2001). Consequently the material in Joshua and Judges is less likely to be historically reliable, whereas the more recent period in the latter part of the books of Kings may be more so.

The important point to notice, however, is that the material does not intend to be historical reportage in any modern sense of the term. We may suggest, rather, two ways of seeing this material that moves away from "historical" claims. On the one hand, the material is *theological testimony*, that is, a believing effort to give an account of faith, an account of God, albeit a God who is said to be engaged in the lived processes of history (Brueggemann 1997, 117–44). To recognize the material as testimony causes us to have expectations very different from those we might have for the genre of "history." On the other hand, it is clear that the literature, especially in the books of Kings, intends to be *interpretive commentary* on historical reportage that is said to be elsewhere available to the reader. Thus the tradition has what amounts to footnotes that refer readers to other materials if they have an interest in history. (See 1 Kgs 11:41; 14:19, 29.) That the text is candid in such citation of other materials eases any modern requirement to make the material "history," and lets us receive it for what it is—a theological advocacy for the meaning of reported history when that history is linked to and reconstrued according to the God of the Torah. It is clear that the imposition of the category of "history" on this material is a failure to recognize what is offered or what is intended in the traditioning process.

Second, if we ask more specifically about the interpretive intentionality that has transposed this textual corpus into a sustained theological testimony, we do best by referring to the dominant critical hypothesis of Martin Noth first published in 1943 (Noth 1981). Noth daringly suggested, against scholarship that had seen the literature of Joshua, Judges, Samuel, and Kings as a collection of many sources, that this extended "historical" narrative is to be understood in canonical form as a *single literary work* written from a *single interpretive angle* as a commentary upon the destruction of Jerusalem in 587 BCE and as a meditation upon the ensuing crisis of exile. Noth urged, moreover, that the theological perspective and assumptions of this corpus of literature are derived from the book of Deuteronomy. Thus the corpus is termed "Deuteronomistic (or Deuteronomic) History," and the assumed author is termed the "Deuteronomist." Noth assumed that this "historian-theologian" used earlier sources but shaped all of the material around the conviction of the covenantal tradition of the book of Deuteronomy that blessing follows obedience and curse follows disobedience (see Deut 30:15–20).

The long historical account of Israel is, in this perspective, largely a story of disobedience; consequently, the destruction of Jerusalem in 587 is to be understood theologically as the enactment of YHWH's curse upon a disobedient people. The long narrative account thus provides a theological basis for understanding the destruction and the consequent deportation. Noth proposed that since the notation of 2 Kings 25:27–30 is dated to 562 BCE ("the thirty-seventh year of the exile of King Jehoiachin"), the corpus was written in 562 in the midst of the exile, as the community pondered its fate as a result of disobedience. Thus Noth proposes to interpret the Former Prophets as

Deuteronomic history, whereby he provides a suggestive clue to the perspective that guided and assured the enormity of the interpretation.

In the time since Noth's proposal in 1943, a number of criticisms and revisions of the hypothesis have been offered by other scholars. (See Knoppers and McConville 2000; Schearing and McKenzie 1999; de Moor and Van Rooy 2000; Campbell and O'Brien 2000.) Two critical revisions in Noth's notion of the unity of the corpus have been proposed: (a) Frank M. Cross and Richard D. Nelson have urged that the pre-587 edition of the history was created only to be adjusted and adapted subsequently in light of the crisis of 587 (Cross 1973, 274–89; Nelson 1981); (b) Rudolf Smend has agreed with Noth's dating, but then has suggested some subsequent editing (Smend 1971). These alternatives are important, but they do not affect the general interpretive intentionality of the corpus as proposed by Noth.

More important for our purposes have been two proposals concerning theological intentionality that seek to move beyond Noth's verdict that the corpus serves only to explain and justify God's judgment upon Jerusalem in 587: (a) Gerhard von Rad has paid attention to the Davidic promise of 2 Samuel 7 as it permeates this text, and suggests that the enigmatic conclusion of 2 Kings 25:27–30 holds open the possibility that the dynasty of David may yet be an opening to the future of Israel (von Rad 1962, 342–47); (b) Hans Walter Wolff has paid particular attention to the notion of repentance, taking special notice of Deuteronomy 4:29–31; 30:10–15; and 1 Kings 8:31–46 (Wolff 1982). Wolff thus proposes that the notion of repentance—and return to Torah obedience—is a way of thinking about the future beyond exile, a way of thinking that eventuates in Judaism as it is shaped in the tradition of Ezra with its intense return to the Torah.

Readers of the Former Prophets will want to take into account the theological intentionality of the whole. In critical conversation that intentionality entails consideration of Noth's hypothesis in one of its variant forms. At the same time, the narrative material in this section of the canon provides some of the most finely crafted and powerful stories from the ancient world, which can be appreciated regardless of their putative historical contexts.

THE LATTER PROPHETS

The term "Latter Prophets" refers to four books, those of the prophets Isaiah, Jeremiah, Ezekiel, and the Twelve (Minor Prophets). In the last case, it is generally understood that these twelve small prophetic books constitute a single scroll and thus a fourth prophetic scroll, so that the four Latter Prophets form a symmetrical complement to the Former Prophets, the two groups together constituting the prophetic canon of eight books. It is with these books that we get to what most people think of as prophecy per se, with public orators issuing passionate critique of the religious and political status quo, or speaking truth to power. As we have seen, an understanding of the Former Prophets (Joshua, Judges, Samuel, and Kings) entails a recognition that this material is not "history" in the sense that we regularly use that term. In somewhat parallel fashion, an understanding of the Latter Prophets (Isaiah, Jeremiah, Ezekiel, and the Twelve) entails a refocus away from a popular notion of prophetic *personalities* to prophetic *books* (Petersen 2002, 1–45 and passim). The prophetic books may have begun in collections of oracles from remembered personalities. In the editorial process, however, the importance and domination of the prophetic personalities recedes almost totally, so that the prophetic books are now the outcome of long-developed traditions that may be seeded by a named personality. In completed form, however, they are the product of an interpretive process that intends to extend the trajectory of faith well beyond the initiating personality.

It is the case that the several prophetic books reflect very different theological trajectories. For example, the book of Isaiah in final form is a meditation upon the *temple-monarchy* tradition of Jerusalem. The book of Jeremiah, influenced by the same circles that produced the Deuteronomic History, is oriented to the centrality of *torah*. The book of Ezekiel, preoccupied with *holiness*, has most affinities with the Priestly tradition of the Torah. Thus it is fair to suggest that the three great prophetic books constitute developing interpretive materials that are committed to and reflect different theological passions in Israel, respectively, royal temple, Torah, and holiness traditions. The three together constitute a compendium of major options in Israel's faith.

Special notice may be taken of the fourth scroll among the Latter Prophets, the Book of the Twelve or, as they are called within the church, the Minor Prophets. In critical understanding, each of these twelve prophets is treated as a distinct entity reflecting a distinct personality, even though they are readily grouped, according to critical judgment, chronologically. Thus Hosea, Amos, and Micah are situated in the eighth century BCE; Nahum, Habakkuk, and Zephaniah in the seventh; Haggai, Zechariah, and Malachi in the Persian period. This leaves Joel, Jonah, and Obadiah, books that are, in critical perspective, understood as later books that are canonically situated in a way that no longer reflects a historical placement.

In more recent scholarship, an effort has been made to understand the Book of the Twelve as a coherent scroll with intentional canonical shape. In particular, James Nogalski and Paul House have made forays into this suggestion, which has the practical effect of loosening each prophetic book from a supposed historical context and instead linking each to the literary-canonical context of the extended scroll (Nogalski 1993; House 1990; Nogalski and Sweeney 2000). This way of thinking is only at its beginning, but it is an important part of the newer scholarship that seeks to pay attention to the final form of the text, in this case the final form of the Scroll of the Twelve.

These four scrolls, rooted in different personalities and in the service of different interpretive interests and commitments, proceed in a variety of different ways. Having noted these differences, it is nonetheless important also to notice that a certain pattern of interpretation is visible in the several scrolls. This is most obvious in the book of Ezekiel, which nicely divides into two parts, chapters 1–24 concerning judgment upon Jerusalem and chapters 25–48 concerning restoration of Jerusalem. The matter is somewhat different in the book of Isaiah with the critical distinction between chapters 1–39 and chapters 40–66, a distinction between judgment and hope. The matter is even less clear in Jeremiah, but even there it is evident that the Book of Comfort (chaps. 30–31; see also chaps. 32–33) and the Oracles against the Nations (chaps. 46–51) are statements of hope. Thus in a variety of ways the final forms of the books acknowledge the destruction and exile that so preoccupied the Deuteronomic Historian, but characteristically they move beyond that acknowledgment to an act of hope for Israel rooted in YHWH's resilient promises. Even in the Scroll of the Twelve, moreover, one can notice hope in the latter parts of the book of Zechariah and in the ultimate paragraph of Malachi (Mal 4:5–6).

Thus it is evident that the Latter Prophets have been more or less programmatically shaped and edited into a twofold assertion of God's *judgment* that brings Israel to exile and death, and God's *promise* that brings Israel to a future that it cannot envision or sense for itself. That pattern has been most clearly seen by Ronald Clements:

> It is rather precisely the element of connectedness between the prophets, and the conviction that they were all referring to a single theme of Israel's destruction and renewal, which has facilitated the ascription to each of them of the message of hope which some of their number had proclaimed after 587 B.C. . . .
>
> In such fashion we can at least come to understand the value and meaning of the way in which distinctive patterns have been imposed upon the prophetic collections of the canon so that warnings of doom and disaster are always followed by promises of hope and restoration. (Clements 1977, 48, 49)

In his summation, Clements makes a claim that the theme of "death and rebirth" pertains to the entire prophetic canon, Former and Latter, as the canonical material is shaped in response to the defining lived experiences of the interpretive community:

> Rather we must see that prophecy is a collection of collections, and that ultimately the final result in the prophetic corpus of the canon formed a recognizable unity not entirely dissimilar from that of the Pentateuch. As this was made up from various sources and collections, so also the Former and Latter Prophets, comprising the various preserved prophecies of a whole series of inspired individuals, acquired an overarching thematic unity. This centered on the death and rebirth of Israel, interpreted theologically as acts of divine judgment and salvation. (Clements 1977, 53)

We are able to see in the Latter Prophets, as in the Former Prophets, that the canonical material has been transposed with great interpretive intentionality. In the Former Prophets, "history" has been transposed into a massive *theological commentary* on Israel's past. In the Latter Prophets what began as personal proclamation has been transposed into a *theological conviction* around YHWH's promise for the future. Both theological commentary (in the Former Prophets) and theological conviction (in the Latter Prophets) became a normative, but at the same time quite practical, resource for a community living in and through the deep fissure of deportation and displacement. The prophetic canon functions as a resource to protect the community of faith from surrendering to the vagaries of historical circumstance. Seen in this way, the prophetic canon that testifies to YHWH's governance of past, present, and future is an offer of a counterworld, counter to denial and despair, counterrooted in YHWH's steadfast purpose for a new Jerusalem, new torah, new covenant, new temple—all things new:

> Thus says the LORD,
>   who makes a way in the sea,
>   a path in the mighty waters,
> who brings out chariot and horse,
>   army and warrior;
> they lie down, they cannot rise,
>   they are extinguished, quenched like a wick:
> Do not remember the former things,
>   or consider the things of old.
> I am about to do a new thing;
>   now it springs forth, do you not perceive it?
> I will make a way in the wilderness
>   and rivers in the desert.
> The wild animals will honor me,
>   the jackals and the ostriches;

for I give water in the wilderness,
    rivers in the desert,
to give drink to my chosen people,
    the people whom I formed for myself
so that they might declare my praise.
                                        (Isa 43:16–21)

12

The Book of Joshua

The move in the Bible from the book of Deuteronomy to the book of Joshua is more than a shift of leadership to a younger generation, though it is that (Deut 31:1–8; Josh 1:1–9). It is as well a leap for the reader to move from the final scroll of the Torah, Israel's normative literature that is dominated by the person of Moses, to the first scroll of the Former Prophets, a corpus preoccupied with the crisis of the land. Thus the move is from more normative literature—normativeness linked to Moses—to the more disputatious literature to follow. This move, moreover, carries Israel from *buoyant anticipation* of the land of promise to *conflictual possession* of the land.

This enormous shift of perspective is signaled in the text itself by the notice of Joshua 5:12: "The manna ceased on the day they ate the produce of the land, and the Israelites no longer had manna; they ate the crops of the land of Canaan that year." As long as YHWH supplied manna to Israel (and we are to believe that the gift of manna initiated in Exod 16 reliably persisted through the remainder of the Torah), Israel could rely on YHWH's gracious sustenance. When Israel enters the land, however, the sense and materiality of sustenance is terminated and Israel is required to secure its life by agricultural effort. This means that whereas the aegis of YHWH's manna kept Israel's life free from the problematics of self-sustenance, the entry into agriculture engaged Israel in all of the realities of life in the land, that is, life in the midst of an indigenous population that did not share its sociotheological perspective. The contemporary novelist Max Apple writes:

> Joshua understands that when he begins the Manna will disappear. A people that can make war is a people that can feed itself. When Joshua acts, Israel's brief protected respite is over. All the dangers and

139

excitements of adult life begin, a life of politics, not myth, a life filled with choices.

The tribes of Israel enter into Canaan as weak and frail and vulnerable as any other Bedouins. The Books of Moses are over, the books of history are beginning. Mythic heroes from now on will be merely soldiers or prophets or judges or kings. The promise of the God of Israel still remains, but His presence is less available.

Because Joshua lives exactly at the tragic moment when myth disintegrates, he may be the first modern man. If he acts, the Manna ceases, the terrible war begins, the tribal squabbling becomes more central than the Ark of the Covenant. If he does not act, he betrays his history and the trust of Moses and God. (Apple 1987, 67)

I

It is conventional to see in the book of Joshua two great clusters of texts plus the introductory and concluding materials that provide a Deuteronomic framework to the whole. The first great section of the text narrates the way in which Israel seized the land from the "Canaanite" population and took possession of it (Josh 2–12). This material is constituted by a collection of what seem to be independent narratives now grouped together to form a whole. The material is quite variegated:

Chapters 3 and 4 tell of the crossing of the Jordan River, an account that appears to be cast as a guideline for periodic liturgical reenactment of the crossing that was the pivotal act of the theological drama of Israel's land entry. That crossing of the Jordan, moreover, is portrayed as a replication and reiteration of the exodus event:

> When your children ask their parents in time to come, "What do these stones mean?" then you shall let your children know, "Israel crossed over the Jordan here on dry ground." For the LORD your God dried up the waters of the Jordan for you until you crossed over, as the LORD your God did to the Red Sea, which he dried up for us until we crossed over, so that all the peoples of the earth may know that the hand of the LORD is mighty, and so that you may fear the LORD your God forever. (Josh 4:21–24)

These chapters are sandwiched by *chapters 2 and 6* that narrate the destruction of Jericho, Israel's first conquest in the land after crossing the Jordan River. While the text celebrates the wonder of the destruction wrought through Yahwistic fervor (6:16), the narrative is also concerned to report a separate peace made with Rahab, thus indicating that relationships with the non-Israelite population are not simple and one-dimensional (6:25). *Chapter*

7 narrates the defeat of Israel in the "Valley of Trouble" (7:26) and portrays the community of Israel under raw and brutal discipline, the kind of discipline that is understood theologically, that is concerned with the loyalty to the community that is under threat. *Chapter 8* narrates a great victory at Ai, a success comparable to the earlier account of the fall of Jericho. *Chapter 9*, in a story parallel to that of Rahab in chapters 2 and 6, tells of coming to terms with the Gibeonites, yet another account of relations with non-Israelites in the land. *Chapters 10 and 11* narrate great victories under Joshua, and chapter 12 provides a summary of the sweep of Israelite military success. The sum of this material indicates that Israel under the leadership of Joshua, at the behest of YHWH, had taken and occupied important parts of the land of Canaan.

This material has been, in recent decades, a matter of immense interpretive dispute. If one grants, provisionally, that the materials portray something of a historical occurrence, one is left with questions about the nature of the "conquest." There are three lively alternatives in current scholarly purview:

1. The conquest was a sweeping, successful onslaught whereby Israel took the land by an invasion of immense military effectiveness. That military effectiveness with all of its accompanying military brutality is credited to YHWH's fidelity. This portrayal has support in some of the great battle narratives and attests to the effectiveness of YHWH's leadership and fidelity. The historical evidence for such a conquest is, in current judgment, quite problematic. Thus the reading of the material, without reference to other data, makes great grist for Israel's faith.

2. The conquest was more of an infiltration whereby smaller groups of Israelites occupied the land here and there and made for themselves what gains they could, all the while being realistic about the indigenous population that

> ### Close Reading:
> ### Joshua as "Half-Moses"
>
> While Joshua inherits the mantle from Moses as leader of Israel ("I will be with you as I was with Moses," God says in Josh 3:7) and achieves the entry into the promised land, it is clear that the tradition understands him as not quite so great as Moses. While Moses leads Israel dramatically through the Red Sea in the book of Exodus, Joshua leads them, less dramatically, through the Jordan River (compare Josh 4:19–24 with Exod 14). Joshua, like Moses, experiences a divine encounter—compare Joshua 5:13–15 with Exodus 3:1–6, where both are instructed to remove their sandals—but whereas Moses encounters God directly, Joshua encounters an angelic "commander of the Lord's army." Perhaps the image that sums it up best is that when Joshua crosses the Jordan River with Israel the waters "stand in a single heap" (3:13), whereas in Exodus 14:22 they form "a wall on their right and on their left." Moses gets two heaps of water, while Joshua gets only one, making him a sort of "half-Moses."

did not simply disappear in the face of Israel. This view, apparently supported by Judges 1:1–2:5, is suggested both by the accommodation made to Rahab's family (Josh 6:25) and by the settlement made with the Gibeonites (9:22–27).

3. A third view, now popular among interpreters and favored in this introduction, is that the conquest narrative reflects an internal struggle in the land of Canaan (without an invasion from the outside) between conflicting elements of the Canaanite population. This internal struggle consists, on the one hand, of the urban elites who excessively taxed and exploited the peasants and, on the other hand, the peasants who under Joshua's leadership and in the name of YHWH mounted an assault upon the exploitative power of the Canaanite city-state system and sought to establish a different socioeconomic order. This hypothesis, most vigorously articulated by Norman Gottwald, is perhaps reflected in the list of cities in 12:7–24, for the cities were both the symbol and reality of huge concentrations of exploitative wealth and power (Gottwald 1979). The movement of Israel, at the behest of YHWH, is understood in this hypothesis as a revolutionary alternative to the conventional pattern of exploitation of the dominant political-economic organizational system.

These hypotheses, variously held by scholars and endlessly reassessed, all proceed on the assumption that the text of Joshua 2–12 reflects a core of historical memory. It is important, however, to reckon as well with the interpretive possibility that this text, in its final form, does not reflect significant rootage in history, but is to be understood as an imaginative creation designed to provide ground for a theological-ideological claim upon the land. An accent upon the ideological intent and force of the material tends not to be concerned with the historical rootage of the material and concludes that, in any case, the historical element of the narrative has little force and occupies little interest for the textual tradition. What counts in this reading is that this corpus of narratives provides a suprahistorical warrant for Israel's claims upon the land. One may recognize in any case that whatever may have been the intent of the material, its subsequent function has certainly been to sustain such a deep claim to the land in a way that means to and serves to override the land claims of any other population.

The second great section of the book of Joshua is chapters 13–19, which contain a long list of boundaries and land assignments whereby Joshua systematically assigns the land, now conquered, to the several tribes that constitute Israel. This detailed list of boundaries purports to be the actual divisions that Joshua made after seizing the land. We have already indicated that the historical claims of the "conquest" narratives are highly doubtful. In the case of this second section of the text, the historical claims for land division are even more dubious. Thus it is more likely, in scholarly judgment, that these boundary texts are belated acts of imagination that perhaps reflect subsequent land arrangements or are perhaps idealizations of how it might have been; either way, the texts function to legitimate land claims, the legitimacy deriving from the immense authority of Joshua, who is in turn authorized by Moses and, in effect, by YHWH, who is the ultimate distributor of land. As Moshe Weinfeld has made clear, it was a practice of royal prerogative in the ancient world to give land grants to the subject whom the sovereign especially favored (Weinfeld 1970). This assumption about the royal capacity for a land grant is evident, for example, in 2 Samuel 9. It is then an easy move to suggest that YHWH, the God of Israel, is exercising sovereign authority in making land grants to YHWH's favorite subject, Israel.

Whatever may lie behind this land-legitimating text—and historical claims may be treated with great skepticism—it is clear that the historical-political-geographical claim receives a theological twist in the ongoing interpretive conversation. This is particularly evident in the specific case of Caleb, Joshua's longtime comrade in noteworthy fidelity. Caleb is promised the land first by Moses and then by Joshua:

> And Moses swore on that day, saying, "Surely the land on which your foot has trodden shall be an inheritance for you and your children forever, because you have wholeheartedly followed the LORD my God." (Josh 14:9)

> Then Joshua blessed him, and gave Hebron to Caleb son of Jephunneh for an inheritance. So Hebron became the inheritance of Caleb son of Jephunneh the Kenizzite to this day, because he wholeheartedly followed the LORD, the God of Israel. (14:13–14)

The theological overlay to the process of land distribution, however, is not immune to what might pass for realism, at least on two counts. In 17:12 it is acknowledged that "Canaanites continued to live in that land," thus anticipating the theme of Judges 1:1–2:5. In Joshua 17:14–18, moreover, the land grant is contested by the "tribe of Joseph." This would suggest that even in a belated idealized version of land entitlement, Israel struggled to get its story straight.

We may particularly notice two efforts at theological closure to the account of land distribution. In 19:51 it is reported that "they finished dividing the land." Joseph Blenkinsopp (1992) has suggested that this formulation is deliberately parallel to the conclusion of the Priestly creation narrative, "Thus the heavens and the earth *were finished*, and all their multitude" (Gen 2:1, italics added), and to the narrative of the construction of the tabernacle: "In this way all the work of the tabernacle of the tent of meeting *was finished*; the Israelites had done everything just as the LORD had commanded Moses" (Exod 39:32, italics added); "So Moses *finished* the work" (Exod 40:33, italics added). If this parallel among the three texts is sustainable, we are permitted the conclusion that creation, tabernacle, and land are treated in the Priestly tradition of the exile as the three elements of order in a lived circumstance of acute disorder. Such a parallel would illuminate why the boundary texts dwell on such detail, a preoccupation with the detail that is not unlike the enormous detail of the tabernacle construction in Exodus 25–31 and 35–40.

More importantly, von Rad has noticed the remarkable concluding formula of Joshua 21:43–45:

> Thus the LORD gave to Israel all the land that he swore to their ancestors that he would give them; and having taken possession of it, they settled there. And the LORD gave them rest on every side just as he had sworn to their ancestors; not one of all their enemies had withstood them, for the LORD had given all their enemies into their hands. Not one of all the good promises that the LORD had made to the house of Israel had failed; all came to pass.

This comment is surely designed to give closure to the account of land distribution, for "rest" means that every tribe and every social group in Israel is given a place of security. This formula, however, is not only a conclusion to the account of land distribution but also to the preceding section on land seizure. But as von Rad suggests, the formula is more than a conclusion to the two great parts of the book of Joshua (von Rad 1966, 70–74). It is also a conclusion to the larger text of the Hexateuch, that is, the long story through six biblical books that began all the way back in Genesis 12 with the initial promise to Abraham. Thus this formula asserts that YHWH's initial promise of land to Abraham, reiterated to the son and to the grandson of Abraham and to the generation of the exodus (Exod 3:7–9), has come to full and wondrous fulfillment. The primal theme of land promise is now fully enacted. YHWH is shown to be faithful and Israel is shown to be fully entitled and thereby safe.

It remains for us to notice that these two extended sections of the book of Joshua concerning land conquest and land distribution are framed, in the final form of the text, by Deuteronomic accents upon Torah obedience. One may entertain the thought that the initial land stories may have focused only upon YHWH's promise and upon Israel's courage. In Deuteronomic traditioning, however, the reception of the land is now framed by and made conditional upon Torah obedience, a primary Deuteronomic accent:

> Only be strong and very courageous, being careful to act in accordance with all the law that my servant Moses commanded you; do not turn from it to the right hand or to the left, so that you may be successful wherever you go. This book of the law shall not depart out of your mouth; you shall meditate on it day and night, so that you

may be careful to act in accordance with all that is written in it. For then you shall make your way prosperous, and then you shall be successful. I hereby command you: Be strong and courageous; do not be frightened or dismayed, for the LORD your God is with you wherever you go. (Josh 1:7–9)

They answered Joshua: "All that you have commanded us we will do, and wherever you send us we will go. Just as we obeyed Moses in all things, so we will obey you. Only may the LORD your God be with you, as he was with Moses! Whoever rebels against your orders and disobeys your words, whatever you command, shall be put to death. Only be strong and courageous." (1:16–18)

The LORD your God will push them back before you, and drive them out of your sight; and you shall possess their land, as the LORD your God promised you. Therefore be very steadfast to observe and do all that is written in the book of the law of Moses, turning aside from it neither to the right nor to the left, so that you may not be mixed with these nations left here among you, or make mention of the names of their gods, or swear by them, or serve them, or bow yourselves down to them, but hold fast to the LORD your God, as you have done to this day. (23:5–8)

These texts serve to transpose and resituate the land texts so that in the final form the land narrative is not about violence and military effectiveness. In the horizon of Deuteronomy the only condition for land is full obedience to the Torah, which in this purview refers precisely to the commandments of the tradition of Deuteronomy.

In Joshua 23, moreover, it is recognized that the threat to Israel in Torah disobedience is that it will be "mixed" with the other nations and thereby have its singular Yahwistic, covenantal identity qualified and compromised (23:7). The danger for disobedient Israel is articulated in characteristic Deuteronomic rhetoric of zeal, whereby "bad things" (23:15) may result from disobedience: "If you transgress the covenant of the LORD your God, which he enjoined on you, and go and serve other gods and bow down to them, then the anger of the LORD will be kindled against you, and you shall perish quickly from the good land that he has given to you" (23:16).

It is clear that in developed Deuteronomic articulation, these latter assertions already have in purview the land loss and deportation that was to come in 587 BCE. Thus the book of Joshua, as Noth saw, serves the larger purpose of the Deuteronomic agenda of commenting on the crisis of 587. From the outset, from the very reception of the land, Israel is put on notice of the acute conditionality of land retention, a conditionality that Israel mocks in wholesale disobedience, according to this reading. It is astonishing then that just as soon as all the promises "[come] to pass" (Josh 21:45), Israel is on notice that "bad things" will come next (23:15).

Finally, special notice of chapter 24 should be taken, for the chapter has been richly appreciated by scholars. It is evident in Deuteronomy 11:29–30; 27:11–13; and Joshua 8:30–35 that the mountains around Shechem—Ebal and Gerizim—are rendered as a place of covenant making. In Joshua 24 the text narrates a covenant-making ceremony whereby Joshua recites the narrative memory of Israel (vv. 2–13), Israel vows loyalty to the requirements of YHWH (vv. 16–24), and on the basis of solemn oaths Joshua makes a covenant, binding Israel to YHWH and to YHWH's commands (v. 25). This text, perhaps liturgically styled, is a summation of all that has preceded and is located here as a marker in Israel's constitution as a peculiar people in the new land. In saying this, it is important to recognize that we may beg historical questions and see this text in any case as a literary, imaginative rendering that is perhaps rooted in historical reality and perhaps is an idealized form of what Israel hopes for at its best. In any case, as the book of Joshua tells it, the people of the Torah are now safely ensconced in the land that YHWH intended them to have. This accomplishment has been wrought through YHWH's fidelity, through Israel's courage, and through a great deal of brutality. In this rendering, all of these factors are held together without comment or reservation. While the convergence is well established, it should not escape us that the convergence of YHWH's fidelity, Israel's courage, and the brutality of the narrative are odd and problematic. The Bible does not blink at either the oddness or its problematic character.

II

Out of this analysis we may observe three dimensions of the book of Joshua that likely will preoccupy the reader:

1. The book of Joshua—concerned with land conquest and land distribution and framed with Torah accents of the theology of Deuteronomy—may originally have been concerned with the reception of the land. In its final form, however, the book of Joshua has been transposed into a theological reflection that arises from and provides a resource to the generation of exiles who can remember the loss of land and who can anticipate reentry into the land. Obviously that possible reentry into the land by returning deportees will not be done by military conquest. Rather, it is the conviction of the traditioning process of the Deuteronomists that land reception and land re-reception are singularly about Torah obedience. For that reason the exilic, postexilic community is focused upon Torah obedience in a way that became

characteristic of emerging Judaism. It is a complex question to ask about the extent to which and the ways in which an older text of violence has been transposed into something else, and the extent to which and the ways in which the transposed material still retains something of the dimension of the text of violence that is an antecedent to the Torah-voiced transpositions of that tradition. The juxtaposition of memories of authorized violence and demanding Torah conditionality constitute the central interpretive problem of the book of Joshua, a problem that admits of no simple or obvious solution.

2. There is no question more troubling for theological interpretation of the Old Testament than the undercurrent of violence that moves through a good bit of the text (Schwartz 1997; Weems 1995; Dempsey 2000). There is, moreover, no part of the textual tradition that is more permeated with violence than the conquest traditions of Joshua. While the land is promised in the ancestral traditions of Genesis, that same land in the implementation of the promise is taken by means of brutal military attack that is characteristic of any military operation and is perhaps especially characteristic of the ancient practices of the Near East. As now, even then, war is hell. There is no warrant for pretending otherwise about war, ancient or contemporary, for war depends upon ruthless aggressiveness that unleashes brutal assaults upon the environment and upon the population, especially the vulnerable population of women and children, who are lightly categorized as "collateral damage."

Thus the book of Joshua in its narrative of the conquest pertaining to Jericho (chaps. 2, 6), Ai (chap. 8), various kings (10:16–43), and Hazor (chap. 11) characterizes the military onslaught of Israel that eventuates in extermination of its enemies. We have already said that these tales of violence are transposed in the traditioning process.

The violence persists, however, and the interpreter must wonder what to make of it. A characteristic explanation is that the narratives of violence are exercises in ideology, that is, in the self-articulation of an intention and right that are taken to be self-justifying and without any critical afterthought. That way of thinking goes a long way in understanding these texts. That explanation, however, is complex because the violence is not simply undertaken on a human initiative, but is understood as a mandate of YHWH as the effective means of keeping YHWH's land promise. It is possible, of course, to say that the ideology is so virulent and self-satisfied that it draws YHWH into the claim of the violence. Even so, however, in the final form of the text YHWH is left as the definitive source of justified violence, justified because the violence is enacted on behalf of YHWH's people. Thus if we take the texts with some theological realism, we are bound to say that YHWH is here implicated in the violence, that YHWH's violence is rooted in the violent propensity in YHWH's own character (Miles 1995).

This is deeply problematic, to say the least, but any other reading is likely to be a dishonest cover-up of the disclosure of YHWH given in these texts. If that were the case, then YHWH, the God of Israel, is seen as the one who is capable of violence against Israel's enemies, but eventually is capable of violence against Israel itself in later contexts. One may argue that in the Christian tradition, anticipated in texts like Hosea 11:8–9, the death of Jesus is a way in which God takes that violence into God's own self. That way of thinking is suggestive—it does not, however, overcome the raw data of YHWH that is deeply etched in the text and that amounts to a deep and abiding problem in Christianity as it has surfaced in the powerful history of violence in the name of God that is characteristically practiced in Western history.

The particular articulation of this violence that appears to be rooted in YHWH is expressed as *herem* (Stern 1991). This is the ancient conviction that things offered to YHWH as booty captured from the enemy must be "utterly destroyed." The verb related to *herem* recurs in the narrative of Joshua 10, where it is repeatedly rendered "utterly destroy":

> From Lachish Joshua passed on with all Israel to Eglon; and they laid siege to it, and assaulted it; and they took it that day, and struck it with the edge of the sword; and every person in it he *utterly destroyed* that day, as he had done to Lachish.
>
> Then Joshua went up with all Israel from Eglon to Hebron; they assaulted it, and took it, and struck it with the edge of the sword, and its king and its towns, and every person in it; he left no one remaining, just as he had done to Eglon, and *utterly destroyed* it with every person in it.
>
> Then Joshua, with all Israel, turned back to Debir and assaulted it, and he took it with its king and all its towns; they struck them with the edge of the sword, and *utterly destroyed* every person in it; he left no one remaining; just as he had done to Hebron, and, as he had done to Libnah and its king, so he did to Debir and its king.
>
> So Joshua defeated the whole land, the hill country and the Negeb and the lowland and the slopes, and all their kings; he left no one remaining, but *utterly destroyed* all that breathed, as the LORD God of Israel commanded. (Josh 10:34–40, italics added)

This notion, well entrenched in Israel, is a way whereby raw military violence and the will of YHWH are intimately linked, wherein the will of YHWH is seen to justify and authorize and legitimate acts of extermination. The rhetoric mandates nothing less than genocide.

3. Whatever the origin of the mandate of violence, and even given the transposition of the text into Torah conditionality, it is clear that the book of Joshua has functioned and continues to function as theologically grounded land entitlement. That is, the "land of Canaan" is thereby transposed into

the "land of promise" and eventually into the "Holy Land." The costly part of this theological-ideological claim is that it makes possible—even easy— the complete write-off of other indigenous populations in the land, either as though they were not there at all or because they have no right to be there. There is no doubt that the text functions to write out of history the Canaanites in the ancient mixed population of the land (Levenson 1985).

There is also no doubt that by extrapolation the same texts of land legitimacy continue to function in contemporary settings in a parallel way. The first, obvious case is the current policy of the State of Israel toward the Palestinian population. Beyond that, however, the same ideology has legitimated European Americans in "discovering" and occupying North America at the unbearable expense of Native Americans. In every part of the world, moreover, European colonial policy toward indigenous populations has received warrant from this text that, if not toxic in intent, has in any case functioned in toxic ways in recent history (Gunn 1998):

> My argument is that the biblical narratives which deal with the promise and gift of land are potentially corrupting in themselves, and have in fact contributed to war crimes and crimes against humanity in virtually every colonized region, by providing allegedly divine legitimation for Western colonizers in their zeal to implant "outposts of progress" in the heart of the darkness. The ongoing identification in subsequent history with the warring scenes of the Hebrew Bible is a burden the biblical tradition must bear. The fact that the particular violence of the Hebrew Scriptures has inspired violence, and has served as a model of, and for persecution, subjugation, and extermination for millennia beyond its own reality makes investigation of these traditions a critical task. Nevertheless, the ethnocentric, xenophobic and militaristic character of the biblical narratives of Israelite origins is treated in conventional biblical scholarship as if it were above any questioning on moral grounds, even by criteria derived from other parts of the Bible. Most commentators are uninfluenced by considerations of human rights, when these conflict with a naïve reading of the sacred text, and appear to be unperturbed by the text's advocacy of plunder, murder, and the exploitation of indigenous peoples, all under the guise of fidelity to the eternal validity of the covenant of Sinai. (Prior 1998, 11)

The book of Joshua is pivotal in our understanding of the Old Testament. The book makes an immense theological affirmation, but, as we have seen, that affirmation is deeply and particularly problematic. The use of this biblical literature requires great care and attentiveness to the unintended effects of our reading.

13

The Book of Judges

If one comes to the book of Judges after reading the book of Joshua, which canonical placement encourages us to do, one immediately notices the oddness of the story's beginning: "The Israelites inquired of the LORD, 'Who shall go up for us first against the Canaanites, to fight against them?'" Its oddness comes from the fact that the book of Joshua has just narrated a complete and final conquest of the Canaanites and possession of the land. Who is there left to fight against? And whereas at the end of the book of Joshua there is peace in the land and the Israelite tribes are united, Judges culminates in the extravagant violence of intertribal warfare (see chaps. 19–21). This discrepancy indicates, from a historical perspective, that we are dealing with different traditions of the conquest of the land, with overlapping stories. But the canonical decision to include both Joshua and Judges creates what is surely an intentional paradox: the taking of the land, and the dispossession of its inhabitants, is presented as *both* easily accomplished *and* forever delayed. We might even see here an ethical conflict of memory: on the one hand Israel, like any nation, wants a clean and decisive story of its origins, but on the other hand it preserves evidence of a messier and more ethically problematic story of origins, one in which the annihilation of a land's inhabitants is not so simple after all. It is not easy to hold these two versions together, but the canon insists that we do.

The book of Judges is part of the Former Prophets, that is, a historical narrative through which Israel reimagines its conflictual life in the land of promise according to the decisive reality of YHWH. The accent in this characterization is upon the act of reimagination whereby the traditioning process takes up (a) old memories and (b) remembered historical facts on the ground, and formulates all of that as data according to the rule of YHWH.

151

In the dominant critical hypothesis, moreover, the book of Judges is part of the Deuteronomic History, a major theological commentary upon the royal past of Israel that is designed to show the ways in which Israel lost the land given by YHWH, and ended as a displaced people in the sixth century BCE (Noth 1981).

I

The first textual unit is *1:1–2:5*. In these verses, according to this rendition, Israel must cope with its new circumstance in the land "after the death of Joshua" (1:1), that is, after the loss of its great war leader and advocate of the Torah. This unit of text is commonly regarded as an early evidence of Israel's life in the land; it may be early, but it functions nonetheless according to the intent of the later traditioning process.

We may identify three accent points in this unit of the text:

1. The narrative continues to be preoccupied with the seizure of the land of promise either from an earlier Canaanite population (if there was an invasion) or from the exploitative power structure of the Canaanite political-economic system (if the matter was an internal social revolution). Either way, Israel is committed to all of the brutality of war: "Adoni-bezek fled; but they pursued him, and caught him, and cut off his thumbs and big toes" (Judg 1:6). That brutality, moreover, is understood as mandated by YHWH (1:2), who is in the payback business: "Adoni-bezek said, 'Seventy kings with their thumbs and big toes cut off used to pick up scraps under my table; as I have done, so *God has paid me back*'" (1:7, italics added).

2. In 1:16–36 the text offers a report on the condition of Israel, the newly established people, who must—even in the land of promise—live with and among Canaanites. Thus the repeated refrain of these verses in many variant forms is that Israel "did not drive out the Canaanites" (1:29). This report is often understood as a note of realism that corrects the extravagant claims of conquest in the narratives of Joshua. If, however, we remember that the traditioning process intends to serve a theological end, then it is not necessary to regard this text as a historical report. It is alternatively possible to note that "Canaanite" (and other parallel terms like "Jebusite") are essentially ideological (not ethnic) terms to identify the "other" who does not share Yahwistic faith and who consequently organizes life differently. Thus the interpretive point is that even in the land of promise the fullness of promise is less than fully established and is compromised by the presence of antipromise peoples. The effect of this acknowledgment, an ideological rather than a historical acknowledgment, is that the ensuing narratives of the book of Judges will

give an account of the incessant compromise of its faith that Israel makes and the incessant seductions and threats posed to Israel's faith by the "other." If in final form this is a sixth-century text, as it is according to the dominant hypothesis, then it may serve the awareness of displaced Israel that it must practice its faith in displacement, in the midst of the "other" who is both threat and seduction.

3. This dangerous challenge of the "other" is evident in 2:1–5, which concludes this unit of text. These verses are commonly taken as a rationale for the continuing presence of the "other" in the land of promise, a presence that is to be regarded as nothing less than an anomaly, given the promises of YHWH. That is, the continuing presence of the "other" is there because Israel did not obey YHWH. Aside from such an explanatory function, however, the clear covenantal requirements stated in symmetrical fashion function as a key marker for all that follows: "I said, 'I will never break my covenant with you. For your part, do not make a covenant with the inhabitants of this land; tear down their altars'" (Judg 2:1b–2a). Both parties to the covenant, YHWH and Israel, are pledged to mutual obedience and loyalty (see Deut 26:16–19). It is as though the entire course of Israel's history in the land is to be an enactment of the first commandment or a refusal of that commandment: "You shall have no other gods before me" (Deut 5:7). The tales that follow in the book of Judges make clear that disobedience to this elemental requirement of covenant is the clue to the endless cycle of disaster that now is to be narrated.

II

The second textual unit in the book of Judges is commonly taken to be the long central section, 2:6–16:31. This material seems to be constituted by old and remembered tales of heroes who intervened in the vexed public life of Israel and who, by their leadership, made possible some extended seasons of ordered well-being in what was a conflictual social environment where Israel was beset on every side by dangerous and demanding adversaries. These stories were likely quite locally remembered and told with great narrative imagination and freedom. As the narratives have been taken up into the larger tradition of Israel, such treasured ad hoc narratives have been ordered sequentially and nationalized to portray a common story of the entire community. The sequencing and nationalizing at the same time permitted the imposition of a certain philosophy of history upon the material that is commonly thought to be Deuteronomic. There can be no doubt that in the traditioning process this formulation of meaning is imposed, because it is done in stereotypical and prosaic fashion. One may suggest at the same time, however, that what is editorially imposed may be a deep discernment of what is the truth of the hero stories even though the vivid telling of them does not move explicitly to such theological rigor until later in the traditioning process. That is, the later traditioning process that did a literary imposition may have discerned what was going on in the narratives.

The hero stories themselves are rich and varied. Among them is a report on Ehud, the left-handed freedom fighter (3:12–30); Abimelech, son of Gideon, who has large political ambitions (9:1–57); and Jephthah, notorious for his primitive oath that evoked the death of his daughter (11:1–40). The variety is rich and imaginative, but we may do well to focus on three stars of the narrative:

1. The Song of Deborah (as the poem is called) in Judges 5 is one of the most important and likely earliest renderings of Israel's faith. (A later narrative account of the same plot is offered in chap. 4.) This poem is a celebration of a mighty victory wrought by Israel over the Canaanites, a celebration in which "the triumphs of [YHWH], the triumphs of his peasantry in Israel," are remembered (v. 11). In the poem it is impossible to distinguish between the triumphs of YHWH and the triumphs of Israelite peasants, for the poem clearly intends that no distinction should be made because both agencies are indispensable to the outcome. The poem details the mighty procession of YHWH from Sinai to lead the troops of Israel (vv. 4–5), the vulnerability of Israel (vv. 6–9), the dissension among the tribes of Israel concerning their respective responsibilities to one another (vv. 13–18, 23), the great battle in which the powers of heaven are mobilized on behalf of Israel (vv. 19–22), the follow-up action of Jael, who killed the despised Canaanite general (vv. 24–27), and the imagined pathos of the wives of the Canaanite generals as the defeat of their men begins to dawn on them (vv. 28–31). At the center of the poem is Deborah, "a mother in Israel" (v. 7). The poem has remarkable rhetorical power. It shows, moreover, the way in which Israel is able to articulate at the same time the palpable reality of YHWH in its life and the lived reality of its historical circumstance. The poem functions as a great testimony to the way in which Israel's life is guaranteed and protected by YHWH.

2. The narrative of Gideon is extended and filled with the sort of detail most appreciated in folk stories (chaps. 6–8). The call of Gideon to be a judge and leader in Israel is told in a way that shows not only Gideon's reticence about the mandate from YHWH, but also his chutzpah in negotiating his terms of call with the angel who recruits him to public service (6:11–27). Once called, Gideon is a vigorous advocate for the most violent kind of Yahwism, destroying both the affrontive religious symbols of "the other" (6:28–32; see Deut 7:5), and violently abusing his enemies, who are taken to be the enemies of both Israel and of Israel's God:

> Gideon replied, "Well then, when the LORD has given Zebah and Zalmunna into my hand, I will trample your flesh on the thorns of the wilderness and on briers." . . . So he took the elders of the city and he took thorns of the wilderness and briers and with them he trampled the people of Succoth. . . . Then Zebah and Zalmunna said, "You come and kill us; for as the man is, so is his strength." So Gideon proceeded to kill Zebah and Zalmunna; and he took the crescents that were on the necks of their camels. (Judg 8:7, 16, 21)

The centerpiece of the Gideon narrative is the great victory he wins over the Midianites, a victory worked through cunning, surprise, and the force of YHWH, whose war Gideon fights. The narrative of Gideon sadly ends in 8:22–28 with an acknowledgment that in the midst of his great fidelity and success, Gideon eventually becomes self-serving, seeking great economic advantage for himself. With both Gideon (8:22) and his son Abimelech (9:1–6), one notices that the principle of dynastic order is in the air in anticipation of the narratives of 1 Samuel, an anticipation that is refused in this narrative. It is perhaps plausible to suggest that Gideon, who rose and fell from faithful advocate for YHWH to self-serving practitioner of ambition, is himself part of the pattern of Israel's life in the narrative, a community always restored to YHWH, but a community always seduced into alternative loyalties. It is, in such a horizon, no surprise that the Gideon narrative ends in compromise: Israel yields to the attraction of the "other," who is endlessly and seductively present in Israel: "As soon as Gideon died, the Israelites relapsed and prostituted themselves with the Baals, making Baal-berith their god. The Israelites did not remember the LORD their God, who had rescued them from the hand of all their enemies on every side; and they did not exhibit loyalty to the house of Jerubbaal (that is, Gideon) in return for all the good that he had done to Israel" (8:33–35).

3. The third narrative to which we give special attention is that of Samson (chaps. 13–16). This narrative takes great care to mark Samson's specialness by attending to his peculiar birth (chap. 13). The primary motif in this narrative, however, is Samson's complex relationship to the Philistines, Israel's paradigmatic enemy, the quintessential "other" whose narrative function is to serve and enhance Israel's own peculiar identity (Jobling 1998, 197–243). On the one hand, Samson is the great Yahwistic warrior who ends his life in a great climactic act as a massive destruction of the Philistines:

> Then Samson called to the LORD and said, "Lord GOD, remember me and strengthen me only this once, O God, so that with this one act of revenge I may pay back the Philistines for my two eyes." And Samson grasped the two middle pillars on which the house rested, and he leaned his weight against them, his right hand on the one and

his left hand on the other. Then Samson said, "Let me die with the Philistines." He strained with all his might; and the house fell on the lords and all the people who were in it. So those he killed at his death were more than those he had killed during his life. (16:28–30)

That powerfully awkward relationship, on the other hand, is made powerfully complex by Samson's marriage to Delilah, a Philistine woman. That relationship is portrayed through a series of dramatic and playful encounters that exhibit the power and the danger of the Philistines to the Israelites:

> Delilah defeated Samson by using the weapon that she had at hand, her tongue. She kept asking him till he couldn't stand it anymore, and by the power of nagging she wore him down. Samson has been here before. Both of his women asked him, over and over. And they accused him of not loving them. Over and over. Samson is susceptible to this combination of persistence and guilt. It would not be fair to say that he had great brawn but little brain, but somehow he does not recognize the tactic and it works again. It is, after all, a very good tactic. According to Proverbs, it is better to live in the desert or a corner of a roof than with a contentious wife (Prov. 21:9, 19; 25:24). Delilah may not have been generally vexatious, but on this matter she was relentless, and Samson could not resist. . . .
>   The Samson-Delilah story is the closest thing the Bible contains to a "Battle of the Sexes," the wars and contests between males and females so common in Greek mythology. (Frymer-Kensky 2002, 82–83)

At the end of the narrative, Samson is faithful to YHWH, the Philistines are defeated, Israel is safe, and YHWH is vindicated. The narrative route to these outcomes, however, is not obvious or easy. Israel endlessly lives in a complex world of the "other," and coming to terms with the "other" is tortuously complicated.

This collection of stories about heroes who made life possible in a challenging environment of powerful Canaanite alternatives evidences a variety of strategies whereby the faithful in Israel responded to that environment with its challenges, threats, and seductions. The traditioning process, here apparently shaped by the Deuteronomists, did not, however, leave the materials in their ad hoc form. Rather, these stories were taken up as vehicles for and in the service of a rather clear and certainly uncompromising theological assertion that is reiterated through this central section of the book of Judges. The simplest articulation of this theological assertion is found in the narrative of 3:7–11, which, once the formula is noticed, is scarcely a narrative at all. We identify four recurring emphases in this theological assertion:

1. "The Israelites did what was evil in the sight of the LORD" (3:7). The beginning point of theological analysis in this tradition is that Israel sinned

by violating the first commandment of exclusive loyalty to YHWH. The text explicitly asserts that Israel violated the exclusive covenant by the embrace of alternative Canaanite gods (see 2:2). This religious enactment, however, is to be understood not simply as cultic deviation, because the Canaanite gods most assuredly served to legitimate Canaanite socioeconomic practices that are characteristically antineighborly. Thus the indictment undoubtedly refers to the entire social system in which life is organized, epitomized by the naming of the gods.

2. In response to that deviation from YHWH, "Therefore the anger of the LORD was kindled against Israel, and he sold them into the hand of King Cushan-rishathaim of Aram-naharaim; and the Israelites served Cushan-rishathaim eight years" (3:8). The daring theological imagination of the Deuteronomists asserts that adherence to YHWH will assure sociopolitical well-being, unencumbered by overlords. Conversely, in negative fashion, failure to adhere to YHWH results in subservience in the political ordering. This is a bold and characteristic linkage whereby the Deuteronomist asserts that theological commitments have immense practical and, in this case, powerful consequences.

3. After enough suffering, Israel comes to its senses, remembers its identity, and makes fresh appeal to the God who it had earlier refused to obey: "But when the Israelites cried out to the LORD . . ." (3:9a). The "cry" is an act of urgent petition (Boyce 1988). But the "cry" of desperate need is also to be understood as an act of repentance, an abandonment of the Canaanite gods upon whom Israel had relied in verse 7, and a return to the rule of YHWH, including new adherence to the Sinai commands of YHWH. It is as though the suffering is recognized as a result of disloyalty, so that the antidote is to renew loyalty, acknowledge primary dependence upon YHWH, and offer a committed resolve to obey the God of the covenant.

4. The fourth element, in response to the "cry" of Israel, is that YHWH answers by providing a "deliverer" who will rescue Israel from oppression and provide a new era of well-being for Israel: "the LORD raised up a deliverer for the Israelites, who delivered them, Othniel son of Kenaz, Caleb's younger brother. The spirit of the LORD came upon him, and he judged Israel; he went out to war, and the LORD gave King Cushan-rishathaim of Aram into his hand; and his hand prevailed over Cushan-rishathaim. So the land had rest forty years. Then Othniel son of Kenaz died" (3:9b–11). It is clear that the "deliverer" is a human agent, elsewhere a "judge," but a human agent who is authorized and empowered by YHWH's own spirit that is the decisive force in rearranging and redeploying political power.

This coherent and symmetrical theological formulation consists in a combination of two already well-established convictions in Israel (Brueggemann

1981, 101–14). First, it belongs to the rigor of covenantal theology that disobedience evokes punishment from YHWH. This connection is elemental to the theology of Deuteronomy, which affirms that there is a moral, covenantal coherence between loyalty and lived outcomes (see Deut 30:15–20). Second, it is long established in the Psalms that the cry of Israel evokes a saving response from YHWH, because YHWH is a God who hears and answers in transformative ways (see Exod 2:23–25; Ps 107:4–32). The full fourfold formula in the book of Judges combines into a single formulation of the two convictions long-standing in Israel of moral symmetry and divine responsiveness.

The imposition of such a theological formula upon the hero narratives is perhaps accomplished in Israel just prior to the crisis of 587 or perhaps just after, in the exile. If we take the latter option, this fourfold formula is readily understood in exile:

1. The indictment of Israel for its sin is a key claim of the preexilic prophets and a continuing accent of Deuteronomic royal history. Israel, up to 587, is fundamentally disloyal to YHWH; that is what the entire recital of Israel's history since land entry is said to exhibit.

2. The punishment is to be given over into enemy hands; in the sixth century this may refer specifically to the hands of the fierce enemy Babylon and its even fiercer king, Nebuchadnezzar. Thus exile is understood in this interpretive tradition as divine punishment for long-term covenantal infidelity.

3. The cry is a proper voice of Israel in exile, a fresh admission of loyalty to YHWH, and a fresh readiness to obey YHWH's commands. It is the compelling thesis of Hans Walter Wolff that the key programmatic concern of the Deuteronomist in exile is repentance, that is, return to YHWH and YHWH's commandments (Wolff 1982). As Wolff has shown, that concern is articulated primarily with the recurrent use of the verb *šub* ("turn, return"), on which see especially 1 Kings 8:31–53. The term means to reverse course and is used in this theological tradition to mean "repentance," to reverse course from recalcitrance and to become obedient to the Torah. In our context in the book of Judges, however, the same motif is expressed by a "cry" that may be taken as an adequate counterpoint to *šub* as an articulation of repentance. Thus the return to YHWH voiced in the purportedly old text may be subsequently reread as a mandate for the exilic community that had also belatedly been given into the hand of the enemy.

4. The fourth element of a "deliverer" powered by YHWH's spirit is not so obviously correlated to an exilic reading. If, however, we remember the poetic anticipation of Cyrus the Persian in Isaiah 41:25; 44:28; and 45:1–7, and if we recall that exilic hopes of a political kind turned to the rise of Cyrus and the

coming of the Persians (as in 2 Chr 36:22–23), then it is not implausible that YHWH's response to Israel's "cry" may be Cyrus who, in poetic idiom, is termed "messiah" (Isa 45:1).

It is not necessary to correlate the formula precisely with exilic experience or exilic articulation. It is enough to see that the accent point of Israel's faith and the cadences of Israel's rhetoric of faith can be reread in a belated crisis in a way that is anticipated in the earlier formulation. The upshot of such a correlation between folk memory and theological formulation is the assertion of YHWH's reliable governance of the historical process of Israel (and the nations) that evokes attentive obedience to YHWH's Torah.

III

The third and concluding textual section of the book of Judges consists in two odd and offensive narratives in *17:1–18:31* and *19:1–21:25*. These two narratives speak in turn of religious idolatry that flourishes even in Israel, and a brutalizing narrative of tribal wars and a brutalizing mistreatment of a concubine. The narratives in sequence bespeak Israel's religious compromise and Israel's social barbarism, and in Israel's horizon these two dimensions of distorted reality are characteristically intimately connected to each other. The two narratives, moreover, are framed by an interpretive formula: "In those days there was no king in Israel; all the people did what was right in their own eyes (17:6; 21:25; see also 18:1; 19:1). This framing formula means to call attention to the disorder of society (religious and moral) and to the fact that the old spirit-driven deliverers are no longer adequate to the crisis. Thus the editorial framing has one eye on the narrative of monarchy soon to follow in the books of Samuel, along with the presupposition that monarchy can maintain an adequate order, as the judges cannot. Such a preference of kings over judges may have been an honest historical judgment at an early time. In its present place in the final form of the text, however, the preference may be a strategic one, in order to let the reader be disillusioned with judges and hopeful about kings, only later to be disillusioned with kings as well. (On the latter see 1 Sam 8 and 12.)

It is remarkable that in these last narratives the traditioning process turns our attention to the coming monarchy. That new institutional engagement, however, is only penultimate in the larger horizon of the sweep of the Deuteronomic tradition. For before kings who are anticipated and behind kings who have failed is the sure rule of YHWH, the one of whom Israel sings even to kings and princes:

Close Reading: Judges 19

This chapter contains one of the most shocking stories in the Bible: the gang rape of a nameless woman, the concubine of a Levite priest, whose body is then cut up into twelve pieces by the Levite (we are never told at what point she dies) and sent to the twelve tribes as a call for vengeance. J. P. Fokkelman (1999, 110) notes the following chiastic structure to the scene leading up to the violence against the woman (vv. 11–14):

> Since they were close to Jebus, and <u>the sun was sinking</u>,
> the attendant said to his master,
>
>> "Let us turn aside to this town of the Jebusites
>> and <u>spend the night</u> in it."
>
>>> But his master said to him,
>>> "We <u>will not turn aside</u>
>>>> to a town of <u>aliens</u>,
>>>> who are <u>not of Israel</u>,
>>> but <u>will continue</u> to Gibeah."
>
>> He also said to his attendant,
>> "Let us approach one of those places
>> and <u>spend the night</u> either in Gibeah or in Ramah."
>
> So they passed on and went their way,
> and <u>the sun went down</u> on them near Gibeah of Benjamin.

Individual readers can decide for themselves how to interpret the possible significance of such a structure, but one notices the irony in the Levite's refusal to stay in a non-Israelite town out of fear for their safety, continuing on to Gibeah, where the violence occurs. The structure lines up a clear contrast between the town of Jebus (the future Jerusalem, not yet Israelite) and the town of Gibeah, only to turn upside down expectations that Gibeah would be the safer place. The moral reversal accords well with the general tone of the ending of Judges, where violence and social chaos reign.

> Hear, O kings; give ear, O princes;
>> to the LORD I will sing,
>> I will make melody to the LORD, the God of Israel.
>>> (5:3)

The penultimate question of "judge or king" is in a larger horizon subservient to the rule of YHWH, whose commands must be obeyed and whose covenant must be kept: "I said, 'I will never break my covenant with you. For your part, do not make a covenant with the inhabitants of this land; tear down their altars.' But you have not obeyed my command. See what you have done!" (2:1b–2).

That Torah practice and covenant keeping, moreover, must be accomplished in the real world of compelling political-theological alternatives. Israel's obedience to YHWH in the face of compelling Canaanite alternatives is not accomplished with great or singular resolve, for in fact Israel's obedience to YHWH's Torah is slipshod, compromised, and characteristically distorted. That is the story the Deuteronomic tradition seeks to tell. The prophetic task of reimagining life (a task so vigorously pursued in the Former Prophets) with reference to YHWH is always upstream, against Israel's easier alternatives that bring threat, subservience, disorder, brutality, and eventually land loss. The Lord of the commands hears the cries of needy Israel. That same Lord who will not be mocked, however, is the singular source of Israel's hope in the contested land of promise.

14

The Books of 1 and 2 Samuel

First and Second Samuel surely represent one of the greatest works of literature to come to us from the ancient world. Bringing together a hard-nosed view of social and political realities, psychologically realistic characters, and a subtle claim for God's providential role in history, the books are a classic example of the complex artfulness of biblical narrative.

Taken as one canonical entry, 1 and 2 Samuel constitute the third element of the Former Prophets, sandwiched between Judges and Kings. Situated in this place, the scroll provides an account of Israel's transition from a *tribal* society (beleaguered by anarchy and barbarism in Judg 17–21) to a *monarchial* society (characterized by a bureaucratic self-aggrandizement in 1 Kgs 1–11). The key character in this transition is David, who, after being a shepherd boy, becomes a tribal chief and ends as king; and the portrait of David as a complex character who changes in dramatic but consistent ways over the course of his life is unmatched in ancient literature. David is surrounded and abetted by a series of other narrative characters—Samuel, Saul, Jonathan, Joab, Bathsheba, Absalom, and so on—all of whom are given the sort of vivid psychological depth that we associate with the best of novelistic fiction. Moving in and through and around these characters and this historical process is God, whose agency is keenly felt but never usurps human agency.

According to the dominant critical hypothesis of Noth, the books of Samuel occupy a place within the Deuteronomic History, an extended narrative designed to trace the life of Israel from *land entry* (in the book of Joshua) to *land loss* (in the books of Kings); but unlike the obvious Deuteronomic theological overlay on the book of Judges, the books of Samuel have little of the characteristic markings of the Deuteronomist (but see Polzin 1989; 1993). The remembered narratives of the books of Samuel may have their

163

origins in the process of folk culture and its celebration of the spectacular personality and remembered historical achievement of David, a figure who dominates much of the social imagination of ancient Israel. Even if the narrative memory arises from folk tradition, however, the story is a sophisticated artistic achievement whereby the narrators in Israel permit the quixotic reality of human choice and human aberration to impinge upon divine intentions.

Earlier critical scholarship judged that by the time of David we have arrived at historically reliable narratives. Now, however, the matter is much more disputed among scholars. The more skeptical assessment of these narratives is that we have here no reliable historical data (Finkelstein and Silberman 2001). The more plausible judgment of many scholars, shared by us, is that we have a historically rooted memory of a tribal chieftain of quite modest proportion, which has been greatly enhanced through artistic imagination (Halpern 2001; McKenzie 2000). One aspect of the dispute over historicity concerns a stela, which archaeologists have found at the excavation at Tel Dan, that perhaps has an inscription, "House of David." This stela is dated by the archaeologists who have discovered it—though it is disputed by others—to the ninth century BCE, a date that would seem to be an authentication of the existence of a Davidic governance, though even such a dated piece of evidence is no verification for any detail of the textual tradition. Whatever may be the "facts of the case," irretrievable as they are, we focus upon the way in which the traditioning process itself intended us to remember and assess the transition from tribal society to monarchy in ancient Israel.

It is a widely held view that the books of Samuel are, in the final form of the text, a compilation of several independent sources that have been arranged to generate a certain perspective on the Davidic transition from tribal society to the modest beginnings of monarchy. We consider in turn several sections of the narrative account that may be the outcome of independent sources that are now edited into something of a coherent unity.

I

First Samuel 1–15 is a narrative of the transition prior to the narrative appearance of David, who is first mentioned in chapter 16. In this pre-Davidic material, we may identify three subunits of text:

1. Chapters 1–3 provide an account of the rise of Samuel to become the most prominent leader in Israel and eventually the kingmaker. The story of the birth of Samuel from a barren mother is part of a narrative strategy designed to show that monarchy arises in Israel *ex nihilo*, that is, as the singular gift of

YHWH. This account of political transformation is staged to indicate that there are no defining antecedents to this wondrous social emergent in ancient Israel. Of particular interest in this unit of text is the Song of Hannah in 2:1–10, a song of thanksgiving and victory placed on the lips of mother Hannah as the "clef sign" for the narrative to follow (see Ps 113; Gordon 1984, 26). In this poem it is particularly noteworthy that mother Hannah anticipates "the messiah" (ostensibly David) long before this theme has been announced in the larger narrative (the NRSV renders the mention of "messiah" in 2:10 as "anointed," which translates the Hebrew word *mašiaḥ* and is in poetic parallel to the word "king"). For Christian readers, moreover, it is unmistakable that the story of Samuel's birth and emergence as a leader in Israel is the model for the story of Jesus as presented in Luke 1 and 2 (R. Brown 1977, 235–499). The focus of the poem, however, is not upon the coming Messiah, but upon the power of YHWH to intervene decisively in public affairs.

2. First Samuel 4:1–7:1 has been dubbed by scholars since Leonhard Rost as the "Ark Narrative" (Rost 1982 [original, 1926]; Miller and Roberts 1977; Brueggemann 2002a), a narrative perhaps continued in 2 Samuel 6. This narrative is peculiar because it relies on no major narrative character, nor on any important human actions. The key "character" is the ark of the covenant, a vehicle to signify the presence of YHWH in the narrative. The narrative as a whole has a dramatic movement from the *defeat of the ark* and then the inscrutable *reassertion of the ark* as YHWH is said to be headed home in glory. The narrative articulates at the same time (a) that the ark and YHWH, who inhabits the ark, will not rescue Israel in war because Israel (through the house of Eli) has been hopelessly corrupt; but (b) that YHWH's own reassertion of sovereign power and freedom cannot be resisted by the Philistines. The dramatic inversion from *defeat* to *reassertion* is perhaps in belated traditioning a pattern that pertains to Israel's own experience of descent into *exile* and anticipated *homecoming* in splendor (the latter as in Isa 40:3–5).

3. First Samuel 7:2–15:35 is an extended narrative that is preoccupied with the vexed question of the rise of the monarchy as a defining social institution in ancient Israel. It is conventional among scholars to identify a promonarchial source (9:1–10:16; 11; 13–14) and an antimonarchial source (7–8; 10:17–27; 12). Whether there were actual literary sources is not important, though it is certainly plausible that there were conflicting opinions on this major reorganization of social power (McCarthy 1973). It is often thought that the promonarchial source that saw the rise of kingship as an act of self-defense congruent with YHWH's intention was perhaps close to the events narrated. Conversely, it is most often thought that the antimonarchial source that views human kingship as an act of defiance to the kingship of YHWH

was later, perhaps a critical reflection on the self-aggrandizing ways of the governance of King Solomon. Thus particularly the negative anticipation of monarchy in 1 Samuel 8:10–18 reflects the usurpatious practice of kingship that was embodied in the regime of Solomon.

While the historical dimension of these texts is problematic, the reality of social conflict over the reconfiguration of power is entirely plausible. Scholars have spent great energy in recent decades on sociological analysis of what may have been the period of the transition that David dominates. In such a context, it is credible that some social interests stood to benefit greatly from centralized authority that would govern economic and political as well as military life. By contrast, some segments of the community would perhaps see the same move toward monarchy as a return to the concentration of power among urban elites, the very ones who dominated the Canaanite city-states that early Israel had so vigorously opposed. In any case, it is important to recognize that the dispute about kingship is not merely a formulaic religious question, but an urgent social issue that reaches down into the most concrete public matters of the community.

The antimonarchial source, likely reflective of peasant consciousness in a segmented society that kept communal decision making quite local, viewed the newly affirmed king as a "taker" who would confiscate the wealth and legacy of the peasant community (see 1 Sam 8). This critical attitude, it is readily recognized, is still alive and well in characteristic resistance to "big government" on the part of many "small-time operators."

The particular narrative character who is the vehicle for this deep dispute over social power is Saul. He is anointed king at the behest of YHWH, but apparently he is never free from dispute enough to function as king. In the retelling of the narrative in 1 Samuel, not only is Saul held in thrall by the dispute, but he is "fated" (see Gunn 1980) to failure by the looming presence of David in the horizon of the narrative, even before David is even mentioned. The narrator twice signals the coming of David as the one who is favored by YHWH, by Israel, and by the narrator:

> Samuel said to Saul, "You have done foolishly; you have not kept the commandment of the LORD your God, which he commanded you. The LORD would have established your kingdom over Israel forever, but now your kingdom will not continue; the LORD has sought out a man after his own heart; and the LORD has appointed him to be ruler over his people, because you have not kept what the LORD commanded you." (13:13–14)

> And Samuel said to him, "The LORD has torn the kingdom of Israel from you this very day, and has given it to a neighbor of yours, who is better than you." (15:28)

It is plausible that Saul functions primarily as a foil to David and never establishes his own right in the narrative as the narrative rushes to David (Gunn 1980; Fretheim 1985).

II

The second great section of the narrative and, according to scholarly judgment, the first of two extended sources in 1 Samuel is the Narrative of the Rise of David. This narrative begins with the lovely account of the introduction of David into the narrative in 1 Samuel 16:1–13 and culminates, according to usual judgment, in 2 Samuel 5:1–5. The flow of the narrative from beginning to end concerns the forceful advance of David from shepherd boy (1 Sam 16:11) to "shepherd king" of Israel (2 Sam 5:2), a rise in power, prominence, and privilege that moves along undeterred so that nothing bad ever happens to David along the way. A theological reading of the Rise is that the narrative evidences the providential intentionality of YHWH, who has willed David's exalted rise to power. Just below the surface of this specific theological presupposition we may see that the rise is also wrought through a series of cunning and ruthless acts of self-advancement on the part of David, acts that are savored and artistically rendered by the narrator, who wants us to notice that the rise is a carefully and perhaps shamelessly engineered advance, humanly crafted in the guise of divine providence. Thus the narrative rendering has multiple layers of telling that admit of an ironic reading. The advance of divine providence is shot through with human vagaries that are relished in their telling and are to be fully appreciated and honored in their reading.

The overall plot of the narrative of the rise is the enduring contestation for power between Saul and David, each of whom has a faithful entourage and each of whom lays claim to divine anointing. The tilt of the narrative from the outset is toward David, who will eventually prevail; Saul, however, does not yield easily. With that dominant plot, we may notice several subthemes:

1. David is related to the house of Saul in delicate, deliberate, and complex ways. In addition to being something of a protégé of Saul, David is deeply engaged with Saul's son, Jonathan, and seems to preempt Jonathan as the anticipated heir of Saul (1 Sam 20:14–17). Notice should also be taken of David's marriage to Michal that would grant him some familial legitimacy (1 Sam 18:20–29). The lament of David over the deaths of Saul and Jonathan, moreover, indicates either a genuine affection for them or at least a theatrical capacity to perform such affection (2 Sam 1:19–27). Clearly David, as given in the narrative, is perfectly capable of such a performance.

2. In 1 Samuel 24–26 we have, in rather playful fashion, a narration of the way in which David's "good fortune" (i.e., providential blessing) protects him in dangerous situations and leads him from one success to another. In chapter 25 David runs a protection racket (see 22:2) and seeks to extort money from a rich landowner, Nabal (meaning "Fool" in Hebrew). Because of Nabal's miscalculation concerning David, he dies; but the narrative is primarily interested in his wife, Abigail, who is a powerful, dramatic match for David. In narrative presentation, Abigail is permitted to utter a classic dynastic oracle concerning David's future: "Please forgive the trespass of your servant; for the LORD will certainly make my lord a sure house, because my lord is fighting the battles of the LORD; and evil shall not be found in you so long as you live" (25:28).

David, moreover, is able to assert his own innocence concerning the death of Nabal through the guise of a commendation to Abigail, an innocence he required in his pursuit of royal power:

> David said to Abigail, "Blessed be the LORD, the God of Israel, who sent you to meet me today! Blessed be your good sense, and blessed be you, who have kept me today from bloodguilt and from avenging myself by my own hand! For as surely as the LORD the God of Israel lives, who has restrained me from hurting you, unless you had hurried and come to meet me, truly by morning there would not have been left to Nabal so much as one male." . . .
>
> When David heard that Nabal was dead, he said, "Blessed be the LORD who has judged the case of Nabal's insult to me, and has kept back his servant from evil; the LORD has returned the evildoing of Nabal upon his own head." Then David sent and wooed Abigail, to make her his wife. (25:32–34, 39)

The Nabal-Abigail narrative of chapter 25 is sandwiched between two parallel narratives concerning the interaction of Saul and David. In each, David spares Saul's life when he has a chance to kill him, in each case evoking in Saul's mouth an affirmation of David's coming kingdom (24:17–20 and 26:25). Thus, even Saul, while he continues to resist David, is made a proponent of David's coming rule. It is possible to read David's sparing of Saul in these chapters as an act of noble magnanimity, as is traditionally done. At the same time, the stories allow for a more cynical reading of David's motives. We notice for example the very particular way that David frames his decision not to kill Saul, in terms of refusing to raise a hand against "the LORD's anointed" (24:10; 26:9). Certainly it is in David's interest to have a precedent against anyone harming the Lord's anointed, since *he* is in fact, since 1 Samuel 16, now the Lord's anointed. And the insertion of chapter 25, with its ruthless and violent portrayal of David, between these two stories shows us that David is far from a model of nonviolence.

3. At the end of the Rise, David is the beneficiary of a series of convenient deaths: Saul (1 Sam 31; 2 Sam 1), Asahel (2 Sam 2), Abner (2 Sam 3), and Ishbaal (2 Sam 4). Each of these deaths removed a major hindrance to David's rise to power. In each case David loudly establishes the guilt of the murderer and thereby asserts his own innocence. David's zeal in his responses could perhaps indicate that he himself is implicated in the deaths and needs to find a way to maintain his innocence in a context where he is heavily under suspicion (see 2 Sam 3:37; 16:7; McKenzie 2000, 111–27; Brueggemann 1990a, 49–85):

> David said to him, "Your blood be on your head; for your own mouth has testified against you, saying, 'I have killed the LORD's anointed.'" (2 Sam 1:16)

> Afterward, when David heard of it, he said, "I and my kingdom are forever guiltless before the LORD for the blood of Abner son of Ner. May the guilt fall on the head of Joab, and on all his father's house; and may the house of Joab never be without one who has a discharge, or who is leprous, or who holds a spindle, or who falls by the sword, or who lacks food!" (3:28–29)

> How much more then, when wicked men have killed a righteous man on his bed in his own house! And now shall I not require his blood at your hand, and destroy you from the earth? (4:11)

However, the very fervency with which David's innocence in this matter is asserted can lead a historian to suspect his complicity. A closer consideration of certain details of the story augments this suspicion. To begin with, David had incentive to get rid of Abner. Abner would have been a constant source of worry for David if he had lived. He was obviously very influential—in the story he persuades both the army and the elders of Israel to go over to David. His dealings with Ishbaal demonstrated that he was independent and would be difficult to control. Moreover, he was a Benjaminite and would always be inclined to keep the kingship within that tribe rather than letting it become the property of David and Judah. Most of all, the Bible makes very clear that Abner was the power in Israel. . . .

As with the earlier killings, the writer claims that David was unaware of and uninvolved in this assassination. The story says David had the two assassins summarily executed and their dismembered corpses displayed in Hebron to show his displeasure at their crime. Once again, however, this contention is difficult to believe. Ishbaal's death came at an extremely convenient time for David, since he represented the last obstacle between David and the throne of Israel. Also, as with Saul's death, David ended up with the incriminating evidence in his possession. Just as the Amalekite's story in 2 Sam 1 may be designed to explain how David got Saul's diadem and bracelets, so this story explains how he came to have Ishbaal's head! (McKenzie 2000, 120, 125–26)

By the management of the narrative, David arrives at the throne of Judah in 2 Samuel 2:1–4 unscathed by the several murders that have occurred on his behalf, and is made king in Israel by covenantal agreement (5:1–5). David's march to power is contested along the way but is never seriously impeded as the narrator presents it. The Rise of David is willed by YHWH, even if accomplished through the rough-and-tumble of politics. It is important to recognize that, just below the surface of such convinced theological affirmation, we are treated to artistic playfulness that enjoys the plethora of ambiguities that mark David's Rise.

III

With the completion of the Narrative of the Rise of David, the movement of the literature pauses to allow for institution building in a series of texts that exhibit the consolidation of the newly established regime (2 Sam 5:6–8:18). For the most part, these chapters lack the vibrant dramatic quality of the preceding narrative and soberly attest, in the purview of the tradition, to the way in which this established chieftain begins nation building. We do not need to adjudicate the question of historicity in these chapters; it is sufficient to recognize that this is the way in which the final form of the tradition wants us to imagine David having established himself.

James Flanagan (1983) has shrewdly observed that the core materials in these four chapters are arranged in a chiastic pattern of three pairs of reports, in each case the first number of the pair reflecting "tribal" considerations, the second member of each pair articulating a "state" action:

> ark (6:1–20) . . . . dynasty (7:1–17)
> Philistine wars (5:17–25) . . . . state wars (8:1–14)
> children (5:13–16) . . . . officials (8:15–18)

The first member of each pair clearly reflects an early social organization when the tribal symbol of the ark and the traditional enemy, the Philistines, were in play as narrative themes. The second triad, including state wars and dynastic oracle plus an emerging bureaucracy, typifies a narrated formation of a state. As Flanagan proposes, the very structure of this text makes a decisive transition in social organization and in the narrated, lived reality of David.

In this collection of texts, special notice should be taken of the divine oracle of 2 Samuel 7:1–17 wherein YHWH, through Nathan, makes a sweeping

unconditional promise to David and to the dynasty to come. It is impossible to
overstate the importance of this divine commitment, which is a crucial theological innovation in Israel, given the conditional character of the Sinai covenant
(as in Exod 19:5–6). This oracular commitment of YHWH will loom large in
the books of Kings and Chronicles as the tradition ponders the durability of
the dynasty and in subsequent prophetic oracles of hope that anticipate a coming Messiah. Even though the oracle no doubt is rendered in the interest of
royal propaganda, it is nonetheless of immense theological importance both
(a) as the taproot of messianic thought in the Old Testament, which became a
hope for an ideal Davidic king yet to come (on which see Isa 9:1–7), and (b) as a
pivotal commitment of unconditional grace by the covenanting God of Israel.
The oracle, moreover, has received important poetic, liturgical articulations in
two very different castings in Psalms 89 and 132.

IV

Second Samuel 9–20 (plus 1 Kgs 1–2 as a presumed addendum and conclusion)
has been much studied and much appreciated in scholarship under the rubric,
"Succession Narrative" (Rost 1982). Rost first gave that name to the narrative in suggesting that the question of a successor to David, posed in 1 Kings
1:27, is the overriding question to which this extended narrative seeks to give
answer. Thus, in the course of the narrative, David's sons Amnon (2 Sam 13),
Absalom (2 Sam 14–19), and Adonijah (1 Kgs 1:41–53; 2:13–25) are eliminated
as Solomon becomes David's ultimate successor (1 Kgs 1:32–40).

This is the second great narrative source in the books of Samuel, so that
the Succession Narrative (2 Kgs 9–20; 1 Kgs 1–2) is a counterpoint to the
Rise of David source (1 Sam 16:1–2 Sam 15:5); consequently, these two very
different kinds of materials taken together constitute an account of the rise
and fall of David. We should note that many scholars doubt Rost's proposal
of the theme of "succession" as the clue to the narrative; the nomenclature
of Succession Narrative, however, continues to be used in critical discussion.

Readers of this narrative should, in any case, be attentive to the fine narrative art exhibited in this text, a narrative art that von Rad has judged to be the
earliest account of human history in which human agents act in freedom, thus
history rendered in exquisite form (von Rad 1966, 166–204). When the true
human character of the narrative plot and its artistic quality are recognized, it
is a likely critical judgment that this narrative account is not mere reportage;
it is rather a particularly imaginative rendering of matters, perhaps rooted in
what happened, but now the creation of a profound narrative generativity.
The narrative goes far to exhibit the hiddenness of YHWH's governance in

an altogether human history, and with equal artistic force gives expression to the immense interplay that characterizes the action of the narrative and the agents who perform it.

The movement of the Succession Narrative toward the enthronement of Solomon as heir goes inexorably through David's sons until it arrives triumphantly at Solomon (see 2 Sam 12:24–25). The narrative account, however, is not a monotonous sequence. Rather, we may suggest that it is arranged around two great climactic moments. In the first, at the end of chapter 11, David must respond to the death of Uriah, a death he has imperiously authorized. In his response to the report of the death, David is presented as an uncaring, unfeeling public figure whose required cover-up nicely converges with the reasons of state (11:25).

The second great climactic moment in the narrative occurs at the death of David's son Absalom (18:33–19:8). This second death is the outcome of a series of events beginning already in chapter 13, wherein Absalom is positioned to avenge the shame of his sister, Tamar, upon the death of his brother, Amnon. Thus the revolt of Absalom against his father in chapters 15–18 derives from the earlier confrontation, and consequently Absalom is killed by Joab—the same Joab who arranged for the death of Uriah—again for reasons of state. Only this time David's response to the killing is profound grief. Indeed, the grief is so profound that Joab must summon David back to his public role as king. That is, Joab visibly overrides David's pathos as a father.

The response of David to the death of Absalom is stunningly contrasted to his response to the death of Uriah. It may be that the narrative is arranged to exhibit these two moments of extremity. In one critical moment David is an unflappable public man, in the other he is moved in a deeply personal way. The interplay of the public and the personal permits this narrative to disclose the deep hiddenness of human reality by taking seriously at the same time intractable public happenings and a profound sense of emotional experience. The reader is summoned by the narrator to a profound appreciation for this most remarkable exhibit of David, Israel's chosen, YHWH's beloved, and in important ways a reliable cipher for what constitutes the ambiguity of humanness in a world ordered by the hidden YHWH of Israel's faith. In sum, this narrative is a remarkable literary, artistic and, consequently, theological achievement in that ancient world.

When these two presumed narratives, the Rise of David and the Succession Narrative, are juxtaposed, together they form a large, intentional commentary on the person, office, and role of David in Israel's self-presentation. Rolf Carlson has proposed that the two narratives together exhibit David "under blessing" (wherein everything fortunate happens to him as he receives advantage after advantage) and "under curse" (wherein David's life, family, and dynasty unravel in violence and deception) (Carlson 1964). The final form of the text nicely juxtaposes the person of David and the force of wonderment that moves through the text.

We may suggest that this double-minded articulation of David is a key intention of the completed tradition. That is, the tradition seeks to assert that for all of the clarity of YHWH's intentionality, the lived reality of that divine intentionality in the life and governance of David is profoundly fluid. Thus the ongoing narrative is a contestation between YHWH's deep commitment and the shabbiness of the human character who tests and jeopardizes that divine commitment. The contestation is nicely epitomized by suggesting an intentional relationship between two texts that loom large in the interpretive intention of the Deuteronomist. In the divine oracle of 2 Samuel 7:14–16, YHWH's resolve is clear: "I will be a father to him, and he shall be a son to me. When he commits iniquity, I will punish him with a rod such as mortals use, with blows inflicted

> ### Close Reading: Absalom's Killing of Amnon
>
> Why does Absalom kill his brother Amnon in 2 Samuel 13? As the subsequent narrative shows, Absalom is politically ambitious and has designs on the throne of David, leading a revolt in chapter 15; and we are encouraged to think that the killing of Amnon is motivated by the fact that it puts Absalom one step closer to the throne (since Amnon was the older of the two). At the same time, the psychological depth and multilayeredness of biblical characters allows for complexity of motivation. So just in case we think we have solved the question with reference to Absalom's political ambition, the narrator gives us one little detail that complicates things: Absalom names his daughter Tamar (14:27), after his sister who was raped by Amnon. This indication of Absalom's real feeling for his sister Tamar encourages us to see the killing of Amnon also as an act of vengeance against him on Tamar's behalf. By giving Absalom this dual motivation, the narrative continues to hold together the *personal* and the *political*.

by human beings. But I will not take my steadfast love from him, as I took it from Saul, whom I put away from before you. Your house and your kingdom shall be made sure forever before me; your throne shall be established forever." In these verses the Hebrew verb *sur* occurs three times:

> I will not *take* [i.e., remove] my steadfast love
> as I *took* [i.e., removed] it from Saul
> whom I *put away* [i.e., remove] from before you

The same verb is used in the divine judgment articulated by Nathan in 2 Samuel 12:10: "Now therefore the sword shall never *depart* from your house, for you have despised me, and have taken the wife of Uriah the Hittite to be your wife" (2 Sam 12:10, italics added). This verdict might also be translated "the sword will never be removed from your house." The important matter to notice is that in both texts the verb *sur* is used negatively. Thus the conclusion of the divine promise via Nathan and the divine judgment via Nathan offer two factors that will never "depart" from David's house: (a) YHWH's stead-fast love and (b) the sword. YHWH's steadfast love sustains the family and dynasty of David. The sword keeps the family and dynasty of David endlessly in jeopardy. The consequence is that the life of the family and the dynasty is an endlessly mixed one, featuring a contest between sustaining divine love and jeopardizing sword. In the full presentation of the Deuteronomic Historian, the divine love sustains the dynasty for a long time, but the sword finally terminates it (see Jer 22:30). In the exile, moreover, there is confidence in that unfailing divine love that leads to a continued expectation of David, even when the dynasty is terminated (Isa 55:3).

In 2 Samuel 21–24 we are offered a collection of random tribal memories that clearly interrupt the flow of the narrative that leaps from 2 Samuel 20 to 1 Kings 1 and that purports to reflect earlier moments in David's life. It is characteristic in scholarship to regard these materials as random and of little moment for the whole. Notice, however, should be taken especially of the poems in 2 Samuel 22:1–51 and 23:1–7. It is to be noted that 2 Samuel 7 is a parallel to Psalm 89, suggesting that the poem is an antecedent liturgical piece belatedly placed here upon the lips of David. The poem of 2 Samuel 23:1–7, also placed in the mouth of David, is a deep assertion of faith, affirming the divine oracle of 2 Samuel 7 and functioning in the final form of a text as a counterpoint to the Song of Hannah in 1 Samuel 2:1–10.

In pondering the chiasmus of 2 Samuel 5:5–8:18, as suggested by Flanagan, we have suggested in turn a chiastic structure for the random texts of chapters 21–24 (Brueggemann 1990, 235–51):

```
narrative (21:1–14) . . . . . . . . . . . . . . . narrative (24:1–25)
    list (21:15–22) . . . . . . . . . . . . . . . . list (23:8–39)
        song (22:1–51) . . . . . . . . song (23:1–7)
```

Whereas the characteristic textual arrangement of chapters 5–8 artistically traces the transition from tribal society to monarchy, we suggest that this little chiastic arrangement in chapters 21–24 serves to deconstruct David, that is, to expose his vulnerability as a king. He is exhibited in such a reading as a flawed human person behind the loud claims of royal legitimacy.

If such a reading is sustainable, then it is yet one more element in this remarkable articulation of a memory in Israel of a major divine initiative in YHWH's commitment to the Davidic monarchy, a major commitment twinned to the quirky, ambiguous human reality of remembered David.

In sum, the books of Samuel bespeak the inexorable transition of Israel from judges to kings, from tribal barbarism to monarchial bureaucracy, accomplished through divine love that is enacted through the force of David as characterized by the narrative. In the midst of that divine resolve, the concrete data of Israel's memory, however, admit of no one-dimensional portrayal of divine governance, for divine governance is endlessly related to the human facts on the ground. History, as remembered and presented here, is an altogether human enterprise with all of the ambiguity and flaws of human character. Thus the books of Samuel attend to the inescapable ways in which the God of the Bible is known and seen to be at work—in, with, and under human life, in quite particular ways, and very often quite subservient to the choices and conduct of human agents. The narrative insists that the divine resolve for steadfast love is decisive for what follows in Davidic history. But such divine resolve is deeply impinged upon by human conduct that evokes a perennially jeopardizing sword. Israel cannot remember otherwise. Israel cannot have its life on any other terms. Eventually, moreover, it becomes clear that the God of Israel is deeply enmeshed in and defined by that vexed performance of human character, human character that defies and submits, that resists YHWH's rule and trusts YHWH's rule, a strange mix of yes and no. It is no wonder, in this tradition, that the disclosure of truth requires artistic narratives in order to sound the odd cadences of Davidic reality, divine fidelity paced by the irregular beat of human assertion.

15

The Books of 1 and 2 Kings

First and Second Kings constitute the fourth element in the Former Prophets, a literature that seeks to reimagine and reinterpret the remembered past of Israel with reference to YHWH, the God who makes promises and who issues commands. According to the dominant critical hypothesis of Martin Noth, 1 and 2 Kings are as well the culmination of the Deuteronomic History, a construal of Israel's life in the land according to the theological assumptions of the traditions of Deuteronomy (Noth 1981). Specifically, the entire literature of the Deuteronomic History seeks to illuminate the destruction of Jerusalem in 587 BCE and the subsequent deportation of leading citizens, an illumination that pivots around the rule of YHWH. Although the books continue the narrative form that we have seen in 1 and 2 Samuel and they show some of the same subtle artfulness, 1 and 2 Kings are more heavily Deuteronomistic in their theology and often more annalistic in their recounting of political events.

The books of Kings, in a surface reading, narrate the course of the united kingdom of Solomon after the death of David (1 Kgs 1–11), the course of the kingdoms of Israel and Judah (1 Kgs 12–2 Kgs 17), and the course of the kingdom of Judah in its last years after the destruction of the northern kingdom (2 Kgs 18–25). Two major awarenesses are important for a critical understanding of this literature that purports to trace the past of the people of God from the death of David (1 Kgs 2:10–11) to the deportation of Judah, ending with a final reference to Jehoiachin, the last Davidic king (2 Kgs 25:27–30). First, this "historian" utilizes a variety of sources to piece together what has become the metanarrative of ancient Israel in the land. The sources appear to include temple archives, royal archives, and folktales. These sources—or perhaps in some cases alleged sources—are of varying degrees of historical reliability, degrees that are most difficult to assess. In the present skeptical

177

mood of scholarship, critical interpreters look quite cautiously upon these materials as historically reliable, though it is common to assume that the later materials—perhaps beginning with the report on Hezekiah—are more reliable than the earlier materials. It is clear that the "historian" does not take much effort to assess the validity of the several sources employed, for the emphasis is completely upon the process of coherently reshaping all kinds of sources and memories together so that they can function as a normative account of the past.

Second, by piecing together these several sources of varying degrees of reliability and significance, the historian has purported to give a sweeping account of that long history in the land. It is crucial to understand that 1 and 2 Kings are not historical reportage and do not intend to be such. Rather, this material is and intends to be a theological and interpretive commentary upon the history that can be otherwise known. Thus this text offers something like footnotes that send the curious reader to the library to check on what are taken to be reliable, sober historical accounts that precede this theological interpretation:

> Now the rest of the acts of Solomon, all that he did as well as his wisdom, are they not written in the Book of the Acts of Solomon? (1 Kgs 11:41)

> Now the rest of the acts of Jeroboam, how he warred and how he reigned, are written in the Book of the Annals of the Kings of Israel. (14:19)

> The rest of the acts of Abijam, and all that he did, are they not written in the Book of the Annals of the Kings of Judah? There was war between Abijam and Jeroboam. (15:7)

These three texts refer to three major sources that were apparently available in the royal library, though none of that alleged source material has survived. In any case, the reader's attention should not be upon the sources but on the interpretive intention and the interpretive imagination whereby this "historian" is able to read out of, or read into, the text a particular, sustained theological angle. This means that the final product of the "historian," already operative in Joshua, Judges, and Samuel but fully explicit in the books of Kings, is a quite particular theological insistence about this long historical sweep.

I

There have been three major attempts to identify the theological program of interpretation in this literature, all from a close circle of astute German interpreters:

1. As already mentioned, Martin Noth, progenitor of the dominant hypothesis about the literature, proposed that the literature was primarily to provide the interpretive grounds whereby the destruction of Jerusalem in 587 BCE is seen to be an act of divine judgment in response to long-term disobedience to YHWH's commands (Noth 1981). That is, Noth thought that the material was singularly focused on an explanation of divine judgment.

2. An alternative was offered by Hans Walter Wolff, who accented the theme of repentance (Wolff 1982). This reading suggests that the literature is not simply a look back from the exile on Israel's long season of disobedience but was addressed to the community of exile about a way forward from exile by the return to and embrace of YHWH's Torah commandments (the same theme is voiced in Ezek 18).

3. Perhaps most influential is the proposal of Gerhard von Rad, who saw this interpretation revolving around two accent points that are in deep tension with each other (von Rad 1953, 74–91; 1962, 334–47). On the one hand, the "history" is dominated by prophetic announcements of judgment that come subsequently to fulfillment. A spectacular case of such prophetic judgment and fulfillment is the harsh, dynasty-ending utterance of Elisha (1 Kgs 21:20–24), which receives its delayed enactment only in 2 Kings 9:36–37: "When they came back and told him, he said, 'This is the word of the LORD, which he spoke by his servant Elijah the Tishbite, "In the territory of Jezreel the dogs shall eat the flesh of Jezebel; the corpse of Jezebel shall be like dung on the field in the territory of Jezreel, so that no one can say, This is Jezebel."'"

Von Rad notices, however, that while the history is preoccupied with such oracles of judgment, matters are not so simple. They are not so simple because alongside such oracles of judgment, on the other hand, there is an element that is "quite undeuteronomic" (von Rad 1953, 82), that is, the sustaining grace of YHWH to this people in disobedience, whereby appropriate divine judgment is remarkably delayed:

> That history, too, appears in the first instance as a story of human disobedience, with the cloud of God's judgement gathering ever thicker. How in this case is the divine forbearance, the much more extended span of divine patience, to be explained? This leads us to mention an element in the Deuteronomist's theology of history which we have so far left out of consideration. (von Rad 1953, 84)

The basis for divine forbearance and grace is in the oracle of 2 Samuel 7:

> By the light which Jahweh promised to David the Deuteronomist means, of course, what is said in the Nathan prophecy in 2 Sam. 7, where Jahweh legitimises and guarantees the Davidic dynasty. It is interesting to see how in the Deuteronomist this prophetic tradition

is fused with the Deuteronomic theology of the cult-place and the name; that is, how two traditional elements of completely different provenance are here united into a whole (cp. especially I Kings 11.36). (von Rad 1953, 85)

Von Rad concludes:

> Finally, the Deuteronomist for his part was only being true to the tradition given to him. There was given to him as a principle creative in history not only the word of Jahweh's curse upon the transgressors of his commandments, as it appears in Deuteronomy, but also the prophetic word of promise in the Davidic covenant. The Deuteronomistic presentation of the history had to reckon with both of these given quantities; the Deuteronomist in fact attributes the form and the course of the history of the kingdom of Judah to their mutual creative power. This enables us to set down an important conclusion: according to the Deuteronomistic presentation, Jahweh's word is active in the history of Judah, creating that history, and that in a double capacity: 1. as law, judging and destroying; 2. as gospel—i.e., in the David prophecy, which was constantly being fulfilled—saving and forgiving. (von Rad 1953, 89)

In the end, in 587 BCE, the prophetic judgments prevailed and destruction came. Except that von Rad notices that the little note on Jehoiachin in 2 Kings 25:27–30 is an open-ended act of hope that is powerfully supported by the dynastic oracle of 2 Samuel 7:1–17: "Thus there can be no doubt, in our opinion, that we can attribute a special theological significance to the final sentences of the Deuteronomist's work, the notice about the release of Jehoiachin from prison" (von Rad 1953, 90).

Von Rad's subtle reading has exercised great influence upon subsequent interpretation. His appreciation of the twinned claims of judgment and hope may not be correct. But in any case his suggestive work, along with that of Noth and Wolff, makes unmistakably clear that what purports to be "history" is a venturesome act of interpretive imagination whereby the will and purpose of YHWH is defining—in judgment and in grace—for the life and memory of this community.

II

The first extended text in Kings is a discussion of the reign of Solomon (1 Kgs 1–11). This reign begins with the death of David and concludes with the death of Solomon (11:41–43); the reign is commonly dated 962–922 BCE. There is no doubt that the "historian" had available some source materials, with particular reference to temple construction, plus some popular legends about Solomon as a wise king.

It is clear that the material concerning Solomon is now intentionally arranged and edited to present a certain perspective on the king. The Deuteronomist has placed 1 Kings 2:1–4 at the beginning of the reign whereby "Deuteronomic David" admonishes the young king to Torah obedience. The whole of the text appears to be organized around two phrases that are in deep tension with each other:

> Solomon loved the LORD, walking in the statutes of his father David; only, he sacrificed and offered incense at the high places. (3:3)

> King Solomon loved many foreign women along with the daughter of Pharaoh: Moabite, Ammonite, Edomite, Sidonian, and Hittite women. (11:1)

The beginning point in 3:3 features Solomon as a good, responsible, faithful king who accomplishes great things. The narrative concludes in chapter 11 with a harsh judgment on Solomon, explaining how most of the territory of the kingdom was lost at his death:

> Then the LORD was angry with Solomon, because his heart had turned away from the LORD, the God of Israel, who had appeared to him twice, and had commanded him concerning this matter, that he should not follow other gods; but he did not observe what the LORD commanded. Therefore the LORD said to Solomon, "Since this has been your mind and you have not kept my covenant and my statutes that I have commanded you, I will surely tear the kingdom from you and give it to your servant. Yet for the sake of your father David I will not do it in your lifetime; I will tear it out of the hand of your son. I will not, however, tear away the entire kingdom; I will give one tribe to your son, for the sake of my servant David and for the sake of Jerusalem, which I have chosen." (11:9–13)

This text nicely exemplifies von Rad's verdict that prophetic judgment and Davidic promise are kept in tension.

At the center of the Solomonic material is placed temple construction (chaps. 5–7) that culminates in the crucial chapter 8 on the dedication of his temple. The material is apparently arranged so that the *good* Solomon is represented in the text prior to the temple construction and the *bad* Solomon is reported in chapters 9–11, after the temple dedication. Everything for the "historian" pivots on the temple as Solomon's most important achievement, an achievement that matters decisively to the "historian" since this account will end in the razing of the temple by the Babylonians (2 Kgs 25:13–17).

The crucial chapter 8 begins with a reported liturgical procession that culminates in an anthem concerning YHWH's palpable presence in the temple (8:12–13). But then critical reflection follows that gives voice to other judgments concerning "real presence," whereby it is insisted that YHWH is attentive to the temple but dwells in heaven: "But will God indeed dwell on the earth? Even heaven and the highest heaven cannot contain you, much less this house that I have built! . . . Hear the plea of your servant and of your people Israel when they pray toward this place; O hear in heaven your dwelling place; heed and forgive" (8:27, 30). This claim is to protect YHWH's freedom from any royal domestication of YHWH that might be accomplished through liturgical or theological means.

Then follows in the chapter a series of prayers in time of distress (vv. 31–45), culminating in a long petition offered from exile (vv. 46–53). It is clear that whatever may be rooted in Solomon's own time continued to be a developing tradition that the "historian" has made serviceable to an exilic community. The point of the chapter is to enhance the temple but also to acknowledge that Israel deported from Jerusalem must have other access points to YHWH without direct presence in the temple. The development of chapter 8 shows the way in which the "historian" characteristically reformulates texts in order to make them pertinent to and authoritative for the generation of the exile.

It is important, and perhaps somewhat ironic, that immediately after the high theology of temple presence and assurance in chapter 8, the "historian" has placed 9:1–9, a characteristic Deuteronomic syllogism:

> obey (v. 4)   prosper (v. 5)
> disobey (v. 6)   trouble (vv. 7–9)

It is worth noting that the negative of verses 6–9 is disproportionately long, suggesting that the negative accent is the point of the whole in the horizon of the "historian."

In 9:10–10:29 it is difficult to know the extent to which the reportage is intended to be ironic. On the face of it, these verses present Solomon as prosperous and effective. Except that in the Deuteronomic horizon, we are to know that the regime *is not working*, is not working because the Torah is being systemically violated in a practice of self-aggrandizement that enacts theological autonomy and thus disregards the ultimate rule of YHWH. Whether these materials are ironic or not, we are caught up short by the vigorous negation of chapter 11. The indictment is that Solomon was led astray from serious covenantal obedience by "many foreign women." We are to notice, however, that his multiple marriages to foreign princesses were part of a larger systematic policy of joining the political-economic apparatus of the globalization of his time, and thereby inevitably forsaking the local tradition of covenantal obedience. In this rendering it is precisely Solomon's policies of ambition that bring success that in turn bring judgment and disaster.

By the time we finish the narrative of Solomon, it is clear that the Solomonic account of 1 Kings 1–11 is a quite intentionally shaped theological statement about the conditionality of Torah obedience for success in the world. This condition is of decisive importance for the larger narrative of the Deuteronomist. It is also important because this conclusion concerning Solomon, inescapable as it seems to this reader, is against the grain of the popular notion of Solomon that mostly celebrates his wisdom, power, and success. The Deuteronomic rendering of this most notable of Judean kings requires of the reader an ironic sense that things in the text are not as they appear. Thus the Deuteronomic rendering witnesses to the nonnegotiable realities of life in the world of YHWH, realities that live just below the surface of what the world sees and values.

III

The long middle section of the books of Kings, 1 Kings 12:1–2 Kings 17:41, provides the prevailing metanarrative of the twinned kingdoms of Israel and Judah after the death of Solomon, a period commonly dated 962–721. The latter date refers to the destruction of the northern kingdom of Israel and its capital, Samaria, at the hands of the Assyrians. For this long period, the "historian" tells, in tandem, the royal account of the two realms, detailing the several kings in both realms. In order to do this, the "historian" has developed a complex strategy of dating each king according to the dates of his counterpart king in the other kingdom. The most important feature of the Deuteronomic editing is the fairly standard formula whereby each king is identified according to the details of his age at the beginning of his reign, the length of his reign, the name of the queen mother, and the formula for the end of reign. The most important detail in the formula is that a verdict is rendered on each king, a verdict according to the theological passions of the "historian" All northern kings are in principle reckoned to be bad kings because they, of necessity, violate commitment to the central shrine in Jerusalem. In the southern Davidic line, most kings are bad, six are qualifiedly approved, and only two (Hezekiah and Josiah) are fully approved. This verdict is rendered in terms of the several kings and their unqualified loyalty to YHWH, to YHWH's commands, and to YHWH's temple.

It should be noted in passing that some scholars hypothesize about a series of editorial procedures whereby different accents are asserted in the ongoing development of the text through different layers of editing. It is, moreover, proposed particularly by U.S. scholars that there was a completed edition of the history in the time of Josiah and only later an exilic adaptation to cope with the new data of destruction (Cross 1973, 274–89; Nelson 1987). This particular hypothesis is a variation upon the hypothesis of Noth, who regarded the whole as an editorial accomplishment of the exile. The differentiation has some importance for a refined reading of the text, but is not important for an introductory approach to the literature.

The most important text in this long sweep for understanding the interpretive perspective of the "historian" is 2 Kings 17:7–41. This long, somewhat tedious statement is a theological reflection upon the destruction of Samaria and the end of the northern kingdom at the hand of Assyrians; it voices important convictions of the Deuteronomists. Whatever may have been the geopolitical, military causes of the Assyrian assault on the northern kingdom, the Deuteronomists single-mindedly insist that the crisis and loss are grounded in YHWH's action and purpose. The statement in chapter 17 opens with the long indictment of Israel's long-term violation of the first commandment of exclusive loyalty to YHWH (vv. 7–12). The verdict is continued in verses 14–17 with only a pause in verse 13 to indicate the conviction that YHWH had sent ample warning by way of a succession of prophets to summon Israel back to YHWH. Thus for the Deuteronomist, the prophets are taken to be key players in the history of Israel and Judah. The long indictment is fulfilled in verse 18 with a terse but absolute sentence of deportation. (See also vv. 20–23.) In verse 19 the "historian" pauses to glance at Judah and to anticipate the future history of chapters 18–25 that will also end in deportation for Judah. In this single verse the "historian" surely knows the outcome of the southern history as well.

The remainder of chapter 17 (vv. 24–41) is a later reflection on the population that Assyria had deported into Samaria. This extended literary assault, from a Jerusalem perspective, characterizes the theological heterodoxy of the northern population in a trajectory of interpretation that is subsequently extended as a diatribe against "Samaritans," that is, northern Jews who are not "Jewish enough" to meet later Jerusalem requirements.

The other most remarkable feature of this extended middle section of the books of Kings is a collection of prophetic narratives in 1 Kings 17–2 Kings 9, featuring Elijah and Elisha, plus a narrative of Micaiah ben Imlah. This collection of narratives bears none of the marks of the Deuteronomic Historian; yet it is surely important that in the final form of the text the Deuteronomic editors gave such prominent and extended place to these narratives.

The narratives themselves exhibit the dramatic larger-than-life characters looming large in the land, enacting spectacular wonders, and in general holding the initiative for this telling of the story, an initiative that otherwise and characteristically belongs to kings. It is conventional to view these stories as folk legends, that is, as stories rooted in some unrecoverable happening but now greatly exaggerated through constant retelling in the most imaginative ways. Such a way of taking this material is adequate, if the conclusion is not drawn from such a labeling and assessment that the narratives are fanciful and therefore are not to be taken seriously. Because they occur in such a prominent and extensive place in the book of Kings (nearly one-third of the whole!), they must be taken with great seriousness as serving the intention of the final interpreters. Most likely the narratives indicate an epistemological crisis and articulate an epistemological alternative in characterizing this royal history. That is, these narratives evidence a way of knowing and living and experiencing reality, plus a way of witnessing to reality, that lies outside the scope and rationality of royal control.

That they are legends of "the folk" means that this was an important and continuing population that did not subscribe to the interpretive categories of the royal establishment and other urban elites, but who were in very different categories able to interpret and manage their lives differently. The work of James C. Scott on the way in which peasant communities develop, transmit, and depend upon "hidden transcripts" to survive the dominant transcript of the landowning community is pertinent to a study of these narratives. Scott suggests that such communities develop narrative strategies for rereading historical reality differently and thereby maintaining nerve and the chance to survive (J. C. Scott 1985; 1990). We suggest that Scott's analysis is pertinent to the origin, survival,

> ### Midrashic Moment: Elijah and the Messianic Age
>
> The vivid story in 2 Kings 2 of Elijah being taken up alive into heaven as he is walking along with his protégé Elisha ("a chariot of fire and horses of fire separated the two of them, and Elijah ascended in a whirlwind into heaven," v. 11) becomes the basis of an expectation, in both Jewish and Christian thinking, that he is waiting to return from heaven to help usher in the messianic age. So Malachi 4:5 has God promise that "I will send you the prophet Elijah before the great and terrible day of the LORD comes." The deuterocanonical book of Sirach proclaims that "at the appointed time" Elijah will "restore the tribes of Israel" (Sir 48:10). The Gospel writers reflect a similar idea (Matt 16:13–14; Mark 6:14–15; Luke 9:7–8), to the extent that John the Baptist is intentionally portrayed as an Elijah-like figure. And to this day, many Jewish Passover meals will include a place setting for Elijah at the table, symbolically representing a hope that he will show up and bring the coming kingdom of God with him.

and intention of these prophetic narratives. It is all the more astonishing that the Deuteronomic Historian preserved these narratives and gave them such prominence in his account of royal history, surely as a strategic means for subverting the pretentious claims of monarchy.

That is, these stories attest to social life that has not been brought under royal control, so that these stories themselves, in their being told and retold and heard yet again, are acts of civil disobedience that affirm that much of life—and the power for life—lies beyond royal control in a world where YHWH's rule is much more immediate and palpable than royal rationality can allow. This alternative sense of lived reality that is close to YHWH's direct governance is exemplified, for example, in large scale in the narrative of Naboth's vineyard wherein the capacity of Jezebel and Ahab to enact a royal land grant according to conventional royal privilege is condemned by Elijah (1 Kgs 21). The same direct governance of YHWH, however, is made dramatically clear in the contest at Mount Carmel in 1 Kings 18 and 19, wherein Elijah is capable of producing rain.

The subversive claim of the story against Ahab serves to assert that a king who cannot cause rain has none of the powers that properly belong to the office. The same sense of an alternatively lived reality is evident in the pastoral act of 2 Kings 4:42–44, wherein Elisha makes food available to hungry people. Moreover, the entire cycle of prophetic narratives is situated in the midst of the northern dynasty of Omri, and exhibits a mode of public life that neither defers to nor depends upon royal governance. Thus it is plausible to suggest that these narratives, in sum, function to delegitimate royal power, at least royal power in the north, and to assert that YHWH as giver of life has other agents and other avenues, outside monarchy, whereby to give the gift of life. Thus the narratives are inherently subversive of royal power, and surely are intended to function so in the final form of the text.

IV

The third and final section of the books of Kings consists in 2 Kings 18–25, an account of the continuing course of the southern kingdom in Jerusalem from the destruction of the northern kingdom in 721 to the destruction of Jerusalem and the Judean kingdom in 587 BCE. As the narrative grows closer to the historian's own time, it stays closely fixed upon materials that lead seemingly inexorably to the destruction of 587. Thus the narrative in this last section is arranged in rather set blocks that amount to almost choreographic rendering to lead the reader to the end.

This material that purports to cover the period from 715 at the beginning of the reign of Hezekiah until 587 focuses upon three kings who epitomize the accent points of the "historian."

1. Hezekiah is reckoned to be a good king who knew YHWH fully and so was able to withstand Assyrian pressure (2 Kgs 18:3–8). (Notice that the material of chaps. 18–20 has a parallel in Isa 36–39.) In the form of several speeches, a prayer of the king, and a responding prophetic oracle by Isaiah, this narrative champions a singular loyalty to YHWH, as practiced by Hezekiah, as the clue to public well-being in Israel. The account of Hezekiah is testimony to the conviction that obedience to YHWH matters decisively in the larger world of geopolitics and perhaps hints, on the way to 587, that an attentive royal policy of adherence to YHWH's Torah might indeed have voided the military debacle that was to come. Thus Hezekiah's loyalty to YHWH in the perspective of the "historian" is the decisive condition for security and prosperity in the public domain. In what follows it will be clear that Judah recalcitrantly resists this single condition and so chooses its own sorry fate.

2. The second king in the final choreograph is Manasseh, son of Hezekiah (1 Kgs 21). He is portrayed as the paradigmatic, quintessential bad king, the one who, at close range, is the cause of the coming destruction of Jerusalem, for he had failed completely on the single requirement of Torah obedience:

> Still the Lord did not turn from the fierceness of his great wrath, by which his anger was kindled against Judah, because of all the provocations with which Manasseh had provoked him. The Lord said, "I will remove Judah also out of my sight, as I have removed Israel; and I will reject this city that I have chosen, Jerusalem, and the house of which I said, My name shall be there." (2 Kgs 23:26–27)

His son Amon merits only a brief mention, for he continued the fated policies of Manasseh: "He did what was evil in the sight of the Lord, as his father Manasseh had done" (2 Kgs 21:20).

3. The third and most important king in this concluding triad is Josiah, heir to the reforms of his great-grandfather Hezekiah and heir as well to the long-term disaster of his grandfather Manasseh. Josiah, along with Hezekiah, is reckoned as the good king in the long history: "Before him there was no king like him, who turned to the Lord with all his heart, with all his soul, and with all his might, according to all the law of Moses; nor did any like him arise after him" (2 Kgs 23:25; see 24:3).

Josiah is of special interest to the "historian" (and to us) because he is the one who witnesses and responds to the scroll found in the temple (22:8–13). It is the surmise of most scholars that the scroll found in the temple is some form of the book of Deuteronomy, out of which Josiah initiated the "Deuteronomic Reform" of 621 (23:1–24). This scroll finding and subsequent reform together constitute the most important element in the long Deuteronomic

History. It may be that the finding of the scroll is an actual historical event, as older scholarship has long thought. Or it may be that the narrative is a fictive creation of the "historian." Either way, the report places the Torah scroll at the center of attention with the best king and establishes Josiah as the model king in the Deuteronomic horizon, the one who submits completely to the Torah. Thus the reported event of the scroll makes the Torah commandments the centerpiece of this history, and establishes Josiah as the champion of what counts most for the "historian." Indeed, Josiah is seen to be the one who embodies the central mandates of Moses to Joshua at the beginning of this history:

> Only be strong and very courageous, being careful to act in accordance with all the law that my servant Moses commanded you; do not turn from it to the right hand or to the left, so that you may be successful wherever you go. This book of the law shall not depart out of your mouth; you shall meditate on it day and night, so that you may be careful to act in accordance with all that is written in it. For then you shall make your way prosperous, and then you shall be successful. I hereby command you: Be strong and courageous; do not be frightened or dismayed, for the LORD your God is with you wherever you go. (Josh 1:7–9)

The connection between Joshua at the beginning of the history and Josiah at the end of this history is surely an intentional strategy for bracketing the royal history by the Torah:

> This Mosaic *torah* becomes, in turn, the mandate for all of Joshua's actions and his legacy to future generations (Josh 1:7, 8; 8:31, 32, 34, 35; 22:5; 23:6; 24:26). . . .
> The Deuteronomistic historian, of course, did not leave the matter at that, but presented Josiah's discovery and implementation of the Mosaic *torah* as the climax of his work (2 Kgs 22:8, 11; 23:24–25a). That he portrayed Joshua as a unique prototype for Josiah's strict obedience to Deuteronomic law is shown by the distribution of the admonition found in Joshua 1:7 regarding that *torah*: "Turn not from it to the right hand or to the left." This admonition to keep to the legal straight and narrow is used four times in Deuteronomy (5:32; 17:11, 20 [the "law of the king"]; 28:14), and again in Joshua's farewell address to Israel (Josh 23:6). It does not recur in the Deuteronomistic History until Josiah is said to have fulfilled it (2 Kgs 22:2).
> Similarly, Joshua "left nothing undone of all that Yahweh had commanded Moses" (Josh 11:15). No such report of complete obedience to Mosaic law occurs again in the Deuteronomistic History until the account of Josiah reaches its climax in 2 Kings 23:25a. (Cheney 1989, 109–10)

Out of this review of Manasseh and Josiah, it is clear that the verdict concerning Josiah given penultimately in 2 Kings 23:25 is positive, but the ultimate verdict in Judah with reference to Manasseh in 23:26–27 is negative and becomes the key pivot point in the entire history. The juxtaposition of *good king* and *bad king* makes clear that Torah *obedience* (as in Josiah) matters decisively, but Torah *disobedience* (as in Manasseh) is so preponderant in royal Israel that long-term Torah disobedience overrides the spectacular Torah obedience of Josiah. Josiah is too little and too late.

Thus the triad of *good* Hezekiah, *bad* Manasseh, and *good* Josiah choreographs the primary intention of the "historian" with the verdict that the end must come to Jerusalem because of disobedience. The remainder of the material in 23:28–25:26 is simply a mop-up action whereby the already given theological verdict becomes embodied as historical consequence. The end comes to Jerusalem in a visible, public way at the hands of Nebuchadnezzar and the Babylonians. Close readers of the history, however, have been able to anticipate this sorry destruction and deportation from the outset:

> But if your heart turns away and you do not hear, but are led astray to bow down to other gods and serve them, I declare to you today that you shall perish; you shall not live long in the land that you are crossing the Jordan to enter and possess. (Deut 30:17–18)

> Then this people will begin to prostitute themselves to the foreign gods in their midst, the gods of the land into which they are going; they will forsake me, breaking my covenant that I have made with them. My anger will be kindled against them in that day. I will forsake them and hide my face from them; they will become easy prey, and many terrible troubles will come upon them. In that day they will say, "Have not these troubles come upon us because our God is not in our midst?" (Deut 31:16–17)

> If you transgress the covenant of the LORD your God, which he enjoined on you, and go and serve other gods and bow down to them, then the anger of the LORD will be kindled against you, and you shall perish quickly from the good land that he has given to you. (Josh 23:16)

With these quite visible connections at the beginning and at the end, it is clear that 1 and 2 Kings are not simply reportage on generations of the monarchy, but a forceful interpretation and a vigorous argument, nothing less than a philosophy of history, upon which this tradition is insistent. The whole, culminating in the three kings noted who are variously marked by theological verdict, is an advocacy for keeping YHWH and YHWH's Torah at the center of public meaning, and that in the face of cynical self-aggrandizement.

It takes little imagination to see that prophetic advocacy is as urgent for our contemporary reading of this history as among that first readership in exile.

The final paragraph of 2 Kings 25:27–30 is a curious notation, offered at some important distance from what precedes. The "thirty-seventh year of exile" is 561 BCE, and that became the key for Noth's dating of the whole of the literature. Scholars are not agreed on the importance or the meaning of this curious paragraph. It may be a mere historical note, except that we know by now that this "historian" is never concerned with mere historical notes. The weightiest and perhaps most influential reading of the paragraph is by von Rad, who takes it as a sign of hope that the Davidic dynasty still survives, so that Israel in exile (and beyond) still has ground for Davidic hope, even in the face of imperial negotiation:

> But the Deuteronomist saw yet another word as active in the history, namely, the promise of salvation in the Nathan prophecy, and it, as well as the threat of judgment, was effectual as it ran through the course of the history. Had it too creatively reached its goal in a fulfilment? The Deuteronomist's history leaves this question open. Yet, closing as it does with the note about the favour shown to Jehoiachin (II Kings XXV. 27 ff.), it points to a possibility with which Jahweh can resume. (von Rad 1962, 343)

That Davidic-messianic hope, here kept only slightly open, loomed large in other exilic texts (see Isa 55:3; Jer 23:5–6; 33:14–16, 17, 23–26; Ezek 34:23–24) and eventually in Christian interpretation of Jesus as well. For this "historian," however, not that much can be claimed. It is contended only that the harsh divine judgment visited upon Jerusalem in 587 BCE is not the final word, though it is in context a decisive word. That word of judgment could not be otherwise, given the nonnegotiable requirements of the Torah, so clearly advocated by the historian, so vividly championed by Joshua, and so boldly enacted by Josiah. In this horizon, kings live in a world of Torah. That is attested by the historian; and when kings are weak on Torah, initiative for public leadership gravitates elsewhere, to such odd characters as Elijah, Elisha, and Micaiah ben Imlah, always an alternative in Israelite imagination to kings who negate the Torah. Readers should in the end notice what an odd royal history this is, intended to be precisely that odd!

16

The Book of Isaiah

The book of Isaiah is the beginning of the Latter Prophets. Consequently it stands, in the Hebrew ordering of the books, back-to-back with Kings, the last book of the Former Prophets. That interface, not visible in the conventional ordering of books in the Christian Bible, is fortuitous because the books of Kings and Isaiah are together preoccupied with the destiny of Jerusalem. The books of Kings end with an account of the sorry end of the destruction of Jerusalem at the hands of the Babylonians and the ensuing deportation and exile. The book of Isaiah, in its turn, is a meditation, albeit in complex configuration, about the destiny of Jerusalem *into* the crises of exile and the promise of Jerusalem *out* of exile into new well-being. The book is also the first book of extended poetry in the Old Testament. Although earlier books had poems inset here and there into the narrative, Isaiah gives us chapter upon chapter of high poetic art.

The book of Isaiah, according to most scholars, is rooted in the actual prophetic personality of Isaiah, son of Amoz, whose conventional dates for life in Jerusalem are perhaps 742 to 689 BCE (1:1):

> There is some support for the traditional scholarly view that Isaiah was an upper-class Jerusalemite who grew up in the city. The prophet seems to have known and had access to members of the royal court (Isa 8:2; 22:15–16), and he apparently had no difficulty gaining an unofficial audience with the king (Isa 7:3). The location of Isaiah within Jerusalem's central social structure may also be suggested by the "wisdom" language that he sometimes uses. At the very least this language may indicate that the prophet was educated at the royal court or in the temple, although our knowledge of Israelite "wisdom circles" is not presently sophisticated enough to permit us to assume

that there was a Jerusalemite "wisdom group" of which Isaiah was a member.

In addition to seeing Isaiah as part of the central social structure, some scholars have argued that he was actually a cultic prophet. These arguments are usually based on the prophet's temple vision (Isaiah 6) and on his general upper-class Jerusalemite background, but the book provides insufficient evidence to establish a cultic setting for his activities. It therefore seems best to accept the traditional view that Isaiah was an upper-class Jerusalemite who was part of the city's central social structure but not necessarily a part of its religious establishment. (R. Wilson 1980, 271)

If we accept such a conventional judgment, Isaiah lived through a series of public crises in Jerusalem related to the pressures of the rising and then powerful Assyrian Empire, and he had important access to the royal establishment in Jerusalem. Isaiah's work there, in both harsh judgment and buoyant promise, was to insist that the public life of Jerusalem could not be properly understood or practiced except by reference to YHWH, who is the ultimate sovereign of public history, the pretenses of Assyrian imperialists notwithstanding.

In the long book of Isaiah, however, the actual words from the eighth-century prophet are judged by scholars to be relatively few; no critical scholar, moreover, believes that the book as a whole is authored by the eighth-century prophet. Rather, the book of Isaiah, while rooted in the person of Isaiah, has emerged only through a long, extensive, and complex traditioning process, perhaps through a continuous succession of disciples of Isaiah who continue to articulate the general interpretative trajectory of the person of Isaiah (see 8:1), but who were themselves powerful interpreters capable of generating new articulations. To some extent the literature of the book of Isaiah is simply a continued meditation upon the destiny of Jerusalem, a meditation that occurred in separated, random acts of responsiveness to new issues of faith in new circumstances; at the same time, however, it is clear that the final form of the text has some rough intentionality that gives the whole of the book a suggestive coherence.

Having given up the notion of the authorship of the eighth-century prophet, as most interpreters have, critical scholarship for over a century has held to the view that the book of Isaiah is constituted into three quite distinct parts that reflect different historical circumstances, different modes of literary articulation, and consequently different theological vistas. In this discussion we will review that long-standing critical discussion because an intelligent read of the book is served by these well-established distinctions. At the same time, however, the reader will want to notice that in more recent scholarship this threefold distinction in the book of Isaiah has been understood in a much more coherent, dynamic, and intentional way. As a result, we will consider in turn the long-standing critical consensus in the book of Isaiah and more recent holistic understandings that depend upon the critical consensus but move beyond it in important ways.

I

In the critical consensus, it has long been held that the literature pertaining to *Isaiah of the eighth century* (then called "First Isaiah") is limited to Isaiah 1–39, because after chapter 39 there is an immense break—literary, historical, and theological—before chapter 40. In sum, we may say that chapters 1–39, rooted in the eighth-century prophet, are concerned with the crises of preexilic Jerusalem in the period 742–701. As soon as we have said that, however, it is clear that the material is much more complex than such a historical connection, for chapters 1–39 contain many other matters as well that are not linked to the eighth century.

In rough outline, we may see that First Isaiah consists in six quite distinct textual units, of which only three are directly connected to First Isaiah: chapters 1–12; 28–31; and 36–39.

The most important materials for the eighth-century prophet are found in chapters 1–12, which harshly anticipate YHWH's judgment upon Jerusalem for Torah disobedience (1:2–6; 2:6–22; 3:1–4:1; 5:1–7, 8–30). Two features in this material are especially noteworthy. First, the harsh judgments announced by the prophet are roughly matched by promises that anticipate that after the judgment of YHWH upon the city, there will be a renewal and restoration. That renewal and restoration does not in any way soften or diminish the judgment to come, but asserts that judgment is not the ultimate prophetic word to YHWH's city. The promises in 2:1–4; 4:2–6; 9:1–7; and 11:1–9 are voiced around a series of different images concerning the Holy City, the temple, the monarchy, and new creation; all of them, however, testify to YHWH's capacity to make new immediately upon judgment. Thus we may imagine that chapters 1–12 are organized in a pattern whereby these four promises become the antidote to the condemnations that precede them.

Second, in chapters 7 and 8 King Ahaz is treated as a *model of unfaith*. The famous dictum of the prophet in 7:9 articulates faith as readiness to trust YHWH in desperate circumstances, in this case the threat of war against Jerusalem by its nearest neighbors. Ahaz is portrayed as a distrusting king who does not have faith in YHWH, but who imagines he can, by his own policies, secure himself. Thus the king stands in total antithesis to the radical form of well-being voiced and offered by the prophet.

It is important to recognize that chapters 1–12 with the patterned variation of *judgment* and *promise* constitute, *in nuce*, the theology of the final form of the book. The whole of the book of Isaiah provides the scenario of the descent of Jerusalem into exile and death and the promised ascent of Jerusalem to new life and well-being. This pattern is already evident in chapters 1–12, in either the prophet's own sense of hope beyond judgment or, more likely, an editorial pattern of the completed tradition.

The second unit of text commonly assigned to the eighth-century prophet is chapters 28–31, with an addendum in chapters 32–33. This text, usually assigned to the time of Hezekiah, Ahaz's son, again features the prophetic voice speaking in the midst of great public issues urging the king to practice policies rooted in YHWH's rule. Especially noteworthy is that the series of oracles regularly begin with *hoy*, conventionally translated "woe" but in the NRSV variously rendered as "Ah," "Oh," or "Alas" (28:1; 29:1; 30:1; 31:1; 33:1; see the same usage in 5:8, 11, 18, 20, 21, 22; 10:1). The term is portentous of coming death. Thus when the oracles are introduced with this startling term, the intent is to place the listening community in jeopardy. This corpus of text, then, concerns the community of Jerusalem when it is not responsive to the will of YHWH. Likely chapters 28–31 represent the rule of Hezekiah in crisis as a counterpoint to the same tone used during the rule of Ahaz.

The third text that is closely linked to the eighth-century prophet is chapters 36–39, a unit that is closely linked to the parallel narrative of 2 Kings 18–20 and is perhaps appropriated from there with only slight variation. This third unit of text, however, is not a series of oracles as are the other two, but a narrative that exhibits quite intentional editorial work. The unit consists in powerful prophetic theology offered as three speeches in the mouths of Assyrian diplomats (Isa 36:4–10, 13–20; 37:8–13). In response to these three political-theological challenges, the text offers a prayer by King Hezekiah (37:15–20) and an oracle by the prophet Isaiah that assures Israel that the Assyrian threat is no match for YHWH (37:22–29; see also vv. 6–7). The outcome of this exchange is an insistence upon YHWH's rule, the specific expression of which is the wondrous rescue of the city of Jerusalem from the Assyrian armies (37:36–38), a rescue rooted in YHWH's loyalty to David as voiced by the prophet:

> Therefore thus says the LORD concerning the king of Assyria: He shall not come into this city, shoot an arrow there, come before it with a shield, or cast up a siege ramp against it. By the way that he came, by the same he shall return; he shall not come into this city, says the LORD. For I will defend this city to save it, for my own sake and for the sake of my servant David. (37:33–35)

This oracle is the most complete expression of YHWH's commitment to the Jerusalem establishment and apparently expresses Isaiah's own deep commitment to that theological claim. It is impossible to know whether these words are from Isaiah or represent the theological intention of the traditioning process. Christopher Seitz has considered the function of this material in the developing tradition of Isaiah, and has proposed that Ahaz and Hezekiah form, for the traditioning process, a contrast of bad king and good king (Seitz 1991). He has also suggested that Isaiah's commitment to Zion theology—the conviction that YHWH will stay faithful to the temple city through thick and thin—has provided the impetus for the continued force of the Isaiah tradition beyond the life of Isaiah and beyond the crisis of Hezekiah:

> The growth of Isaiah tradition was not the consequence of some internal suitability that distinguished Isaiah from other preexilic prophetic collections or made secondary supplementation intrinsically more appropriate. Rather, it was the existence of *Heilsprophetie* in the form of oracles (1) limiting the role of Assyria as agent of divine wrath and (2) expressing final divine concern for Zion, that set Isaiah traditions off as unique among preexilic prophetic collections. (Seitz 1991, 146)

It is clear in all three units of text (Isa 1–12; 28–31 plus 32–33; and 36–39) that the tradition of Isaiah insists upon the powerful rule of YHWH in the midst of deeply problematic public affairs. As much as any of the prophets of ancient Israel, Isaiah is the voice of an insistent public theology, an assertion that YHWH's rule matters consistently to policy and to practice.

Alongside these three sections of First Isaiah that are connected to the person of Isaiah, the corpus also includes three other units of text that may be understood as growths in the tradition that are congruent with Isaiah's perspective, in particular the conviction concerning YHWH's commitment to Jerusalem. It means that judgment is not the last word, but that YHWH will bring *shalom* in the environs of Jerusalem:

1. Chapters 13–23 constitute a distinct corpus, which, as we shall see, is closely paralleled by oracles against the nations in the other prophetic books as an assertion of YHWH's sovereignty over all the nations. The pattern for this genre of text is the naming of a number of nation-states and the pronouncement of a prophetic lawsuit against them, thus insisting that even non-Israelite peoples are fully subject to the rule of YHWH and are under judgment when they do not conform to that rule. John Barton has nicely suggested that such oracles against the nations assume that all nations know about YHWH's rule and demands, and need not appeal to the commands of Sinai, thus issuing in some form of "natural law" (Barton 1979). The ground for judgment against the nations appeals to the knowledge of all concerning

the will of the Creator God without reference to Sinai, a tradition that in later Judaism is connected to the covenant of Noah. (See Isa 2:1–4 as the "Torah of Zion" as distinct from the "Torah of Sinai" as a guide for all nations.)

The corpus of Isaiah 13–23 concerns a range of nations, but the most important is the oracle of chapters 13 and 14 concerning Babylon. The oracle is an assertion that even Babylon, that great superpower, is subject to the will of YHWH. This is of particular interest because Babylon was not and could not have been on the horizon of eighth-century Isaiah. In a later time (the sixth century), however, and in the latter part of the book of Isaiah, Babylon is the great oppressor against Israel (chaps. 46 and 47) and the great defier of YHWH. Thus chapters 13 and 14, already in First Isaiah, look ahead to the later part of the book and offer the passionate assurance that even barbaric Babylon is subject to the will of YHWH. Thus the oracle, along with a series of poems concerning other peoples, asserts YHWH's rule and thereby offers hope for Israel that the God who loves Israel is the God who will judge all barbarian nations, including especially those who abuse Israel.

2. The second textual development beyond the eighth-century Isaiah is in chapters 24–27, often termed "Fourth Isaiah" or the "Little Apocalypse of Isaiah" (commonly thought to be the latest development of tradition in the book of Isaiah). The distinguishing feature of this material is that it lacks all reference to context and dating and makes sweeping cosmic claims for YHWH, the effect of which is to assert YHWH's sovereignty, both as harsh judgment (24) and then as hope (25–27). While the rhetoric is well beyond that assigned to the prophet himself, it is easy to see how this radical insistence on sovereignty is congruent with the claims of the prophet himself, even though the material surely comes later.

The most remarkable feature of this material is that it articulates a conviction of the resurrection of the body, thus the sure vindication of those who suffer faithfully, so that not even the reality of death can match the power and fidelity of YHWH. In 25:6–8 YHWH is portrayed as the great rival of "death" who will defeat and swallow death:

> On this mountain the LORD of hosts will make for all peoples
>   a feast of rich food, a feast of well-aged wines,
>   of rich food filled with marrow, of well-aged wines strained clear.
> And he will destroy on this mountain
>   the shroud that is cast over all peoples,
>   the sheet that is spread over all nations;
>   he will swallow up death forever.
> Then the Lord GOD will wipe away the tears from all faces,
>   and the disgrace of his people he will take away from all the earth,
>   for the LORD has spoken.

In Isaiah 26:19, moreover, the poetry anticipates joyous resurrection:

> Your dead shall live, their corpses shall rise.
>   O dwellers in the dust, awake and sing for joy!
> For your dew is a radiant dew,
>   and the earth will give birth to those long dead.

These assertions constitute a *novum* in Israel; they are, however, consistent with the Isaianic conviction that YHWH's sovereignty finally cannot be defeated, not even by the enemies of YHWH in the world or the enemies of YHWH in the cosmos.

3. The third unit of text in Isaiah in 1–39 that goes beyond the prophet is found in chapters 34–35, which anticipate the recovery of Jerusalem and the glad return of exiles from the deportation. It is clear that the envisioned return of chapter 35 has parallels to chapter 40 and following chapters, so that the material is regularly seen as an introduction to the material of 40–55 that celebrates restoration and the homecoming of Israel.

It is clear in these texts (Isa 13–23; 14–27; and 34–35) that the tradition has moved well beyond Isaiah of the eighth century. That prophet had evoked and voiced the miraculous deliverance from Assyria in 701, but this belated section has moved past the cries of 701 to the greater crisis of 587:

> One approach to understanding the growth of the book of Isaiah as a whole involved the possibility that a correlation was seen to exist between 701 and 587 events. . . . It is appropriate at this juncture to return to the puzzle of Isaiah's growth, with the possibility that a correlation between 701 and 587 events gave rise to the extension of Isaiah tradition beyond the lifetime of the prophet to the events of the exile and beyond. (Seitz 1991, 118)

The prophet in the eighth century had shown that the deliverance of Jerusalem in 701 from the threat of the Assyrians was a gift of YHWH. Now the faith of the prophet is turned to the more difficult case of 587. Even here, insists the tradition of Isaiah, YHWH's will for the good of Jerusalem will last through the crisis of 587 to effect a coming glorious well-being. Thus the crisis of 701 is taken to prefigure in an inchoate way the greater crisis of 587. While the loss cuts deeper in the latter crisis, as Israel generally conceded, the assurance is the same: the same God who was faithful in 701 stands faithful yet again.

It is this deep conviction that evokes the extension of the book of Isaiah beyond the dire prediction of 39:5–8 concerning the power of Babylon. The good news of 40:1 that follows immediately after 39:5–8 in the text did not come soon or immediately. It did, however, come next as divine promise after the oracle of threat. It was spoken because YHWH's ultimate will for well-being in Jerusalem is pervasive in the tradition of Isaiah. The book in its final form does not dwell ultimately on judgment; it looks beyond judgment to coming well-being that is the gift of YHWH. The anticipation of that coming gift of well-being from YHWH is the work of the remainder of the book—well beyond the eighth century—to which we now turn.

Thus First Isaiah (chaps. 1–39) is a complex body of text, rooted in Isaiah of the eighth century (1–12; 28–31; 36–39), but with an ongoing tradition that moves past the crisis of 587, anticipating homecoming for exiles (34–35), the reassertion of YHWH's rule over the nations (13–23), and ultimately the vigorous exercise of YHWH's sovereignty over all recalcitrant forces—including the power of death (24–27). While the tradition rooted in eighth-century Isaiah concerns the judgment of YHWH upon Jerusalem, the developed tradition looks beyond that judgment to the rule of YHWH that assures *shalom* for Jerusalem and for the entire earth over which the God of Israel—the Creator of heaven and earth—reigns.

II

This developing tradition of anticipated well-being prepares the way for "Second Isaiah" (also termed "Deutero-Isaiah"), the middle portion of the book of Isaiah in chapters 40–55. It is a long-held view of scholarship that these chapters constitute a quite distinct tradition that is

- different in literary style and genre wherein this text is much more lyrical in its articulation than First Isaiah
- different in historical circumstance as this text is preoccupied with the fall of Babylon (46–47) and the rise of Cyrus the Persian (44:28; 45:1)
- different in theological vista as this text moves decisively toward monotheism, voicing the God of Israel as the sole God, the Creator of heaven and earth

The scholarly title "Second Isaiah" recognizes that this material is in the book of Isaiah and perhaps is connected to First Isaiah. The title also asserts by "Second," however, that this is very different material addressed as the word of YHWH to Israel in very different circumstances.

The text likely reflects the great upheaval in the Fertile Crescent as the Neo-Babylonian Empire (present-day Iraq) of Nebuchadnezzar came to its rapid demise at the hand of the rising eastern power of Persia (present-day Iran) under the leadership of Cyrus. This text is conventionally dated to 540 BCE, with the claim that the Persians will defeat Babylon and that consequently Cyrus will soon thereafter permit the first Jerusalem deportees to return home (in 537; see 2 Chr 36:22–23; Ezra 1:2–4). Thus the *theological anticipation* of this poetry that YHWH would enact a mighty miracle that permitted the end to exile is fully commensurate with the *historical occurrence* of Cyrus, who initiated new colonial policies that restored aspects of local autonomy and local governance. This convergence of theological claim and historical happening is characteristic of the Bible. In this case, moreover, this literature poetically asserts that it is precisely YHWH who has summoned, evoked, authorized, and dispatched Cyrus, so that the new Persian policy is said to be at the behest of YHWH's own intentionality for the restoration of Israel after exile (Isa 44:28; 45:1). As Brevard Childs has suggested, the "new thing" that YHWH does here is restoration after the "former thing" of destruction and deportation (see 43:16–21; Childs 1979, 325–33).

The poetry of Isaiah 40–55, in a variety of daring rhetorical strategies, gives voice to the new historical intervention of YHWH. Thus we may understand 40:1–11 as an assertion that YHWH, in divine counsel among many angels and other heavenly messengers, has declared of Jerusalem that "her penalty is paid" (40:2), and so dispatches a "herald"—perhaps the poet, Second Isaiah—who will announce the "good tidings" (or "gospel") that "your God" is taking an initiative (40:9), that "your God reigns" (see 52:7). Thus we are to understand that between 39:5–8, which anticipates deportation to Babylon, and 40:1–11, which anticipates restoration from Babylon, there has been a long historical caesura. In the gap between these texts have come (a) the destruction of Jerusalem anticipated by the prophet already in the eighth century, and (b) the deportation of Jerusalem citizens. The gap between 39:5–8 and 40:1–11 is deeply freighted with the reality of loss, suffering, and dismay; that gap, moreover, is elemental for understanding the book of Isaiah, for it is the dramatic, dynamic connection between *displacement* and *restoration* that gives structure to the book of Isaiah (respectively in chaps. 1–39 and 40–66) and that articulates the fundamental message of the book, namely, that the judgment of YHWH is real but penultimate and is followed by YHWH's will for restoration that will follow according to YHWH's "plan." (See Isa 55:6–9 on the "plan" of YHWH that entails restoration and well-being.)

The poetry of Isaiah 40–55 is designed, with immense imagination, to give credible lyrical articulation to the resolve of YHWH to enact restoration for Israel and well-being for Jerusalem. To that end, the articulation of 44:21–45:7 is perhaps the centerpiece, focusing upon Cyrus as YHWH's agent for rescue. Prior to this text, the poetry includes *great doxologies* that celebrate YHWH's singular power as Creator (40:12–23; 42:10–13; 43:16–21); *lyrical assaults* upon and humiliation of rival gods, who are shown to be impotent (41:21–29), presumably the gods of Babylon, who would keep Israel enthralled but who are unable to do so; and *pastoral assurance* of YHWH in the form of salvation oracles guaranteeing that YHWH will be with and for Israel (41:8–13; 43:1–7). The cumulative effort of this poetry is to establish YHWH as powerful and compassionate toward Israel, and to expose the other gods who will ill for Israel as impotent and irrelevant. The poetry creates a world of stunning possibility for Israel, a world that counters in powerfully imaginative ways the presumed world of Babylon that seeks to keep Israel helpless and in despair.

After the pivotal Cyrus texts of 44:21–45:7, there are vigorous assertions of YHWH's power and sovereignty, celebrations in anticipation of the defeat and humiliation of Babylon (chap. 46) and the defeat and humiliation of Babylonian gods (chap. 47), and a vigorous announcement of YHWH's fresh resolve to act boldly and in new ways on behalf of Israel after a time of dormancy, silence, and absence (51:9–16; 54:1–17). The upshot of the whole is to arouse Israel in exile to new hope and possibility (51:17–23; 52:1–12), and to initiate a departure from Babylon that will match the earlier exodus departure from Egypt (52:11–12). It is conceded that YHWH has indeed abandoned Israel (54:7–8), but now, after that hiatus, YHWH is back in engagement on behalf of Israel.

It is worth noting that in 40:9 and 52:7, the poetry uses the term *basar* ("good tidings"), which the Septuagint translated by a Greek term related to the decisive New Testament term for "gospel." It is in this literature related to this particular historical crisis that the poet begins usage of the notion of "gospel," that is, news of the reassertion of YHWH's governance, news that is good for this community, helpless and in despair, now enlivened by God's intended intervention. This usage is fully congruent with the usage made in the New Testament concerning Jesus' announcement of the new rule of God (Mark 1:14–15) and Jesus' persistent enactment of that new rule of God.

We may notice in particular one element of this poetry upon which many interpreters comment. There is no doubt that in this poetry "Israel" as the addressee is named and regarded as YHWH's "servant," as the one in covenant with YHWH and so bound in obedience to YHWH. Scholars have, however, identified four poems dubbed "Servant Songs" that came to be regarded as distinct from the usage of the term "servant" in the rest of the poetry (42:1–9; 49:1–6; 50:4–9; 52:13–53:12). Many scholars have thought that the person designated as "servant" in these poems (and only in these poems) is a special figure with a special relationship to YHWH and a special vocation from YHWH, quite different from Israel as "servant." Scholars have used much energy to offer various hypotheses concerning this special agent, and Christians have found it convenient to suggest that the character in the poetry is Jesus in anticipation (North 1956; see Childs 2001, 422–23).

More recent scholarship, however, has moved to a consensus that these four poems are not to be separated from the rest of the poetry, and are to be taken in context along with the rest of the poetry. The important implication of this critical judgment is the conclusion that the "servant" in these four poems, like the "servant" elsewhere in the poetry of Second Isaiah, is none other than Israel (Mettinger 1983). Moreover, Israel with its special relationship to YHWH is also given a special assignment:

> I am the LORD, I have called you in righteousness,
>   I have taken you by the hand and kept you;
> I have given you as a covenant to the people,
>   a light to the nations,
>   to open the eyes that are blind,
> to bring out the prisoners from the dungeon,
>   from the prison those who sit in darkness.
>   (42:6–7)

> I will give you as a light to the nations,
>   that my salvation may reach to the end of the earth.
>   (49:6b)

That mandate, however, is not a *novum* in Israel's self-understanding, but is fully congruent with the mandate already given to Father Abraham to be "a blessing" to the nations. (See Gen 12:3; Isa 51:1–3.)

Given that emerging interpretive consensus, it is nonetheless important to recognize that Isaiah 49:6 constitutes something of a problem for that interpretation:

> It is too light a thing that you should be my servant
>   to raise up the tribes of Jacob
>   and to restore the survivors of Israel.

The verse is a problem because if Israel is the servant, it as servant has a mandate to "raise up, restore" Israel. Thus it is a commission for Israel to serve Israel. It is possible, while keeping this identity of the servant, to imagine a "pure, obedient, faithful Israel" with a mandate to a more inclusive Israel that needs rescue and restoration. While the point is awkward and leaves a bit of an enigma, this problematic is not an obstruction to the identity of the servant in these four songs as Israel. Childs has rearticulated the connection made in the tradition between this text and the church's claim for Jesus (Childs 2001, 420–23).

It is sufficient in general to know that Israel now displaced and soon to be restored is the primary subject of Second Isaiah. The hints of a larger mandate to Israel in 42:6 and 49:6 situate Israel as a vehicle and agent in the service of

YHWH's larger governance of all peoples. Thus the anticipated restoration of Israel is for the well-being of Israel, but an Israel always related to the larger intentions of YHWH for the world.

> ### Close Reading:
> ### Isaiah 49:14–15
>
> It is often fascinating to see how certain biblical texts quote or allude to earlier biblical texts, an example of which we see in this passage. Much of the burden of Second Isaiah (chaps. 40–55) is to convince the exiles that God is aware of their suffering and is engaged to act for their restoration. To that end, the poet here cites one of the bleakest of Israel's laments and endeavors to reverse it. The cited text is Lamentations 5:20, "Why have you forgotten us forever, abandoned us without end?" The poet picks up the crucial word pair from that verse—"abandoned" (*'azab*) and "forgotten" (*šakah*)—and admits that this is what Zion has said in the past. But now comes the answer from YHWH: "Can a woman forget her nursing child? Or have no pity for the child of her womb? Even these may forget, but I will not forget you" (Isa 49:15). In a remarkable metaphorical turn, God is presented as a nursing mother who will not forget her child. God longs for the return of Israel from exile as a nursing mother longs for her child, and it may well be that the metaphor plays on the physical discomfort that such a mother feels in the absence of the baby's nursing: God simply cannot forget Israel; it is almost physically impossible.

It is clear, according to critical judgment, that Isaiah 40–55 constitutes a quite distinct literature. It is equally clear, however, that this distinct corpus is to be related, in the final form of the text, to Isaiah 1–39. That relationship is a literary achievement. That artistic achievement of the final form of the text is not only literary, however, for the twinning of chapters 1–39 and chapters 40–55 constitutes a core Isaianic assertion concerning *inescapable judgment* reliably followed by *generous restoration*. Thus the two themes together constitute both Israel's lived memory and Israel's defining theological conviction. The shape of the book of Isaiah, as Clements and Childs have shown so clearly, is a theological shaping (Clements 1982; 1985; Childs 1979, 325–38). It is nonetheless a theological shaping that is completely resonant with Israel's lived memory.

III

The third section of the book of Isaiah comprises chapters 56–66, which for reasons now obvious are termed by scholars "Third Isaiah." It is the judgment of most scholars that this material reflects a community occupied with issues very different from those in chapters 40–55, and so it is judged to be a later literature. The apparent context of this literature is after the return and restoration anticipated in Second Isaiah, in a context where the community had to work out disputed internal questions of social life and religious practice. It is common to locate this literature somewhere between the building of the Second Temple (520–516), on which see Haggai and Zechariah, and the restoration of Ezra and Nehemiah after 450 BCE. Most scholars prefer a date earlier rather than later, thus soon after 520. That date is not very long after the hypothetical date of Second Isaiah, but places the literature in a very different sociohistorical circumstance.

Whereas Second Isaiah is preoccupied with emancipation from Babylon, Third Isaiah is concerned with internal communal life and the tensions that must have arisen among the parties that we might label "liberal and conservative." In chapter 56, for example, there is a dispute about inclusion and exclusion in the community, and in chapter 58 there is a debate about what constitutes a proper practice of religious fasting. The chapters apparently reflect disputed negotiation in the community that became the earliest form of Judaism after the great restoration from exile had been accomplished. It turned out that the facts on the ground in restored Jerusalem were modest and shabby when contrasted with the lyrical anticipations of Second Isaiah. The community reflected in Third Isaiah had to deal with the frustrations and disappointments that so sharply contrasted with the earlier lyrical expectations.

In the midst of Third Isaiah, one might give special attention to chapters 60–62, which voice a lyrical power that compares favorably with that of Second Isaiah. These chapters in grand lyrical fashion anticipate future well-being for Israel. These chapters include familiar formulations, most especially 61:1–4, which is reiterated in Luke 4:18–19:

> The spirit of the Lord GOD is upon me,
>   because the LORD has anointed me;
> he has sent me to bring good news to the oppressed,
>   to bind up the brokenhearted,
> to proclaim liberty to the captives,
>   and release to the prisoners;
> to proclaim the year of the LORD's favor,
>   and the day of vengeance of our God;
>   to comfort all who mourn;
> to provide for those who mourn in Zion—
>   to give them a garland instead of ashes,
> the oil of gladness instead of mourning,
>   the mantle of praise instead of a faint spirit.
> They will be called oaks of righteousness,
>   the planting of the LORD, to display his glory.
> They shall build up the ancient ruins,
>   they shall raise up the former devastations;
> they shall repair the ruined cities,
>   the devastations of many generations.
>
> (Isa 61:1–4)

Beyond these expectations, the lyrical promise of 65:17–25 voices the most sweeping anticipation of the "new age" when YHWH's rule is fully established, a promise that is the basis for the immense and final promise of the New Testament in Revelation 21: "Then I saw a new heaven and a new earth; for the first heaven and the first earth had passed away, and the sea was no more. And I saw the holy city, the new Jerusalem, coming down out of heaven from God, prepared as a bride adorned for her husband" (Rev 21:1–2).

While the cosmic scope of "new heaven and a new earth" is the furthest reach of biblical hope, along with them is the promise of a "new Jerusalem" that will be ordered by YHWH's presence in terms of justice, compassion, and neighborliness. The culmination of the book of Isaiah with "new Jerusalem" (65:17–25; see 66:10–13 as well) brings closure to the Jerusalem theme that dominates the entire book of Isaiah. Thus First Isaiah, in sum, bespeaks the destruction of Jerusalem as the judgment of YHWH; Second Isaiah anticipates restoration of Jerusalem, and Third Isaiah struggles with the shaping of the Jerusalem to come. The sequence of First, Second, and Third Isaiah attracts the interpreted memory of Jerusalem as *destroyed*, *expected*, and *reorganized*. The traditioning process thus has ordered material into a coherent interpretive pattern that has risen out of, and with respect to many different circumstances. Having noted the sequence of First, Second, and Third Isaiah, however, it is equally important to notice that in the final form of the book an overture articulates all of these themes at the very outset:

How the faithful city
   has become a whore!
   She that was full of justice,
righteousness lodged in her—
   but now murderers!
Your silver has become dross,
   your wine is mixed with water.
Your princes are rebels
   and companions of thieves.
Everyone loves a bribe
   and runs after gifts.
They do not defend the orphan,
   and the widow's cause does not come before them.

Therefore says the Sovereign, the LORD of hosts, the Mighty One of Israel:
Ah, I will pour out my wrath on my enemies,
   and avenge myself on my foes!
I will turn my hand against you;
   I will smelt away your dross as with lye
   and remove all your alloy.

And I will restore your judges as at the first,
    and your counselors as at the beginning.
Afterward you shall be called the city of righteousness,
    the faithful city.

Zion shall be redeemed by justice,
    and those in her who repent, by righteousness.
(1:21–27)

This brief précis traces the entire history of Jerusalem as it is to be lined out in what follows in the book. The entire book of Isaiah concerns YHWH's love-hate relationship with Jerusalem, a city punished by YHWH in anger and then (but not until then) loved to newness by this same YHWH.

IV

Critical study of the book of Isaiah characteristically attends to the details of specific texts that have arisen from many hands in many circumstances. Such critical study, however, offers an understanding of the book of Isaiah that is fragmented and piecemeal. As a consequence, the major and demanding interpretive issue of the book of Isaiah concerns the relationship of the parts to the intent of the whole. The parts show the community of Israel in a series of crises. The whole brings all of those parts into coherence in terms of YHWH's governance. When taken all together, it is clear that the gap between 39:5–8 and 40:1–11 is the pivot point between YHWH's judgment and YHWH's generous mercy. When taken in this way, we are able to see that the book of Isaiah is an unmistakable embodiment of Ronald Clements's thesis concerning the thematic shaping of prophetic books:

> In such fashion we can at least come to understand the value and meaning of the way in which distinctive patterns have been imposed upon the prophetic collections of the canon so that warnings of doom and disaster are always followed by promises of hope and restoration. . . .
> We must see that prophecy is a collection of collections, and that ultimately the final result in the prophetic corpus of the canon formed a recognizable unity not entirely dissimilar from that of the Pentateuch. As this was made up from various sources and collections, so also the Former and Latter Prophets, comprising the various preserved prophecies of a whole series of inspired individuals, acquired an overarching thematic unity. This centered on the death and rebirth of Israel, interpreted theologically as acts of divine judgment and salvation. (Clements 1977, 49, 53)

The relationship between *critical* attentiveness to the parts and *canonical* attentiveness to the whole constitutes a major interpretive opportunity. Having said that, we conclude by commenting on three texts that have exercised important influence on Christian interpretation of Jesus. As John Sawyer has made clear, the book of Isaiah has been an important biblical textual source for Christian interpretation (Sawyer 1996). It is for that reason important to notice the particular reinterpretive moves characteristically made in Christian interpretation:

1. The text of Isaiah 7:14 has been an indispensable basis for the New Testament assertion of the virgin birth of Jesus that has loomed so large in Christian tradition. The text of Isaiah 7:14 itself concerns Isaiah's word to King Ahaz in a particular political-military crisis. The prophet wants to communicate to the king that within two years (the time when the baby born to the "young woman" can tell right from wrong) the threat to Jerusalem from the north will pass. In context, the prophetic word has no particular interest in the young woman or in the mode of the birth of the child, but only in the age of the baby in order to indicate the passage of time. As is often noticed, the Hebrew term for "young woman" in the verse does not of itself indicate "virgin," so the text itself is not germane to the later theological claim of "virgin birth."

It is the case, however, that the Hebrew term *'almah* ("young woman") was rendered in the Greek translation (well before the Christian era) as *parthenos*, that is, "virgin." From that rendering it was an easy step for the Gospel of Matthew to take up the Greek version and reread the text with reference to Jesus and his birth from a "virgin." The move from the Old Testament to the New Testament via a Greek translation means that the text has taken on new, christological meanings that are nowhere present in the intent or on the horizon of the eighth-century prophet. As a consequence, the text has taken on a quite different second meaning that has served the church in powerful ways, but that stands at a distance from the Hebrew of the book of Isaiah. It is important to appreciate that the text is capable of a second meaning, but especially important to distinguish that second meaning from what is appropriately a first meaning in the crisis of King Ahaz. It is not necessary to deny the force of such a second meaning, but great confusion and mischief have been wrought by an uninformed propensity to merge these two quite different meanings into one, whereby doctrinal needs have blatantly overridden historical readings. By honoring such double meanings it becomes unnecessary (a) to have doctrinal readings that override historical meanings or, conversely, (b) to have historical readings that deny doctrinal meanings. The text is deep enough to carry both options, provided we are thoughtful and critical enough to host them both.

2. Isaiah 40:3–5 stands at the very beginning of Second Isaiah with its promise of return and restoration, just after the gap of destruction following 39:5–8. These verses in 40:3–5 are part of the initial act of poetic imagination whereby it is declared that Jerusalem has "served her term" of punishment (40:2). In order to move the imagination of Israel beyond exile in Babylon, the poet imagines a great triumphal procession home on a newly constructed road (already anticipated in 35:8–10). The procession led by the victorious YHWH who has just defeated the gods of Babylon is a procession out of exile and into well-being. The metaphor of procession bespeaks a complete reversal from suffering to well-being, from displacement to homecoming, a turn in historical circumstance effected by the powerful reality and intentionality of YHWH.

It is remarkable that this vision of homecoming is taken up as an introductory formula for all four Gospels in the New Testament (Matt 3:3; Mark 1:3; Luke 3:4–6; John 1:23). In each case the quotation is used to situate John the Baptizer as a forerunner of Jesus. By placing this text at the beginning of the gospel narrative, the tradition clearly interprets the coming of John and then of Jesus as a mighty reassertion of the rule (kingdom) of God who will lead God's people out of exile into well-being. Unquestionably Isaiah 40:3–5 did not have the New Testament figures in purview. In the reuse of the text in the New Testament, nonetheless, the church's testimony to Jesus attests Jesus as the one who will lead God's people safely to well-being. In that movement, moreover, all flesh will see the glory of YHWH disclosed in the person of Jesus.

3. The so-called Servant Song in Isaiah 52:13–53:12, as argued above, features Israel as the one who suffers and who saves through suffering. The identity of the servant, however, is covert and enigmatic enough to allow for another reading. This emancipated possibility of alternative interpretation was, not surprisingly, taken up by the early church, which found in the text an anticipation of Jesus (Acts 8:32–33): "The eunuch asked Philip, 'About whom, may I ask you, does the prophet say this, about himself or about someone else?' Then Philip began to speak, and starting with this scripture, he proclaimed to him the good news about Jesus" (Acts 8:34–35). The faith of the early church, here voiced through Philip, found the Servant Song to be an acceptable characterization of the person and vocation of Jesus. The early church exercised immense interpretive imagination and was able to make connections between the compelling reality of Jesus and the poetic openness of the Isaiah text. The resultant interpretive use of Isaiah 53 went well beyond what might have been intended in the historical articulation of the text.

All three of these texts, 7:14; 40:3–5; and 52:13–53:12, have particular meanings in historical context that are reasonably clear. In canonical usage, nonetheless, the text moves readily beyond such historical intentionality to make the illumination of Jesus that the early church found credible in terms of Jesus and available in terms of the book of Isaiah. Thus it is clear that in its canonical shape, and in its subsequent appropriation by the early church in the New Testament, the book of Isaiah is particularly generative of new waves of interpretation, each of which has been received in the interpretive community as a legitimate future from the text. It is clear that the text itself provides some of the impetus for such generativity, an impetus readily seized upon by the community of the continuing interpretive process. Even though the text itself is boldly venturesome in new meanings and even though the subsequent Christian community moved even further in new meanings, it is clear that on the whole the interpretive tradition has not moved far from the initial intentionality of the Isaiah tradition itself. That tradition is focused on YHWH's judgment against Jerusalem and against the people of Israel, and then on the restoration of Jerusalem and the reconstitution of the people of Israel as the people of covenant. This twofold tradition of judgment and promise appears in many modes in subsequent interpretation but continues with the fundamental conviction that the judgment and rescue of YHWH continually impinge upon the historical reality that is lived in the world over which YHWH the Creator presides.

17

The Book of Jeremiah

The book of Jeremiah is a multivoiced meditation of faith occasioned by the crisis of the destruction of Jerusalem in 587 BCE and the ensuing crises of deportation and loss (see Brueggemann 2002b). It is a book filled with deep feeling, primarily of grief and mourning, but also with hope for the future. The second book of the Latter Prophets is exceedingly complicated and multilayered, put together through a complex traditioning process.

The book is rooted in the utterance of the prophet Jeremiah in Jerusalem at the end of the seventh century (perhaps as early as 626 or perhaps as late as 609 BCE). There is little doubt that the book of Jeremiah, especially in chapters 1–20, contains the well-remembered poetic utterances of the prophet Jeremiah. It is evident that his poetic utterances were shaped, albeit in quite imaginative ways, as speeches of judgment that served to indict Jerusalem for its disobedience to YHWH's Torah and to sentence Jerusalem to the punishments that follow upon Torah disobedience. Expressed in rich imagery and venturesome metaphor, these prophetic oracles of judgment anticipate the destruction of Jerusalem in an enemy assault that is an enactment of the will of YHWH, who will not be mocked or disobeyed.

While the core of "prophetic lawsuit" is commonly shared among Israel's prophets in the eighth and seventh centuries, the poetic utterances of Jeremiah reflect a particular angle of vision. In terms of tradition, Jeremiah belongs to the Ephraimite (northern) tradition, for whom Hosea is an antecedent, a tradition that claims to reach back into Mosaic tradition:

> Jeremiah's links with the Ephraimite tradition are apparent not only in his language and theology but also in his concept of his prophetic role. A number of scholars have pointed out that in the prophet's call he was not simply appointed as a prophet but he was specifically

designated a *Mosaic* prophet. In reply to Jeremiah's objection to Yahweh's original call, God touches the prophet's lips and declares, "I have put my words in your mouth" (Jer 1:9). This phrase is almost identical to the one used in Deut 18:18, where Yahweh says of the promised Mosaic prophet, "I will put my words in his mouth." As a Mosaic prophet, Jeremiah is told to speak only the divine word that God gives: "Whatever I command you, you shall speak" (Jer 1:7); "say to them everything that I command you" (Jer 1:17). Similar instructions were also given to Moses and his prophetic successors: "He shall speak to them all that I command him" (Deut 18:18). It is, of course, impossible to know whether Jeremiah actually quoted the words of Deuteronomy in describing his call or whether the quotations were added by later editors in the Jeremiah tradition. In either case, the call narrative places the prophet clearly in the distinctive Ephraimite prophetic tradition. As a Mosaic prophet, he is to speak the pure word of God to the people, who are required to obey the word that comes through such a prophet. (R. Wilson 1980, 237)

We may, however, be more specific about the rootage of the prophet Jeremiah. He is identified as being "of the priests in Anathoth in the land of Benjamin" (1:2). That particular pedigree refers us back to 1 Kings 2:26–27, where Abiathar the priest is banished by King Solomon back to his village of Anathoth (see 1 Sam 22:20–23). The linkage of Jeremiah to the banishment of Abiathar—both rooted in the village of Anathoth—suggests that Jeremiah's home base and theological perspective is as an outsider to the royal reality of Judaism. He is thus capable of sharp and elemental critique of the monarchial establishment, perhaps not untinged by long generations of resentful brooding since the expulsion of the ancestor Abiathar in the long-ago time of Solomon. In any case, Jeremiah positions himself to utter the "words" when "the word of the LORD" is given to him (1:2), words anticipating the end of the royal-temple establishment in Jerusalem.

I

In the long poetic section of Jeremiah 1–20, we may notice in particular two clusters of texts. First, in chapters 4–6, a series of poems anticipate that Jerusalem will be assaulted by an ominous foreign invader who remains unnamed in the text. Older scholarship called these poems the "Scythian Songs," because it was assumed that the invading force was the Scythians known to us from the Greek historian Herodotus. Readers will find such a designation in the older critical studies. That identification is surely not correct; it is, rather, crucial that the poetic articulation of threat sustains its ominous overtone precisely by remaining elusive and not naming the invader:

I am going to bring upon you
 a nation from far away, O house of Israel,
says the LORD.
It is an enduring nation,
 it is an ancient nation,
a nation whose language you do not know,
 nor can you understand what they say.
Their quiver is like an open tomb;
 all of them are mighty warriors.
They shall eat up your harvest and your food;
 they shall eat up your sons and your daughters;
they shall eat up your flocks and your herds;
 they shall eat up your vines and your fig trees;
they shall destroy with the sword
 your fortified cities in which you trust.
(5:15–17)

Thus says the LORD:
See, a people is coming from the land of the north,
 a great nation is stirring from the farthest parts of the earth.
They grasp the bow and the javelin,
 they are cruel and have no mercy,
 their sound is like the roaring sea;
they ride on horses,
 equipped like a warrior for battle,
 against you, O daughter Zion!
(6:22–23)

As the book of Jeremiah evolves, after 20:1–6, it is clear that the invader is Babylon (Hill 1999). But to name the invader too soon is to dissipate the taut intention of the text. The point of this poetry is to voice the concrete way in which YHWH's harsh purpose is eventuated in the real world of the nations, a connection between *YHWH's purpose* and *worldly power* made precisely through poetic, prophetic utterance.

Second, in chapters 11–20, scholars have located a series of texts (11:18–12:6; 15:10–21; 17:14–18; 18:18–23; 20:7–13, 14–18) in which the poet engages in prayer to YHWH as an intimate, combative exchange (O'Connor 1988; Diamond 1987). These poems are patterned after conventional laments known in the book of Psalms, but they seem peculiarly poignant in the vexed circumstance of the prophet. These poems may perhaps be understood as personal articulations of faith when the prophet discovers that his prophetic assignment from YHWH is more than he can bear. Or it may be that these lamentations, though cast as quite personal in a first-person voice, are utilized to express the communal grief of Judah at its suffering and dismay in the face of historical threat. Either way, these poems are deeply moving articulations of grief and consternation that are brought to speech in powerful ways. (This collection of poems established the identity of Jeremiah as the one who laments, an identification that led belatedly to the tradition that Jeremiah is the author of the book of Lamentations; these poems in chaps. 11–20 are popularly termed the "Lamentations of Jeremiah.")

> ### Midrashic Moment: Jeremiah 4:23–27
>
> This passage offers a bleak vision of the undoing of God's creation, explicitly referencing Genesis 1 (and anticipating Job's even more radical curse in Job 3). About verse 25, "I see, and look, there is no human left, and all the birds of the sky have fled," the Holocaust survivor, author, and Nobel laureate Elie Wiesel (1981, 126) writes: "As for the birds of the sky that have fled, I understood the prophet's imagery only when I returned to Auschwitz and Birkenau in the summer of 1979. Then and only then did I remember that, during the tempest of fire and silence, there were no birds to be seen on the horizon: they had fled the skies above all the death-camps. I stood in Birkenau and remembered Jeremiah."

There is no doubt in critical study that in the book of Jeremiah we have poetic utterance from the person of Jeremiah. There also is no doubt, however, that we do not have direct and immediate access to the person of Jeremiah, because whatever may have been the produce of that person has now been refracted through a vigorous and sustained traditioning process (Brueggemann 1987). Thus attention must be turned from the *person* of Jeremiah (to whom we have no access) to the *book* of Jeremiah, which is, in its final form, our proper subject of study. That vigorous and sustained editorial process has effectively transposed what has been retained of the person of Jeremiah into the book of Jeremiah. It is a long-held view of scholarship that that traditioning has been accomplished by advocates of Deuteronomic theology, that is, interpreters committed to the Torah theology of the book of Deuteronomy who are intimately connected to (or perhaps identified with) the Deuteronomic historians of the books of Joshua, Judges, Samuel, and Kings.

II

The relationship of the *poetic oracles* in the book of Jeremiah (judged to be from the person of Jeremiah) and the *prose* (acutely marked by Deuteronomic assumption and vocabulary) is a difficult question in Jeremiah studies. A conservative scholarly view is that the prose sections are only another version of the same and so authentically reflect the prophet (Holladay 1986–1989). A more radical view is that the prose is an imposition of a very different theology that came later and was perhaps intended to serve the community that had experienced the first Babylonian deportation in 598 (see 2 Kgs 24:10–17), or perhaps had even survived the second and major deportation of 587 (Carroll 1986). Either way, as Louis Stulman has shown, the prose Deuteronomic materials have been strategically placed to give shape to the whole. We may particularly mention five such strategically placed materials (Stulman 1998):

1. The "call of Jeremiah" in 1:4–10 may perhaps be Deuteronomic. If so, then its purpose is to assert the themes of 1:10:

> See, today I appoint you over nations and over kingdoms,
> to pluck up and to pull down,
> to destroy and to overthrow,
> to build and to plant.

With this approach, the book is to exhibit the way in which the prophet is (a) "to pluck up and to pull down" into exile and (b) "to build and to plant" out of exile, thus a theological shaping of *judgment* and *restoration* that is an influence on the final form of the book of Jeremiah as it is in much of the prophetic literature. We do well to recall again Clements's estimate of this editorial achievement that imposed a particular theological pattern on many prophetic traditions:

> In such fashion we can at least come to understand the value and meaning of the way in which distinctive patterns have been imposed upon the prophetic collections of the canon so that warnings of doom and disaster are always followed by promises of hope and restoration. . . .
>
> We must see that prophecy is a collection of collections, and that ultimately the final result in the prophetic corpus of the canon formed a recognizable unity not entirely dissimilar from that of the Pentateuch. As this was made up from various sources and collections, so also the Former and Latter Prophets, comprising the various preserved prophecies of a whole series of inspired individuals, acquired an overarching thematic unity. This centered on the death and rebirth of Israel, interpreted theologically as acts of divine judgment and salvation. (Clements 1977, 49, 53)

2. The text of 7:1–8:3, commonly termed the "Temple Sermon," places Jeremiah in a public place summoning Judah to "amend" its ways according to Torah requirements (vv. 3–7), and threatening Jerusalem with destruction and extinction (like the ancient shrine of Shiloh) if it does not repent (vv. 13–15). The call to repent is characteristic of Deuteronomic theology, except that in the latter verses the time for repentance seems past. In any case, the sermon constitutes a frontal assault on the claims and pretensions of the temple apparatus.

3. In the chapter 11 narrative the prophet is presented as a vigorous public advocate for "this covenant," presumably the Torah covenant of the

Deuteronomic tradition (v. 2). Jeremiah's preaching of "this covenant" is at the same time a vigorous summons to "obey" (the Hebrew word is *šemaʿ*, which also means "hear") reflecting Deuteronomy (vv. 4, 5, 7) and a harsh condemnation for Israel's failure to listen (v. 8). Thus the appeal to repent is stated along with a recognition that it is too late for repentance. This agile juxtaposition contributes to the ominous tone of the whole; it also permits a glance to the future, when repentance may yet open a new possibility.

4. Chapter 26 reports Jeremiah's trial as an enemy of the Jerusalem establishment, apparently with direct reference to the sermon of chapter 7. Jeremiah is condemned to death by religious leaders (v. 11), but continues, in the face of his conviction, to be relentless concerning the urgency of repentance (v. 13). In the end, Jeremiah is rescued from the death sentence by appeal to an earlier prophetic precedent (26:18 and the citation of Mic 3:12).

5. Chapter 36 purports to describe the way in which the scroll (book) of Jeremiah was written. According to this narrative, the scroll was made public through Baruch, Jeremiah's friend and secretary (v. 10); received by Jerusalem officialdom (vv. 11–19); read and destroyed by the king, who resisted the scroll (vv. 20–27); but then reiterated in a new, expanded version (v. 32): "Then Jeremiah took another scroll and gave it to the secretary Baruch son of Neriah, who wrote on it at Jeremiah's dictation all the words of the scroll that King Jehoiakim of Judah had burned in the fire; and many similar words were added to them." It is clear that the scroll, in its completed Deuteronomic form, stood as a powerful challenge and, therefore, threat to royal Jerusalem, a challenge and threat that might be rooted in the old priestly tradition of Abiathar of Anathoth, who stood over against the self-aggrandizing monarchy. (Other prose texts connected to these include 18:1–12 and chap. 24.)

If we ask more specifically about the circle of traditionists who fostered the scroll, we may notice that in 26:24 it is a son of Shaphan who protected the prophet, and in chapter 36 powerful officials, also connected to Shaphan, urged Jeremiah and Baruch to hide from the threat of the state (v. 19), an urging tersely enacted in verse 26. In 2 Kings 22:8–14, moreover, there is yet another mention of Shaphan in connection with the scroll. While there is a lack of clarity about the identity of Shaphan (perhaps there are several men of that name), it is clear that in Jerusalem a cadre of powerful officials were sympathetic to Jeremiah's assault on the monarchy, and themselves represented a loyal opposition to the king inside the royal government. It is likely that Jeremiah, in the name of YHWH, became a spokesperson for that opinion and received surreptitious support from those in the hazardous enterprise of exposing and opposing the foolish policies of the king. It is also plausible that in this cadre of advocates may be found the scribes who edited the traditional words of Jeremiah into the book of Jeremiah. Thus a variety of data suggest that the book of Jeremiah, rooted in the words of Jeremiah, became a vehicle and rallying form for Torah-based policies that stood in profound opposition to royal policies in Jerusalem. If the several data permit such a conclusion, then we are able to see that at least some parts of the book of Jeremiah are an intensely subversive element in the crisis of Jerusalem.

If we understand that opposition to royal policy, we may see that it is theologically based as "the word of the LORD." Such opposition, however, also has immediate political force—this tradition asserts that it is the will of YHWH that Jerusalem should surrender to Babylon, and this against royal policy that was determined (hopelessly determined) to resist Babylon. (On a proposed policy of submission and surrender to Babylon, see 21:3–10; 27:4–8; 37:9–10, 17; 38:2–4, 17–23.) It is important to recognize that prophetic urging, while deeply rooted theologically, characteristically (and certainly here) concerns real and dangerous policy decisions that have real and dangerous concrete consequences. Thus the dispute between the prophetic visions of Jeremiah and Hananiah in chapter 28 is about the most urgent question of the day. The Jeremiah-Shaphan advocacy is one that urged, "Better to be Red than dead"—better to submit to the empire than to be destroyed by the empire. It is as though this tradition in loyal opposition to monarchy takes a very long view of political history, and can imagine the restoration of Jerusalem in radically new form, assured that Babylonian victory is not termination for Jerusalem. The traditioning process, with its immense theological passion and political courage, found the tradition of Jeremiah a most important voice for a subversive alternative in Jerusalem.

The remainder of the book after the poetry of Jeremiah (chaps. 1–20) and after the several prose imperatives begins to look beyond the destruction of the city (which is now an accomplished reality), and certainly beyond the horizon of the lifetime of the person of Jeremiah. Thus the book of Jeremiah moves on to new circumstance, new issues, and new possibilities that William McKane terms "a rolling *corpus*" (McKane 1986, l). The ongoing tradition serves to vindicate Jeremiah, for the "plucking up and pulling down" did happen. That reality, however, left the question, What now, if anything? What can be said of the future?

III

As the corpus of the book of Jeremiah "rolls" on past 587 and into deportation (on which see chap. 24), we may identify four literary forays into the future that constitute the remainder of the book.

1. Most scholars take chapters 37–45 as a sustained historical narrative that tells of the final days before the destruction of 587 and of the anarchic time after that date. There is a scholarly tradition that this material was written by Baruch. While that may not be so, it is clear that the narrative reflects an emerging *scribal vision* for which Baruch is a convenient representation.

This narrative tells of the final, failed days of the last, pitiful king in Jerusalem, Zedekiah (chaps. 37–39), and of the abuse heaped upon Jeremiah, who was perceived as a traitor (see 38:4). Beyond that, the narrative tells of the fall of the city at the hands of the Babylonians, and of the appointment of Gedaliah—grandson of Shaphan!—as Babylonian governor as part of an interim arrangement for the victorious empire after the failure of kingship. Gedaliah's appointment reflects imperial recognition that the clique of officials around Shaphan are pro-Babylonian, a clique of officials no doubt viewed by others in Jerusalem as accommodators who sold out to the empire and who now, in this appointment, reap personal advantage of wealth and power for their political sellout. Consequently, the accommodator, Gedaliah, is assassinated by the proponents of a revived monarchy who were never persuaded of Jeremiah's proposal of surrender (41:1–3). Thus the narrative concerns a first attempt at an organized future after the fall of the monarchy that failed completely.

We may notice that in the brief narrative of chapter 45 Baruch is commended for his faithfulness to Jeremiah and to Jeremiah's vision, and so receives his life "as a prize of war" (v. 5). This brief note may suggest that Baruch—and his scribal ilk—are the wave of the future, the ones who will reconstitute Jerusalem as a scribal community in the face of imperial hegemony, Babylonian or Persian. This long narrative of chapters 37–45 thus culminates in a quite modest image of Israel's future in the real world of the nations, in the midst of which Israel is profoundly vulnerable.

It is entirely possible that these words in chapter 45 at some point constituted the end of the book of Jeremiah, for, as we shall see, some traditions locate chapters 46–51 in the midst of chapter 25, thus removing them from the end of the book. Such a scenario would suggest that the book of Jeremiah ended with a reference to the faithful scribal remnant as the future of Judaism. In that scenario, Baruch is a metaphor for the scribes, that is, the bookmen and scroll makers who will reconstitute Judaism as the scroll people par excellence.

2. A second scenario about the future is found in the oracles against the nations in chapters 46–51. While this material is highly stylized and seems almost extraneous to the book of Jeremiah, in the final form of the book these chapters no doubt are connected to Jeremiah's call to be a prophet to the nations (1:10). In its final form, the book of Jeremiah is preoccupied with the rise and fall of the nations, the decisive sovereignty of YHWH, and the outcome of such sovereignty for the future of Israel.

While this entire corpus of chapters 46–51 may be quite stylized, it is of immense importance that the corpus culminates in a long unit concerning the fall of Babylon, the empire that has preoccupied the tradition (Bellis 1995):

> Declare among the nations and proclaim,
>   set up a banner and proclaim,
>   do not conceal it, say:
> Babylon is taken,
>   Bel is put to shame,
>   Merodach is dismayed.
> Her images are put to shame,
>   her idols are dismayed.
>
> For out of the north a nation has come up against her; it shall make her land a desolation, and no one shall live in it; both human beings and animals shall flee away. (Jer 50:2–3)

The lyrical celebration of the anticipated demise of Babylon at the hands of YHWH becomes the culmination of the book of Jeremiah. How far we have come in the "rolling corpus" from Jeremiah's hard words against Jerusalem! Now the word of the prophetic tradition is good news for Jerusalem and for Israel. Babylon had been YHWH's useful tool in the termination of disobedient Jerusalem. As such, Nebuchadnezzar, king of Babylon, has been "servant of YHWH" (25:9; 27:6). But neither Nebuchadnezzar nor Babylon is a permanent ally of YHWH. In the end, YHWH moves against arrogant Babylon in a way that makes a new future open for Israel (a new future imagined in the poetry of Second Isaiah).

The oracles against the nations culminating in the demise of Babylon have as their climactic statement the brief narrative of 51:59–64. This remarkable narrative might well have been the ending of the book of Jeremiah at one time, as indicated in the final words of verse 64. In such a reckoning, the decisive defeat and fall of Babylon is the final word that needs to be spoken: "Thus shall Babylon sink, to rise no more, because of the disasters that I am bringing on her" (51:64a). The fall of Babylon implies the release, homecoming, and restoration of Jerusalem, that is, the "planting and building" that negates the "plucking up and pulling down" of Jerusalem that YHWH has accomplished through Nebuchadnezzar.

This narrative reports one of Jeremiah's characteristic acted parables or symbolic actions. In such symbolization, the thing done symbolically is done effectively. Thus the sinking of the scroll into the Euphrates River is the effective sinking of the empire in the imaginative vista of prophetic action. Further, this entire symbolic-effective act of sinking scroll and empire is accomplished by Seraiah of the scribal family of Baruch; it is a scroll that signifies the ending, and the scroll is the trademark of scribal reality. This remarkable convergence of features suggests that in the corpus of Jeremiah, a corpus developed through Deuteronomic-scribal activity, it is the scribe who is championed as the conqueror of the empire, the scribe who survives— scroll in hand—to live another day and to accomplish the future of which the prophet had spoken. Thus the oracles against the nations are a mighty victory of YHWH that makes room for Israel's new future:

> I will restore Israel to its pasture, and it shall feed on Carmel and in Bashan, and on the hills of Ephraim and in Gilead its hunger shall be satisfied. In those days and at that time, says the LORD, the iniquity of Israel shall be sought, and there shall be none; and the sins of Judah, and none shall be found; for I will pardon the remnant that I have spared. (50:19–20)

It is worth noting that in a scenario wherein Jeremiah 45 ends the book of Jeremiah and in a scenario wherein 51:64 ends the book of Jeremiah, both versions bespeak a scribal future, in one case represented by Baruch, in the other by Seraiah and his scroll. Either way, the completed book of Jeremiah recognizes and anticipates that the restored Judaism will take on a wholly new form, a form brought to fruition by the scribe Ezra (see the book of Ezra).

3. Chapters 30–33, anticipated by 29:10–14, constitute yet another way into the future in the tradition of Jeremiah. The traditioning process has gathered in these chapters most of the explicit promises in the Jeremiah tradition. In 29:10–14 we are offered a prose anticipation that clearly assumes an exilic context. The most important promises are gathered in chapters 30–31, commonly referred to by scholars as the "Book of Comfort," nomenclature appealing to the reference to the "book" in 30:2. In a variety of rich promises the tradition moves beyond prophetic speeches of judgment and beyond Deuteronomic imperatives to repentance, and anticipates a wholly new action of YHWH that unilaterally, graciously, and without restraint restores Israel to land and to well-being.

These two most powerful chapters are reinforced by the narrative of Jeremiah 32 wherein the prophet is said to invest in the future in a concrete real estate transaction, an action linked to deep and sure promises of future well-being in the land:

> For thus says the LORD of hosts, the God of Israel: Houses and fields and vineyards shall again be bought in this land. (32:15)

> Fields shall be bought for money, and deeds shall be signed and sealed and witnessed, in the land of Benjamin, in the places around Jerusalem, and in the cities of Judah, of the hill country, of the Shephelah,

and of the Negeb; for I will restore their fortunes, says the Lord.
(32:44)

The finished tradition is unambiguously certain that deportation and displacement are not the last word for Israel. This certitude, moreover, is sec-
onded by the collection of brief promise oracles in chapter 33. In all these
variations, the leitmotif is "restore the fortunes" (29:14; 30:18; 32:44; 33:7,
11, 26). This repeated formula reiterates the foundational conviction of the
completed tradition that an act of YHWH's sovereignty will reestablish
the people of Israel as God's own people in their own secure land. Although
the texture of this promise in the book of Jeremiah is very different from the
ideological force of the land claim in the book of Joshua, and the contexts are
different, readers will want to note that the claim is fundamentally the same:
God's people are assured by God of well-being *in the land.*

4. Chapter 25 stands alone in the center of the book of Jeremiah as perhaps
the most remarkable anticipation of the future in the entire tradition. The
first part of the chapter is a conventional prose bid for repentance (v. 5) and
a conventional anticipation of the conquest of Jerusalem by Nebuchadnezzar
(vv. 8–11). But then the prose takes a fresh direction and looks beyond Babylon hegemony to Babylonian termination:

> Then after seventy years are completed, I will punish the king of
> Babylon and that nation, the land of the Chaldeans, for their iniquity,
> says the Lord, making the land an everlasting waste. I will bring upon
> that land all the words that I have uttered against it, everything writ-
> ten in this book, which Jeremiah prophesied against all the nations.
> (25:12–13)

This anticipation of YHWH's wrath upon "many nations and great kings"
(v. 14) unleashes the remarkable vision of world judgment in verses 15–29
wherein the tradition of Jeremiah moves in the direction of the sweeping
radicality of apocalyptic. It is important to notice that in the Greek tradition of the book of Jeremiah, the entire cluster of oracles against the nations
in chapters 46–51 is inserted here, thus removing those oracles from the
end of the book, as noted above. The practical effect is to line out concretely the prophetic mandate of 1:10 wherein YHWH's fierce rule over
all the nations is accomplished. The culminating oracle of chapter 25 is as
though the ferocious imagination of the tradition has unleashed its deep
resentment about the vulnerability and suffering of little Israel and coupled
that deep resentment to a sure conviction about YHWH's power and fidelity. This may be the ultimate statement of the Jeremiah tradition, a statement that envisions in boldest fashion YHWH's rule of all nations, before
whom Nebuchadnezzar's readily observed hegemony is made pitifully and

trivially penultimate. This grand vision given by the one made "prophet to the nations" is a sweeping vision characteristic of apocalyptic interpretation, a vision closely and necessarily paralleled with a christological addendum in Revelation 11:15:

> Then the seventh angel blew his trumpet, and there were loud voices in heaven, saying,
>
> "The kingdom of the world has become the kingdom of our Lord
>   and of his Messiah,
> and he will reign forever and ever."

The final notice of hope in the Jeremiah tradition that we will mention here is 52:31–34, a passage closely parallel to and likely appropriated from 2 Kings 25:27–30. In our earlier discussion of 2 Kings 25:27–30, we noted that the passage is deeply and perhaps intentionally ambiguous, affirming the present survival of the Davidic heir, but claiming nothing beyond that.

It is worth noting that in what is surely an earlier poetic utterance, the Jeremiah tradition had anticipated and acknowledged the sorry end of Jehoiachin and with him the royal line:

> Is this man Coniah a despised broken pot,
>   a vessel no one wants?
> Why are he and his offspring hurled out
>   and cast away in a land that they do not know?
> O land, land, land,
>   hear the word of the LORD!
> Thus says the LORD:
> Record this man as childless,
>   a man who shall not succeed in his days;
> for none of his offspring shall succeed
>   in sitting on the throne of David,
>   and ruling again in Judah.
>   (Jer 22:28–30)

But then in 33:14–16, 17, 19–22, and 23–26 the tradition affirms the durability of the Davidic line. When we consider 52:31–34 in light of all these texts, it is clear that there was no consensus in the community about the future of the monarchy. In the ending of the book of Jeremiah as we have it, the future of the monarchy is open, continuation possible but not assured. This potential royal future is surely in important tension with the apocalyptic assertion of chapter 25 that depends upon no royal institution and with the scribal ending of 45:5 or 51:64. It is clear that the makers of the book of Jeremiah did not know the way ahead. It is equally clear, however, that they did not doubt that there was a way ahead. Thus the book of Jeremiah "rolls" toward the future that is in detail completely inchoate but as sure as the God who "plants and builds."

Christian readers will want to pay particular attention to one passage, 31:31–34, the promise of the new covenant. In conventional Christian reading, the new covenant is understood as the covenant God makes through Christ, a claim that seems supported by the fact that in the Old Latin translation, "covenant" is translated *testamentum* (testament), thus the "New Testament." This reading is reinforced by appeal to the Jeremiah text in Hebrews 8. After quoting the text in verses 8–12, the Christian writer adds: "In speaking of 'a new covenant,' he has made the first one obsolete. And what is obsolete and growing old will soon disappear" (Heb 8:13). This dismissive judgment of the new covenant promised to Israel thus enshrines in the New Testament a piece of unembarrassed supersessionism that affirms that the Christian faith—faith in Christ—has superseded Judaism and made Judaism "obsolete." Such a reading is of long-standing authority and influence in the Christian tradition. The text in Hebrews 8 is part of the polemic against Judaism that is increasingly recognized in contemporary interpretation to be deeply problematic (Soulen 1996).

In the case of Jeremiah 31:31–34, it is clear that such a supersessionist reading is an astonishing misreading, for the "new covenant" is precisely "with the house of Israel and with the house of Judah," and with none other. There are, to be sure, complex issues concerning theological claims of Judaism and Christianity, as recognized in all their complexity in the argument of Paul in Romans 9–11. Given Paul's alertness to the complexity of the question, it is important for Christian reading of the text to recognize that the supersessionist claim of the New Testament made in Hebrews 8 is a misreading of the new covenant passage, for the text in Jeremiah 31:31–34 looks not to a displacement of Judaism but to a reconstitution of Judaism in a mode of glad obedience to the God of the Torah.

Because of a long history of conventional supersessionism, it is clear that Christians have a great deal of unlearning to do with reference to this text. Attention should be paid in particular to the study by Norbert Lohfink, nicely titled *The Covenant Never Revoked* (1991). Lohfink's work, informed and supported by the new teaching in the Vatican, critiques the old practice of supersessionist interpretation and asserts that the covenant God has made with Israel is in effect and not revoked, not displaced in Christ:

> I lean therefore to a one-covenant theory, which however embraces Jews and Christians, whatever their differences in the one covenant, and that means Jews and Christians of today. This is "ecumenism" at its most basic, to introduce the word so often used today. One is thus very close to the biblical view, for all the variety of biblical language, especially in the matter of "covenant." (Lohfink 1991, 84)

While making a claim for the community of Christ as God's people, Christian readers will need to reflect much more on the way in which Jews also continue to be YHWH's covenant people. Such a study lies well beyond a critical introduction to the book of Jeremiah. Clearly, nonetheless, the issue of "Jew and Christian" is deeply linked to the horizon of the future with which the book of Jeremiah is complexly preoccupied. It is remarkable that after the poignant prophetic oracles of the book of Jeremiah looking to the judgment of 587, the late development of the book moves readily beyond the catastrophe to new possibilities. The book, in its final form, is not very clear about the future. It was and is clear, nonetheless, that YHWH, the durable, persistent force in Israel's horizon, is the durable, persistent force who will prevail when all other forms of rule are exhausted. Because of YHWH's durability, the future is opened and awaits embrace. That much the book of Jeremiah knows, though it struggles and disputes about how to speak that future (Seitz 1989). The book of Jeremiah has options about the future:

> the scribal remnant (45:5)
> the sinking of Babylon at scribal hands (51:64)
> the new planting and building by God (chaps. 30–33)
> the large sovereignty of YHWH in apocalyptic mode (chap. 25)
> the ambiguous awareness of a surviving king (52:31–34)

It is easy enough to see concretely the "plucking up and pulling down" that has come upon Jerusalem. "Building and planting" are sure but not easily observed, and so receive and generate more tentative, multivoiced articulation.

18

The Book of Ezekiel

Like the books of Isaiah and Jeremiah that precede it in the canon of the Latter Prophets, the book of Ezekiel is concerned with the crisis of 587 BCE in
Jerusalem and the consequent season of deep displacement and disarray in the
exile. Thus the three great prophetic books (a) share a focus on this *crisis*, (b)
refer the crisis to the defining reality of *YHWH*, and (c) construe the crisis as
one of YHWH's *judgment* that produces the crisis and YHWH's *fidelity* that
makes possible a hope for the future of Israel beyond exile.

With the commonality noted, however, Christian readers of the book of
Ezekiel are likely to find the articulations of the book at least unfamiliar, if not
peculiar and difficult to follow. There is no doubt that the book of Ezekiel is
cast in a mode that is foreign to most contemporary readers, certainly most
contemporary Christian readers. And if the book of Ezekiel casts common
themes in uncommon modes, the outcome is that the book voices a quite
distinctive sense of Israel's faith in crisis.

In part, that distinctiveness may be because of the traumatic events that
provide the context for the book, for all familiar stabilities in the life of the
community are taken away. In part, that radical distinctiveness may be related
to the peculiar personality of Ezekiel, and a great deal of study has been
devoted to what appears to be his peculiar or disordered personality:

> Not surprisingly, Ezekiel has been the subject of numerous psycho-
> analytical studies. While prophets were known often to act and speak
> erratically for rhetorical purposes, Ezekiel is in a class of his own. The
> concentration of so many bizarre features in one individual is with-
> out precedent: his muteness; lying bound and naked; digging holes
> in the walls of houses; emotional paralysis in the face of his wife's
> death; "spiritual" travels; images of strange creatures, of eyes, and of

creeping things; hearing voices and the sounds of water; withdrawal symptoms; fascination with feces and blood; wild literary imagination; pornographic imagery; unreal if not surreal understanding of Israel's past; and the list goes on. It is no wonder that Karl Jaspers found in Ezekiel an unequalled case for psychological analysis. E. C. Broome concluded that Ezekiel was a true psychotic, capable of great religious insight but exhibiting a series of diagnostic characteristics: catatonia, narcissistic-masochistic conflict, schizophrenic withdrawal, delusions of grandeur and of persecution. In short, he suffered from a paranoid condition common in many great spiritual leaders.

This psychoanalytic approach has been rejected by commentators and psychiatrists alike. (Block 1997, 10)

In the end, however, we may judge that the distinctiveness of this prophetic articulation is rooted in the particular locus of Ezekiel and his traditionists in an identifiable interpretive tradition, that of the Priestly tradition that we have already considered concerning the Torah. That tradition interpreted the faith of Israel through a preoccupation with YHWH's holiness and with the *crisis of presence* when this Holy God could no longer be present in the midst of an impure, profane people. These concerns are not unknown in the traditions of Isaiah and Jeremiah, but they are not the focus there as they are here in the book of Ezekiel.

Given the crisis of presence, we may see that the book of Ezekiel is almost systematically arranged in two parts. The first part, chapters 1–24, concerns *impending judgment* upon Jerusalem; and the second part, chapters 25–48, concerns *anticipated restoration* for Jerusalem. To be sure, the development of these two themes is not a simple, neat package, because there are variations of genre and of accent; the reader nonetheless will do well to begin with the awareness of a twofold message of judgment and hope.

I

The first half of the book (chaps. 1–24) begins in chapters 1–3 with an enigmatic vision that eventuates in Ezekiel's call to be a prophet. This initiating confrontation with YHWH is located "in the land of the Chaldeans by the river Chebar" (1:3), that is, among the exiles. The encounter is situated, moreover, in "the fifth year of the exile of King Jehoiachin" (1:2), that is, in 593 BCE. These data indicate that Ezekiel was among the exiles of the first deportation of 598 (see 2 Kgs 24:10–17; Jer 24:1–10; 52:28), and that he addressed that population of deported people with his radical pastoral concern (as did Jeremiah in chaps. 24 and 29). The initial vision of God reported in chapter 1 is exceedingly enigmatic. Very likely it intends to testify to the mobility of YHWH, who is not confined to the Jerusalem temple but can come and go in a way that permits YHWH's presence even among exiles in a foreign and impure land. It is evident that Ezekiel is preoccupied with the problem of divine presence in Israel, a concern resolved in 1:28 and 3:23 with an appearance "like the glory," thus echoing a Priestly theme resolved in Exodus 40:34. This initial encounter, however, does not dwell excessively on divine presence, but focuses upon the call of Ezekiel, the mandate to "eat this scroll" (3:1) and to be a "sentinel for the house of Israel" (3:16–21). Thus the effect of the opening chapters is to authorize and dispatch this odd voice of testimony in Israel in its profound crisis.

The call of chapters 1–3 is followed by chapters 4–10, which exhibit the theme of judgment as the primary theme of the first half of the book. Chapters 4–6 report on the prophet's peculiar actions that bespeak impending judgment on Jerusalem; chapter 8 characterizes the "abomination" that has been committed in the temple of Jerusalem that must evoke YHWH's wrath and, subsequently, YHWH's absence. It is characteristic that the affront to YHWH in this Priestly tradition is a violation of the holiness of the temple; that is, the horizon of Ezekiel is singularly sacerdotal. The upshot of these narratives of denunciation is that in chapter 9 the idolaters are marked for destruction because they have committed "abominations," and in 10:15–19 the prophet envisions the glory of YHWH—the sign of YHWH's temple presence—departing from the temple, making it a place of absence:

> Then the glory of the LORD went out from the threshold of the house and stopped above the cherubim. The cherubim lifted up their wings and rose up from the earth in my sight as they went out with the

---

Midrashic Moment: Ezekiel and Poetic Tradition

Ezekiel is famous for his extravagant visions, and becomes a sort of patron saint for visionary poets as a result, including John Milton and William Blake (who claimed to have dined with Ezekiel and Isaiah). In the opening stanzas of T. S. Eliot's long poem *The Wasteland*, the speaker alludes to Ezekiel's call narrative, when God commands the cowering prophet, "Son of man, stand upon thy feet, and I will speak unto thee" (2:1): "What are the roots that clutch, what branches grow / Out of this stony rubbish? Son of man, / You cannot say, or guess, for you know only / A heap of broken images. . . ." *The Wasteland* is often thought to be the quintessential *modern* poem, representing a radical break with tradition, which makes it even more striking for the poet to draw on Ezekiel. But if the past is envisioned in *The Wasteland* as rubble, either real or symbolic, Ezekiel is a natural choice for a poetic predecessor, living as he did through the destruction of Jerusalem and of the temple and presenting a clear-eyed vision of it, while nevertheless holding out hope for a future restoration.

> wheels beside them. They stopped at the entrance of the east gate of the house of the LORD; and the glory of the God of Israel was above them. (10:18–19)

The material that follows in chapters 11–24 is characteristically a reiteration of condemnation of abominable Israel and the harsh judgment that must follow from such affrontive disobedience to YHWH. We may in particular note the following:

1. In chapter 13 the prophet delivers a harsh condemnation against prophets who "whitewash" reality and falsely proclaim "Peace" (*shalom*) over the city of Jerusalem (13:10). This indictment is reminiscent of the strictures of Jeremiah against false assurances (Jer 6:13–15; 8:10–12; 23:9–22; 28:1–17). It is most likely that these false prophets were those who believed that Jerusalem was inviolate because of YHWH's promises and presence, thus reflecting a high Zion theology. It is remarkable that Ezekiel, so inured in the categories of temple theology, should reject such a high claim for the temple. He does so, clearly enough, because he senses that YHWH's sovereignty, of which he has a very sweeping sense, cannot be reduced to or contained in the temple.

2. Ezekiel 22:23–31 is a characteristic indictment against all of the leadership of Judah, a failed leadership—princes, priests, officials, prophets, people of the land—that has brought corruption and pollution upon the land in a way that will cause YHWH's indignant absence from the land. The critique is sweeping and wholesale. We single out for attention, however, the particular indictment of the priests: "Its priests have done violence to my teaching and have profaned my holy things; they have made no distinction between the holy and the common, neither have they taught the difference between the unclean and the clean, and they have disregarded my sabbaths, so that I am profaned among them" (22:26).

This particular condemnation reflects Ezekiel's priestly horizon, for in such a horizon it is precisely mixing what must be kept apart that causes confusion and therefore threat. The function of such priests, according to this teaching, is to protect holy things, for the maintenance of holy things makes possible the abiding presence of YHWH. This vigilant sorting out and maintenance of distinctions is a primary preoccupation of the Priestly tradition of Leviticus, with which Ezekiel has strong affinities. For example, Ezekiel would have had great empathy with this primitive teaching: "You shall keep my statutes. You shall not let your animals breed with a different kind; you shall not sow your field with two kinds of seed; nor shall you put on a garment made of two different materials" (Lev 19:19). In this preoccupation the coming deep crisis in Jerusalem is because of the failed leadership that created a cultic environment completely inhospitable to the reliable residence of YHWH.

3. In three extensive and remarkable chapters, Ezekiel traces the history of Israel with YHWH as a history of failure and obscene violation of trust (16; 20; 23). These are remarkable rereadings of that long history, not only because it is a history of failure (a theme differently articulated in Ps 106), but because the relationship of YHWH and Israel is imagined as an intimate relationship that became erotic, and that in turn became obscene in ways that display all of the distortions and betrayals of which an erotic relationship is capable. The impression given us of this rhetoric is that the prophet must find the most extreme and offensive imagery in order to voice what he knows to be the most extreme and offensive distortion of a relationship that began in generosity and compassion. The negation of the relationship is unspeakable in its abhorrence, and so Ezekiel finds a way to speak the unspeakable:

> You played the whore with the Egyptians, your lustful neighbors, multiplying your whoring, to provoke me to anger. Therefore I stretched out my hand against you, reduced your rations, and gave you up to the will of your enemies, the daughters of the Philistines, who were ashamed of your lewd behavior. You played the whore with the Assyrians, because you were insatiable; you played the whore with them, and still you were not satisfied. You multiplied your whoring with Chaldea, the land of merchants; and even with this you were not satisfied. (16:26–29)

> And the Babylonians came to her into the bed of love, and they defiled her with their lust; and after she defiled herself with them, she turned from them in disgust. When she carried on her whorings so openly and flaunted her nakedness, I turned in disgust from her, as I had turned from her sister. Yet she increased her whorings, remembering the days of her youth, when she played the whore in the land of Egypt and lusted after her paramours there, whose members were like those of donkeys, and whose emission was like that of stallions. Thus you longed for the lewdness of your youth, when the Egyptians fondled your bosom and caressed your young breasts. (23:17–21)

The affront against YHWH is not moral but concerns emotions and passions that are well beneath any morality and that evoke in YHWH the rage befitting a betrayed, humiliated lover:

> I will deliver you into their hands, and they shall throw down your platform and break down your lofty places; they shall strip you of your clothes and take your beautiful objects and leave you naked and bare. They shall bring up a mob against you, and they shall stone you and cut you to pieces with their swords. They shall burn your houses and execute judgments on you in the sight of many women; I will stop you from playing the whore, and you shall also make no more

payments. So I will satisfy my fury on you, and my jealousy shall turn away from you; I will be calm, and will be angry no longer. Because you have not remembered the days of your youth, but have enraged me with all these things; therefore, I have returned your deeds upon your head, says the Lord GOD. (16:39–43)

It is remarkable that a prophetic tradition so preoccupied with symmetry and right ordering should articulate such elemental and seemingly uncontrollable passion. The reason given for that hostile reaction from YHWH is because YHWH's holy name has been profaned, and YHWH must act decisively to rescue YHWH's reputation in "the sight of the nations" (5:8 [cf. v. 14]; 20:9, 14, 22, 41; 22:16; 28:25; 39:27): "Then I bathed you with water and washed off the blood from you, and anointed you with oil. . . . And in all your abominations and your whorings you did not remember the days of your youth, when you were naked and bare, flailing about in your blood" (16:9, 22).

4. Given the power of such imagery, we are not prepared for the fact that already in this first half of the book there are anticipations of restoration that look beyond the sure devastation to come and that promise YHWH's restorative activity. Among these anticipations are 11:14–21; 16:60–63; and 17:22–24. Such promises in the context of harsh judgment may be a result of careless editing. More likely they serve to indicate that even the harshest condemnation and the fullest judgments against Jerusalem that can be voiced are, in the final form of the text, penultimate. Harsh judgment is important and inescapable; it is not, however, the last word. Thus these promissory passages bind the harshness of chapters 1–24 to the visions of restoration that are to follow in chapters 32–47. In these harbingers of that restoration, then, it is clear that the theological shape of Ezekiel's voice is parallel to that of Isaiah and Jeremiah, and establishes what became a normative pattern of discernment in emerging Judaism that shaped the final form of the text in these voices of prophetic anticipation.

The first half of the book of Ezekiel ends with a notice (24:25–27) that is as enigmatic, albeit in a different way, as the initial vision of chapter 1. The prophet's awareness of the impending doom upon the city of Jerusalem has reduced him to silence, a traumatic personal embodiment of the public trauma to come upon Jerusalem in its final days to mark the end when Jerusalem will lose "their joy and glory, the delight of their eyes and their heart's affection, and also their sons and their daughters" (24:25).

Thus the extended text of judgment runs out in silence, but the silence itself is an unmistakable articulation of the depth of loss, alienation, and abandonment. Characteristically, however, the prophetic tradition cannot leave it at the dismal end in verse 25. Thus the new formulation in verse 26, "on that day," moves beyond the devastation anticipated in verse 25. The new day sure to come is the day when Ezekiel receives "the news." The news toward which the literature has moved is the word that Jerusalem has been destroyed. When that news comes, a radical reversal is in order, for YHWH's holiness will have been vindicated and Ezekiel's own articulation will have been confirmed:

> The moment of Ezekiel's deepest alienation from his community (due to their contrasting estimations of the disaster) would mark the turn toward his identification with them. Inhibitions upon his intercourse with them entailed by their hostility would be removed at a stroke. Their calamity would be the start of his fortune—his and God's—as the people would eventually realize the redemptive significance of Jerusalem's fall. (Greenberg 1997, 516)

When the city falls—as surely it must—the prophet is ready to turn to newness. The prophet can turn to newness, however, only because YHWH can now turn to newness when YHWH's holy name is vindicated by the destruction of that which caused the profanation of the name—the distorted and polluted temple. The first half of the book of Ezekiel ends with a decisive and ringing declaration that "I am the Lord [YHWH]" (24:27). The newness from YHWH and from YHWH's prophet is explicit. Implicit in this vigorous assertion, but carefully left unsaid, is that when YHWH and YHWH's prophet move on, so also Israel's rescue now becomes thinkable and speakable. Thus 24:25–27 is a major hinge in the book of Ezekiel that moves in a radical reversal, away from condemnation.

II

The second half of the book, chapters 25–48, consists in a rich variety of articulations of hope for the future of Jerusalem; these chapters thus constitute a fairly precise counterpoint to the judgment issued in chapters 1–24 and make clear the twofold movement in prophetic imagination of judgment and hope as they swirl around the defining crisis of Jerusalem and of Judaism.

We may identify four distinct units of material concerning the future and take up each in turn. Before taking up these units, however, we may take particular notice of 33:21:

> In the twelfth year of our exile, in the tenth month, on the fifth day of the month, someone who had escaped from Jerusalem came to me and said, "The city has fallen."

The message comes from Jerusalem in the twelfth year of the exile of Jehoiachin, that is, in 586 BCE. The messenger had escaped the city as it suffered

its final destruction at the hands of Babylon, and brought succinct news of
the battle report to the exilic community in Babylon: "The city has fallen!"
This utterance is a characteristic battle report, on which see the parallel in
Jeremiah 50:2 concerning Babylon.

The news of the destruction of Jerusalem is devastating; the Holy City is
captured. In the categories of Ezekiel, however, the news that is otherwise
devastating is a great release. The devastation constitutes the vigorous reassertion of YHWH's holiness for all the world to see. It represents at the same
time vindication of Ezekiel's long, peculiar announcement of woe. And more
specifically, it ends Ezekiel's silence that was imposed by YHWH. Ezekiel
is now free to speak! That speech still contains leftovers of judgment but, in
large part, is a visionary anticipation of restoration.

1. The first textual unit concerning Israel's restoration is in chapters 25–32.
We have leapt in our analysis from 24:25–27 to 33:21. These two passages
are, of course, closely connected. Between them, however, the traditioning
process has placed the first textual unit of hope, chapters 25–32. These chapters are something of an intrusion between 24:25–27 and 33:21, but they are
an effective beginning on hope and restoration, the primary theme for what
follows in the book of Ezekiel. These chapters are a collection of oracles
against the nations, parallel to the corpus of oracles against the nations in
Isaiah 13–23 and Jeremiah 46–51, in each case asserting the rule of YHWH
over the nations and in each case making room for the restoration and future
well-being of Israel.

The cast of characters in the roster of nations is of great interest when
compared with the parallel texts in Isaiah and Jeremiah. This corpus begins
with brief oracles against four nations in chapter 25. But then Tyre, a great
economic center, receives three chapters of condemnation and lament (26–28)
while Egypt receives four chapters, a remarkably extended treatment (29–32).
These accent points likely reflect the geopolitical realities of the time, and are
of particular interest because of the mythopoetic language of condemnation
and lament. Thus the lament over Tyre appeals to a tradition about the garden of Eden (28:11), and Egypt is portrayed in an autonomy of immense and
defiant proportion, imagining itself to be self-made (29:3).

Two other features of this corpus are noteworthy. First, it is often remarked
that Ezekiel's strictures against the nations include no reference to Babylon,
unlike the text of Jeremiah 50–51. It is frequently speculated that this silence
concerning the great destroyer of Jerusalem is for prudential, pragmatic reasons for the prophet who was himself situated in Babylon among the exiles:

> Nowhere in the book of Ezekiel, in all the oracles against foreign
> nations, is there any oracle against Babylon. This seems remarkable

in view of all that Judah suffered at Babylonian hands over the period which the book of Ezekiel covers. It is not remarkable, however, if Ezekiel is prophesying in Babylonia, where such oracles, if they had come to public notice, would doubtless have involved the prophet in immediate and serious trouble. (McKeating 1993, 121–22)

Second, the brief unit in 28:25–26 indicates a celebrated by-product of YHWH's defeat among the nations:

> Thus says the Lord GOD: When I gather the house of Israel from the peoples among whom they are scattered, and manifest my holiness in them in the sight of the nations, then they shall settle on their own soil that I gave to my servant Jacob. They shall live in safety in it, and shall build houses and plant vineyards. They shall live in safety, when I execute judgments upon all their neighbors who have treated them with contempt. And they shall know that I am the LORD their God.

The defeat of the nations is to enhance YHWH's sovereignty. Alongside that theocentric enhancement, however, is the opportunity for Israel to be restored to its land. It is a peculiar nuance in the tradition of Ezekiel that the rescue of Israel is nothing more than a strategy for manifesting YHWH's holiness. Thus the terrible judgment worked on Israel's enemies (YHWH's enemies?) is to the singular benefit of Israel.

2. Chapters 33–37 constitute some of the most interesting and most moving promise passages in the Ezekiel tradition. This unit of text is introduced in chapter 33 by a disputatious word that perhaps reflects the disputatious environment of exilic Israel. The judgment on the disobedient continues in 34:1–10 with a harsh condemnation of kings in Israel, for whom the metaphor of "shepherd" is used. The simple calculus of 34:1–10 is that self-aggrandizing kings have caused the "scattering" (exile) of Judah. By 34:11, however, the oracle of judgment against the king turns to hope. The remainder of the chapter portrays YHWH's willingness to be the "good shepherd," that is, the good king who enacts compassion and governance for all members of the society. Thus the prophet enacts a radical turn in the prospects of Israel that is to be effected by YHWH's own resolve and self-announcement. This text offers a vision of society that is perhaps reflected in the teaching of Jesus in Matthew 25:31–46, and surely in the "good shepherd" passages of Luke 15:3–7 and John 10:1–18.

Still in the interest of a new future, the tradition offers a most remarkable statement in 36:22–32. In this text, YHWH promises a radically new future for Israel:

> I will take you from the nations, and gather you from all the countries, and bring you into your own land. I will sprinkle clean water upon you, and you shall be clean from all your uncleannesses, and from all

> your idols I will cleanse you. A new heart I will give you, and a new spirit I will put within you; and I will remove from your body the heart of stone and give you a heart of flesh. I will put my spirit within you, and make you follow my statutes and be careful to observe my ordinances. Then you shall live in the land that I gave to your ancestors; and you shall be my people, and I will be your God. (36:24–28)

The rhetoric asserts that YHWH has the capacity to work a transformative newness on behalf of YHWH's people. It is astonishing, however, that this new resolve of YHWH is framed in verses 22 and 32 with a decisive denial of YHWH's concern for Israel:

> Therefore say to the house of Israel, Thus says the Lord GOD: It is not for your sake, O house of Israel, that I am about to act, but for the sake of my holy name, which you have profaned among the nations to which you came. . . . It is not for your sake that I will act, says the Lord GOD; let that be known to you. Be ashamed and dismayed for your ways, O house of Israel.

In some other traditions, especially Hosea and Jeremiah, such newness from YHWH is rooted in YHWH's compassion for and fidelity to Israel. But not here! Here the newness is "not for your sake," that is, not because YHWH loves Israel. Rather, in this tradition, YHWH is preoccupied with YHWH's own self and YHWH's reputation among the nations. Thus YHWH's actions are designed only to enhance YHWH and, if we may say so, to appeal to YHWH's vanity:

> The ultimate motive of Yahweh's activity is found in his desire to vindicate his "name," the primary content of which is, it seems, not his reputation as a compassionate, forgiving or even a just God, but rather in his reputation as a powerful deity. It would not be inaccurate to say that in Ezekiel Yahweh does indeed in a sense act out of "divine self-interest." (Joyce 1989, 103)

The rescue of Israel is a happy by-product of YHWH's self-vindication, but nonetheless only a by-product (see also 39:26–29). This nuance of motivation is important, because it exhibits in the Ezekiel tradition a very different Yahwistic grounding for Israel's future, a hope rooted not in love but in holiness.

The third remarkable text in this section of the book of Ezekiel is 37:1–14, a vision of the future that is popularly known in the song "Dry Bones." In this text, the "Valley of Dry Bones" is a metaphor for Israel in exile with no prospect for the future. After intense dialogic exchange between YHWH and YHWH's prophet, the text ends in a divine oracle promising new life and restoration in the land: "I am going to open your graves, and bring you up from your graves, O my people; and I will bring you back to the land of Israel. And you shall know that I am the LORD, when I open your graves, and bring you up from your graves, O my people" (37:12–13).

This oracular reassurance is totally God-centered. The future of Israel depends upon a fresh decree by YHWH, who will commit an act of life-giving power. The rhetorical force of the passage is due to the interplay between the concrete concern for reentry into the land and the image of the resurrection of the dead. It is important that the divine announcement moves between these two themes so that even later Christian thought about resurrection of the dead is not removed from the concrete bodiliness of land issues. This interplay assures that the Bible's concern for the future is intensely bodily, a dimension that requires rhetorical agility in the Pauline exposition of the resurrection in 1 Corinthians 15 and that eventuated in the church's conviction about "the resurrection of the body and the life of the world to come." In Israel's expectation, the old promise of and entitlement to land continues to be powerful among the belatedly landless in the sixth century.

In 37:14 the ultimate promise of YHWH is to give life by the divine gift of the spirit (or breath). The news of the book of Ezekiel is that YHWH wills life and has power to grant it (see 33:11). Finally, however, the gift of new life is for the enhancement of YHWH, who thereby establishes YHWH's own prestige and credibility: "I will put my spirit within you, and you shall live, and I will place you on your own soil; then you shall know that I, the LORD, have spoken and will act, says the LORD" (37:14). As David Noel Freedman has noted:

> Yahweh's commitment to Judah's covenant is almost completely overshadowed by his commitment to the principles of that covenant. In the valley of bones, Yahweh says he animates the bones not so that they can live, but so they can know that he is the Lord. Yahweh acts only for the sake of his name. (Freedman 1975, 181)

Thus chapters 34–37 are a vigorous promise for the future of Israel, taking full account of present dire circumstances and referring the future to the powerful good intention of YHWH.

3. Chapters 38–39 constitute a peculiar pair of chapters in the tradition of Ezekiel. These chapters have much in common with the oracles against the nations, except that the rhetoric here is much more extreme and the identity of "the enemy" is unclear. As a result, it is most likely that these chapters show the Ezekiel tradition turned in an apocalyptic direction, so that the "enemy" is ominous and nearly cosmic, and the power of YHWH is mobilized in extreme

measure to defeat that ominous enemy and so to rescue Israel from threat. The plot line is not unlike that of the Oracles against the Nations:

a. The enemy (here Gog) is seen to be a brutalizing threat against "my people":

> Therefore, mortal, prophesy, and say to Gog: Thus says the Lord GOD: On that day when my people Israel are living securely, you will rouse yourself and come from your place out of the remotest parts of the north, you and many peoples with you, all of them riding on horses, a great horde, a mighty army; you will come up against my people Israel, like a cloud covering the earth. (38:14–16a)

b. YHWH will move against the enemy that defies YHWH and that threatens YHWH's people:

> I will summon the sword against Gog in all my mountains, says the Lord GOD; the swords of all will be against their comrades. With pestilence and bloodshed I will enter into judgment with him; and I will pour down torrential rains and hailstones, fire and sulfur, upon him and his troops and the many peoples that are with him. (38:21–22)

c. The intent of such a show of force by YHWH is to enhance YHWH:

> So I will display my greatness and my holiness and make myself known in the eyes of many nations. Then they shall know that I am the LORD. (38:23)

> My holy name I will make known among my people Israel; and I will not let my holy name be profaned anymore; and the nations shall know that I am the LORD, the Holy One in Israel. (39:7)

d. The happy by-product of such self-enhancing action by YHWH is the well-being of Israel:

> Therefore thus says the Lord GOD: Now I will restore the fortunes of Jacob, and have mercy on the whole house of Israel; and I will be jealous for my holy name. They shall forget their shame, and all the treachery they have practiced against me, when they live securely in their land with no one to make them afraid, when I have brought them back from the peoples and gathered them from their enemies' lands, and through them have displayed my holiness in the sight of many nations. (39:25–27)

The enhancement of YHWH and the well-being of Israel are inescapably linked. YHWH cannot be enhanced except by rescuing Israel; Israel has no hope except from an enhanced YHWH.

It is commonly noted that Gog and Magog are impossible to identify as historical enemies, a fact that has opened the way to endless interpretive speculation. Because the pattern of defeat of Gog and the consequent rescue of Israel is not unlike YHWH's treatment of Babylon in the book of Jeremiah, it is not impossible that Gog and Magog are intended to be surreptitious code names for Babylon: "What more likely, then, than that the land of Gog is a cypher for Babylon itself, and the prophecies of Gog's destruction a heavily coded message predicting the demise of the Babylonian power?" (McKeating 1993, 122).

Thus the most extreme *rhetoric* is matched to the most extreme *enemy* in anticipation of YHWH's most extreme *deliverance* that eventuates in Israel's well-being. The entire dramatic development so characteristic of Ezekiel is for the sake of YHWH's self-interest: "Be ready and keep ready, you and all the companies that are assembled around you, and hold yourselves in reserve for them" (38:7).

4. The final, quite extended textual unit on hope in Ezekiel is chapters 40–48, a vision of the restoration of the temple and the restored presence of YHWH in the Jerusalem temple. The rebuilt temple is the pivotal vision of loss and return already voiced in the traditions of Isaiah and Jeremiah. This vision of the temple is closely informed by priestly expertise, thus a vision rooted in known reality but projected into the future. The vision is remarkably precise in construction, a kind of carefulness often associated with a priestly sensibility that pays close attention to sacerdotal detail.

We may suggest that in this vision of a promised, soon-to-be-given priestly restoration, the text has two pivot points. First, in 43:1–5 the glory of YHWH returns to Jerusalem and takes up residence in the newly purified temple that is envisioned in this priestly tradition:

> Then he brought me to the gate, the gate facing east. And there, the glory of the God of Israel was coming from the east; the sound was like the sound of mighty waters; and the earth shone with his glory. The vision I saw was like the vision that I had seen when he came to destroy the city, and like the vision that I had seen by the river Chebar; and I fell upon my face. As the glory of the LORD entered the temple by the gate facing east, the spirit lifted me up, and brought me into the inner court; and the glory of the LORD filled the temple.

The return of the glory of YHWH, a decisive component of priestly hope, is made possible by the careful reordering of cultic life through a series of provisions and regulated practices in chapters 40–42 and 45. This priestly vision of the newly given divine presence is obviously deeply instructed by what is known and remembered of the past so that the renewed temple is an important continuity with the past. The dramatic return of YHWH's glory in 43:1–5, a glory now permanently secured for the temple in 44:1–3, is the decisive antidote to the departure of YHWH's glory in chapters 9 and 10. Thus the supreme punishment of YHWH, in priestly purview, is absence; the supreme resolution of crisis, in priestly purview, is restored cultic presence.

This newly given divine presence, moreover, is to be presided over by priests with whom the Ezekiel tradition is directly aligned. Thus the presiders and guarantors of the renewed divine presence are the "descendants of Zadok" (43:15–44:31), who are contrasted to the Levites, here taken to be a lower caste of priests (44:9–14). Frank Cross has proposed that this text, along with others, reflects a deep dispute in exilic and postexilic Israel between competing priestly communities (Cross 1973, 195–215). We suggest that this tension reflected in chapter 44 may illuminate the contrasting rhetorical styles and theological perspectives of the traditions of Jeremiah and Ezekiel. While twinned in judgment and hope, Jeremiah stays close to the Deuteronomic perspective with its basis in Levitical traditions, whereas the book of Ezekiel is close to the priestly project of the book of Leviticus and its focus on the priesthood of Aaron. Thus the text, in its overriding theological claim, is at the same time an advocacy, a deeply contested position that concerns not only theological truth but also social power.

The priestly tradition to which Ezekiel bears witness bets everything on the temple. This is especially evident in chapter 47 wherein the rivers of life flow "from below the threshold of the temple" (47:1). It is clear that in priestly imagination, the rivers of Eden in Genesis 2:10–14 have now been resituated in a liturgical context so that the anticipated temple guarantees not only the presence of YHWH but life-giving sustenance for all of creation. Thus the Ezekiel tradition holds an immensely high view of the temple as the epicenter of the new creation.

The temple itself is the entry point for newness in the Ezekiel tradition. The priests who form the tradition, however, know that the temple does not exist in a geopolitical vacuum; rather, the temple is the entry point for the recovered and reentered land. Thus the second pivot point in this vision of restoration begins in 47:13: "Thus says the Lord GOD: These are the boundaries by which you shall divide the land for inheritance among the twelve tribes of Israel. Joseph shall have two portions." This formulation parallels the formulations we have found in Joshua 13–19, so that this tradition imagines a redeployment of the old promises of land, tribe by tribe, in an exile-ending reapportionment. Both the temple reconstruction and the land redistribution are visionary, but for their visionary quality no less concretely important.

In her important study, Kalinda Stevenson has noted the "territorial rhetoric" of Ezekiel that aims at a real social situation and aims at reordering of territory, social power, and social authority so that all are included in a just and humane social ordering:

> Re-storation refers to re-vival, re-turn, re-building, re-making, re-newing, re-pairing, re-formation—to making something the way it was. However, what the Rhetor sees is not re-storation or re-formation but trans-formation. There is no trace of nostalgia in this Rhetor's view of the world. The goal of the ideology of the Book of Ezekiel is not restoration to what was, but transformation to a new thing. The power of a book is that it can create a new world. . . .
> What is truly remarkable about the priestly vision of the reorganized society of Israel is the balance of power inherent in it, and its concern for the well-being of everyone in the society. It is true that the priests are the ones who control access to the holy place. It is also true that the priests do not own land. I find that single fact extraordinary. Unlike the monarchy, which both controlled the temple and controlled the land, this social plan creates a balance of power. The very existence of the priests, their subsistence and livelihood, depends upon the support of the people who do possess land. It is a system which is characterized by justice, a reorganization of society in which everyone has enough. No one is displaced and no one is wronged by a rapacious central government out of control. (Stevenson 1996, 149, 158)

The restoration program of chapters 40–48 envisioning both a revisited temple that is now an adequate residence for YHWH and a redistributed land culminate in the ultimate affirmation of the book of Ezekiel: "And the name of the city from that time on shall be, The Lord is There" (48:35b). The city and the temple that were abandoned are now the place made holy, a suitable habitat for a holy God vindicated before the nations, a welcome habitat for a restored holy people. Thus the great drama of judgment and hope culminates in Ezekiel in a powerful theocentric anticipation. The God who judges and terminates is the God who restores and abides permanently and securely in the midst of well-ordered people, now completely at peace:

> When he is harsh, he seems pitiless; when he is kind, his graciousness spills over. In his outbursts of extreme severity, he declares his own nation ugly and repugnant; but, then, all of a sudden, he recovers his compassion, and everything and everybody radiate sunshine and serenity.
> He oscillates between the shame of sin and the grandeur of salvation—for him there is nothing in between. Ezekiel is the man of extremes. . . .
> Exaggeration of sin must be matched by exaggerated divine rescue. Here Ezekiel disagrees with Jeremiah, who believed in repentance that would generate redemption. Ezekiel believed in redemption that

would come outside of repentance. Jews would be redeemed, not because they would deserve it, but because God would choose to be merciful. (Wiesel 1987, 167–68, 183–84)

III

Finally, we will give attention to one text that is of special importance and that is frequently misread. Ezekiel 18 is a summons to failed Israel to repent and return to Torah obedience. It should be noted that the chapter is framed by a proverb at the outset that is refuted by what follows (18:2–3), and at the end with the assurance that YHWH wants life and not death (v. 32). This text is often misread because the refutation of the folk proverb in verse 2 seems to suggest that the individual suffers for his or her disobedience, and not the community for the disobedience of the individual, so that the text is taken to be an assertion of moral individualism. Such a reading is erroneous because it seeks to turn the text into a universal moral principle, when the text must be understood in context, locally and pastorally:

> It is easy enough to see how this section of Ezekiel 18, picturing the three men, could be misread as an argument for "individual responsibility." However, whilst Ezekiel certainly rejects the idea that the present disaster is a punishment for the sins of previous generations, he is not concerned here with the moral independence of contemporary individuals. He takes for granted the general principle of "individual responsibility" in the realm of legal practice (and employs it in considering his three hypothetical cases), but the possibility of Yahweh judging individuals in isolation from their contemporaries is not considered. This is because the question at issue is a different one, namely, "Why is this inevitably communal, national crisis happening?"
>
> The corporate nature of the concerns of Ezek. 18.1–20 has not been taken sufficiently seriously by scholars. (Joyce 1989, 46)

When taken locally and pastorally, the text has a very different meaning. The body of the text is organized into three generations:

the first generation of a righteous man (vv. 5–9)
the second generation of a wicked man (vv. 10–13)
the third generation of a righteous man (vv. 14–18)

In each case, the destiny for and verdict upon each generation depends upon adherence to the Torah in terms of (a) avoiding idolatry and serving only YHWH, (b) obedient sexuality, and (c) obedient economics. It is likely that three generations are not a theoretical case, but refer in turn to (a) Josiah the good king (2 Kgs 23:25), (b) Jehoiakim the bad king (2 Kgs 23:36–37), and (c) Jehoiachin the third king (2 Kgs 24:8–12). That is, the verdict is still out on the third king, who is in exile, the leader of the exilic community, the king upon whom the Ezekiel tradition has based its chronology (Ezek 1:2). Thus it is probable that this text in Ezekiel 18 concerns the destiny of and the theological verdict upon the third generation, the generation of exiles led by Jehoiachin.

The good news announced in this text is that the third generation may indeed repent and be obedient in the three key areas of (a) YHWH's sovereignty, (b) sexuality, and (c) economics. The assurance of the text is that the exilic generation need not be kept enthralled by the sins of the previous generation of Jehoiakim, but is free to start again in repentance and new obedience; this same theme of repentance is one characteristic of the exilic Deuteronomists, as in Deuteronomy 4:29–31 and 30:1–10, and is reflected in Isaiah 55:6–9 and Jeremiah 29:10–14.

As Jacqueline Lapsley has clearly established, this rigorous call for repentance belongs to a particular point in the argument of the Ezekiel tradition (Lapsley 2000). It is equally clear in the second half of the book, as Lapsley has demonstrated, that an appeal for Israel's repentance is no adequate basis for a future of Israel, for the repentance is not forthcoming in adequate measure. Thus the second half of the book of Ezekiel moves beyond the imperative requirement of chapter 18 to an indicative assertion of YHWH's own resolve as a basis for Israel's future. The promise of a future is unilateral and unconditional; YHWH no longer waits for Israel's repentance. Instead, what is offered is an act of radical grace toward Israel that is rooted in and motivated by YHWH's own self-regard:

> And the nations shall know that I am the LORD, says the Lord GOD, when through you I display my holiness before their eyes. I will take you from the nations, and gather you from all the countries, and bring you into your own land. I will sprinkle clean water upon you, and you shall be clean from all your uncleannesses, and from all your idols I will cleanse you. A new heart I will give you, and a new spirit I will put within you; and I will remove from your body the heart of stone and give you a heart of flesh. I will put my spirit within you, and make you follow my statutes and be careful to observe my ordinances. Then you shall live in the land that I gave to your ancestors; and you shall be my people, and I will be your God. (36:23–28)

The book of Ezekiel is a demanding reflection upon the crisis of the loss and the prospect of newness in ancient Jerusalem. The loss, in Priestly purview, is because of ritual contamination. The future is grounded in the will of the Holy God to be present in restored Israel, a will that sovereignly creates the conditions that make renewed presence possible. The tradition of Ezekiel proceeds in a rigorous, starchy way without much offer of generosity or graciousness on YHWH's part. The gift of newness for Israel in this tradition is very sure, because it is rooted in nothing short of YHWH's self-regard. Israel is the beneficiary of YHWH's own intentionality to be well regarded, sovereign, and present to Israel.

19

The Minor Prophets (1)

<hr>

The fourth scroll of the Latter Prophets—after Isaiah, Jeremiah, and Ezekiel—is that of the Twelve (or Minor) Prophets. These four scrolls together constitute an exact counterpoint to the four books of the Former Prophets, Joshua, Judges, Samuel, and Kings. This last scroll of the prophetic canon brings together a series of shorter prophetic collections, the twelve juxtaposed without explanation. (They are traditionally termed "minor" only because these books that bear prophetic names are relatively brief compared to the "major prophets," Isaiah, Jeremiah, and Ezekiel. It is important to recognize that the term "minor" does not mean unimportant or less important.) That there are twelve named prophetic "books" on this scroll seems to make it a very different kind of scroll from those of Isaiah, Jeremiah, and Ezekiel. We have seen, however, that these scrolls from the Major Prophets are themselves also collections and subcollections of material brought together in dynamic interpretive processes. The ultimate theological intention of the completed shape of the book is not always clear. Thus, fragmented as this final scroll is, it is not all that different from the three quite complex traditions that precede it in the books of Isaiah, Jeremiah, and Ezekiel.

By way of introduction to this scroll and its twelve elements, we may observe that there are currently two approaches to the material, historical-critical and canonical, which we will consider in turn.

The *historical-critical approach* has long dominated the interpretive discussion and takes each of the twelve books on its own without consideration of its literary context among the Twelve. As elsewhere with historical criticism, this approach seeks to identify the sociohistorical context of the book and to trace the editorial process by which the book reached its final form. When we summarize the consensus position of historical-critical study, we may observe that of the Twelve, we can identify three groups of three books that are located in three quite distinct and fairly secure historical contexts:

1. Hosea, Amos, and Micah are situated in the eighth century and so are related as "minor" partners to the "major" prophetic book of Isaiah. The defining contextual matter for this literature is the imposing reality of Assyrian imperial hegemony that threatened, in turn, the northern kingdom of Israel and the southern kingdom of Judah. These three prophets, along with Isaiah, seek to relate the Assyrian threat to divine judgment wrought by YHWH upon the two kingdoms because of internal distortions in the community that are understood as covenantal disobedience that takes various forms: religious, political, and economic. The imaginative capacity of these prophets is representative of the prophetic tradition in its capacity to relate internal distortion and external threat as indictment and sentence, the two held together by the insistent governance of YHWH.

2. Nahum, Habakkuk, and Zephaniah are situated in the midst of the late seventh century and so are related as "minor" partners to the "major" prophetic book of Jeremiah. The defining contextual matter for these books is the waning reality of Assyrian hegemony, the soon-to-arrive Babylonian Empire, and the general disarray in Jerusalem attributable to poor royal leadership and a general disregard of the requirements of Judah as YHWH's covenanted people. Of these three prophets, Zephaniah most closely continues the traditional agenda of the eighth-century prophets, Nahum focuses exclusively and shrilly upon the demise and destruction of the Assyrian empire, while Habakkuk takes up emerging questions of theodicy. All three books attend to the great movement of rise and fall, and construe that movement with reference to YHWH, who rules over the nations and over Judah, albeit in hidden or enigmatic ways.

3. Haggai, Zechariah, and Malachi form a third triad that is in the wake of the exilic prophetic promises of Jeremiah 30–31, Ezekiel 40–48, and Isaiah 40–55. These high expectations from the exilic period were quickly transposed into the mundane reality of "small things" involved in the restoration of the land at the beginning of the Persian hegemony of the late sixth century under the leadership of Cyrus and then Darius (see Zech 4:10). The defining contextual reality for this literature is the new, more benign imperial policies of Persia that, unlike the policies of Babylon, permitted some reassertion of local religious and political traditions under the more general aegis of the empire. Haggai and Zechariah are specifically dated to the first wave of temple rebuilding in 520 to 516, whereas Malachi comes somewhat later and reflects upon the malaise of the community of Judah as it lost the sharp edge of theological self-consciousness and intentionality. In the context of Persian

oversight that was benign but unyielding, the issue for Judaism was how to enact the kinds of institutional and symbolic modes of life that would sustain a distinct identity as the people of YHWH's covenant:

> To theologize from the perspective of the exiles, however, is to start from a radically different assumption about the nature of the people of God, an assumption perhaps foreign to modern Christian theologians outside the minority traditions. From the perspective of the "Fourth World," such conflicts between the "world" (and its threat of impurity) and the "true fellowship," or the "remnant," are necessary for continued survival. (D. Smith 1989, 197)

4. It is clear with these three groups of three books that the scroll of the Twelve is roughly organized in a chronological fashion. Of the nine books we have mentioned, Hosea, Amos, and Micah are from the eighth century; Nahum, Habakkuk, and Zephaniah from the seventh century; and Haggai, Zechariah, and Malachi from the fifth century.

This analysis leaves three of the books without placement in such a scheme:

1. The book of Joel is surely the most enigmatic of the Twelve, and perhaps the most puzzling book of the entire Old Testament canon.
2. The book of Obadiah is a reiteration of a text from the book of Jeremiah. The data of the book itself seem to be best placed in the fifth century, a time of acute tension for Judah with the Edomites.
3. The book of Jonah is distinguished as the only one of the Twelve that is offered as narrative.

We will give attention below to these three books, though, as we shall see, the critical consensus does not take us very far in interpreting them.

A second, more recent approach to the scroll of the Twelve is *canonical*. After doing what can be done through historical-critical analysis, scholarship has turned to ask about the final form of the text and the arrangement of these twelve seemingly disconnected pieces into a larger and intentional whole. This way of interpretation is only at its beginning and thus far has only produced a general understanding and suggested some lines of investigation. The material itself is somewhat intractable and does not easily yield to larger patterns of interpretation. Brevard Childs has considered the "canonical shape" of each of the books of the Twelve, but has not gone very far in his analysis of the Twelve as a canonical unit (Childs 1979, 373–498). More venturesome have been the studies of Paul House and James Nogalski (House 1990; Nogalski 1993).

House has suggested that one can see in the Twelve definite patterns around three theological themes: sin, punishment, and restoration.

> A close analysis of the Twelve reveals some definite patterns in the posi-
> tioning of the minor prophets. It appears that the books are ordered as
> they are so that the main points of the prophetic message will be high-
> lighted. In fact, the Twelve are structured in a way that demonstrates
> the sin of Israel and the nations, the punishment of the sin, and the
> restoration of both from that sin. These three emphases represent the
> heart of the content of the prophetic genre. (House 1990, 68)

He further develops this scheme by assigning each of the Twelve to one of
these themes:

Chart 1
The Structure of the Twelve

Hosea Joel Amos Obadiah Jonah Micah	Sin: Covenant and Cosmic
Nahum Habakkuk Zephaniah	Punishment: Covenant and Cosmic
Haggai Zechariah Malachi	Restoration: Covenant and Cosmic

(House 1990, 72)

Moreover, House follows Northrop Frye (2000, 207–9) in suggesting that
"comic action" is narrated by a U shape that descends to the bottom, pauses
at the bottom, and then ascends to a new condition of well-being. He suggests
the following for the "comic plot" of the Twelve:

1. Introduction to the Downward Trek: Hosea and Joel
2. Complication of the Plot's Problem: Amos–Micah
3. Crisis Point of the Twelve: Nahum and Habakkuk
4. Climax and Falling Action: Zephaniah
5. Resolution (Denouement) of the Plot: Haggai, Zechariah, and Malachi
   (House 1990, 124–62)

Our sense is that House's proposal is excessively schematic and cannot be
sustained through a careful examination of the text. To the extent that his
analysis is sustainable, it is clear that *the pattern of dissent and then resolution* is

not unlike *the pattern of loss and hope* that we have seen in Isaiah, Jeremiah, and Ezekiel. Or again, as Ronald Clements proposes:

> In such fashion we can at least come to understand the value and meaning of the way in which distinctive patterns have been imposed upon the prophetic collections of the canon so that warnings of doom and disaster are always followed by promises of hope and restoration. . . . We must see that prophecy is a collection of collections, and that ultimately the final result in the prophetic corpus of the canon formed a recognizable unity not entirely dissimilar from that of the Pentateuch. As this was made up from various sources and collections, so also the Former and Latter Prophets, comprising the various preserved prophecies of a whole series of inspired individuals, acquired an overarching thematic unity. This centered on the death and rebirth of Israel, interpreted theologically as acts of divine judgment and salvation. (Clements 1977, 49–53)

It may be, however, that House's primary contribution is that he, among others, has taught us to ask a different kind of question about the scroll of the Twelve. That question assumes a historical-critical understanding of each book of the Twelve, but then recognizes that the traditioning process has transposed these several quite distinct books into a more coherent statement. That coherent statement, not surprisingly, serves to articulate primary theological convictions about Israel and about YHWH, namely, that in the world of YHWH's rule *judgment* comes in historical processes, but judgment is penultimate and leaves open postjudgment *well-being*. We begin to see the gain of such study whereby specifically located prophetic traditions become normative articulations to which the community endlessly returns.

The other important study of the Twelve in canonical form is the work of Nogalski. In a very close reading, he has traced the way in which a system of "catchwords" has served to piece the several books together. That is, a term in one text is placed next to the same term in another text, and the texts are thereby placed back-to-back. Nogalski's study has permitted him to trace (a) the Deuteronomic editing of the corpus (which fits well with the prominent themes identified by House), and (b) the extensive editing that goes beyond Deuteronomic theology in the process of creating a canonical unity. The current state of the question is well summarized in a recent book edited by Nogalski and Marvin Sweeney (Nogalski and Sweeney 2000). It is our judgment that this is an altogether welcome interpretive venture. At the same time, it is important to recognize that the investigation of the canonical shape of the corpus of the Minor Prophets is only at its beginning. At the moment we have, for the most part, only suggestive speculation that has not at all reached acceptance in the scholarly community, nor has it arrived at a consensus. While the reader should be aware of that emerging scholarly perspective, we believe that such work is much too provisional to claim attention in this introduction. Thus we will, in our brief comments concerning the Twelve, review the primary learning of the older historical-critical analysis; we will at the same time, however, be aware that after historical matters are traced, we still must attend to the ways in which the literature has been taken up in intentional theological reinterpretation. Through that process what is initially specific has been transposed into a normative statement regarded in faith communities as revelatory of divine will and purpose.

THE BOOK OF HOSEA

The book of Hosea stands first among the Minor Prophets. It announces the initial accent of indictment and sentence from the broken covenant that provides the access point for the theological thematics of the Twelve. It is apparent that the book of Hosea is rooted in the life and words of the northern prophet in the eighth century (R. Wilson 1980, 225–31). It is not clear precisely when the work of the prophet is to be dated, but it is clearly related to the rise of Assyrian power and the abiding threat of Assyrian power against the northern kingdom. Robert Wilson has made the case that Hosea is situated among the prophets in the northern kingdom who are rooted in the covenantal traditions that claim to go back to Moses, perhaps filtered through what became the Deuteronomic tradition. The accent on broken covenant causes the prophet to speak particularly oracles that are "prophetic lawsuits" that indict Israel and announce a divine judgment against Israel (Westermann 1967). A clear example is found in Hosea 4:1–3:

Verse 1a—A call to court:

Hear the word of the LORD, O people of Israel;
	for the LORD has an indictment against the inhabitants of the land.

Verses 1b–2—Indictment:

There is no faithfulness or loyalty,
	and no knowledge of God in the land.
Swearing, lying, and murder,
	and stealing and adultery break out;
	bloodshed follows bloodshed.

Verse 3—Sentence:

Therefore the land mourns,
	and all who live in it languish;

together with the wild animals
    and the birds of the air,
    even the fish of the sea are perishing.

The daring argument made by the poem is that the violation of the Torah commandments, herewith an allusion to the Decalogue, will result in divine judgment, here *the undoing of creation* through a drought. It is the insistence of this most recurring form of prophetic speech in the eighth century that the world is covenantally coherent and must answer to the covenant Lord. Hosea, in most imaginative form, can articulate that thematic point in endless poetic variation with extreme images and daring metaphors. While 4:1–3 articulates drought as the divine judgment, more likely the punishment is historical, in this case the threat of Assyrian invasion and conquest that is understood, as in Isaiah 10:5, as YHWH's action of punishment for the broken covenant (see Hos 10:6).

It is conventional to divide the book of Hosea into two unequal parts, chapters 1–3 and 4–14. The second, larger section is filled out with prophetic lawsuits. The first part is famously about divorce and remarriage, that is, infidelity and fidelity and the crisis of broken covenant and renewed covenant. Chapter 1 purports to be a report on the prophet's personal experience, and chapter 3 purports to be a first-person testimony of the prophet. While the particularities are in dispute, the text clearly testifies that Hosea's bold theological articulation is deeply rooted in a personal experience of broken and restored relationship that the prophet receives and reports on as revelatory of the divine character and divine intentionality.

Whatever may be the connection between personal experience and prophetic proclamation, chapter 2 is among the most important presentations of covenantal theology in all of the Old Testament. Verses 2–13 portray the broken covenant of Israel with YHWH that eventuates in rejection and divorce. The theme of Israel's infidelity is reported through a triangle of husband (YHWH), lover (Baal), and wife (Israel), who has forsaken husband YHWH in order to cohabit with lover Baal. This betrayal of the covenant evokes YHWH's anger and eventual termination of the relationship. (The theme is not unlike the one we have seen in Ezek 16; 20; and 23.)

The difference in Hosea's presentation is that in Hosea 2, verses 2–13 are followed, astonishingly enough, by verses 14–23, in which the wounded and forsaken husband YHWH woos Israel again and remarries her, a new marriage that causes the earth to flourish again (vv. 21–23). The bold theme of remarriage is as graphic as a new set of wedding vows that are the outcome of YHWH's courting: "And I will take you for my wife forever; I will take you for my wife in righteousness and in justice, in steadfast love, and in mercy.

I will take you for my wife in faithfulness; and you shall know the LORD"
(2:19–20).

The report on divorce (vv. 2–13) and remarriage (vv. 14–23) concerns the
broken and restored covenant. David Clines has shown how the two parts
of the completed poem are designed to be symmetrical and commensurate
(Clines 1998). Two observations about this wondrous poetic foray are to be
noticed. First, Hosea seems to regard religious, cultic infidelity to YHWH
through preoccupation with Baal as "fertility god" as the besetting sin of
Israel. Second, given that fact, it is remarkable that the poetry of Hosea utilizes the rhetoric of "fertility" (vv. 16–18, 21–23) in order to combat the
seductions of Baal. Thus the argument is not that fertility religion—that is,
appreciation of the juices of new life that occur in creation—is in principle
bad, but that YHWH, not Baal, is the authoritative, reliable fertility God
(Harrelson 1969). That is, the tradition of Hosea employs precisely the rhetoric of Baalism in order to combat Baalism, and to make the claim that the
power for life is administered only by YHWH the Creator, who is also the
God of the Torah and who must be obeyed. It is most remarkable that Hosea
casts the gravitas of covenantal faith in the categories of the most intimate
relationship of fidelity.

It is common now to recognize that the initial words of the prophet Hosea
(to which we have no direct access) became a "text" on which the ongoing
traditioning process continued to reflect and to extend. We may identify two
characteristic maneuvers in this traditioning process of Hosea. First, the tradition of Hosea was situated in and addressed to the religious-political crisis
of the north in the last days of the northern kingdom. It is clear, however, that
this northern material was subsequently taken up by and found useful to the
continuing life of Judah after Assyria had terminated the kingdom of Samaria
in 721 BCE. For example, 2:7 recognizes the end of the northern kingdom
but anticipates the continuation of the southern kingdom:

> She shall pursue her lovers,
>   but not overtake them;
> and she shall seek them,
>   but shall not find them.
> Then she shall say, "I will go
>   and return to my first husband,
>   for it was better with me then than now."

In other texts Judah is now twinned with Israel in disobedience, judgment,
and punishment in a way that was not likely on the horizon of eighth-century
Hosea. Thus the continuing tradition found (and made) his words addressed
to northern Israel pertinent to the kingdom of Judah:

Israel's pride testifies against him;
    Ephraim stumbles in his guilt;
    Judah also stumbles with them.
                 (5:5)

Israel has forgotten his Maker,
    and built palaces;
and Judah has multiplied fortified cities;
    but I will send a fire upon his cities,
    and it shall devour his strongholds.
          (8:14; see 6:4; 10:11; 12:2)

In 6:11 the reference to Judah appears to be an editorial afterthought, making the editorial process more transcendent. Thus we are able to see how it is that the tradition continues to develop in ways that keep the remembered words of the prophet contemporary to new crises.

The second editorial maneuver, which may or may not be directly related to the eighth-century prophet, is that the devastating message of judgment concerning the unbearable infidelity of Israel toward YHWH is matched, answered, and overcome by assurances about a future for Israel that follows judgment. It is not impossible that the eighth-century prophet entertained such expectation. It is in any case unmistakable that the completed book of Hosea offers assurance for Israel's survival and well-being beyond the deep dislocation of judgment. As we have seen, 2:14–23 answers 2:2–13. It is not clear that the second half of the poem belongs to the eighth-century prophet; it is, however, quite clear, in the final form of the text, that the final word for Israel is restored well-being.

Second, we may notice the final oracle of assurance in 14:4–7 (followed only by a redactional signature of editorial scribes in 14:8–9):

I will heal their disloyalty;
    I will love them freely,
    for my anger has turned from them.
I will be like the dew to Israel;
    he shall blossom like the lily,
    he shall strike root like the forests of Lebanon.
His shoots shall spread out;
    his beauty shall be like the olive tree,
    and his fragrance like that of Lebanon.
They shall again live beneath my shadow,
    they shall flourish as a garden;
they shall blossom like the vine,
    their fragrance shall be like the wine of Lebanon.

The theme of YHWH as "healer" is already known in Hosea (6:2). In this passage, however, the healing anticipated is a complete divine resolution of all suffering and judgment that has been visited upon YHWH's people. The imagery through which the healing is announced, moreover, is itself the rhetoric of fertility, "blossom," "root," "shoot," and so on. We may take this final affirmation of the book of Hosea as a characteristic editorial act that we have already seen in the books of Isaiah, Jeremiah, and Ezekiel. The prophetic corpus is framed to move the community of faith into and out of the crisis of displacement. While the theme of restoration becomes more vigorous in the latter parts of the Twelve, the traditioning process cannot leave even the first of the Twelve unresolved.

Finally, we call attention to 11:1–9, among the most remarkable oracles in the entire prophetic literature. The oracle falls into three parts:

1. Verses 1–4 review YHWH's initial kindness to Israel under the rubric of attentive parent to a small child.
2. Verses 5–7 voice YHWH's profound indignation toward recalcitrant Israel, and YHWH's resolve to permit Israel to be devastated by the sword, proper punishment for profound disobedience.
3. But then, in an inexplicable rhetorical maneuver not unlike the break between 2:13 and 2:14, it is as though YHWH reverses field and breaks from the anger of verses 5–7:

> How can I give you up, Ephraim?
>   How can I hand you over, O Israel?
> How can I make you like Admah?
>   How can I treat you like Zeboiim?
> My heart recoils within me;
>   my compassion grows warm and tender.
> I will not execute my fierce anger;
>   I will not again destroy Ephraim;
> for I am God and no mortal,
>   the Holy One in your midst,
>   and I will not come in wrath.
>   (11:8–9)

It is as though YHWH, through the daring of the poet, reaches deeper into YHWH's own sensibility. There YHWH discovers, so the poet dares to say, a deep passion and, consequently, deep compassion for Israel that precludes the destruction just announced in verses 5–7. In this text the anticipated and legitimate punishment of Israel is foresworn; this divine resolve is different from and much more radical than 14:4–7, where healing comes after devastation. Here the devastation is averted. The ground for averted devastation, moreover, is YHWH's own sense of self. YHWH is not "a man" to react in anger; YHWH, rather, is "God." More than that, YHWH is "the Holy One in Israel," the God whose holy character is profoundly qualified by loyalty to Israel. This sense of self on YHWH's part is the ground for well-being in Israel, even when Israel's shabby treatment of YHWH merits otherwise. Thus the poetic tradition of Hosea reaches down into the poetic-rhetorical-emotional depths that move past any simple formula of disobedience and punishment or any other quid pro quo. We cannot trace how this depth perception has come about; the tradition of Hosea is indeed a disclosure of YHWH's deep capacity for grace, a grace rooted in YHWH's own life, but defining for Israel as Israel finds its recalcitrant way through the vagaries of historical crisis. It is no wonder that the ongoing traditioning process found the memory of Hosea particularly compelling and peculiarly pertinent in the recurring reality of displacement and loss in Judaism. The tradition in its final form denies nothing of that loss, nor the ground of such loss in Israel's infidelity.

It refuses, however, to permit such loss to have the final word in the tradition. This conclusion may be an editorial achievement remote from the personal experience of the prophet. It is easy to see, nonetheless, how the tradition understood itself to be rooted in the intimate personal suffering of this anguished prophet who received the mandate: "The LORD said to me again, 'Go, love a woman who has a lover and is an adulteress'" (3:1a). That articulation of intimate reality moves immediately to become revelation of YHWH: ". . . just as the LORD loves the people of Israel, though they turn to other gods and love raisin cakes" (3:1b). This poetic venture stands close to the lived reality of infidelity; the rhetoric, moreover, makes possible the life of YHWH in the midst of the defining infidelity that endlessly marks the life of Israel. The prophetic word is that such infidelity is indeed defining for Israel—but not finally so.

THE BOOK OF JOEL

Joel, the second book of the Twelve, is profoundly enigmatic. Nothing is known of the prophet Joel or of the historical context of the book. It is clear that the book of Joel quotes from older texts, and on that basis it is conventionally taken to be as late as the Persian period. Any historical-critical judgment that is made, however, is more than a little speculative.

The book divides into two parts. Chapters 1–2 deal with some profound historical or natural crisis. (Here the difference between Hebrew and English versification is notable; 2:28 in English is 3:1 in Hebrew, and it is at this point that the second part of the book begins.) The poetry characterizes some kind of immense onslaught on Israel that puts the community in deep crisis and evokes great terror (1:2–2:11). That immense "invasion" is as a season of locusts. But the season of locusts that jeopardizes the agricultural community—real as it may have been in that community—becomes the ground from which the poet offers in hyperbole the profound military threat under which the community lives:

> The rhetoric is cranked up; the sound is turned up to its highest, acrosonic. Those who hear are to tremble. An alarm is being sounded. We move to a day of darkness, thick darkness. And as the section gathers velocity and sharpness, we begin to see, through the pervasive darkness, the avenging and sharpness, we begin to see, through the pervasive darkness, the avenging army. . . .
> . . . This is the description of a blitzkrieg, though it be of locusts. . . .
> . . . The invading locusts have not the immediacy of recent history or of an immediately threatened future. But for the modern reader the locust army is still more terrible than the human army because it combines aspects of a science-fiction horror film—enlarged bugs ravaging our planet, grinding us all to bits—and an archetypal terror that indeed this will be so, the smallest particles of moving life that we live among, step on, destroy by the millions when it suits our purposes, when the judgment is finally meted out—and, after all, that's what this poem is about—will be in the saddle (have the appearance of horsemen) and we will be those who flee as before a devouring flame.
> (H. Shapiro 1987, 202, 203, 204)

The rhetoric of locusts—here made larger than life—shades over into an invading army. For the alert reader, however, the jeopardy of either locusts or army is only an instant in the awesome "Day of the Lord" whenever YHWH works hard sovereignty in the world and over YHWH's people:

> Alas for the day!
> For *the day of the* LORD is near,
>   and as destruction from the Almighty it comes.
>   (1:15, italics added)

> Blow the trumpet in Zion;
>   sound the alarm on my holy mountain!
> Let all the inhabitants of the land tremble,
>   for the *day of the* LORD is coming, it is near—
>   (2:1, italics added)

> The LORD utters his voice
>   at the head of his army;
> how vast is his host!
>   Numberless are those who obey his command.
> Truly *the day of the* LORD is great;
>   terrible indeed—who can endure it?
>   (2:11, italics added)

Thus the poetry makes characteristic connections between lived public reality and the rule of YHWH, the God who places all in jeopardy. The community is helpless, so that the only appropriate response is public grief as unto the grief of death:

> How the animals groan!
>   The herds of cattle wander about
> because there is no pasture for them;
>   even the flocks of sheep are dazed.
>   (1:18)

> Put on sackcloth and lament, you priests;
>   wail, you ministers of the altar.
>   (1:13a)

By the third mention of the "Day of the Lord" in 2:11, the poem turns to invite a response of repentance (2:12–17):

> Yet even now, says the LORD,
>   return to me with all your heart,
> with fasting, with weeping, and with mourning;
>   rend your hearts and not your clothing.
>   (2:12–13a)

To provide ground for repentance, the poet offers Israel's classic assurance of YHWH's generosity, a quote from Exodus 34:6:

> Return to the LORD, your God,
>   for he is gracious and merciful,
> slow to anger, and abounding in steadfast love,
>   and relents from punishing.
>   (Joel 2:13b)

That is, the repentance is not motivated by fear, but is offered on the basis of comfort and confidence. We are invited to infer that repentance will cause an end to the threat.

Then in 2:18 the poem turns yet again, so that now YHWH has compassion for land and people, will end the threat, and will restore the land to productivity (grain, wine, oil) and the people to well-being. The culmination of this assurance is the reassertion and re-recognition of YHWH's sovereignty:

> You shall know that I am in the midst of Israel,
>   and that I, the LORD, am your God and there is no other.
> And my people shall never again
>   be put to shame.
>   (2:27)

Thus the first two chapters of the book of Joel move through characteristic accents of *judgment, repentance,* and *mercy.* It is not said in the shift of 2:18 whether Israel has repented and so receives mercy from YHWH, or whether the motivation for YHWH's new governance is without regard to Israel's repentance. Either way, these two chapters that follow sound yet again the themes of judgment and rescue.

The latter half of the book, beginning at 2:28 (Hebrew 3:1), speaks of "afterward," an interpretation of a coming future in much larger scope. The language of 2:30–32 moves in the direction of apocalyptic; such rhetorical usage is in the service of large visioning prospects for the future that are rooted not in visible circumstance, but in nothing other than the unencumbered freedom of YHWH's own creative spirit that can infuse the land and the people with newness. The conclusion of the poem includes an anticipation of restoration from exile (3:1–3), YHWH's assault upon the peoples that oppress Judah (3:4–8), and the launching of war by YHWH the warrior so that YHWH takes as enemy all those who are enemy of Judah (3:9–10).

By the end of the poem (3:17–21) YHWH, as the main character of the poetry, has done a complete about-face: the one who had placed people and land under attack is now the guarantor of both land and people. Thus the land will produce (3:18), and the people will be safe (3:20). Jerusalem, so recently under assault, will be YHWH's place of residence (3:21). All will be well and all will be well!

The poem of Joel thus juxtaposes a reflection on what seems to be a historical crisis (1:2–2:27) together with a visionary anticipation that outruns the historical in making a larger point about YHWH's goodness toward Israel (2:28–3:21). In our estimate it is futile to try to decode the rhetoric and unhelpful to overstate the distinction between the "historical" in chapters 1 and 2 and the "apocalyptic" in the last part of 2 and 3, as though the poet pressed buttons to produce alternative genres. Rather, the entire corpus is a dramatic reflection on the force of YHWH's rule amid the vagaries of lived reality and all of its problems. It is easy enough to see the U shape that House has appropriated from Northrop Frye (House 1990). The poem begins in savage descent and culminates with wonderful ascent to well-being. The movement in the U is marked in 2:28 by "Then afterward," when the poetry moves beyond observable reality, entertaining what cannot be seen and trusting what cannot be seen to the Lord of all that is, visible and invisible.

If we understand the book of Joel to be a highly stylized articulation of YHWH's rule expressed as *judgment* and rescuing *mercy,* then we may notice three texts that are of particular interest to Christian readers, each of which attests to YHWH's rule:

1. Joel 2:12–13 is a text often used in Christian tradition in Lent as a summons to repent. The text in Joel is initially a summons to a ritual of repentance. Nonetheless, the Christian use of the text, in the midst of Lenten ritual, is congruent with the Joel text, for the summons is to reengage with the Lord of grace and mercy.

2. Joel 2:28–32 is a text, cast as apocalyptic, quoted in Peter's sermon at Pentecost (Acts 2:17–21). In this usage, the massive incursion of God's Spirit that is anticipated is no ecclesial function, but refers to the prospect of the entire population now propelled by God's emancipated Spirit. The connection of the Joel text to Pentecost assures that Pentecost, in the tradition of the book of Acts, is no domesticated ritual. It is, rather, an access point whereby God will undo all that has failed and act to protect that remnant aligned with God. Thus the usage in Acts 2:17–21 faithfully reads the Joel text as an invitation to the cataclysmic turn in the world that amounts to nothing less than the full assertion of YHWH's sovereign power.

3. The mandate in 3:10 is of particular interest because it is a counterpoint to the better-known peace vision of Isaiah 2:4 and Micah 4:4. In conventional Christian reading, the Isaiah-Micah reading is much preferred. This text, however, without being politically correct, regards YHWH's role as warrior as essential to the rescue of Israel from the nations.

All three of these texts witness to the decisiveness of YHWH for the lived processes of Israel. Israel must come to terms with YHWH (repentance) and, when Israel is fully congruent with YHWH, then YHWH's own support on behalf of Israel is welcome and decisive.

THE BOOK OF AMOS

It is impossible to overestimate the importance of the book of Amos and the attention given to it in recent interpretation. Older critical scholarship (now eclipsed) held that Amos was the first articulation of Israel's "ethical monotheism," that is, the prophet articulated the rule of one God over all peoples, one God who had a moral purpose of justice for the whole world. More recent critical study has seen Amos as the beginning of a prophetic tradition that would create the matrix in which were generated the narratives and commands that came to constitute the Torah. In current context, moreover, the book of Amos functions to assert the sharp divine judgment that begins the Book of the Twelve in Hosea, with only a glimpse to the newness upon which the Twelve will culminate in its latter books (9:11–15).

The book of Amos is rooted in the work of Amos the prophet. He is commonly dated to the middle of the eighth century, perhaps about 752 BCE, in the midst of the prosperous reign of Jeroboam II in the northern kingdom, matched by the equally prosperous reign of Uzziah in the southern kingdom (1:1; see 2 Kgs 14:23–29 and 15:1–7, where Uzziah is cited by his other name, Azariah). In prophetic perspective, it was clear that this immense prosperity enjoyed in both kingdoms was based on a disastrous practice of the rich against the poor that was sure to be unsustainable. It is the burden of the prophet to assert the illegitimacy of such social practice and to anticipate a coming judgment from YHWH, as it turned out, in the form of Assyrian devastation:

> The breakdown in traditional values was particularly striking among the wealthiest in the society, who cultivated and enjoyed considerable luxury. While some were losing their land and homes and family, others had both winter and summer houses (3:15), lived in homes of ashlar masonry (5:11), or enjoyed furnishings decorated with fine ivory work (3:15, 6:4; excavations have produced numerous examples of Samarian ivories). In 6:1–6 there is a graphic description of the sybaritic banquets enjoyed by the elite of the society, with choice meats, wine (*cf.* 4:1b), unguents, and music.
>
> Amos castigates those who enjoy a life of carefree luxury and remain at the same time oblivious to the violence and oppression on which it is based. Indeed, having lost sight of the right direction for the society (3:9–10), the elite are said to "hoard violence and oppression for themselves" (3:10–11). The core of Amos' message, then, is that because of these misdeeds, God will destroy this society. The finality and thoroughness of this coming disaster, as well as its inescapability, are a persistent theme. (Parker 1989, 368)

Thus the prophet, apparently from Judah but at work in the northern kingdom (see 7:12), articulates a powerful social critique that is rooted in a vigorous Yahwistic sense of what is required and what is possible in a covenantal society. The judgment that is sure to come is voiced as the Day of the Lord when YHWH's governance will be fully and harshly enacted (5:18–20).

From the beginning point in the prophet himself, the book of Amos has emerged through an editorial process whereby the remembered oracles and poems of Amos have been shaped, revised, and supplemented to form a coherent and fairly symmetrical whole. The book of Amos is divided into three parts:

1. Chapters 1 and 2 are constituted as oracles against the nations, a genre we have already seen in Isaiah 13–23, Jeremiah 46–51, and Ezekiel 25–32. This genre is a rhetorical means whereby YHWH's full sovereignty over all peoples is voiced. Two particular notes should be observed in this corpus. First, the small neighboring states are listed as coming under the horizon of

YHWH's governance. This list of small neighboring states is in contrast to the oracles against the nations we have seen in the Major Prophets, which are characteristically concerned with the "great powers." In Amos 2:4–5 and 2:6–16, Judah and Israel are also named among the peoples who are soon to be subject to YHWH's harsh sovereignty. That is, the "chosen peoples" are here treated like all other peoples, subject to the same requirements and marked for the same judgments, without exception for special status:

> For Israel this is a complete overturning of its values, a reversal of its theology. Yahweh's "eye," hitherto fixed benevolently on Israel, is now fixed malevolently on it (9:4b). The Day of Yahweh, eagerly awaited as the time when Yahweh would intervene among the nations on Israel's behalf to give it victory over its enemies, would be a day not of light but of darkness, not of victory but of defeat, as Yahweh fights not for but against Israel (5:18, 20). The motif of Yahweh turning light to darkness recurs in two of the hymnic passages (4:13a, 5:8a), and the same reversal opens the announcement of disaster in 8:9–10. (Parker 1989, 369)

Second, as John Barton has noted, the divine indictment of the nations is not according to the Torah of Sinai, nor is it assumed that the nations know of such a set of commandments. Rather, the appeal is to a much more general ethical requirement to which all nations are held, a requirement that Barton identifies as something like "natural law" (Barton 1979). That is, the oracles against the nations assume that all peoples are subject to the will and limit of YHWH the Creator, and need not know the commands of Sinai in order to know what is required. (In subsequent Judaism, this more general knowledge of the will of YHWH the Creator is subsumed under the covenant of Noah, and all nations are held accountable to the Noachide covenant.)

2. Chapters 3–6 are a collection of prophetic oracles, characteristically expressed as indictments for disobedience and sentences that will be enacted as divine punishment. These oracles form the central materials for what is popularly regarded as "the prophetic," that is, they articulate the urgency of a failed society that does not measure up to covenant requirements. In joining together *indictment* (through a process of astute social analysis) and *sentence* (as anticipation of divine gravitas), the prophetic tradition boldly makes connections between God and world, or God and society. It is the insistence upon this connection through what Klaus Koch calls "metahistory" that is the heart of prophetic proclamation (Koch 1983b).

3. The third section of the book in chapters 7–9 is ordered around five "visions" that initially arise out of observed natural phenomena but that move intensely toward a threatening divine future (7:1–3, 4–6, 7–9; 8:1–3; 9:1).

The sense of the sequence of vision is to assert that a time for repentance is now passed and a time for divine judgment is both near and ominous. Thus the injustices and failure to obey divine requirements delineated in the oracles of chapters 3–6 evoke an anticipation of coming catastrophe, an anticipation that specifically refers to the onslaught of the Assyrians who, at the behest of YHWH, terminated the northern kingdom in 721 BCE. Thus in moving from oracles against the nations (chaps. 1–2) to prophetic oracles (chaps. 3–6) to visions of the end (chaps. 7–9), the book of Amos creates a mighty articulation of YHWH's massive sovereignty, a ruler who will finally tolerate no long-term recalcitrance. The rapid demise of Israel in the northern kingdom in the eighth century at the hands of the Assyrians gave concreteness to the poetic scenario of this prophetic tradition.

> ### Close Reading: Amos 1–2
>
> To catch the full impact of Amos's oracles against the nations in chapters 1 and 2, it helps to have a map of the biblical world at hand. One notices that the speeches are ordered in a very intentional, geographic way, so that the prophet's fierce indictments begin away from Israel and gradually zero in, moving directionally from the northeast (1:3–5) to the southwest (1:6–8) to the northwest (1:9–10) to the southeast (1:11–12) to two close-by locations directly to the east of Judah (1:13–2:3). The prophet then rhetorically moves to the west, delivering an indictment of the southern kingdom of Judah (2:4–5), before finally culminating in the real source of his concern, the northern kingdom of Israel (2:6–16). Once landing on the map on Israel, we notice that the speech lengthens and becomes more detailed, as Amos hits his stride. We also notice that while the foreign nations are indicted for, essentially, obvious war crimes, Israel is indicted for violation of Torah ethics (compare vv. 6–8 with the laws against economic exploitation in Exod 21–22 and Deut 24). The rhetorical point seems clear: in Israel, economic exploitation and social injustice is on equal footing with the worst of violent crimes, because Israel (unlike the other nations) has the Torah to guide them.

In reading the book of Amos, we clearly have moved well beyond the person of Amos, though there is no doubt that the person Amos stands at the outset of what became the book. There is also no doubt that the formation of the book of Amos is through an interpretive process, the purpose of which is to shape, preserve, and transport prophetic cadences into new contexts. Most clearly, the book of Amos has been redacted in order to make the proclamation in the north pertinent to Judah, likely after the northern kingdom had been terminated. We have already cited the oracle of 2:4–5 concerning Judah, an oracle that most scholars believe is a late development in the tradition. Even more important than that, the oracles against the nations in chapters 1 and 2 are now introduced by a Jerusalem reference in 1:2 that has the effect of resituating all of the oracles against the nations in the Jerusalem temple, thus as a detailing of the great claim of Psalm 96:10:

> Say among the nations, "The LORD is king!
>   The world is firmly established; it shall never be moved.
> He will judge the peoples with equity."

Amos, in sync with the great Jerusalem liturgy, is made to assert the rule of the God of Jerusalem over all the nations.

The most persistent critical question in the book of Amos concerns the concluding promise of 9:11–15. Because this promise is so incongruent with Amos's own insistent theme of judgment, many scholars take this promise as a later addition. We may grant that it is a later addition, but are able to see nonetheless that in a belated (canonical) coherence, the concluding promise serves to give even Amos a characteristic prophetic accent of judgment and hope, the same twofold pattern of articulation that we have seen elsewhere in the prophetic tradition. It is probable that the twofold pattern is part of the traditioning process and not the work of Amos the prophet in the eighth century. That is simply more evidence why we must attend not only to the person of Amos but to the book of the prophet.

For a piece of literature so brief, the book of Amos has thoroughly occupied the imagination of the church. Here I mention four texts that serve to carry the thread of the book that are endlessly important to the ongoing theological interpretation of the prophetic tradition:

1. Amos 3:2 in a powerful way links the immediacy of the prophetic judgment to the ancient traditions of promise:

> You only have I known
>   of all the families of the earth;
> therefore I will punish you
>   for all your iniquities.

The verb "know" is the verb used in Genesis 18:19 (there rendered "have chosen" in the NRSV) to indicate Abraham's special relationship to YHWH. Now in the eighth century that special relationship that distinguishes Israel from "all the families of the earth" (see Gen 12:3) becomes the ground for the particular judgment against disobedient Israel. This particular citation in Amos 3:2, with reference to the Abraham text of Genesis 12:3 and 18:19, is a particular way in which the prophetic corpus alludes back to and depends upon the Torah traditions.

2. Three times Amos utilizes the defining phrase "justice and righteousness" as the core prophetic concern (Amos 5:7, 24; 6:12; see Gen 18:19). In the second of these usages, the prophet utters what has become the decisive summons of all prophetic faith:

But let justice roll down like waters,
  and righteousness like an ever-flowing stream.

A characteristic use of this phrasing is by Martin Luther King Jr., a familiar cadence of his rhetoric later utilized in his memorial in Montgomery. This phrasing of Amos has become the impetus for prophetic faith and the ground for prophetic critique of social systems that disregard and violate this most elemental command of YHWH.

3. In three uses the book of Amos reiterates what must have been characteristic doxologies, perhaps used in the Jerusalem temple that celebrated YHWH's sovereignty as Creator (Amos 4:13; 5:8–9; 9:5–6). These texts ground the Amos traditions in Israel's liturgy, and evidence the way in which the sovereignty of YHWH governs the horizon of the book of Amos. It is also thinkable that this doxological creation tradition is the horizon of the oracles against the nations, for the nations are treated as creatures who must obey the Creator. It is this incredible sovereign power of YHWH that is the ground of judgment and eventually the ground of hope in the final promise of 9:11–15. YHWH uttered in sweeping doxology is the one who will not be domesticated by any particular policy, ideology, or intellectual presupposition.

4. The tradition affirms Israel's glorious memory of exodus, and then abruptly in Amos 9:7 deconstructs that claim with the assertion that the God of the exodus does many exoduses even for Israel's sworn enemies, Syria and the Philistines (Brueggemann 1998). Israel has no monopoly on YHWH's saving deeds and therefore cannot claim privilege or imagine itself exceptional. Rather, Israel stands exposed, like every other people, to the demands of this God. As in 3:2 or even 5:18–20, 9:7 plays down Israel's exceptionalism in drastic ways of threat. Given the doxology of 9:5–6, which signals the book's ending, the reader has been ill prepared for the astonishing claim of verse 7 as well as what follows it. After 9:7 the tradition moves quickly toward what stands now as the conclusion, the promise of restoration of monarchy and of all creation (9:11–15). Clearly this sequence is designed to make a rhetorical assault upon Israel's convictions held too long in complacency and without critical or obedient engagement.

THE BOOK OF OBADIAH

This briefest of prophetic books is rooted in a postexilic antipathy of Judah against its neighbor, Edom. In the fifth century, when Judah was a weak political colony of Persia, the Edomites to the east and south impinged upon Judean territory in hostile and aggressive ways. Such action, not surprisingly, evoked resentment and hostility that is here brought to speech. The book of Obadiah is in genre an oracle against the nations, not unlike the more extended collections of Isaiah 13–23, Jeremiah 46–51, Ezekiel 25–32, and Amos 1–2. This genre characteristically articulates YHWH's judgment upon a nation and then, in a commensurate way, anticipates good for Israel when the enemy is defeated by YHWH. This particular oracle in Obadiah against Edom must have had a wide currency—suggesting that resentment against Edom was widespread—for the same material also appears in Jeremiah 49:9–10, 14–16. The double usage of the same material may suggest that it was popular and well known, though we are unable to determine its particular source.

The oracle against Edom in verses 1–14 characteristically identifies pride and arrogance of the enemy people that has eventuated in aggressive policies, here plundering and pillaging (vv. 5–6). In response, the prophetic oracle anticipates the coming Day of the Lord that will be a day of judgment in Edom, when Edom will be harshly treated (v. 8).

The oracle reiterates the Day of the Lord in verse 15. In that verse and thereafter, however, the concern for Edom is now broadened into a generic pronouncement against all nations that are enemies of YHWH and enemies of YHWH's people. In what follows, the poem vacillates between a continued reference to Edom and a generic reference to all nations: "The effect of the new framework is to ensure that Edom is now understood as a representative entity, namely, the ungodly power of this world which threatens the people of God. The canonical shape of the book addresses Edom as an example of what lies ahead for the pagan world" (Childs 1979, 415).

With reference to either hated Edom or to all nations under judgment, the outcome is one of the soon-to-be-given well-being for Mount Zion, which will take possession of enemy territory:

> But on Mount Zion there shall be those that escape,
>   and it shall be holy;
> and the house of Jacob shall take possession of those who dispossessed them.
> The house of Jacob shall be a fire,
>   the house of Joseph a flame,
>   and the house of Esau stubble;
> they shall burn them and consume them,
>   and there shall be no survivor of the house of Esau;
> for the LORD has spoken.
>
> (Obad 17–18)

Insofar as this oracle concerns Edom—and before it becomes generic toward all nations—this poetry focuses on a particular crisis between neighboring states and recognizes that Israel and Edom are peoples deeply linked historically and culturally. Thus in Amos 1:11 the two peoples are "brothers" bound in covenantal loyalty (Fishbane 1970). And behind these prophetic texts the narrative memory of Israel concerning Jacob and Esau has understood a common inheritance, so that the conflict is one between siblings (Gen 32–33). In Deuteronomy 2:1–8, moreover, it is recognized that "Esau" is entitled to land upon which Israel must not encroach because this is an entitlement of "your kindred" (Deut 2:4; see Miller 2000, 593–602). Thus the relationship is one of ambiguity, but not one that is predictably or uniformly hostile.

The articulation of the book of Obadiah is unambiguous in its judgment upon Edom and in its promise to Israel. For the most part, commentators leave it at that. A reading of Obadiah at the outset of the twenty-first century, however, must surely take into account the present immense conflict between Israel and the Palestinians. The latter are not quite "Edomites," but they do fall within the general category of "Arab." There is no doubt that behind the present conflict over territory and water, there is traditional impetus for hostility between Israel and Arabs that is fed by a sense of inordinate entitlement on the part of Israel, whereby Israel readily triangulates with YHWH against Israel's enemies. Thus one must not read this anti-Edomite (anti-Arab) polemic innocently, but must recognize that such an ancient text can feed present conflict with old, sacral guarantees that still have firepower, even if they are quite removed from political reality. The book of Obadiah is a clear example of the way in which theological conviction serves political agenda in a powerful way. Such a notion of the Day of the Lord to the unmitigated benefit of Israel (as in v. 15) is exactly the kind of usage against which Amos polemicizes in Amos 5:18–20, for Obadiah anticipates such a "day" to be for Israel a day of "light, not darkness."

THE BOOK OF JONAH

The book of Jonah is unique among the Twelve because it is the only one that is in the genre of a narrative. The lead character in the narrative, Jonah, seems to be rooted in the textual reference of 2 Kings 14:25, but the narrative character is not in any way linked to the character in that historical reportage except by literary allusion. The book of Jonah may be reckoned to be "prophetic," both because the lead character who is sent by YHWH is a prophet and because the book itself seems to carry a prophetic message, given not by the character Jonah but by the narrator.

The beginning question of interpretation of the book of Jonah concerns the genre of the narrative. Critical scholarship has long since given up any notion that the story of Jonah is historical. Rather, it is an artistic, imaginative creation designed to carry a message, but one that is delivered in an artistic way that is not excessively didactic. Thus the narrative is offered as a parable, a fable, or a didactic novel, though any of these labels must not be taken with too much precision. The narrative must be taken on its own terms, and since we can make no historical or even few historical-critical judgments about the book, we can say very little with certitude about it other than to comment on its content. The book of Jonah is conventionally dated to the Persian period and, as with much literature from that later period, it contains allusions to earlier texts.

Two specific questions have dominated much of the interpretive discussion. The first concerns the identity and meaning of the "big fish" in chapter 2. It is clear that the "fish" is elemental to the narrative, but it may be taken in the narrative for what it is; consequently, it is not necessary to interpret allegorically as though the fish were an image suggesting Israel's exile. It is enough to see the "fish" as a vehicle whereby Jonah is put deeply at risk to the power of chaos (the sea), and is rescued by the power of the Creator (who presides over chaos) through the creature, the fish. Thus the rescue of Jonah is also a demonstration of the power of the Creator, who will not have the mission of the prophet thwarted. Even the fish, consequently, serves the prophetic mission intended by YHWH.

The second critical question, more intrinsic to the narrative itself, is the issue of whether the psalm in Jonah 2:2–9, a song of thanksgiving, is intrinsic to the narrative or is inserted. There need be little doubt, because of its genre, that the psalm existed apart from the narrative. That, however, does not make the psalm extraneous to the narrative, but rather it is a vehicle for the advance of the narrative. Thus George Landes has insisted that the psalm becomes pivotal for the working of the narrative in its theological intentionality (Landes 1967). In this perception, the prayer of thanksgiving on the lips of Jonah articulates the traditional trust of Israelite prayer and functions as a counterpoint to Jonah's prayer in 4:2 that acknowledges YHWH's great mercy (which Jonah himself has received in chap. 2); Jonah, however, in chapter 4, resents and resists the very mercy that YHWH has shown to Nineveh, which he himself has received in chapter 2:

> In his prayer and worship relationship to Yahweh, as well as in his experience of the divine deliverance, Jonah is on the same plane with the pagans. But in his refusal to repent and change his mind about the destruction of Nineveh, his attitude is in striking contrast to that of the Ninevites. By his question in 4:4, Yahweh hopes Jonah will confess the error in his predilection for confining the divine mercy and salvation to persons like himself. But Jonah misunderstands the purpose of Yahweh's query, taking it to imply, not that he should

revise his thinking about what God has refused to do to Nineveh, but that his own prophecy of doom for the city may yet be vindicated. When he goes out and constructs the shelter for himself, it is with the intention of viewing what will happen in the city, that is, in his hopeful expectation, the prophesied cataclysm. . . .

Despite the fact that everything seems to be against Yahweh's overthrowing the city—the inhabitants have repented, and Yahweh has acknowledged this by refusing to destroy it—Jonah desperately holds to the hope that judgment will prevail. It is only when his cherished *qiqayon* [castor bean plant] has withered and he feels the blasts of the desert wind and the merciless beat of the sun, that he realizes his expectation will not be fulfilled—and more than this—that a fundamental conviction by which he has lived has been shattered: he had believed that God's wrath to judge those outside Israel should outweigh his mercy to save them. He does not object to the divine compassion and salvation directed to those like himself, but when it is also effective for the wicked, he cannot abide it. Yet he is unwilling to live without his old belief; and because he refuses to let Yahweh transform his anger into love, his pity for plants into pity for people, his conception of what the object of the divine mercy ought to be into what Yahweh has shown him it actually is, he desperately longs to die. (Landes 1967, 27, 29)

The plot of the whole concerns YHWH's resolve to save Nineveh if Nineveh will repent. It is important to recognize that "Nineveh"—the hated imperial city of the hated Assyrian Empire—has here become a cipher for all foreign nations who have abused Israel but who nonetheless fall under the aegis of YHWH's governance. Thus the narrative of Jonah appeals to the genre of oracles against the nations as we have just seen in the book of Obadiah and as we will see in the hate song of the book of Nahum against Nineveh. The narrative of Jonah, however, instead of responding polemically against Nineveh, as do most of the examples of the genre of oracles against the nations, portrays YHWH as ready to rescue Nineveh, that is, to save it (Jonah 3). The character of Jonah—and consequently the entire plot of the narrative—is a presentation of the way in which the gracious God who rescues Israel (and Jonah in 2:9) is the God who intends to rescue Nineveh as well.

The plot turns on YHWH's resolve to save Nineveh; YHWH's strategy is a prophetic summons via Jonah to Nineveh to repent, a summons that the king of Nineveh unexpectedly embraces. Thus the hated foreigner repents and turns to YHWH; while the Israelite insider, Jonah, acknowledges YHWH's mercy and resists its offer to the outsider. As a parable, the narrative exposes Israel (Jonah) as the great and dependent recipient of YHWH's mercy who resists the extension of that same mercy beyond Israel to other peoples who also are recipients of that mercy. Israel (Jonah) fully acknowledges the merciful character of YHWH in most traditional language (4:2; see Exod 34:6–7), but wishes most passionately that the truth of YHWH's mercy did not extend beyond Israel.

It is conventional to interpret the narrative of Jonah in relation to the harsh antiforeign policies of Ezra and Nehemiah in the condemnation of mixed marriages and in their general animosity toward non-Jews (see Ezra 9:1–4; Neh 13:23–27). While the narrative plot of Jonah readily witnesses against that sort of xenophobia by evidencing the embracive mercy of YHWH toward the foreigner, it is less likely that the narrative of Jonah is deliberately a response to that particular political crisis. Rather, the book of Jonah concerns a recurring and endlessly powerful resistance to reduce YHWH's character, so large in mercy and comprehensive in compassion, to the local convenience of the insider community of Israel. While the Ezra-Nehemiah reference constitutes one case study in such an inclination to reduce the character of YHWH, the problem is a perennial one that is inescapably endemic to the tradition (Levenson 1996). In the character of Jonah, the narrative presents an Israel who must inevitably rely on YHWH's generosity but who, in the very act of relying upon that generosity, resists the awareness that the same generosity extends to "the other," who is unlike "us" in many ways, but exactly like "us" in relying on YHWH's gracious mercy.

Finally, the narrative of Jonah is an artistic achievement of considerable power in which patterns of words and phrases give the narrative a remarkable and cunning depth. After one has read the narrative of Jonah for the plot line, a reread for artistic nuance is worth the effort. By attending to a close reading of the narrative, the reader can begin to see how artistic sensibility permits biblical material to be more than a simple offer of truth, for truth given artistically has a narrative thickness that resists reductionist domestication. The reader will find a rich, reliable, and persuasive guide for a close reading of Jonah, and more generally the learning of good method, in the perceptive study by Phyllis Trible (1994).

THE BOOK OF MICAH

The name "Micah" in Hebrew can be taken as a vigorous affirmation of YHWH in the form of a question, "Who is like Yahweh?" to which the vigorous implied answer is: no one! The question is posed exactly that way in Micah 7:18 where it is affirmed, at the conclusion of the book of Micah, that there is *none like YHWH*:

> Who is a God like you, pardoning iniquity
>   and passing over the transgression
>   of the remnant of your possession?
> He does not retain his anger forever,
>   because he delights in showing clemency.

Thus the book of Micah may be understood as a doxological meditation upon the character of YHWH as understood and evidenced in a series of critical moments in the life of Israel.

The book of Micah is rooted in the utterance of the prophet Micah, who is commonly dated at the end of the eighth century, perhaps as late as 715 BCE. This prophet thus lived in the same context of crisis as the prophet Isaiah and they have much in common; at the same time, however, they have very different perspectives. Whereas Isaiah was a resident of Jerusalem and perceived Yahwistic reality through the claims of urban Jerusalem, Micah is from Moresheth, a village to the southeast of Jerusalem, and so he brings a rural, agrarian perspective to his task and is not enamored of the high religious claims of Jerusalem (Wolff 1978).

It is a common judgment of scholars that most of chapters 1–3 derive from the prophet Micah, perhaps along with some of the harsh indictment of Judah in chapter 6 that resonates with other eighth-century prophets, notably Amos and Isaiah. Specifically, the prophet Micah accents the rapacious economic practices of the landed community that exploit the vulnerable, and so violate the will of YHWH for economic justice in the community. The affronts committed against YHWH include aggressive land practices (2:1–2) and exploitative policies that generated urban wealth at the expense of the vulnerable (3:9–11). As a consequence, the ones able and willing to enact systemic economic violence are the ones who become economically advantaged and well-off (6:9–12). Characteristic of such prophetic indictment, there follow in Micah's oracles dire threats against the city and its leadership, for finally political and economic practice must answer to the Lord of all public processes.

From that rootage in the eighth-century prophet, it is clear that the tradition has continued to develop beyond the eighth-century crisis and beyond the person of Micah from Moresheth. Indeed, the continued development of the book of Micah extends into the crisis of the sixth century and around the characteristic accents we have already encountered in other prophetic literature. The promise in 2:12–13 appears to be a belated oracle that is in the context of exile and resonates with the fuller articulation of Ezekiel 34 of YHWH as the "gathering" shepherd.

The promissory passages of chapters 4 and 5, introduced by the formula "in days to come," are surely later and reflect a recurring prophetic conviction that the *God who punishes* is the *God who will restore*. Thus Micah 4:1–5 is a promise that parallels Isaiah 2:1–5, though with variation that an agrarian setting might evoke (this with particular reference to "vines and fig trees" in v. 4). In verse 6 a second promissory formula is used, again to anticipate restoration from exile (4:6–13). The theme of the restoration of the lame and afflicted echoes the great vision of return in Isaiah 40:1–11. The parallels to Isaiah of the exile support the claim that this material is likely exilic.

The second wave of material begins in 6:1, so that chapters 6–7 offer something of a parallel to chapters 1–5 with twin accents of judgment and restoration. Both units of text begin in *judgment*, in each case likely from the eighth-century prophet (chaps. 1–3; 6:1–7:7), and both units culminate with promises of *restoration* that reflect a later circumstance and a later need of the community (chaps. 4–5; 7:8–20). These latter promissory visions of restoration are not from the eighth-century prophet, but are a product of the ongoing tradition that constituted the final form of the book of Micah.

Thus chapter 6 begins in a speech of judgment that is characteristic of eighth-century prophets and continues with a series of indictments and sentences concerning a distorted social practice that is unacceptable to the God of Israel. In chapter 7 the first voice that speaks is the voice of one who has been victimized by exploitative social practice, one who must wait for God's saving intervention (v. 7). A new textual unit begins in 7:8 and continues to the end of the book, a unit that has liturgical markings and that ponders a future yet to be given by the generosity of YHWH. The poem, in characteristic fashion, acknowledges the burden of the present, but does not doubt God's coming intervention (v. 9). That time of divine intervention will be "a day for building" (v. 11). The anticipated well-being for Israel, surely an allusion to restoration from exile, will be a day of infamy for the abusive nations (7:16–17). Thus the text anticipates a great show of divine power on behalf of Israel. That power is rooted, moreover, in God's *compassion, faithfulness*, and *loyalty* (vv. 18–20). These three characteristic markings of YHWH—the same three that are enumerated in Lamentations 3:22–23—are decisive for the incomparability of YHWH, an incomparability that is to be mobilized on behalf of needy, abused Israel. These final verses of the book of Micah constitute one of the most remarkable poetic, prophetic characterizations of the God of the Bible. In this utterance, the tradition takes up old and familiar formulae and brings them together in response to the particular need in the community.

Three texts in particular might be noted:

1. Micah 3:9–12 constitutes a characteristic eighth-century speech of judgment made up of indictment and sentence, the latter introduced by "Therefore" (Westermann 1967). Quite clearly, the rural peasant Micah had no investment in the Jerusalem claims and promises that are paramount to his contemporary Isaiah. This oracle is of special interest because it functions as

an important precedent in the trial of Jeremiah, who is apparently rescued from a judicial sentence of death by appeal to this text that establishes the legitimacy of prophetic critique of the Jerusalem establishment (Jer 26:17–19). Thus the texts of Micah and Jeremiah together are a marvelous example of the Bible quoting the Bible.

2. Micah 5:2–6 is of interest in Christian reading because the text is quoted in Matthew 2:6 at the outset of the gospel narrative and recurs in Christian reading in Advent. The text anticipates a new ruler of Judah from Bethlehem, a village near Moresheth, the prophet's home. Thus the oracle anticipates a rural savior who is not beholden to the urban establishment of Jerusalem, who will have the capacity to rescue Judah and confound the great power of Assyria. The Bethlehem connection would seem to be a Davidic allusion, but nothing is made of that connection here. The church's reading of the text understands Jesus as the one anticipated from Bethlehem, a rootage that in the Gospel of Matthew confounded the Eastern "wise men" (Matt 2:1–12).

3. Micah 6:1–8, a classic prophetic speech of judgment, is well known because of the culminating teaching of verse 8:

> He has told you, O mortal, what is good;
>   and what does the LORD require of you
> but to do *justice*, and to love *kindness*,
>   and to *walk humbly* with your God?
> (italics added)

This verse is widely taken to be a summary of prophetic ethics, which requires justice, steadfast love, and intimate responsiveness to YHWH. In context, this imperative requirement is contrasted to cultic offerings that are here devalued (vv. 6–7), and is understood as a response to the accusation of infidelity that YHWH lodges against Israel in verses 3–5.

The sum of the book of Micah demonstrates the way in which an originary prophetic utterance is transformed into a fuller, coherent theological statement. The text is rooted in the harsh articulation of Micah. The continuing tradition, however, with awareness of the needs of a later context, will not let the harsh judgment of Micah be the last word. The last word, rather, concerns the God who pardons, the God who is unlike any other in *compassion*, *faithfulness*, and *loyalty*. The book of Micah has a notable dynamism; clearly its framers felt no need to sort out the tensive relationship between the initial harshness of the tradition and the culminating pardon. Both belong to the defining relationship with YHWH that Israel came to understand and articulate only through the extended vagaries of their lived experience.

20

The Minor Prophets (2)

If the first six books of the Minor Prophets tend to focus on *sin* against covenant and cosmos, the next six can be divided into two groups of three, with Nahum, Habakkuk, and Zephaniah tending to focus on *punishment* for such sin, and Haggai, Zechariah, and Malachi tending to focus on the *restoration* that follows punishment. We say "tending" because, as noted at the beginning of the last chapter, things are not quite so schematic as that makes it seem. Nevertheless, there is at least a rough canonical shaping of the material to evince this typical prophetic move from indictment to punishment to the hope for restoration.

THE BOOK OF NAHUM

The book of Nahum is one of three books of the Minor Prophets (the other two being Habakkuk and Zephaniah) regularly dated to the late seventh century, the time of the rise and fall of the great superpowers to the north and the impending demise of Jerusalem. Nothing is known of Nahum, though the proper name means "Comfort," and the poetry of the book offers comfort to Israel by celebrating the defeat of Israel's enemies.

The poetry of Nahum, according to its general theme, is not unlike the oracles against the nations we have encountered in Isaiah 13–23, Jeremiah 46–51, Ezekiel 25–32, Amos 1–2, and most recently in the book of Obadiah. This genre celebrates the wrathful judgment of YHWH against foreign powers who, in arrogance and assumed autonomy, have defied YHWH and mocked YHWH's sovereignty. Now, according to the poetry of this genre, YHWH is provoked by such defiance and mockery, and acts through extraordinary military power to crush the recalcitrant subject and creature (Brueggemann 1995). The predictable by-product of such violent assertion of YHWH's sovereignty against recalcitrant subjects is release, joy, and new well-being for Israel; characteristically the way in which foreign powers mock YHWH is to abuse Israel. And therefore the reassertion of YHWH's rule is characteristically a benefit to Israel. Thus the oracles against the nations in general and Nahum in particular celebrate both the *defeat* of the foreign powers and the *release* of Israel as consequence of YHWH's reassertion of sovereignty.

The superscription of 1:1 resituates the generic words of the opening poem so that the poetry refers to the fall of Assyria in 612 BCE (see also 3:18). This particular connection makes the poetry of Nahum into a celebration of the fall of Nineveh as the capital of Assyria, though on its own terms the poetry is quite generic and lacks such specificity. Assyria had been the dominant imperial power in the Near East for more than a century and an endless threat to Israel. We know from Assyria's own royal records, moreover, that Assyrian imperial military power was uncommonly harsh and brutal. Thus the undoing of the empire and the fall of its capital city of Nineveh must have evoked great relief and joy, a relief and joy that here are gladly linked to the reality of YHWH. We may imagine the glad release of long-pent-up resentment, the kind of hostility readily channeled into theological indignation, but surely based upon political debasement that is unbearable.

The assault on Assyrian governance and the affirmation of YHWH's rule together offer an opportunity to consider prophetic notions of history that Klaus Koch has termed "metahistory" (Koch 1983b). It was voiced already in the Isaiah tradition that Assyria was a vehicle of YHWH's rule (10:5). Assyria, however, exploited that role assigned by YHWH for its own aggrandizement and so in turn became an enemy of YHWH who is subject to YHWH's wrath (10:7–19). Thus the prophetic tradition can imagine that such a power as Assyria may be allied with YHWH—even against YHWH's own people— but such alliances are always provisional and transient (Brueggemann 1997, 492–527).

The book of Nahum is divided into two parts. In 1:2–8, verses that preserve the semblance of an acrostic poem, the decisive character of YHWH is announced as the one who will seek "vengeance" (vv. 2–3) and who will "make a full end" to those who resist YHWH's sovereignty (v. 8). Here, as elsewhere in the oracles against the nations genre, YHWH is the key character and the decisive force; indeed, the entire book attests to YHWH's rule and to YHWH as powerful and capable of harsh governance. Thus "vengeance" is not arbitrary violence on the part of YHWH, but an imposition of divine sovereignty on a recalcitrant subject. In speaking of the term *nqm* (vengeance), George Mendenhall proposes:

the words for "vengeance" even in ancient pagan texts are used characteristically only of actions carried out by the highest of social and
political authority—the gods and the king—and the action is virtually restricted to warfare beyond the body politic. . . . [A] study of the
various uses of the Hebrew/Canaanite root *NQM* demonstrates an
almost precise analogy to the uses of its semantic equivalents in other
ancient languages, but with the most significant contrasts which well
illustrate the peculiar sophistication of ancient biblical thought. Fur-
thermore, those uses illustrate with particular cogency the main thesis
of this collection of essays, namely, that early Israel can be conceived
of as a functioning social organism only as the actual dominion of
Yahweh. (Mendenhall 1974, 72)

The second part of the book, beginning at 1:9, continues to give expression to YHWH's wrathful initiative against Nineveh, thus asserting YHWH's
remarkable continued rule that has been only modestly challenged by the
aggressiveness of that empire. In the service of Yahwistic affirmation, the
poetry employs a series of genres—a woe oracle in 3:1–7, a taunt song in 3:8–
13, an oracle portraying Nineveh's defeat in 3:14–17, and a final funeral dirge
in 3:18–19. All of these several forms serve the key theological point that is,
in context, also the key political point, namely, that Israel is given breathing
space in a world governed by YHWH.

Two notations may be added. First, it is common to notice that this poem
of threat against Nineveh has as a counterpoint the narrative of Jonah that
offers the king of Assyria an opportunity to repent, a chance taken by the
king of Nineveh. In the narrative of Jonah, the prophet himself is portrayed
as one disappointed by YHWH's mercy to Nineveh. Thus the character
of Jonah, who does not want Nineveh forgiven or saved, is at one with the
mood of the poetry of Nahum. The narrative of Jonah, as distinct from
the character of Jonah, testifies against such a narrow chauvinism that
wants only trouble and death for the enemy and no mercy at all. In a world
increasingly prone to nationalistic barbarism, as is our contemporary world,
a counterpoint of the narrative of Jonah helps us read the poem of Nineveh
with critical alertness.

Second, it is common for interpreters of Nahum to take the words of
Nahum as a powerful theological witness to the sovereign capacity of YHWH.
In reading the literature on the book of Nahum, we have been surprised that
interpreters take the polemic against Nineveh at face value as a vigorous theological affirmation. Surely it is to be recognized, without denigrating that
theological point, that the poetry is, at the same time, self-serving Israelite
glee and perhaps even self-congratulations as beneficiary of YHWH's action.
We may perhaps read Nahum with critical alertness if we attend to Israel's
capacity to equate *my* enemies with *YHWH's* enemies:

Do I not hate those who hate you, O Lᴏʀᴅ?
  And do I not loathe those who rise up against you?
I hate them with perfect hatred;
  I count them my enemies.

(Ps 139:21–22)

The psalm does not speak of enemies in international scope. The point, however, is readily extrapolated so that the shrill glee of the poetry has no trouble presenting Assyria as an enemy of YHWH, the empire that was surely an enemy of YHWH's people. Since the poetry is preponderantly threat with very little indictment, there is no guilt of Nineveh named that is related to Israel. The indictment, rather, concerns arrogant autonomy, and the tone of the whole poem readily aligns YHWH and Israel against Assyria. Such a ready alignment of YHWH and YHWH's people against a common enemy might give pause to readers of the poetry who are citizens of the "last super-power." Such a superpower may evoke resentment from many subordinated peoples and may also live close (in arrogant autonomy) to profound affront against this God so capable of ferocious reassertion of governance. The last act in this scenario is YHWH's hard rule against Assyria. The last word voices the superpower run amok, beyond recall:

Your shepherds are asleep,
  O king of Assyria;
  your nobles slumber.
Your people are scattered on the mountains
  with no one to gather them.
There is no assuaging your hurt,
  your wound is mortal.
All who hear the news about you
  clap their hands over you.
For who has ever escaped
  your endless cruelty?

(3:18–19)

THE BOOK OF HABAKKUK

In ancient Israel, events of great depth and large scope evoked poetic-prophetic-imaginative generativity. The defining international reality of the prophetic tradition featured the demise of the long-resented Assyrian Empire, a demise celebrated by Nahum as a triumph of YHWH. The demise of Assyria, however, only made way for the emergence of the Babylonian Empire, a force that was to become a profound and decisive threat to the political reality of Jerusalem. Thus the end of the seventh century BCE featured acute political turmoil in Jerusalem, a turmoil matched by prophetic generativity (see 2 Kgs 24–25).

As the book of Nahum marked the end of Assyrian hegemony, so the prophetic book of Habakkuk, in the Babylonian period of Jerusalem's history, mobilizes a rich variety of extant liturgical traditions into a roughly coherent statement of faith that features *cries of need* that are ultimately resolved in a *hymn of triumph*. The liturgical pieces taken up in the book of Habakkuk are commonly thought to be the following:

1. The book of Habakkuk opens with a dialogic exchange of *lament* and *divine response*, a characteristic liturgical interaction familiar from the book of Psalms. The initial complaint of 1:2–4, with echoes of Jeremiah 12:1–4, raises the acute question of theodicy, Why do the wicked prosper at the expense of the righteous? While this question, as raised by Jeremiah and Job, characteristically concerns internal relations in the community between the righteous and the wicked, here it is transposed into international affairs, thus reflecting a scope of concern not unlike that of Obadiah and Nahum. In these verses, one cannot determine the identity of the wicked; the cruciality of Babylon (the Chaldeans) in the divine response of 1:5–11 would suggest that the wicked who are to receive divine judgment are the Assyrians, thus drawing the opening of the book of Habakkuk into the orbit of Nahum. The divine response of verses 5–11 features an invasive foreign army in which the rhetoric is not unlike the war poetry of Jeremiah 4–6.

In the ongoing dialogic exchange, the second complaint of 1:12–17 discloses in detail for YHWH the abusive arrogance of the invasive force. Because this rhetoric has much in common with Psalms 74 and 79, which describe the Babylonian assault on the temple in Jerusalem, it is possible that this complaint pertains to Babylon:

> Habakkuk's second lament, in which he complains of the injustice of the Babylonian oppression, implies some experience of Babylonian rule and thus must be dated sometime later than the first lament. Here one must distinguish between the presumed oral setting of the original independent units and their present literary juxtaposition. Obviously the book as a whole dates from the period after Babylon had imposed its yoke on Judah, and the bitterness of Habakkuk's lament suggests the period after the Babylonians first sacked Jerusalem in 597 B.C.E. (Roberts 1989, 393)

If the reference is indeed to Babylon, then the successive complaints of 1:2–4 and 12–17 portray an international context that is out of control; the appeal to YHWH is thus an urgent petition for YHWH to reassert sovereignty against such enemies, a reassertion already voiced in Nahum.

The second divine response in 2:1–4 asserts the decisive importance of the prophet, who will receive the answer from YHWH (2:1). The divine answer is that the faithful must wait for a future in which faithfulness will be vindicated by YHWH. In due course, in a time sure to come, "the arrogant do not endure" (2:5), that is, the arrogant wicked, whether Assyrian or Babylonian. Thus the provisional resolution to the issue of *theodicy* is *eschatology*, that is, the future is secure in YHWH's governance even if the present is unbearably out of control. The assurance of YHWH's ultimate sovereignty is given very different nuance from that of the book of Nahum, but the end result is the same: YHWH will rule!

2. The second rhetorical strategy of the book of Habakkuk is a series of five oracles that begin, in the NRSV rendering, with "Alas," a marker of trouble to come. This series, which has much in common with Isaiah 5:8–23, issues a warning against autonomous behavior that is self-serving and self-advancing but that cannot succeed. The warnings concern, in turn, acquisitiveness (2:6–7), evil gain (2:9–10), exploitation characterized as "bloodshed" (2:12), destabilization of neighbors by strong drink (2:15), and appeal to dead idols (2:19). Each of these is a characteristic prophetic indictment that initially pertained to antineighborly acts in the Torah community. Such acts are condemned because they destroy community and in the long run are unsustainable. In the present usage, however, these more local reflections have been transposed to serve the large international vista of Habakkuk, so that the interpretive extrapolations of a domestic agenda of neighborliness can now pertain to "many nations" (2:8), "many peoples" (2:10), "peoples" (2:13). In 2:16, moreover, the "cup" of staggering is reminiscent of Jeremiah 25:15–28, in which all nations vomit and reel before the ferocious sovereignty of YHWH. Prophetic imagination is able to transfer conventional communal concerns to the large horizon of international upheaval, thus making the oracles congruent with the concerns of the two complaints in 1:2–4 and 12–17.

The concluding formula of 2:20, perhaps congruent with the claim of Amos 1:2, has YHWH address the nations from the Jerusalem temple. The silencing of "all the earth" before the temple-residing presence of YHWH is a response and antidote to the clamor of upheaval and conspiracy that the nations seek to conduct against YHWH, against YHWH's city, and against YHWH's people (see Ps 2:1–3). These five oracles warn the arrogant, autonomous power—whether Assyria or Babylon—and 2:20 provides a fitting divine edict that puts the nations in the proper place as silently subservient to the ultimacy of YHWH's sovereignty (see Zeph 1:7).

3. The book of Habakkuk ends in chapter 3 with an extended hymn that voices vexation at present trouble, but concludes with complete confidence in the ultimate triumph of YHWH. The chapter begins with a petition that

the promised vindication of YHWH over the nations should come soon, "in our own time" (v. 2). In what seems to be a response to that plea, verses 3–15 take up a very old hymn that traverses the massive coming of YHWH in lordly theophany from Mount Sinai in military splendor in order to crush opposition and establish governance. It is widely agreed that these verses constitute one of the oldest liturgical uses in Israel; in context, however, that dramatic royal progress of YHWH is brought into play in the present seventh-century emergency, so that the speaker of verses 1–2 may have confidence in YHWH:

> In Habakkuk, as in Nahum, the hymn helps to relocate the contingent of historical action at the core of the book. Against the turmoil and uncertainty of human affairs—the world of existential immediacy which is the traditional scene of prophecy—the compilers set the elemental features of the phenomenal world (light and darkness; earth, sea, and sky) in their timeless sublimity. The two orders so juxtaposed have almost nothing in common except the dominion of YHWH, personified in the hymns where the approach is descriptive, and represented in the oracular forms by the dynamic force of the word, a dramatic figure for the grammatical modes of command, dread, and desire, as for the principle of causal succession. It is for the reader to specify more precisely the relation between cosmology and history, and thereby to define the nature of their common terms. But since no simple formula (inside-outside, above-below, whole-part, cause-effect) can explain the relation, one is thrown back on the human motives generally associated with the different genres, alternating between the willful impulses of desire and fear expressed in the oracles and the contemplative impulse to praise, accept, and enforce magnified in the hymn. (Marks 1987, 218)

In verse 16 the speaker acknowledges disease as the present circumstance, but then declares readiness to "wait quietly," thus in complete congruity with the mandate of 2:3, "wait for it."

The poem, and finally the entire book of Habakkuk, culminates in a massive assertion of complete confidence and hope in YHWH:

> Though the fig tree does not blossom,
>   and no fruit is on the vines;
> though the produce of the olive fails,
>   and the fields yield no food;
> though the flock is cut off from the fold,
>   and there is no herd in the stalls,
> yet I will rejoice in the LORD;
>   I will exult in the God of my salvation.
>   (3:17–18)

The threefold "though" of verse 17 anticipates a dreadful circumstance of failure, defeat, drought, and death. The poet voices the most unbearable circumstance possible. The threefold "though" is then answered by a powerful "yet" that is rooted in profound faith, the faith acknowledged in 2:4. The faithful will not give in to unbearable circumstance, but will face circumstance in uncompromising confidence in YHWH. The final verse 19 articulates complete confidence in YHWH, who will make one "trembling" and "quivering" completely buoyant, no matter the circumstance (v. 16).

In considering the coherence of the book of Habakkuk, we may identify three considerations:

1. The book consists in already existing liturgical pieces that are woven together here in a fresh way: dialogue of complaint and responding oracle, "alas" oracles, and theophanic resolution in a hymnic voice.

2. This material has all been mobilized to voice and respond to the crisis in Israel in the late seventh and early sixth century when all old certitudes were coming unglued and the Yahwistic coherence of the world appeared to be deeply in jeopardy.

3. While the book of Habakkuk is thus context-specific, its durable theological claim is a message of profound hope in a circumstance of profound despair. The posing of the issue of theodicy posed in the first complaint (1:2–4) is answered by eschatological anticipation expressed as theophany (3:3–15). The reader must not, however, be so preoccupied with genre analysis as to minimize the theological point to which the several genres adhere, namely, the ultimate, utter reliability of YHWH and YHWH's sure triumph. Thus the "yet" of 3:18 is completely Yahwistic in its buoyant affirmation, an affirmation that resolves in theological conviction the deep vagaries of the historical moment.

Christian readers may pay particular attention to the divine response of 2:4: "but the righteous live by their faith." This particular statement, along with Genesis 15:6, is taken up by Paul in his argument concerning justification by faith:

> For in it the righteousness of God is revealed through faith for faith; as it is written, "The one who is righteous will live by faith." (Rom 1:17)

> Now it is evident that no one is justified before God by the law; for "The one who is righteous will live by faith." (Gal 3:11; see Heb 10:38)

The theological grounding provided in these texts via Paul figured heavily in Luther's strong theological insight. Paul, and after him Luther, gave very different nuances in very different contexts to this notion of life in faith. Taken all together, nevertheless, it is clear that these Christian extrapolations from the tradition of Habakkuk understood rightly and utilized in faithful ways the primary affirmation of the tradition. The claim culminating in the great "yet" of 3:18 that invites "waiting quietly" is that hope in any circumstance is in "no other save in thee alone" (Calvin 1990).

THE BOOK OF ZEPHANIAH

The book of Zephaniah is commonly grouped with the books of Nahum and Habakkuk at the end of the seventh century, thus in the environment of Jeremiah, during the reign of Josiah, likely before the reform of 621 (on which see 2 Kings 22–23) and thus only a few decades before the destruction of Jerusalem (Zeph 1:1). Nothing is known of the person of Zephaniah; the mention of Hezekiah in the superscription of 1:1, however, has led to speculation that the Hezekiah named here may be the eighth-century king. If this were so, it would situate the prophet in the environs of Jerusalem and cause him to be acutely alert to the coming Jerusalem crisis.

The book of Zephaniah articulates the most familiar and defining themes of preexilic prophecy, and thus is a close parallel, for example, to Amos:

> In sum, the book of Zephaniah deploys many Israelite images and traditions in formulating its speeches. Day of the Lord, creation, Zion, and covenant traditions are only the most prominent of such rhetoric. Moreover, Zephaniah provides a comprehensive picture of Yahweh's interactions with Israel by offering indictments of Israel, judgments on foreign nations, and a vision of the time beyond punishment—a rather remarkable package for so brief a book. (Petersen 2002, 205)

Chapter 1 articulates a massive judgment against the city of Jerusalem. The poem begins with a cosmic sweep concerning the undoing of all creation (see Jer 4:23–26). That large vista, however, moves promptly to focus upon the city of Jerusalem. The key rhetorical figure for the coming harsh judgment is the Day of the Lord, when YHWH will fiercely establish YHWH's own governance (1:7, 10, 14–16).

Chapter 2 concerns YHWH's equally harsh judgment against the nations, here in sequence the Philistine cities, Moab, Ammon, Ethiopia, and Assyria. None of them can withstand YHWH's rule. The initial part of the sequence concerning smaller neighboring peoples is not unlike the oracles against the nations of Amos 1–2. The culmination with Assyria in 2:13–15, however, is more resonant with the book of Nahum, and securely places the poem at the end of the seventh century.

Zephaniah 3:1–7 resumes the attack upon Jerusalem from chapter 1, with particular reference to the leadership (as in Mic 3:9–11; see also Jer 6:13–15).

The shrill attack on Jerusalem leaves the reader quite unprepared for the concluding poetic unit beginning in 3:8 that anticipates YHWH's generous rescue of devastated Jerusalem and the gathering of exiles back to the homeland. The beginning point in 3:8 is quite parallel to the hope of Habakkuk 2:3 and 3:16. While the promise is in the future and Israel is to wait for YHWH to keep that promise, the tone of the poem invites expectation that the decisive turn wrought by YHWH's rescue is to come very soon. In context, the "very soon" apparently refers to the homecoming of the exiles from Babylon.

The themes in this unit suggest an exilic context, thus indicating that the book of Zephaniah has moved beyond the seventh-century person of Zephaniah to serve the community in a new context. As we have seen in other prophetic books, the corpus develops to meet a quite new need. Notice should be taken of the themes that serve that later context, which one would not expect from the seventh-century prophet:

1. Acknowledgment of exile:

   From beyond the rivers of Ethiopia
       my suppliants, my *scattered* ones,
       shall bring my offering.
                     (3:10, italics added)

2. Focus upon a remnant:

    the *remnant* of Israel;
   they shall do no wrong
       and utter no lies,
   nor shall a deceitful tongue
       be found in their mouths.
   Then they will pasture and lie down,
       and no one shall make them afraid.
                     (3:13, italics added)

3. Promise of gathering even the disabled in homecoming:

   I will deal with all your oppressors
       at that time.
   And I will save the lame
       and *gather* the outcast,
   and I will change their shame into praise
       and renown in all the earth.
   At that time I will bring you home,
       at the time when I gather you.
                     (3:19–20a, italics added)

4. The conclusion with the formula "restore your fortunes" is a tag word for dramatic reversal, homecoming, and well-being (see also Ps 126:4; Jer 29:14; 30:18; 32:44; 33:7, 11, 26; Job 42:10):

> for I will make you renowned and praised
>   among all the peoples of the earth,
> when I *restore your fortunes*
>   before your eyes, says the LORD.
>   (3:20b, italics added)

Thus the book finishes with a mighty affirmation that the future will be a good one for Israel, because that future is in the generous and powerful hands of YHWH.

The book of Zephaniah traverses the now familiar two-phase drama of demise and restoration. The themes are familiar enough that one must pay attention in order not to miss the rhetorical force of Zephaniah's particular articulation. It is worth suggesting that the rhetoric of the book of Nahum pivots on the theme of the Day of the Lord. Rolf Rendtorff has shown how that theme recurs in the Book of the Twelve (Rendtorff 2000). Nowhere is the theme more crucial and central than it is in this book:

> The great *day of the LORD* is near,
>   near and hastening fast;
> the sound of the *day of the LORD* is bitter,
>   the warrior cries aloud there.
> That day will be a day of wrath,
>   a day of distress and anguish,
> a day of ruin and devastation,
>   a day of darkness and gloom,
> a day of clouds and thick darkness,
>   a day of trumpet blast and battle cry
> against the fortified cities
>   and against the lofty battlements.
>   (Zeph 1:14–16, italics added)

The "day," articulated in the violence of military assault that is cosmic in force, is the occasion of YHWH's full sovereignty. That harsh sovereignty fiercely moves against YHWH's own people; it also moves, eventually, against the other nations to the great benefit of Israel. In the end, it is the same "warrior" who makes a future for Israel who had terminated Israel's present (Miller 1973):

> The LORD, your God, is in your midst,
>   a warrior who gives victory;
> he will rejoice over you with gladness,
>   he will renew you in his love.
>   (3:17a)

The warrior who is decisive for world history and for the history of Israel is the one already known in Israel since the exodus:

> Then Moses and the Israelites sang this song to the LORD:
>
> "I will sing to the LORD, for he has triumphed gloriously;
>   horse and rider he has thrown into the sea.
> The LORD is my strength and my might,
>   and he has become my salvation;
> this is my God, and I will praise him,
>   my father's God, and I will exalt him.
> The LORD is a warrior;
>   the LORD is his name."
>
> (Exod 15:1–3)

THE BOOK OF HAGGAI

With the book of Haggai, the rough chronology of the Twelve enters the Persian period. Persia (modern Iran), a newly emergent power to the east of the old Semitic powers of Assyria and Babylonia, overthrew the vestiges of Babylonian power in 540 BCE and began its imperial expansion westward, finally only checked by Alexander the Great in 333 BCE. Since the late twentieth century, scholars have given the Persian period of Israelite history immense attention, because it is now thought likely that the major accomplishments of canonization were completed in the Persian period when Judah was a small client state of the Persians (Berquist 1995). Haggai and Zechariah are together dated at the beginning of the Persian period (520–516 BCE), and Malachi is dated soon thereafter. From the prophetic poetry of Isaiah 40–55, the Persians, and especially Cyrus, were understood as YHWH's salvific agent who would permit Israel to return from exile to Jerusalem (2 Chr 36:22–23; Isa 44:28; 45:1).

The prophetic poetry of Isaiah 40–55 in lyrical fashion had anticipated a glorious, exultant homecoming of Jews from exile. The facts on the ground, however, fell far short of such poetic exuberance, for the city was a residue of shabby ruins left by the Babylonians. It is in this context that the book of Haggai is to be understood: "The book of Haggai is a compact witness to a coherent theological view of the relationship among Yahweh's universal sovereignty, the Temple as the site from which that rule is to be exercised, and the welfare of the restored Jewish community" (Ollenburger 1989, 408).

The book of Haggai consists in four units, each of which is dated to the time of Darius, the third Persian leader, after Cyrus and Cambyses. So far as we know, this material, dated 520–516, indicates the first sustained effort at restoration of Jerusalem after the debacle of 587 BCE. It is clear that Haggai is situated in a priestly matrix, so that all of the anticipations and awaited action of the oracles by Haggai are sacerdotal in nature. Indeed, Haggai's name means "my festival," thus referring to a cultic celebration.

The first quite extended oracle concerns the rebuilding of the temple (1:1–15). After initial resistance, Haggai is able to mobilize the remnant community led by Zerubbabel the governor and Joshua the priest—the two faces of communal authority to rebuild the temple. The second oracle further concerns the rebuilding of the temple, again by the two leaders and the remnant community (2:1–9). This second oracle includes three additional notes of interest:

1. The imperatives of 2:4 are not unlike the imperatives issued to Joshua in Joshua 1:6–7, 18, perhaps suggesting a Deuteronomic influence in the Haggai tradition.
2. The rhetoric of 2:5–6 asserts the decisive work of "my spirit" in the public process, whereby YHWH will "shake" the world order. The verb refers to an immense upheaval; in this case, moreover, the drastic upheaval anticipated will be to the benefit of Jerusalem. The revamped world order will cause Jerusalem to be the focal point of a new economy, whereby "the treasure of all nations" will flow and adorn the newly constructed temple in Jerusalem. The vision of a revised economy caused by YHWH's spirit is not unlike the vision of Isaiah 60:5–7.
3. It is anticipated in 2:9 that the new temple now to be constructed will outclass even the glorious temple of Solomon that exhibited the wealth, prestige, and magnificence of Solomon (see 1 Kgs 6:14–22; 7:48–50). The new temple will be invested by YHWH as a place of *shalom* (v. 9).

The third oracle in 2:10–19 reflects further on the significance of the temple. The priestly teaching on "clean" and "unclean" is, according to priestly ordering, a requirement in order to make possible the residence of the Holy God, for the Holy God cannot and will not remain in a place that is polluted and defiled. The faithful, disciplined practices of the priests will assure YHWH's presence. The oracle then contrasts this new era presence with the "before" that was a time of poverty and misery, because YHWH's power for life was not present in Jerusalem. The concluding statement of verse 19, paralleled to that of verse 9, asserts that the rightly ordered temple will become a source of blessing.

These three oracles together make a sustained point, so crucial in sacerdotal perception, that the temple is sine qua non for the well-being, prosperity, and blessing that come from YHWH's guaranteed sacramental presence in the temple. Cautious Protestant interpretation, fearful of making the temple presence into a magical guarantee that detracts from the personal sovereignty of YHWH, wants to minimize the importance of the temple in order to enhance the personal sovereignty of YHWH. Such a caution is in order, but it should not be overstated, because in priestly perception the function of the temple as YHWH's place of residence is indispensable for the divine gift of life. Claus Westermann has seen that the power of blessing is peculiarly concentrated in the temple, and Fredrik Lindström has more fully shown that in the Psalter YHWH's power for life is concentrated in the temple so that access to the temple is pivotal for well-being:

> The individual's God is the God of the temple: "So I have looked upon you in the sanctuary, beholding your power ('z) and glory (kbwd)" (Ps 63:3). The liturgy of the temple does not provide the sufferer with a "mystical" experience as a compensation or a wage for the accidents of life. Rather, the petitioner in the temple of YHWH is seeking assurance of a presence of God which encompasses all of life and thereby causes the affliction which now plagues him to cease ("in the sanctuary"//"as long as I live," Ps 63:3a, 5a). Such assurance is given to the one who cries to "his God" (Ps 3:3, 8) by the answer from YHWH's "holy hill" (Ps 3:5). This reference, like the divine epithet mlky w'lhy, "my King and my God" (Ps 5:3), implies the traditio-historical background for the classical individual complaint psalm, namely, the monarchial theology which was cultivated in connection with the temple on Zion during the monarchy. The King, enthroning in the sanctuary of Jerusalem, is the God of the individual (cf. Ps 23:1, 6: yhwh r'y, "YHWH is my shepherd"—šbty bbyt-yhwh, "I shall dwell in the house of YHWH"). . . .
>
> The protection of the individual is also formulated by the temple theologians through the image of how man is crowned like an earthly king by YHWH: tsk 'lyw kṣnh rṣwn t'trnw, "You protect him as with a shield, you crown him with favor" (Ps 5:13). According to this monarchial theology, the heavenly King shares his royal dignity and receives the individual into his saving presence (see also Ps 8:6). The conception of how YHWH of the temple establishes his relationship with man threatened by Death by providing him with protection and royal dignity is also apparent by the divine epithet kbwdy, "(You are) my glory" (Ps 3:4, par. with mgn, "shield"). This divine epithet probably means "you are the one who gives me my kbwd, my honor," i.e., YHWH establishes the individual's existential (as in Ps 7:6) as well as religious (Pss 3:4; 57:9) foundations. By sharing the honor and glory which really only belong to the King himself, he presents his salvation as a free gift to the individual. It is this divine and for man unclaimable gift which according to the temple theologians gives the individual his human dignity and establishes his relationship with God. The divine presence is salvific, both in the sense that it is protective from the threat of the evil powers, and that it, like life itself, is given to man as a free gift. (Lindström 1994, 436)

Appreciation of the book of Haggai invites appreciation of the priestly perceptual field. The temple is a first-order gift of YHWH as the pivot point of blessing, prosperity, and life; without the temple, moreover, as Haggai observes in 2:15–19, Israel is deficient in all the resources necessary for life.

The fourth oracle of 2:20–23 goes in a quite different direction. It is now not concerned for the temple, but returns to the theme of "shake" from 2:6, and anticipates a cosmic shaking that will overthrow all established order, political and military. The outcome of such shaking will be that Zerubbabel of the line of David will return to power. Thus the oracle evidences that the dynastic promise to David in 2 Samuel 7 (see also Ps 89) is still powerful, and that political agitators continue to swirl in Jerusalem concerning the restoration of the monarchy. The reestablishment of the Davidic house would not be permitted by Persian hegemony, so that this oracle, without being specific or concrete, includes in its shaking the Persian rule that was relatively benign toward recovering Jerusalem.

The most important phenomenon of the Haggai tradition is that it holds together a realized eschatology of the temple that assures prosperity, peace, and blessing in the present time (in the first three oracles) and a futuristic eschatology of Davidic restoration (in the fourth oracle). The tradition itself does not ponder or comment on what seems to be a tension between these two, twin accents that no doubt reflect lively and competing advocacies in the community under restoration.

We may suggest two ways in which to understand this seeming tension. First, temple and monarchy are profoundly twinned in the Jerusalem tradition:

> He rejected the tent of Joseph,
>   he did not choose the tribe of Ephraim;
> but he chose the tribe of Judah,
>   Mount Zion, which he loves.
> He built his sanctuary like the high heavens,
>   like the earth, which he has founded forever.
> He chose his servant David,
>   and took him from the sheepfolds;
> from tending the nursing ewes he brought him
>   to be the shepherd of his people Jacob,
>   of Israel, his inheritance.
>
>   (Ps 78:67–71)

The king is in fact the high priest of the temple and guarantees the right ordering of the temple. The temple, in turn, provides the matrix of symbols that causes the king to be not only a political operator but a guarantor of a viable cosmic order (see Ps 72). Thus the celebration of *present temple* and *anticipated king* assures important liturgical ideological continuity (Ollenburger 1987).

Second, the temple is a gift from YHWH to make the present life of Jerusalem prosperous. The anticipated monarchy will come by the stirring of YHWH's spirit. Thus both present temple and anticipated king are works of YHWH that provide to Jerusalem stability and well-being "in this age and in the age to come" (Matt 12:32). YHWH has the will and power to destabilize the entire earth for the benefit of a chosen city and chosen people. Whereas the temple guarantees *blessing*, kingship provides *power* for the new order. In Christian thematics, YHWH is thus *Creator* and *Redeemer*. The book of Haggai attests to YHWH's sovereign goodwill for Jerusalem; it attests with equal insistence that that good divine will is in, with, and under, and not apart from, viable social structures that are indispensable vehicles now and for time to come. The concrete realities of social construction and maintenance form the venue for the spirit that stirs in this crisis moment toward well-being.

THE BOOK OF ZECHARIAH

Sandwiched as it is between Haggai and Malachi, Zechariah constitutes one of three of the Minor Prophets located in the Persian period. The book of Zechariah is commonly divided into two quite distinct parts.

The first part, chapters 1–8, is linked to the context and concerns of the book of Haggai, namely, the return of exiles to Jerusalem and the reconstitution of the Jerusalem temple as a pivot point for a more general restoration of Israel in the territory in and around Jerusalem. It is the case at the same time, however, that the text of Zechariah 1–8—while linked to the reign of Darius (520–516 BCE; on which see 1:1; 7:1)—that Zechariah has an agenda very different from that of Haggai. The text is introduced in 1:1–6 in a familiar way that reflects the cadences of Deuteronomy and seems clearly related to Jeremiah 18:1–11 with its emphasis upon repentance. This textual corpus of chapters 1–8 concludes in 7:1–8:23 with a series of oracular assertions that offer traditional themes appropriate to a postexilic context. The oracle of 7:8–14 presents a characteristic prophetic sequence of (a) imperatives summoning to obedience that echo Deuteronomy (vv. 9–10), (b) a report on disobedience to those imperatives (vv. 11–12a), and (c) a consequent divine judgment that justifies the "scattering" of Israel into exile (vv. 12b–14).

That speech of judgment, however, is primarily a foil for what follows concerning (a) YHWH's return to Zion in a way reminiscent of Ezekiel (8:1–3), (b) a reassertion of the covenantal relationship of YHWH and Israel (8:8), (c) a remnant that will prosper in the land (8:12–13), culminating in a salvation oracle, (d) a promise of "good" for Jerusalem marked by festal joy that compels "truth and peace" (8:14–19), and (e) an envisioned streaming of the nations to Zion (8:20–23) that echoes the poetic scenario of Isaiah 2:1–4 and Micah 4:1–4. Thus this unit of text ends with a great articulation of hope that celebrates Jerusalem in a way that transcends Israel.

Between the introductory paragraph of 1:1–6 and the concluding statement of hope in 7:1–8:23, the body of the text is constituted by a series of visions, each of which includes a symbolic sighting that is characteristically enigmatic, followed by an interpretive commentary. While this series of visions is indeed quite complex, it is clear that the sum of the visions concerns the deliverance of Israel from exile and restoration to land and city:

> Thus says the LORD of hosts; I am very jealous for Jerusalem and for Zion. And I am extremely angry with the nations that are at ease; for while I was only a little angry, they made the disaster worse. Therefore, thus says the LORD, I have returned to Jerusalem with compassion; my house shall be built in it, says the LORD of hosts, and the measuring line shall be stretched out over Jerusalem. (1:14b–16)

The promise is that those who are scattered will escape Babylon and return home:

> Up! Escape to Zion, you that live with daughter Babylon. For thus said the LORD of hosts (after his glory sent me) regarding the nations that plundered you: Truly, one who touches you touches the apple of my eye. . . . The LORD will inherit Judah as his portion in the holy land, and will again choose Jerusalem. (2:7–8, 12)

The restoration includes ritual cleansing (3:4–5). This oracle pertains to priestly authority (3:1–3), but passing attention is also given to monarchial pretensions in the person of Zerubbabel (on whom see Hag 2:20–23). It is clear that restoration is understood to be led by the priestly hierarchy (6:11–14) in connection with the rebuilt temple, so that the future envisioned, as in Ezekiel and Haggai, is sacerdotal. The primary theme of the visions is evident, but the particularities—including the reference to Satan (3:1–2) and to "Wickedness" (5:8)—are not obvious. The movement toward the visionary is clearly part of the beginning of apocalyptic rhetoric that attends especially to powerful picturesque imagery:

> The strategy of the prophets Haggai and Zechariah was masterful; to the priestly tradition of the Zadokites they welded the eschatological fervor, which was the hallmark of the prophetic group. Thus the detailed, pragmatic plans representing the interests of the hierocrats were cast into the visionary forms of the prophets, orchestrating the impulses of the visionaries and the realists into one passionate message, a message whose appeal was enhanced by an international

> situation which fanned the burning embers of nationalistic hope into the brilliant flames of an allegedly attainable eschatological plan; build the temple and the kingdom of blessedness would arrive. (Hanson 1975, 245)

This unit of text in Zechariah 1–8 offers a large vision of restoration accomplished by the God who is passionate for Jerusalem. That visioning possibility is kept close to the facts on the ground, for the future clearly concerns the city and, more particularly, the temple over which the legitimated priesthood presides with weighty authority.

The second part of the book of Zechariah—sometimes termed "Second Zechariah"—concerns the materials of chapters 9–14, materials that are usually divided into two subunits, chapters 9–11 and chapters 12–14, each section of which (along with Malachi) is introduced by a terse formulary, "An oracle." Chapters 9–11 begin with fairly common prophetic themes, including oracles against the nations in 9:1–8 juxtaposed to promised restoration for Judah in 9:9–10:12. As we have seen in other oracles against the nations, these oracles serve as a counterpoint to the restoration of Israel's well-being. Thus the two prophetic utterances of 9:1–8 and 9:9–10:12 sound familiar themes that yield a twofold structure of hope, much as we have seen in the book of Zephaniah. As is characteristic of prophets who anticipate the later period of Israel's life, the destruction of Jerusalem and deportation is acknowledged, but the accent is upon restoration. A fine epitome of this claim is voiced in 10:8–10 with its focus upon "scatter" and "gather," a movement made possible by the judgment against the nations that have enacted the "scattering" (see Jer 31:10):

> I will signal for them and gather them in,
>> for I have redeemed them,
>> and they shall be as numerous as they were before.
> Though I *scattered* them among the nations,
>> yet in far countries they shall remember me,
>> and they shall rear their children and return.
> I will bring them home from the land of Egypt,
>> and *gather* them from Assyria;
> I will bring them to the land of Gilead and to Lebanon,
>> until there is no room for them.
>> (italics added)

Chapter 11, beginning at verse 4, picks up the theme of "shepherd" from 10:3 and offers an enigmatic rumination on "shepherds," that is, on kings and rulers. The text appears to be something of a commentary upon the "bad shepherds" of Ezekiel 34, except that YHWH's own role as shepherd here is much more negative and condemnatory. The intention of this unit is elusive and no doubt reflects tensions in the later period over the ordering of power in the community.

The second part of Second Zechariah is constituted by chapters 12–14, a distinct unit with its own heading, "An Oracle." This text is dominated by the repeated formula "on that day" (12:3, 4, 6, 8, 9, 11; 13:1, 2; 14:6, 8, 13), assuring a focus upon a future to be enacted and imposed solely by YHWH. This material is a strange mix of prophetic *judgment* upon Jerusalem and prophetic *hope* for Jerusalem. The judgment here is uttered severely and given extensive expression:

> See, a day is coming for the LORD, when the plunder taken from you will be divided in your midst. For I will gather all the nations against Jerusalem to battle, and the city shall be taken and the houses looted and the women raped; half the city shall go into exile, but the rest of the people shall not be cut off from the city. (14:1–2)

The hope is as powerful as the judgment:

> On that day the LORD will shield the inhabitants of Jerusalem so that the feeblest among them on that day shall be like David, and the house of David shall be like God, like the angel of the LORD, at their head. And on that day I will seek to destroy all the nations that come against Jerusalem. (12:8–9)

> And it shall be inhabited, for never again shall it be doomed to destruction; Jerusalem shall abide in security. (14:11)

The two themes of judgment and hope are interwoven rather than lined out in sequence, so that hope follows judgment, as in a traditional formulation. The effect of the extreme imagery is to create an environment of profound instability that reflects the sovereign assertion of YHWH, the one who "make[s] weal and create[s] woe" (Isa 45:7). In the end, the promised future of Jerusalem and Judah is at the behest of YHWH. The unit ends with a great vision of Jerusalem as the place to which all nations come in pilgrimage (Zech 14:16; see 8:20–23), a place marked as "Holy to the LORD" (14:20).

It is clear that the tradition of Zechariah is rooted in particularities linked to the reign of Darius the Persian (see 1:1; 7:1). It is equally clear that the tradition of Zechariah moves freely and imaginatively beyond historical circumstances to a vivid future given by YHWH, so vivid that the movement from chapters 1–8 through chapters 9–11 to chapters 12–14 is a development that is regularly labeled "apocalyptic," that is, a vision of a world destabilized and restabilized and governed by YHWH. The reader of this material should not be excessively disappointed or frustrated by a failure to understand, for this literature has defied clear understanding even among the most careful critical scholarship. What is clear is that as the text tradition becomes more futuristic, the tradition reimagines the world and especially Jerusalem in radically Yahwistic terms.

William McKane has referred to the book of Jeremiah as a "rolling *corpus*," by which he means that the tradition of Jeremiah "developed" in new directions over time to make interpretive responses to new circumstances (McKane 1986, l). It is possible that we may think of the Book of the Twelve as a "rolling corpus," that is, a tradition that develops in fresh interpretive directions in new contexts. Nowhere, we suggest, is that more evident than in the apocalyptic impulse of the book of Zechariah whereby the tradition "rolls" from the Haggai crisis in the reign of Darius (520–516 BCE) to an unspecified future under YHWH's sovereignty.

The "roll" of the tradition is in effect an immense act of imagination, what Herbert Marks terms "a form of imaginative vision akin to dreaming, the superior imagination" that moves beyond circumstance (Marks 1987, 227). That "superior imagination" imagines worlds made and unmade by the power of YHWH (see Collins 1987). In all of the enigmatic imagining of this act of alternative construal, the constant is the rule of YHWH who makes and unmakes and remakes Jerusalem, and who dispatches and then rejects other nations as agents in the unmaking and remaking of Jerusalem. This "superior imagination" is not bound by historical circumstance, but only by the extremity of YHWH, who surges beyond circumstance in prophetic revelation. Thus, like an interpreter of dreams, the reader of this text should not seek to decode, but may follow the imagistic suggestions of the text in order to see what lines of interpretation are released by attending to the "vision akin to dreaming." The alternative world of revelatory visioning is a world of YHWH, but the world of YHWH is always linked to some conjured Jerusalem in anticipation that "a day is coming for the LORD" (14:1):

> The transcendent world may be expressed through mythological symbolism or celestial geography or both. It puts the problem in perspective and projects a definitive resolution to come. This apocalyptic technique does not, of course, have a publicly discernible effect on a historical crisis, but it provides a resolution in the imagination by instilling conviction in the revealed "knowledge" that it imparts. The function of the apocalyptic literature is to shape one's imaginative perception of a situation and so lay the basis for whatever course of action it exhorts. (Collins 1987, 32)

Christian readers may want to notice in particular two texts in this book. First, the claim of the tradition concerning the decisive rule of YHWH is asserted with reference to Zerubbabel:

> He said to me, "This is the word of the LORD to Zerubbabel: Not by might, nor by power, but by my spirit, says the LORD of hosts." (4:6)

Although Zerubbabel is a political figure, this statement eschews worldly power and counts only on the power of YHWH's spirit, the power of life in the world. (This rejection of worldly power is congruent with the apocalyptic assertion in Dan 11:34 that human agency is "a little help," but not help enough to matter.) The formula of Zechariah 4:6 thus celebrates YHWH's decisive power in a way that makes all other power irrelevant, even in the public arena of Zerubbabel.

Second, special note should be taken of Zechariah 9:9:

> Rejoice greatly, O daughter Zion!
>> Shout aloud, O daughter Jerusalem!
> Lo, your king comes to you;
>> triumphant and victorious is he,
> humble and riding on a donkey,
>> on a colt, the foal of a donkey.

This text appeals to an image of a triumphant Davidic king and so reflects continuing Davidic-messianic hope for restoration that pervades the tradition of Zechariah, although the imaging of hope here is noticeably inchoate and lacks a political concreteness:

> The author of Zech. 9:9 is presenting a highly nuanced form of political expectation. This is no standard royal or messianic expectation, namely, the return of a real or ideal Davidide. This expectation has little in common with the hope for a prince (Ezekiel 40–48), a crowned Zerubbabel (Hag. 2:23); a Davidide à la the oracles of Zechariah (Zech. 4:6–10). Instead, the poet focuses on collectivities, addressed through the technique of personification. (Petersen 1995, 59)

That poetic anticipation, moreover, is quoted in Matthew 21:5 and is utilized for the coming of the victorious Jesus into the city of Jerusalem. Matthew has famously misunderstood the poetic parallelism in Zechariah 9:9 and, consequently, presents Jesus as riding on two animals. In Christian reading, the large expectations of this tradition are gathered specifically to Jesus who, in the gospel narrative, carries all of the large hopes of God's coming rule in Israel and in the world:

> A book which, as we have already seen, was arguably of great influence on Jesus, and which contained dark hints about the necessary suffering of the people of YHWH, is of course Zechariah, particularly its second part (chapters 9–14). The writer promises the long-awaited arrival of the true king (9.9–10), the renewed covenant and the real return from exile (9.11–12), the violent defeat of Israel's enemies and the rescue of the true people of YHWH (9.13–17). At the moment, however, Israel are like sheep without a shepherd (10.2); they have shepherds, but they are not doing their job, and will be punished (10.3) as part of the divine plan for the return from exile (10.6–12).
> (Wright 1996, 586)

Thus Jesus' primal articulation that "the kingdom of God has come near" is rooted in these expectations (Mark 1:15). It is no wonder that current New Testament scholarship accepts that the origins of the Christian movement are set deep in the kinds of apocalyptic expectations that are front and center in the tradition of Zechariah.

THE BOOK OF MALACHI

The book of Malachi concludes the Book of the Twelve. The book of Malachi itself provides few clues concerning its author, audience, or context. It is commonly linked to the books of Haggai and Zechariah, and forms with them a triad of prophetic books from the Persian period. This connection to Haggai and Zechariah is reinforced by the beginning phrase of Malachi 1:1, "An oracle," a formula that suggests a parallel to Zechariah 9:1 and 12:1. Within the Persian period, Malachi is conventionally dated somewhat later than Haggai and Zechariah, closer to the reform movement of Ezra, when the initial zeal for restoration and rebuilding reflected in Haggai and Zechariah had waned and the community is inattentive to its Yahwistic responsibilities.

Nothing is known of the prophetic voice that speaks here, though that voice is rooted in the older traditions and particularly attends to the priestly order of Levi, thus suggesting, perhaps, the ongoing tradition of Deuteronomy. It is possible, moreover, that the name "Malachi" is not even a proper name referring to a particular individual, for the Hebrew is readily translated, as in 3:1, as "my messenger." Thus with little to go on concerning context or authorship, we must in any case pay primary attention to the material of the book itself.

The book begins with an introduction in 1:1–5 that asserts, "Great is the LORD beyond the borders of Israel!" (1:5b). The particular way in which the claim for YHWH is made in this introduction concerns YHWH's fierce sovereignty over the hated Edomites, thus a theme reminiscent of the book of

Obadiah. The accent, however, is not upon the Edomites but upon the power of YHWH, who must be taken with great seriousness, a seriousness neglected in Judah's evident laxness concerning cultic and neighborly obedience.

The main body of the book of Malachi concerns a series of disputatious comments, each of which asks a question, allegedly quotes the ones addressed who regularly fail to grasp it, and moves to a divine oracle of resolution. The subjects of these disputes vary somewhat, but for the most part they concern inattentiveness to cultic requirements, an inattentiveness that profanes, pollutes, and defiles, making Jerusalem inhospitable to YHWH. Attention is focused upon the Torah responsibility of the Levites (2:5–7) and the corresponding faithlessness of Judah (2:14).

In chapter 3 the tradition turns to eschatological hope for the coming of YHWH in YHWH's "day," which will be a day of judgment. On the basis of that impending threat of YHWH, the tradition appeals for repentance in terms much like the tradition of Deuteronomy (see Deut 4:29–31; 30:1–10). Thus the disputatious indictments of Malachi 1 and 2 form the ground for the threat and the summons to repent in chapter 3. In 3:16–18 a subcommunity of the faithful is recognized as those spared by YHWH. It is evident that this disputatious text no doubt reflects competing claims in the postexilic community.

The theme of "the day" is continued in chapter 4. The conclusion of the book in 4:1–3, congruent with 3:16–18, makes an important distinction between the "evildoers" who will be destroyed and the "righteous" who will exult in well-being. This sharp and uncompromising contrast in the face of anticipated judgment is not unlike Psalm 1, which also reflects the disputatious character of the postexilic community through which the authentic character of the community is contested:

> Therefore the wicked will not stand in the judgment,
>   nor sinners in the congregation of the righteous;
> for the LORD watches over the way of the righteous,
>   but the way of the wicked will perish.
>   (Ps 1:5–6)

It is plausible that Malachi 4:1–3 provided a conclusion to the book in some stage of transmission. To that conclusion, however, were added two additional notations, the interrelationship of which is particularly telling:

1. In 4:4 the focus is upon the Torah of Moses from Mount Sinai, thus a theme already noted in 2:5–7.

2. In 4:5–6 the focus is upon Elijah, and therefore the prophetic tradition. It is important to note that Elijah, in the narrative tradition of Israel, did not die but "ascended" into heaven (2 Kgs 2:11). Consequently, in the elaborated

tradition, Elijah continues to be alive and may come again to the earth in order to effect the "turn" already urged in 3:7.

This threefold conclusion to the book of Malachi—and to the Book of the Twelve—is of immense interest and importance. The first conclusion (4:1–3) posits a profound contrast between the wicked and the righteous, a contrast that was to be endlessly important in the Torah traditions of Judaism. The second (4:4) and third (4:5–6) conclusions taken together draw into unity the *Torah of Moses* and the *prophetic tradition* represented by Elijah, thus "the law and the prophets." Whereas the Torah asserts the requirement of *obedience*, a primary concern in the tradition of Malachi, the prophets invite *hope* for YHWH's future effected by this human agent, the messenger. The upshot is that the two together yield a characteristic biblical accent on obedience and hope on the basis of the two canons of "law and prophets."

The conclusion of the prophetic canon in Malachi 4:5–6 thus ends in hope, for the Latter Prophets characteristically have been preoccupied with hope beyond the destruction of Jerusalem and the exile. As such, this hope becomes a grounding for emerging Judaism that anticipates restoration of temple, city, and people. This conclusion that is formed according to the fidelity of YHWH, moreover, is nicely congruent with the conclusion of the Torah in Deuteronomy 34:1–8, with its celebration of Moses in 34:10–12, and the introduction of Joshua in 34:9 as the carrier of Mosaic faith into the future. Thus the completed Torah is short of arrival and lives in anticipation of YHWH's promises yet to be enacted. In parallel fashion, the prophetic canon also ends short of arrival and lives in anticipation of YHWH's promises yet to be enacted. In this way both "the law and the prophets" are deeply rooted, but end in hope that still awaits fruition.

For Christian readers, three additional comments are in order. First, it is crucial for Christian faith that this text in Malachi 4:5–6 not only concludes the Latter Prophets, but in Christian reading concludes the entire canon of the Old Testament. Thus the Christian Old Testament—in a way very different from the Hebrew Bible (as we shall see)—ends in prophetic hope. This ending made it relatively easy to make connections to the Jesus movement and its harbinger, John the Baptist, who as "forerunner" is linked to Elijah (see Mark 1:2–8; Wink 2000). Second, the particular promise of Malachi 4:5–6 is taken up in the Gospel of Luke (with some variation), so that the work of John the Baptist is explicitly understood as connected to a return of Elijah: "He will turn many of the people of Israel to the Lord their God. With the spirit and power of Elijah he will go before him, to turn the hearts of parents to their children, and the disobedient to the wisdom of the righteous, to make ready a people prepared for the Lord" (Luke 1:16–17). More than that, it is clear that the fingerprints of "Elijah returned" are all over the gospel narration, suggesting (a) that hope for returned Elijah was in the air, and/or (b) that the Christian community intentionally connected the Jesus movement to that tradition of expectation (see Matt 11:14; 16:14; 17:3–12; 27:47–49).

Third, particular attention may be paid to the narrative of transfiguration (Matt 17:1–13; Mark 9:2–8; Luke 9:28–36). In this narrative, both Moses and Elijah appear to and with Jesus. When Moses is recognized as the *carrier of the Torah* (as in Mal 4:4) and Elijah as *representative of the prophetic tradition* (as in Mal 4:5–6), it is clear that the two are present to Jesus as "the law and the prophets," so that Jesus is the embodiment and fulfillment of Israel's normative revelatory literature through whom all of Israel's hopes now come to bodily fruition.

It is evident that the culmination of the prophetic canon (and the entire Christian Old Testament) in Malachi 4:4–6 is of immense importance for the way in which the early church, in its narrative account of Jesus, was able to claim deep and defining continuity between the Israelite tradition and the narrative of Jesus. A more critical and distanced reflection might make it possible to see that Jesus is understood as one fruition of the durable expectation of Israel's hope, but only one fruition alongside a fruition in Judaism that is mediated through Ezra. The openness left by the expectation of the prophetic canon surely requires no single one-on-one match between expectation and fruition, a single match too much insisted upon in conventional authoritarian and triumphalist interpretation. Rather, the openness of the promissory tradition easily permits the awareness that God's promises admit of more than fruition, an openness congruent with the claim that this God generates futures well beyond all of our designed and controlled categories. That is the theological significance of promise: the promise permits open futures that exist only upon God's initiative. Thus the promissory conclusion to the canon is a rhetorical feature, but a rhetorical offer that has profound theological significance. Such a promissory openness tells against every interpretive attempt to reduce, control, capture, or domesticate the future that always belongs only to God, and is given only in God's mercy and generosity.

21

Reprise on the Prophets

The prophetic canon of the Hebrew Bible comprises eight books: the four books that constitute the Former Prophets: Joshua, Judges, Samuel, and Kings (note that Ruth is not included in this sequence in the Hebrew Bible); and the four books that constitute the Latter Prophets: Isaiah, Jeremiah, Ezekiel, and the Twelve (note that Lamentations and Daniel are not included in this sequence in the Hebrew Bible).

1. The four books of the Former Prophets (Joshua, Judges, Samuel, and Kings) constitute a sustained narrative account of Israel from the entry into the land of promise until the deportation from Jerusalem out of the land into exile. While popular Christian understanding treats these books as "history," we have seen that the category of "prophet" indicates that a more or less historical narrative is prophetic in the sense that it retells or reimagines the past from a quite particular perspective, namely, the rule of YHWH with an abiding insistence on Torah obedience and an abiding fidelity to the Davidic promise. We have seen, moreover, that the dominant hypothesis of a Deuteronomic History makes clear that this extended narrative, written from a particular perspective with a particular passion, makes use of a variety of older and traditional materials that had been shaped into a roughly coherent theological vision. This Yahwistically oriented vision is that Israel's life in the land is eventually forfeited because of disobedience to the Torah that has been, from the outset, the condition of entering into and enjoying the land of promise.

It remains to consider the way in which the Former Prophets as a canonical unit cohere with the five books of the Torah. There can be no doubt that according to canonical formation the four books of the Former Prophets constitute a corpus for the faith community that is quite distinct from the five books of the Torah.

In current scholarship, however, there is an important impulse to treat the nine books of the Torah and Former Prophets together as one extended, coherent narrative that stretches from creation to exile (Freedman 1991, 1–39). The hypothesis of such a coherent narrative must disregard the long-standing canonical distinction between Torah and Prophets in order to appreciate the narrative continuity of the whole, a continuity that has the creation of the earth (*'eres*) culminate in loss of land (*'eres*). This impulse to read the whole as a continuous narrative, termed the "Primary Narrative," eschews older historical-critical distinctions and particularly eschews the fragmentation that has become the hallmark of source analysis.

If we can for now consider the claim of such a hypothesis, it is nonetheless important to notice the distinction between the first five books and the last four books of what is termed the "Primary Narrative," a distinction important not only because of canonical markers, but because of the decisive turn of plot between the two units of material. We may say that the Torah concerns a promise of and eventual entry into the land of promise, a coherent statement that Gerhard von Rad has characterized as a movement from promise to fulfillment (von Rad 1966, 1–78). This movement toward and into the land of promise culminates with the crossing of the Jordan. Thus Israel, according to this narrative, arrives at the Jordan River at the beginning of Deuteronomy (see Num 33:48; Deut 1:5), pauses at the Jordan for the long interpretive instruction of Moses in the book of Deuteronomy, and then crosses the Jordan in Joshua 3:14–17, an act replicating the exodus:

> [Joshua said] to the Israelites, "When your children ask their parents in time to come, 'What do these stones mean?' then you shall let your children know, 'Israel crossed over the Jordan here on dry ground.' For the LORD your God dried up the waters of the Jordan for you until you crossed over, as the LORD your God did to the Red Sea, which he dried up for us until we crossed over, so that all the peoples of the earth may know that the hand of the LORD is mighty, and so that you may fear the LORD your God forever." (Josh 4:21–24)

Thus the Jordan River functions not only as a geographical marker, but as a literary-canonical-theological marker as well.

The Former Prophets (Joshua, Judges, Samuel, and Kings) tell the narrative of land loss once the Jordan River has been crossed. In bold strokes this narrative details the sustained and recurring disobedience of Israel that culminates in the loss of the land, a disobedience elsewhere sketched in Psalm 106. Thus these four books rooted in Deuteronomy constitute a tale of *land loss* that is commensurate with the Torah narrative of *land gift*. The dual themes of land gift and land loss constitute a single primary narrative, but the Jordan

River marks two quite distinct themes within that larger narrative. The land is given, so it is affirmed, according to YHWH's generous fidelity. The land given, however, is not Israel's unconditional possession; rather it is held in trust according to the stipulations of the Giver, conditions of the land grant that Israel has failed to meet. The outcome is that the community summoned to venture to a new land in Genesis 12:1 is at the end yet again landless and yet again reliant on the old promises that keep open the chance for a new land entry, a reentry that is anticipated in the Latter Prophets. It is instructive that the Primary Narrative in the two themes of land gift and land loss makes no explicit move beyond land loss, unless the singular role of 2 Kings 25:27–30 is read as a move beyond.

2. The Latter Prophets (Isaiah, Jeremiah, Ezekiel, and the Twelve) make the move beyond land loss. Because the Book of the Twelve constitutes a particular problem, we shall comment first upon the three great scrolls of Isaiah, Jeremiah, and Ezekiel, which, for all their variation, are shaped in close parallel around the themes of judgment and restoration:

a. The book of Isaiah is clearly edited so that chapters 1–39 and chapters 40–66 concern, as Brevard Childs has suggested, "old things" under judgment and "new things" of restoration (Childs 1979, 325–38).

b. The book of Jeremiah is more raggedly edited. It is clear that chapters 1–20 are about "pluck[ing] up and . . . pull[ing] down" (1:10). The "building and planting" of the Jeremiah tradition is not very clear or well-ordered literarily. We can, nonetheless, observe that the Book of Comfort (Jer 30–31) plus the narrative of chapter 32 and the collection of promises in chapter 33 constitute a tradition whereby Israel may have "a future with hope" (29:11). In addition to that cluster, we may notice the postcrisis affirmation of (a) a promise to the Baruch remnant (chap. 45); (b) an anticipated demise of oppressive powers (chaps. 46–51), especially the "sinking" of Babylon (chaps. 50–51); and (c) the continuing significance of the exiled Davidic king (52:31–34). Thus in its own way, the book of Jeremiah reiterates the two themes of judgment and hope in broad parallel to the structure of the book of Isaiah.

c. The book of Ezekiel is symmetrically ordered, so that chapters 1–24 and chapters 25–48, respectively, articulate judgment and hope around the priestly accents of absence and restored divine presence.

All three scrolls together pivot around the loss of city and temple in 587; all three, each in a distinctive dialect, move decisively beyond loss to focus on the future that YHWH will give. It is worth noting, then, that while the warnings and condemnations concerning the failure of the urban system of Jerusalem are harsh, uncompromising, and unrelenting in these three traditions, the completed form of the text is not focused on judgment. Rather, the articulation of judgment, in each case no doubt rooted in words of the historical person of the prophet, becomes the launching venue for focus on the future to be given in YHWH's promises through YHWH's fidelity. Thus the old stereotype of "prophetic" as connoting righteous indignation and rage is at best a partial truth and likely a caricature, because the prophetic books finally concern the future.

If it is correct that all three prophetic traditions focus on the same themes of judgment and move determinedly toward hope, we may consider why canonical formation included three articulations of the same claim. We may find a clue to this canonical reality by asking again about the relationship of the Prophets to the Torah. To be sure, source analysis in the Torah traditions is now most problematic. While leaving many things undecided in the current state of the question of source analysis, it is nonetheless clear that the two definitive sources of the Torah are the Priestly tradition that gives shape to the Tetrateuch (Genesis–Numbers) and Deuteronomy, which provided the themes for the Former Prophets (Deuteronomic History). Alongside a recognition of the Priestly and Deuteronomic sources, it seems clear that there is a third, perhaps early, source that may still be identified as the Yahwist (J), that is, the source that uses the name of YHWH from the outset of the beginning in Genesis.

These three sources, it is now clear, are not to be understood in terms of unilinear religious development in Israel. Rather they are coexisting advocacies for certain interpretive perspectives in ancient Israel. On the assumption that the interpretive advocacies in the Torah are closely linked to interpretive advocacies in the Prophets, we may suggest that the three great traditions of Isaiah, Jeremiah, and Ezekiel correlate with and are informed by the interpretive advocacies in the Torah:

> It is evident that *Ezekiel* is clearly linked to the *Priestly* traditions of the Torah.
> It is equally evident that *Jeremiah* is closely linked to the traditions of *Deuteronomy*.
> It is not so obvious that *Isaiah* is closely related to the *Yahwist tradition*. But it may at least be suggested that the Abrahamic memories that are central to J yield the Davidic and Zion foci so crucial for the Isaiah tradition.

Thus it is possible to see that these prophetic traditions move through judgment and into hope precisely in connection to the Torah sources, whether the sources fund the prophetic tradition or vice versa. Either way, the connections between the two provide an important and suggestive heuristic entry point for interpretation. The relationship between Torah and Prophets is a very old question in Old Testament studies (Zimmerli 1965). It is important to recognize in critical study that the two units of canonical material do not flow in a simple sequence, but may be related in quite interactive ways. Thus the interpretive advocacies in the several sources of the Torah show up in these three prophets as interpretive advocacies about the ways to understand divine judgment upon Israel in Jerusalem and, more important, the ways to imagine futures that will yet be given by YHWH. The prophetic canon more explicitly meditates upon the abyss of exile than does the canon of the Torah; the same issues, however, pertain to the Torah traditions as well. Both Torah and Prophets reflect passionately upon the reality of loss and the promise of futures that pertain through and beyond the loss.

3. The Book of the Twelve (Minor Prophets) constitutes a particular concern in canonical consideration, and so merits a particular comment. An older historical-critical approach to the Twelve continues to be important. On that basis, as indicated above, one can with some confidence assign three prophets to the eighth century (Hosea, Amos, Micah), three prophets to the late seventh century (Nahum, Habakkuk, Zephaniah), and three prophets to the early Persian period (Haggai, Zechariah, Malachi). The dating of Obadiah is secure in the Persian period, and that leaves Joel and Jonah somewhat ill defined. The historical placement of the prophets in these several historical locations gives the sequence of the Twelve a rough chronological ordering. More than that, it also hints of early entries that provide *warning and judgment* and late entries on *hope and restoration*. Thus the sequence that is roughly chronological also provides a theological pattern of judgment and hope.

It is clear in present scholarship that such historical-critical understandings are important but not adequate in themselves for reading this material. Thus the newer scholarship seeks to move beyond historical criticism to ask about the corpus of the Twelve and the particular way in which these originally distinctive literary units have been combined. On the one hand, scholars have noticed that within most of the books there is a developing tradition that moves beyond the historical person of the prophet in order to be related to later contexts and crises. On the other hand, scholars are now inclined to consider the Twelve as one canonical statement. Such explorations are only at the beginning, and more work remains to be done. It is already apparent, in any case, that the several elements of the Twelve have developed according to familiar themes of judgment and restoration, so that the eighth-century prophets focus more on judgment and the prophets of the Persian period focus much more on hope. And because hope is "the conviction of things not seen" (Heb 11:1), it is not surprising that hope moves in an apocalyptic direction, that is, toward expectations that move beyond known historical categories.

In completed form it is possible, as with Isaiah, Jeremiah, and Ezekiel, to see that the Twelve is constituted as a meditation about the crisis into the abyss of 587 (or earlier in 721 BCE in northern Israel) and expectations of newness from YHWH beyond the abyss. Thus the traditioning process has taken these diverse materials and shaped them into some theological coherence. It is to be recognized at the same time, however, that the several subunits do not readily or completely yield themselves to a new, larger theological scheme. As we have seen elsewhere, the traditioning process is only partially successful. As a result, the development of the tradition appears to be a tensive, ongoing negotiation between the already extant materials and the interpretive vision that is more or less imposed and that eventuated in the canonical shape of the literature. The success of the canonical enterprise should not be overstated, but must surely be recognized so that historical-critical understandings are seen to be only partially adequate for the material. The outcome of the traditioning is a literary entity that is a mixed lot that holds together in ragged fashion *initial utterances* that have their own say and an *interpretive coherence* that both respects and overrides such initial say.

In the lived reality of Israel, the two moves of entry *into the abyss of exile* and movement *beyond the abyss of exile* are defining. One must recognize the exile as the indispensable matrix for Israel's self-understanding so that the historical reality of exile becomes paradigmatically definitional for Israel (Voegelin 1956). That adherence to historical facts on the ground, however, is further decisively defined by the claim that it is YHWH who presides over both the scattering and the gathering (as in Zech 10:9–10). While the facts on the ground about history are held to be decisive, the inscrutable reality of YHWH is ultimately the singular agent of both scattering and gathering. Thus the Twelve, as elsewhere in the prophetic literature, is an effort to imagine the vagaries of history with reference to the reality of YHWH. Rolf Rendtorff has suggested one motif that pervades the Twelve that makes YHWH the defining character, namely, the Day of the Lord. He comments cautiously:

> I tried in this essay to find out whether definable lines run through the Book of the Twelve, indicating common themes or conceptions. Obviously the Day of the Lord is one of the dominating themes. The question is whether there are deliberate interrelations among the different writings that deal with this theme. Observing the compositional relationships among Joel, Amos, and Obadiah has proven very fruitful. In following the insights gained by study of the highly complex interrelationships, many more common elements appeared. I mention in particular the complex of repentance and salvation in the face of the Day of the Lord. . . . In many cases where the term "day" appears, be it alone or in certain combinations, the reader of

the Book of the Twelve should associate it with something like the Day of the Lord. The outcome is far from unified; on the contrary, in the Book of the Twelve we find a number of controversies, and even contradictions, that are characteristic of the Hebrew Bible in general. (Rendtorff 2000, 86)

Thus the "Day of the Lord," the time of YHWH's vigorous assertion of sovereignty, is a day of *disaster and scattering*:

> The great day of the LORD is near,
>   near and hastening fast;
> the sound of the day of the LORD is bitter,
>   the warrior cries aloud there.
> That day will be a day of wrath,
>   a day of distress and anguish,
> a day of ruin and devastation,
>   a day of darkness and gloom,
> a day of clouds and thick darkness,
>   a day of trumpet blast and battle cry
> against the fortified cities
>   and against the lofty battlements.
>   (Zeph 1:14–16)

But "the day" also becomes a *time of gathering*:

> And the LORD will become king over all the earth; on that day the LORD will be one and his name one.
>   The whole land shall be turned into a plain from Geba to Rimmon south of Jerusalem. But Jerusalem shall remain aloft on its site from the Gate of Benjamin to the place of the former gate, to the Corner Gate, and from the Tower of Hananel to the king's wine presses. And it shall be inhabited, for never again shall it be doomed to destruction; Jerusalem shall abide in security. (Zech 14:9–11)

Thus the reiteration of "the day" in this literature brings the whole of Israel's lived experience under the aegis of YHWH's governance. In the end YHWH "will be one and his name one" (Zech 14:9). The enhancement of YHWH is accomplished, in the large vista of the Twelve, by the restoration of Jerusalem. Jerusalem has no future apart from YHWH, but YHWH has no way of enhancement apart from the well-being of the city and the people for whom YHWH is jealous. Clear to the end of the Twelve, the pervasive themes of repentance, obedience, and hope persist. It cannot be otherwise because the world is imagined with reference to YHWH and YHWH's characteristic markings persist through all of the losses in the life of Israel into all of the futures that YHWH will yet give. These themes are the very themes that arise in the Moses tradition and that are entrusted to Joshua at the beginning of the prophetic corpus:

> Only be strong and very courageous, being careful to act in accordance with all the law that my servant Moses commanded you; do not turn from it to the right hand or to the left, so that you may be successful wherever you go. This book of the law shall not depart out of your mouth; you shall meditate on it day and night, so that you may be careful to act in accordance with all that is written in it. For then you shall make your way prosperous, and then you shall be successful. I hereby command you: Be strong and courageous; do not be frightened or dismayed, for the LORD your God is with you wherever you go. (Josh 1:7–9)

This imaginative insistence on history under the rule of YHWH persists until the last urging of Malachi to Torah obedience (Mal 4:4) and Malachi's last promise for future well-being (4:5–6).

PART III

The Writings

22

Introduction to the Writings

The third canon of the Hebrew Bible is termed the "Writings." The term most likely reflects (a) an awareness that Judaism had devolved to scroll making in a context where it was peculiarly vulnerable, and (b) a recognition that the primal scroll makers are scribes who preserve old traditions and interpret them by way of commentary:

> The most important social group in this period would appear to be the sages. This group—with its concern for right living, its theological perspective so in tune with Deuteronomic thinking, its close connection to the central institutions and texts, its growing importance as interpreters and transmitters—comes as close as any to being the common denominator in a social analysis of the Writings. Although the diverseness of literature and agenda prevents any simple and homogeneous description of the sages in post-exilic literature, their particular interests and abilities will become increasingly important to all, especially with the emergence of a community of the book. (Morgan 1990, 55)

Thus the nomenclature "Writings" itself goes far to characterize the Judaism that is reflected in this third canon.

The actual settlement on the books included in the third canon continues to be a debatable, debated matter, and even the concluding date for the framing of the list is very much open to question. The usual reference point of a council at Jamnia (Jabneh) is much in question, not only about the date and character of such an assembly, but about the historicity of the event. Thus the recognition of these books as scripturally normative for the community is an unstable affair reflected, moreover, in that the Greek version of the books,

unlike the Greek version of the Torah and the Prophets, takes extreme lib-
erties in translation, or even better to say, reflects a quite alternative textual
tradition. This immense variation suggests that the traditioning community
had great freedom in the formation and transformation of these books, a latitude attesting that they were not, in practice, perceived as possessing high
scriptural authority of the kind reflected in the authoritative view of Mosaic
Scripture (on which see Deut 4:2; 12:32). Indeed, it is impossible to imagine
such a stricture as that given by Moses about these books in the third canon.
Conversely, the freedom reflected in the formation and transmission of this
canon—in every dimension of it—is peculiarly appropriate to the circumstance of Judaism that required flexibility and interpretive imagination of the
highest order.

Without doubt, this third canon has a miscellaneous quality to it. We must
seek to understand it nonetheless, as best we can, as a serious scriptural phenomenon. The most accessible (if somewhat rambling) discussion of this issue
is by Donn Morgan (1990). His discussion revolves around three points that
are worth notice:

1. What we have termed the "miscellaneous" character of the collection Morgan rightly understands as *pluralism*. The third canon consists in
a pluralism of genre, topic, and perspective befitting the pluralistic character of Judaism. The older view of Second Temple Judaism, perhaps especially favored by Christians, tended to think of "normative Judaism," which
revolved around Ezra's preoccupation with the Torah, thus a Judaism that
Christians could treat dismissively in terms of the "Law." Against such an
uninformed reductionism, it is now clear that Judaism in and through the
period of the rise of Christianity was a vibrant, complex, interpretive community, so that the only way in which Judaism of the period could desig-
nate "Holy Writings" was bound to embody pluralism (Stone 1980). (Of
course, the Torah is also an achievement of pluralism, there accomplished by
different voices or traditions that are incorporated into the Mosaic whole.)
Thus in studying this third canon, the reader is invited to recognize that each
of the writings included in this more or less normative collection sounds a
voice of advocacy and interpretation that some in the ongoing community
took with utmost seriousness. We dare imagine, moreover, that the voices
included were powerful enough or taken seriously enough that they could
not be omitted. Thus the collection is something of an ecumenical achievement, a big-tent enactment of Judaism.

2. Morgan helpfully shows that the writings are in dialogic continuity with
the older traditions of the Torah and the Prophets. Indeed, this *dialogic continuity* with the older traditions is important, for Morgan concludes that the

valuing of older traditions is all that the several books of the Writings have in common:

> When the hermeneutics used by the Writings in their use of Torah and Prophets are surveyed, we are unable to find one particular approach to Torah and Prophets that is shared by all and able to win the day. All post-exilic communities are concerned to determine how best to live faithfully in difficult times, but such a common goal does not suggest one way to view Torah and Prophets theologically, socially, or otherwise. Yet, all these textual traditions take the authority of the central texts seriously. In the final analysis, when viewed *together*, it is only this that the Writings share.
>
> [A]lthough we believe the function and message of the Writings are illuminated by the presupposition of a shared response to Torah and Prophets in this period, we also recognize that no conceptual system adequately explains all of the textual and historical evidence; that is, no "system" or hermeneutical paradigm is adequate to the task, for always something does not quite fit, and defies all our attempts to synthesize and explain. Such a recognition, of course, is congruent with both the history and the literature itself. The diversity of the Writings, however successfully we may organize it, still witnesses to the lack of consensus, the inability to agree upon what should be central to Judaism, in this period. This lack of consensus, always in dialogue with a basic and common story, ultimately becomes the theological and hermeneutical gift of the Writings to the biblical communities that follow. (Morgan 1990, 71, 40)

3. As the writings are in dialogue with the older, more basic traditions, so the writings are *in dialogue with cultural-historical context* as well. It is important to recognize that the exile and the termination of Israelite political independence, the resulting Diaspora of Jews, and the encircling cultural hegemony of the Greeks after the relatively benign hegemony of the Persians left the Jewish community in a fragmented situation. In that context, immense courage and interpretive flexibility were required in order to sustain Jewish canonical coherence and identity, the task of sustenance undertaken in many ways by many subcommunities:

> When the Writings are viewed as a whole, it seems inappropriate to suggest that the history of this period is a history of solitary and homogeneous communities, each with their clearly defined agendas. Rather, the perspectives and concerns of the psalmists must be related to the sages and the community builders, the storytellers must be related to the sages, and so on. The Writings vividly demonstrate a process of cross-fertilization between Diaspora and non-Diaspora communities and between those who are concerned to build social

structures in Jerusalem and those concerned to provide paradigms for
faithful living in the Diaspora. (Morgan, 1990, 53)

Thus *pluralism*, *dialogue with tradition*, and *dialogue with context* help to provide an integrated perspective on this literature. Our own way of seeing this
pluralism whole is to suggest four textual groupings in the material:

1. The three great books of Psalms, Job, and Proverbs together constitute
a sustained liturgical-sapiential reflection on God-given order in the world
and the inescapable posing of the question of theodicy to which Israel gives
faithful answer in hymn and lament.

2. The Five Scrolls, or the Megilloth (Song of Songs/Song of Solomon,
Ruth, Lamentations, Ecclesiastes/Qoheleth, Esther), evidence the way in
which various voices of the community were drawn into the liturgical calendar. For in the end it is the liturgical calendar that will provide socialization
into and sustenance of a distinctive community (Neusner 1987).

3. The apocalyptic book of Daniel perhaps reflects a compromise whereby,
from a great plentitude of apocalyptic texts that were available, the canonizing
tradition was able to exclude from the sacred books all but this apocalyptic
book (and the latter part of Zechariah). It is clear that the book of Daniel,
in canonical form, is the quintessential book of hope in the Hebrew Bible,
hope that invites courage and freedom in the enactment of a singularly Jewish
identity. Thus as the books of Psalms, Job, and Proverbs pose the question
of theodicy, the book of Daniel is a characteristic voice of hope that is totally
sure of YHWH's triumph over all threats to Jerusalem and all threats that
would dismantle the world of YHWH's creation.

4. This third canon ends by a presentation of the historical books of Ezra,
Nehemiah, and Chronicles. But of course they are not "history" in any modern sense of the term, any more than the Deuteronomic History is "history,"
a text that is a predecessor to the Chronicles. The four books of Ezra, Nehemiah, and 1 and 2 Chronicles represent a theological-ideological insistence for
a particular shape and mode of Judaism; it is important to recognize, however,
that as powerful as that advocacy is, it did not and was not able to claim the
field in the third canon, for its advocacy is placed alongside the other advocacies already mentioned. It is of particular interest that taken historically, Ezra
and Nehemiah should follow Chronicles, as is evident in the overlap and reiteration of Ezra 1:2–3 from 2 Chronicles 36:23. The inversion of the sequence
from what we might have expected is apparently so that the third canon, and
thus the entire Hebrew Bible, can end with the edict of Cyrus the Persian
with its project of a return from exile (2 Chr 36:22–23). Thus the canon ends
with an expected recovery, for Judaism—with its preoccupation with exile—is
always returning home again, always yet again recovering YHWH's promise

of the land, always again working beneath the radar of imperial hegemony according to its own distinctive identity.

These four groupings, then, evidence Judaism at work in a variety of ways, coming to terms with its circumstance. By many acts of imagination Judaism comes to terms with a necessary flexibility; in the end, however, it finally never yields the core of its theological identity. Given this fourfold articulation, we note that Morgan somewhat differently articulates five basic perspectives in the third canon that enabled the traditionists to respond to the same five perspectives of the Torah and the Prophets (Morgan 1990, 72, 85):

1. Sapiential literature (Job, Proverbs, Ecclesiastes, Song of Songs)
2. Liturgical literature (Psalms, Lamentations)
3. Historical literature (Ezra, Nehemiah, 1 and 2 Chronicles)
4. Apocalyptic literature (Daniel 7–12)
5. Edifying literature (Ruth, Esther, Daniel 1–6)

The distinctions between our fourfold delineation and Morgan's fivefold grouping are not important, except that Morgan's delineation does not follow the canonical groupings as such. Taken either way, the point is the same concerning *pluralism* and *dialogue*.

We digress in the midst of the pluralism of the third canon in terms of theme, perspective, and the several advocacies represented in these books to call attention to the "hermeneutics of testimony" proposed by Paul Ricoeur. In his effort to be nonfoundational, Ricoeur has proposed that testimony is the claim of epistemology that dominates the Old Testament (Ricoeur 1980, 119–34; see Brueggemann 1997, 117–45 and passim). More specifically, however, Ricoeur has paid attention to the several genres of testimony in the textual tradition and lists the following:

1. Prophetic discourse
2. Narrative discourse
3. Prescriptive discourse
4. Wisdom discourse
5. Hymnic discourse

It is worth noticing the correlations between Ricoeur's inventory and that of the third canon, in either Morgan's delineation or our own. The correlation and overlap in these several delineations are sufficient to suggest that the third canon is a peculiar way in which polyvalent testimony is given concerning both the God who is the focus of Israel's faith and the distinctive community related to that God. Jack Miles has observed that by the end of the third canon, the God of Israel is for the most part silent and absent (Miles 1995; see Friedman 1995). But then, given that silence and absence, everything for this God depends upon the answering of Israel. The third canon is an answer whereby the community is sustained and YHWH is kept available in a community that has become politically marginal but confessionally resolved and sure of the will and identity that belongs to it in a dangerous circumstance. The answer turns out to be, in canonical traditioning, *revelatory* of this God who is offered according to the resolve given in the answer of Israel.

23

The Book of Psalms

If, as the great German scholar Gerhard von Rad has suggested, the magnificent poetry of Psalms, Job, and Proverbs is a "response" to God's miraculous interventions as Creator and covenant maker, then it is not a surprise that the book of Psalms comes first in the third canon of Scripture (von Rad 1962, 355–459). For the Psalms constitute the quintessential articulation of Israel's faith in the primal utterance of Israel to YHWH in affirmation and in distress, and in testimony to the world concerning the wonders of YHWH. The book of Psalms is an ancient mapping of Israel's life with YHWH, a mapping that has continued through the centuries to be the primary guide for faith and worship in both the synagogue and the church (Holladay 1993).

In its present, canonical form, the book of Psalms is organized into five "books" (Pss 1–41; 42–72; 73–89; 90–106; and 107–150), with each book culminating in a doxology and the whole culminating in a collection of doxologies in Psalms 145–150. This arrangement is a late canonizing articulation and appears to be designed as a liturgical counterpoint to the "Five Books of Moses" that constitute the Torah. The final form of the text into these five parts is perhaps instructive in linking the whole of the Psalter to the faith of the Torah. It is nonetheless necessary to consider the way in which the parts of the Psalter together constitute the sum of the whole that now makes up the book of Psalms.

It is clear that the collection of Psalms that constitute the book of Psalms is formed by earlier, smaller collections that may come from many hands in many contexts. For example, Psalms 120–134 are each designated "A Song of Ascents," suggesting a small collection of songs perhaps used in a particular liturgical context. In Psalms 73–83 there is a series of psalms related to Asaph, matched in Psalms 84, 85, and 88 by psalms related to Korah (Goulder 1982). These little groups of psalms are perhaps related to particular guilds of choirs in the Persian period, wherein each such guild related to temple worship might have developed its own manual of worship—or hymnal—which was to be subsequently incorporated into the larger collection (see 2 Chr 25). Behind these smaller collections, there is a long history of psalm-like materials in older collections that have been borrowed from other cultures or imitated in Israel, so that Israel's Psalter is part of a much larger cultural-liturgical inheritance in which Israel is a participant as a relative latecomer (Miller 1994, 5–31). Thus it is possible to understand the Psalter as a long editorial-traditioning process whereby many songs and poems from many sources were formed into collections for usage in a variety of contexts, until finally the several collections were shaped into a grand scheme of the present Psalter in five books. Anyone who knows anything about the formation of a church hymnal will understand that this process in Israel was in part intentional and in part accidental and haphazard, no doubt shot through with competing advocacies and political compromises along the way. In the end, the Psalter is evidence of a long practice of Israel in finding poetic, artistic ways to voice faith, but poetic, artistic ways that were being impinged upon, no doubt in decisive insistence, by vigorous theological intention and urgent ideological advocacy. We may imagine that the end result is an ecumenical achievement in Israel that sought to bring many diverse traditions together into a generally accepted poetic and theological coherence.

Over time, interpretation of the Psalter has pursued several paths. One approach has been to try to situate each psalm *in a particular historical context*. Such an approach is not very helpful because it is likely that only Psalm 137 can, with any reasonable certainty, be connected to a particular circumstance. Attention should be given, with reference to issues of historical context, to the superscriptions that characteristically link psalms to historical events in the life of David (Childs 1971). (Psalm 51 is the best known of these, wherein it is linked to David's crisis after the events relating him to Uriah and Bathsheba.) In general scholars judge that these superscriptions that situate the psalms in a particular way are not to be taken with historical seriousness, but rather constitute an interpretive guideline from a later community about how to understand the particular psalms. In this connection, it is also useful to recognize that the formula "A Psalm of David" (as in Pss 3, 4, 5, etc.) is not a note on authorship, so that Davidic authorship of the Psalms is not held credible in critical study. More likely, the formula should be translated "for David," that is, "for the king," in a way that may suggest liturgical usage in the royal environs.

A second approach to the Psalter among Christians is an inclination to read *christologically*, as though Jesus were either the speaker of the psalm, as in Psalm 22, or the one who speaks as the righteous sufferer, or the subject of the psalm, as in the royal psalms such as Psalm 2. Such an approach was taken with great seriousness in the early centuries of the church and was championed by Augustine; with the rise of critical study, however, it is clear that no direct link can be made to Jesus. That does not preclude a second christological interpretive move once the Psalter has been taken seriously in its own Old Testament context. This latter move is especially important in the interpretive work of Dietrich Bonhoeffer (Bonhoeffer 1970; see Miller 2000, 345–54).

If we recognize that neither a historical nor a messianic approach is sustainable in psalm interpretation, we may focus upon the singular contribution of Hermann Gunkel, a scholar of the early twentieth century who has decisively influenced all subsequent psalm study. Gunkel came to see that the psalms recur in a fairly limited number of rhetorical patterns (genres) and that the several genres reflect social settings so that *genre* and *setting* are characteristically twinned. As a consequence, the psalms tend not to be free and innovative speech, but are highly stylized and predictable in form, presumably in traditional societies that counted on the regularity of rhetorical patterns to shape and sustain life in certain ways: "Accordingly, *genre research* in the Psalms is nonnegotiable, not something one can execute or ignore according to preference. Rather, it is *the foundational work* without which there can be no certainty in the remainder. It is the firm ground from which everything else must ascend" (Gunkel and Begrich 1998, 5).

The work of psalm study, then, is to pay attention to the most distinctive rhetorical patterns that characteristically carry certain content appropriate to specific contexts. Such patterns may be voiced with great imaginative variation, but the variations typically adhere to a constant pattern. This way of understanding the psalms means that they arise in community usage, so that it is largely futile to try to date the psalms or to identify authorship. In that regard, the psalms are not unlike "Negro spirituals" that have no author or identifiable place or origin, but simply arise in the life and practice of the community and are found to be recurringly adequate to many different usages over time.

Gunkel identified a series of recurring genres (Gerstenberger 1974; Anderson 1983, 239–42). Here we may identify the most prominent types of recurring rhetorical patterns:

1. *The Hymn.* The term "psalm" means "hymn," an exuberant act of praise that exalts and celebrates either the person of YHWH or the characteristic actions of YHWH. Psalm 117 is a short example of a hymn that includes two parts:

a. A *summons* to praise with evocative address:

> Praise the LORD, all you nations!
>   Extol him, all you peoples!
>   (117:1)

b. A *reason* for praise, in this case YHWH's most identifiable characteristic of fidelity:

> For great is his steadfast love toward us,
>   and the faithfulness of the LORD endures forever.
>   (117:2)

The concluding formula, "praise the LORD," often reiterates the opening summons in a hymn. The pattern can be endlessly expanded in liturgical usage. Thus in 147:1b–6, 8–11, 13–20, the reasons for praise are numerous, each section introduced by a summons (vv. 1a, 7, 12), all concluded with the doxological formula of verse 20.

2. *Communal Lament.* While the hymn is positive and celebrative, its counterpoint is a lament that concerns the entire community. This genre may be evoked by any number of public crises, notably drought or defeat in war. Psalms 74 and 79 focus upon the destruction of the temple in Jerusalem, the quintessential public crisis in the Old Testament. In Psalm 74, for example, we may identify three characteristic rhetorical elements:

a. A *description of the disaster*, apparently to evoke YHWH's interest and intervention (vv. 4–11):

> Your foes have roared within your holy place;
>   they set up their emblems there.
> At the upper entrance they hacked
>   the wooden trellis with axes.
> And then, with hatchets and hammers,
>   they smashed all its carved work.
>   (74:4–6)

b. A *doxology* celebrating YHWH's immense power, apparently to mobilize YHWH to act in a situation in which Israel finds itself helpless (vv. 12–17):

> Yet God my King is from of old,
>   working salvation in the earth.
> You divided the sea by your might;
>   you broke the heads of the dragons in the waters.
> You crushed the heads of Leviathan;
>   you gave him as food for the creatures of the wilderness.
>   (74:12–14)

c. A series of *imperative petitions*, seeking YHWH's decisive, transformative intervention (vv. 18–23):

> Rise up, O God, plead your cause;
>   remember how the impious scoff at you all day long.
>   (74:22)

It is obvious that each of these elements of description, doxological motivation, and imperative petition can be variously expanded in a variety of uses.

3. *Individual Lament.* This genre of speech, a frequent one in the Psalter, is the voice of an individual person who speaks personal distress (such as sickness, abandonment, or imprisonment) to YHWH, and asks YHWH to intervene and deliver. While the genre developed in complex ways, Psalm 13 is a clear example of the main elements of the rhetorical pattern (Westermann 1965, 64 and passim).

a. A *complaint* that describes for YHWH the vexation in which YHWH is implicated:

> How long, O Lord? Will you forget me forever?
>   How long will you hide your face from me?
> How long must I bear pain in my soul,
>   and have sorrow in my heart all day long?
> How long shall my enemy be exalted over me?
>   (13:1–2)

b. A *petition* that seeks YHWH's intervention:

> Consider and answer me, O Lord my God!
>   Give light to my eyes . . .
>   (13:3a)

c. *Reasons* given to YHWH for YHWH's intervention:

> . . . or I will sleep the sleep of death,
> and my enemy will say, "I have prevailed";
>   my foes will rejoice because I am shaken.
>   (13:3b–4)

d. A statement of glad *resolution* with a promise to praise YHWH:

> But I trusted in your steadfast love;
>   my heart shall rejoice in your salvation.
> I will sing to the Lord,
>   because he has dealt bountifully with me.
>   (13:5–6)

It is commonly noticed that this pattern of rhetoric moves dramatically, even abruptly, from plea to praise:

> In my opinion, this fact that in the Psalms of the O.T. there is no, or almost no, such thing as "mere" lament and petition, shows conclusively the polarity between praise and petition in the Psalms. The cry to God is here never one-dimensional, without tension. It is always somewhere in the middle between petition and praise. By nature it cannot be mere petition or lament, but is always underway from supplication to praise. . . .
>
> The fact that lamentation and petition can change into praise in the same Psalm has as a consequence a development which is peculiar to the Israelite Psalms, i.e., that praise is already heard in the conclusion of lament and petition, and that it forms the basis for the vow of praise. . . .
>
> This transition is the real theme of the Psalms which are being discussed here. *They are no longer mere petition, but petition that has been heard. They are no longer mere lament, but lament that has been turned to praise.* (Westermann 1965, 75, 79, 80; italics original)

While the movement from plea (including complaint and petition) to praise is accomplished in ways not readily explainable, the dominant scholarly hypothesis is that at the turn from plea to praise (as in Ps 13 between v. 4 and v. 5), a trusted, authorized official uttered a salvation oracle, not unlike the "fear not" formula of Isaiah 43:1:

> But now thus says the LORD,
>   he who created you, O Jacob,
>   he who formed you, O Israel:
> Do not fear, for I have redeemed you;
>   I have called you by name, you are mine.

That utterance, taken as YHWH's own assurance, dramatically changes reality for the petitioner that makes praise possible:

> As far as the lament of the individual is concerned we must reckon in every case with the possibility that the content is not only the lament and petition of the one who comes before God, that is, that he not only "pours out his heart" before Yahweh, but in some instances it is to be assumed that an oracle of salvation was given in the *midst* of the Psalm and that the Psalm also includes the words that follow the giving of the oracle. (Westermann 1965, 65; italics original)

The two statements of God in Lamentations 3 and Psalm 35 give us the main parts of a form of divine speech that we hear frequently in the Old Testament and also in the New. It has come to be called the oracle of salvation, though that is merely a modern designation. It means that a divine speech is transmitted through some agency, that is, an oracle, and its basic character is an announcement of salvation and deliverance. It is fundamentally a word of assurance, and we will also use that way of referring to this divine speech. . . .

The heart of the oracle of salvation and its effective and performative word is the simple *assurance, "Do not fear."* It occurs in most of the salvation oracles and is the most characteristic single feature of this divine word. Lamentations 3:57, as we noted above, identifies these words, "Do not fear," or "Fear not," as the response of God to the prayer for help:

> You came near when I called on you;
>   you said, "Do not fear!"

This word of assurance is often repeated poetically, "Do not be dismayed," or "Do not be discouraged." Its performative character is suggested in the way that these assuring words have the capacity to remove the fear and anxiety that are at the center of the trouble and distress of those who cry out to God. Over and over again the prayers of the Psalms express the fear of death or the terror in the mind and heart of the petitioner in the face of enemies. In the expressions of trust and confidence or songs of thanksgiving, the afflicted one bears witness to the power of this word of assurance to quell the fear that has evoked the prayer. (Miller 1994, 141–42, 144)

Thus the dramatic movement of lament is genuinely interactive between YHWH and the speaker:

> Can we therefore conclude that the Hebrew term "meditation" suggests something like romantic self-consciousness—a self-consciousness that expresses itself essentially in monologue? The answer is that the Psalms are not monologues but insistently and at all times dialogue-poems, poems of the self but of the self in the mutuality of relationship with the other. . . .
>
> To speak of relationality pure and simple is, however, misleading. The Psalms are not exercises in existential philosophy; we are not speaking of an encounter for the sake of merely discovering the existence of the other and of the self in relation to the other. The "Thou" answers the plea of the "I" and that answer signals a change in the opening situation. The Psalms are in this sense dynamic, they involve action, purpose. W. H. Auden said in his elegy on the death of Yeats, "For poetry makes nothing happen." This is not true of the Psalms. In nearly every psalm something does happen. The encounter between the "I" and the "Thou" is the signal for a change not merely in the inner realm of consciousness but in the realm of outer events. (Fisch 1988, 108–9)

This genre of speech articulates what is perhaps most definitional and elemental in Israel's faith that is ordered in an interaction of *cry-hear-thank*, the same pattern that is given in the narrative of the exodus:

> After a long time the king of Egypt died. The Israelites groaned under their slavery, and cried out. Out of the slavery their cry for help rose up to God. God heard their groaning, and God remembered his covenant with Abraham, Isaac, and Jacob. God looked upon the Israelites, and God took notice of them. (Exod 2:23–25)

> And Miriam sang to them: "Sing to the LORD, for he has triumphed gloriously; horse and rider he has thrown into the sea." (Exod 15:21)

4. *The Individual Song of Thanksgiving.* This song has the rhetorical pattern of an individual expressing a lament, YHWH answering, so that the vexation voiced has been resolved by the decisive intervention of YHWH, and then the individual praising YHWH: "The main part is then the *narrative account of God's deed*, almost always divided into a review of the crisis and an account of the rescue. Here trouble is often described as being enslaved or being in death, while rescue is correspondingly described as liberation from death" (Westermann 1980b, 76).

Psalm 30 constitutes a good example of this genre:

a. The speaker *reports the unexpected trouble*:

> You hid your face;
>　　I was dismayed.
>　　　　(30:7b)

b. The speaker *reports on the prayer of complaint* that was previously uttered:

> To you, O LORD, I cried,
>　　and to the LORD I made supplication:
> "What profit is there in my death,
>　　if I go down to the Pit?
> Will the dust praise you?
>　　Will it tell of your faithfulness?
> Hear, O LORD, and be gracious to me!
>　　O LORD, be my helper!"
>　　　　(30:8–10)

c. The speaker *affirms YHWH's decisive intervention*:

> You have turned my mourning into dancing;
>　　you have taken off my sackcloth
>　　and clothed me with joy. . . .
>　　　　(30:11)

d. The speaker *promises praise and thanks to YHWH*:

> . . . so that my soul may praise you and not be silent.
> O LORD my God, I will give thanks to you forever.
>   (30:12)

Thus the individual Song of Thanksgiving reiterates the previous lament, but then celebrates restoration. The outcome is thanks (*todah*), whereby the speaker promises to testify in the congregation by utterance and by material offering to YHWH's powerful, life-giving intervention.

These four genres provide a useful map for Israel's life before YHWH, in speech patterns whereby Israel answers to YHWH in every season of its life:

	Celebration:	Protest and Petition:
Communal:	Hymn	Communal Lament
Personal:	Song of Thanksgiving	Individual Lament

While there are other important genres, these four show Israel in its extremities of ecstasy and agony, telling the truth to YHWH—and before the congregation—the truth of deep need in Israel and of deep, attentive generosity by YHWH.

We may identify the following themes that are important for current psalm study:

1. There is no doubt that the Psalter has a heavy *Jerusalem accent*, suggesting both that the Psalter has been compiled and shaped in the environs of Jerusalem and that Jerusalem is the key theological focus of the Psalms. More specifically, the Jerusalem focus is made the culmination of the faith recital of Israel in Psalm 78:67–72, wherein Jerusalem displaces an older alternative sanctuary. Three theological accent points pertain to the Jerusalem focus of the Psalter:

a. *The temple* is celebrated as the place of YHWH's residence and therefore is the guarantee of the safety of the city and of all who reside there. Particular attention should be paid to the Songs of Zion that celebrate the city, of which Psalm 46 is the most familiar:

> God is our refuge and strength,
>   a very present help in trouble.
> Therefore we will not fear, though the earth should change,
>   though the mountains shake in the heart of the sea;
> though its waters roar and foam,
>   though the mountains tremble with its tumult.
>   (46:1–3; see also Pss 48, 76, 84, 87)

These psalms celebrate the abiding presence of YHWH in the Jerusalem temple:

> As the dwelling-place of Yahweh, creator of the cosmic order and defender of Israel, Zion functions pre-eminently as a symbol of security. This component of Zion symbolism has been traditionally viewed as the predominant aspect of the Zion tradition, leading scholars to speak of the inviolability of Zion/Jerusalem. For our present purposes it is sufficient to note that the security symbolized by Zion is rooted first of all in *Yahweh's presence*. (Ollenburger 1987, 66)

b. In the Jerusalem temple, *YHWH is celebrated as Creator and King*, a claim particularly expressed in the enthronement psalms (Pss 47, 93, 96–99):

> Say among the nations, "The LORD is king!
>   The world is firmly established; it shall never be moved.
>   He will judge the peoples with equity."
>
> > (96:10)

> The LORD is king! Let the earth rejoice;
>   let the many coastlands be glad!
> > (97:1)

This rule of YHWH in Jerusalem is constituted in justice, righteousness, equity, and mercy.

c. Jerusalem as YHWH's city is the place of the *Davidic king*, YHWH's regent, a claim celebrated by the royal psalms (Pss 2, 18, 20–21, 45, 72, 89, 101, 110, 144). Of these, especially Psalms 2 and 110 are taken up by the early church to articulate the Davidic claims of Jesus of Nazareth:

> It is clear that in early Christianity several Old Testament psalms were extremely important. They were quoted again and again and cited as "star witnesses" in the proclamation that the promises of God had been fulfilled. These are Psalms 2; 22; 69; 110; 118. It seems appropriate to begin with Psalms 2 and 110, two "royal psalms," because these two songs stand at the center of the messianic message of the New Testament and are used as witnesses to the messiahship of Jesus of Nazareth. (Kraus 1986, 180)

> I will tell of the decree of the LORD:
> He said to me, "You are my son;
>   today I have begotten you."
> > (2:7; see Mays 1994, 108–16)

> The LORD has sworn and will not change his mind,
>   "You are a priest forever according to the order of Melchizedek."
> > (110:4)

2. The strong Jerusalem accent of the completed Psalter focuses upon *cosmic themes of creation*, with a rhetoric that invests city and temple with unconditional permanence. There is no doubt that the promotion of these claims in the city through the royal apparatus was a major liturgical effort. It is evident that such promotion and investment in the city and its royal entourage live in some tension with the old Torah traditions of Sinai that made all institutional claims penultimately dependent upon Torah obedience. Consequently, the Jerusalem focus (of Zion, divine kingship, and Davidic kingship) is in profound tension with the Torah traditions of Moses (Levenson 1987).

While the Jerusalem accent is crucial for the Psalter, it is clear that in its final form the Psalter has received a "Torah editing" with particular reference to Psalm 1, which sets the tone for reading and using all that follows in the Psalter:

> The first psalm, by echoing these texts, applies the instruction and lesson of that record to wisdom's question about how life is to be lived. The torah of the Lord replaces wisdom and its human teachers. The responsibility that once was primarily that of Israel's leaders is laid squarely on the shoulders of the pious. In its introductory role, Psalm 1 is a signal of the importance of the Psalter for that piety and of torah-piety for the book of Psalms. All the categories by which the psalmists identify themselves and their circle—servants, humble, fearers of the Lord, devoted ones—are to be understood in light of the first psalm. (Mays 1987, 4–5)

Thus the placement of Psalm 1, matched by Psalm 119, evidences the way in which the traditioning process curbed and balanced the Jerusalem usage by giving weight to the normative countertradition of the Torah. A reading of the Psalter must take into account the twinned opening of Psalms 1 and 2, respectively, concerning the Torah and the king, as the way to read all that follows (see Miller 1993).

3. Because so much of the Psalter reflects the usage of the Jerusalem temple, it is certain that the Psalter reflects *liturgic usage*. Indeed, Sigmund Mowinckel, Gunkel's most important student, proposed that the Psalter reflects liturgic usage in which, by careful design, the worship in the temple on New Year's Day reconstituted the world as a viable creation for another year with YHWH as the presiding Creator-King. Mowinckel urged that the worship in the temple "effectively" generated a new world (Mowinckel 1961).

Such an accent on the generativity of liturgy has in other quarters, especially among Calvinist interpreters, been resisted. Such scholarship proposes that while the Psalms in earlier usage may have been closely related to actual worship, in canonical form what was *liturgical* has now become *instructional*, thus in a later environment dominated by scribes whose work is instruction in and commentary upon old traditions. This view is particularly reinforced by the decisive placement of Psalm 1 at the outset of the collection that urges the study of the Torah "day and night."

Whether the Psalter is to be understood as directly related to worship or as removed from worship for purposes of instruction largely depends on the predilection of the scholarly interpreter. In the end, we suggest, the matter is not solvable and is not even very important. For as worship (sacrament) or as instruction (word), the community that uses these Psalms regularly is up to a simple but important matter, namely, "the social construction of reality" whereby the community affirms its peculiar "world," attests to that world among "outsiders," and inculcates its own young into that world (Berger 1966; Brueggemann 1988, 1–28). As either liturgy or instruction, the Psalms function to reveal, authorize, and imagine a world in which YHWH is the key player and in which all other players (Israel and the nations) are inescapably engaged in dialogic interaction with YHWH, who is the Lord of the nations and the Savior of Israel. Thus in the two options of liturgy and instruction, the Psalms mediate an alternative world, alternative either to the notion that the world is morally incoherent and therefore unsafe, or that the world is given over to human autonomy and aggrandizement. The world mediated by the Psalter, amid the tensions of Torah conditionality and Jerusalem unconditionality, is a world always at risk but on which the community gathered around the Psalter bets its entire destiny.

4. We want to suggest (following Brueggemann 1995b, 3–32) that Gunkel's normative genre analysis can be related to the immediate dynamics of lived human reality. The relationship of Psalms and life, in our reckoning, is greatly illuminated by the simple grid we have appropriated from the work of Paul Ricoeur, namely, *orientation–disorientation–new orientation*.

a. Many of Gunkel's hymns (concerning Torah, wisdom, creation) can be identified as "psalms of orientation," which assure the reliable coherence of the world and that command conformity to normative teaching as a condition of maintaining a viable, livable world. These psalms function, at the same time, to affirm and enact the most treasured claims of Israel's faith, but also to effect social conformity and control.

b. The psalms of lament and protest we understand to be articulations of faith amid dislocation when the promises and guarantees of hymnic orientation have failed, thus "psalms of disorientation." The astonishing reality of the Psalter is that Israel did not hesitate to give full voice to its fear, anger, and dismay, which are palpably present in life and in speech, and which contradict the settled claims of faith. It is remarkable that while these psalms of disorientation occupy fully one-third of the Psalter, they have largely been lost in the practice of the church. Indeed, it is the church's propensity, in its large and long-standing cultural accommodation, either to deny disorientation and to continue to voice orientation or to reduce disorientation to guilt, as though all bad things are punishment for disobedience:

> One of the more important reasons that the scheme of retribution has played such an important role in the exegesis of the descriptions of affliction in the individual complaint psalms, is undoubtedly the strong position which the *idea of* "YHWH's *pancausality*" in connection with calamities has among biblical scholars. Keel, for instance, in one of the most thorough-going studies of the individual complaint psalms, maintains that Israel did not want to explain calamity through the activity of evil powers, so that affliction must instead be projected onto either humans or God; YHWH's "pancausality" would prohibit anything else. (Lindström 1994, 13)

The tendency to reduce disorientation to guilt has, in turn, caused the church to abandon the lament psalm, because these psalms and prayers refuse to accept a morally simplistic world. Fredrik Lindström has most vigorously proposed, as an alternative to retributive punishment, the recognition that the Psalms concern the assault of "the enemy" upon the petitioner: "The absolutely most important motif in the individual complaint psalms' interpretation of suffering is the *enemy motif*. The motif is the most important in the sense that it is found in and throughout the psalms in question" (Lindström 1994, 6). Lindström makes the point that either the enemy has overpowered the petitioner and therefore the trouble, or YHWH has been neglectful and therefore the enemy has occupied the vacuum of space and power. Either way, it is the work of the enemy and not the guilt of the sufferer that is the cause of the trouble.

Claus Westermann opines that the loss of the lament in church practice is a consequence of modern stoicism:

> It would be a worthwhile task to ascertain how it happened that in Western Christendom the lament has been totally excluded from man's relationship with God, with the result that it has completely disappeared above all from prayer and worship. We must ask whether this exclusion is actually based on the message of the New Testament or whether it is in part attributable to the influence of Greek thought, since it is so thoroughly consistent with the ethic of Stoicism. (Westermann 1994, 25)

Thus the recovery of the psalms of disorientation (complaint, protest, and lament) is a major enterprise in valuing the full spectrum of Israel's faith rhetoric.

c. Psalms of new orientation—of which the salvation oracle is already a harbinger—celebrate the new world that is given in YHWH's powerful generosity. In such psalms as those of thanksgiving (for example, Ps 107) and divine enthronement (for example, Ps 96), YHWH is credited with a radical *novum* in the life of the world that is not derived from antecedents but is a fresh miracle of YHWH. This scheme of orientation–disorientation–new orientation is, we propose, a useful way to see the interaction of the several genres of the Psalms that Gunkel has identified, and the way in which the genres contribute to the construction and maintenance of a world that is alternative to the facts on the ground and yet always dialogically referred to YHWH. Calvin's famous statement that the Psalms are "the anatomy of all parts of the soul" nicely relates to the grid of orientation–disorientation–new orientation. Seen in this way, the Psalter brings to speech the wonder and risk of life in faith that must be voiced candidly in every season of Israel's life.

5. Finally, readers should be aware that near the end of the twentieth century a new impetus in Psalms study concerned the *canonical placement* of the psalms (G. Wilson 1985). For the most part, psalms study had considered the psalms *ad seriatim* without reference to the placement of the psalms in relationship to one another. More recent study has proposed that there are patterns of arrangement of the psalms, perhaps especially signaled by the placement of torah psalms and royal psalms that

---

Midrashic Moment: Psalm 22 and Jesus

The opening line of Psalm 22 will be familiar to many Christian readers as the words Jesus cries out from the cross: "My God, my God, why have you forsaken me?" (Mark 15:34; Matt 27:46). Although Jesus is presented as uttering only the first line of this psalm of lament, clearly the reader of the gospel is supposed to recall the psalm as a whole, as the author works in several other references to it, including the dividing of the garments (Ps 22:18), the piercing of hands and feet (22:16), and the mocking of passersby (22:7–8). The idea of Jesus being "forsaken" by God is of course a powerfully tragic effect of using Psalm 22 in the passion scene. At the same time, we are surely to note that the lament of Psalm 22 eventually turns toward salvation and praise (vv. 22–31), thus presaging Jesus' eventual resurrection. Indeed, the gospel story as a whole mirrors the basic psalmic pattern of *orientation* (Jesus's initial ministry), *disorientation* (the passion and death), and *new orientation* (the resurrection). As both the psalmist and the gospel writer affirm, however, the new orientation can be had only by traveling through the disorientation. There is no shortcut through the pain.

---

indicate a theologically acute traditioning process (G. Wilson 1985; McCann 1993). While that line of study is still in its early stages, it offers yet more evidence of the lively traditioning process that has led to and produced the canon.

A case study of such canonical analysis is that offered by Patrick Miller in his study of Psalms 15–24 (Miller 2000, 279–97). He shows that this section of the Psalter appears to be arranged in a chiastic fashion:

```
        a 15 entrance liturgy . . . . . . . . . . . . . . . . . . . . . . a' 24 entrance liturgy
         b 16 song of trust . . . . . . . . . . . . . . . . . . . . . . b' 23 song of trust
          c 17 prayer for help . . . . . . . . . . . . . . . c' 22 prayer for help
           d 18 royal psalm . . . . . . . . . . . . .d' 20–21 royal psalms
                            e 19 torah psalm
```

Miller shows that the linguistic connections in these psalms are very "thick," culminating with Psalm 19, a torah psalm at the center.

It is likely that such canonical investigations will continue to refine our awareness of the theological shaping of the tradition of the Psalter. It is clear that the Psalter is a rhetorical exercise (as either worship or instruction), a "limit expression" that is artistic and intentional (Ricoeur 1975). The ability to participate in this rhetorical practice is the process by which the faithful live in an alternative world defined by issues of fidelity and infidelity about which the dominant world knows very little. The God to whom the Psalter "answers" is the one "from whom no secrets are hid" (*Book of Common Prayer*). In this dialogical engagement, Israel regularly *claims* for itself the fidelity of YHWH and *cedes* over to YHWH its life in (as Charles Wesley's hymn "Love Divine, All Loves Excelling" puts it) "wonder, love, and praise." One way to see in sum the dialogical quality of this corpus is to see that it begins in a summons to obedience (Ps 1) and ends in a lyrical summons to praise (Ps 150) (Brueggemann 1995b, 189–213). The dramatic movement from *obedience* to *praise* is in and through the vagaries of fidelity and infidelity that are articulated all through the Psalter. All seasons of this voiced life are held determinately to the God of the tradition to whom the Psalter answers sometimes in gladness and sometimes in shrillness, characteristically and incessantly truth telling before the God of all truth.

24

The Book of Job

It is no overstatement to say that the book of Job is a towering classic of the human literary and theological imagination. The great novelist Victor Hugo went so far as to say, "Tomorrow, if all literature was to be destroyed and it was left to me to retain one work only, I should save Job." Few books of the Bible are as challenging as Job, and few offer rewards as great for sustained engagement, reflection, and discussion. As a poetic achievement, it is the high-water mark of ancient Hebrew verse; as a theological document, it is unmatched for its honesty about the problems raised by human suffering for any account of God's workings in the world. One could spend a lifetime reading and rereading the book of Job, and it would be a life well spent.

The book of Job lives—rhetorically and theologically—at the edge of the Old Testament. Rhetorically the book takes up older genres and patterns of speech, and fashions them into the most artistic and urbane statement of faith in the Old Testament. Theologically the book takes up old covenantal and sapiential presuppositions, challenges basic premises of Israel's faith, and refuses any easy resolution of the most difficult theological questions that appear on the horizon of Israel's faith. It is, moreover, appropriate that the book of Job should follow the book of Psalms in the Hebrew canonical order, for the book of Job takes up the primary genres of the Psalms, especially lament and hymn, weaves them into a new coherent dialogue, and pushes both lament and hymn to an emotional, artistic, and theological extremity.

Concerning the genre of the book of Job, Claus Westermann has suggested that the basic material is that of lament that characteristically engages three parties—the speaker, YHWH, and the adversary; that the lament has been arranged in the book of Job as a dialogic disputation, a disputation that stands "within the lament"; and that the dialogic dispute (expressed in forensic language) amounts to a drama wherein we are offered "a dramatizing of the lament" (Westermann 1981, 11–12).

Such an analysis of genre indicates that we are dealing with an immensely sophisticated artistic work that is removed from any particular historical context or crisis, and that it stands on its own as a daring explication of the most difficult questions of faith. The book of Job is not for everyday use among the faithful, but is an artistic extremity that is peculiarly matched to the most extreme crises of life lived in faith. In this artistic achievement, it is clear that the dramatist who produced the book of Job did not start from scratch, but was informed by and drew upon already well-established cultural reservoirs of Job-like materials from elsewhere in the ancient Near East.

I

The centerpiece of the book of Job is the long poetic work of 3:1–42:6, a dispute in two parts (chaps. 3–28 and 32:1–42:6) that are connected by an extended soliloquy in chapters 29–31. In the dispute, the several speeches engage the most unbearable questions of faith. While it is commonly said that the poem of Job deals with the "problem of evil," or the "problem of theodicy," it is important at the outset to recognize that the issues taken up here are not speculative or cerebral, but are rooted in and driven by the immediate facts of Job's suffering. The issues concern the most intense and immediate existential issues of faith, morality, and fidelity that grow out of Israel's older traditions of the Torah (as in the book of Deuteronomy) and wisdom (as in the book of Proverbs), but they never lose sight of the emotional and physical toll of being human.

The first part of the dialogic dispute concerns Job's engagement with his three friends, Eliphaz, Bildad, and Zophar, who are representatives of older, settled, traditional faith. The literature of chapters 3–27 is not a discussion, but rather a series of speeches—alternating between Job and his friends—that deal with the same issues but do not directly engage each other. In chapters 3–27 the pattern is to have Job's utterances alternate with speeches by his three friends:

Job 3	Eliphaz 4–5
Job 6–7	Bildad 8
Job 9–10	Zophar 11

This series of speeches constitutes one cycle of exchange, and the process is repeated two more times, though in the third cycle of speeches the pattern is left incomplete.

In this exchange, Job and his friends mostly talk past each other. Job speaks existentially of his dismay and despair due to his inability to understand why he suffers unbearably in view of the unquestioned reality of his obedience to God's requirements. His passionate articulation concerns the unbearable interface between *obedience* and *suffering*, an interface that ought not to occur according to conventional categories of Israel's faith. Partly, Job is adamant to state his innocence; more precisely, he wants to know the reason for his suffering, for he, like his friends, can only imagine that suffering is rooted in guilt.

Whereas Job speaks with existential passion, albeit in measured artistic cadences, his friends do not engage him, but simply reiterate the primary claims of Israel's covenantal-sapiential tradition that the world governed by God is morally reliable, wherein obedience yields prosperity as disobedience yields adversity. The impeccable logic of his friends leads inescapably to the conclusion that Job suffers, and his suffering can only be grounded in disobedience. Job, for the most part, accepts this premise himself, but then insists that he is entitled to know the charges of disobedience made against him. And his friends do not answer, because they do not know. Thus the dispute concerns an unbearable mismatch between *lived reality* and *traditional explanations* that proceed by their own logic without reference to lived reality.

> ### Close Reading: Job 3
>
> The prologue to Job sets up the question of whether Job will "curse God," and the poetic section begins in chapter 3 with the statement that Job "cursed the day of his birth" (3:1). This cannot count as a curse of God—or can it? Although Job begins by saying "perish the day on which I was born," the curse quickly becomes a curse of all of creation. This is signaled already in verse 3, as Job poetically sets the clock moving backward from the day of his *birth* to the night of *conception*. And when Job says in verse 4, "That day—let there be darkness!" the allusion is clearly to the very first reported words of God in Genesis 1, "Let there be light!" Job 3 then becomes a poetic dismantling of God's creation, as Job calls on darkness to reclaim created light, and even calls up God's old adversary, the anticreation chaos monster Leviathan (v. 8). Some commentators argue that a curse on God's creation is functionally a curse on God, while others say that it obviously is not; but either is too simple a reading. If Job *either* clearly curses God *or* clearly refuses to curse God, then the plot of the book is essentially over. So the author has come up with this brilliant ploy: let Job get as close as possible to cursing God without literally doing so, and thus we are pushed forward into the book to see how this will play out.

For his part, Job's *integrity* is such that he will not deny his own lived reality in order to preserve the tradition of orthodoxy or to maintain the reputation of God. (See 4:6; 27:5; 31:6.) Job's integrity requires truth telling about his own lived experience, even if that truth telling clashes with settled traditional explanations that relieve God of responsibility and exposes such explanations as inadequate if not fraudulent. This exchange between Job and his friends ends without resolution, for the drama intends to make clear that there is no way in which to accommodate settled orthodoxy to the wretchedness of Job's life. The friends finish their speech without yielding to Job's anguish; Job finishes unpersuaded by the heavy-handed insistence of his friends:

> Far be it from me to say that you are right;
>   until I die I will not put away my integrity from me.
> I hold fast my righteousness, and will not let it go;
>   my heart does not reproach me for any of my days.
>   (27:5–6)

It is precisely the integrity of Job that God celebrated in the opening verses of the book that will not allow Job to admit trumped-up sins in order to let God off the hook.

At the end of this dispute with the friends, the book of Job provides an interlude in chapters 28–31. Chapter 28 is a quite distinctive text, and it certainly rewards a closer analysis than we can give it here. This poem is a meditation on the reality that human wisdom—that is, the wisdom of both Job and his friends—cannot penetrate the ultimate mystery of creation, which only God knows. The poem does not belittle human knowledge or ingenuity; indeed, it celebrates them with Godlike language in the first twelve verses of the poem. But, the poem seems to claim, mastery of the physical world, for all its rewards, does not yield the sort of wisdom that would help one to explain the underlying nature of reality. Wisdom is not "out there" to be found or acquired, as the more traditionally minded book of Proverbs would suggest (4:5; 8:17), but is rather an extraordinarily elusive quality that was first discerned by God during acts of creation. Wisdom is not a *thing*, the poem seems to claim, but is rather an active mode of being. God embodies wisdom in *creation*, but wisdom, Job 28:28 seems to say, is available to human beings in the *everyday*, in acts of social and moral creation.

> Truly, the fear of the LORD, that is wisdom;
>   and to depart from evil is understanding.

One notes, and we think we are *supposed* to note, that these twin qualities of piety ("fear of the LORD") and morality ("depart from evil") are precisely what Job is said to possess in the opening lines of the book. Whether this means that we are back to where we started or that the terms have taken on a different meaning after 28 chapters of intense dispute and rethinking is up to individual readers to decide. Perhaps Job's mistake has been to think, with the friends, that there is some other more abstract and explanatory principle of wisdom to be found "out there" rather than in the concrete living of a life.

The other material in this interlude is found in Job's extraordinary soliloquy in chapters 29–31. Job contrasts his wondrous past when he was socially significant and socially responsible (chap. 29) with his present state of powerlessness and social humiliation (chap. 30). Chapters 29 and 30 form a basis for the magnificent chapter 31, in which Job articulates in sweeping fashion his own innocence as a man who has singularly acted according to the best ethical norms. In making this case of innocence for himself, Job moves to refute decisively the traditional assumption of his friends that his suffering is rooted in guilt. Job's bold self-assertion is a denial of guilt and an insistence on his right. This remarkable self-declaration is a "high point of Old Testament ethics" (Fohrer 1974, 14). The statement culminates, moreover, in Job's defiant insistence in verses 35–37 that he be given particular charges of guilt that are, as his friends allege, the cause of his suffering:

> Oh, that I had one to hear me!
>   (Here is my signature! let the Almighty answer me!)
>   Oh, that I had the indictment written by my adversary!
> Surely I would carry it on my shoulder;
>   I would bind it on me like a crown;
> I would give him an account of all my steps;
>   like a prince I would approach him.

In this remarkable challenge to the God of heaven, Job still operates on the moral assumption of his friends that suffering is or should be tied to disobedience and guilt. Job has made his most vigorous case inside the rhetoric of the courtroom. In what follows, it will be clear that according to the larger drama of the book, Job has missed the point as radically as have his friends, even if he has done so in a more honest way.

Chapters 32–37 continue the first cycle of disputes in chapters 3–27, this time with a fourth friend, Elihu, now introduced for the first time. It is a consensus judgment of scholars that this material is a disruptive intrusion into the work, so that in an earlier version of the poetry the concluding formula of 31:40, "The words of Job are ended," may have been followed immediately by the utterance of YHWH in 38:1.

In any case, in 38:1 the second dispute begins, this time between Job and YHWH, a dispute that is continued through the poetry until 42:6. (It is worth noting that in 38:1 the God who speaks is termed "YHWH," a name for God that has been used in the initial prose of chaps. 1–2, but withheld in the poetry of chaps. 3–37. The reintroduction of the name YHWH suggests that the dramatist now wants to call attention to the claim that the God with whom Job struggles—the God of Israel—is no ordinary God of religion but is the true God, Creator of heaven and earth, known in all inscrutable mystery in the faith of Israel.)

In this second dispute, YHWH speaks twice (38:1–39:30; 40:6–41:34). Two times YHWH addresses Job in an invitation, perhaps a taunting invitation, to engage the dispute (38:2–3; 40:1–2). In response Job also speaks twice (40:3–4; 42:1–6). It is evident that YHWH's utterance is completely disproportionate to that of Job, clearly dominating the dispute. Conversely, it is evident that before the power, mystery, and eloquence of YHWH, Job has very little to say. That is, Job's capacity to speak in the first dispute with his three friends is now contrasted with his inability to defend his case before the ultimate disputant.

The whirlwind speeches of YHWH portray YHWH with massive power as sovereign Creator and with an artistic appreciation for the beauty and wonder of the special creatures whom God has created. The self-praise implied in these speeches is an assertion of the immense power of YHWH the Creator that lies well beyond the capacity of Job. It is to be noticed that YHWH, in these lyrical utterances, pays no attention to Job's defiant demands and exhibits no interest in Job's troubles. Indeed, Job, and even all of humanity, seem a profound irrelevance in the large vista of creation. It is not at all clear how this second dispute—a dispute between completely incommensurate parties—is related to the earlier dispute that Job has with his friends. Between the dispute of 3:1–27:23 (plus chaps. 32–37) and the dispute of 38:1–42:6, there is a dramatic disconnect. It seems plausible, moreover, that this dramatic disconnect is exactly the point of the sequence of speeches. Perhaps we are to accept, as traditional interpretation mostly does, the idea that the God of these speeches is rightfully understood as beyond human criticism. Or perhaps, as some more recent commentators have suggested, we are to see God's response as unjust and obfuscating and are to continue to take Job's side in the dispute.

Job's first response (40:3–5) to the speeches of YHWH is terse and concedes only that he will speak no more in the face of YHWH's inscrutable magnificence. The second response of Job (42:1–6) is more enigmatic. With particular reference to verse 6, conventional interpretation has concluded that Job submits to YHWH, and so by implication retracts his earlier defiance and settles for life as YHWH's trusting creature:

> According to the majority of commentators, the general meaning of the passage seems clear: Job stands now as a creature before his God, as a child before his Father. His complaints and protests had in fact never outweighed his hope and trust. He does not now withdraw his claim of innocence, for his conviction on this count is as great as his

faith in God. Nor does he have to withdraw it, for Yahweh has not repeated the accusations of the three friends. Neither does Job accept with resignation something he regards as unjust. God, however, has now made known to Job a plan and the meaning of a justice that cannot be contained in the straitjacket of the doctrine of retribution. Job, for his part, has come to see that his language had perhaps been disrespectful. He therefore repents and humbly proposes to do penance in dust and ashes. (Gutiérrez 1987, 86)

But Gustavo Gutiérrez himself qualifies this conventional reading:

> The text in Job thus means: "I repudiate and abandon (change my mind about) dust and ashes."
>
> The phrase "dust and ashes" is an image for groaning and lamentation; in other words, it is an image befitting the situation of Job as described before the dialogues began (see 2:8–12). This, then, is the object of the retraction and change of mind of which this key verse speaks. Job is rejecting the attitude of lamentation that has been his until now. The speeches of God have shown him that this attitude is not justified. He does not retract or repent of what he has hitherto said, but he now sees clearly that he cannot go on complaining. . . .
>
> . . . This means that in his final reply what Job is expressing is not contrition but *a renunciation of his lamentation and dejected outlook*. Certain emphases in his protest had been due to the doctrine of retribution, which despite everything had continued to be his point of reference. Now that the Lord has overthrown that doctrine by revealing the key to the divine plan, Job realizes that he has been speaking of God in a way that implied that God was a prisoner of a particular way of understanding justice. It is this whole outlook that Job says he is now abandoning. . . .
>
> Job's answer, of which the new translation just expounded gives a better understanding, represents a high point in contemplative speech about God. Job has arrived only gradually at this way of talking about God. At one point he had even felt God to be distant and unconnected with his life; he had then confronted this God in a bitter lawsuit. Now, however, he surrenders to Yahweh with renewed trust. (Gutiérrez 1987, 86–87)

It is generally recognized, however, that 42:6 is immensely problematic, perhaps loaded with irony, and likely intentionally ambiguous. Several words in the statement of Job admit of more than one nuance, and the grammar is elusive. As a consequence, it is possible that Job's final statement is no concession to YHWH at all, but an act of defiance that concedes nothing, but only acknowledges the greater power of the Creator. It is possible, even likely, that the dramatist intends no clear resolution—he offers only the disputation about insoluble matters with the Inescapable Dialogue Partner as the ultimate practice of faith. Jack Miles offers a thorough and suggestive review of the problem of 42:6 that perhaps culminates only in "a final perseverance" (Miles 1995, 428). Miles concludes:

> What is primary is whether or not God succeeds in forcing Job's attention away from God and back upon Job himself. If God can force Job somehow to stop blaming God and start blaming himself, God wins. If God cannot do that, God loses. In contemporary political language, the question is whether God can make his opponent the issue. Despite spectacular effort, God, in my judgment, fails in his attempt to do this, and Job becomes as a result the turning point in the life of God, reading that life as a movement from self-ignorance to self-knowledge.
>
> If God defeats Job, in short, Job ceases to be a serious event in the life of God, and God can forget about his garrulous upstart. But if Job defeats God, God can never forget Job, and neither can we. The creature having taken this much of a hand in creating his creator, the two are, henceforth, permanently linked. (Miles 1995, 429–30)

In the end Job and YHWH, creature and Creator, are "permanently linked" in an unequal relationship. YHWH is preoccupied with Job's own grandeur, Job with his own troubles. And there they are . . . endlessly.

II

The *poetry* of 3:1–42:6 is framed by the *prose* narrative of 1:1–2:13 (the prologue) and 42:7–17 (the epilogue). It may be that these verses are an older folktale into which the disputatious poetry has been inserted, as many scholars hold; or it may be that the prose material is a late literary construction designed to contain the poetic dispute. Either way, chapters 1–2 as a literary frame present a man who is "blameless [that is, with integrity] and upright," who is indeed framed in the collusion between YHWH and YHWH's disputatious agent, Satan (1:1, 8; 2:3). It is worth noting that Job and his fellow disputants are completely unaware of the collusion of YHWH and Satan, setting up a classic case of dramatic irony wherein the readers have access to crucial information that is withheld from characters within the story world.

The corresponding prose narrative of 42:7–17 provides a resolution of the trouble whereby YHWH "restored the fortunes" of Job in 42:10; that verse employs a technical phrase much used in exilic literature to bespeak YHWH's radical inversion of historical circumstance (see Jer 29:14; 30:18; 32:44; 33:7, 11, 26). It is to be noted that Job is affirmed by YHWH as the one, in contrast to his "orthodox" friends, who has spoken "what is right" (42:7–8). This divine verdict may refer to Job's alleged capitulation in 42:6; or it may refer to

Job's larger defiant discourse, suggesting that this disputatious God delights in disputatious human dialogue. Either way, Job the disputer receives divine approbation.

The narrative suggests *full restoration* for Job by YHWH, the Creator God:

> The LORD blessed the latter days of Job more than his beginning; and he had fourteen thousand sheep, six thousand camels, a thousand yoke of oxen, and a thousand donkeys. He also had seven sons and three daughters. He named the first Jemimah, the second Keziah, and third Keren-happuch. In all the land there were no women so beautiful as Job's daughters; and their father gave them an inheritance along with their brothers. After this Job lived one hundred and forty years, and saw his children, and his children's children, four generations. And Job died, old and full of days. (42:12–17)

The matter is nearly symmetrical, so that the *final* state of Job is fully commensurate with the *beginning* state of this blessed man. It is as though the long poetic disruption of his life were as nothing and Job experiences a return to normalcy. Except that we may notice a few differences. First, surely we are to recognize that one cannot simply replace lost children with new ones. They are (surely!) of a different order than Job's possessions. Emil Fackenheim connects this fact with Jeremiah 31:15 and Rachel, who "refuses to be comforted" for her lost children. Fackenheim proposes that among the lost children of Job are six million at "Auschwitz and Ravenbruck." Then Fackenheim, following A. S. Peake, comments that "no lost child can be replaced":

> Our "annoyance" with and "outrage" at the text—the stern refusal of Rachel to be comforted—is focused, then, on one single fact. This fact haunts, or ought to haunt, the religious consciousness of Jews and Christians alike. To Job sons and daughters are restored; but they are not the same sons and daughters. Children of Rachel have returned from exile; but they are not the same children. (Fackenheim 1980, 202)

Job received new children; but he could never receive back what he had lost. The restitution of 42:7–17 is crucial for the whole of the narrative; the new well-being, however, should not be overstated, because the last state is not exactly the first state recovered. The last state of restoration is marked by durable loss; and Job, like mother Rachel, may do well not to be excessively comforted, even by his brothers and sisters (42:11), who apparently do better with comfort than the three friends at the outset (see 2:11–13; see also Jer 31:15).

Second, we notice that Job's possessions are restored two times over. The attentive reader might notice that in the Torah this is the prescription for a thief who has been caught stealing: he must restore what he took *twice over* (Exod 22:7). It is just possible then that this most radical of ancient Hebrew authors intended for readers to catch that allusion to the Torah and to apply it to God! God has been caught stealing Job's life, and so God must restore that life twice over.

III

The book of Job in its three parts of *narrative-poetry-narrative* is a daring, majestic fugue that renders theological trouble and submissiveness in all of its immense complexity. The whole of the drama is to be fully appreciated in its inexhaustible artistry, and not interpreted so that it is made to conform to any of our ready-made theological packages. A conventional reading of the book brings the crisis of Job to a full restoration, a resolution likely reflected in Ezekiel 14:14, 20, and James 5:11. A more likely reading of the book of Job, however, suggests no such easy resolution, it being, rather, a witness to the enigmatic dimension of faith whereby Job—the man of faith—is endlessly in a relationship with God the Creator that admits of no ready fix. The dramatic power of the book of Job attests to the reality that faith, beyond easy convictions, is a demanding way to live that thrives on candor and requires immense courage. Faith of this kind that pushes deeply beyond covenantal quid pro quos or sapiential consequences that follow from deeds is no enterprise for wimps or sissies.

If we consider the dramatic flow from narrative (1:1–2:13) to poetry (3:1–42:6) to narrative (42:7–17), it is possible to see a pattern that we have already suggested for the book of Psalms, a pattern of orientation, disorientation, and new orientation:

1:1–2:13	a fully oriented life of faith that is moving toward disorientation
3:1–42:6	a practice of dispute that is fully marked by disorientation
42:7–17	a new orientation that is wrought by YHWH that has within it persistent traces of loss

Thus the book of Job is a large, imaginative drama of life with God that is inescapable for those who live life in full awareness and voice it with candor, for the savage reality of loss eventually spares none.

Because the book of Job is an artistic construction by artists who know the tradition of Israel and who move beyond the tradition in an enormous act of imagination, it is not possible to suggest any historical context for the book. There are linguistic clues to possible datings, but they are only suggestive. It is possible, for a variety of reasons, to suggest that the book of Job is a meditation upon the defining crisis of the exile in ancient Israel, so that the refutation of easy explanations of suffering as a consequence of guilt is a response to the easy explanations for the exile in the conventional faith of Israel, most especially on the horizon of the Deuteronomists. The connection between Job and the exile is suggestive, but it should not be pressed too far, for the book of Job resists any simplistic historical placement.

It is better to say that the book of Job in an artistic way is endlessly contemporary because the inability to reduce raw life to explanation is a perennial human reality. Gutiérrez suggests, out of his mystical sensibility, a way for Job beyond every scheme of explanatory retribution:

> Inspired by the experience of his own innocence, Job bitterly criticized the theology of temporal retribution as maintained in his day and expounded by his friends. And he was right to do so. But his challenge stopped halfway and, as a result, except at moments when his deep faith and trust in God broke through, he could not escape the dilemma so cogently presented by his friends: if he was innocent, then God was guilty. God subsequently rebuked Job for remaining prisoner of this either-or mentality (see 40:8). What he should have done was to leap the fence set up around him by this sclerotic theology that is so dangerously close to idolatry, run free in the fields of God's love, and breathe an unrestricted air like the animals described in God's argument—animals that humans cannot domesticate. The world outside the fence is the world of gratuitousness; it is there that God dwells and there that God's friends find a joyous welcome.
>
> The world of retribution—and not of temporal retribution only— is not where God dwells; at most God visits it. The Lord is not prisoner of the "give to me and I will give to you" mentality. Nothing, no human work however valuable, merits grace, for if it did, grace would cease to be grace. This is the heart of the message of the book of Job. (Gutiérrez 1987, 88–89)

At the outset of the twenty-first century, as things become unglued on a large scale, the artistry of the book of Job invites faith to face the dangers of a connection to a Creator God who is immense in glory but who offers no easy comfort. Such a practice of faith, if honest, may anticipate comforts and settlements here and there; mostly, however, life and faith in a disputatious mode do not shrink from truth telling that offends friends who comfort and that defies the God who self-congratulates.

25

The Book of Proverbs

The book of Proverbs is the third great poetic book that stands at the beginning of the third canon, the Writings. It is the baseline for all that follows in Judaism concerning the wisdom tradition, a theological trajectory that is an alternative to the more traditional theology of covenant (Crenshaw 1981; Murphy 1990; von Rad 1972). The book of Proverbs, moreover, provides a consensus teaching that is the foil for dissenting sapiential statements of the books of Job and Ecclesiastes, for those books represent challenges to the settled teaching of the book of Proverbs.

I

The book of Proverbs is a collection of earlier collections that the traditioning process has brought together. Thus the larger collection has been formed through an editorial process, a process that has yielded a canonical book whose completed form is not evidently intentional. While the first collection of chapters 1–9 appears to be a theological introduction to the whole, what follows has a random quality. James Crenshaw, among others, has nicely summarized the several collections that constitute the book:

1. The proverbs of Solomon, David's son, king of Israel (chaps. 1–9)
2. The proverbs of Solomon (10:1–22:16)
3. The sayings of the wise (22:17–24:22)
4. More sayings of wise men (24:23–34)
5. More proverbs of Solomon transcribed by the men of the Judean king, Hezekiah (chaps. 25–29)
6. The sayings of Agur, Jakeh's son, from Massa (30:1–9 [or 1–4 or 4–14])

7. Maternal instructions to Lemuel, king of Massa (31:1–9)
Two other divisions, 30:10–33 and 31:10–31, lack external identification.
(Crenshaw 1989, 223)

Each of these several collections has its own history. It is, however, impossible to know anything certain about the context or date of the collections that constitute the book of Proverbs. In the canonical editing, three collections are linked to Solomon with his reputation for wisdom (1:1; 10:1; 25:1), and the introduction of 25:1 also refers to King Hezekiah. These references are likely to be understood as interpretive markers rather than historical connections, though scholars are more inclined to take the Hezekiah references with more historical seriousness than the references to Solomon (Brueggemann 1990b).

Moreover, the wisdom collections partake of a more general sapiential tradition that pervaded ancient Near Eastern culture (Day, Gordon, and Williamson 1998, 17–52; Gammie and Perdue 1990, 3–92). Thus 30:1 and 31:1 refer to non-Israelites, and 22:17–24:22 is a collection that is evidently closely linked to the Egyptian Instruction of Amen-em-opet (Pritchard 1969, 421–25). More generally, it is regularly noticed that wisdom teaching, in the book of Proverbs as elsewhere, completely lacks the primary marks of Israel's history or of Israel's covenantal tradition. As a consequence, in this teaching Israel stands alongside its non-Yahwistic neighbors in pondering the inscrutable mystery of life, even as that mystery permeates the most concrete and mundane dimensions of daily existence.

Primary attention has been given to the rhetorical forms in which proverbial teaching is cast (Crenshaw 1989). While chapters 1–9 offer more extended poetic units that are more theologically self-conscious, for the most part wisdom teaching in the book of Proverbs is offered in short units, often two lines that are in tension with each other, which may then be expanded in artistic fashion (Alter 1985, chap. 7). In the brief proverbial sayings, two forms predominate: (a) the "sentence," which is simply an observation about lived reality (as in 10:1–32), and (b) the "instruction," which is cast as an imperative (as in 22:9–10, 12). These forms are undoubtedly old and were well established long before the canonical process of the Old Testament.

Scholars are not agreed upon the original context of such teaching, but the recurring candidates for context are (a) family nurture in which children are socialized into a certain world by the reiteration of folk sayings; (b) schools where instruction is more formal, though the existence of schools in Israel is itself a problematic question; and (c) the royal court wherein the sons of the politically well connected were inducted into the protocols and arts of governance (see Gammie and Perdue 1990, 95–181, especially Lemaire; Day, Gordon, and Williamson 1998, especially G. Davies). It is evident, we believe, that no single social context can be identified as a place of origin for all of these materials; we must allow for the probability that in many different contexts, critical and artistic reflection on the order and meaning of life were practiced. Consequently, these several forms of articulation may have arisen and been employed wherever questions of meaning were raised, questions that are intrinsically theological in character.

It is likely that the eventual collection of collections and the canonical codification of these collections into the book of Proverbs reflect the sustained work in the postexilic community of scribes who became important in the emergence of Judaism. Indeed, scribal-sapiential teaching embodies one of the most important trajectories in pluriform Judaism that emerged after the restoration from exile (G. Davies 1998). These scribes were rooted in and familiar with older covenantal traditions; in a sociopolitical environment where Jewish claims for Torah religion were marginal and vulnerable, however, it was essential that the crucial teaching of Judaism be cast in modes that were intellectually credible in a larger, non-Jewish

> ### Close Reading: Proverbs 13:24
>
> Translating any poetry into another language is always a difficult task, since so much of what makes something "poetry" resides in the play and sound of the words themselves. But the translations of Proverbs have suffered more than most, largely because of how hard it is to capture the pithy conciseness of the Hebrew in a more expansive modern language such as English. Robert Alter points out that the famous proverb against sparing the rod (Prov 13:24) is made up of only two lines, with just four Hebrew words in the first line and three in the second: ḥosek šibto sone' beno / we'ohabo šiḥaro musar (Alter 1985, 166). The King James Version turns these seven words into sixteen, and the NRSV turns them into eighteen ("Those who spare the rod hate their children, / but those who love them are diligent to discipline them"). It is not that these translations are inaccurate, but rather that they lose the rhetorical punch that comes with the brevity of the original. Though less accurate, the traditional English paraphrase of the first line, "Spare the rod, spoil the child," is, as Alter points out, truer to the spirit of the Hebrew.

environment. Thus we may regard the codification of sapiential instruction that issued in the canonical book of Proverbs as a major theological, intellectual achievement, nothing short of the capstone of what Norman Whybray has termed "the intellectual tradition," a tradition that casts the claims of Israel's faith in terms credible to a larger, quite sophisticated intellectual environment that may have regarded the historical-covenantal traditions of ancient Israel as somewhat primitive (Whybray 1974).

This remarkable intellectual achievement cast the faith of Israel in categories that in large part are not distinctly Israelite, but accommodate broader intellectual assumptions. (The relationship of *sapiential* theology to *covenantal* theology in ancient Israel is not unlike the theological work of Paul Tillich in relationship to the theological work of Karl Barth in the twentieth century. Barth worked with classical categories of theology and Tillich sought to make compelling contact with those whom Schleiermacher termed "the cultured despisers of religion.") Thus after we take into account the critical assumptions about the book of Proverbs stated above, we will give primary attention to the theological assumptions and affirmations of the literature. We may suggest five themes that pertain to the character of sapiential theology:

1. Wisdom theology in the book of Proverbs is thoroughly theological. That is, it refers every aspect of life to the rule of God. William McKane has famously proposed that there was a secular, prudential tradition of wisdom teaching that only subsequently developed into theological awareness (McKane 1970). But this is surely wrong. In that ancient world, a secular approach to life was not intellectually or socially possible; thus the disputatious issue always revolved around idolatry (the wrong God) and not atheism (the absence of God). It is unmistakably the case that while the proverbs are preoccupied with daily life, the interesting and defining point of reference— sometimes implicit, sometimes explicit—is the role of God, whose intentionality pervades every detail of human life.

2. If we begin with the focus on God, the implicit or explicit subject of sapiential teaching, we may go further to say that the God of Proverbs is the Creator God who in hidden ways has ordered the world and presides over that order (Boström 1990). Or as Walther Zimmerli has famously articulated, "Wisdom thinks resolutely within the framework of a theology of creation" (Zimmerli 1964, 148). That is, the particular observations in the book of Proverbs are aimed at discerning the connections between matters that are intractably given in the nature of things, the "nature of things" being understood as the ordering of reality toward life, the disregard of which leads to death. The reasoning of the wisdom teachers is characteristically inductive, so that they reason case by case and eventually generalize about inescapable connections, for example, between idleness and laziness, or between foolishness and poverty, or between righteousness and well-being. Eventually such convictions become established consensus positions. They are, however, based in the evidence of facts on the ground and are subject to revision as new, concrete data occur. Thus there is an empirical base to this creation theology that is quite in contrast to the revelatory, top-down mode of disclosure known at Mount Sinai. That the teaching is inductive and established case by case, however, makes the teaching no less formidable theologically, because wisdom asserts that the God who decrees and maintains a particular ordering of reality toward life is a sovereign beyond challenge whose will, purpose, and

order cannot be defied or circumvented with impunity. The brief sayings and imperatives that constitute much of the book of Proverbs stay very close to concrete cases. But the more extended, more lyrical poetry of Proverbs 1–9 escalates the claims in doxological fashion to assert that YHWH's ordering capacity pervades all of creation:

> The LORD by wisdom founded the earth;
> > by understanding he established the heavens;
> by his knowledge the deeps broke open,
> > and the clouds drop down the dew.
>
> > > > > > (3:19–20)

3. The aim of wisdom instruction is that the young be educated to discern the world rightly. While the talk of the teachers is characteristically of money and food and friends and sexuality, for example, all of these concrete matters are referred to YHWH. Thus creation theology here proceeds from the premise that:

> The fear of the LORD is the beginning of knowledge;
> > fools despise wisdom and instruction.
>
> > > > > > (1:7)

Of this programmatic assertion, Gerhard von Rad comments:

> There is no knowledge which does not, before long, throw the one who seeks the knowledge back upon the question of his self-knowledge and his self-understanding. Even Israel did not give herself uncritically to her drive for knowledge, but went on to ask the question about the possibility of and the authority for knowledge. She made intellect itself the object of her knowledge. The thesis that all human knowledge comes back to the question about commitment to God is a statement of penetrating perspicacity. . . . In the most concise phraseology it encompasses a wide range of intellectual content and can itself be understood only as the result of a long process of thought. It contains in a nutshell the whole Israelite theory of knowledge. In the almost abrupt way in which it is expressed, it gives the impression that some form of polemic might be involved. Why the repetition of this firm assertion that all knowledge has its point of departure in knowledge about God, if the pupil's range of vision did not contain other possible ways of acquiring knowledge which were being firmly repulsed? . . . At any rate, there lies behind the statement an awareness of the fact that the search for knowledge can go wrong, not as a result of individual, erroneous judgments or of mistakes creeping in at different points, but because of one single mistake at the beginning. One becomes competent and expert as far as the orders in life are concerned only if one begins from knowledge about God. To this extent, Israel attributes

> to the fear of God, to belief in God, a highly important function in
> respect of human knowledge. She was, in all seriousness, of the opin-
> ion that effective knowledge about God is the only thing that puts a
> man into a right relationship with the objects of his perception, that
> it enables him to ask questions more pertinently, to take stock of rela-
> tionships more effectively and generally to have a better awareness of
> circumstances. (von Rad 1972, 67–68)

There is a divine ordering of creation that must be honored. That divine
ordering, however, is not easy or obvious. Its observation requires attentiveness, discernment, and a right orientation in order to perceive. Thus right
discernment of life begins with an obedient discernment of YHWH the Creator. This is indeed "faith seeking understanding."

It is perhaps worth noting that this same ordering of right knowledge is the
judgment with which John Calvin begins his *Institutes*:

> Again, it is certain that man never achieves a clear knowledge of him-
> self unless he has first looked upon God's face, and then descends
> from contemplating him to scrutinize himself. For we always seem
> to ourselves righteous and upright and wise and holy pride is innate
> in all of us—unless by clear proofs we stand convinced of our own
> unrighteousness, foulness, folly, and impurity. Moreover, we are not
> thus convinced if we look merely to ourselves and not also to the Lord,
> who is the sole standard by which this judgment must be measured. . . .
>
> Yet, however the knowledge of God and of ourselves may be mutu-
> ally connected, the order of right teaching requires that we discuss
> the former first, then proceed afterward to treat the latter. (Calvin
> 1994, 37–39)

The referral of life to God makes for a right ordering of life through obedience that issues in happiness:

> For until men recognize that they owe everything to God, that they
> are nourished by his fatherly care, that he is the Author of their every
> good, that they should seek nothing beyond him—they will never
> yield him willing service. Nay, unless they establish their complete
> happiness in him, they will never give themselves truly and sincerely
> to him. (Calvin 1994, 41)

It is particularly instructive that in beginning his argument, Calvin casts his
statements with reference to "divine wisdom" that resonates with the book of
Proverbs and that focuses fully on "fear of the LORD":

> There are innumerable evidences both in heaven and on earth that
> declare his wonderful wisdom; not only those more recondite mat-
> ters for the closer observation of which astronomy, medicine, and all

natural science are intended, but also those which thrust themselves upon the sight of even the most untutored and ignorant persons, so that they cannot open their eyes without being compelled to witness them. Indeed, men who have either quaffed or even tasted the liberal arts penetrate with their aid far more deeply into the secrets of the divine wisdom. . . . Even the common folk and the most untutored, who have been taught only by the aid of the eyes, cannot be unaware of the excellence of divine art, for it reveals itself in this innumerable and yet distinct and well-ordered variety of the heavenly host. It is, accordingly, clear that there is no one to whom the Lord does not abundantly show his wisdom. (Calvin 1994, 53)

While the book of Proverbs permits us to infer more particularly Israelite truth claims (and while Calvin will move beyond general assertions of divine providence to particularly Christian claims), it is clear that the book of Proverbs (as also Calvin) intends that such right discernment of the divine ordering of reality is available for all to see. In contrast to the claims of revelation at Mount Sinai, it is the wisdom teachers who understood that the faithful knowledge of Israel is offered to all, thus a ground for natural theology, and eventually a ground for scientific knowledge, which is the study of regularities whereby the vagaries of reality are ordered, seem to be constant, and therefore are in some sense predictable. Indeed, the wisdom teachers proceed by what we might term "scientific method": they collect data and propose generalized hypotheses from the data of many cases. All of that learning, however, is for these teachers in a context where the will and purpose of YHWH for life are primarily in every aspect of knowing.

4. The ordering of the world by the Creator makes certain behavioral choices productive of life and other choices productive of death:

> And now, my children, listen to me:
>   happy are those who keep my ways.
> Hear instruction and be wise,
>   and do not neglect it.
> Happy is the one who listens to me,
>   watching daily at my gates,
>   waiting beside my doors.
> For whoever finds me finds life
>   and obtains favor from the LORD;
> but those who miss me injure themselves;
>   all who hate me love death.
>   (8:32–36)

There is no escape from these connections. Such a recognition has caused Klaus Koch to formulate the sapiential teaching as a system of "Deeds-Consequences" (Koch 1983a; see also Miller 1982). That is, "deeds" have connected to them inescapable consequences, so that deeds create their own "sphere of influence" with their own "built-in consequences" that the Creator God guarantees without slippage:

> Up to this point, our investigation has shown that in the book of Proverbs there is not even a single convincing reference to suggest a retribution teaching. What we do find repeated time and time again is a construct which describes human actions which have a built-in consequence. Part of this construct includes a conviction that Yahweh pays close attention to the connection between actions and destiny, hurries it along, and "completes" it when necessary. The wisdom literature reflects on and articulates the close connection between the Good Action-Blessings-Construct and the Wicked Action-Disaster-Construct as this applied to individuals. (Koch 1983a, 64)

Thus, for example, "slackness" causes "poverty" (10:4). It is as though the wisdom teachers have observed many cases of slackness and have noticed that, without exception, such conduct eventuates in poverty. The data are so constant and—critically—so predictable that the conviction may be taken as part of YHWH's structuring of creation. There is no exception because it is YHWH's intention that diligence, an antithesis to slackness, is a condition of well-being.

It is most important for Koch's argument that in this sequence of deeds-consequences discerned by the wisdom teachers, there is no punishment, no divine intervention, and no divine anger or agency. That is why Koch insists that there is no "retribution" in a direct sense as an act of God. Rather, the Creator has ordered the creation so that things simply work this way.

5. The wisdom teachers, on the basis of much data and acute discernment, concluded that the linkage between deed and consequence guaranteed by the Creator allowed no slippage. Such a teaching moves in the direction of deism and allows none of the force of grace or forgiveness. This teaching readily conformed to the general ancient Near Eastern wisdom teaching that is inherently conservative in defense of stable order and, lamentably, is congruent with popular moralism that is characteristically unforgiving. That is indeed a primary thrust of wisdom teaching; in some ways it is that thrust that has evoked the powerful dissent of the book of Job.

Given the preponderance of this argument in the book of Proverbs, it is of immense importance that von Rad has identified six proverbs that move beyond a simple deeds-consequences program to allow for the inscrutable freedom of YHWH:

> A man's heart thinks out a way for itself,
> but Jahweh guides its step.
> (Prov. XVI. 9)

Many are the plans in the heart of a man,
but it is the purpose of Jahweh that is established.
(Prov. XIX. 21)

Every way of a man is right in his own eyes,
but the one who tests the heart is Jahweh.
(Prov. XXI. 2, XVI. 2)

A man's steps come from Jahweh,
but man—how could he understand his way?
(Prov. XX. 24)

There is no wisdom, no understanding, no counsel
over against Jahweh.
The horse is harnessed for the day of battle,
but the victory comes from Jahweh.
(Prov. XXI. 30f.)
(von Rad 1962, 439)

These six sayings, even though only few, assert the freedom of YHWH even from the system of creation ordered by the Creator, a freedom that permits futures that are not derived from deeds:

> Its aim is, rather, to put a stop to the erroneous concept that a guarantee of success was to be found simply in practicing human wisdom and in making preparations. Man must always keep himself open to the activity of God, an activity which completely escapes all calculation, for between the putting into practice of the most reliable wisdom and that which then actually takes place, there always lies a great unknown. Is that a dangerous doctrine? Must not—we might ask—as a result of this great unknown factor, a veil of resignation lie over all human knowledge and action? This question can be answered only by the degree of trust which man is capable of placing in that divine activity which surpasses all planning. . . .
>
> Thus, it is not the quantitative limitation of human capabilities which forbids self-confidence and self-glorification; it is, rather, something which can be explained only in theological terms: self-glorification cannot be combined with trust in Yahweh. Even the ability of wisdom to master life must inevitably come up against this alternative. Thus, in this case too, the teaching of the wise men is rooted in ultimate, basic convictions about faith in Yahweh. A disparagement of wisdom would be the last thing with which one could reproach these teachers; but the limit is drawn surprisingly sharply. Wisdom itself can never become the object of trust, never become that upon which a man leans in life. (von Rad 1972, 101, 102–3)

These statements serve to make wisdom penultimate, for it is YHWH, the Lord of wisdom, who is ultimate. Thus, finally, these teachers produce not a system of moral calculation; rather, they attest to a *relationship* that is characterized by inscrutability and mystery, but that has immense concrete implications. That is why, in Job 28, after all of the acknowledgment of divine mystery, the teaching concludes in a tone much like Proverbs:

> And he said to humankind,
> "Truly, the fear of the LORD, that is wisdom;
>   and to depart from evil is understanding."
>   (Job 28:28)

That is what even the most sophisticated can finally say, in a teaching that surely evokes the motto of the book of Proverbs:

> Do not be wise in your own eyes;
>   fear the LORD, and turn away from evil.
>   (Prov 3:7)

This simple teaching that combines (a) a relationship to God with (b) a practical imperative, and (c) a promise of life, is not unlike the response Mother Teresa gave to Henri Nouwen when he asked about the meaning of life. She responded: "Pray every day and do not hurt anyone." Thus the wisdom teaching: "Fear the LORD, shun evil." Action counts, but it is action based on a relationship to the one who presides over all actions: YHWH.

II

The reader of the book of Proverbs in the end might be dazzled by the capacity of wisdom teachers to hold together the primary testimony of Israel to the God who rules in firmness but in inscrutability (the inscrutability of freedom and grace) with an urbane mode of discourse that exhibits none of the sectarian markings of Israel's covenantal tradition. It is most unfortunate that for a very long time Old Testament interpretation has treated wisdom as a stepchild or an outsider, when it is a major project of faith and reason held together in supple and sophisticated ways:

> Thus here, in proverbial wisdom, there is faith in the stability of the elementary relationships between man and man, faith in the similarity of men and of their reactions, faith in the reliability of the orders which support human life and thus, implicitly or explicitly, faith in God who put these orders into operation. If one understands those sentences which are expressed in wholly secular terms against their total intellectual background, then they, too, are undoubtedly dependent both on knowledge and on faith in God. Indeed, it was precisely

because this knowledge of Yahweh was so strong, so unassailable, that Israel was able to speak of the orders of this world in quite secular terms. (von Rad 1972, 62–63)

The wisdom teachers know about sin. It is worth noticing, however, that their preferred way to speak of destructive choices is not "sin" but "foolishness." They ponder the stupidity of living against the grain of creation as ordered by the Creator. None has commented more eloquently on the interface of *God* and *world* in this testimony than David Shapiro:

> One's face is rubbed in *the near*, as Leo Baeck has put it—the nearness of the divine, the nearness of the world, the nearness of the uncanny fusion of world and divinity. There is no wisdom without the fear of God, but also no wisdom without the fear at home, the fear of home, since we are those who may be exported in haste to a dim underworld, as materialist an underground as has been conceived, a world called Sheol, derived etymologically from the small cramped grave. . . . Proverbs is a cadenza of prudential severity, and it may indeed be misconceived as the authoritarian necklace, chain, or crown to which it refers. Actually, it may come to seem closest to a book of dreams or jokes, with the kind of prudence we feel in Freud when he suggests that children should not be sent to the Arctic with summer clothing and maps of the Italian lakes. Proverbs, said to be the most sublimating book in the Bible, is, rather, an eruptive text of a restless shrewdness that does more than balance the idealism of priests and prophets with the cunning of the "elders." Commandments are finite; the Proverbs are infinite and remind us that attention must be so. (D. Shapiro 1987, 320)

This is indeed literature for grown-ups:

> the book is a constant critique of infantilism. If there are no constants, there is the drive toward constancy. The book may, at least, be seen as an anthology of utopian and, paradoxically, materialist idealizations. These ideals, as William James has said, create the real. The real world depends upon a comparison. (D. Shapiro 1987, 324)

Two other textual matters warrant notice. First, Christian readers may want to pay particular attention to the poetry of Proverbs 8:22–31. This text speaks of "wisdom" as the "ordering power" of creation whereby creation is permitted to function in abundant, life-giving ways. This text is significantly related to the creation traditions of Genesis 1 (see Landes 1974; Yee 1992). In Proverbs 8 several words—notably what the NRSV translates as "created" (*qnn*) in verse 22 and "master worker" (*'amon*) in verse 30—are particularly difficult. These difficulties, however, do not detract from the primary lyrical claim that "wisdom" as an agent of YHWH the Creator has definitively determined the shape of creation.

This text is of special interest because it is widely thought that the themes voiced here are taken up, albeit in a transposed way, in the poetic opening of the Gospel of John (John 1:1–3; O'Day 1995, 519). In transposition into Christian affirmation, wisdom as the "ordering force" of the creation has become the *logos*, the logic of creation that pervades the world, and that has "become flesh" in Jesus of Nazareth. It is clear that the claim voiced in John 1 has moved well beyond the affirmation of Proverbs 8. It is equally clear, however, that the statement of John 1 is understandable precisely with reference to Proverbs 8. The trajectory of wisdom toward John 1 opens a theological articulation that in the Old Testament is radically alternative to covenantalism and in the New Testament is radically alternative to the most familiar dimensions of Paul's thought.

Second, great attention has been paid—given the impetus of a feminist hermeneutic—to the wise woman and the woman of folly in Proverbs 1–9 and 31:10–13 (see 2:16–19; 5:1–11; 6:23–25; 7:14–20; 9:16–17). A variety of proposed interpretations of the "woman of folly" have been offered, including (a) that she is an adulteress who will endanger, (b) that she is a foreigner, thus a threat in the world of Ezra, or (c) that she is articulated out of a generalized male anxiety (Camp 2000). While these various options need to be considered, here I wish to commend the exquisite study of Christine Yoder (2001). On the basis of the economic thrust of 31:10–31, Yoder proposes an economic reading of the two women. It is clear from the Persian documents that Yoder cites that it was a practice of upper-class Persian men to seek out a woman who had good business sense who could provide financial security for the husband, who did not need to be productive: "In sum, Wisdom is the key to socioeconomic privilege. Hers is a wealth of quality, perpetuity, and abundance that secures for her husband a position of honor and well-being in the community" (Yoder 2001, 99–100).

Conversely, the "Strange Woman" may put everything valued in the economic world at risk:

> The sage of Proverbs 1–9, a proponent of Ezra-Nehemiah's ideological strategy, incorporated this economic concern in his crafting of the composite figure of the "Stranger" Woman. In 2:12–22, for example, the father warns his son that association with the "Stranger" Woman results in the alienation of land. In 5:7–14, he cautions that involvement with her carries a double penalty: bankruptcy at the hands of foreigners and utter disgrace in the community. In short, the description of the "Stranger" Woman in Proverbs 1–9 in part reflects anxiety about the socioeconomic power of foreign women in Persian-period Palestine. As H. Washington states, the "Stranger" Woman became "technical terminology" for "outsider" women with power, specifically economic power, to endanger the stability of the community. . . .

... The choice between death and life, [the sage] proposed, is like the choice between two women. On the one hand, there is the sexually attractive (6:25), smooth-talking (e.g., 2:16; 5:3; 6:24; 7:21) Woman of Folly (or "Stranger" Woman), a composite figure of women whose socioeconomic power *endangered* a young man's economic stability. To choose her, the sage warned, was to forfeit every economic advantage: land (2:12–22), wealth, and honor (5:7–14). It was even to lose life itself (7:27). (Yoder 2001, 73–74, 102)

Wisdom instruction is characteristically about choices:

Woman Wisdom, like her negative counterpart, is also a composite figure of women—affluent and royal Persian-period women whose socioeconomic power *ensured* economic prosperity. To choose her was to gain every economic advantage: business profits, imported delicacies, fine clothing, real estate, a mansion complete with staff, treasury-storehouses filled to the brim, perpetual wealth, and social prominence. It is no wonder that the youth was urged to marry such a Woman of Substance. She offered to him an abundant, secure life. (Yoder 2001, 102)

Yoder's compelling argument is an interesting exercise in method, because it makes clear that when fresh questions are asked of difficult texts, different answers become available. Beyond issues of method, however, Yoder's argument places the text back into the concrete world of sapiential instruction that was characteristically preoccupied with real-life issues (such as economics). Yoder's sound judgment warns against "an idealistic seduction" in interpretation that turns away from the real world of creation. Here, as elsewhere in Proverbs, issues of faith are held close to daily life. Yoder's reading nicely fits with Shapiro's verdict: "One's face is rubbed in *the near*" (D. Shapiro 1987, 320). It is a "near" governed by the God who permeates the concrete world with which the wisdom teachers are endlessly occupied, thus keeping together "the experience of Yahweh" and an "experience of the world" (von Rad 1972, 62).

26

The Five Scrolls

In the third canon, the Writings, the three great poetic books of Psalms, Job, and Proverbs come first. As we have seen, the three are deeply interrelated, for the sapiential teaching of Proverbs becomes a foil for the book of Job, and both are connected to the normative liturgical-textual tradition of the Psalms. After these three great books, next in the canonical sequence come five small "scrolls" that are grouped together in the canon and in the liturgical practices of Judaism as the Megilloth (scrolls). The Five Scrolls (which are expressed in different genres and are concerned with different themes and issues) undoubtedly originated in a variety of contexts, though they were early on grouped canonically.

By way of introduction, we make only two observations. First, while the five are characteristically grouped together, different sequences of the five occur in different textual traditions, so that there was not a fixed order among the five. It is possible that the ordering is thought to be roughly chronological, beginning with Ruth "in the days when judges judged" (1:1) and culminating with Esther from the Persian period. Such a historical sequence, however, is not to be taken with much seriousness. Second, in the liturgical practice of Judaism, the Five Scrolls are now linked to and utilized in five festal occasions, so that the liturgical use impacts the angle from which they are to be read and heard:

Song of Songs/Song of Solomon	Passover
Ruth	Festival of Weeks
Lamentations	The Ninth of Ab
Ecclesiastes	Festival of Booths
Esther	Festival of Purim

The collection of the five reflects the vitality of Judaism in the late canonizing period with its capacity to take up older materials for new use; further, it demonstrates the generative freedom of the tradition in claiming and repositioning texts to meet contemporary needs in the community. Consequently, when the scrolls are pressed into liturgical service they are situated to perform in ways that may be very different from the intent of the initial formulators of the texts.

It is important to recognize that in the Greek canon, the basis of the Christian canon, the Five Scrolls are variously distributed among other books. In this usage each such scroll is to be read in context without reference to any group of five, for such a grouping has been voided in this sequence that is familiar to us in Christian Bibles.

THE BOOK OF RUTH

The book of Ruth must be appreciated as a story. The story includes in its telling and being heard all the range of narrative entertainment, including the possibility of humor and of light-handed instruction. The plot is a simple one: an Israelite family incorporates into its midst a Moabite daughter-in-law, Ruth, who is a model of faithfulness, courage, and cleverness. In the plot she becomes a mother in Israel and eventually a progenitor of King David (4:17b, 18–20), a traditional claim kept current in the genealogy of the Gospel of Matthew (Matt 1:5). Whereas a brief summary of the plot of the book of Ruth is simple, the literary, rhetorical articulation of the plot is immensely subtle and is indeed a wondrous artistic achievement (Trible 1978, 166–99; Linafelt 1999).

The setting of the book itself is in the period of the judges, which illuminates why, in familiar Christian sequence, the book follows the book of Judges (1:1). Common critical judgment, however, takes the story as much later, long after the exile and with no connection to the historical period of the judges.

For a very long time scholarship has focused on historical questions. In view of that perspective, it was most important that Ruth the Moabite, a foreigner, was accepted into the community of Israel. Out of that claim voiced in the plot, scholars have suggested that the narrative was a fifth-century affirmation of legitimacy of foreigners in the community (on which see Isa 56:3–7), so that the narrative is designed to challenge and polemicize against the policies of Ezra and Nehemiah in their rejection of marriages of Jews to foreigners (see Ezra 10:6–44; Neh 13:23–27). On this reading, the narrative of Ruth advocates an open and generous Judaism.

That conventional reading of the narrative has become much less important—and less credible—as scholars have turned away from historical questions to literary-rhetorical matters. When we read the book of Ruth on its own terms and without respect to a hypothesized context, we not only appreciate the shrewd and artistic way in which the narrative is wrought, but become aware that we know less of the context than we imagined. Thus current interest in the narrative of Ruth makes few judgments about context and seeks to stay inside the narrative and take it on its own terms. Taken in this way, the story of Ruth is about the careful negotiation between a vulnerable outsider woman and a man of substance in the community, a negotiation that has to do with honor and shame, but that is also self-conscious about economic issues in the exchange.

Particular attention has been paid to the narrative by those interested in feminist hermeneutics, for it is possible to see that Ruth is a daring model of a woman who acts decisively to create a future for herself in a patriarchal social context where no good future was on offer for her:

> On my reading, Ruth the obedient and submissive recedes before a Ruth who demonstrates a fierce solidarity with Naomi, but who is far from obedient and never entirely forthcoming. She clearly demonstrates a strong agency in the narrative, pushing Boaz to drop his veneer of social acceptability by her verbal sparring in which she employs subtle yet recognizable double entendres. (Linafelt 2000, xv)

Given the recognition of the human initiative that is championed in the narrative through the agency of Ruth, it is at the same time important to recognize that the God of Israel is, at best, hidden in the narrative. Jack Miles goes further than that in his dismissive judgment about God in the narrative:

> The Book of Ruth, however, pays only very modest attention to the Lord God. It is far more concerned with a change in the dignity and mutual respect of women. The underlying polemic over the decency and orthodoxy of foreign wives translates with some difficulty into a statement that God himself has grown more tolerant of them. Whether the Lord God is tolerant or intolerant, he is, with respect to the action of this story, almost otiose. In the cast of characters of the Book of Ruth, he is a bystander. Happy and unhappy outcomes are routinely attributed to him, good wishes are delivered with reference to him, but the references, the pronouncements, seem purely pro forma. The Lord God says nothing, as already noted; and, for all practical purposes, he also does nothing. (Miles 1995, 343)

Against such a dismissive verdict, Phyllis Trible allows for a God at work in and through the lives of the women:

> As a whole, this human comedy suggests a theological interpretation of feminism: women working out their own salvation with fear and

trembling, for it is God who works in them. Naomi works as a bridge between tradition and innovation. Ruth and the females of Bethlehem work as paradigms for radicality. All together they are women in culture, women against culture, and women transforming culture. What they reflect, they challenge. And that challenge is a legacy of faith to this day for all who have ears to hear the stories of women in a man's world. (Trible 1978, 196)

The different judgments of Miles and Trible, for example, indicate the playful, artistic options that are available in interpretation when the story is left to make its own case without reference to a supposed historical context. In its artistic force the narrative is not only subtle but seems deliberately to articulate many ambiguities for readers to resolve as best they can. It is clear that by the time of this narrator, Israel's sense is that YHWH is best understood at work in and through social interactions, or perhaps we should say in and through rhetorical operations—either way now a God intrinsic to the lived processes of the human community.

The liturgical linkage Judaism has made of this book to the Festival of Weeks is to the fact that in the narrative the primary action occurs on the threshing floor (3:1–18). It may be that the reference to the harvest festival is enough for a connection. It may also be, however, that in the imaginative horizon of the narrator the threshing floor, the defining venue for the festival, is understood as a most generative arena in which radical newness is given that opens futures for Israel. On that basis, every celebration of the Festival of Weeks is an occasion for divinely given newness that opens futures for the community.

The placement of the book of Ruth in the Christian canon between the book of Judges and the books of Samuel seeks to connect the book historically rather than liturgically. Against usual scholarly preference for the later canonical placement of the book according to the practices of Judaism, it is quite possible that the book is designed precisely to connect the books of Judges and Samuel and to provide a transition from tribe to monarchy with the final pointer to King David in 4:17–20 (see Linafelt 1999, xviii, xix–xx). The traditional scholarly view of the process of canon formation held that the Septuagint ordering of the books was a later development among hellenized Jews who rearranged a previously existing Palestinian canon. Such a view would make Ruth's placement between Judges and 1 Samuel secondary and derivative. More recent scholarship, however, has demonstrated that the process of canonization is much more complex and uncertain than this scenario allows, particularly in the relationship between Jews of Palestine and Hellenistic Jews; it is simply no longer tenable to assume the Septuagint order to be late and derivative. This has opened up the possibility that Ruth was not moved to its position between Judges and 1 Samuel because it seemed to fit there, but that it has a more intrinsic connection with those books. Indeed, it becomes possible to speculate that the book of Ruth was written as and intended to be a connector between these two books.

The book of Ruth shows convincing evidence of a connection to the ending of the book of Judges. What has not been noticed—and what opens up a new line of interpretation that we want to pursue—is that the book of Ruth also shows convincing evidence of a connection to the books of Samuel. If this is the case, then rather than thinking of the book of Ruth as a coda to the book of Judges, it is more appropriate to see it as a connector between Judges and Samuel.

By noting the alternative canonical placements, it is evident that the Jewish and Christian orderings provide very different reading opportunities. Either way, the book of Ruth is a subtle artistic scenario of the ways in which human courage and divine hiddenness cause Israel to entertain futures beyond any patriarchal or ethnocentric present tense. Any theological reflection on the book must start with the recognition that human action is of primary importance, and that human actors have the ability, indeed perhaps the responsibility, to resist and challenge social systems that tightly circumscribe such action but that are never entirely free from ideological gaps. The hope is that God will in turn respond to such initiative and bring to fruition what human actors have worked toward. To the extent that the book of Ruth has a theology, it is one that is less traditional but also less simplistic than has generally been recognized. It is a theology that refuses to see the human characters in the drama as puppets of God's providence and that, because of this refusal, may ultimately prove more relevant to the modern world than we might suppose.

THE SONG OF SONGS

The Song of Songs (also known as the Song of Solomon) is ancient Israel's contribution to the literature of love. If it were not for the fact that this sequence of ancient Hebrew erotic love poems was preserved in Scripture, one might be given to believe that only Israel, among all peoples, wrote no love poetry. But the Song of Songs *was* included as part of the biblical canon and so was saved from the oblivion suffered by other ancient Hebrew literature, since nearly all writings from ancient Israel not preserved in the Bible simply disappeared over the course of the centuries. It seems likely that there would have been other examples of love poetry in Israel—how could there not have been?—but whether any other examples would have matched the poetic art of the Song seems less likely. For in the Song we find one of the very finest examples of ancient Hebrew poetry coupled with a distinctive vision of the nature of love.

Although the superscription to the book, "The Song of Songs, which is Solomon's," associates it with King Solomon (who lived in the tenth century BCE), the language of the poetry represents a much later form of Hebrew, indicating that Solomon was not the author. The poems were probably written between the fifth and third centuries BCE, and its author or authors are anonymous. Although many scholars treat the book as an anthology of short poems by different hands, a strong consistency of diction, theme, voice, and poetic technique suggests a single author behind most of the poetry. The book became associated with Solomon perhaps because of his dual reputation as both an extravagant lover of women (1 Kgs 11:1–3) and a prolific composer of poetry (1 Kgs 4:32).

There is a long history, among both Jewish and Christian commentators, of reading the Song as if it were a theological treatise, and a significantly shorter history, among biblical scholars, of reading it as if it were a treatise on love or sexuality; but the book is neither: the Song is not a treatise of any sort, but is rather lyrical poetry. Indeed, the Song is arguably one of the highest achievements of ancient Hebrew poetry, and to do it justice means to read it *as poetry*, rather than turning it into something it is not. In reading and appreciating the Song we should not look for information about or a representation of God's relationship to Israel (it is not theology), nor should we look for a story with plot and real characters (it is not narrative), and neither should we look for explicit reflection on the sources and nature of love (it is not philosophy). Rather, to appreciate fully the Song requires that one pay close attention to its poetic art, including the structure of both individual lines and larger poems, word choice, sound play, metaphor, tone, and voice. Some of these elements, most especially sound play, are less obvious or even unavailable in translation, but one can still get a very strong sense of how the Song works as poetry even in translation.

Like nearly all ancient Hebrew poetry, the Song makes primary use of short parallel lines, which mostly occur in a couplet form with the second line often heightening emotionally, making more concrete, or otherwise modifying the first; occasionally a third line is added to complement or extend the image or metaphor. Thus, to the two classically parallel lines in 6:4, "You are beautiful as Tirzah, my love, / comely as Jerusalem," is added a third line, "terrible as an army with banners" (NRSV). Elsewhere the poetry of the Song exhibits a greater freedom than most ancient Hebrew poetry in relating the parallel lines. In 2:2, for example, as a male voice describes his female lover, the poet pairs a simile in the first line with its referent in the second: "As a lily among brambles, / so is my love among maidens." Part of the task—and the fun—of reading and interpreting the poetry of the Song is to ponder and to try to work out the relationship between the lines.

The book alternates between a male voice and a female voice, with occasional interruptions by a female group voice (e.g., 5:9; 6:1) and a male group voice (e.g., 8:8–9). The primary male and female voices represent two young, apparently unmarried lovers, who spend most of the poem expressing their erotic yearnings and describing each other's physical attractions in lush, sometimes hyperbolic imagery. Thus, a quote from the male voice in 4:5–6:

> Your breasts are like two fawns,
>   twins of a gazelle,
>   that feed among the lilies.
> Until the day breathes
>   and the shadows flee,
> I will hasten to the mountain of myrrh
>   and the hill of frankincense.

And from the female voice in 2:3:

> As an apple tree among the trees of the wood,
>   so is my beloved among young men.
> With great delight I sit in his shadow,
>   and his fruit was sweet to my taste.

As these quotes indicate, much of the poetic imagery is drawn from the natural world, and it often seems to contain double entendres (e.g., "his fruit was sweet to my taste"; or "Let my beloved come to his garden, / and eat its choicest fruits" [4:16]). But even though the poetry is frankly erotic, it is never graphic or crassly explicit, preferring to rely on suggestion and metaphor to convey its erotic charge.

Despite the presence of alternating voices, the poetry is not fundamentally dramatic—there is no overarching plot, and little narrative development— but rather remains squarely within the realm of lyric, a form of poetry that works with anonymous voices or personae rather than attempting to represent full-blooded, identifiable characters. And one should not mistake the poetic voices of the young speakers as representing the real voices of ancient Israelite adolescents. No, clearly this is the language of a master poet who has chosen to represent what it is like to be young and in love by inventing the voices of two speakers who are young and in love. It is not unlike Shakespeare putting his highly polished poetry into the mouths of Romeo and Juliet. Teenagers, whether in Shakespeare's day or in ancient Israel, did not speak this way, no matter how in love they might have been.

One striking consequence of the alternation of female and male voices in the Song is an underscoring of the egalitarian nature of erotic love with regard to gender roles (see especially Trible 1978). The intermingling of voices works against the gender stereotypes that would assign the active role of "lover" to the man and the passive role of "beloved" to the woman. The two voices are given roughly equal amounts of space in the book, each describes the body of the other, and each expresses the desire felt for the other. This mutuality is exhibited also in the range of imagery with which the lovers are imagined: both lovers (not just the young woman) are associated with the beauty and grace of doves, lilies, and fawns or gazelles; and both lovers (not just the young man) are described in terms of power and strength, the man being associated with marble columns and cedar trees (5:15) and the woman with ramparts and towers (8:10).

The poetry of the Song is, for the most part, a positive celebration of the pleasures of erotic love. Yet it does acknowledge, if only briefly, the dangers of Eros—not only those dangers that arise from outside the erotic relationship and threaten the young lovers, but also those dangers that are inherent to the nature of Eros itself. With regard to the former, see especially 5:2–8, where the young woman imagines herself wandering the streets at night searching for her lover, only to be met and beaten by the "sentinels of the walls." With regard to the latter, see 8:6:

> Set me as a seal upon your heart,
>   as a seal upon your arm;
> for love is strong as death,
>   passion fierce as the grave.
> Its flashes are flashes of fire,
>   a raging flame.

Though thoroughly rooted in the body, Eros here takes on near-cosmic dimensions. The language of the body, elsewhere in the Song so positive, teeters in this instance on the brink of obsession.

Given that the Song is preserved as a part of Jewish and Christian Scripture, the question is often asked, Where is God in all this? Indeed, God is never mentioned in the book. Nevertheless, for centuries complex allegorical interpretations of the poetry—in which the two young lovers are taken to be ciphers for God and humanity—have prevailed. In traditional Jewish interpretation, Israel is cast as the female lover and God as the male lover. For Christian interpreters the lovers of the biblical book are taken to refer variously to God and the church, or Christ and the individual soul, or even to Jesus and the Virgin Mary. Modern scholars have tended to dismiss these allegorical interpretations, since they obviously do violence to the literal sense of the text.

It is true that such a mode of interpretation *spiritualizes* the Song and thus tames its potentially subversive role in a Bible that has often been taken as shoring up borders and fencing in sexuality. It is also no less true that such interpretation *eroticizes* theological discourse, with potentially very interest-ing results for doing theology, especially if one is willing to imagine God as not only an object of desire but subject to its throes as well. Although it seems clear that the poetry was not written with a theological intent, it is worth pondering why later interpreters found the erotic metaphor to be such a compelling way of talking about God and how the lyrical presentation of Eros that we find in the Song might contribute to such God-talk.

Although it is true that God is never mentioned in the Song, there are some close calls, places where the poet seems to come intentionally very near to naming God, without quite doing so. For example, in the twice-repeated oath, "I adjure you, O daughters of Jerusalem, / by the gazelles or the wild does: // do not stir up or awaken love / until it is ready" (2:7; 3:5), there would seem to be a pun or wordplay on two com-mon epithets for God. "Gazelles" in Hebrew is *ṣeba'ot*, which puns on *Yahweh ṣeba'ot*, or "LORD of

> ## Midrashic Moment: On the Holiness of the Song of Songs
>
> It is reported that, in the first century CE when Jewish religious leaders were debating the holiness of certain ancient writings and whether they should be considered part of Scripture, the great Rabbi Akiba declared that "while all the Scriptures are holy, the Song of Songs is the Holy of Holies." The "Holy of Holies" is that innermost part of the Jerusalem temple, where God's holiness is thought to be most palpable. On the one hand, Akiba is punning, perhaps playfully, on the title of the book: the "Song of Songs" is the "Holy of Holies," or in Hebrew, *šir ha-širim* is *qodeš ha-qodešim*. But he is also making a serious statement about the central importance of the Song in Scripture, which is here being imagined as the Bible's innermost sanctum. The Song is read once a year in most Jewish synagogues, as part of the Passover Festival, but by all evidence it is read only rarely in Christian churches. It is interesting to imagine how different our view of the Bible might be if we took Akiba's statement seriously and gave the Song the sort of attention it deserves as part of Scripture.

hosts." And "wild does" in Hebrew is *be'ayelot ha-sadeh*, which puns on *'el šadday*, or "God Almighty." By having her companions swear on these eroti-cally charged animals (gazelles and wild does are frequently associated with the goddess of love in ancient Near Eastern iconography and inscriptions) rather than on a name or title of God, the female speaker both celebrates the natural world as a primary source for erotic symbolism and makes an indirect theological claim. The nature of this claim depends on how one construes the tone of the speaker here. It is certainly possible to take the tone as ironic and intentionally subversive of theological claims, with erotic love pointedly replacing God as ultimate referent. But it is also possible that, rather than subverting piety in favor of love, the poet is vaunting the power of love precisely by associating it with God.

We find the same ambiguity of tone with the second instance of a near-miss in naming God, found in 8:6. This famous verse represents a crescendo of sorts for the poetry, offering for the first time a second-order reflection on the nature of love, even the metaphysics of love, rather than the first-person declarations and descriptions that fill the rest of the book. Here the female voice declares: "love is strong as death, / passion fierce as the grave. // Its flashes are flashes of fire, / a raging flame." We may note how, in a move typical of Hebrew poetry, the second term of each of the three syntactically matched pairs in the first couplet ("love/passion," "strong/harsh," "death/grave") serves to intensify, specify, or concretize the first. The next couplet makes this heightening of terms even more acute with the progression from "flashes" to "fire" to "a raging flame." In Hebrew the final line, translated in the NRSV as "a raging flame," is a single word, *šalhebetyah*. Given the equally weighted lines that precede it and their syntactical parallelism, this abbreviated final line pulls the reader up short, causing one to pause and dwell on the effect of that "raging flame," love. The sense of emphasis on this final line is bolstered by the occurrence here of a fragment of the divine name: *–yah*, the last syllable of the last word of the verse, is a shortened form of Israel's personal name for God, Yahweh, and serves grammatically as an intensifying particle; it is what justifies the translation "a *raging* flame."

The question is whether this fragmentary allusion to God is *only* a grammatical intensifier, or whether it might represent a genuine, if muted, theological claim. If the latter, one still must negotiate the tone of the claim, in the same way as the punning oath in 2:7 and 3:5: is it a theologically subversive replacement of God with erotic love, or an attempt to exalt human love by adding a poetic whiff of divinity? One need not finally decide, since with poetry—unlike theology or philosophy—lack of precision is often a virtue, and the ambiguity may well be intended by the poet.

THE BOOK OF ECCLESIASTES

The third of the "scrolls" is Ecclesiastes. The name in Hebrew (*Qohelet* or *Kohelet*) is a feminine participle referring to "an assembly" or the one who "assembles" the "assembly," thus "the preacher." This "preacher," moreover, is given as Solomon, so that this sapiential teaching that reflects upon the inscrutable mystery of life in the world is drawn into the Solomonic tradition of wisdom, as in 1 Kings 3:16–28 and 4:29–34. The linkage of this teaching to Solomon (as in the books of Proverbs and the Song of Songs) was perhaps instrumental in the canonization of the book of Ecclesiastes, which was accomplished only with difficulty. The Solomonic connection in the book, however, is a secondary, traditional maneuver that is not related to the material of the book itself—unless we can imagine that the self-indulgent Solomon by the end of his reign had come to a sad awareness of his life, a sad awareness that is voiced in the book.

The substance of the book is a collection of wisdom sayings and teachings that ponder the mystery of creation and life in the world, and find that mystery much more inscrutable and much less user-friendly than the old affirmative wisdom teaching of the book of Proverbs. The relationship of this material to the older tradition as known in the book of Proverbs is, as Roland Murphy suggests, a dissenting "yes, but" (Murphy 1979, 235). It is a "yes, but" that takes the old teaching of moral coherence seriously, but finds it less than persuasive or credible. It is entirely plausible that the disillusionment with the old buoyant sapiential teaching reflected in this material is context driven, though the matter of historical, social context is less than certain. It is conventional to place this material, amorphous as it is, in the late Persian period or in the Hellenistic period, perhaps in a context of economic failure or disillusionment, when candor made affirmation no longer possible:

> The determining factor in the new situation is, of course, the national disaster suffered by Israel, even if the wisdom literature does not reflect on it explicitly. Israel and thus the landowning classes are now among the immensely rich and thus in a quite different degree the object of history. The social and political balance between the free peasantry and the monarchy that was characteristic of preexilic Judah has ceased to exist. Taxes and duties are levied by outside forces, bringing heavy burdens and serious causes of insecurity. The pressure is intensified by the fact that the economy is increasingly based on money and then on coinage, and the self-sufficiency of the individual farm and village is significantly undermined. Increasing pressure for productivity leads to the conversion of farmland to olive orchards and vineyards, which are geared to export. Because the productive forces remain essentially unchanged, the inevitable result is a reduction in the number of units (families) that are productive. The great and rapid economic changes, especially of the Hellenistic age, cause insecurity; they cannot be understood or controlled. . . .
>   It can hardly be denied that there is a correlation between this kind of thinking and the orientation of all activity in the Ptolemaic state (of which the aristocratic class in Judah was now a part) toward purely economic profit and productivity. The quest for gain undermines all

traditional human relations. Koheleth's thinking, taking gain as its criterion, perceives everything as *hebel*, a stirring of the air. (Crüsemann 1984, 62–63, 66)

The teaching of the book is variously summarized by scholars, though all such summaries necessarily gloss over the power of concrete rhetoric. Gerhard von Rad suggests the central themes are these:

> If we first let him speak for himself, there emerge three basic insights round which his thoughts continually circle. 1. A thorough, rational examination of life is unable to find any satisfactory meaning; everything is "vanity." 2. God determines every event. 3. Man is unable to discern these decrees, the "works of God" in the world. It is clear that these insights are all interconnected, that even if the emphasis of a statement lies only on one of them, they nevertheless belong indissolubly together. (von Rad 1972, 227–28)

James Crenshaw puts the matter slightly differently:

> According to the thematic statement in 1:2 and 12:8, he sought to demonstrate the claim that life lacked profit and therefore was totally absurd. In support of this thesis, Qoheleth argued: (1) that wisdom could not achieve its goal; (2) that a remote God ruled over a crooked world; and (3) that death did not take virtue or vice into consideration. Hence (4), he advocated enjoyment as the wisest course of action during youth before the cares of advancing years made that response impossible. (Crenshaw 1995, 509)

Daphne Merkin voices the theses of the book in a refreshing way:

> The cornerstones of Koheleth's philosophy seem to be the concepts of consolation (*menachem* or *nachas*), futility or vanity (*hevel*) and profit (*yitron*). Within this triad of possibilities, consolation is at best fleeting, vanity is a constant, and profit is difficult to show. Ultimately, the reader is presented with the cunning collapse of two of the terms into the third, and we find ourselves with the triumph of contingency over forethought. (In diagram form this system would reveal an upside-down triangle, with the vectors of consolation and profit meeting at the inverted apex of vanity and futility.) . . .
> . . . Koheleth seems to be talking far more than the usual Biblical protagonist for the *real* rather than the *ideal* self in all of us. (Merkin 1987, 397)

It is clear that Ecclesiastes stands as a lively dissenter from what is generally the consensus of Old Testament faith. This teaching does not deny that God is sovereign, but only that this Sovereign is inaccessible to human faith and is indifferent to human destiny (Brueggemann 1997, 393–98). It is not possible to harmonize this teaching into what is usually taken as the core of Israel's faith. At the most we may recognize that this material is a remarkable statement of candor that is expressed with great courage. By the time of Ecclesiastes, what had been the dangerous probes of the book of Job has now become a settled commonplace in a theological environment that no longer wants to struggle with the old consensus.

As is usual in church usage, the conventional practice of the church is to select a few texts from the book that resonate with the church's consensus, take this material out of context, and ignore the rest. We may particularly observe four texts that have been important, even if they are distorted when out of context.

1. Ecclesiastes 3:1–8 is a familiar and much-quoted text that recognizes that life comes in many times and many seasons, and that one must act in ways appropriate to the times:

> For everything there is a season, and a time for every matter under heaven:
> a time to be born, and a time to die;
> a time to plant, and a time to pluck up what is planted;
> a time to kill, and a time to heal;
> a time to break down, and a time to build up;
> a time to weep, and a time to laugh;
> a time to mourn, and a time to dance;
> a time to throw away stones, and a time to gather stones together;
> a time to embrace, and a time to refrain from embracing;
> a time to seek, and a time to lose;
> a time to keep, and a time to throw away;
> a time to tear, and a time to sew;
> a time to keep silence, and a time to speak;
> a time to love, and a time to hate;
> a time for war, and a time for peace.

This poetic probe is a powerful attestation against absolutism and invites a kind of flexible, existential approach to life that aims to be contextual, appreciative of interpretive agility, and open to contingency. Von Rad, however, observes that the old perspective of contingency and contextuality was hardened by Ecclesiastes so that by this time it was "bound up with a theological determinism" (von Rad 1972, 143). Thus even this text is not as open to an urbane, poetic easiness as many uses of it may suggest.

2. Ecclesiastes 9:7 seems to be a warrant for self-indulgence:

> Go, eat your bread with enjoyment, and drink your wine with a merry heart; for God has long ago approved what you do.

Taken in context, however, it is more likely that this statement seeks to provide a curb to excessive self-aggrandizement, and counsels the pupil to enjoy what is at hand in order to remain free of social conflict, excessive guilt, or destructive ambition. It is plausible that the parable of Jesus in Luke 12:19 alludes to this text, for it contains the same triad of "eat, drink, and be merry." If the connection of the proverb to the parable is valid, perhaps Jesus' parable is a curb to the satiation that seems to be warranted by the proverb; or, more likely, the parable is a reminder of the permit of the proverb that never intended what the "fool" in the parable has made of it.

3. Ecclesiastes 11:9–12:7 offers a meditation upon youth and age. The opening lines of 11:9 and the statement of 12:1 are a celebration of youth when one should "seize the day":

> Qoheleth urges young persons to seize this period and make the most of it, daring to do the forbidden, and throwing caution to the wind. In a time of sensual gratification, one obeys the dictates of sight and imagination, leaving no place for responsible thought or physical pain. Such is the conduct that Qoheleth recommends before the deterioration of the body begins. (Crenshaw 1995, 542)

Youth should live life to the hilt.

This affirmation, however, is immediately followed by a characterization of old age that affirms that old age is not for wimps. Thus disillusionment that seems appropriate to old age in this teaching seeps over into youth, for even youth stands under the harsh honesty that it is only a relative good and cannot last:

> For Qoheleth, youth was preferable to old age because in the early years one had the capacity to enjoy life. But the advantage was a relative one, like that of sages over fools. In terms of absolute profit, which was the measure of all things for Qoheleth, youth and old age alike were futile, absurd, and without substance. (Crenshaw 1995, 544)

4. Finally, careful attention should be given to 12:13–14. Brevard Childs, following Gerald Sheppard, suggests that this epilogue provides a clue for a canonical reading of the entire book, so that the whole is subsumed under a generalized wisdom perspective (Childs 1979, 584–86; Sheppard 1977). Or it may be that given the disillusionment that pervades the tradition of Ecclesiastes, the writer finally settles in these verses for the replication of faith that is adequate for the day, even if such an attitude will no more venture into the deeper mysteries of life that have now, in the writer's own context, become so problematic.

Even if Childs is right about a canonical clue provided by these verses, it is our judgment that such traditional closure to the book must not be permitted to silence the troubled restlessness given in the rest of the material. As the teaching of the book of Ecclesiastes is in profound tension with the older sapiential instruction, so it is also in deep tension with the canonical closure of its own last verses. What is at issue is not that canonical closure overcomes the vexations that precede in the text, but that the two remain in tension. It is a tension voiced here as a literary articulation.

We can imagine, however, that the tension is true to life and articulates a social reality that should not be explained away in favor of a settled piety. In a quite personal embrace of the book, Merkin sees how contemporary the book of Ecclesiastes is in a society in trouble as she publishes her essay in 1987: "He is a man for the eighties, a private-sectorite. But being a personality who wears contradictions without discomfort, he has another side, one that suits another realm—the realm of the artist, where a restless spirit of inquiry soars beyond the walls of the *status quo*" (Merkin 1987, 401–2). It is easy enough to sink into the status quo as do the final verses, and the older teachers urge just that. But here is an artist with a restless spirit, restless not to voice easy ways, but resolved to articulate hard truth.

It remains to comment on canonical placement. In the Jewish liturgical utilization of the Megilloth, Ecclesiastes is linked to the Festival of Booths (Tabernacles), a day of deep rootage and joy. Such a book as Ecclesiastes for such a day:

> As is true of so much of Jewish life, the specific occasion designated for its reading—the festival of *Succot*, or Tabernacles, which falls, in our hemisphere, in the brilliant days of early autumn—evokes a dialectic and therefore a deliberate state of tension. It is part of the constant righting of balances that is at the heart of this religion's approach. Set against the gaiety and plenty of the holiday, which commemorates the ingathering of the harvest, the shadows cast by the book of Koheleth lengthen and darken. (Merkin 1987, 398)

The shadow tells powerfully even in the face of the season of brilliance in a community that will have no easy way of self-deception.

In some Christian Bibles, the book of Ecclesiastes is resituated in a section of "poetry." This book stands between Proverbs and the Song of Songs, all linked to Solomon, who is the traditional patron of wisdom. If the book is drawn toward wisdom, one can make a central focus for the book out of "fear God and keep the commandments." One can also suggest, however, that the knowing witness of Ecclesiastes has long since appreciated youthful erotic love (as in the Song of Songs) and knows that it will not last. As a consequence, the jaded wisdom of Ecclesiastes warns the reader not to absolutize either the buoyancy of Proverbs or the eroticism of the Song of Songs. Time moves and time bears away every season. The eternal one, in silent indifference, brings closure to every scene. It is all one: "For the fate of humans and the fate of animals is the same; as one dies, so dies the other. They all have the same breath, and humans have no advantage over the animals; for all is vanity. All go to one place; all are from the dust, and all turn to dust again" (Eccl 3:19–20).

Soberness belongs, in Jewish usage of the book, in the context of the exuberance of the Festival of Booths. Soberness belongs, in Christian usage, between the buoyancy of the book of Proverbs and the eroticism of the Song of Songs. As even this teacher knows, such soberness is not the whole truth; but it is the truth and it must be heard.

THE BOOK OF LAMENTATIONS

Of the five scrolls of the Megilloth, the book of Lamentations is most clearly tied to a specific event. The book is constituted by five poems of lament and grief over the destruction of the city of Jerusalem at the hands of the Babylonians in 587 BCE. That event is the defining moment of loss in the faith of the Old Testament, a loss that continues to be definitional in the imaginative processes of Judaism: "no other event in the history of Israel has been transmitted to us as vividly and concretely as the fall of Jerusalem and its consequences for the survivors" (Westermann 1989, 305).

The theological implication of the destruction of the city that produced such profound grief is that the liturgical tradition of the inviolability of the city—a notion fostered in temple-monarchy ideology—is shown to be false. (On that ideology see Isa 37:33–35 plus the "Songs of Zion" as in Pss 46, 48, 76, 84, 87.) The deep sense of displacement evoked by the loss led to the conclusion in some quarters that all the old promises of YHWH to Israel— and consequently Israel's status as YHWH's people and Jerusalem's status as YHWH's city—were placed in deep jeopardy.

The capacity to give public articulation to grief over the suffering and humiliation of the city is not undertaken de novo in Jerusalem. Behind the book of Lamentations stand other examples of the genre of lament over the city that provided the context for Israel's peculiar voicing of grief. Nonetheless, a proper study of the book, after taking into account the already extant genre of lament over a fallen city, requires close attention to Israel's distinctive utilization of the conventional genre of lament over the city. Thus the book offers five poems of grief that were evoked by the crisis of 587, poems that were formulated soon after the crisis, likely by the population of Jews that remained in the shattered city. All but the last of the five poems are voiced in acrostic fashion, that is, they are structured according to order of the Hebrew alphabet. Thus poems 1, 2, and 4 have twenty-two verses, one for each letter of the alphabet. The third, longer poem is constituted by sixty-six verses, in which each letter in succession begins three consecutive lines. Even the fifth poem continues in the pattern, with twenty-two verses, although the discipline of the acrostic is not continued in that poem. It is possible that the discipline of the acrostic arrangement is in order that the loss and grief of Israel could be expressed in totality and completeness, from A to Z.

The poetry proceeds, albeit under great artistic discipline, to bring to speech the deep emotive reality of loss, suffering, and abandonment. A preferred strategy in the poetry is to create a number of rhetorical personae in interaction with each other in order to intensify the dialogical density of the poetry. Particular attention is paid to the role of the children in the dying city:

> The survival of Zion's children occupies a privileged and critical role in this rhetoric of persuasion, representing a key to the literary and emotional structure of Lamentations 1 and 2. As the drive for life becomes more apparent in the shift in genre from the dirge to the lament and in the increasing emphasis on the function of persuasion, the drive for life also becomes more apparent in the content of Zion's lament. The laments of both Zion and the poet culminate in a concern for the lives of the children who are dying in the streets. . . .
>
> The cause of the brokenness of Zion is identified as the children collapsing like the wounded in the squares of the city. Thus it is Zion's presentation of the plight of her children that has recruited the poet so forcefully. Since the lament as a genre is concerned to get a response from God to the suffering it describes, the poet is modeling the response to Zion's lament that should come from God. (Linafelt 2000, 50, 53)

Specifically, the poetry offers the voices of a suffering, dying, abandoned woman as the voice of the city, a woman who is dying and who continues to die, but who does not finally die—in order that her voice of bereavement is kept continually alive as the city suffers and dies without relief. This commingling of dying and living is accomplished by the mixture of the genres of *dirge* (for death) and *lament* (by the living):

> We have in chapters 1 and 2 of Lamentations a certain mixture or combination of genres: the more common lament (whether understood as individual or communal) and the dirge or funeral song. What is less clear, and what I will argue now, is that the combination of the genres is not haphazard or confused. Rather it evinces the fundamental dynamic of survival literature identified above: the paradox of life in death and death in life. . . .

While Zion survives in the dirge of the poet, the import of this really becomes apparent only in the second half of chapter 1. It is here that Zion emerges most forcefully as a speaking subject, and it is here that elements of the funeral song increasingly give way to the elements of lament. The scene of death implied by the dirge, already undercut by the presence of Zion, begins to open out toward life even more. Not only is the one who should be dead alive, but she is speaking, and speaking vigorously. The genre of lament, like the dirge, arises out of pain and knows much about death. Yet unlike the dirge, its primary aim is life. . . .

The voice of Zion holds sway for most of the second half of Lamentations 1, effectively excluding the elements of the dirge, based as they are in the finality of death. (Linafelt 2000, 37, 38, 40)

The lament of Israel over the city admits of a poetic instability that is appropriate to the loss that is beyond explanation, beyond explanation in a way that the poetry so well voices. One such evidence of instability, for example, is 3:40–66. At the beginning of this poetic unit, Israel is a guilty perpetrator who confesses transgression and whose sin has caused the destruction:

> We have transgressed and rebelled,
>   and you have not forgiven.
>   (3:42)

The poem moves on; by verse 52 the *perpetrator* of verse 42 has become the *victim* of suffering that is enacted "without cause":

> Those who were my enemies without cause
>   have hunted me like a bird;
> they flung me alive into a pit
>   and hurled stones on me;
> water closed over my head;
>   I said, "I am lost."
>   (3:52–54)

The poetry does not worry about such a logical contradiction, for the logic of loss is not governed by explanation.

There is no doubt that this poetry pertains precisely to this city in this moment. Any compromise of this concreteness is excluded. Having said that, however, it is clear that the power of this concrete poetry causes the lament to extend this tearful eloquence beyond Jerusalem to many other losses that are experienced by others with the same acuteness that Jews know in this loss:

> There is one way of reading Lamentations that does satisfy my sense of history. And that is to see Jerusalem as a symbol for *all* cities cap-

tured and destroyed. After all, we have no words handed down to us from the agony of Troy. Silence from Herat, which Genghis Khan obliterated with its million and a half inhabitants; silence from Montezuma's Tenochtitlan; silence from ten thousand African villages whose existence we don't even know about. And from the Canaanite cities, Jericho, Hazor, Ai, and the rest, where our own exemplary Joshua, for the greater glory of God, "butchered every creature in the city, all the men and women, all the babies and old people, all the oxen and sheep and donkeys": a terrible silence. Only these words of lament for the destruction of Jerusalem remain. Why shouldn't they be given to all the other cities as well? We Jews are rich in words. We can afford to be generous. (Mitchell 1987, 385)

Thus the poetry is at the same time concrete and paradigmatic. No one has understood the paradigmatic power of this poetry of grief as well as has Kathleen O'Connor. She shows the way in which these poems are to be taken up for many uses, and in every use she urges that Lamentations is

1. An act of *truthfulness*:

Because Lamentations' speakers proclaim unvarnished truth before God, the book is full to overflowing with worshipful fidelity. Truth-telling is faithful to the "Other" because speakers of truth hold the relationship open from their side. They keep communicating as if the Other might finally respond. Of course, the speakers persistently express distrust of God's intentions. They accuse God of doing outright evil against them. Only the speaker in chapter 3 uses explicit language of trust, but even he does so with intermittent, unsteady confidence. Lamentations' speakers pray anyway. They proceed with the shaky hope that God hears them, that God is still open to them, that God can be persuaded to see. The lament form, more bleakly employed here than anywhere else in the Old Testament, is still prayer, desperate prayer, prayer abandoned to truth. (O'Connor 2002, 126)

2. An act of *impassioned hope*:

Speakers in Lamentations tenaciously persist in trying to engage God. They make claims on God, demand attention, and beg for a future. They do this even as God walks away and silently closes the door on them. God may be unfaithful, but they are faithful. God may hide, but they stand in plain view. They berate God, protest God's work, and dare to ask for more than patent cruelty. Lamentations is a bare act of hope and a plea for life.

Even in the face of God's silence, the speakers persevere. Their hope resides in the strongman's words for whom, at least briefly,

God's mercies are "new every morning" (3:22–23). Hope resides in the broken, desperate pleas of Daughter Zion, who begs God to see (1:9c, 11c, 20; 2:20); in the urgings of the narrator, who tells her to weep day and night (2:18–19); and in the voices of the community, who plead with God to "return us to yourself" (5:21). (O'Connor 2002, 127)

3. A *wish for justice*:

Unlike other biblical prayers of praise and thanksgiving, laments announce aloud and publicly what is wrong right now. Laments create room within the individual and the community not only for grief and loss but also for seeing and naming injustice. Laments name the warping and fracturing of relationships—personal, political, domestic, ecclesial, national, and global. The point of lamenting is not to confess sin, though such confession deserves an honored place in liturgy, but to name injustice, hurt, and anger.

Prayers of lament are not about what is wrong *with us* but about wrong done *to us*. They tell in specific ways how sin, evil, and deprivation harm human life and the earth itself. They point to all that destroy our abilities "to survive, dream . . . and to flourish." . . . When people live in conditions that deprive them of dignity, of control of their bodies, of what they need to eat and clothe themselves, or of what they need to flourish in mind and spirit, they need to lament. Laments make "spaces of recognition and catharsis" . . . that prepare for justice. (O'Connor 2002, 128)

4. A *political act*:

But the tears of Lamentations are of loss and grief, abandonment and outrage. They are a flag, a sign, a revelation of injury and destruction, an expression of resistance to the world's arrangements. They are also a release, an emptying, a cleansing of body and spirit. . . . Lamentations validates tears. It has the power to gather bitter pain and bring tears to the surface. Then it accepts them.

Tears can give watery birth to hope. They can wash out space once occupied by despair, fury, or sorrow, and in that space hope can emerge uninvited. Hope comes apart from human will, decision, or optimism. (O'Connor 2002, 130)

5. The *teaching of resistance*:

By urging truth telling before the powerful, and providing language, form, and practice of defiance, Lamentations encourages resistance and promotes human agency. But what can this mean in a wealthy, secure country where as a people we suffer from an excess of power?

My answer is simple. Without coming to grips with our own despair, losses, and anger, we cannot gain our full humanity, unleash our blocked passions, or live in genuine community with others. Lamentations untangles complex knots of grief, despair, and violent anger that pervade this society—a society that refuses woundedness, weakness, and hurt. We need to access our passions to become true moral agents. By calling us both inward and outward, Lamentations can melt frozen and numbed spirits. (O'Connor 2002, 131)

In the end, tears have in them the *power of newness*:

Lamentations in particular and laments in general can unleash tears. They mirror suffering and expose wounds. They bring painful memories to light and provoke the unbidden bodily response of weeping. . . . But in the dominant culture of the United States, we generally consider public and private stoicism to be a sign of strength and dignity, no matter the loss. . . . We often belittle tears as a sign of weakness and inadequacy, allowing them only to women and children. This may be because if men were encouraged to weep, if men and women in power positions were to weep, they would then have access to their full humanity and the world would change. Tears are powerful, not weak. (O'Connor 2002, 129)

These tears-to-power are nowhere more poignant than in this book. Thus the event of 587 required a deep relinquishment of what was and a lively readiness beyond what was lost. But the event of 587 could not of itself accomplish either relinquishment or readiness. That could be done only on the lips of the poet whose words then come to the lips of the community, and whose words then, belatedly, have been shared in the Jewish generosity with many other quivering-lipped communities that go *deep beyond denial* and that go *new beyond despair*, but only by utterance that is disciplined, unrestrained, honest, and entailing openness to newness—but not soon.

Special attention should be given to two texts. First, 3:21–24 is the text to which readers seeking hope—especially Christians who want the loss to be over and done with—inevitably turn. These verses articulate the only hope for the future that is present in the entire book; this hope is based, for the poet, on appeal to the old credo traditions articulated in Exodus 34:6–7, an assertion of YHWH's fidelity through every negating circumstance, including that of exile. Thus the text voices the durability of YHWH's commitment to Israel in and through the abyss and into some good future. It is no wonder that Christian readers have gravitated to this text, for it is an affirmation like Easter faith in the midst of Friday death. Indeed, Brevard Childs has taken these verses as an interpretive clue for the whole of the book:

> In vv. 22–24 the psalmist confesses his faith in God's mercy in a formulation which makes free association with Israel's traditional "creeds" (Ex. 34.6–7; Num. 14.18; Ps. 86.15). There follows in vv. 25–30 another confessional statement more akin to the wisdom saying of Ps. 37. Again the theme of God's mercy is picked up in the form of instruction not uncommon to the lament and concludes with a series of rhetorical questions (vv. 37–39).
>
> The function of chapter 3 is to translate Israel's historically conditioned plight into the language of faith and by the use of traditional forms to appeal to the whole nation to experience that dimension of faith testified to by a representative figure. The promises of God to Israel have not come to an end, but there are still grounds for hope (3.22ff.). (Childs 1979, 594–95)

That interpretive judgment is unexceptional, given Christian practice.

However, we might suggest that the Christian habit of putting these verses of triumph over the unmitigated suffering of the rest of the poetry is to reach a resolution that is too easy and characteristically triumphalistic.

> The "good news" that the Christian reader can expect to find in Lamentations comes on the heels of the "rejection of grumbling" in favor of accepting the "message of salvation" found in the overcoming of suffering. If even so well respected a critical scholar as Kraus can import this much Christian language and imagery into his treatment of Lamentations, one can safely surmise that a Christian bias in favor of chapter 3 based on Christological considerations is operative elsewhere as well, even when not so explicit as the above examples. As stated earlier, this bias in modern times is less likely to take the form of a simple identification of the suffering man with Christ, as it may have in precritical exegesis. Nevertheless, to the extent that the theological imagination of Christian biblical interpreters has been shaped by the notion of a suffering individual, who serves in some way as a model of redemption for others, their attention is understandably drawn to what is perceived as a similar figure in the masculine figure rather than the figure of Zion.
>
> More subtly, when Gottwald articulates what he calls the "theology of hope" found in Lamentations he writes that the book "inculcates" in its readers a "submissive spirit." Gottwald goes so far as to claim that "in Lamentations we come upon the most outspoken appeals for submission to be found anywhere in the Old Testament." But all the examples he cites as support for such a far-reaching claim come from 3:25–33. Gottwald admits briefly that the figure of Zion does not quite fit this characterization, "for she is much more concerned with the bitterness of suffering and the pangs of sin," but in the same paragraph he nevertheless asserts that "an intimation of suffering that is purposeful is the central teaching of Lamentations, the axis around which all the confessing and lamenting revolves." Such a

central teaching can only be gleaned from chapter 3, for in chapters 1 and 2, and especially in those sections attributed to the figure of Zion, the notion that suffering may have a purpose is scarcely on the horizon (Linafelt 2000, 9, 12–13).

And even beyond such a propensity among Christians, we may note that both Jewish and Christian readers tend to be biased toward male figures, which we may help to correct by paying attention to Zion as an alternative female figure.

Second, the ending of the book of Lamentations in 5:19–22 is worthy of special notice. In sequence, verses 19–22 include a doxology (v. 19), a pair of haunting rhetorical questions (v. 20), and an imperative petition (v. 21). And then in the final verse an enigmatic acknowledgment: "unless you have utterly rejected us, and are angry with us beyond measure" (v. 22). (See O'Connor 2002, 77; Linafelt 2000; Provan 1991, 133–34.) On this verse O'Connor comments:

> the people close their prayer with a dispirited modification of their request: "Return us to yourself . . . unless you have utterly rejected us and are angry with us forever" (5:21–22). This verse has driven translators to their lexicons, concordances, and other ancient versions in search of a more positive translation. Hillers . . . and Linafelt . . . delineate numerous possible translations, ranging from turning the line into a question, "Or have you utterly rejected us?" . . . , to making God's rejection a past event over and done with, "Even though you greatly despised us and had been angry with us!"

But the book's final verse yields a happy ending only by distorting the Hebrew text.

> The text expresses the community's doubt about God's care and about God's character. It utters the unthinkable—that God has utterly and permanently rejected them, cast them off in unrelenting anger. The verse is fearsome, a nightmare of abandonment, like a child's terror that the only ones who can protect her and give her a home have rejected her forever. Such is the ending of this book, and I think it is wonderful. (O'Connor 2002, 78–79)

This last utterance of the poetry is a wistful awareness that YHWH may indeed reject. This ending destabilizes the better claim of 3:22–24, and since canonical reading most often pays attention to endings, this one must be taken with great seriousness.

It is surely intentional that the verbs of 5:20 are reiterated in Isaiah 49:14 in what looks like a quote from Israel's liturgy of lament. Thus Second Isaiah offers a resolution to Lamentations, poetry that resolves exile in hope and possibility. Given the mood of the book of Lamentations, however, it is important that Second Isaiah should not be permitted to solve the grief of the lament too soon or too completely. In poetry as in life, the grief lingers in an open-ended way. Faith answers such grief, but faith must not run rough-shod over the lived reality that depends upon candor, out of which may come newness. This candor will not be silenced by any moralism that is rooted in Deuteronomy, nor will it give in to the Zion tradition of inviolability, for it pays heed, endless heed, to the fact of pain on the ground. It turned out that there was a life for Jews after 587, after exile, and after Lamentations. The loss, however, is not erased from life or from faith. The book of Lamentations survives to witness to the durability of loss. An analogue to this durability of the poetry of pain may be expressed in christological rhetoric that affirms that the "Risen One" remains the "Crucified One."

It remains to comment on the canonical location of the book of Lamenta-tions. In Jewish sequence, the book is among the five liturgic scrolls, this one linked to the ninth of Ab, the day in the Jewish calendar when Jerusalem was destroyed. That day is a weighty day of remembering, a synagogue celebra-tion, for that event—through which many other events of loss are voiced—lingers as the supreme act of candor in Judaism. It must be enacted over and over again that Jews live faith in a world where silence is not fully answered and where absence looms up daily in many forms of violence.

In Christian canonical sequence, the book of Lamentations is placed along-side the book of Jeremiah, likely on the basis of 2 Chronicles 35:25: "Jeremiah also uttered a lament for Josiah, and all the singing men and singing women have spoken of Josiah in their laments to this day. They made these a custom in Israel; they are recorded in the Laments." The connection of the poetry to Jer-emiah is a credible one, even if not historical, for it is this prophet above all who invites grief over the city that could not learn the things that make for peace.

Taken either way, the locus of the Ninth of Ab or alongside Jeremiah, this text invites us to grieve in our own time and place, especially as taxpayers in the last superpower with endless ambitious visions of control, victory, and success. The book of Lamentations knows, from the ground up (and down), that his-tory does not happen as easily as hegemony might imagine. History happens, rather, in the midst of silence that is at the edge of absence. It happens first of all in tears that are long and salty, that yield only late, very late, to hope.

THE BOOK OF ESTHER

The final book of the Five Scrolls is the book of Esther, a *tale of Jewish courage* amid the threats and risks of the *Persian Empire*. This opening sentence of our analysis of the book indicates the three primary accent points of interpretation that we judge to be important:

1. The book of Esther is set in the midst of the *Persian Empire*, a power that was pervasively definitional for Jews through the fifth and fourth centuries BCE. The Jewish community had endlessly to come to terms with Persian rule, and apparently the Jerusalem community of Jews was in some important way economically dependent upon the empire. While the story is set in the Persian period and while the narrative evidences some familiarity with Persian cultural and political practices, the story in the book of Esther may well date later in the Hellenistic period. In either the Persian or Hellenistic period, the critical problem of coming to terms with political or cultural hegemony is the same.

2. The book of Esther is a *tale*, that is, an imaginative act of narration designed, perhaps, for both entertainment and instruction. While the book is rooted in historical, political, and cultural reality, critical scholars do not regard it as historical reportage, but as novelistic imagination rooted in historical awareness. This critical judgment means that the book requires a certain mode of reading that is committed to imaginative instruction of a world of Jewish courage through narrative performance.

3. The book of Esther is quintessentially *Jewish*, that is, it is preoccupied with the status of Jews in the empire who at the same time (a) maintain an intense self-consciousness as Jews, and (b) with pragmatic wisdom come to terms with the reality of imperial power. The tale portrays this tricky Jewish task of identity maintenance that avoids both a *sellout* of Jewishness for the sake of imperial advancement and *sectarian withdrawal* into a private Jewish world. Thus it is an articulation, in concretely Jewish terms, of how a distinct religious community practices public theology without giving away its distinctiveness. The convergence of *Persian power* and *Jewish self-consciousness* is perhaps best articulated in the daring and climactic resolve of Esther in her famous self-announcement:

> After that I will go to the king, though it is against the law; and if I perish, I perish. (Esth 4:16)

The entire story turns on Esther's cunning way in the empire in order to save the Jews. The outcome of her risky effort is that Mordecai, the quintessential Jew, is honored (8:15; 10:2–3); and Haman, the quintessential enemy of the Jews, is hanged on the authority of the Persian king (7:9–10).

The conclusion of the book in 9:20–32 is of special interest in understanding the canonical, institutional form of the tale of Esther. These verses authorize the regular celebration of the Festival of Purim, an occasion of joy and elation over the sheer Jewishness of life and faith. The actual relationship of the festival to the book of Esther is not at all clear; the text as it stands, however, presents the Festival of Purim as the occasion for the reiteration and representation of the story of Esther. The result of such a practice is that every generation of Jews has opportunity to engage again in the daring task of Jewish particularity in the public life of the world.

Four studies of the book of Esther may be of particular interest in the theological appropriation of this book:

1. David Clines has carefully traced the complex traditioning process of the Esther story through what he terms "Five Esther Stories" that eventuated in the settled Hebrew and Greek textual versions (Clines 1984, 139). It is particularly important that the text that we have in the Hebrew Bible likely had narrative antecedents, as well as subsequent developments in the Greek rendering. This continuing development in the traditioning process—not very different from the continuing development that we have seen in both the Torah and the Prophets—indicates the lively interest in this book, as it became material for endless reflection on the problematic of Jewish specificity amid many hegemonic cultural forces. Clines shrewdly observes of the Greek additions to the book that the effect "of making the book unlike its Hebrew original was to make it more like its nearest counterparts within the Hebrew Bible. A transformation of its canonical shape had the effect of affirming its canonical status" (Clines 1984, 174).

Close Reading: Esther 3:1

In this verse Haman is identified as an "Agagite." Why are we given that information? What does it mean? Consistent with the tendency in biblical narrative to refrain from explaining things overtly, we are not told by the narrator if there is any significance to the fact. Instead, the reader has to catch the allusion to the story, in 1 Samuel 15, of Saul's failure to annihilate the Amalekites, including their King Agag, and to destroy all the spoils from battle, for which he loses his claim to the throne of Israel. Haman, then, is presented as a descendant not only of the ancient enemies of Israel, the Amalekites, but also of this very Agag who was the undoing of King Saul. With 1 Samuel 15 in mind, we notice that Mordecai is identified as a Benjaminite (Esth 2:5), or a member of Saul's tribe. The stage is being set for a latter-day showdown between a descendant of Saul and a descendant of Agag, and we are not surprised when Mordecai refuses to bow down to Haman (3:2), thus escalating the tension and leading to Haman's plot to do away with the Jews. Of course, this version of the Agagite-Benjaminite conflict ends differently than that in 1 Samuel, with Haman and all his sons impaled. However, the narrator is careful to repeat three times in chapter 9 (vv. 10, 15, 16) that in this instance the Jews "did not touch the plunder," thus symbolically redeeming Saul's failure.

2. Daniel Smith-Christopher, following W. Lee Humphreys, has seen that the book of Esther—along with the narratives of Daniel and Joseph—are stories designed to teach "a lifestyle for the Diaspora" (Smith-Christopher 2002). These several stories, and Esther in particular, function to foster an endlessly negotiated social status in a cultural environment that was not overly hospitable to Jewishness. Smith-Christopher's analysis is important because it makes clear that the story of Esther is not only a telling but a doing; that is, it actually generates a certain kind of Judaism that is given articulation in a public festival, but that is nurtured and sustained wherever the narrative is retold and reheard.

3. Jack Miles has traced the "biography of God" to the concluding observation that God is no longer an active character in the book of Esther:

> Neither Mordecai nor any of the Jews now in peril for their lives calls on the Lord in prayer.
> The omission is stunning because this decree of extermination so closely resembles that earlier decree of Pharaoh against the male infants of the Israelites. Whether or not, when they cried out, the Israelites in Egypt were consciously crying to their God, "their cry for help rose up to God," and he heard it and came to their rescue. The cry of the Jews in Persia does not rise up to God, God takes no action on their behalf, and they give no indication whatsoever that they expect him to do so. . . .
> . . . Israel is back, as we might put it, now calling itself "the Jews," still speaking Hebrew, still beyond confusion with any other nation, but, amazingly, without its God. . . .
> . . . Years may go by in which no discussion is permitted of why they may not be spoken, but the silence continues and is "heard" at every moment. Whatever the intent of the silence about God in the Book of Esther, this is its effect. Esther and Mordecai are not God incarnate. . . . They do for the Jews under Ahasuerus what the Lord did for Israel under Pharaoh. They do what the Lord's anointed was once expected to do again for a restored Israel. . . .
> . . . [A]ccording to the Book of Esther, the Jews have become, as it were, God's ex-wife now responsible for her own debts only, God's former client now representing herself, God's grown-up child moved out of the house. The Jews' world is sometimes hostile, but with talent, courage, and a little luck, they are making a go of it. As for God, he is, to all seeming, no longer any concern of theirs. (Miles 1995, 358, 361, 362)

The gist of Miles's analysis is that in the late period of the Hebrew Bible, God has ceased to be an active player or even a subject of narrative interest. It may be that this absence of God is the outcome of a jaded secularism in which had come to know that they were on their own, or perhaps the God of the late period is so transcendent as to be beyond narrative engagement. Either way, history has now become a human enterprise wherein it is Jews, not the God of the Jews, who makes the decisive difference.

4. Timothy Beal understands the narrative of Esther as a narrative of ambivalence in which nothing of roles or relationships is settled or stable, but in which roles and relationships are open and subject to endless dynamic modification. Beal understands this both in terms of the relationship of Jews and non-Jews and the relationship of men and women. The weight of the narrative is about the assertion of Jewish authority in a context where Jews lack all authority:

> Jewish identity is shored up and reinforced toward the objective mastery of power, to such an extent that "fear of the Jews" and "fear of Mordecai" falls on people throughout the kingdom (8:17; 9:3). . . .
> Whatever the performance might entail (perhaps one simply begins calling oneself a Jew), Persians everywhere are suddenly "jewing." Earlier, to be identified as Jewish was to be marked for death; now for some Persians it seems to have become a matter of "to jew or die." Then and now, there appears in Esther to be no particular core to Jewish identity. Rather, the book plays—often with deadly seriousness—on Jewish identity as a matter of appearances, disclosures, and withholdings. (Beal 1997, 102–3)

The deliberate ambiguity of the narrative presentation is profoundly subversive of all settled social relations, a subversion that makes hope possible in a context of hopelessness, and power available in a context of powerlessness:

> The book of Esther is about surviving dead ends: living beyond the end determined for those projected as quintessentially not-self, the privileged representatives of divergence, marked as sacrifices for the furtherance of a vision of identity and political homogeneity. . . .
> . . . In my readings of Esther and contemporary theory, I have focused particularly on ambiguities in representations of the other Jew and the other woman, arguing such ambiguities can be used to sabotage the very politics of anti-Judaism and misogyny that rely on these representations of otherness. . . .
> The book of Esther plays on the borderlines between the ostensible and the inostensible: between overt power and covert power, between the public and the private, between identity and difference, between sameness and otherness, between the determined and the accidental, between disclosure and hiding. (Beal 1997, 107–8, 123)

While the narrative itself serves this function, the Festival of Purim is itself a carnival performance of misrepresentation that prevents powerless Jews from being cornered and trapped in conventional power relations:

This is also where Purim plays. As carnival performance, Purim is a communal embodiment of the book *par excellence*, subverting authority, inebriating sobriety, blurring the lines between self and other, and laughing in the face of chillingly real historical possibilities. . . .

Purim is not simply a reiteration of Esther. Rather, it is a *survival* of Esther. That is, Purim lives beyond Esther, supplementing it in ways that make it meaningful in today's world. Through the masking and the transvesting of Purim, one may recognize ways that one's own self is inextricably mixed with otherness, and otherness with one's self. Purim invites us to recognize, and even to celebrate, the otherness within us that we so often try to repress or hide. Purim is, in this sense, a coming-out party. Purim crosses boundaries, and invites others to do the same. (Beal 1997, 123, 124)

Carnivals like Purim and carnivalized literature like Esther are expressions of festive outbreak against the structures and norms of moral, economic, ethnic, and sexual hierarchies which structure relationships between individuals and groups in a society. In carnival, those structures are radically undermined. Social and symbolic norms and privileges are thrown into a wild slide, identities within the normal order of things blur, and life and death cocontaminate—a time of "pregnant death," highlighting "the ambivalent nature of life itself: destruction and uncrowning are related to birth and renewal; death is linked to regeneration. . . . Symbols of change and renewal highlight the rejection of prevailing truths and authorities." This is the carnivalized, radically unbelievable and morally disturbing world of reversal in Esther 9—a new beginning fraught with death. (Beal 1999, 113–14)

It remains only to observe that the book of Esther as a narrative of elusiveness and Purim as a festival of performance are in the service of an intense Jewishness, a Jewishness that is always an awkwardness and embarrassment to every hegemonic culture. As hegemony always seeks a "final solution" to the particular, so the book and the festival, in their dynamism, elusiveness, and restlessness, are primal refutations of a "final" anything, most especially a "final solution." No wonder the book of Esther continues its dynamic development in the tradition, for Jewishness under assault must continually reinvent and reenact itself.

It will be evident that the book of Esther (a) belongs to the Persian literature in the context of hegemony (as do Daniel, Ezra, Nehemiah, and Chronicles, the remainder of the third canon), and (b) voices Jewishness that prevails by wit and courage. The book of Esther is to be read with fresh attentiveness and force in light of the attempted "final solution" of the Shoah, for it is characteristic of the Old Testament to refuse finality, and nowhere more than here.

The book of Esther is intractably and wondrously Jewish. At the most, Christians may ponder the mystery of Jewishness in an understanding of Christian faith, with reference to Romans 9–11 (Soulen 1996). Beyond that and without in any way softening the Jewish concreteness of the book of Esther, Christians in the West, in a now increasingly deprivileged situation, may be instructed by the book of Esther. The book of Esther invites readers—contemporary and ancient, Christian and Jewish—away from the certitudes of modernity that have long been an instrument of Christendom. It instructs to the fragile strategies of drama and narrative by which to maintain a distinct identity. The point at which characteristic Judaism (short of the State of Israel) and contemporary Christianity (now deabsolutized) may read together concerns narrative strategies and playful futures that generate particular identity out beyond the leveling, generic humanity of military consumerism. The cases of Judaism and Christianity are not at all symmetrical, but there is now enough of a crisis in Western Christianity to ask about the practice of subversion in the interest of communal survival.

The book of Esther is a huge act of subversive, dissenting imagination. Of such generative Jewish imagination exemplified in the book of Esther, Jacob Neusner has commented:

> *We are Jews through the power of our imagination.* To be a Jew is at its foundations an act of art. It is to perceive the ordinary as simile and the received as metaphor. It is through will and heart and soul to turn what we are into something more than we imagine we can be. The Jews' task is to make ourselves, souls, lives, into works of art. This surpassing act of art we do through art: poetry, drama, music, dance, the arts of the eye and the arts of the soul and the arts of the folk alike. Setting the Sabbath table is an act of art. Carrying the Torah in the synagogue processional is an act of dance. Composing a prayer and reciting a prayer are acts of poetry and drama. The memorial and commemoration of the murder of six million Jews in Europe take the form of film and fiction even now. All of these point the way in which we must go.
>
> It is the arts' enchantment of Jewish existence, worked through poetry not prose, through music not uncadenced speech, that transforms one thing into something else. For our human existence as Jews requires us to turn one place, in the here and now, into another place, in time to come or times past and always, a thing into a different thing: humanity into God's image and after God's likeness, the ultimate transformation of creation. Time becomes a different time; space, a different place; gesture and mime, more than what they seem; assembled people, a social entity, a being that transcends the human beings gathered together: a nation, a people, a community. Scripture, prayers, formulas of faith—these form mere words, define categories other than those contributed by the here and now.
>
> To be a Jew is to live both *as if* and also in the here and now. By *as if* I mean that we form in our minds and imaginations a picture of ourselves that the world we see every day does not sustain. We are

more than we seem, other than we appear to be. To be a Jew is to live a metaphor, to explore the meaning of life as simile, of language as poetry and of action as drama and of vision as art. For Scripture begins with the judgment of humanity that we are "in our image, after our likeness"; and once humanity forms image and likeness, we are not what we seem but something different, something more. And for Israel, the Jewish people, the metaphor takes over in the comparison and contrast between what we appear to be and what in the image, after the likeness of the Torah, we are told we really are. (Neusner 1987, 208–9)

It is worth noticing that the book of Esther, the most uncompromisingly Jewish book in the canon, is the one that most fully discloses the playful openness of Israel's faith, a faith that refuses any closure wrought by power.

A Christian reader of the book might entertain the thought that deabsolutized Christianity now has an opportunity to "create worlds" by acts of imagination, worlds that do not echo and reiterate the closed world of dogmatism, moralism, chauvinism, or any other excessive certitude, but worlds that live by artistry in which characters perform and futures emerge against all the conventions of every hegemony. It is a long stretch from the Jewishness of Purim and its joyous freedom to the church's celebration of Easter concerning death and life. I do not suggest a linkage—except to note that the enacted narration of life outside dominant categories is a task commonly entrusted to Jews and Christians. To entertain and enact such subversion requires the gritty resolve of Esther, "If I perish, I perish." So it always is in these commonly dangerous traditions of faith.

27

The Book of Daniel

The book of Daniel is among the most peculiar and most difficult books in the Old Testament, an expression of faith voiced in genres that are unusual in Old Testament rhetoric. The book was formulated late in the Old Testament period, and has exercised immense influence in ongoing interpretive work. There is a broad critical consensus about the primary matters in the book but, as we shall see, much remains enigmatic and beyond critical discernment.

The book, according to genre, is divided into two parts: chapters 1–6 constitute a series of *narratives* about the hero, Daniel, a wise Jew. Chapters 7–12 offer a series of *visions* of the future and constitute the fullest articulation of apocalyptic literature in the Old Testament. The relationship between the narratives and the visions is particularly problematic, made even more problematic by the alternating pattern of Hebrew text (chap. 1), Aramaic text (chaps. 2–7), and Hebrew text (chaps. 8–12).

The narratives of chapters 1–6 give an account of the way in which Daniel the Jew exercises immense influence in the kingdom of Nebuchadnezzar of Babylon. The narrative clusters around Daniel, whose name means "God has judged." There is no doubt that in these narratives Daniel is a representative Jew who has learned to sustain and enact his *distinctive Jewish identity* in the presence of *indifferent or hostile imperial power*, a task required of every serious Jew in the Persian and Hellenistic periods. These stories may well be rooted in the sixth century in the time of Nebuchadnezzar; in any case, Nebuchadnezzar now functions in the narratives as a metaphorical foil for Jewish faith and for the Jewish community, and as an enemy of the God of Israel who is "the Most High," Creator of heaven and earth. (It is this same Nebuchadnezzar, moreover, who earlier was "YHWH's servant" in destroying Jerusalem [see Jer 25:9; 27:6].) Thus the narratives may preserve actual memories of and rootage in the sixth-century exile. It is clear nonetheless that Nebuchad-nezzar has now become a symbolic, representative figure before whom the Jewish faith must be enacted with intentional courage and freedom. Philip Davies has observed that while the several narratives have peculiar plots (most familiarly Daniel in the fiery furnace [3:19–30] and Daniel in the lion's den [6:16–24]), the narratives have a recognizable pattern that varies only in the two forms of "narratives of interpretation" or "narratives of deliverance":

interpretation story
(a) the king has a vision or dream
(b) the wise men of his court cannot interpret its meaning
(c) the hero emerges and gives the interpretation
(d) the hero is rewarded
(e) the king learns that the hero's god is all-powerful

deliverance story
(a) the king issues an order that commands Jews to worship an idol
(b) the hero or heroes are discovered disobeying
(c) they refuse to comply with the order and are prepared for execution
(d) they are delivered
(e) they are rewarded, their enemies punished
(f) the king learns that the hero's god is all-powerful
(P. Davies 1998, 51–52)

In the narratives of interpretation, as in chapter 4, Daniel the Jew has wis-dom and insight to do dream interpretation after the intelligence community of the empire has failed. In the narratives of deliverance, the Jews are placed in jeopardy by the Gentile king, but are saved by the hidden, miraculous power of the Most High God before whom the Gentile king is completely help-less. These narratives may be rooted in historical memories. They are now, however, acts of imagination that seek to nurture and instruct Jews, likely in a context later than the Babylonian period. These Jews are skilled in the tricky practice of faith wherein truth speaks to power; such speaking is characteristi-cally an act of daring and cunning and sometimes a risky act of defiance. Thus Daniel, as the key character and as the representative Jew, is a model for Jew-ish truth in the midst of Gentile power, a truth that is deeply and passionately fixed on the God of Israel, who is said to be and shown to be reliable in every circumstance of risk and threat.

W. Lee Humphreys, followed by Daniel Smith-Christopher, has shown the way in which these narratives tell of a Jewish courtier, who functions agilely in a foreign court, respecting and acknowledging the authority of that court, but without compromising faith in the Most High God of Jewishness. Some of these narratives are what Humphreys terms "contests" (Davies's "interpretation") and some are "conflicts" (Davies's "deliverance") (Humphreys 1973, 220). Humphreys allows that long before the use of these narratives in the second century BCE (on which see below), Jews struggled with the cultural reality that was for them demandingly redefined by the reality of "the Most High God":

> Certainly Jews of the diaspora and prior to the period of the Maccabees knew adversity and even the danger of persecution at pagan hands. However, the situation was fluid. A close intermixing with foreign cultural forces on all levels of life and a full interaction with one's pagan environment could result in hostility directed toward individual Jews—and, rarely, toward Jews in general—and the point of contention could in part be one's Jewishness. However, such adversity could be met and overcome through this same interaction. One could, as a Jew, overcome adversity and find a life both rewarding and creative within the pagan setting and as a part of this foreign world; one need not cut himself off from that world or seek or hope for its destruction. (Humphreys 1973, 222–23)

These narratives feed the imagination of faith in any circumstance. As U.S. society grows more deathly in its dominant contemporary trajectory, and as the church in the United States grows more marginal in that society, these narratives may have peculiar resonance for the practice of faith. It is clear in current church practice that Christians, like these ancient Jews, cannot simply collude with the state—or with the corporate economy—in its brazen antihuman commitments, but must speak of "righteousness, and . . . mercy to the oppressed" in many venues of power (Dan 4:27). Conversely, the church in such a society cannot retreat into a safer sectarian mode of life, but must be present to public reality. These narratives invite a negotiated, negotiating presence that weaves its way in the tricky demand of truth in the face of overwhelming power.

The second half of the book of Daniel is of a completely different genre, offering *visions* that bespeak an apocalyptic horizon (chaps. 7–12). Indeed, these chapters are the primary representative (along with Zech 9–14) of apocalyptic literature in the Hebrew Bible, the visionary dimension of faith that was so crucial in the emergence of the Christian movement. The visions gather together historical memories and present awarenesses into a massive act of theological imagination whereby present time, present circumstance, and present generation are identified as a break point in human history. In that break point, the raw sovereignty of God impinges decisively and even violently upon human history in order to overwhelm all competing powers, and in order to create a new world as a hospitable place where the small community of the faithful will prosper and be safe. The accent is upon the inbreaking of divine power that no longer pays any attention to the political realities featured in the earlier narratives; unimpeded by such realities, the inbreaking causes the decisive end of what was and, by implication, generates an entirely new beginning of a new world for the faithful. That characteristic apocalyptic articulation, sketched out by a number of scholars, is utilized in Daniel 7–12 for a quite particular purpose, namely, to comment upon and interpret the crisis of 167–164 BCE that so threatened Jews and Jewishness (Collins 1987, 68–92). Thus apocalyptic rhetoric is here linked to a particular historical reality, so that apocalyptic faith is not in a vacuum, but concerns real people in real circumstances.

In this instance, the crisis of faith to be faced is the onslaught of Hellenism through the initiative of Antiochus IV (Epiphanes) of the Seleucid regime of Syria who sought to establish his political as well as his cultural domination over Jerusalem by overriding and eradicating Judaism. Thus the vision of "the end" concerns the profound threat in these years to Judaism, a threat symbolized by the "abomination of desolation" that Antiochus imposed upon the Jerusalem temple, a defiant pollution of the holy place of Judaism (9:27; 11:31; 12:11). This same crisis is understood and reported upon "historically" in the narrative account of 1 Maccabees; here, however, the same crisis is presented apocalyptically, so that the counter to Antiochus is not the armies of the Jews (as in the case of the Maccabean horizon), but the direct intervention of the God of Israel, who needs not even "a little help" from human agents (11:34). These visions offer a complex history of the world whereby a succession of worldly powers are indicated, culminating in the "little horn" of 8:9 who has acted arrogantly and who has "cast truth to the ground," and is opposed by the Holy God (8:9–14) (see Noth 1967, 194–214). That "little horn" is commonly understood to be Antiochus, who enacted the ultimate defiance of the Holy God but who in the end cannot prevail. Thus the dispute between Antiochus and the Jews in Jerusalem is by this rhetoric escalated into a cosmic contest that the Most High God is sure to win—to the advantage of the faithful.

Most scholars think that the visions of chapters 7–12 are later than the narratives of chapters 1–6. The *narratives* may be rooted as early as the sixth century with reference to Nebuchadnezzar, but the *visions* pertain precisely to the second-century crisis of Antiochus; the traditioning process has worked so that the visions have been able to draw the older narrative materials into the second-century crisis. Thus the narratives are given a new read, and Nebuchadnezzar is reread as Antiochus, who cannot prevail in the midst of divine power upon which the Jews can trust confidently and completely.

The combination of narratives and visions thus together form something of a coherent theological statement, though, as elsewhere in the Old Testament, the new coherence does not overrun all the earlier textual particularities. Specifically, chapters 2–7 are transmitted in Aramaic, whereas chapters 1 and 8–12 are in Hebrew. It is easy to recognize that this twofold pattern of language (2–7; 1, 8–12) does not conform to the twofold pattern of genres (1–6; 7–12), so that the traditioning process is more complex than we are able to explain. Given that odd outcome of the traditioning process, it is clear nonetheless that both narratives and visions (in both Aramaic and Hebrew) attest to a single theological claim, namely, that the God of Israel is the defining agent in human history and in world history, an agent the Jews can fully trust in and before whom the Gentiles finally must yield. Thus the sum of the theological claim is a great assertion of hope that empowers responding Jews to great acts of courageous obedience in the face of alien powers that grow even more alien and ominous as we move from narrative to vision. However odd the imagining offered here and however difficult the critical questions, the focus is upon the same hope that is given us in these several genres, hope that matters in the real world of hostile power, hope that is situated beyond historical processes in the holy mystery of God, who presides over heaven and earth but who has disclosed the time of ending and beginning only to God's beloved people. Thus the process of hope for Jews is to let Jews know about the divine intention for the future that remains completely hidden from obtuse Gentiles, who trouble and posture but who finally face harsh judgment and ultimate failure.

In the vision section of the book of Daniel, chapters 7–12, we may note four particularly important texts.

1. In 7:13–14 a poetic interpretation of the "coming one" is voiced that has been immensely important in subsequent interpretation. The "Ancient of Days" (so RSV; rendered in NRSV as the "Ancient One") refers to the high, transcendent God. But interpretive interest has focused rather upon the phrase "a son of man" (so RSV; rendered in NRSV as "a human being"). The juxtaposition of these two figures—"Ancient of Days" and "son of man"—is a promise that the high transcendent God whose sovereignty is completely sure will have dominion and kingship established in the earth through an agent, the "son of man." Interpretation, however, has struggled with the intention of and identification of the "son of man."

Two issues are important. First, W. Sibley Towner has helpfully explored the issue of whether "coming with the clouds" means a descent of a heavenly being in a *theophany* or an ascent of a human agent in an apotheosis; he argues for the latter, that the coming one is a human agent, "a figure for a fifth human monarchy" (Towner 1984, 104). But if human, then the second question is whether this royal figure is an individual and thus a king, or whether the phrase refers to the entire kingdom as a collective entity. Towner opts for the latter and concludes:

> if we assume the intended identification of the son of man with the group called the saints of the Most High in this chapter, and if, based on verse 13, we conceive of the son of man not as an angelic figure but as a human figure lifted up by the clouds of heaven to receive the heavenly gift of dominion, then the saints of the Most High must refer to a human group. The most logical group are, of course, those *hasidim* by and for whom the Book of Daniel itself was written and for whom the apocalyptic expectation of vindication was a source of particularly crucial comfort. These are the saints who even as the book was being written were experiencing the pangs of persecution at the hands of the Syrian king. It is they who expect the reward of their devotion in the form of everlasting dominion. (Towner 1984, 105–6)

Such an interpretation indicates the quite direct way in which this promise for the future is made to a particular group of Jews with the urging that they should remain obedient, faithful, and trusting in the midst of adversity. It is likely that this particular group of the pious is to be contrasted with the militant Zealots of the Maccabean movement who sought to establish an earthly kingdom of their own. Here the imagery and the expectation are wholly on being *receptive* to the new order that God would give.

While I find Towner's reading cogent, it is important to recognize that we are dealing with highly metaphorical, poetic phrases that are rooted in older mythic traditions, so that the meanings are not clear and likely are not stable. It is important to notice that the history of interpretation has been open to rich alternative readings in various contexts, as Towner's own commentary makes clear. It is important for Christian readers to recognize how this particular text in 7:13–14 was taken up in the earliest Christian proclamation that was rooted in apocalyptic horizons (Nickelsburg 1992, 142–50). It is clear that in order to proclaim (a) the coming of God's new regime, and (b) Jesus as the bringer of that new regime, the attestation of the early church utilized the Daniel traditions that were mythically rooted but, as in the book of Daniel, linked to a quite historical moment, in this case the moment of Jesus through whom the kingdom is "at hand" (Mark 1:14–15; see especially Mark 13:14–27 for a primal Christian use of the tradition).

2. Whereas 7:13–14 links together "son of man" and the "Ancient of Days" who will enact the new kingdom, 7:18, 21, and 25 speak of "the holy ones of the Most High" who "shall receive the kingdom and possess the kingdom forever—forever and ever" (7:18). The identity of this community has been the subject of important critical reflection. There is no doubt that this visionary material is rooted in a mythic tradition that imagined God in the heavenly court surrounded by legions of angels who attend to the heavenly king (Miller 1978, 9–26). Out of that appeal to a much older mythic, liturgical

tradition, Martin Noth has argued that the "holy ones" are "divine beings." Noth concludes:

> It does seem that in the main part of *Dan*. VII "the holy ones of the Most High" are thought of as the heavenly associates of God, and that only subsequently did a change in meaning take place, so that Mowinckel's assertion that "the holy ones" in the Old Testament are divine beings is confirmed in *Dan*. VII, and therefore, just as the basis of the dream in *Dan*. II is the expectation of an eschatological "kingdom of God," the vision of *Dan*. VII amounts basically to a proclamation of the imminent "heavenly kingdom." (Noth 1967, 228)

Given that rootage, however, it is equally clear that the tradition has transposed this phrasing so that it now refers to the human community of the faithful who adhere in obedience to the "Most High," and who shall receive the new rule of God. Thus the tradition has taken old mythic imagery about heavenly matters and has connected them to a historical crisis. Taken together then, "son of man" and "holy ones" now concern the community that has acted defiantly against established powers and according to the will of the "Ancient of Days." This cluster of images, given through these visionary texts, concerns a new community of the faithful who live in hope. And while they hope, they act in radical obedience, in order to receive what the Most High God will give, namely, a new world of well-being.

3. Special attention should be given to the prayer offered in Daniel 9:4–19. This prayer (which has particular resonance with long prayers also set in the Persian period in Ezra 9 and Neh 9) is odd in context. It does, however, focus on two particular matters: (a) Israel's petitions for and dependence upon God's forgiveness in a circumstance of persecution where compromise and accommodation must have been powerful seductions, and (b) the reliability of God as a keeper of covenant. Thus the prayer may be understood as an actual transaction between God and Israel. It is also, however, an important piece of theological affirmation that serves as a grounding of hope:

> Further, the prayer also makes a particular contribution with respect to the question of Jerusalem's future. The Lord is the "great and awesome God who keeps covenant and steadfast love." This proclamation grounds not only the hope for forgiveness but also the promise of ultimate restoration. God is a "keeper of covenant." With Gabriel's announcement that the desolations must run their allotted time "until the decreed end" (v. 27), the full meaning of God's covenant fidelity is defined in terms of the present crisis. God *will* maintain the covenant, not because of Daniel's prayer of penitence but for God's own sake. By so functioning as a literary vehicle proclaiming God's self-vindication, the prayer is appropriately linked, as G. Bornkamm

suggests, with the *Gattung* of Doxology. Towner affirms this point: the prayer is "first and foremost a proclamation of God's being and a celebration of his power." Such a proclamation is not out of place in Daniel 9. What better way to confirm that the promise of Jerusalem's restoration is in safe hands? (Balentine 1993, 108–9; see Greenberg 1983; Miller 1994; and Newman 1999)

4. Daniel 12:1–3 is one of two texts in the Old Testament that clearly attest to the resurrection of the dead (the other is Isa 26:19, but see also Isa 25:6–10a). In Daniel 12:1–3 a double resurrection is anticipated, some to everlasting life and some to everlasting shame and contempt. (The vision of that twofold judgment is replicated in the parable of Matthew 25:31–46.) Beyond the joyous promise of Isaiah 26:19, which speaks of resurrection only in terms of joy, this text in the book of Daniel contemplates both joy and judgment beyond death. It is clear that this affirmation of life-beyond-death, which is only at the fringes of the Old Testament, is able to speak of resurrection as a function of *the end* (12:13) that is also the *beginning* of *new life*. That is, resurrection is a vehicle for radical apocalyptic thought that bespeaks fearful endings and amazing beginnings, all of which are wrought by the power of God.

It is clear that the resurrection in early Christian preaching was also a function of a world-ending and world-beginning proclamation. It is an immense loss for the church that this deep understanding has been largely trivialized and privatized so that the resurrection is timidly taken to be resuscitation or restoration to one's loved ones, either notion of which minimizes the large hope claimed in God's sovereignty, a sovereignty that at the end will judge and save.

It is unfortunate that apocalyptic has been taken over in popular usage by religious "crazies," for this visionary language is a rhetorical strategy for articulating deep hope that lies beyond the vagaries of historical reality. This is not a world-escaping hope; rather it is a summons to obedience that refuses accommodation to the rulers of the old age. Thus the narrative is witness to the rule of God, who sustains the practitioners of truth in the presence of power, and the visions intensify the claim for God's rule that is so powerful, so majestic, and so mysterious that none can resist. This rhetoric of hope in the resurrection links the most sweeping mystery of God to the most concrete practice of a nameable community. That connection amounts in poetic imagery and in disciplined practice to a dismissive disregard of the rulers of this age who will be terminated at "the end."

The book of Daniel represents a daring and outrageous invitation to hope in a God who is not ordered or domesticated or generated by historical facts on the ground. This text invites believers to wager everything on that which is not in hand but surely promised. Mark Mirsky has offered, from a Jewish perspective, the intimate solace of such a personal hope:

> It is for this reason that the voice of the angel in the Book of Daniel has such authority for us. It seems to speak out of the soft assurance of a parent, my mother bending over the bed, singing in her lovely, throaty voice, "Close your eyes, / And you'll have a surprise. / The sandman is coming. / He's coming, he's coming." It is the voice which urges one down into sleep in the hope not of extinction but of joy. To hear that voice one second after death would redeem all earthly pain. (Mirsky 1987, 454)

In Christian parlance, Douglas John Hall, after offering an acute analysis of contemporary despair, identifies the practice of hope as the most difficult and most demanding requirement of contemporary faith:

> Human despair is notoriously hard to counter—especially when it is a despair whose whole energy is concentrated upon denying its own reality! According to Christian faith, it has taken the entire wisdom and generosity of God to begin—even to begin!—to transform the soul of restless, alienated humankind. Utopian solutions, even when they are clothed in the language of the sacred, are therefore to be avoided. Hope remains hope, not "sight" (Heb. 11), and Christian hope remains hope "against hope"—against all final solutions.
>
> Given that eschatological caveat, however, it is not so hard to discern at least the kind of *challenge* to which the foregoing reflections must lead: human despair can be obviated only by a renewal of genuine hope, and *repressed* human despair can be prepared to hope again only if it is first enabled to admit itself and to face the impossibility of the artifice by which it thinks to survive the consequences of its loss of meaning. Those who despair, if they are not given some cause to think that the admission of their despair could be a means to its overcoming, will resist the confession of it so long as their material and psychic circumstances insulate them from the cold shock of reality. To repeat, only a new system of meaning can provide the permission that repressed despair needs if it is to name and attempt to replace the bogus goals and cheap hopes that are the residue of modern Prometheanism. False and unworthy as they are, those goals and hopes are all that is left of the bright visions of the architects of modernity. We fear to lose them and, besides, they are firmly entrenched. Meaning has departed; the system remains.
>
> The question for serious Christians is this: Can Christian faith, especially in its Protestant mode, sufficiently *extricate itself* from modernity to enucleate such an alternative system of meaning? Can the Christian movement distinguish itself from Christendom with enough imagination and daring to help humanity find a way into the

future beyond the demise of the modern vision and the spent imperi-
alism of the "Christian" West? (Hall 2001, 92–93)

Despair in the contemporary world is evident among the marginal, who do
not believe the system can yield well-being for them. But despair among the
well-off is perhaps more profound, because many of the well-off also believe
that the system is not adequate for one's deepest needs and deepest yearnings.
In such a context, it is the shared work of Jews and Christians to eschew the
violence wrought of despair in order to articulate a God who evokes radical
futures, albeit through agents, but only as God's own gift. Such hope will no
doubt be rooted in texts. And for such work, no text is more powerful than
the narratives in Daniel of contest and conflict and the visions in Daniel of
endings and new regimes.

In the Hebrew ordering of the canon, the book of Daniel is placed after
Esther, the last of the Five Scrolls, and just before the cluster of materials in
Ezra, Nehemiah, and Chronicles. That is, the book of Daniel is situated in the
midst of the Persian literature, suggesting that Jewishness-amid-empire is the
characteristic context for Jews at the end of the Hebrew canon. It is the challenge for Jews in a Persian milieu—or extrapolated into the Hellenistic environment of Antiochus—to see if Jewishness can yield futures in and through
and beyond the capacity of the empire. In some instances the book of Daniel
sees the hegemony of the empire in the person of Nebuchadnezzar as a way to
the future. More often it sees God's newness in spite of the empire, which must
end. Either way, hope is linked to lived reality, for God's newness will be given
in a world of power where truth may be fragile but endlessly insistent. Clearly
the process of canon did not intend to keep this material tied to the Persian
context. In the dynamism of the tradition, the text moves beyond Persian realities to the defining Jewish reality of trusting in a future-generating God.

In the ordering of the Christian Bible, the book of Daniel is resituated
among the Prophets. This alternative canonical location accents the point
that the book of Daniel anticipates God's new future and so is congruent with
the great literature of prophetic hope. It is surely the case that the hope given
in the book of Daniel is offered in a different genre of narrative and vision and
thus in important ways differs from the most characteristic prophetic genres.
The accent on the future, however, is enough to assert, now in a prophetic
context, the newness of the God who cannot be resisted and who invites a
trusting obedience in the present for the soon-to-come newness of God's
future. It is on the basis of such future that the church endlessly prays, "Thine
is the kingdom and the power and the glory."

In such a prayer of anticipation, the church evokes the phrasing of
Daniel 7:14:

> To him was given dominion
>   and glory and kingship,
> that all peoples, nations, and languages
>   should serve him.
> His dominion is an everlasting dominion
>   that shall not pass away,
> and his kingship is one
>   that shall never be destroyed.

The surging of apocalyptic cadence, moreover, does not stop until that future is voiced doxologically:

> Then the seventh angel blew his trumpet, and there were loud voices
>   in heaven, saying,
> "The kingdom of the world has become the kingdom of our Lord
>   and of his Messiah,
> and he will reign forever and ever."
>
>   (Rev 11:15)

The singing church waits. It waits confidently. And while waiting, it obeys in confidence, unimpressed by the alternative obedience always imposed by the "little horn" and often resisted by a "little help." In the end, neither the "little horn" that resists nor the "little help" that assists matters much because, finally, it is God alone who gives futures according to this subversive tradition.

28

The Books of Ezra and Nehemiah

The books of Ezra and Nehemiah are familiarly presented as two distinct books in contemporary Bibles. But in the long textual tradition, both Hebrew and Greek, the two books are treated as one. While we may treat them in the familiar way as two books, it is clear that the literary form and the interpretive intention of the two books is all of a piece; together they present with great intentionality the formation of the late community of Judaism, led by leadership from the Persian deportation, as the legitimate community occupying Jerusalem that practices the Torah of YHWH.

A great deal of scholarly energy has been used upon historical issues related to the texts of Ezra and Nehemiah. In general, the historicity of the leaders and their movements is granted, though much remains unclear. Nehemiah, the self-glorifying entrepreneur, is commonly dated around 444 BCE and credited, through Persian legitimization and financial support, as the decisive force in rebuilding of the city of Jerusalem that Nebuchadnezzar had left in shambles. Ezra, "the self-effacing teacher of Torah," is commonly dated around 458 BCE, just prior to Nehemiah, as the one who reconstitutes Judaism as a community committed to Torah obedience (Eskenazi 1988, 154). Thus the literature purports to trace the careers and the decisive leadership of these two, who perform very different but complementary tasks for the future of Judaism. Indeed, the Ezra-Nehemiah movement is the single biblical "historical report" from the long Persian period that is given to us in the Old Testament. Its importance both for its own theological intentionality and for subsequent theological interpretation is quite disproportionate to the brevity of the literature.

It should be noticed in passing that Ezra-Nehemiah in contemporary Bibles follows immediately upon 1 and 2 Chronicles; the two pieces of literature, moreover, appear to be intentionally linked by the fact that the decree of Cyrus that ends the Chronicler's account in 2 Chronicles 36:22–23 also provides the beginning point of the literature of Ezra-Nehemiah in Ezra 1:2–4. Consequently, there is a long-held scholarly assumption that the books of Chronicles, Ezra, and Nehemiah constitute a single corpus that functions as a third history after the Torah and the Former Prophets. That assumed linkage of Ezra-Nehemiah to Chronicles, however, has been more recently reviewed and decisively rejected by leading scholars. It is now judged most probable that Ezra-Nehemiah is not at all connected to the book of Chronicles, except in very late traditioning, as suggested by the sequence of the Hebrew Bible in which Ezra-Nehemiah precedes Chronicles (Japhet 1993; Eskenazi 1988; Williamson 1985; 1987).

I

The book of Ezra, reflecting the formative events in Jerusalem in the midst of the Persian period in the fifth century, is divided into two parts. Ezra 1–6 reports on—or purports to report upon—the initial return of Babylonian exiles immediately after the permit granted by Cyrus and the events that ensued in the first years of restoration. These events are connected to the work of Haggai and Zechariah, who are specifically named in 5:1. The narrative report concerns the culminating event of the rebuilding of the temple and the consequent celebration of the Passover (6:19–22), a celebration that marks the dramatic restoration of worship in Jerusalem, that is, a restoration that is taken to be legitimate by the returnees. There had been continuing worship in Jerusalem, as evidenced in Jeremiah 41:4–5; that continuing practice, however, was not regarded as legitimate by the returnees, who had exclusionary notions of what constituted legitimate worship.

These six chapters are framed at the outset by the decree of Cyrus (1:2–4) and at the conclusion by the decree of Darius (6:1–12), concerning whom one should refer to Haggai 1:1; 2:1, 10. This bracketing by these two Persian decrees establishes the premise of the literature that the restoration undertaken by the returnees enjoys Persian imperial support and approval.

Within that framework, we should note two other points. First, the long list in Ezra 2 indicates a concern for communal legitimacy in general and priestly pedigree in particular. The list indicates a choice for purity that pervades the entire Ezra movement. Second, the narrative report of chapter 4 indicates a contested situation among different groups in the community; in this presentation, it is clear that the rebuilding is to be undertaken only by exilic returnees who have enough clout and influence in the empire to preclude activity by others in Jerusalem:

Close Reading:
Ezra 3:10–13

The first temple in Jerusalem was destroyed, as we have seen, in 587 BCE by the Babylonian conquerors of Judah. Close to seventy years later, after Babylon had in turn fallen to Persia, the temple was rebuilt in Jerusalem. The rebuilding is recounted in this passage, and if one looks closely at the description of the scene, it is clear that the author intends it to convey a genuine ambivalence about the Second Temple. The scene describes the "great shout" that goes up upon the laying of the foundation, but it is a shout composed of equal parts weeping and joy. All the "elders," who had seen the first temple with their own eyes, wept loudly at the sight of the new temple; while others "shouted joyously at the top of their lungs" (au. trans.). The point would seem to be that those who remember the glory of the great first temple are disappointed in this new, smaller, and less impressive replacement; while those who never saw the first are content with the second. In the end, "the people could not distinguish the shouts of joy from the sound of the people's weeping, for the people shouted so loudly that the sound was heard far away" (v. 13).

But Zerubbabel, Jeshua, and the rest of the heads of families in Israel said to them, "You shall have no part with us in building a house to our God; but we alone will build to the LORD, the God of Israel, as King Cyrus of Persia has commanded us." (4:3)

Therefore issue an order that these people be made to cease, and that this city not be rebuilt, until I make a decree. (4:21)

This contested reality, alongside the pedigrees of purity in chapter 2, provides a defining clue for the angle of vision advocated in this literature.

The second part of the book of Ezra, chapters 7–10, features the leadership of Ezra, who himself has a full and detailed pedigree. These chapters indicate that Ezra has the full backing of Persian authorities as indicated by the decree of Artaxerxes in 7:11–27. This decree, saturated with conventional covenantal rhetoric, identifies Ezra's primary work as that of "a scribe of the law of the God of heaven" (7:12). Thus Ezra reconstitutes the Jerusalem community as one intensely committed to the Torah. In this work,

1. Ezra enjoys the full backing of Persia. The empire has no resistance against an intentional theological community, one that is obviously in general political conformity to the empire.

2. Ezra is supported by "selected men" who were in full agreement with his leadership (10:16–44).

3. Ezra undertakes radical reforms designed to preserve the "holy seed" of Israel that has "not separated" from the "peoples of the land" but has "mixed" with them (9:1–4). Consequently, Ezra undertakes a remarkable and costly

reform by requiring Jewish men to send away the "foreign women" whom they had married, marriages that in their own contexts had not been perceived as at all problematic. Thus the Ezra movement is one of Torah purification that was exclusionary, not only toward non-Jews, but toward other Jews who were thought to be less Jewish than the small group of returnees who presented themselves as the real Jews who were qualified in pure Torah obedience. This passion for an exclusionary policy is part of a larger dispute concerning the limits of inclusiveness in the worship of emerging Judaism, on which see Deuteronomy 23:1–8 and Isaiah 56:3–8.

This radical reform of Ezra will reappear in the work of Nehemiah (Neh 13:23–27). It was an act of immense authority that readily terminated marriages and disrupted families for the sake of a particular religious passion rooted in a particular notion of Israel as "holy seed," that is, as a community with a particular pedigree of purity. This exclusionary propensity is a hallmark of the returnees from Babylon. This intense religious passion may be understood as a response to the felt jeopardy of the community, for as Mary Douglas has evidenced, communities in *danger* perceive *purity* as the great antidote to threat (Douglas 1996). Two suspicions about this religious propensity, however, may be registered. First, it is clear, as Fernando Belo has shown, that purity is not the only issue in the Torah that might have been taken as a leitmotif for reform, for *debt* is an alternative agenda of comparable importance:

> I have only read the modern French translations of these texts and tried to find therein a logic that guides the organization of the two systems and that may later serve in the reading of Mark's gospel narrative.
>
> It is with the same intent and in the same perspective that I now carry the argument forward. The next step is to compare the two systems in order to determine their points of likeness and difference.
>
> Purity, as we have seen, brings fruitfulness and multiplication; that is, it brings Yahweh's blessing and gift. In the system based on debt, what I have called the principle of expansion or of gift is at work. Pollution, on the contrary, brings corruption, death, destruction, diminution; in other words, a principle of restriction is at work. (Belo 1981, 53)

Alongside a purity system that is a practice of restrictiveness, the Torah also champions a debt system that moves against restrictiveness. Thus we may appreciate that the reform of Ezra was one option among others that might have been chosen as a strategy for reconstitution of the community. Indeed, the debt system is evident as well in Nehemiah 5, but not in a way that is definitional for the entire movement as is the preoccupation with impurity.

The list of returnees (2:3–70), Ezra's own pedigree (7:1–5), and the list of select men (10:16–44) suggest a community dominated by those who were self-conscious about social status and social standing. It is clear that the purity system is not only a religious passion to those of high social standing, but that the system is also a benefit to them, a way of maintaining authority and power as the "best" of the population. Thus if the Torah offered option strategies for reform and if the Ezra community chose the option of purity, we entertain the awareness that that chosen option is not a disinterested one, but one that sustains a practice of domination to which this text attests and which this reform movement embodied.

II

The book of Nehemiah contains many of the same themes as the book of Ezra, though now the text clusters around the leadership of Nehemiah. It is of great importance that much of the book is a first-person report by Nehemiah (chaps. 1–2; 4–6; 7:1–5; 12:31–43; 13:4–31). In recent scholarship this material is regarded as a residue of the "Memoir" of Nehemiah, perhaps a more extensive document than we have in hand that was designed to enhance the reputation and role of Nehemiah, not unlike autobiographies written by political figures. This Memoir is most often taken for the most part as historically reliable. It accomplishes several things:

1. It reports on Nehemiah's commission from the Persians and his decision to rebuild the walls of the city of Jerusalem (chaps. 1–2).

2. It narrates Nehemiah's vigorous leadership on behalf of his own community and his vigorous, stern resistance to his detractors, who try to impede his work (chaps. 4–6). Nehemiah's leadership indicates his remarkable economic sensitivity to the unjust economy of the community wherein powerful Jews were exploiting vulnerable Jews (5:1–13). (In this act of Nehemiah it seems likely that he was appealing to the debt motif of the Torah noted above, perhaps with the particular reference to the "year of release" in Deut 15:1–18.)

3. It defends Nehemiah's defense of the city and his initiative toward repopulation (7:1–4).

4. It exhibits Nehemiah's organization of a great procession celebrating the completion of the walls that will restore safety to the city (12:31–43).

5. It evidences that his administration was concerned with produce for the temple, attentiveness to the Sabbath, and his intervention into marriages with foreign women (13:4–31). In this last regard Nehemiah's work is congruent with that of Ezra noted above (Ezra 9:10).

This material exhibits Nehemiah as a determined and successful administrator who brought viability to the civic life of the city, an account markedly different from the instructional focus of Ezra. In addition to the Memoir, other material in the book of Nehemiah includes a report on urban construction (chap. 3), and a list of returnees, again evidencing a preoccupation with legitimacy and pedigree (7:5–60; see 10:1–27; 12:1–26). Notice should be taken of 7:61–64, which gives the names of the "unclean" who were precluded from the priesthood and from "the most holy food."

We should pay particular attention to the remarkable cluster of materials in chapters 8–10. Chapter 8 is a most suggestive narrative report that has received great attention. In this chapter, Ezra leads the community through careful Torah instruction, and provides interpretation of the Torah so that it can be understood and received as relevant to the life of the community (see especially vv. 7–8). The text narrates a determinative act that (a) evidences the existence of some canonical text, perhaps the Torah (Pentateuch), that is by this time authoritative in the community; (b) demonstrates the practice of Torah interpretation that will become the hallmark of Judaism and that assures the endless dynamism of the Torah through a durable imaginative traditioning process; and (c) marks the community of Judaism as the people of the book-cum-interpretation. That is, Ezra here reconstitutes Israel as the community initially convened by Moses and now reconstituted with great intentionality concerning the Torah.

The dramatic moment of chapter 8 is followed in chapter 9 with the great prayer of confession (on which see also Ezra 9 and, less directly, Dan 9), which seeks to reconnect the community to YHWH, from whom the community has become alienated.

These two acts together—*reading of the Torah* in Nehemiah 8 and *confession of sin* in chapter 9—provide the context for the remarkable act of covenant making in 9:38–10:39 whereby Israel is reconstituted as a community of intentional obedience to YHWH's Torah. It is to be noticed that Nehemiah's role in this series of texts is minimal (8:9; 10:1), for these acts of religious reconstruction belong credibly to the work of Ezra the scribe, who reconstitutes the community of the Torah.

The main accents of this literature are not difficult to identify. The work of Ezra—supported by Nehemiah as urban planner—is the creation and nurture and sustenance of a distinct *community of Torah obedience* in the midst of the *Persian Empire* that is benign toward and supportive of such a community, so long as it adheres to the large imperial expectations, most notably the utilization of the temple as a tax-collecting agency for the empire. This interface of *distinct community* and *imperial hegemony* means that this literature reflects a community that must endlessly negotiate between the two, a negotiation we have also noticed in the narratives of Esther and Daniel (Smith-Christopher 2002). The text itself accents the cause of the distinct Torah community. It is important, however, not to miss the imperial side of the equation:

> The Persian Empire formed itself as a state and expanded itself into neighboring states in order to fulfill its own internal needs as an imperial power. Through its intrusion into neighboring nonstate organized regions, such as the Jerusalem area, it produced secondary states for the purposes of exploitation of resources. Yehud was such a colony, operated for the benefit of the Persian Empire. Yehud thus organized itself as a state, but its statehood operated within the limits imposed upon it by the empire.
>
> Yehud's organization involved the presence of political leaders such as Zerubbabel, Ezra, and Nehemiah. These officials received their power on the basis of Persian appointment and fulfilled administrative tasks for the purpose of strengthening Persian influence and gain from Yehud. They also possessed ties to Yehudite culture and shared their allegiance with the goal of preserving Yehud as a state of its own, albeit a secondary state dominated by Persia. These governors managed the Persian program of intensification to increase the imperial use of resources. (Berquist 1995, 144)

It is the negotiating practice—and the literature of negotiation—that become the hallmark of Judaism as it has over a long time had to make its distinctive way in the midst of hegemonic powers that have sometimes been benign toward this distinctiveness, but more often indifferent or hostile to its claims. Daniel Smith-Christopher, following Joel Weinberg, has suggested that the community of Jerusalem's liturgic practice, termed in the text *Bet 'Abot*, was attentive to both internal and external social relations. As a consequence, Ezra's achievement concerns both internal community formation and also a viable settlement concerning the empire (Smith-Christopher 2002, 27–73).

III

It seems likely that scholarship has spent far too much time on historical questions, without recognizing what Tamara Eskenazi terms "fictive actions" in these texts (Eskenazi 1988, 7). Whatever may have been the history, the books of Ezra and Nehemiah are to be recognized, in a way we have already seen in other texts, as ideological statements. Thus the books offer an imaginative construal of reality designed as advocacy in the context of other competing advocacies. The ideological advocacy of these texts is to insist upon a singular legitimacy of a small community of Babylonian returnees as the only real Jews, a claim based in *pedigree* and sustained by practices of *purity* for which the other, "lesser" Jews were excluded in principle. By this time it should not surprise us that the biblical literature is theological advocacy that is accompanied by social-political-economic interest, though perhaps the point is especially acute in this particular literature.

It remains to consider how this literature might be entertained, appreciated, and appropriated as Scripture in Christian reading. We suggest the following:

1. At the outset we must recognize that in conventional Christian practice this literature is either skipped over completely or heavily caricatured as Jewish legalism, without any appreciation of the lived reality that evoked such an interpretive vision. Thus it is important to pay attention to the literature and to recognize that it is there as serious Jewish Scripture but also as serious Christian Scripture.

2. The rigorous reform and restoration undertaken by Ezra and Nehemiah, jarring as they seem to us, are to be understood in a context of profound social extremity. That is, the reassertion and establishment of the "holy community" may be understood as a necessary undertaking if the communal identity is to survive at all. This urgency would be true under Persian hegemony, more so if Claudia Camp, for example, is correct in her judgment that this literature reflects Hellenistic culture, thus reflecting a Jewish crisis known very well in the Maccabean period (Camp 2000). A community of faith grounded in the book, when communal identity is threatened, must undertake jarring disciplines for the sake of survival.

3. Given that reality, it is nonetheless deeply shocking to ponder the exclusionary practices that led to the breakup of marriages for the sake of communal purity, a practice credited to both Ezra and Nehemiah. This act has been noticed, in feminine critiques, as a heavy-handed patriarchal maneuver that regards women as threats to faith and to the social order, a threat that must be controlled, if not eliminated:

> Whether Ezra's attempt at social engineering was carried out at all, much less with the success recorded in Ezra 9–10, its image is boldly stamped onto the face of the emerging canon, whether in texts of compliance or resistance; it will provide a point of departure for all the biblical literature considered in this book. For good reason, then, a number of recent scholars have argued for a relationship between Ezra and Nehemiah's reported attempts to get rid of wives taken from outside the *golah* group and the depiction of the Strange Woman in Proverbs. . . . It will be my contention . . . that the Strange Woman figure is too multidimensional to be univocally linked to one historical moment. To the extent, however, that Ezra–Nehemiah's "foreign wives" already represent a complicated linkage between gender and nationality in the construction of "Jewish" identity, this material

points in the direction that my analysis of the Strange Woman, both inside and outside Proverbs, will take. (Camp 2000, 32)

Ezra is concerned with foreign wives in particular. Female returnees who married the "peoples of the land" have already joined those people, and to Ezra they are not part of Israel. But the women that the male returnees have married are adulterating the *gôlah*, which Ezra considers a "holy seed." They have to be expelled together with their children, a deviation from the normal divorce pattern of the ancient world in which the woman left and the children, who were their father's lineage and posterity, stayed with him. Ezra does not want these children, even though their fathers were of the "pure seed." The reason may very well be economic; indeed the division of the community into the *gôlah* and the "peoples of the land" may very well reflect struggles over who owned the land that the people abandoned when they went into exile, land that had been worked in the interim by those who remained. But he never mentions such causes, speaking only the theological language of Deuteronomic law, the pollution language of Leviticus, and the ontological polarity of "holy seed" and "foreign women." As with any politician, we are tempted to ask whether Ezra was using theological language to justify economically motivated actions or whether he truly believed he was defending the "holy seed" from adulteration. But whatever his motives, his argument was successful, and the community of former exiles expelled its wives. . . .

This association of the foreign woman with all kinds of otherness makes her the very symbol of the "Other." (Frymer-Kensky 2002, 289–91)

This act of Ezra and Nehemiah can be taken ideologically as the quintessential act of exclusivism, an ideological act that is representative of an endless sequence of exclusions that have marked both Judaism and Christianity (see Ezra 10:6–44; Neh 13:1–3). In their anxious attempts to maintain purity, both Judaism and Christianity, in various ways, have undertaken to assure a communal homogeneity and to maintain the status quo of current power arrangements.

4. Camp can speak of the "annihilation of the other" as a prominent priestly act in these traditions (Camp 2000, 343). This I judge may be the most pertinent theological point in the contemporary use of this material. It is not to be denied that communities under threat must practice discipline. When the discipline is propelled primarily by anxiety that causes core commitments of the community to be surrendered for the sake of anxiety-assuaging disciplines, however, then the community asserts secondary matters at the cost of primary commitments. The question posed by this literature is how to maintain disciplines and boundaries without sacrificing core commitments in the process.

The felt threat of the "other" is of course a durable one, even if it takes many forms. There is a rich philosophical base for critical reflection on the "other":

> Few issues have exercised as powerful a hold over the thought of
> this century as that of "the Other." It is difficult to think of a second
> theme, even one that might be of more substantial significance, that
> has provoked as widespread an interest as this one; it is difficult to
> think of a second theme that so sharply marks off the present—admit-
> tedly a present growing out of the nineteenth century and reaching
> back to it—from its historical roots in the tradition. To be sure, the
> problem of the Other has been thought through in former times and
> has at times been accorded a prominent place in ethics and anthropol-
> ogy, in legal and political philosophy. But the problem of the Other
> has certainly never penetrated as deeply as today into the foundations
> of philosophical thought. It is no longer the simple object of a specific
> discipline but has already become the topic of first philosophy. The
> question of the Other cannot be separated from the most primordial
> questions raised by modern thought. (Theunissen 1984, 1)

The matter of the "other" does not remain abstract and cognitive. It bites
into real life, as it did in the Persian period. Thus from a Jewish perspective,
Jacob Neusner opines:

> Then what of the other? Jews were driven to the East, to the more
> tolerant pioneering territories of Poland, Lithuania, White Russia,
> the Ukraine; Islam would then be ignored; and Christians would
> spend centuries killing other Christians. Some theory of the other!
> Some theory of the social order! . . .
>   The case of Judaism tells us when and why a religion must frame a
> theory of the other. It is when political change of a fundamental char-
> acter transfigures the social world that a religious system addresses,
> thus imposing an urgent question that must be addressed. In the case
> of Judaism that change, at once political and religious, came about
> when in the fourth century Christianity became the religion of the
> Roman Empire. At that moment, the new faith, long ignored as a
> petty inconvenience at best, required attention, and more to the point,
> the fundamental allegations of the new faith, all of them challenges
> to Judaism, demanded response. Christians had long told Israel that
> Jesus is Christ, that the Messiah has come, and that there is no fur-
> ther salvation awaiting Israel; that Christians were now bearers of the
> promises of the Old Testament, and in them, the Israelite prophets'
> predictions were realized; that Christians were now Israel and Israel
> was now finished. The political change in government made it neces-
> sary for the people of Israel, particularly in the Land of Israel ("Pales-
> tine"), to respond to Christianity as in the prior three centuries they
> had not had to.
>   What they did by way of response was not to form a theory of
> Christianity within the framework of Judaism, but to re-form their
> theory of Judaism—of who is Israel and what is its relationship,
> through the Torah, with God. To that theory, Christendom was
> simply beside the point. Within that theory—that religious system

defining the holy way of life, world view, and social entity that was Israel—Christianity did not find any explanation at all. Nor has it ever since. (Neusner 1991, 108, 111–12)

Every community of meaning tries either to assimilate the "other" or to eliminate the "other." In the case of Ezra and Nehemiah, the strategy was one of elimination by declaring the "other"—non-Jews or not "good enough" Jews—to be disqualified. In contemporary practice, the same issue of the "other" concerns religious pluralism and how to credit claims of religion other than our own. More immediately, the threatening "other" in conventional capitalist society are gays and lesbians, who are imagined to be a threat to the dominant bourgeoisie, capitalist order. The particular identity of the "other," however, does not matter for making a connection to Ezra and Nehemiah; it may be any presence of gender, race, class, or whatever that produces anxiety and threatens the dominance of the homogeneous population. Judaism, to be sure, has other vistas than that of exclusion; but in Ezra and Nehemiah this exclusionary principle derives from and serves an interpretive monopoly. Our use of the text makes it possible to imagine our own voice of unity in like terms, and to imagine how it is and what it costs to submit the reality of human relations to the unbending insistence of forceful ideology.

With a later rabbi, it is Sabbath (that is, religious practice) for the sake of humankind: "Then he said to them, 'The sabbath was made for humankind, and not humankind for the sabbath; so the Son of Man is lord even of the sabbath'" (Mark 2:27–28). When the "other" threatens, however, it is humankind given to serve the *Sabbath*; it is marriage enacted to serve *purity*; it is whatever is vulnerable and treasured given over to maintain *sameness*. In this moment of rigorous reform, the Torah is now the text, the scroll utilized by Ezra (see Neh 8:7–8). In this particular context, however, it is the purity trajectory that dominates, while the God of the Torah awaits other readings from other parts of the same scroll.

We finish with an astonishing reflection on the book of Ezra by Jay Neugeboren. He reports that as a teenager he went to Camp Winsoki, where he summered with serious, practicing Orthodox Jews, he being a Jew but not one from a yeshiva. He pursued, as one does in summer camp, a young woman and was finally ready to kiss her. She resisted his approach and said: "'It's just'—she said—'it's that you're not Jewish enough for me'" (Neugeboren 1987, 458). Neugeboren comments:

> The Book of Ezra is not so much a hymn to the rebuilding of the Temple—to one of the most glorious moments in Jewish history—as it is an accounting of how the Jewish people respond to adversity, to the attempts to hinder the rebuilding of the Temple as they work to

re-establish the Jewish community in the Holy Land. It is a narrative that is obsessed with purity and impurity. . . .

Ezra's response is clear: the Jewish people must be as wary of assimilation as of the Samaritans; we must keep ourselves separate and pure, morally, religiously, physically. Although, of course, as modern Jews, we may try to gloss over the literalness of the injunctions against mingling with the Gentiles and choose to interpret the text metaphorically (we should keep ourselves separate only from the abominations and evil *ways* of the Gentiles, of impure and immoral Jews), the text itself is unequivocal; if we Jews are to be true to our Covenant with God as His chosen people, we must guard always against the slightest physical or moral union with those unlike ourselves, with those not chosen by God. To judge from Ezra, this includes not only Gentiles, but also those Jews who are corrupt because their lineage or faith is questionable. The young women who spurned me at Camp Winsoki would have been as praised by Ezra as by their parents. (Neugeboren 1987, 460, 461)

Neugeboren's reflection leaves the question for Jews, a question now much more acute than when the essay was written: How much Jewishness is enough Jewishness? And for Christians: How much Christianity is enough Christianity? And for whites, how much whiteness is enough? And for men, how much maleness is enough? And for Americans, how much patriotism is enough? And for Calvinists, how much Calvinism is enough? And so on. For the insiders in any crisis over sameness, there is never enough—except for our own. All around the edges of that sameness, moreover, are the disqualified waiting, along with the Lord of the Torah, for an alternative reading of the scroll that permits more than one reading. Indeed, the scroll permits many other readings that keep intruding upon the power of sameness.

29

The Books of 1 and 2 Chronicles

The books of Chronicles occupy the final position in the Hebrew Bible, and so provide an important culminating assertion of faith. It is ironic that the books are placed so propitiously and with great self-consciousness, and yet have been almost completely neglected in Christian study and Christian usage. That neglect is no doubt part of a long-standing Christian caricature of the postexilic period of the Hebrew Bible that has characteristically viewed these texts in anti-Semitic stereotypes as narrowly Jewish and irrelevant for Christian readers. With the current cautious but important rapprochement of serious Jewish readers and serious Christian readers of the Bible, it is important for Christian readers to pay attention to the books of Chronicles, both for their explicit theological voice and for the suggestive interpretive practices enacted in them.

The books of Chronicles trace the history of the world and the history of Israel from "Adam" (1 Chr 1:1) to the brink of the postexilic restoration in 539 BCE (2 Chr 36:22–23). In so doing, the text makes a wondrous sweep of the entire past and drives it freely and imaginatively into the historical specificity of postexilic Judaism upon which the text wants to reflect and to which it wants to bear witness. Thus the books are a revised version of Israel's memory in the context and under the impact of the Persian context of Judaism; in the context of Persia as a dependent colony of the empire, Judaism's only chance for freedom of thought, faith, and action is through the maintenance of a liturgical practice and sensibility.

The process of formulating this extended redescription of the Jewish past is the same as we have witnessed almost everywhere in Scripture, namely, the mobilization of old sources to be reformulated into a fresh, coherent, theological, interpretive statement that is accomplished with immense imagination.

That is the process that is apparent everywhere in the Old Testament text. Only here the process is of particular interest because it includes a great deal of scriptural material that is now available for the traditioning process, so that we are able to observe *Scripture using Scripture*. Most specifically, the long review of the monarchial period in Chronicles draws upon the monarchial history given in the books of Kings.

The books of Chronicles are of special interest because they provide a case study of interpretation with the control of the books of Kings. We must, however, enter a caveat upon the relationship of the books of Kings as "source" and Chronicles as "interpretation." It is a long-standing bias of scholarship to assume that the books of Kings are a more or less reliable history, whereas Chronicles is an imaginative project that is not historically reliable. As indicated in our discussion of the books of Kings, however, the monarchial history there also is not and does not purport to be reliable history, but is a generatively presented, self-conscious interpretation of history. Thus the books of Chronicles are an interpretation of a remembered past that makes use of an earlier interpretation that itself acts upon the memory with enormous interpretive freedom. As a consequence, the books of Kings should not in principle be given automatic priority over Chronicles in terms of historical reliability, for both histories are interpretive advocacies, though somewhat different from each other in emphasis, each reflecting its own circumstance and its own passionate conviction.

It is clear that Chronicles offers a quite free and unencumbered replay of the past, so free and unencumbered that Herbert Tarr can judge: "Now, this is not history, it is grand opera" (Tarr 1987, 508). Tarr's imagery is especially pertinent, because so much of the presentation shows Israel as a *choir* that sings its way through historical crisis, no doubt at the behest of various postexilic temple musical guilds. The acknowledgment of this remarkable recycling of the past is to make a connection between past and present upon which the legitimacy, credibility, and viability of contemporary Judaism depended:

> However, together with the increasing sanctification of the past by later generations, there developed a gap—which also steadily increased—between their own complex reality and the reality they found described in the Bible. A gap of this sort, the inevitable result of historical development, undermines the stability of both realities. First, early history becomes incomprehensible to the present generation and the norms of the formative period are in fact no longer appropriate to contemporary needs and aspirations. Second, present-day institutions, religious tenets, and ritual observance are severed from their origins and lose their authoritative source of legitimation.
>
> The book of Chronicles represents a powerful effort to bridge this gap. By reformulating Israel's history in its formative period, the

Chronicler gives new significance to the two components of Israelite life: the past is explained so that its institutions and religious principles become relevant to the present, and the ways of the present are legitimized anew by being connected to the prime source of authority—the formative period in the people's past.

Thus, Chronicles is a comprehensive expression of the perpetual need to renew and revitalize the religion of Israel. It makes an extremely important attempt to affirm the meaningfulness of contemporary life without severing ties between the present and the sources of the past; in fact, it strengthens the bond between past and present and proclaims the continuity of Israel's faith and history. (Japhet 1993, 49)

I

The books of Chronicles are readily divided into four clear sections. First, 1 Chronicles 1–9 astonishes and delays the reader by offering the most extended genealogy in the whole of the Bible. The genealogy is a way of summarizing a great deal of the past. Beyond that, it is also a way to establish deep rootage in the past that gives a connection to the present and so validates the present through continuity with the past. Among the noted features of this genealogy are the following:

1. First Chronicles 1:1–24 has rooted the human story in Adam, thus in congruity with Genesis 5:1–2, a picture reiterated by the Gospel of Luke, which roots the story of Jesus back to Adam (Luke 3:23–37). The genealogy proceeds by reference to the three sons of Noah in a way congruent with Genesis 10:1–32 and 11:10–26, culminating with Abraham and the beginning of the history of Israel.

2. It is remarkable that the genealogy that will trace the community through Isaac pauses over the lineage of Ishmael (1 Chr 1:29–31), which also belongs in the full story (1:28–54). This is of particular interest if we remember the animosity shown, for example, to Edom in the Persian period, as in the book of Obadiah (see 1 Chr 1:43–54).

3. Not surprisingly, special attention is given to the family of David and Solomon, who will become the primary actors in the later narrative (3:1–24).

4. Chapter 6 is devoted to the "sons of Levi" (see also 9:14–33). This is of particular importance because the Levites emerge later in the chapter as "temple singers," with particular reference to Korah (6:37; cf. also vv. 44–49) and Asaph (v. 39; cf. also vv. 74–83), who are credited in the book of Psalms (Pss 42; 44–49; 50; 73–83) with series of hymnody. As Gerhard von Rad (e.g., 1966, 267–80) and Jacob Myers (1965) have demonstrated, moreover, the "sermons" of the Levites provide some of the most important theological

material of the books of Chronicles; the connection between the books of Chronicles and Levitical circles of interpretation is especially important.

5. Remarkably, 1 Chronicles 9:35–44 traces the genealogy of Saul, even though this literature has no interest in northern kings. Evidently Saul is noted here and in chapter 10 as a transitional first king in Israel to prepare the way for David, and to contrast the faithlessness of Saul with the coming splendor of David. Saul must be mentioned, but is quickly disposed of as "unfaithful," and thus opens the way for David (10:13). The whole of the genealogy moves tersely toward the rule of David, the one who is the proper subject of the entire history.

The second large unit of Chronicles is the extended narrative of David in 1 Chronicles 11–29, with the transitional comments on Saul in chapter 10. It is evident that the Chronicler provides an account of David's reign that is quite alternative to the more familiar one in the books of Samuel. First we observe how much of the older narrative account has been omitted because this tradition wishes to paint a very different picture concerning David and Solomon: "all is wartless" (Tarr 1987, 498). All of the struggle between David and Saul is omitted, as are all of the vagaries of David's rise to power, and all of the belated struggles that David had with his sons. In this account, David is completely free of struggle in acquiring the throne and retaining it. He is now the untroubled, unchallenged ruler and carrier of YHWH's eternal promises to dynasty and to community. Of special interest in this presentation is the "eternal promise" given in chapter 17. But more spectacularly important is the long account of the preparation for the temple in Jerusalem, a preparation for which David receives full credit, even if the implementation must await his son (chaps. 22–26). In these chapters David is preoccupied with the elaborate detail of the coming temple and makes special allowance for the Levites and the Aaronides, the temple musicians and the gatekeepers. That is, the story of David revolves around the establishment of legitimate cultic practice.

Particular attention is given in this tradition to the connection between David and Solomon, for Solomon's work will be to build the temple for which David has made careful and extended preparation (28:2–29:30). Although the books of Chronicles begin the narrative account of Solomon only in 2 Chronicles, Solomon is actively present at the end of 1 Chronicles in order to make the point of continuity between father and son. The David account culminates in 29:10–22 with David's own lavish offerings to YHWH, an act that has produced the widely used offertory formula of 29:14: "For all things come from you, and of your own have we given you."

The third section of the Chronicler concerns Solomon the temple builder (2 Chr 1–9). The account of Solomon offered here is like that of 1 Kings

3–11, in which the temple material is sandwiched between other materials. In 1 Kings the arrangement is:

other materials	1 Kings 3–4
temple materials	1 Kings 5–8
other materials	1 Kings 9–11

In 2 Chronicles it is:

other materials	2 Chronicles 1
temple materials	2 Chronicles 2:1–7:11
other materials	2 Chronicles 7:12–9:31

Thus the temple materials occupy a central and more extended place in this account because the temple and its legitimated cultic practice are decisive for this narrator. After the temple materials, it is noteworthy that unlike 1 Kings 11:1–9, this version has no negative verdict to render on the third king.

The final section of the book concerns the Davidic dynasty from Rehoboam in 962 until the end of the city of Jerusalem in 587 BCE (2 Chr 10:1–36:23). This material traces the Davidic dynasty over the same path as 1 and 2 Kings, with occasional new material added. The most prominent feature of this material is the general disregard of the northern kings, the mention of which occurs only when those kings play upon the southern dynasty. This omission means as well the omission of the prophetic narratives of Elijah and Elisha, Elisha being mentioned only in 21:12 with reference to Jehoram. (See also Micaiah ben Imlah in 18:4–27.) This material, moreover, does not deviate from the earlier account in the books of Kings in tracing the ruin of Judah as the inescapable outcome of infidelity toward YHWH's Torah.

II

It is clear that this presentation of Israel's past is boldly revisionist. The past is bent, tilted, tweaked to serve present needs. The tradition makes no claim to historical accuracy, and scholarship of a modernist kind has misunderstood the character of the text by asking questions in the service of objectivity. From this it is possible for Christian readers to notice that presentations of the past, in Jewish purview, are characteristically supple and imaginative (Yerushalmi 1982; Brueggemann 1991). "History writing" is an endless process of negotiation, as is evidenced in the New Testament with its fourfold account of Jesus. It is worth pondering how wrongheaded much modernist Scripture study has been to imagine a "meant" that can be kept apart from "means" and therefore innocent (Stendahl 1962, 418–20). The Chronicler knew better than that. We might be instructed by the Chronicler in this regard and, consequently, free our energies for better imagining.

At the end of this fourth section and after the account of the demise of Jerusalem in 36:15–21, we should pay particular attention to the culmination of the book in 36:22–23. These two verses have spectacularly displaced the Deuteronomic ending of 2 Kings 25:27–30 (which is reiterated in Jer 52:31–34). This displacement may be even more noteworthy because the textual tradition of Jeremiah is important to the concluding report on Jerusalem in 2 Chronicles 35:25; 36:12, 21, and then in verse 22. The tradition omits the famous enigmatic reference to the survival of Jehoiachin in 2 Kings 25:27–30, because the future in this purview is not a royal, Davidic, messianic future. Now it is the foreign king Cyrus, the benign Persian, who opens the way for the future of Jews. Indeed, with reference to Isaiah 45:1, which calls Cyrus YHWH's "anointed," or "messiah," it seems apparent that Cyrus has now come to occupy the role and place of David in the imagination of Israel. This is noteworthy in light of the earlier preoccupation in the narrative with David. Now, in acute recognition of its concrete circumstance, Israel must reckon with Persian reality, a reckoning that is indispensable if Judah is to have any future at all.

Thus it is by the good offer of Cyrus (who is stirred up by YHWH) that Judaism has a future and a prospect of restoration to the land, a restoration that is crucial to the returnees, who now occupy center stage and define Judaism. In these verses, in the mouth of the Persian, it is "the God of heaven" who governs all nations and who wills Judah's restoration, thus linking this most concrete act to the story of Adam, which has been signaled at the outset of the literature. World history, the history of humanity, devolves to this Jewish project for the future.

The narrative of 36:22 continues the repeated citation of Jeremiah: "The LORD has stirred up the spirit of the kings of the Medes, because his purpose concerning Babylon is to destroy it, for that is the vengeance of the LORD, vengeance for his temple" (Jer 51:11; see also Isa 41:2–4, 25; 45:13). The restoration of Jerusalem now anticipated is initiated by YHWH. Its proximate agent, however, is Cyrus, so that movement of return is legitimated, permitted, and likely financed by Persia, who acts at the behest of YHWH. It is apparent that the leaders of the restoration movement, notably Ezra and Nehemiah, never forgot their own Persian connection, and so the restoration that followed was an act of *self-conscious Jewish faith* but also an act of *self-conscious accommodation* to the empire. It could not have been otherwise.

Christian readers may particularly ponder the last two verses of 2 Chronicles, which turn out to be the last two verses of the third canon of the Writings and, consequently, the last two verses of the Hebrew Bible. The people who were led to produce this text "through many toils and snares had already come"—the toils of deportation and the snares of imperial hegemony. The culmination of the book—and therefore of the Bible—is nonetheless an act of defiant faith. The old promises are in effect and Jewishness will act as the clue and culmination of world history. Thus, in its present form, the biblical text is profoundly given over to the demands and possibilities of Persian hegemony. Jewishness may suffer, but it has not been defeated, due here to the capacity of YHWH to move empires on behalf of Judaism. Tarr ponders the remarkable capacity of Jews in the midst of every imperial reality:

> So the devastating Babylonian conquest, the destruction of the Temple, and the exile of Judeans to Babylonia were followed by an unparalleled phenomenon—a miracle wrought by the Judeans themselves. They were the only people in antiquity exiled from their homeland and national religion who maintained their religious and social identity in captivity. All other exiled peoples assimilated, as did the "Ten Lost Tribes of Israel." . . . Then, still another miracle: in response to King Cyrus' edict, a substantial number of Judeans, though established now in Babylonia, did return and erect the Second Temple (completed ca. 516 B.C.E.). (Tarr 1987, 510)

It is impossible to overestimate the significance of this steadfast reality:

> Is it any wonder that this peculiar people has driven philosophers of history like Arnold Toynbee mad? For the Jews, themselves living in accordance with the law, have always shattered the laws of systematic philosophers of history, none of whose theories satisfactorily explain the Jews' continued existence. An unfathomable mystery!
>
> Whereas the Greeks invented the art form of tragedy, the Jews have lived it—and endured. Whereas the ancient mystery religions worshipped deities who died only to be resurrected, the people Israel, to whom such a concept is anathema, have lived that, too. They should have died out countless times, vanished; all other ancient civilizations did. The Jews alone persisted in returning again and again to life. And not only to life: to creativity as well, serving as a kind of yeast within other nations and contributing a disproportionate share to whatever progress mankind has made throughout the ages. (Imagine how much more they'd have contributed if allowed to live in peace!)
>
> No wonder the Jews spook people. Irritatingly, brazenly, provocatively, spitefully, bafflingly, they have refused to stay dead, or even permanently embittered. Does that account in large part for the anti-Semitism? A people whom you've subjugated, pillaged, slandered, raped, maimed, tortured, exiled, crucified, cremated—what else can you do except try to annihilate them once and for all? Or perhaps,

what's even harder, acknowledge at last this people's peculiar link to the divine?

So, perhaps the Jewish Bible is correct, after all, and it is God, who has kept the people Israel alive and productive all these millennia, fulfilling His part of the Covenant, as promised. (Tarr 1987, 510–11)

It is not difficult then to see how this act of hope and possibility given in these final two verses is definitional for Jews. It is not difficult, moreover, to see how this act of hope and possibility has been transposed in contemporary life into a rationality for the contemporary state of Israel. This is a state of a peculiar kind that is able in its anxiety to remember, but in that same anxiety is tempted to forget what else it must also remember.

In any case, the culmination of the Hebrew Bible in 36:22–23 is a profound contrast to the culminating promise of the Christian Bible in Malachi 4:5–6. Both endings concern futures—but futures staged very differently. It is important that this difference be honored and taken seriously, Judaism in a particular focus on land and Torah, Christianity with its focus on a Messiah for both Gentiles and Israel:

> Master, now you are dismissing your servant in peace,
>   according to your word;
> for my eyes have seen your salvation,
>   which you have prepared in the presence of all peoples,
> a light for revelation to the Gentiles
>   and for glory to your people Israel.
>   (Luke 2:29–32)

The difference is important and must not be softened. In the midst of that difference, however, our judgment is that Jews and Christians must read together as long as we are able and as far as we can (Brueggemann 2003). Because both Malachi 4:5–6 and 2 Chronicles 36:22–23 end in anticipation, it is clear that God may yet do for the peoples of the book what we cannot yet imagine (see 1 John 3:2). It remains for us to keep reading, aware of distinctions, respectful of differences, grateful for what is held in common, a future with many shapes given by the God of all futures.

30

Reprise on the Writings

Having reviewed the rich diversity of this third canon of the Hebrew Bible, we may return to Donn Morgan's thesis that the third canon reflects a "dialogic" response to the first two canons of Torah and Prophets in the context of postexilic Judaism (Morgan 1990). It is an unsettled question the extent to which context should be decisive for our interpretation, but it is clear in any case that the postexilic context (a) cast Judaism in a marginal role in the midst of political and cultural hegemony, and (b) evoked immense imaginative variation in Judaism. This casting and evocation are important for understanding what is before us in the third canon. That is, the diversity of literature in the canon is reflective of the diversity of life and faith that the context of postexilic Judaism both permitted and required. That period of Judaism lacked—either as deficit or as benefit—overarching institutions such as ruling monarchy or commanding temple that could impose a certain singularity upon the community. Consequently, the third canon, which arose in such a context, reflects many efforts at truth telling and many initiatives in sense making in the community, no one of which could predominate but, of equal importance, no one of which could be silenced or eliminated by other voices of advocacy. Thus the recognition of pluralism in the canon is of great importance, especially in contemporary church interpretation when a variety of anxieties propel uniformity that seeks to squelch diversity. (In other castings of canon, the Torah also reflects diversity in its several interpretive "sources"; in comparable fashion, moreover, the prophetic canon also reflects diversity, as, for example, the certainty that the great scrolls of Isaiah, Jeremiah, and Ezekiel represent alternative and perhaps competing interpretive trajectories.)

Beyond the recognition of diversity in the literature that bespeaks diversity in community and in interpretive vistas, it is not easy to draw general conclusions about this third canon. Nonetheless, we will risk three other observations, with the recognition that they only proximately apply to the entire third canon:

1. In his fanciful "biographical" characterization of God in the Old Testament, Jack Miles ponders the fact that in the later Old Testament there are not as many of "God's mighty deeds" as in the earlier texts (Miles 1995). He observes that with the dramatic closure of the book of Job, much less is given by God to earth. In his rather coded references to God, Miles judges: "At length, the Israelites took charge of their own lives. Eloh and Yah were still honored, but their home was understood to be in heaven now; little was expected of them on earth. The law of Sab was codified and copied, but it was now a law in firm human custody. Annually, a religious drama was celebrated recalling the epic of Israel and the gods" (Miles 1995, 401). In his terse citation of "Eloh," "Yah," and "Sab," Miles alludes to "the gods" and takes these as representative of all "the gods" who have withdrawn from the arena of human life. Miles opines that in the Song of Songs, "a secular spirit pushes not just Israel but also God himself to the margin" (405). In his judgment, moreover, the book of Ruth confirms and solidifies "the new mood":

> Thus is the otherwise deathly silence of the Lord God covered over by the rising bustle and hum of real life. Through Lamentations, Ecclesiastes, Esther, and Daniel, the silence of God may continue; but thanks to Proverbs, Song of Songs, and Ruth, the silence *merely* continues. It acquires no new momentum. It does not become deafening. The relationship between God and mankind does not again reach the fatal pitch of the last chapters of the Book of Job. (Miles 1995, 405–6)

Miles does, to his credit, not permit his notion of God's withdrawal to override the claim of the text. He acknowledges that in Ezra, Nehemiah, and Chronicles,

> then, suddenly, as a motionless, long-beached boat may begin to rock back and forth again on a rising tide, we find ourselves again in a historical narrative. The Lord God has an honored place in the narrative, but he is now a motivating force rather than an actor. His "precious thoughts," so cherished by the Psalmist and linked by the Psalmist to the Lord's still-remembered and acknowledged role as the master of the physical universe, are objectified and placed in the possession of every member of the community—as their constitution, the written law to which they all swear solemn allegiance and in which some actually sign their names. Israel's immediate neighbors are hostile, but they do at least acknowledge that there is no god but the Lord God; and the king of Persia comes close to doing the same.

Nehemiah, significantly, shuttles back and forth between Jerusalem and Shushan, the Persian capital. The sons of Israel in their promised land have been succeeded by world Jewry. (Miles 1995, 406)

Miles identifies Nehemiah, in a quite playful way, as "the first day of the rest of the Lord God's life":

> Though Nehemiah is male, he has about him the energetic practicality of Lady Wisdom on creation morn. He lacks something in self-consciousness. He is inclined to act first and reflect later (if ever). He tends to recognize a sin only after he sees it committed. He becomes a warrior only when pushed to it. In all this, however, he merely recalls what his creator was in his time of greatest vigor. Nehemiah is not divine. He is not the son of God. But in key regards he is the perfect reflection, the comprehensive self-image, the quasi incarnation, of the young *yahweh 'elohim*. (Miles 1995, 406)

It is not necessary to approve of Miles's artistic mode of expression in order to be instructed by his observation. It is the case that in the third canon Israel does not attest as it did earlier in the same way to the God who is at the center of historical activity. It seems likely that as Judaism's own life is driven from the center of political reality, so the God of the Jews in the same way moves from the active center to the reflective margin, as Jacob Neusner has noticed in the later Judaism of the second century CE (Neusner 1973). Thus the third canon has a sustained tendency to *reflection* that is at some distance from *direct divine activity*, a *distance* in contrast to the *immediacy* of YHWH in some earlier texts. Such a distancing was perhaps essential to the realism of Judaism in its marginal context; that same distancing, moreover, may be essential to Christian faith in a cultural context where immediacy often takes the form of pious superstition: "I ask no dream, no prophet ecstasies, // No sudden rending of the veil of clay, // No angel visitant, no op'ning skies; // But take the dimness of my soul away" (Croly 1982). The book of Daniel dissents from such a mood, for Daniel traffics in dreams and perhaps "prophetic ecstasies." That, however, only reminds us of the diversity of the canon that refuses simplicity. On the whole, Miles's point seems correct: the late canon is restrained about the innocence of Israel's older memories.

2. For that reason, Miles can judge, "At length, the Israelites took charge of their own lives" (Miles 1995, 401). It follows that if later Israel can no longer rely upon the direct action of YHWH, as did the remembered ancients, then the matter of shaping human history devolves upon human agency and human responsibility undertaken in faithful courage and freedom. If Scripture now is in a pensive, pondering mode, and if the God of this Scripture is motivator and legitimator but not actor, then human agents must take their

own risks. The quintessential human agent, the model for publicly engaged Jewish action, is Esther. Of her, Richard Howard writes:

> Just as I knew that human beings, not Jehovah, delivered the Jews, so my delight in the Scroll of Esther, by the time I could read, was a delight that there was a power disparate from that of politics, a power that inheres in Wisdom literature, though that literature might well be called the literature of folly. For that power is merely and magically that of showing forth, apparition, epiphany of the person, of the poor, defenseless, and, as I could determine now, invincible human body. . . . That story was a much cruder, much earlier, much more primal one. It was no longer the matter of the deliverance of the Jewish people through a brave woman. It was a reminder, urged as by a tidal undulation from an unacknowledged depth, of the body's power, beyond argument, beyond art, to beguile. (Howard 1987, 416–17)

Esther is the extreme case of human risk. And again, after Esther the book of Daniel comes next in a dissenting way to remind Judaism of the futility of "a little help" (Dan 11:34).

Given Daniel's dissent, however, history has become increasingly *human* history. As Gerhard von Rad has shown, the emergence of the human in history is very old in Israel (von Rad 1966, 166–204). But now as YHWH is more remote and hidden, the sphere of human responsibility and possibility is very large. Indeed, Job, in his nerviness, may be the harbinger of Jewishness that is to come. The human accent in the Persian period is crucial for the way in which everything devolves upon Cyrus and his ilk (see Isa 44:28; 45:1; Dan 1:21; 6:28; 10:1; many times in Ezra; 2 Chr 36:22–23; and the successors of Cyrus mentioned in Haggai, Zechariah, Daniel, and Ezra). As long ago as Moses, the divine resolve of "I, I, I" turns at the pivotal point in Exodus 3:10 to "I send *you* to Pharaoh" (italics added). If we stretch the case into the New Testament, moreover, it is clear that Jesus of Nazareth, "truly man," is of course the carrier of all that belongs to "truly God," the one whom we say is "fleshed word." Thus the cruciality of human agency is not peculiar to the third canon but it is noteworthy there, surely a requirement of a God who stays mostly in the shadows. The third canon is important evidence for the way in which these trusting Jews—and many after them—became subjects of their own history.

3. Finally, we want to consider the way in which Psalm 1 functions not only as an introduction to the Psalter but as an introduction to the entire third canon, mindful yet again that every such judgment can only be proximate, given the diversity of the literature. Psalm 1 is a clear and unambiguous advocacy of the study and practice of the Torah as the guide and sine qua non for a life of well-being. That psalm, moreover, is able to make a complete and unaccommodating contrast between the righteous who keep Torah—and so

prosper—and the wicked who despise Torah—and so are blown away in the day of judgment. This Torah advocacy with its single assumption that Torah obedience generates its own "sphere of influence" (Koch 1983a, 77) has rootage in the Deuteronomic theological tradition. By way of critical assumption, we observe the proposal of von Rad that Deuteronomy and its interpretive tradition are rooted in the teaching of the Levites, a Torah tradition that stands in deep contrast to the more establishment perceptions of the Aaronides (von Rad 1953).

It is easy enough to imagine that this Deuteronomic-Levitical teaching of Torah exercised immense influence in the postexilic period, clearly culminating in the work of Ezra, who is "the scribe of the law of the God of heaven" (Ezra 7:12; see Neh 8:7–8). That is, the dominant stance of postexilic Judaism is committed to Torah teaching as the way to well-being, a well-being on offer from the God of heaven.

It is clear that in its final form the book of Psalms is shaped to serve such Torah advocacy (Miller 2000, 318–36). More than that, it is fair to say that the great books of Proverbs and Job address the same issues, though Proverbs does so with reference to wisdom rather than Torah. As Moshe Weinfeld has shown, however, wisdom and Torah are not to be sharply distinguished, for both of them hold to a "deeds-consequences" understanding of reality (see Deut 4:7–8; Weinfeld 1972). The book of Job, moreover, struggles with the consequences of such a theology, whether one understands that book in terms of a critique of Torah or of sapiential teaching.

At the conclusion of the third canon, we may suggest that the interpretive reference point of the Deuteronomic-Levitical Psalm 1 exercises important influence. The book of Daniel has a very different texture from the world of Psalms, Proverbs, and Job. Yet we may observe three points that are germane:

1. In Daniel 1 it is clear that Daniel is portrayed as a Jewish man under Torah discipline who refuses to violate the rules of purity and defilement.

2. In 4:27 Daniel admonishes the Babylonian king in cadences of Israel's covenant-prophetic tradition.

3. Most important is that in the prayer of Daniel 9 the Torah is pivotal to Israel's confession and Israel's hope:

> To the Lord our God belong mercy and forgiveness, for we have rebelled against him, and have not obeyed the voice of the LORD our God by following his laws, which he set before us by his servants the prophets.
> All Israel has transgressed your law and turned aside, refusing to obey your voice. So the curse and the oath written in the law of Moses, the servant of God, have been poured out upon us, because we have sinned against you. He has confirmed his words, which he spoke

> against us and against our rulers, by bringing upon us a calamity so great that what has been done against Jerusalem has never before been done under the whole heaven. Just as it is written in the law of Moses, all this calamity has come upon us. We did not entreat the favor of the LORD our God, turning from our iniquities and reflecting on his fidelity. (Dan 9:9–13)

While the Torah accent is not overriding in the book of Daniel, it is clearly a powerful premise of the literature.

In the traditions of Ezra, Nehemiah, and Chronicles, of course, adherence to Torah is taken to be the condition of a life of well-being. More specifically, von Rad has isolated a series of interpretive homilies that appeal to older texts and that summon to contemporary obedience (von Rad 1966, 267–80). It is not necessary to consider these sermons in detail, except to notice that the summons and appeals for obedience do indeed concern Torah obedience. The homilies, moreover, are characteristically on the lips of the Levites.

Consequently, we wish to suggest that both the central focus of Ezra the scribe and the interpretive trajectory of the Chronicler live very close to the Deuteronomic-Levitical teaching of Psalm 1 (von Rad 1962, 347–54). The books of Chronicles, moreover, culminate, as does their Deuteronomic forerunner, with a celebration of Josiah, the quintessential Torah keeper who perfectly enacts Psalm 1:

> While they were bringing out the money that had been brought into the house of the LORD, the priest Hilkiah found the book of the law of the LORD given through Moses. Hilkiah said to the secretary Shaphan, "I have found the book of the law in the house of the LORD"; and Hilkiah gave the book to Shaphan. . . .
> When the king heard the words of the law he tore his clothes. . . .
> . . . Now the rest of the acts of Josiah and his faithful deeds in accordance with what is written in the law of the LORD, and his acts, first and last, are written in the Book of the Kings of Israel and Judah. (2 Chr 34:14–15, 19; 35:26–27)

The leap from the two reports on Josiah (2 Chr 35:26–27) and the termination of Jerusalem (36:15–21) to the promise of 36:22–23 is made without comment, even as the parallel leap is made in 2 Kings 25:1–21 without comment. Nonetheless, it is evident that the tradition thinks in terms of the Torah as a door to a future, so that Ezra's teaching, almost predictably, is next after the promise of 2 Chronicles 36:22–23, even though the tradition of Ezra is quite distinct from that of the Chronicler. Thus we propose that Psalms-Proverbs-Job at the outset and Daniel-Ezra-Nehemiah-Chronicles at the conclusion provide the framing of the third canon. They focus characteristically, moreover, upon the *Torah as the clue to the future*.

We have no wish to impose such a Torah focus on the five scrolls of the Megilloth. If, however, "Torah" is understood not as law or even as commandments, but as guidance and lore of the most comprehensive kind, then even the Five Scrolls are materials through which a marginalized community may foster and sustain a distinct identity in the world as the people of YHWH.

Thus, with Torah at its center, the third canon serves the evocation and maintenance of a community with a distinct identity, evoked and maintained by a counterethic and by a counterimagination that makes this community characteristically awkward in the world, a community that endlessly subverts all hegemonic judgments (Neusner 1987). To the extent that the Western church is now disestablished and must pay attention to a counteridentity in a world of military consumerism, these texts of the third canon, mutatis mutandis, might freshly serve the church as they have long since scripted Judaism in its alternative identity and practice in the world.

Concluding Reflection

31

The Hiddenness of God and the Complexities of Interpretation

The foregoing discussion will have made clear that the processes through which the Bible received the shape and substance of its final form are complex and largely hidden from our view. They are complex, most of all, because a great variety of practitioners of faith in ancient Israel and in emerging Judaism had a decisive role in those processes. That great company of faithful practitioners, moreover, worked in many contexts, responding to many issues of faith, and did so from many perspectives and on behalf of many advocacies. The outcome of such complex processes, inevitably, is a text that lacks complete coherence. More than that, it is a text that has many facets that strike our modern sensibility as profoundly problematic. This text with all of its oddness has been for the most part without revisions that we could regard as solutions to the problems that defy all conventional explanations.

The processes of Bible formation are, moreover, mostly hidden from us. In some great measure, those processes are hidden because these bold practitioners of faith either were not eager to give explanations for their text-framing work and preferred to remain submerged in the processes themselves; or, while not seeking to remain hidden, they had no appreciation for the modern accent upon "individual" authorship and were content to be a part of the great, ongoing, text-making work of the community.

We may, however, suggest a quite different reason—a theological reason—for the hiddenness of the processes of text formation. The subject of the text in all of its parts is YHWH, Creator of heaven and earth and God of Israel. In the faith of the church, YHWH is not only the one attested and revealed by the text of Scripture; YHWH is also, in ways we firmly believe but can never adequately characterize, a decisive agent in the formation of the text. Thus the hiddenness of the processes of text formation is congruent with

427

the character of YHWH, who is hidden and revealed, but who in free sovereignty and sovereign freedom never conforms to our explanation of Scripture or expectation of Scripture. Thus the hiddenness of the canonical process arises not only from the complex work of faithful Israel in creating the Bible, but also from the character of the God who is here disclosed in ways that preclude explanatory clarity. Of God's hiddenness in the faith of Israel, Sam Balentine writes:

> It is not basically a reflection of man's inability to understand or even to perceive God's presence in the world. It is manifest in both these ways, but it is not restricted to them. It is rather an integral part of the nature of God which is not to be explained away by theological exposition of human failures or human limitations. God is hidden just as he is present; he is far away just as he is near. Once this fact is given due consideration, then it is possible to understand the Old Testament's witness to the absence of a present God: "Truly thou art a God who hidest thyself, O God of Israel, the Savior" (Isa 45:15). (Balentine 1983, 175–76)

Learning to "trust and obey" the God revealed in the Bible requires acknowledgment of this hiddenness that cannot be explained away.

1. It is right to say that in the interpretive community of the church to which this book is addressed, the primary approach to the appropriation of the Bible has been to ask *historical questions*. This approach has been concerned with both the history of what is *reported* in the Bible (did it happen?) but also, and more important, the history of the biblical text *itself*. It is important to recognize that preoccupation with historical questions of both kinds arose in the intellectual world of the European Enlightenment, an intellectual stance that was an important alternative to the traditional absolutism of church teaching that was based on a certain reading of Scripture. Thus "history" became an alternative to biblical-doctrinal absolutism, and had the effect of deabsolutizing (relativizing) Scripture.

a. To ask about the *historicity of events reported* in the text is to exercise an Enlightenment suspicion over the conventional practice of simply accepting at face value the historical reportage of the Bible; and indeed that suspicion has helped careful students of the Bible make judgments concerning the historical reliability of the Bible (Dever 2001; Finkelstein and Silberman 2001).

b. To ask about the *history of the textual tradition* is to seek to situate each text in a particular historical context, and to assume that the text can be explained by and understood in terms of context. The clear implication of such a procedure is that apart from that context, the text loses much of its claim to authority.

The sustained attentiveness given in the Western church to historical questions—concerning both reported events and the text itself—has been immensely valuable and instructive. The impact of such study is to make clear that the Bible arose in and through the lived processes of Israel's life, and that the Bible can never again be treated as an undifferentiated, contextless absolute authority.

In more recent times, however, this almost complete commitment to historical perspectives and questions has come under severe criticism. It has become clear that the historical questions that have preoccupied interpreters are not innocent questions but easily carry their own interpretive baggage, whether of a fideistic or skeptical kind. Thus in current discussion, "historical methods" have come to be countered by or supplemented by (depending on one's stance) other methods that are not preoccupied with historical questions. Among the most prominent of these is *rhetorical criticism*, which focuses upon the artistic dimension of the text, and the approaches of the *social sciences* and particularly sociology, which seek to understand the text in terms of the field of social forces that are operative in, with, and under the processes of text formation (Brueggemann 1997, 61–89; Trible 1994; R. Wilson 1984). A study of these emerging methods is of crucial importance, but we will not pursue the matter here.

2. In contemporary Old Testament scholarship, the primary antidote to historical criticism is the focus upon the canon of the Old Testament, that is, the normative list of books and the normative teaching contained in those books. The artistic and dynamic facets of canon have been particularly appreciated by Ronald Clements (1977; 1982; 1985) and James A. Sanders (J. Sanders 1972; 1976). It is important to note, however, that the primary program of canonical study is that of Brevard Childs, who, in a series of books (e.g., Childs 1979), has developed an argument about the Old Testament that seeks to bracket out conventional historical questions and to focus upon the canonical (normative) teaching intention of the text, which he finds congruent with the *Rule of Faith* that emerged in the early centuries of the church's theological enterprise (Childs 1993).

It would be evident to any reader of Childs's important work that this present book has been greatly impacted and influenced by his argument. It will also be clear that our own approach differs in important ways from that of Childs: (a) We do not believe that the "canonizing process" was everywhere as completely successful as Childs suggests in overcoming what he dismisses as noncanonical data in the text. We believe that much of that material that lies outside the conventional scope of church interpretation is powerfully evidenced in the text and has refused to be silenced and cannot be silenced simply by an appeal to canonical authority. (b) We do not believe that even in its most intentional and normative canonical achievement does the text serve so easily and so readily what subsequently became the church's *Rule of Faith*. Thus we believe that the canonizing process was a vigorous one, but not as singular as Childs thinks and in the end not as reductionist toward "church truth" as Childs insists (see Olson 1998). Thus in our judgment Sanders is correct in speaking of a "tendency," but a tendency that did not run roughshod over ancient textual claims and one that did not completely impose itself upon the ongoing textual tradition. The matter of the completeness and comprehensiveness of the canonizing process is one that will remain contested and under adjudication. We suspect that for all parties to that contestation, the conclusions we draw reflect more the perspective of the interpreter than they reflect upon the text itself. Our own inclination is to think that the Old Testament is "canonical" in its rich variegation and that the polyvalence of the text itself is an important part of the canonical claim. It matters whether one believes that such variegated textual realities threaten the core of truth or if they in an important way understood something of the truth, that is, a refusal to excessive closure that characteristically runs the risk of settled idolatry.

3. The text-forming process that eventuated in the Old Testament is one of bold, ongoing *interpretation*, and interpretation is never mere reportage. It is rather a creative process that identifies and articulates meaningfulness that is in part *discovered* in old nuances and that is in part *invented* in the struggle from older meaning to newer text. Thus, for example, it is clear that the layering of tradition in the Torah (characteristically articulated as the Documentary Hypothesis) was a process whereby a new generation of text makers took up older tradition and reshaped it according to the horizons and needs of the contemporary in a new circumstance. Any attention to the text makes clear that the dynamic of the text that became canon is a process of locating new meanings from older texts, new meanings that themselves are belatedly taken to be reliable and normative.

It is equally the case that the framing of the final form of the text did not end the interpretive process. Rather, the ongoing work of church and synagogue is to continue to interpret the text so that it has pertinence in contemporary life. There is, to be sure, an important difference in the interpretive process that produced the canon and the interpretive process that derives from the canon. It is nonetheless important to recognize that in ongoing interpretive work, the faithful church continues in its own time and place the same interpretive processes that were operative among the text makers, being clear that the text receives interpretation each time it is reread. The ongoing interpretive process in Judaism includes the "oral Torah" (Neusner 1998); in Christian practice it includes the old scholastic conviction about the "fuller sense" of the text (R. Brown 1955) that received a different articulation in what came to be called the "New Hermeneutic" (Robinson and Cobb 1964). All of these ongoing practices whereby new meanings are received in the text fall under the famous dictum of the Pilgrim leader John Robinson in the U.S. colonial period, "the Lord hath more truth and light yet to break forth from his holy word." Interpretive issues concern not only the reiteration of old meanings, important as they are, but also attentiveness to new meanings that arise in careful, diligent study.

4. The complex and hidden processes through which we have received the Old Testament make inexplicably clear the recognition that the formation of the final form of the text, along with its subsequent interpretation, is never a venture of flat objectivity and cold facticity. The Bible is never simply reportage and description, but is always interpretive commentary that pushes beyond the observable to the constructed, that is, imagination beyond the given. We may think of *imagination* as the generation of images that lie beyond the socially acceptable consensus and socially guaranteed:

> Kant offers a surprisingly simple definition: "*Imagination* is the faculty of representing in intuition an object that is *not itself present.*" Imagination re-presents what is absent; it makes present through images what is inaccessible to direct experience. As a point of departure for a conceptual grammar of *imagination* in ordinary usage, Kant's straightforward definition is useful, as long as his emphasis on representation is not taken too literally. The point is that imagination makes accessible what would otherwise be unavailable to us; whether *representation* is the best way to express this function is open to question. (Green 1989, 62)

We may see this imaginative construal of the data at hand articulated in many ways. At the most elemental level, the claim that YHWH "enacts" observable events (for example, the exodus) clearly goes beyond the observable to construe the event toward YHWH rather than to characterize the event without an agent or with reference to other agents. At a second level, the endless traditioning process through which the same narrative plot is variously given in different sources exhibits the capacity of the tradition to reimagine the claimed memory in many different circumstances. In a third way, the old imagined event becomes a type, whereby new experiences are imagined differently in light of the older extant types. For example, the exile is reimagined according to the memory of the flood (Isa 54:9), or homecoming from exile is reimagined as a new exodus (Isa 43:16–21). The effect of such imagination is to see that the data that became Scripture are thick with many meanings that leave open many possible readings and that the text itself authorizes these many new acts of imagination.

It is through the work of faithful imagination that the text of Scripture has been produced. In a quite similar way, it is clear that interpretation of Scripture (that is, readings beyond the final form of the text) continues in faithful church practice to be an act of imagination that is congruent with the imaginative character of the text itself. It is for that reason that the interpretive task is always undertaken again. It is also for that reason that many church teachers, pastors, and scholars turn to the text yet again and find newness there.

This is not to suggest that every imaginative extrapolation of Scripture is as good as any other. Garrett Green has explicated the notion of "canonical imagination" or "paradigmatic imagination" that interprets texts and reality according to the normative patterns and models of Scripture:

> The primary job of theology (like its counterparts in science and literary criticism) is precisely the systematic articulation of the analogical metaphors, myths, and paradigms that constitute the primary "data" of the enterprise. Theology is in just this sense a hermeneutical inquiry, a disciplined interpretation of imaginative texts. (Green 1989, 70)

Green goes far in the direction of suggesting that faithful imaginative interpretation of Scripture is according to the patterns of faith that are given in the creeds and normative teachings of the church. This implies that faithful imaginative interpretation "reads past" some of the text in the service of paradigmatic claims. Green goes further in this direction than we would, but the matter remains unsettled. Very often a fragment of Scripture may disclose new faithful insight, even if that fragment does not manifestly fit what we may regard as "paradigmatic claims." Thus we suggest that imaginative freedom and fidelity in interpretation constitute a dialogic process of adherence to paradigmatic claims that at the same time honors fragments of texts that may challenge paradigmatic claims and require rearticulations of those claims when the fragments have been incorporated into the interpretation. (It is evident, for example, in current liberation hermeneutics that we are invited to notice important matters in the text that in a more settled, hegemonic reading were not noticed.)

It is, moreover, clear that an accent upon imagination may sound like an invitation to wild fantasy in any direction. There is, however, an important and extensive literature on imagination as faithful interpretation that sharply distinguishes imagination from undisciplined, uncritical fantasy (R. Kearney 1988; Bryant 1989). It is possible, beyond that distinction, to suggest that imagination is not only an act of initiation but also an act of receptivity through which new interpretations come to us and are given to us in ways that lie beyond our own generativity. Thus it is possible to see that imagination is a fertile arena in which God's self-disclosing power calls us beyond our own interpretive horizon so that new truth may arise in interpretation. Thus, for example: "And Jesus answered him, 'Blessed are you, Simon son of Jonah! For flesh and blood has not revealed this to you, but my Father in heaven'" (Matt 16:17). The processes whereby God's disclosing work is channeled through human imagination—both in text formation and in text interpretation—are beyond explanation. But clearly processes of disclosure function in that way. Even such a centrist, judicious scholar as Bernhard Anderson states:

> We must, in a sense, be poets in order to understand poetry, drama-tists in order to appreciate drama, musicians in order to enjoy music. So the Spirit must meet with our spirit for Scripture to become "God-breathed" or inspired. The Word of God, insofar as it is Scrip-ture or literature, calls for genuine literary appreciation and the kind of involvement between text and reader that awakens poetic, literary imagination. God speaks to his people today through Scripture at the point of our imagination, that is, where the "inspired writing" meets the "inspired reader" and becomes Word of God. (Anderson 1979, 35)

The contemporary appreciation of imagination that goes beyond objective interpretation and positivistic perspective moves in the direction of inspira-tion, a move that leads us to our next point.

5. We have considered the ways, albeit complex and hidden ways, in which human imagination and human fidelity have produced the text of Scripture. In the context of the church, that full acknowledgment of the human produc-tion of the text—warts and all—does not detract from the church's conviction that in the text of Scripture we have something more and something other than the outcome of human imagination and human fidelity, which we signal by the term "inspiration." That is, the church takes Scripture as a gift of God and God's own self-disclosure, even if humanly mediated. For that reason the church, upon hearing Scripture, characteristically responds, "The Word of the Lord . . . thanks be to God."

The church is very sure of this claim and knows that in the Bible there is disclosure that is beyond us, that is given us in the mercy and mystery of God. It has not been easy, however, for the church to find ways to articulate this conviction. At the outset we must acknowledge that, in a centrist Reformed tradition, scholastic notions of inspiration that suggest a mechanical or dicta-tion theory of God's gift of the text are unhelpful. That is, God's way of giv-ing Scripture is not in any narrow sense a private transaction with a human author; it is rather a sustained giving of God's self in and through commu-nity that feeds, guides, corrects, and sustains human creativity in the entire process of Scripture from initial articulation through transmission and into subsequent interpretation and utilization (Bauckham 2002, 50–77). It is likely unhelpful, in the modern world, to speak of God as "author" of Scripture and more helpful to reflect on God's *authorizing* of the text that is produced by human agents in a believing human community. Thus the human documents of Scripture carry divine authority, so that the claim for God's authorship of Scripture is not a literary one, but rather a theological one. In the end, it is adequate to say, "We love these books." We in the church have found them trustworthy, true, and reliable.

We may pay attention to two formidable attempts to speak of the authority of Scripture in a "modern" world where that claim is odd. In his famous essay "The Strange New World of the Bible," Karl Barth has declared:

> Within the Bible there is a strange, new world, the world of God. This answer is the same as that which came to the first martyr, Stephen: Behold, I see the heavens opened and the Son of man standing on the right hand of God. Neither by the earnestness of our belief nor by the depth and richness of our experience have we deserved the right to this answer. What I shall have to say about it will be only a small and unsatisfying part of it. We must openly confess that we are reaching far beyond ourselves. But that is just the point: if we wish to come to grips with the contents of the Bible, we must dare to reach far beyond ourselves. The Book admits of nothing less. (Barth 1957, 33)

In his characteristically high theological claim, Barth concludes his essay without any compromise concerning the agendas of history, morality, or religion; rather he gives a theological grounding to Scripture and thus makes a claim for God's Spirit as the energy and validator of Scripture:

> But God is also that spirit (that is to say, that love and good will) which will and must break forth from quiet hearts into the world outside, that it may be manifest, visible, comprehensible: behold the tabernacle of God is with men! The Holy Spirit makes a new heaven and a new earth and, therefore, new men, new families, new relationships, new politics. It has no respect for old traditions simply because they are traditions, for old solemnities simply because they are solemn, for old powers simply because they are powerful. The *Holy* Spirit has respect only for truth, for itself. The Holy Spirit establishes the righteousness of earth and will not stop nor stay until all that is dead has been brought to life and a new *world* has come into being.
>
> This is within the Bible. It is within the Bible for us. For it we were baptized. Oh, that we dared in faith to take what grace can offer us! (Barth 1957, 49–50)

In a parallel, closely contemporary statement, Martin Buber gives like answer about the Bible, albeit from a Jewish perspective. He notes the "strangeness" of the Bible and concludes that a "modern person" must yield to it:

He must read the Jewish Bible as though it were something entirely unfamiliar, as though it had not been set before him ready-made, as though he has not been confronted all his life with sham concepts and sham statements that cited the Bible as their authority. He must face the Book with a new attitude as something new. He must yield to it, withhold nothing of his being, and let whatever will occur between himself and it. He does not know which of its sayings and images will overwhelm him and mold him, from where the spirit will ferment and enter into him, to incorporate itself anew in his body. But he holds himself open. He does not believe anything a priori; he does not disbelieve anything a priori. He reads aloud the words written in the book in front of him; he hears the word he utters and it reaches him. Nothing is prejudged. The current of time flows on, and the contemporary character of this man becomes itself a receiving vessel.

In order to understand the situation fully, we must picture to ourselves the complete chasm between the Scriptures and the man of today. (Buber 1968, 5)

Buber's affirmation of the Bible as revelation affirms that Scripture offers a word from beyond us that comes to us from God's own self in a way that addresses and transforms us. In both Barth and Buber, it is clear that the Bible is known to be other than our words, other than human words, words grounded in the otherness of God, an otherness that moves toward us and against us in order to make all things new.

6. The recognition that the Bible is marked, indeed, saturated, by *ideology* creates a deep tension with the claim just made for divine inspiration. We may understand "ideology" as an assertion of truth that contains covert dimensions of vested interest, an attempt to pass off a partial claim of reality as a whole. When we recognize that the Bible is a product of many persons situated in many various sociopolitical-economic contexts, it is not surprising if these contexts and the several interests reflected in those contexts should inevitably show up in the most serious attempts to articulate God's self-disclosure. Thus current scholarship may recognize that the Bible itself is shot through with partisan advocacy. The first level of such partisanship that is offered as the claim of truth includes ethnicity that tilts toward racism (Jobling 1998, 197–243) and patriarchal practice that endlessly casts women in subservient roles (Schüssler Fiorenza 1984; 2001). The partly hidden commitments of ethnocentrism and patriarchalism move in the direction of violence in a variety of forms (Schwartz 1997; Dempsey 2000; Weems 1995). Beyond that, there is no doubt that ideological commitments, for example, to the Jerusalem establishment and its dynasty and temple, pervade the text. In addition, there is no doubt that what began as land promise has become an enormous ideological claim that continues to operate in the contemporary world (Prior 1999).

It is evident, moreover, that ideology not only *pervades the text* so that the text before us in the Old Testament is no innocent text. It is equally clear that ideology *pervades interpretation of the text* so that there are no innocent interpretations and no innocent interpreters. Presently scholars are noting the long-standing practice of hegemonic interpretation, which sustains white, male, Western, colonial ways of articulating the text that have been clearly allied with dominant social interests and have made use of historical criticism to serve those ends (Sugirtharajah 2002). Of course, neither the text makers nor subsequent interpretation of the text can fully step outside the interests and passions of those engaged in such work. A recognition of ideology in interpretation nonetheless invites (a) self-critical awareness of how much interest shapes reading, and (b) recognition that our most passionate readings are partisan and have no claim to absoluteness (Dube Shomanah 2000).

The reader will, in the end, ponder the odd reality that the biblical text is recognized to be *inspired by God* and *permeated by ideology*, two claims that live in deep and inescapable tension. It is possible to approach the text in a precritical innocence and take the text as it comes, simply as God's inspired word. It is possible, conversely, to take the text skeptically as a statement of ideology that is not to be trusted. To be sure, some interpreters operate, respectively, either in innocence or in skepticism. The tradition of Reformed theology reflected in this book takes the more demanding work of acknowledging the reality of both God's inspiration and human ideology. Such an interpretive tradition understands that *imaginative interpretation* is an endless critical process of seeking to hear faithfully God's word of address as it is mediated in, with, and under human interest-saturated utterance.

We may notice that Jeremiah 1:1–2 is a clear acknowledgment of this problematic that permeates Scripture:

> The words of Jeremiah son of Hilkiah, of the priests who were in Anathoth in the land of Benjamin, to whom the word of the Lord came in the days of King Josiah son of Amon of Judah, in the thirteenth year of his reign.

It is said first that the book of Jeremiah that follows is "the words of Jeremiah," that is, human speech from the prophet. But the prophet is one "to whom the word of the Lord came." This twofold formulation seems to make clear that the book of Jeremiah that follows the superscription is itself not "the word of the Lord," but is a human word from one addressed by a divine word. We may imagine (!) that Jeremiah was addressed, summoned, and dispatched by the inscrutable utterance of YHWH (see 1:4–10); what Jeremiah uttered on the basis of divine address, however, is human utterance filtered through and shaped by human reality, in this case that the prophet is "of the priests who were in Anathoth" (R. Wilson 1980, 231–51). In the case of Jeremiah as everywhere else in Scripture, that is what is given to us in the text. The interplay of human speech and divine word requires a faithful attentiveness matched by human critical awareness, both of which are indispensable for receiving what is given in the text as new truth.

It is clear that all four of these dimensions—interpretation, imagination, inspiration, and ideology—pertain both to the *formation of the text* as it reached canonical completion and the *interpretive practice of the text* in the ongoing community of faith.

The framers of the text kept interpreting and reinterpreting in order to make new texts; subsequent church practice in preaching and teaching, moreover, is endlessly interpretive. The framers of the text practice immense imagination in making new connections given the repertoire before them; and church practice in preaching and teaching is endlessly imaginative, even by those who propose that they are neither interpretive nor imaginative, but only "giving the plain meaning of the text."

The framers of the text are led by God's Spirit, we confess, to go beyond self into God's truth; we confess as well that faithful, imaginative interpretation is led by the same spirit of truth.

The framers of the text are human persons permeated with context, perspective, interest, and passion through which divine inspiration receives concrete articulation; no less so, subsequent interpretation is shot through with ideology. Thus the complexity of the process of framing the text is matched by the complexity in the interpretive processes, both complexities inescapable because the Bible is a gift of the Holy God, who escapes all our explanatory possibilities.

7. The canon is a consensus presentation of the way in which YHWH's self-disclosive truth has been and is articulated among us. The canon in principle bespeaks a norm for church practice in interpretation. We must recognize, however, that the normative canon is immensely open and allows for great latitude and diversity in church interpretation and practice, a fact powerfully attested in the life of the church (Albertz 1994; Gerstenberger 2002). There is indeed a normative quality to the canon, but a quite open one. We might wish the canon were more disciplined and unambiguous, but it is not. And the reason it is not is that the inscrutable God given here in the text does not fully conform to any of our certitudes, even those of the most settled orthodoxy.

The canon is a gift from God that mediates God's self-disclosure to us. While the canon is a book we hold in our hands, the self-disclosure of God given there is not so readily held and possessed by us, for that self-disclosure is a personal, interpersonal matter that is not fully reduced to any exacting formulation. Thus if we take the Bible seriously on its own terms, we must reckon with clear teaching that reflects the certain will of YHWH, but a clear teaching always elusive because the God whom we trust remains hidden even in self-disclosure.

In the end, then, the Bible yields no flat certitudes of the kind that can be found in modern, technological society. The Bible yields the truthfulness of YHWH, a truthfulness that insists, demands, and transforms, and therefore Bible study is a life-changing, life-risking venture. That strange truthfulness of God is not given flatly, but only by living with and attending to the One who is attested in the text. The Bible is not a drop-in activity; rather it requires a dwelling and a tending over time, a dwelling done in trustful innocence, an attending done in critical awareness. Raymond Brown has nicely situated serious, ready engagement with the Bible: "After all, in the Scriptures we are in our Father's house where the children are permitted to play" (R. Brown 1955, 28).

The Reformed tradition of theological interpretation understands that the church is always being *re-formed*. One aspect of that venture is to *re-read* Scripture, for *re-forming* and *re-reading* inescapably go together. For the sake of the church and its mission, readers in this tradition dwell in and attend to Scripture—innocently, critically, obediently, and hopefully.

Bibliography

Albertz, Rainer. 1994. *A History of Israelite Religion in the Old Testament Period.* Translated by John Bowden. Old Testament Library. Louisville, Ky.: Westminster John Knox.

Alter, Robert. 1981. *The Art of Biblical Narrative.* New York: Basic Books.

———. 1985. *The Art of Biblical Poetry.* New York: Basic Books.

———. 1996. *Genesis: Translation and Commentary.* New York: Norton.

———. 2004. *The Five Books of Moses: Translation with Commentary.* New York: Norton.

Anderson, Bernhard W. 1962. "Exodus Typology in Second Isaiah." In *Israel's Prophetic Heritage: Essays in Honor of James Muilenburg,* edited by Bernhard W. Anderson and Walter Harrelson, 177–95. New York: Harper.

———. 1976 . "Exodus and Covenant in Second Isaiah and Prophetic Tradition." In *Magnalia Dei, the Mighty Acts of God: Essays on the Bible and Archaeology in Memory of G. Ernest Wright,* edited by Frank Moore Cross, Werner E. Lemke, and Patrick D. Miller, 339–60. Garden City, N.Y.: Doubleday.

———. 1979. *The Living Word of the Bible.* Philadelphia: Westminster.

———. 1983. *Out of the Depths: The Psalms Speak for Us Today.* 2nd ed. Philadelphia: Westminster.

———, ed. 1989. *The Books of the Bible.* Vol. 1, *The Old Testament/The Hebrew Bible.* New York: Scribner's.

———. 1994. *From Creation to New Creation: Old Testament Perspectives.* Overtures to Biblical Theology. Minneapolis: Fortress.

Apple, Max. 1987. "Joshua." In *Congregation: Contemporary Writers Read the Jewish Bible,* edited by David Rosenberg, 61–69. San Diego: Harcourt Brace Jovanovich.

Auerbach, Erich. 1953. "Odysseus' Scar." In *Mimesis: The Representation of Reality in Western Literature,* translated by Willard Trask, 3–23. Princeton: Princeton University Press.

Bailey, Lloyd R. 1989. *Noah: The Person and the Story in History and Tradition.* Columbia, S.C.: University of South Carolina Press.

Bal, Mieke. 2008. *Loving Yusuf: Conceptual Travels from Present to Past.* Chicago: University of Chicago Press.

Balentine, Samuel E. 1983. *The Hidden God: The Hiding of the Face of God in the Old Testament*. Oxford Theological Monographs. Oxford: Oxford University Press.

———. 1993. *Prayer in the Hebrew Bible: The Drama of Divine-Human Dialogue*. Overtures to Biblical Theology. Minneapolis: Fortress.

———. 1999. *The Torah's Vision of Worship*. Overtures to Biblical Theology. Minneapolis: Fortress.

Barr, James. 1968–1969. "The Image of God in the Book of Genesis: A Study of Terminology." *Bulletin of the John Rylands Library* 51:11–26.

———. 2000. *History and Ideology in the Old Testament: Biblical Studies at the End of a Millennium*. New York: Oxford University Press.

Barth, Karl. 1957. *The Word of God and the Word of Man*. Translated by Douglas Horton. Reprint, New York: Harper & Row.

Barton, John. 1979. "Natural Law and Poetic Justice in the Old Testament." *Journal of Theological Studies* 30:1–14.

———. 1980. *Amos's Oracles against the Nations: A Study of Amos 1.3–2.5*. Society for the Study of the Old Testament Monograph Series 6. Cambridge: Cambridge University Press.

———. 1988. *Oracles of God: Perceptions of Ancient Prophecy in Israel after the Exile*. New York: Oxford University Press.

Bauckham, Richard. 2002. *God and the Crisis of Freedom: Biblical and Contemporary Perspectives*. Louisville, Ky.: Westminster John Knox.

Beal, Timothy K. 1997. *The Book of Hiding: Gender, Ethnicity, Annihilation, and Esther*. Biblical Limits. New York: Routledge.

———. 1999. "Esther." In *Ruth and Esther*, by Tod Linafelt and Timothy K. Beal, v–121 [second pagination]. Berit Olam. Collegeville, Minn.: Liturgical Press.

———. 2011. *The Rise and Fall of the Bible: The Unexpected History of an Accidental Book*. Boston: Houghton Mifflin Harcourt.

Bellis, Alice Ogden. 1995. *The Structure and Composition of Jeremiah 50:2–51:58*. Lewiston, N.Y.: Mellen Biblical Press.

Belo, Fernando. 1981. *A Materialist Reading of the Gospel of Mark*. Translated by Matthew J. O'Connell. Maryknoll, N.Y.: Orbis.

Berger, Peter L. 1966. *The Social Construction of Reality: A Treatise in the Sociology of Knowledge*. Garden City, N.Y.: Anchor.

Berlin, Adele. 1985. *The Dynamics of Biblical Parallelism*. Bloomington: Indiana University Press.

———. 2000. "Numinous *Nomos*: On the Relationship between Narrative and Law." In *"A Wise and Discerning Mind": Essays in Honor of Burke O. Long*, edited by Saul M. Olyan and Robert C. Culley, 25–31. Brown Judaic Studies 325. Providence: Brown Judaic Studies.

Berquist, Jon L. 1995. *Judaism in Persia's Shadow: A Social and Historical Approach*. Minneapolis: Fortress.

Bird, Phyllis A. 1981. "Male and Female He Created Them: Genesis 1:27b in the Context of the Priestly Account of Creation." *Harvard Theological Review* 74:129–59.

———. 1997. *Missing Persons and Mistaken Identities: Women and Gender in Ancient Israel*. Overtures to Biblical Theology. Minneapolis: Fortress.

Blenkinsopp, Joseph. 1977. *Prophecy and Canon: A Contribution to the Study of Jewish Origins*. Notre Dame, Ind.: University of Notre Dame Press.

———. 1992. *The Pentateuch: An Introduction to the First Five Books of the Bible*. Anchor Bible Reference Library 5. New York: Doubleday.

Block, Daniel I. 1997. *The Book of Ezekiel 1–24*. New International Commentary on the Old Testament. Grand Rapids: Eerdmans.

Bonhoeffer, Dietrich. 1970. *Psalms: The Prayer Book of the Bible*. Translated by James H. Burtness. Minneapolis: Augsburg.

Børresen, Kari Elisabeth. 1995. *The Image of God: Gender Models in Judaeo-Christian Tradition*. Minneapolis: Fortress.

Boström, Lennart. 1990. *The God of the Sages: The Portrayal of God in the Book of Proverbs*. Coniectanea Biblica Old Testament Series 29. Stockholm: Almqvist & Wiksell International.

Boyce, Richard Nelson. 1988. *The Cry to God in the Old Testament*. Society of Biblical Literature Dissertation Series 103. Atlanta: Scholars Press.

Bright, John. 2000. *A History of Israel*. 4th ed. Louisville, Ky.: Westminster John Knox.

Brooks, Roger, and John Joseph Collins. 1990. *Hebrew Bible or Old Testament? Studying the Bible in Judaism and Christianity*. Notre Dame, Ind.: University of Notre Dame Press.

Brown, David. 1999. *Tradition and Imagination: Revelation and Change*. New York: Oxford University Press.

———. 2000. *Discipleship and Imagination: Christian Tradition and Truth*. Oxford: Oxford University Press.

Brown, Raymond E. 1955. *The Sensus Plenior of Sacred Scripture*. Baltimore: St. Mary's University Press.

———. 1977. *The Birth of the Messiah: A Commentary on the Infancy Narratives in Matthew and Luke*. Garden City, N.Y.: Doubleday.

Brueggemann, Walter. 1981. "Social Criticism and Social Vision in the Deuteronomic Formula of the Judges." In *Die Botschaft und die Boten: Festschrift für Hans Walter Wolff zum 70. Geburtstag*, edited by Jörg Jeremias and Lothar Perlitt, 101–14. Neukirchen-Vluyn: Neukirchener Verlag.

———. 1984. *The Message of the Psalms: A Theological Commentary*. Augsburg Old Testament Studies. Minneapolis: Augsburg.

———. 1987. "The Book of Jeremiah: Portrait of a Prophet." In *Interpreting the Prophets*, edited by James Luther Mays and Paul J. Achtemeier, 113–29. Philadelphia: Fortress.

———. 1988. *Israel's Praise: Doxology against Idolatry and Ideology*. Philadelphia: Fortress.

———. 1990a. *First and Second Samuel*. Interpretation. Atlanta: John Knox.

———. 1990b. *Power, Providence, and Personality: Biblical Insight into Life and Ministry*. Louisville, Ky.: Westminster/John Knox.

———. 1990c. "The Social Significance of Solomon as a Patron of Wisdom." In *The Sage in Israel and the Ancient Near East*, edited by John G. Gammie and Leo G. Perdue, 117–32. Winona Lake, Ind.: Eisenbrauns.

———. 1991. *Abiding Astonishment: Psalms, Modernity, and the Making of History*. Literary Currents in Biblical Interpretation. Louisville, Ky.: Westminster/John Knox.

———. 1992. *Old Testament Theology: Essays on Structure, Theme, and Text*. Edited by Patrick Miller. Minneapolis: Fortress.

———. 1995a. "Pharaoh as Vassal: A Study of a Political Metaphor." *Catholic Biblical Quarterly* 57:27–51.

———. 1995b. *The Psalms and the Life of Faith*. Minneapolis: Fortress.

———. 1997. *Theology of the Old Testament: Testimony, Dispute, Advocacy*. Minneapolis: Fortress.

———. 1998. "Exodus in the Plural." In *Many Voices, One God: Being Faithful in a Pluralistic World: In Honor of Shirley Guthrie*, edited by Walter Brueggemann and George W. Stroup, 15–34. Louisville, Ky.: Westminster John Knox.

———. 2001a. *Deuteronomy*. Abingdon Old Testament Commentaries 1. Nashville: Abingdon.

———. 2001b. "Introduction." In *Old Testament Theology*, by Gerhard von Rad, ix–xxxi. Reprint, Louisville, Ky.: Westminster John Knox.

———. 2001c. "Dialogue between Incommensurate Partners: Prospects for Common Testimony." *Journal of Ecumenical Studies* 38, no. 4:383–98.

———. 2002a. *Ichabod toward Home: The Journey of God's Glory*. Grand Rapids: Eerdmans.

———. 2002b. "Meditation upon the Abyss: The Book of Jeremiah." *Word and World* 22:340–50.

Brueggemann, Walter, Sharon Parks, and Thomas H. Groome. 1986. *To Act Justly, Love Tenderly, Walk Humbly: An Agenda for Ministers*. New York: Paulist Press.

Brueggemann, Walter, William C. Placher, and Brian K. Blount. 2002. *Struggling with Scripture*. Louisville, Ky.: Westminster John Knox.

Bryant, David J. 1989. *Faith and the Play of Imagination: On the Role of Imagination in Religion*. Studies in American Biblical Hermeneutics 5. Macon, Ga.: Mercer University Press.

Buber, Martin. 1968. *On the Bible: Eighteen Studies*. Edited by Nahum N. Glatzer. New York: Schocken.

Bultmann, Rudolf. 1963. "The Significance of the Old Testament for the Christian Faith." Translated by Bernhard W. Anderson. In *The Old Testament and Christian Faith: A Theological Discussion*, edited by Bernhard W. Anderson, 8–35. New York: Harper & Row.

Callaway, Mary. 1986. *Sing, O Barren One: A Study in Comparative Midrash*. Society of Biblical Literature Dissertation Series 91. Missoula, Mont.: Scholars Press.

Calvin, John. 1990. "I Greet Thee Who My Sure Redeemer Art." In *Presbyterian Hymnal: Hymns, Psalms, and Spiritual Songs*, 457. Louisville, Ky.: Westminster/John Knox.

———. 1994. *Institutes of the Christian Religion*. 2 vols. Library of Christian Classics. Reprint, Philadelphia: Westminster, 1960.

Camp, Claudia V. 2000. *Wise, Strange, and Holy: The Strange Woman and the Making of the Bible*. Journal for the Study of the Old Testament Supplement Series 320. Sheffield: Sheffield Academic Press.

Campbell, Antony F., and Mark A. O'Brien. 2000. *Unfolding the Deuteronomistic History: Origins, Upgrades, Present Text*. Minneapolis: Fortress.

Carlson, Rolf August. 1964. *David, the Chosen King: A Traditio-Historical Approach to the Second Book of Samuel*. Stockholm: Almqvist & Wiksell.

Carroll, Robert P. 1986. *Jeremiah: A Commentary*. Old Testament Library. Philadelphia: Westminster.

———. 1991. *Wolf in the Sheepfold: The Bible as a Problem for Christianity*. London: SPCK.

Cheney, Marvin L. 1989. "Joshua." In *The Books of the Bible*. Vol. 1, *The Old Testament/The Hebrew Bible*, edited by Bernhard W. Anderson, 103–12. New York: Scribner's.

Childs, Brevard S. 1971. "Psalm Titles and Midrashic Exegesis." *Journal of Semitic Studies* 16:137–50.

———. 1979. *Introduction to the Old Testament as Scripture*. Philadelphia: Fortress.

———. 1993. *Biblical Theology of the Old and New Testaments: Theological Reflection on the Christian Bible*. Minneapolis: Fortress.

———. 2001. *Isaiah*. Old Testament Library. Louisville, Ky.: Westminster John Knox.

Clements, Ronald E. 1977. "Patterns in the Prophetic Canon." In *Canon and Authority: Essays in Old Testament Religion and Theology*, edited by George W. Coats and Burke O. Long, 42–55. Philadelphia: Fortress.

———. 1982. "The Unity of the Book of Isaiah." *Interpretation* 36:117–29.

———. 1985. "Beyond Tradition-History." *Journal for the Study of the Old Testament* 31:95–113.

Clines, David J. A. 1984. *The Esther Scroll: The Story of the Story*. Journal for the Study of the Old Testament Supplement Series 30. Sheffield: JSOT Press.

———. 1994. "Why Is There a Song of Songs and What Does It Do to You If You Read It?" *Jian Dao* 1:3–27.

———. 1998. "Hosea 2: Structure and Interpretation." In *On the Way to the Postmodern: Old Testament Essays 1967–1998*, 1:293–313. Journal for the Study of the Old Testament Supplement Series 292–93. Sheffield: Sheffield Academic Press.

Coats, George W., and Burke O. Long, eds. 1977. *Canon and Authority: Essays in Old Testament Religion and Theology*. Philadelphia: Fortress.

Cochrane, Charles Norris. 1957. *Christianity and Classical Culture: A Study of Thought and Action from Augustus to Augustine*. New York: Oxford University Press.

Collins, John Joseph. 1987. *The Apocalyptic Imagination: An Introduction to the Jewish Matrix of Christianity*. New York: Crossroad.

Crenshaw, James L. 1974. "Wisdom." In *Old Testament Form Criticism*, edited by John H. Hayes, 225–64. San Antonio: Trinity University Press.

———. 1981. *Old Testament Wisdom: An Introduction*. Atlanta: John Knox.

———. 1989. "Proverbs." In *The Books of the Bible*. Vol. 1, *The Old Testament/The Hebrew Bible*, edited by Bernhard W. Anderson, 223–30. New York: Scribner's.

———. 1995. *Urgent Advice and Probing Questions: Collected Writings on Old Testament Wisdom*. Atlanta: Mercer University Press.

Croly, George. 1982. "Spirit of God, Descend upon My Heart." In *Lutheran Book of Worship*, 486. Minneapolis: Augsburg.

Cross, Frank Moore. 1973. *Canaanite Myth and Hebrew Epic: Essays in the History of the Religion of Israel*. Cambridge, Mass.: Harvard University Press.

Crüsemann, Frank. 1984. "The Unchangeable World: The 'Crisis of Wisdom' in Koheleth." In *God of the Lowly: Socio-Historical Interpretations of the Bible*, edited by Willy Schottroff and Wolfgang Stegemann. Translated by Matthew J. O'Connell, 57–77. Maryknoll, N.Y.: Orbis.

———. 1996. *The Torah: Theology and Social History of Old Testament Law*. Translated by Allan W. Mahnke. Minneapolis: Fortress.

Davies, G. I. 1998. "Were There Schools in Ancient Israel?" In *Wisdom in Ancient Israel: Essays in Honour of J. A. Emerton*, edited by John Day, Robert P. Gordon, and H. G. M. Williamson, 199–211. Cambridge: Cambridge University Press.

Davies, Philip R. 1998. *Daniel*. Old Testament Guides. Sheffield: Sheffield Academic Press.

Davies, Philip R., and David J. A. Clines, eds. 1993. *Among the Prophets: Language, Image and Structure in the Prophetic Writings*. Journal for the Study of the Old Testament Supplement Series 144. Sheffield: JSOT Press.

Day, John, Robert P. Gordon, and H. G. M. Williamson, eds. 1998. *Wisdom in Ancient Israel: Essays in Honour of J. A. Emerton*. Cambridge: Cambridge University Press.

Dempsey, Carol J. 2000. *The Prophets: A Liberation-Critical Reading.* A Liberation-Critical Reading of the Old Testament, ed. Alice Laffey. Minneapolis: Fortress.

Dever, William G. 2001. *What Did the Biblical Writers Know, and When Did They Know It? What Archaeology Can Tell Us about the Reality of Ancient Israel.* Grand Rapids: Eerdmans.

Diamond, A. R. 1987. *The Confessions of Jeremiah in Context: Scenes of Prophetic Drama.* Journal for the Study of the Old Testament Supplement Series 45. Sheffield: JSOT Press.

Dobbs-Allsopp, F. W. 2002. *Lamentations.* Interpretation. Louisville: John Knox.

———. 2009. "Poetry, Hebrew." Pages 550–58 in vol. 4 of *The New Interpreter's Dictionary of the Bible*, edited by Katharine Doob Sakenfeld. Nashville: Abingdon.

Douglas, Mary. 1996. *Purity and Danger: An Analysis of the Concepts of Pollution and Taboo.* 1966. Reprint, London: Routledge.

———. 1999. "Justice as the Cornerstone: An Interpretation of Leviticus 18–20." *Interpretation* 53:341–50.

Dozeman, Thomas B., and Konrad Schmid, eds. 2006. *A Farewell to the Yahwist? The Composition of the Pentateuch in Recent European Interpretation.* Society of Biblical Literature Symposium Series 34. Atlanta: Society of Biblical Literature.

Dresner, Samuel H. 1994. *Rachel.* Minneapolis: Fortress.

Dube Shomanah, Musa W. 2000. *Postcolonial Feminist Interpretation of the Bible.* St. Louis: Chalice Press.

Eskenazi, Tamara Cohn. 1998. *In an Age of Prose: A Literary Approach to Ezra-Nehemiah.* Society of Biblical Literature Monograph Series 36. Atlanta: Scholars Press.

Fackenheim, Emil. 1980. "New Hearts and the Old Covenant: On Some Possibilities of a Fraternal Jewish-Christian Reading of the Jewish Bible Today." In *The Divine Helmsman: Studies on God's Control of Human Events*, edited by Lou H. Silberman, James L. Crenshaw, and Samuel Sandmel, 191–205. New York: Ktav.

Fewell, Danna Nolan, and David Gunn. 1993. *Gender, Power, and Promise: The Subject of the Bible's First Story.* Nashville: Abingdon.

Finkelstein, Israel, and Neil Asher Silberman. 2001. *The Bible Unearthed: Archaeology's New Vision of Ancient Israel and the Origin of Its Sacred Texts.* New York: Free Press.

Fisch, Harold. 1988. *Poetry with a Purpose: Biblical Poetics and Interpretation.* Indiana Studies in Biblical Literature. Bloomington: Indiana University Press.

Fishbane, Michael. 1970. "The Treaty Background of Amos 1:11 and Related Matters." *Journal of Biblical Literature* 89, no. 3:313–18.

———. 1979. *Text and Texture: Close Readings of Selected Biblical Texts.* New York: Schocken.

Flanagan, James. 1983. "Social Transformation and Ritual in 2 Samuel 6." In *The Word of the Lord Shall Go Forth: Essays in Honor of David Noel Freedman in Celebration of His Sixtieth Birthday*, edited by Carol L. Meyers and Michael Patrick O'Connor, 361–72. Winona Lake, Ind.: Eisenbrauns.

Fohrer, Georg. 1974. "The Righteous Man in Job 31." In *Essays in Old Testament Ethics (J. Philip Hyatt, In Memoriam)*, edited by James L. Crenshaw and John T. Willis, 3–22. New York: Ktav.

Fokkelman, J. P. 1999. *Reading Biblical Narrative.* Louisville, Ky.: Westminster John Knox.

Freedman, David N. 1975. "Son of Man, Can These Bones Live?" *Interpretation* 29:171–86.

———. 1991. *The Unity of the Hebrew Bible*. Distinguished Senior Faculty Lecture Series. Ann Arbor: University of Michigan Press.

Fretheim, Terence E. 1985. "Divine Foreknowledge, Divine Constancy, and the Rejection of Saul's Kingship." *Catholic Biblical Quarterly* 47:595–602.

———. 1991. "The Plagues as Ecological Signs of Historical Disaster." *Journal of Biblical Literature* 110:385–96.

Friedman, Richard Elliott. 1995. *The Disappearance of God: A Divine Mystery*. Boston: Little, Brown.

———. 1997. *Who Wrote the Bible?* 2nd ed. San Francisco: HarperSanFrancisco.

———. 1998. *The Hidden Book in the Bible*. San Francisco: HarperSanFrancisco.

Frye, Northrop. 2000. *Anatomy of Criticism: Four Essays*. 1957. Reprint, Princeton, N.J.: Princeton University Press.

Frymer-Kensky, Tikva. 2002. *Reading the Women of the Bible*. New York: Schocken.

Gammie, John G. 1989. *Holiness in Israel*. Overtures to Biblical Theology. Minneapolis: Fortress.

Gammie, John G., and Leo G. Perdue, eds. 1990. *The Sage in Israel and the Ancient Near East*. Winona Lake, Ind.: Eisenbrauns.

Gerstenberger, Erhard. 1974. "Psalms." In *Old Testament Form Criticism*, edited by John H. Hayes, 179–223. San Antonio: Trinity University Press.

———. 2002. *Theologies in the Old Testament*. Translated by John Bowden. Minneapolis: Fortress.

Gordis, Robert. 1974. *The Song of Songs and Lamentations: A Study, Modern Translation, and Commentary*. New York: Ktav.

Gordon, R. P. 1984. *1 and 2 Samuel*. Old Testament Guides. Sheffield: JSOT Press.

Gottwald, Norman K. 1979. *The Tribes of Yahweh: A Sociology of the Religion of Liberated Israel, 1250–1050 B.C.E.* Maryknoll, N.Y.: Orbis.

Goulder, M. D. 1982. *The Psalms of the Sons of Korah*. Journal for the Study of the Old Testament Supplement Series 20. Sheffield: JSOT Press.

Green, Garrett. 1989. *Imagining God: Theology and the Religious Imagination*. San Francisco: Harper & Row.

Greenberg, Moshe. 1983. *Biblical Prose Prayer: As a Window to the Popular Religion of Ancient Israel*. Taubman Lectures in Jewish Studies, Sixth Series. Berkeley: University of California Press.

———. 1997. *Ezekiel 21–37: A New Translation with Introduction and Commentary*. Anchor Bible 22A. New York: Doubleday.

Gunkel, Hermann. 1997. *Genesis*. Translated by Mark E. Biddle. Macon, Ga.: Mercer University Press.

Gunkel, Hermann, and Joachim Begrich. 1998. *Introduction to Psalms: The Genres of the Religious Lyric of Israel*. Translated by James D. Nogalski. Mercer Library of Biblical Studies. Macon, Ga.: Mercer University Press.

Gunn, David. 1980. *The Fate of King Saul: An Interpretation of a Biblical Story*. Journal for the Study of the Old Testament Supplement Series 14. Sheffield: JSOT Press.

———, ed. 1991. *Narrative and Novella in Samuel: Studies by Hugo Gressmann and Other Scholars 1906–1923*, translated by David E. Orton. Journal for the Study of the Old Testament Supplement Series 116. Sheffield: Sheffield Academic Press.

———. 1998. "Colonialism and the Vagaries of Scripture: Te Kooti in Canaan (a Story of Bible and Dispossession in Aotearoa/New Zealand)." In *God in the Fray: A Tribute to Walter Brueggemann*, edited by Tod Linafelt and Timothy K. Beal, 127–42. Minneapolis: Fortress.

_____. 2005. *Judges*. Blackwell Bible Commentaries. Oxford: Blackwell.

Gutiérrez, Gustavo. 1987. *On Job: God-Talk and the Suffering of the Innocent*. Translated by Matthew J. O'Connell. Maryknoll, N.Y.: Orbis.

Hall, Douglas John. 2001. "Despair as Pervasive Ailment." In *Hope for the World: Mission in a Global Context: Papers from the Campbell Seminar*, edited by Walter Brueggemann, 83–93. Louisville, Ky.: Westminster John Knox.

Halpern, Baruch. 2001. *David's Secret Demons: Messiah, Murderer, Traitor, King*. Bible in Its World. Grand Rapids: Eerdmans.

Hamilton, Jeffries M. 1992. *Social Justice and Deuteronomy: The Case of Deuteronomy 15*. Society of Biblical Literature Dissertation Series 136. Atlanta: Scholars Press.

Hanson, Paul D. 1975. *The Dawn of Apocalyptic*. Philadelphia: Fortress.

_____. 1977. "The Theological Significance of Contradiction within the Book of the Covenant." In *Canon and Authority: Essays in Old Testament Religion and Theology*, edited by George W. Coats and Burke O. Long, 110–31. Philadelphia: Fortress.

Harrelson, Walter J. 1969. *From Fertility Cult to Worship*. Garden City, N.Y.: Anchor Books/Doubleday.

Hayes, John H., and James Maxwell Miller, eds. 1977. *Israelite and Judaean History*. Old Testament Library. Philadelphia: Westminster.

_____. 1986. *A History of Ancient Israel and Judah*. Philadelphia: Westminster.

Haynes, Stephen R. 2001. *Noah's Curse: The Biblical Justification of American Slavery*. New York: Oxford University Press.

Heschel, Abraham Joshua. 1962. *The Prophets*. New York: Harper & Row.

Hill, John. 1999. *Friend or Foe? The Figure of Babylon in the Book of Jeremiah*. Leiden: Brill.

Hillers, Delbert R. 1992. *Lamentations: A New Translation with Introduction and Commentary*. 2nd ed. Anchor Bible 7A. New York: Doubleday.

Holladay, William. 1986–1989. *Jeremiah: A Commentary on the Book of the Prophet Jeremiah*. Hermeneia. 2 vols. Philadelphia: Fortress.

_____. 1993. *The Psalms through Three Thousand Years: Prayerbook of a Cloud of Witnesses*. Minneapolis: Fortress.

Homer. 1990. *The Iliad*. Translated by Robert Fagles. New York: Penguin.

House, Paul R. 1990. *The Unity of the Twelve*. Bible and Literature Series 27. Sheffield: Almond Press.

Howard, Richard. 1987. "Esther." In *Congregation: Contemporary Writers Read the Jewish Bible*, edited by David Rosenberg, 406–17. San Diego: Harcourt Brace Jovanovich.

Humphreys, W. Lee. 1973. "Life-Style for Diaspora: A Study of the Tales of Esther and Daniel." *Journal of Biblical Literature* 92, no. 2:211–23.

Hurston, Zora Neale. 1991. *Moses, Man of the Mountain*. Reprint, New York: Harper-Collins, 1939.

Japhet, Sara. 1993. *1 and 2 Chronicles: A Commentary*. Old Testament Library. Louisville, Ky.: Westminster/John Knox.

Jobling, David. 1998. *1 Samuel*. Berit Olam. Collegeville, Minn.: Liturgical Press.

Johnson, Marshall D. 1988. *The Purpose of the Biblical Genealogies*. 2nd ed. Cambridge: Cambridge University Press.

Joyce, Paul. 1989. *Divine Initiative and Human Response in Ezekiel*. Journal for the Study of the Old Testament Supplement Series 51. Sheffield: JSOT Press.

Kaufman, Stephen A. 1978–1979. "The Structure of the Deuteronomic Law." *Maarav* 1/2:105–58.

Kawashima, Robert. 2004a. *Biblical Narrative and the Death of the Rhapsode*. Bloomington: Indiana University Press.

———. 2004b. "*Homo Faber* in J's Primeval History." *Zeitschrift für die alttestamentliche
Wissenschaft* 116:483–501.

———. 2010. "Sources and Redaction." In *Reading Genesis: Ten Methods*, edited by
Ronald Hendel, 47–70. Cambridge: Cambridge University Press.

Kearney, P. J. 1977. "The P Redaction of Exodus 25–40." *Zeitschrift für die alttestamentliche Wissenschaft* 89:375–86.

Kearney, Richard. 1988. *The Wake of Imagination: Toward a Postmodern Culture*. Minneapolis: University of Minnesota Press.

Knohl, Israel. 1995. *The Sanctuary of Silence: The Priestly Torah and the Holiness School*.
Minneapolis: Fortress.

Knoppers, Gary N., and J. Gordon McConville, eds. 2000. *Reconsidering Israel and
Judah: Recent Studies on the Deuteronomistic History*. Sources for Biblical and
Theological Study 8. Winona Lake, Ind.: Eisenbrauns.

Koch, Klaus. 1983a. "Is There a Doctrine of Retribution in the Old Testament?"
Translated by Thomas H. Trapp. In *Theodicy in the Old Testament*, edited by
James L. Crenshaw, 57–87. Issues in Religion and Theology 4. Philadelphia:
Fortress.

———. 1983b. *The Prophets I: The Assyrian Period*. Translated by Margaret Kohl. Philadelphia: Fortress.

Koosed, Jennifer. 2011. *Gleaning Ruth: A Biblical Heroine and Her Afterlives*. Columbia:
University of South Carolina Press.

Kraus, Hans-Joachim. 1986. *Theology of the Psalms*. Translated by Keith Crim. Minneapolis: Augsburg.

Kugel, James. 1981. *The Idea of Biblical Poetry: Parallelism and Its History*. Baltimore:
Johns Hopkins University Press.

Lacocque, André, and Paul Ricoeur. 1998. *Thinking Biblically: Exegetical and Herme-
neutical Studies*. Translated by David Pellauer. Chicago: University of Chicago
Press.

Landes, George M. 1967. "Kerygma of the Book of Jonah: The Contextual Interpretation of the Jonah Psalm." *Interpretation* 21:3–31.

———. 1974. "Creation Tradition in Proverbs 8:22–31 and Genesis 1." In *A Light
unto My Path: Old Testament Studies in Honor of Jacob M. Myers*, edited by Howard N. Bream, Ralph D. Heim, and Carey A. Moore, 279–93. Philadelphia:
Temple University Press.

Lapsley, Jacqueline E. 2000. *Can These Bones Live? The Problem of the Moral Self in the
Book of Ezekiel*. Beihefte zur Zeitschrift für die alttestamentliche Wissenschaft
301. Berlin: de Gruyter.

Lemaire, André. 1990. "The Sage in School and Temple." In *The Sage in Israel and
the Ancient Near East*, edited by John G. Gammie and Leo G. Perdue, 165–81.
Winona Lake, Ind.: Eisenbrauns.

Levenson, Jon D. 1985. "Is There a Counterpart in the Hebrew Bible to New Testament Antisemitism?" *Journal of Ecumenical Studies* 22, no. 2:242–60.

———. 1987. *Sinai and Zion: An Entry into the Jewish Bible*. San Francisco: Harper &
Row.

———. 1988. *Creation and the Persistence of Evil: The Jewish Drama of Divine Omnipo-
tence*. San Francisco: Harper & Row.

———. 1993. *The Hebrew Bible, the Old Testament, and Historical Criticism: Jews and
Christians in Biblical Studies*. Louisville, Ky.: Westminster/John Knox.

————. 1996. "The Universal Horizon of Biblical Particularism." In *Ethnicity and the Bible*, edited by Mark G. Brett, 143–69. Leiden: Brill.

Linafelt, Tod. 1999. "Ruth." In *Ruth and Esther*, by Tod Linafelt and Timothy K. Beal, v–90 [first pagination]. Berit Olam. Collegeville, Minn.: Liturgical Press.

————. 2000. *Surviving Lamentations: Catastrophe, Lament, and Protest in the Afterlife of a Biblical Book.* Chicago: University of Chicago Press.

————. 2001. "The Refusal of a Conclusion in the Book of Lamentations." *Journal of Biblical Literature* 120, no. 2:340–43.

————. 2002. "Biblical Love Poetry (. . . and God)." *Journal of the American Academy of Religion* 70, no. 2:323–45.

————. 2006. "The Wizard of Uz: Job, Dorothy, and the Limits of the Sublime." *Biblical Interpretation* 14, nos. 1/2:94–110.

————. 2008. "Prolegomena to Meaning, or, What Is 'Literary' about the Torah?" *Theological Studies* 69, no. 1:62–79.

————. 2008. "Private Poetry and Public Eloquence in 2 Samuel 1:17–27: Hearing and Overhearing David's Lament for Jonathan and Saul." *Journal of Religion* 88, no. 4:497–526.

————. 2010. "Narrative and Poetic Art in the Book of Ruth." *Interpretation* 64:117–29.

Linafelt, Tod, Claudia V. Camp, and Timothy K. Beal, eds. 2010. *The Fate of King David: The Past and Present of a Biblical Icon.* New York: T & T Clark.

Lindström, Fredrik. 1994. *Suffering and Sin: Interpretations of Illness in the Individual Complaint Psalms.* Coniectanea biblica: Old Testament Series 37. Stockholm: Almqvist & Wiksell International.

Little, Sara. 1983. *To Set One's Heart: Belief and Teaching in the Church.* Atlanta: John Knox.

Lohfink, Norbert. 1982. "Distribution of the Functions of Power." In *Great Themes from the Old Testament*, 55–75. Translated by Ronald Walls. Edinburgh: T. & T. Clark.

————. 1991. *The Covenant Never Revoked: Biblical Reflections on Christian-Jewish Dialogue.* Translated by John J. Scullion. New York: Paulist Press.

Longman, Tremper. 2001. *Song of Songs.* New International Commentary on the Old Testament. Grand Rapids: Eerdmans.

Lowth, Robert. 2005. *Lectures on the Sacred Poetry of the Hebrews.* 1839. Reprint, Port Chester, N.Y.: Elibron Classics.

Marks, Herbert. 1987. "The Twelve Prophets." In *The Literary Guide to the Bible*, edited by Robert Alter and Frank Kermode, 207–33. Cambridge, Mass.: Belknap Press of Harvard University Press.

Mays, James Luther. 1987. "The Place of the Torah-Psalms in the Psalter." *Journal of Biblical Literature* 106, no. 1:3–12.

————. 1994. *The Lord Reigns: A Theological Handbook to the Psalms.* Louisville, Ky.: Westminster John Knox.

McBride, S. Dean. 1987. "Polity of the Covenant People: The Book of Deuteronomy." *Interpretation* 41:229–44.

McCann, J. Clinton. 1993. *The Shape and Shaping of the Psalter.* Journal for the Study of the Old Testament Supplement Series 159. Sheffield: JSOT Press.

McCarthy, Dennis J. 1973. "Inauguration of Monarchy in Israel: A Form-Critical Study of 1 Samuel 8–12." *Interpretation* 27:401–12.

McKane, William. 1970. *Proverbs: A New Approach.* Old Testament Library. Philadelphia: Westminster.

————. 1986. *A Critical and Exegetical Commentary on Jeremiah.* Vol. 1, *Introduction and Commentary on Jeremiah I–XXV*. International Critical Commentary. Edinburgh: T. & T. Clark.

McKeating, Henry. 1993. *Ezekiel*. Old Testament Guides. Sheffield: JSOT Press.

McKenzie, Steven L. 2000. *King David: A Biography*. New York: Oxford University Press.

McKim, Donald K., ed. 1998. *Historical Handbook of Major Biblical Interpreters*. Downers Grove, Ill.: InterVarsity Press.

Mendenhall, George E. 1973. *The Tenth Generation: The Origins of the Biblical Tradition*. Baltimore: Johns Hopkins University Press.

Merkin, Daphne. 1987. "Ecclesiastes." In *Congregation: Contemporary Writers Read the Jewish Bible*, edited by David Rosenberg, 393–405. San Diego: Harcourt Brace Jovanovich.

Mettinger, Tryggve N. D. 1983. *A Farewell to the Servant Songs: A Critical Examination of an Exegetical Axiom*. Scripta Minora 3. Lund, Swed.: Gleerup.

Miles, Jack. 1995. *God: A Biography*. New York: Simon & Schuster.

Milgrom, Jacob. 1989. "Leviticus." In *The Books of the Bible*. Vol. 1, *The Old Testament/ The Hebrew Bible*, edited by Bernhard W. Anderson, 63–70. New York: Scribner's.

———. 2004. *Leviticus: A Book of Ritual and Ethics*. Continental Commentary. Minneapolis: Fortress.

Miller, Patrick D. 1973. *The Divine Warrior in Early Israel*. Harvard Semitic Monographs 5. Cambridge, Mass.: Harvard University Press.

———. 1978. *Genesis 1–11: Studies in Structure and Theme*. Journal for the Study of the Old Testament Supplement Series 8. Sheffield: JSOT Press.

———. 1982. *Sin and Judgment in the Prophets: A Stylistic and Theological Analysis*. Society of Biblical Literature Monograph Series 27. Chico, Calif.: Scholars Press.

———. 1993. "The Beginning of the Psalter." In *The Shape and Shaping of the Psalter*, edited by J. Clinton McCann, 83–92. Journal for the Study of the Old Testament Supplement Series 159. Sheffield: JSOT Press.

———. 1994. *They Cried to the Lord: The Form and Theology of Biblical Prayer*. Minneapolis: Fortress.

———. 1995. "Creation and Covenant." In *Biblical Theology: Problems and Perspectives: In Honor of J. Christiaan Beker*, edited by Steven John Kraftchick, Charles Davison Myers, and Ben C. Ollenburger, 155–68. Nashville: Abingdon.

———. 2000. *Israelite Religion and Biblical Theology: Collected Essays*. Journal for the Study of the Old Testament Supplement Series 267. Sheffield: Sheffield Academic Press.

Miller, Patrick D., and J. J. M. Roberts. 1977. *The Hand of the Lord: A Reassessment of the "Ark Narrative" of 1 Samuel*. Baltimore: Johns Hopkins University Press.

Mirsky, Mark. 1987. "Daniel." In *Congregation: Contemporary Writers Read the Jewish Bible*, edited by David Rosenberg, 435–55. San Diego: Harcourt Brace Jovanovich.

Mitchell, Stephen. 1987. "Lamentations." In *Congregation: Contemporary Writers Read the Jewish Bible*, edited by David Rosenberg, 383–92. San Diego: Harcourt Brace Jovanovich.

Moberly, R. W. L. 1992. *The Old Testament of the Old Testament: Patriarchal Narratives and Mosaic Yahwism*. Overtures to Biblical Theology. Minneapolis: Fortress.

Moor, Johannes C. de, and Harry F. van Rooy, eds. 2000. *Past, Present, Future: The Deuteronomistic History and the Prophets*. Oudtestamentische Studiën 44. Leiden: Brill.

Morgan, Donn F. 1990. *Between Text and Community: The "Writings" in Canonical Interpretation*. Minneapolis: Fortress.

Mowinckel, Sigmund. 1961. *Psalmenstudien*. Vol. 2, *Das Thronbesteigungsfest Jahwäs und der Ursprung der Eschatologie*. 1924. Reprint, 2 vols. in 1. Amsterdam: P. Schippers.

Murphy, Roland Edmund. 1979. "Qohelet's 'Quarrel' with the Fathers." In *From Faith to Faith: Essays in Honor of Donald G. Miller on His Seventieth Birthday*, edited by Dikran Y. Hadidian, 235–45. Pittsburgh: Pickwick.

———. 1990. *The Tree of Life: An Exploration of Biblical Wisdom Literature*. Anchor Bible Reference Library. New York: Doubleday.

Myers, Jacob M. 1965. *I Chronicles*. Anchor Bible 12. Garden City, N.Y.: Doubleday.

Nelson, Richard D. 1981. *The Double Redaction of the Deuteronomistic History*. Journal for the Study of the Old Testament Supplement Series 18. Sheffield: JSOT Press.

———. 1987. *First and Second Kings*. Interpretation. Atlanta: John Knox.

Nemo, Philippe. 1998. *Job and the Excess of Evil*. Pittsburgh: Duquesne University Press.

Neugeboren, Jay. 1987. "Ezra." In *Congregation: Contemporary Writers Read the Jewish Bible*, edited by David Rosenberg, 456–72. San Diego: Harcourt Brace Jovanovich.

Neusner, Jacob. 1973. *From Politics to Piety: The Emergence of Pharisaic Judaism*. Englewood Cliffs, N.J.: Prentice-Hall.

———. 1987. *The Enchantments of Judaism: Rites of Transformation from Birth through Death*. New York: Basic Books.

———. 1991. *Jews and Christians: The Myth of a Common Tradition*. Philadelphia: Trinity Press International.

———. 1998. *What, Exactly, Did the Rabbinic Sages Mean by "the Oral Torah"? An Inductive Answer to the Question of Rabbinic Judaism*. South Florida Studies in the History of Judaism 196. Atlanta: Scholars Press.

Newman, Judith H. 1999. *Praying by the Book: The Scripturalization of Prayer in Second Temple Judaism*. Early Judaism and Its Literature 14. Atlanta: Scholars Press.

Newsom, Carol. 2002. "The Book of Job as Polyphonic Text." *Journal for the Study of the Old Testament* 97:87–108.

———. 2003. *The Book of Job: A Contest of Moral Imaginations*. Oxford: Oxford University Press.

Nickelsburg, George. 1992. "Son of Man." Pages 142–50 in vol. 4 of *Anchor Bible Dictionary*, edited by David Noel Freedman. New York: Doubleday.

Nissinen, Martti. 1998. *Homoeroticism in the Biblical World: A Historical Perspective*. Minneapolis: Fortress.

Nogalski, James. 1993. *Redactional Processes in the Book of the Twelve*. Beihefte zur Zeitschrift für die alttestamentliche Wissenschaft 218. Berlin: de Gruyter.

Nogalski, James, and Marvin A. Sweeney, eds. 2000. *Reading and Hearing the Book of the Twelve*. Society of Biblical Literature Symposium Series 15. Atlanta: Society of Biblical Literature.

North, Christopher R. 1956. *The Suffering Servant in Deutero-Isaiah: An Historical and Critical Study*. 2nd ed. London: Oxford University Press.

Noth, Martin. 1967. *The Laws in the Pentateuch, and Other Studies*. Translated by D. R. Ap-Thomas. Philadelphia: Fortress.

———. 1972. *A History of Pentateuchal Traditions*. Translated by Bernhard W. Anderson. Englewood Cliffs, N.J.: Prentice-Hall.

———. 1981. *The Deuteronomistic History*. Journal for the Study of the Old Testament Supplement Series 15. Sheffield: JSOT Press.

Nygren, Anders. 1969. *Agape and Eros*. Translated by Philip S. Watson. 1953. Reprint, New York: Harper & Row.

O'Connor, Kathleen M. 1988. *The Confessions of Jeremiah: Their Interpretation and Role in Chapters 1–25*. Society of Biblical Literature Dissertation Series 94. Atlanta: Scholars Press.

————. 2002. *Lamentations and the Tears of the World*. Maryknoll, N.Y.: Orbis.

O'Connor, M. 1980. *Hebrew Verse Structure*. Winona Lake, Ind.: Eisenbrauns.

O'Day, Gail R. 1995. "The Gospel of John: Introduction, Commentary, and Reflections." Pages 491–865 in vol. 9 of *The New Interpreter's Bible*, edited by Leander Keck. Nashville: Abingdon.

O'Day, Gail R., and David Petersen, eds. 2009. *The Theological Bible Commentary*. Louisville, Ky.: Westminster John Knox.

Ollenburger, Ben C. 1987. *Zion, the City of the Great King: A Theological Symbol of the Jerusalem Cult*. Journal for the Study of the Old Testament Supplement Series 41. Sheffield: JSOT Press.

————. 1989. "Haggai, Zechariah, Malachi." In *The Books of the Bible*. Vol. 1, *The Old Testament/The Hebrew Bible*, edited by Bernhard W. Anderson, 405–14. New York: Scribner's.

Olson, Dennis T. 1985. *The Death of the Old and the Birth of the New: The Framework of the Book of Numbers and the Pentateuch*. Brown Judaic Studies 71. Chico, Calif.: Scholars Press.

————. 1998. "Biblical Theology as Provisional Monologization: A Dialogue with Childs, Brueggemann, and Bakhtin." *Biblical Interpretation* 6:162–80.

Parker, Simon B. 1989. "Amos." In *The Books of the Bible*. Vol. 1, *The Old Testament/The Hebrew Bible*, edited by Bernhard W. Anderson, 367–74. New York: Scribner's.

Perdue, Leo G. 2008. *The Sword and the Stylus: An Introduction to Wisdom in the Age of Empire*. Grand Rapids: Eerdmans.

Petersen, David L. 1995. *Zechariah 9–14 and Malachi: A Commentary*. Old Testament Library. Louisville, Ky.: Westminster John Knox.

————. 2002. *The Prophetic Literature: An Introduction*. Louisville, Ky.: Westminster John Knox.

Pinsky, Robert. 2005. *The Life of David*. New York: Schocken.

Pixley, Jorge V. 1987. *On Exodus: A Liberation Perspective*. Translated by Robert R. Barr. Maryknoll, N.Y.: Orbis.

Plastaras, James. 1966. *The God of Exodus: The Theology of the Exodus Narratives*. Milwaukee: Bruce.

Polzin, Robert. 1989. *Samuel and the Deuteronomist: 1 Samuel*. San Francisco: Harper & Row.

————. 1993. *David and the Deuteronomist: 2 Samuel*. Bloomington: Indiana University Press.

Prior, Michael. 1997. *The Bible and Colonialism: A Moral Critique*. Biblical Seminar 48. Sheffield: Sheffield Academic Press.

————. 1998. "A Land Flowing with Milk, Honey and People (the Lattey Lecture 1997)." *Scripture Britain* 28:2–17.

————. 1999. *Zionism and the State of Israel: A Moral Inquiry*. London: Routledge.

Pritchard, James B., ed. 1969. *Ancient Near Eastern Texts Relating to the Old Testament*. 3rd ed. Princeton, N.J.: Princeton University Press.

Provan, Iain W. 1991. *Lamentations*. New Century Bible Commentary. Grand Rapids: Eerdmans.

Rad, Gerhard von. 1953. *Studies in Deuteronomy*. Translated by David Stalker. Studies in Biblical Theology 1/9. Chicago: Regnery.

————. 1962. *Old Testament Theology*. Vol. 1, *The Theology of Israel's Historical Traditions*. Translated by D. M. G. Stalker. New York: Harper & Row.

————. 1965. *Old Testament Theology*. Vol. 2, *The Theology of Israel's Prophetic Traditions*. Translated by D. M. G. Stalker. New York: Harper & Row.

————. 1966. *The Problem of the Hexateuch and Other Essays*. Translated by E. W. True-
man Dicken. New York: McGraw-Hill.

————. 1972. *Wisdom in Israel*. Translated by James D. Martin. Nashville: Abingdon.

Rendtorff, Rolf. 1993. *Canon and Theology: Overtures to an Old Testament Theology*.
Overtures to Biblical Theology. Minneapolis: Fortress.

————. 2000. "How to Read the Book of the Twelve as a Theological Unity." In *Read-
ing and Hearing the Book of the Twelve*, edited by James Nogalski and Marvin A.
Sweeney, 75–87. Society of Biblical Literature Symposium Series 15. Atlanta:
Society of Biblical Literature.

Ricoeur, Paul. 1975. "Biblical Hermeneutics." *Semeia* 4:29–148.

————. 1980. *Essays on Biblical Interpretation*. Philadelphia: Fortress.

Roberts, J. J. M. 1989. "Habakkuk." In *The Books of the Bible*. Vol. 1, *The Old Testament/
The Hebrew Bible*, edited by Bernhard W. Anderson, 391–96. New York:
Scribner's.

Robinson, James McConkey, and John B. Cobb. 1964. *The New Hermeneutic*. New
York: Harper & Row.

Rosenberg, David, ed. 1987. *Congregation: Contemporary Writers Read the Jewish Bible*.
San Diego: Harcourt Brace Jovanovich.

Rost, Leonhard. 1982. *The Succession to the Throne of David*. Translated by Michael D.
Rutter and David M. Gunn. Historic Texts and Interpreters in Biblical Scholarship 1. Sheffield: Almond Press.

Sanders, E. P. 1977. *Paul and Palestinian Judaism: A Comparison of Patterns of Religion*.
Philadelphia: Fortress.

Sanders, James A. 1972. *Torah and Canon*. Philadelphia: Fortress.

————. 1976. "Adaptable for Life: The Nature and Function of Canon." In *Magna-
lia Dei, the Mighty Acts of God: Essays on the Bible and Archaeology in Memory of
G. Ernest Wright*, edited by Frank Moore Cross, Werner E. Lemke, and Patrick
D. Miller, 531–60. Garden City, N.Y.: Doubleday.

Sanders, Seth. 2009. *The Invention of Hebrew*. Urbana: University of Illinois Press.

Sawyer, John F. A. 1996. *The Fifth Gospel: Isaiah in the History of Christianity*. New
York: Cambridge University Press.

Schearing, Linda S., and Steven L. McKenzie. 1999. *Those Elusive Deuteronomists: The
Phenomenon of Pan-Deuteronomism*. Journal for the Study of the Old Testament
Supplement Series 268. Sheffield: Sheffield Academic Press.

Schipper, Jeremy. 2011. *Disability and Isaiah's Suffering Servant*. Biblical Refigurations.
Oxford: Oxford University Press.

Schleiermacher, Friedrich. 1988. *On Religion: Speeches to Its Cultured Despisers*. Translated by Richard Crouter. New York: Cambridge University Press.

Schulman, Grace. 1987. "The Song of Songs." In *Congregation: Contemporary Writers
Read the Jewish Bible*, edited by David Rosenberg, 346–60. San Diego: Harcourt
Brace Jovanovich.

Schüssler Fiorenza, Elisabeth. 1984. *Bread Not Stone: The Challenge of Feminist Biblical
Interpretation*. Boston: Beacon.

————. 2001. *Wisdom Ways: Introducing Feminist Biblical Interpretation*. Maryknoll,
N.Y.: Orbis.

Schwartz, Regina M. 1997. *The Curse of Cain: The Violent Legacy of Monotheism*. Chicago: University of Chicago Press.

Scott, James C. 1985. *Weapons of the Weak: Everyday Forms of Peasant Resistance*. New
Haven, Conn.: Yale University Press.

————. 1990. *Domination and the Arts of Resistance: Hidden Transcripts*. New Haven,
Conn.: Yale University Press.

Scott, James M. 1997. *Exile: Old Testament, Jewish, and Christian Conceptions.* Journal for the Study of Judaism Supplement 56. New York: Brill.

Seitz, Christopher R. 1989. *Theology in Conflict: Reactions to the Exile in the Book of Jeremiah.* Beihefte zur Zeitschrift für die alttestamentliche Wissenschaft 176. Berlin: de Gruyter.

———. 1991. *Zion's Final Destiny: The Development of the Book of Isaiah: A Reassessment of Isaiah 36–39.* Minneapolis: Fortress.

Seow, Choon-Leong. 1997. *Ecclesiastes: A New Translation with Introduction and Commentary.* Anchor Bible 18C. New York: Doubleday.

Shapiro, David. 1987. "Proverbs." In *Congregation: Contemporary Writers Read the Jewish Bible,* edited by David Rosenberg, 313–30. San Diego: Harcourt Brace Jovanovich.

Shapiro, Harvey. 1987. "Joel." In *Congregation: Contemporary Writers Read the Jewish Bible,* edited by David Rosenberg, 197–209. San Diego: Harcourt Brace Jovanovich.

Sheppard, G. T. 1977. "The Epilogue to Qoheleth as Theological Commentary." *Catholic Biblical Quarterly* 39:182–89.

Smend, Rudolf. 1971. "Das Gesetz und die Völker: Ein Beitrag zur deuteronomistischen Redaktionsgeschichte." In *Probleme biblischer Theologie: Gerhard von Rad zum 70. Geburtstag,* edited by Hans Walter Wolff, 494–509. Munich: C. Kaiser.

Smith, Daniel L. 1989. *The Religion of the Landless: The Social Context of the Babylonian Exile.* Bloomington, Ind.: Meyer-Stone.

Smith, Morton. 1987. *Palestinian Parties and Politics That Shaped the Old Testament.* 2nd ed. London: SCM.

Smith-Christopher, Daniel L. 2002. *A Biblical Theology of Exile.* Overtures to Biblical Theology. Minneapolis: Fortress.

Soulen, R. Kendall. 1996. *The God of Israel and Christian Theology.* Minneapolis: Fortress.

Stendahl, Krister. 1962. "Biblical Theology, Contemporary." Pages 418–32 in vol. 1 of *The Interpreter's Dictionary of the Bible,* edited by George Arthur Buttrick. Nashville: Abingdon.

Stern, Philip D. 1991. *The Biblical Ḥerem: A Window on Israel's Religious Experience.* Brown Judaic Studies 211. Atlanta: Scholars Press.

Stevenson, Kalinda Rose. 1996. *Vision of Transformation: The Territorial Rhetoric of Ezekiel 40–48.* Society of Biblical Literature Dissertation Series 154. Atlanta: Scholars Press.

Stone, Michael E. 1980. *Scriptures, Sects, and Visions: A Profile of Judaism from Ezra to the Jewish Revolts.* Philadelphia: Fortress.

Stulman, Louis. 1998. *Order Amid Chaos: Jeremiah as Symbolic Tapestry.* Biblical Seminar 57. Sheffield: Sheffield Academic Press.

Sugirtharajah, R. S. 2002. *Postcolonial Criticism and Biblical Interpretation.* Oxford: Oxford University Press.

Tarr, Herbert. 1987. "Chronicles." In *Congregation: Contemporary Writers Read the Jewish Bible,* edited by David Rosenberg, 497–512. San Diego: Harcourt Brace Jovanovich.

Theunissen, Michael. 1984. *The Other: Studies in the Social Ontology of Husserl, Heidegger, Sartre, and Buber.* Studies in Contemporary German Social Thought. Cambridge, Mass.: MIT Press.

Towner, W. Sibley. 1984. *Daniel.* Interpretation. Atlanta: John Knox.

Tracy, David. 1981. *The Analogical Imagination: Christian Theology and the Culture of Pluralism.* New York: Crossroad.

Trible, Phyllis. 1973. "Depatriarchalizing in Biblical Interpretation." *Journal of the American Academy of Religion* 41, no. 1:30–48.

———. 1978. *God and the Rhetoric of Sexuality*. Overtures to Biblical Theology. Philadelphia: Fortress.

———. 1989a. "Bringing Miriam out of the Shadows." *Bible Review* 5:14–25.

———. 1989b. "Subversive Justice: Tracing the Miriamic Traditions." In *Justice and the Holy: Essays in Honor of Walter Harrelson*, edited by Douglas A. Knight and Peter J. Paris, 99–109. Atlanta: Scholars Press.

———. 1994. *Rhetorical Criticism: Context, Method, and the Book of Jonah*. Guides to Biblical Scholarship: Old Testament Series. Minneapolis: Fortress.

Voegelin, Eric. 1956. *Order and History*. Vol. 1, *Israel and Revelation*. Baton Rouge: Louisiana State University Press.

Walzer, Michael. 1985. *Exodus and Revolution*. New York: Basic Books.

Weems, Renita J. 1995. *Battered Love: Marriage, Sex, and Violence in the Hebrew Prophets*. Overtures to Biblical Theology. Minneapolis: Fortress.

Weinfeld, Moshe. 1970. "The Covenant of Grant in the Old Testament and the Ancient Near East." *Journal of the American Oriental Society* 90:184–203.

———. 1972. *Deuteronomy and the Deuteronomic School*. Oxford: Clarendon.

Wellhausen, Julius. 1994. *Prolegomena to the History of Israel*. 1885. Scholars Press Reprints and Translations Series. Atlanta: Scholars Press. Original German publication, 1878.

Westermann, Claus. 1965. *The Praise of God in the Psalms*. Translated by Keith R. Crim. Richmond: John Knox. Reprint in *Praise and Lament in the Psalms*, 1–162. Atlanta: John Knox, 1981.

———. 1967. *Basic Forms of Prophetic Speech*. Translated by Hugh Clayton White. Philadelphia: Westminster.

———. 1974. "The Role of the Lament in the Theology of the Old Testament." Translated by Richard N. Soulen. *Interpretation* 28:20–38. Reprint in *Praise and Lament in the Psalms*, 259–80. Atlanta: John Knox, 1981.

———. 1980a. *The Promises to the Fathers: Studies on the Patriarchal Narratives*. Translated by David E. Green. Philadelphia: Fortress.

———. 1980b. *The Psalms: Structure, Content, and Message*. Translated by Ralph D. Gehrke. Minneapolis: Augsburg.

———. 1981. *The Structure of the Book of Job: A Form-Critical Analysis*. Translated by Charles A. Muenchow. Philadelphia: Fortress.

———. 1989. "Lamentations." Translated by Bernhard W. Anderson. In *The Books of the Bible*. Vol. 1, *The Old Testament/The Hebrew Bible*, edited by Bernhard W. Anderson, 303–18. New York: Scribner's.

———. 1994. *Lamentations: Issues and Interpretation*. Translated by Charles A. Muenchow. Minneapolis: Fortress.

White, Lynn. 1967. "The Historical Roots of Our Ecological Crisis." *Science* 155:1203–7.

Whybray, R. N. 1974. *The Intellectual Tradition in the Old Testament*. Beihefte zur Zeitschrift für die alttestamentliche Wissenschaft 135. New York: de Gruyter.

Wiesel, Elie. 1976. *Messengers of God: Biblical Portraits and Legends*. New York: Summit.

———. 1981. *Five Biblical Portraits*. Notre Dame, Ind.: University of Notre Dame Press.

———. 1987. "Ezekiel." In *Congregation: Contemporary Writers Read the Jewish Bible*, edited by David Rosenberg, 167–86. San Diego: Harcourt Brace Jovanovich.

Wilder, Amos N. 1983. "Story and Story-World." *Interpretation* 37:353–64.

Williamson, H. G. M. 1985. *Ezra, Nehemiah*. Word Biblical Commentary 16. Waco, Tex.: Word.

———. 1987. *Ezra and Nehemiah*. Old Testament Guides. Sheffield: Sheffield Academic Press.

Wilson, Gerald H. 1985. *The Editing of the Hebrew Psalter*. Society of Biblical Literature Dissertation Series 76. Chico, Calif.: Scholars Press.

Wilson, Robert R. 1977. *Genealogy and History in the Biblical World*. New Haven, Conn.: Yale University Press.

———. 1980. *Prophecy and Society in Ancient Israel*. Philadelphia: Fortress.

———. 1984. *Sociological Approaches to the Old Testament*. Guides to Biblical Scholarship: Old Testament Guides. Philadelphia: Fortress.

Wink, Walter. 2000. *John the Baptist in the Gospel Tradition*. Eugene, Or.: Wipf & Stock.

Wolff, Hans Walter. 1966. "The Kerygma of the Yahwist." Translated by Wilbur A. Benware. *Interpretation* 20:131–58. Reprint in *The Vitality of Old Testament Traditions*, by Walter Brueggemann and Hans Walter Wolff, 41–66. 2nd ed. Atlanta: John Knox, 1982.

———. 1978. "Micah the Moreshite—the Prophet and His Background." Translated by Charles E. Weber. In *Israelite Wisdom: Theological and Literary Essays in Honor of Samuel Terrien*, edited by John G. Gammie et al., 77–84. Missoula, Mont.: Scholars Press for Union Theological Seminary.

———. 1982. "The Kerygma of the Deuteronomic Historical Work." Translated by Frederick C. Prussner. In *The Vitality of Old Testament Traditions*, by Walter Brueggemann and Hans Walter Wolff, 83–100. 2nd ed. Atlanta: John Knox.

Wright, N. T. 1996. *Christian Origins and the Question of God*. Vol. 2, *Jesus and the Victory of God*. Minneapolis: Fortress.

Wybrow, Cameron. 1991. *The Bible, Baconianism, and Mastery over Nature: The Old Testament and Its Modern Misreading*. American University Studies: Series 7, Theology and Religion 112. New York: P. Lang.

Yee, Gale A. 1992. "The Theology of Creation in Proverbs 8:22–31." In *Creation in the Biblical Traditions*, edited by Richard J. Clifford and John Joseph Collins, 85–96. Washington, D.C.: Catholic Biblical Association of America.

Yerushalmi, Yosef Hayim. 1982. *Zakhor, Jewish History and Jewish Memory*. The Samuel and Althea Stroum Lectures in Jewish Studies. Seattle: University of Washington Press.

Yoder, Christine Elizabeth. 2001. *Wisdom as a Woman of Substance: A Socioeconomic Reading of Proverbs 1–9 and 31:10–31*. Beihefte zur Zeitschrift für die alttestamentliche Wissenschaft 304. Berlin: de Gruyter.

Zimmerli, Walther. 1964. "The Place and Limit of the Wisdom in the Framework of the Old Testament Theology." *Scottish Journal of Theology* 17:146–58. Reprint in *Studies in Ancient Israelite Wisdom*, edited by James L. Crenshaw, 314–26. New York: Ktav, 1976.

———. 1965. *The Law and the Prophets: A Study of the Meaning of the Old Testament*. James Sprunt Lectures, 1963. Oxford: Blackwell.

Zornberg, Avivah Gottlieb. 2009. *The Murmuring Deep: Reflections on the Biblical Unconscious*. New York: Schocken.

Index of Scripture

Index of Names

Index of Subjects

Aaron, 21–22, 75, 86–87, 93, 102, 236
Aaronides, 412
Aaron's sons, 21–22, 93, 102
Abel, 51
Abiathar, 210, 214
Abigail, 168
Abihu, 21–22
Abijam, 178
Abimelech, 154, 155
Abner, 169
Abraham
  death of, 73
  and God's blessing on Israel generally, 105
  and God's mandate to be "a blessing" to
    the nations, 201
  God's promise of land and offspring to, 25,
    67–71, 144
  Hagar and, 73
  obedience of, and faith in God, 73
  origins of Israel and, 53, 65, 411
  Paul on, 70
  sacrifice of Isaac and, 19, 22–24
  Sarah's death and, 21
  special relationship generally between God
    and, 259
Absalom, 163, 171, 172, 173
Adam, 53, 55–60, 65, 411, 414
Adoni-bezek, 152
Adonijah, 171
Advent, 268
Agag, King, 378
Agur, 339
Ahab, 186

Ahaz, 194, 195, 206
Alexander the Great, 280
Amalekites, 378
Amen-em-opet, 340
American Revolution, 77
Ammon, 277
Amnon, 171, 172, 173
Amon, 187
Amos, book of
  close reading of, 258
  connections between Torah traditions and,
    259
  on ethical monotheism, 255
  on God's sovereignty as Creator, 260
  historical context and dating of, 134, 242,
    243, 255–56, 299
  on Israel's lack of privilege in relation to
    God, 260
  on justice and righteousness, 30, 259–60
  oracles against the nations in, 256–60, 261
  prophet Amos and, 255–56, 258, 259
  prophetic nature of, 257–60
  on sin and judgment, 244, 257–60
  social critique in, 256
  theological themes of, 242, 244, 255–60
  traditioning process in, 259
anger of God
  in Exodus, 81
  in Ezekiel, 227–28
  in Genesis, 53
  in Hosea, 250
  in Jeremiah, 219, 414
  in Judges, 157

Ethiopia, 277
etiologies, 51
Eve, 53, 55–60. *See also* Adam
evolution versus creation debate, 57
exile
  of ark of the covenant, 165
  entry into and movement beyond abyss of,
    300
  female imagery for God and, 202
  homecoming from, as new exodus, 77–78,
    431
  in Kings, 182
  Rachel's grief and, 72, 335
  Tarr on, 415
  theologizing from perspective of exiles, 243
  Torah and, 41–47
  See also Babylonian exile; exodus story
Exodus and Revolution (Walzer), 77
exodus story
  ark of God and, 77
  and burning bush as theophany, 79
  and covenant between God and Israel,
    83–88, 318
  crossing of Jordan River as replication of,
    77, 140, 141
  deaths of firstborn in Egypt in, 46, 75
  God's destruction of Pharaoh's army at
    Red Sea, 25, 75, 80, 140, 141
  historical dating of, 76
  homecoming from exile as new exodus,
    77–78, 431
  initial impetus for, from slaves, 79–80, 318,
    379
  interval in the wilderness before arriving at
    Sinai, 81–83, 102–4
  liberation of Israelites from Egypt in,
    25–26, 75–81
  and liberation trajectories of interpretation,
    81
  manna and, 139
  midrash on, 77, 79
  Moses in, 25–26, 75, 79–80, 141, 280
  paradigmatic reading of, 76–78
  Passover and, 45–46, 75–76, 80, 185
  Pharaoh of Egypt and, 25–26, 75–76, 77,
    80, 87–88, 112, 379, 420
  plagues against Egypt and, 26, 78–79
  presence of Holy One in, 85–86, 88
  Priestly tradition of, 82–83, 85, 88
  significance of, for later political move-
    ments, 77
  Sinai experience, 83–88, 171
  Song of Moses and, 80

Ten Commandments and, 75, 83–84
theological themes of, 87–88
Ezekiel, book of
  on anticipated restoration for Jerusalem,
    135, 224, 228–40
  apocalyptic rhetoric in, 233–35
  Babylonian exile and, 223, 224–25
  on boundaries of land for twelve tribes,
    236–37
  call of Ezekiel to be prophet in, 224
  Christian response to, 223
  concluding comments on, 297–99
  and crisis of presence of God, 224
  on destruction of Jerusalem, 229–30
  distinctiveness of, 223–24
  divine self-interest in, 231–32
  on false prophets, 226
  Gog and Magog in, 234–35
  historical context and dating of, 224,
    229–30
  on holiness, 134
  on impending judgment on Jerusalem, 135,
    224–29
  on indictment against leadership of Judah,
    226
  loss and hope in generally, 245
  midrash on, 225
  oracles against the nations in, 230–31, 256,
    257, 261
  personality of Ezekiel in, 223–24
  Priestly tradition and, 134, 224, 225, 235–
    37, 239
  prophetic nature of, 133–37
  on relationship of God and Israel, 227–28
  on repentance, 237–40
  on restoration of temple, 235–38
  on resurrection of the body, 233
  on Torah obedience/disobedience, 238–40
  "Valley of Dry Bones" metaphor in,
    232–33
Ezra (scribe), 218, 397, 399–404
Ezra, book of
  Christian interpretation of, 404–8
  close reading of, 399
  completion of Torah during time of Ezra,
    7, 41
  on debt system, 400
  God's presence in, 418
  historical context of, 308, 309, 397
  ideology in, 403–7
  introduction to, 308
  links between Nehemiah and, 397–98
  otherness and, 404–7

CPSIA information can be obtained
at www.ICGtesting.com
Printed in the USA
LVOW12s1252030816
498849LV00004B/96/P

9 780664 234584